Philadelphia JEWISH LIFE
1940–2000

This book is sponsored by the Feinstein Center for American Jewish History at Temple University, The Jewish Federation of Greater Philadelphia, and the Philadelphia chapter of the American Jewish Committee.

Philadelphia JEWISH LIFE
1940–2000

Edited by MURRAY FRIEDMAN

Illustrations provided by
The Urban Archives at Temple University
and The Philadelphia Jewish Archives Center

Temple University Press
Philadelphia

Temple University Press, Philadelphia 19122

⊖ The paper used in this publication meets the requirements of the
American National Standard for Information Sciences—
Permanence of Paper for Printed Library Materials, ANSI Z39.48-1984

*All attempts were made to locate the owners of the photographs published
in this book. If you believe you may own one of them, please contact the publisher
at Temple University Press, 1601 North Broad Street, Philadelphia, PA 19122.
The publisher will be sure to include appropriate acknowledgment in subsequent
editions of the book.*

Library of Congress Cataloging-in-Publication Data
Philadelphia Jewish Life, 1940–2000/Murray Friedman, editor
p. cm.
Includes biographical references and index.
ISBN 1-56639-999-8 (cloth)
1. Jews—Pennsylvania—Philadelphia—History—20th century.
2. Jews—Pennsylvania—Philadelphia—Politics and government—20th century.
3. Philadelphia (Pa.)—Ethnic relations. I. Friedman, Murray, 1926–

F158.9J5 P5 2003
974.8'11004924–dc21   2002026604

2 4 6 8 9 7 5 3 1

Designed and composed by CHRISTINE CANTERA DESIGN, Medford, New Jersey, ccantera@aol.com

For Eve and Marsha,
who have shared and enriched Philadelphia Jewish life for me

Contents

Foreword ≈

E. Digby Baltzell

I was honored when my old friend, Murray Friedman, asked me to write a few lines by way of a preface to this volume on the changes in the Philadelphia Jewish community during the almost half-century since 1940, the year John F. Kennedy graduated from Harvard and the year following my own graduation from the University of Pennsylvania. The essays in this book cover a period in Philadelphia Jewish history that exactly spans my own adult life.

I was raised in Chestnut Hill among a class of people who took anti-Semitism for granted. Several years of service in the armed forces, where privileges were based on functional rank rather than class or ethnic ancestry, were bound to challenge the traditional values of my generation. Both gentile and Jewish officers and gentlemen of the United States Navy, for the first time in their lives, shared leisurely intimacies in the wardroom as well as common dangers at their respective battle stations. Although country-club anti-Semitism was the overwhelming rule before the war, it would have seemed entirely out of place in the first-class officers clubs at the Naval Air Stations at Norfolk, Quonset, or Corpus Christi, to say nothing of those more primitive bastions of privilege in the South Pacific, at Espietu Santo, Guadalcanal, and Guam. And many if not most of my fellow officers and friends returned to civilian life far less willing to tolerate the traditional, often dehumanizing, ethnic snobberies of our pre-war years. One of my South Pacific shipmates and a close friend, for instance, played an important role in eliminating the categorical exclusion of Jewish alumni from membership in the Harvard Club of New York City. I myself gave up a pre-war business career to become a sociologist, receiving a Ph.D. from Columbia and then spending my entire academic career at the University of Pennsylvania. I did not join the Lenape Club, a private faculty club whose older members tended to be anti-Semitic. Instead I became an enthusiastic member of our present Faculty Club, whose membership by now is as heterogeneous in background as the United Nations. There was surely little or no anti-Semitism among my generation of faculty members at Penn, and the same was true of the Philadelphia College of Art, where my wife, Jane Piper, taught for three decades.

Outside of academic life, my wife and I confined our social life largely to the art and academic worlds, especially among a kind of countercultural elite of reform Democrats centering in the Americans for Democratic Action, who took the lead in bringing Joseph S. Clark and Richardson Dilworth into the mayor's office in the 1950s. Of importance here is the fact that the leading members of this reform counterculture were tacitly but emphatically agreed on the evils and destructiveness of anti-Semitism.

In the meantime, my writing and research interests paralleled my academic and social life. My first book, *Philadelphia Gentleman* (1958), examined the historical background and contemporary structure of Philadelphia's leadership class in 1940, a date purposely chosen because it preceded the post-war social changes, such as those discussed in the essays in this volume. My second book, *The Protestant Establishment: Aristocracy and Caste in America* (1964), was an analysis of the history of anti-Semitism within the American WASP establishment in the years between the assassination of Czar Alexander of Russia in 1881, and the assassination of John F. Kennedy in 1963.

The first and most important thing to be said about elite anti-Semitism in the years since the end of World War II, especially since 1963, is that while Philadelphia was a familistic and class society in 1940, it is a relatively individualistic and bureaucratic society today. In 1940, a class of WASP gentlemen still dominated the business and cultural life of the city as their ancestors had since colonial days. For instance, Edward Hopkinson, Jr., the senior partner of Drexel and Company, was probably the most powerful man in the city. He had graduated from both the college and the law school at Penn; was a partner in one of the city's major law firms (100 percent WASP until the 1960s) for many years before going to the Drexel firm; was a descendant of a member of the first class to graduate from the College of Philadelphia; was a great-great-great grandson of a founder of the American Philosophical Society; and was a great-great grandson of a signer of the Declaration of Independence. In that same year, Benjamin Rush, whose namesake was a signer of the Declaration and the city's most famous physician, was chairman of the board of the Insurance Company of North America (he had been president from 1916 to 1939). The Pennsylvania Railroad and the famous Baldwin Locomotive Works had a president and a majority of board members who were listed in the *Social Register*. The University of Pennsylvania was entirely run by such proper Philadelphia gentlemen as Lippincotts, Cadwaladers, Merricks, Whartons, and Peppers. Senator George Wharton Pepper, a life trustee, was Penn's most eminent alumnus and unofficial dean of the Philadelphia Bar. Penn's president, Thomas S. Gates, the senior Drexel partner before Hopkinson and a birthright Quaker-turned-Episcopal Philadelphian, served without pay. And finally, the presidents of all the major banks in the city and a vast majority of their directors were listed in the *Social Register*.

At the same time, and most important, the class cohesion of the WASP leadership in 1940 was consolidated in an elaborate complex of city men's clubs and various exclusive cricket and golf clubs out in the suburbs, in all of which the anti-Semitic line was firmly drawn. In Center City, the members of the Philadelphia Club dominated the upper-class leadership in both business and culture. Like President Gates at Penn, most of the cultural institutions—the Art Museum, the Historical Society, the Academy of Fine Arts, the Philadelphia Orchestra, and so forth—were headed by amateur volunteers (gentlemen of independent means) who served at minimal or no salaries.

All that has changed since the Second World War and especially since President Kennedy's assassination in 1963 and his brother's in 1968. One must always bear in mind that the sixties, which peaked between 1968 and 1970, was the most egalitarian and atomizing era in American history. It was largely a revolt from the top: the 1969 "Bust" at Harvard was led first by the sons of successful and even affluent Jewish intellectuals, and then by the WASP and preppy children of privilege who made up the majority of the three hundred or so undergraduates who occupied University Hall on April 9, 1969.

The sixties accelerated a secular trend in America from a pre-war social structure dominated by a relatively open class system (despite ethnic barriers) to a more or less classless bureaucracy, based largely on educational achievement. John F. Kennedy's entering class at Princeton in 1935, for instance, ranked below the national average in IQ and included a handful of Jews (2 to 3 percent); the entering class today is at the very top levels of the nation academically and is composed of a third or more Jewish students. The school for gentlemen has been replaced by a school for preprofessional men and women. In those pre-war days, moreover, it was the colleges (especially Harvard, Yale, and Princeton) that educated a class of leaders, whereas it is the graduate and professional schools that are now training bureaucrats; hence the preprofessional "A" has now replaced the upper-class "gentleman's C" of the old undergraduate days.

It is no accident that the revolutionary trend of the sixties was centered on the prestige campuses of the nation, such as Berkeley, Columbia, and Harvard. For, as Max Weber observed in bureaucratic Germany before the First World War, the certificate of education finally replaced the test for ancestors after the Second World War, even in Philadelphia. Thus, the largest private employer in the city today is the huge bureaucracy that is the University of Pennsylvania. Martin Meyerson, quite unlike Thomas Gates, not only was the first Jewish president of a major American university, but also had spent a lifetime as an agile academic bureaucrat of the first rank. The trustees were no longer primarily high-born Philadelphia Gentlemen, but persons of merit from all over the nation—Jew and gentile, black and white, female and male.

The Drexel firm, always allied with the Pennsylvania Railroad and the heavy industries, such as the Baldwin Locomotive Works, which marked the pre-war city, is no longer a major Proper Philadelphia institution; the prestigious and traditional name has been retained by the largely Jewish and very successful New York firm of Drexel Burnham Lambert Incorporated (and Mr. I. W. Burnham II became a Penn trustee under the Meyerson regime). Today, there is no man or woman of informal and traditional dominance in the city's life to compare with Edward Hopkinson, Jr. Nor is there an unofficial dean of the bar to compare with Senator Pepper. The official position as head of the Philadelphia Bar Association, moreover, is no longer a mark of personal prestige, but is more likely to be rotated from firm to firm as a duty to be discharged rather than strictly an honor. While the most prestigious law firms in the city in 1940 were small and homogeneous partnerships (all save the German Jewish firm of Wolf, Block, Schorr & Solis-Cohen), entirely old stock and Protestant in membership, they are today becoming larger and larger bureaucracies with partners—men and women—of varying ethnic backgrounds, including Jewish. Some would also say that the law is increasingly becoming a business rather than a profession (just as Penn is now in the "education business," as members of the administration are so fond of saying).

While the traditional class authority of men like Hopkinson and Gates in 1940 emanated from the halls of the Philadelphia Club (the oldest of its kind in the nation), the elite Union League club, far more likely to include the big industrial and financial leaders of newly achieved status, has now become the focus of most of the important bureaucratic power struggles in the city. While the members of the League were almost entirely WASP and supporters of the Republican party in 1940, today one meets men of mannerly power and often new money, of all races and ethnic backgrounds (and convictions, even including confessed supporters of the Democratic party). As I write, the League has just voted to accept women members, after years of threats from City Hall and prodding from the media. Similarly, the Philadelphia, Racquet, and Rittenhouse clubs, more upper class than the League, have recently let down anti-Semitic barriers to membership and presumably will soon accept women (the Racquet already has).

What I have been saying here is that, in the three post-war decades, elite anti-Semitism and ethnic prejudice have declined to a considerable degree. But what are the prospects for the future in an atomistic and elitist bureaucratic society as against the traditional class society that marked pre-war America and Philadelphia? In the first place, the present Philadelphia (and American) leadership structure has never been so justly chosen and meritocratically based; at the same time, it is my contention that it has never been so prone to atomization and disorder. There is, for example, no organic and historically rooted center of authority or responsibility in Philadelphia or in America today. A WASP establishment such as we had in Philadelphia in 1940 is no longer possible or desirable today. Some sort of authoritative establishment, however, may be a prerequisite for the ordered freedom that we and the British have enjoyed to a greater extent than any other nation in modern times.

This is especially so in contrast to post-Bismark and pre-Hitler Germany, which was extremely bureaucratic compared with the Anglo-American class systems of that period. There were no upper-class educational institutions in Germany that melded the sons of the old nobilities, such as the agricultural and militaristic Junkers, and the sons of the rising upper-bourgeois into one coherent class ethic. There has never been anything to compare with the colleges of Oxford and Cambridge in England, or with the undergraduate colleges at Harvard, Yale, and Princeton in this country, where the sons of the aristocracy, gentry, and high middle classes in England, or of the old professional gentry and the new industrialists here, were molded in a single gentlemanly ethic. On the contrary, the great universities, such as of Heidelberg, Bonn, or Berlin, have always been engaged in educating scholars and scientists and in training professional bureaucrats. We imported the Ph.D. from Germany and the Bachelor of Arts from Oxbridge. Similarly with secondary education, in Germany, the Gymnasium, a total community school run by the state, was much like our public high school or the British grammar school. There have never been national class schools such as Eton, Harrow, or Rugby in England, or Groton, St. Paul's, Exeter, and Andover in America. Organized games and the gentlemanly sportsmanship ethic for which they once stood have never been a part of either Gymnasium or university education in Germany. There are no class rituals to compare with the Eton-Harrow cricket matches at Lords each spring or the Harvard-Yale football games at the end of each fall. I have often thought, how different modern history might have been had Karl Marx captained his (nonexistent) college football team at Bonn or Berlin, or had the Nazi leadership been schooled in some German equivalent of the playing fields of Eton. All this is not to say that the positive values of the Anglo-American sportsmanship ethic were not correlated with a gentlemanly anti-Semitism. But on the other hand, there have been no Dreyfus cases or concentration camps, and ultimately no permanent barriers, as the current Jewish experience makes clear.

At any rate, just as the shallow forms of socially humiliating anti-Semitism did not exist in liberal and permissive Weimar Germany to anywhere near the extent they did in America during that era, so today our permissive society has never seen so little manifest anti-Semitism. And yet . . . perhaps it has never been so structurally weak at the top levels of leadership and consequently, so I contend, never so vulnerable should some new anti-Semitic movement take hold in America. Nothing in this life comes without a price, and our atomized age of total (even intolerant) tolerance must pay the price of weakened authority and social cohesion. The decline of anti-Semitism discussed in the course of these essays is, of course, all to the good. Let us hope that my reflections here on the unanticipated consequences of undoubted progress will never be tested.

Acknowledgments

This volume completes a project that initially began with a volume during the tercentenary of the founding of Philadelphia by William Penn, covering an earlier period of Philadelphia Jewish life. The essays in the two books represent less a history of the Jewish experience in Philadelphia than a series of building blocks necessary for the writing of such a definitive history. I know better than almost anyone that there are important omissions in subject areas. And because this particular volume covers what to many is contemporary history, there will be those who will remember things differently or find errors of fact. Wiser people suggested that the job could not be done, or at least that I should not undertake it. I can only ask the reader to approach this book with a degree of charity reserved for either the young (which I am not) or those who live perhaps unwisely.

As always in such matters, I had a great deal of advice and assistance from friends and colleagues. I would like to thank them and apologize to those I have inadvertently neglected. They include Dr. Dennis J. Clark, Daniel C. Cohen, Maurice B. Fagan, Robert A. Klein, Dr. Ernest Kahn, Robert Price, Burt Siegel, Emily W. Sunstein, Lily Schwartz, and Edwin Wolf II. Of course they are not responsible for the material contained in this volume—and, indeed, may be somewhat surprised at what they find here.

In closing, the editor wishes to thank the countless people too numerous to name individually who helped create this volume. Singled out for special recognition must be the Federation of Jewish Agencies of Greater Philadelphia, whose generous grant made it possible, and Micah Kleit, the senior acquisitions editor at Temple University Press, who originated the idea for this new edition and guided it through the intricacies of publication.

THE EIGHTIES TO A NEW CENTURY

Murray Friedman · Andrew Harrison

When the research and writing for the first edition of this volume began about twenty-five years ago, the Introduction posed a question: Had Jews become insiders in the life of the community? The matter was still in doubt. True, the signs were promising. Still, one had some hesitation in announcing that Jews had been fully accepted when the book was first conceived and written. Almost a quarter of a century later, the matter is no longer in doubt: Jews are insiders.

The evidence is clear by any reasonable measurement of success. It is illustrated by the career of David Cohen, Esquire. Cohen served as Mayor Ed Rendell's much-admired chief of staff. When Cohen resigned in 1997, he returned to an elite law firm as its managing partner. In the early 1960s, virtually none of the older-stock Philadelphia law firms would have hired him, let alone move him into a high-level position.

True enough, anti-Semitic incidents such as the torching of Beit Harambaum, a Sephardic Orthodox congregation in Northeast Philadelphia several years ago, occur occasionally. These incidents, however, are rare; they do not reflect any long-term patterns and are widely condemned. Jews have "made it" as full citizens in community life, but at what cost? Here we are reminded of a joke that makes the rounds of the Jewish community: Two Jewish women are talking, and one admires a gem on the finger of the other. The woman wearing the ring tells her proudly that it has a name. It is called the Plotnick gem, but it comes with a curse. Impressed, her friend asks, "What is the curse?" "Mr. Plotnick," the other replies.

The gains that Jews have made here in the last quarter of a century do not come with a curse, but they are a mixed blessing. But we are getting ahead of the story.

In the decades immediately following World War II, a series of Working Papers published by the American Jewish Committee charted the decline in anti-Semitism.[1] This has been accompanied by growing affluence. Virtually no area of community life is barred to Jews today.[2] The results are evident in the ease of movement of Jews from older sections of the city and the suburbs in line with demographic patterns of the population generally.[3]

Jewish communal agencies, however, continue to grapple with pockets of poverty. Attacking poverty was a central theme in the Federation's 2001 fundraising campaign.

The change can be seen most dramatically in South Philadelphia. In 1920, South Philadelphia contained approximately 100,000 Jews, making it the largest concentration of Eastern European Jews in the city. By the close of the twentieth century, the Jewish population of the area had dwindled to about four hundred. Most are over the age of 70 and often in need of communal assistance.[4]

When this book was first published, a majority of Jews lived in Philadelphia proper.[5] No longer. The Jewish Federation of Greater Philadelphia's Jewish Population Study of 1996–1997 revealed that of the 99,300 Jewish households in the five-county Philadelphia region, a majority no longer reside in the city. The number of people in Jewish households in Bucks County went from 24,000 in 1984 to 43,600, a 10 percent increase. Chester County experienced the largest growth, starting with 3,700 people in Jewish households in 1984 and rising to 13,400, an incredible 250 percent increase.[6] Anecdotal reports suggest that these trends are increasing.

The Northeast, which gained the greatest number of Jews in the post-war years, suffered the greatest losses. Only Center City, with a high proportion of older professionals and empty nesters eager to enjoy the rich cultural resources of the area, saw an increase.[7] "We no longer can think of our Federation as a Philadelphia Federation, but as a Federation for all the Jews living in the five-county area," former Federation president Michael R. Belman has observed.[8]

As a whole, the region lost Jewish households (from 103,100 in the 1983–1984 Federation survey to 99,300 Jewish households in the 1996–1997 survey.) In terms of actual numbers, the figures show a decline from 256,000 in 1984 to 241,000 in 1996–1997, a drop of more than 14 percent. If one counts such areas of Southern New Jersey as Cherry Hill (not included in this book), however, Philadelphia Jewry may be holding its own more or less.[9]

While the dispersion of Jews is a sign of the growing middle- and upper-middle-class character of the Jewish community and its success, *it reduces,* nevertheless, communal coherence. Dr. Gary Tobin, the president of the Institute for Jewish and Community Research in San Francisco and a consultant to the 1996–1997 Jewish population study, characterized the Philadelphia Jewish community in the late 1980s as "lacking institutional glue."[10] The byline of a *Philadelphia Inquirer* story on February 24, 2001, reported, "In the Lower Northeast, synagogues are struggling."

In the fall of 2000, a number of representatives of the remaining congregations in the Northeast came together with the assistance of the Federation to chart their future. It was agreed that despite territorial issues, within ten years the five synagogue buildings must be consolidated into one centrally located site, with each congregation still having the option of remaining a separate entity.[11] In turn, the newly emerging Jewish areas struggle to create new organizational and religious networks.[12]

When one of the authors of this Introduction first came to Philadelphia in the early 1960s, the executive suites of the major industrial and financial institutions were closed to Jews. Jews are now employed by, serve on the boards of, and operate many of the city's largest and important corporations.[13] Joseph Neubauer heads Aramark Corporation; Ralph and Brian Roberts, Comcast; and Jack Farber, CSS Industries. Jews increasingly also enjoy leadership roles in the city's major cultural institutions. Neubauer, for example, served as chairman of the Philadelphia Orchestra board, and the late Philip Berman, an Allentown businessman, headed the Philadelphia Museum of Art. It is no longer unusual to see Jewish names like the Steinberg/Dietrich Hall at the Wharton School and the Annenberg School of Communication, as well as the Van Pelt Library at the University of Pennsylvania.

The prominence of Jews in civic philanthropy, of course, is a reflection of growing affluence and civic acceptance or, as one wag put it, "the democracy of the dollar." Leading the list of generous donors over the years have been Leonore and Walter H. Annenberg. The latter made a gift in 2000 of $10 million to endow permanently a chair for the music director of the Philadelphia Orchestra (added to a gift in the same amount in 1994 toward the renovation of the Academy of Music) and $20 million to the Philadelphia Museum of Art, the largest cash gift in its 125-year history. Raymond G. Perelman also donated $15 million to help the museum expand.[14] The largest single gift that has come to our attention is the $100 million given by Madeline and Leonard Abramson to the cancer center of the University of Pennsylvania.

In the winter of 2001, the Sydney Kimmel Regional Performing Arts Center, which houses the city's famed orchestra, was opened; it is named after the founder and head of Jones Apparel, the largest private donor, with a gift total of 30 million. Raymond G. and Ruth Perelman also helped to expedite the building of the center by contributing $5 million.

Such largesse, however, is a measure, too, of the enthusiasm with which Jews have thrown themselves into the educational and cultural life of the community. It is no exaggeration to suggest that they have altered the cultural landscape of the city. Moe Septee (who died in 1997 at age 71), Philadelphia's version of New York's famed impressario Sol Hurok, emerged as the driving force behind the creation of the city's Avenue of the Arts performing arts district along Broad Street. Philadelphia lawyer Stephanie W. Naidoff took Septee's vision and turned it into a reality. When she accepted the post as president of the Kimmel Center Regional Performing Arts Center, many doubted a performing arts center would ever be built. Naidoff navigated and built consensus through some intense conflicts between Mayor Ed Rendell and developer William Rouse III. Her vision and tenacity helped to make the Kimmel Regional Performing Arts Center a showplace on Philadelphia's Avenue of the Arts.[15]

At his death in 2001, Meyer P. Potamkin, a banker, and his wife Vivian had assembled one of the finest private collections of American art in the United States, with special emphasis on masters like Georgia O'Keeffe, Red Grooms, Winslow Homer, Mary Cassatt, and John Sloan.[15] They donated to the Art Museum seven oil paintings and one watercolor by members of the artist group known as The Eight, which museum director Anne d'Harnoncourt has described as "clearly stars" among its holdings.[16]

Nor have the interests of Jewish philanthropists and businessmen been limited to fine arts. Ray Posel, a lawyer-businessman with a passion for films, offers patrons high-quality movies in the Ritz movie theaters he opened. "Almost single-handedly, Posel has turned the Philadelphia market from a foreign and art film backwater into one of the country's premier markets," a movie columnist for the *Philadelphia Inquirer* wrote.[17]

Through an aggressive campaign against graffiti, Jane Golden, director of the Philadelphia Mural Arts Program, has helped beautify the city, particularly poorer areas. Under her guidance, more than 100,000 inner-city children have helped to transform their neighborhoods and the city itself. "The most successful thing we did for these kids," Golden says, "was to take them out of the cycle of crime." Her efforts have enabled Philadelphia to feature the largest number of murals of any city in the United States.[18]

The heightened role of Jews in philanthropy, however, has had a downside. "Well-to-do Jews are giving ever larger gifts to institutions outside the Jewish community," Jack Wertheimer, provost and chief academic officer of the Jewish Theological Seminary, reports. "Their gifts to Jewish institutions, if they exist at all, are a fraction of what they are bestowing upon nonsectarian institutions or institutions outside of the Jewish community. When there are families that do give some of their wealth to Jewish institutions, the size of those gifts are dwarfed by those to the university, the museum, or the hospital."[19] Jewish philanthropists still support Jewish institutions, but there is little doubt that the big gifts are going elsewhere.

Part of the reason for this, Tobin suggests, is that "Jews are fully integrated into the larger society; where they go to school, where they work, who they do business with. They generally follow the giving patterns of society as a whole."[20] The 1996–1997 study indicated that less than half of the respondents making gifts of more than $100,000 made a contribution to the Federation, the central vehicle for communal planning and welfare purposes.[21] Moreover, as one communal official points out, some of the younger "dot comers" are new to the process of philanthropy. They were raised often in families not accustomed to charitable giving. This, together with the fact that Philadelphia is a community with little economic and industrial growth, defines one of the more serious challenges to the Jewish philanthropic process.

Another indication of the broader acceptance of Jews is their continuing and increasing role in politics despite their small numbers in the population. Senator Arlen Specter, a moderate Republican who makes his home in Philadelphia, and was first elected in 1981, continues to win reelection with strong support from parts of the state known for their lack of affection for the city. In 1995, sensing a vacuum and anxious to keep the GOP from falling into the hands of the Far Right, he launched a bid to gain the Republican presidential nomination. The campaign failed, but his candidacy suggests how high Jewish aspirations could now reach.[22] Several years earlier (in 1991), Ed Rendell was elected as the first Jewish mayor of Philadelphia. Further north and west in Montgomery County, Jon Fox, a Republican, and Marjorie Margolies Mezvinsky, a Democrat, have represented that area in Congress. Another Jewish politician who appears to have a bright career ahead of her is State Senator Alyson Schwartz, a Democrat whose district encompasses Philadelphia and Montgomery Counties, including Cheltenham Township West and East Mount Airy, West Oak Land, Fox Chase, and Chestnut Hill.

In their study, *The Jew Within: Self, Family and Community in America,* authors Steven N. Cohen, associate professor at the Melton School for Jewish Education at the Hebrew University in Jerusalem, and Arnold M. Eisen, professor of religious studies at Stanford University, describe the system of belief and behavior among the baby boomer generation of Jews: "Their connection to Israel . . . is weak, as is the connection they feel to the organized Jewish community in America. They take for granted the compatibility of being both Jewish and American: this is simply not an issue anymore. . . . They want to be Jewish because of what it means to them personally—not because of obligation to the Jewish group . . . or the historical destiny of the Jewish group." Asked about their emotional attachment to Israel, just 9 percent of respondents answered "extremely attached" (as opposed to 13 percent in a similar survey in 1988). Only 20 percent in the survey thought it was essential for a good Jew to support Israel, and even fewer (18 percent) had similar views with regard to visiting Israel in the course of one's life.[23]

On matters involving religious observance, Cohen and Eisen found "an unprecedented exercise of autonomy." Three quarters of the Jews who participated in their national study agreed, "I have a right to reject those Jewish observances that I don't find meaningful." The principal authority for contemporary American Jews, the authors write, is "the sovereign self."[24] In Philadelphia, the 1996–1997 study reported that area Jews gravitated toward family- and child-centered behavior that is not labor intensive and did not differentiate them too much from their non-Jewish cohorts. Thus, 74 percent took part in a Passover seder, and 71 percent lit Hanukkah candles.[25]

Not surprisingly, interfaith marriage—the ultimate test of broader acceptance—is a fact of life among Jews. Between 1984 and 1997, the intermarriage rate among respondents in the five county areas nearly doubled. In the Cohen–Eisen national study of broader Jewish population currents, 80 percent agreed that "intermarriage is inevitable in an open society."[26] Some 50 percent said it was "racist" to oppose marriages between Jews and non-Jews.[27] While the 1996–1997 Jewish Population Study reports that intermarried couples did express some interest in Jewish rituals, culture, and education, most reported a lower level of Jewish engagement than partners born or raised Jewish.[28]

The problem of lessening Jewish identification is found especially among younger Jews. They have had no experience with World War II, the Holocaust, Israel's creation and struggle for survival, and, in most instances, prejudice and discrimination. Driving issues of the past, such as the Soviet Jewry movement and the threat of anti-Semitism, no longer exist or have been sharply reduced. The Federation 1996–1997 study indicates that only 21 percent of Jews ages 35 and younger contribute to the Federation. In turn, two-thirds of that group donate to non-Jewish causes.[29]

Jews, in short, are becoming like other Americans. An example may be in their political responses. There are indications that Jews may be moving to the right, in line with more conservative tendencies Americans have manifested recently. Since the days of Franklin D. Roosevelt, of course, Jews have been prototypical liberals. Jews still vote heavily Democratic in national elections. However, at local and state levels where the here-and-now problems of crime and social disruption are felt most acutely, Democrats can no longer take their votes for granted.[30]

The first indication of this in Philadelphia occurred in the aftermath of the turbulent 1960s. The latter brought with them racial disorders and widespread destruction of property along Columbia and Ridge Avenues (see Chapter 5). Jewish businesses were particularly hard hit. Former police commissioner Frank L. Rizzo, a "tough cop" and a conservative, received a considerable number of Jewish votes in his two races for mayor, but this vote was divided along class lines. More affluent Jews tended to cast their ballots more heavily for his opponents. In marked contrast, in middle- to lower-middle-class divisions in the Northeast and elsewhere, Jews gave a majority of their votes to Rizzo.[31] In 1983 and again in 1987, W. Wilson Goode, an African American and a Democrat, received only 30 percent and 25 percent of the Jewish vote, respectively. However, Jews cast more votes for him than did any other white group in the city.[32]

The election of former district attorney, Ed Rendell, a Democrat who is Jewish and who served two terms, brought Jews back to their normal Democratic moorings. However, in the 1999 mayoral race, Jews cast ballots overwhelmingly for Sam Katz (82 percent), a Republican running against John Street, who narrowly squeaked by to victory.[33] Katz is Jewish and a moderate. However, in the presidential race the following year, a curious dichotomy became apparent, as reported in an exit poll of local Jewish voters conducted for the *Jewish Exponent* by the Zogby International polling firm. While Jews as a whole supported the Gore-Lieberman ticket overwhelmingly (almost 78 percent), a sharp split developed among older and younger Jews. Broken down by age, the results showed a steady decline among the generations in the rate of Jewish support for the Democratic presidential ticket, from 95 percent among voters age 65 years and older, down to 82 percent among voters age 30 to 49. Thereafter, support for Gore plummeted among voters ages 18 to 29. Gore received only 41 percent of that vote. The remaining 59 percent polled supported Bush.[34] Significantly, Rick Santorum, the Republican senatorial incumbent, widely seen as a hard-line conservative, received some 41 percent of the Jewish vote, according to the Zogby-*Exponent* poll.

The argument that Jews are moving to the right, however, can be pressed too far. As David Hyman, president of the local chapter of the American Jewish Committee, who is active in local Philadelphia politics, declared in an election postscript, "The gross numbers show the news remains the same. Seventy-five to 80 percent of the Jewish community continued to support the Democratic nominee for president. It's a pretty steady baseline for as long as I can remember."

It is noteworthy, too, that in every instance in which African American candidates have run for high office here, Jews have voted in higher proportions for them than have other whites. Jews have played a significant role in the Street administration. In this respect, tensions between blacks and Jews, which were at a height when the first edition of this book went to press—Jesse Jackson had made his famous "Hymietown" remark, characterizing New York, in his presidential race in 1984—have calmed considerably. Strong lines of communication continue to exist between leaders in the two communities. Following Jackson's "Hymietown" remark, blacks and Jews closed ranks through the creation of Operation Understanding, founded by former Congressman Bill Gray and George Ross, a former chair of the local American Jewish Committee chapter. Now in its sixteenth year, OU, which is also sponsored by the Urban League, sends incoming African American and Jewish high school seniors to Africa and Israel and other areas of the country each summer to explore each other's histories and traditions. The Jewish Community Relations Council also has worked closely with African American leaders through the Black-Jewish Coalition. A momentary flair-up occurred in 1997, following a confrontation between whites and blacks in the Grays Ferry area of the city. Some Jewish leaders were infuriated when Mayor Rendell joined with the head of the Nation of Islam, Louis Farrakhan, widely viewed by Jews as anti-Semitic, in an effort to calm things. The episode, however, quickly blew over.

Having reported a weakening of the ties that have bound Jews together over the years, it is also important to note the existence of countervailing forces or tendencies. The demographic losses Philadelphia Jewry has sustained have been lessened somewhat by an infusion of Jews from the former Soviet Union. Beginning in the 1970s and accelerating heavily in the late 1980s following the collapse of the Soviet Union, some 35,000 Russians, virtually all Jewish, have arrived in Philadelphia.

Most have settled in the Northeast in Bustleton, Fox Chase, Somerton, and other sections west of Roosevelt Boulevard. Their attraction to Philadelphia grew in part because of the contact many had had with a number of Philadelphia Soviet Jewry advocacy networks prior to their departure.[35] Most, of course, have had little or no exposure to Judaism in the Soviet Union, but vigorous efforts have been undertaken by the Jewish Family and Children's Service, the Klein Branch of the Jewish Community Centers of Greater Philadelphia, and other communal bodies to enhance their sense of Jewish identification.[36] The presence of so many Russian Jews has pumped new energy into Northeast Philadelphia's Jewish community, even as many, following the trajectory of their co-religionists here, are moving into Lower Bucks or Eastern Montgomery counties.[37]

Recent years also have witnessed the growth of new pockets of Jewish energy. Chief among these is the spurt in religious Orthodoxy and Orthodox activity here. An older generation that often did not live a religious life has died off and been replaced by younger Orthodox Jews who are showing greater commitment to following *halacha,* Jewish law.

A case in point has been the experience of Lower Merion Synagogue. In 1981, the Orthodox community in the area had grown to about one hundred families, and a separate wing had to be constructed to offer more space for services and programs. Twenty years later, however, growth in size and participation at the synagogue has inspired a $3.5 million building campaign to replace the worn-down, three-story house on Old Lancaster Road in Bala Cynwyd with a new, modern facility. "Younger people are coming to study [on the Main Line], to do medical school rotations," David Lebor, co-president of the synagogue says, "They like the community well enough to stay on."[38]

In addition to being better educated Jewishly, the 30-something Orthodox are more secure in Orthodoxy, and more confident in their practice, than previous generations. Lower Merion Synagogue is only one of a handful of growing congregations ranging from modern Orthodox to *haredi* (more intensely) Orthodox. The locale—if one includes Overbrook Park as well—includes two *eruvim* (an artificially constructed boundary usually denoted by a wall or wires, in which Jews who are strictly observant can perform work, such as pushing a stroller, without violating the Sabbath), *mikvahot* (or ritual baths) for men and women, and the Torah Academy of Greater Philadelphia. In addition, Akiba Hebrew Academy, a community school, thrives in the area. There is also a sizable Orthodox community across the Delaware River in Cherry Hill, New Jersey, and growing activity in Bucks County. In 2001, the *Jewish Exponent* reported plans being made to construct an *eruv* in Center City. Another eruv was being constructed in West Philadelphia to serve the Orthodox community at the University of Pennsylvania.[39] The *eruf* that presently exists in Elkins Park was established with the help of Conservative and Reform rabbis.

Although we have reported the Jewish population in the Northeast is declining, one exception is the Orthodox community in Rhawnhurst. The neighborhood has an eruv; two schools, the Politz Hebrew Academy of Philadelphia and the Stern Hebrew High School; mikvahot; a handful of kosher restaurants and markets; and a number of synagogues.

Two outreach groups, Aish Hatorah Philadelphia and Lubavitch of the Main Line, have set up two storefronts on Montgomery Avenue to provide entry-level activities into the community for non-observant Jews. The growth of the Orthodox community is reflected not only in the number of institutions, but also in the greater availability of kosher food. Genuardi's Family Markets has three kosher food counters in the Philadelphia area—in their Wynnewood, St. David's, and Rockledge locations. Business is booming, the director of food services there reports. Acme Markets, Inc., has also opened a kosher food counter in its Bala Cynwyd site; Shop Rite has done the same in the Northeast.[40] "The fact that these companies [Genuardi's, Acme Markets, and others] have seen the benefit to their bottom line in providing kosher products to their customers suggests that Jewish observance is no longer relegated to the margins of American society," the *Jewish Exponent* editorially exults.[41]

Kosher Jewish fast-food restaurants also are flourishing, creating a new mix of modern American marketing and ancient tradition. It is true that one cannot order a Philly cheese steak at Safta's, the new kosher takeout in Bucks County, but this has not slowed the more than one-third of the 12,000 community members who follow strict dietary laws of the Torah and patronize the facility. "I love getting a break from cooking," Harriet Shamis, 48, a Bensalem resident who keeps kosher in her home, says. "Being kosher in Bucks County is impossible because you can't run to McDonald's with the kids when you're tired. You always have to cook. . . . When Safta's opened, I was thrilled that I could get a break."[42]

In addition, the Reform and Conservative religious movements are experiencing an intensification of Jewish educational and other programs. Large suburban congregations are reaching out more to intermarried couples. The Reform congregation in Bucks County has a *mikvah,* as does Beth Hillel–Beth El, a Conservative synagogue in Wynnewood.[43] Alternate Jewish services to accommodate special Jewish interests both within and outside of synagogues are growing. The Reform movement, as has been widely noted, has introduced more traditional forms of ritual, including Hebrew, in its services. The Reconstructionist movement and the Reconstructionist Rabbinical College, which is located in Wyncote just outside Philadelphia, have been particularly active.

As Dr. Ernest Kahn indicates in his new essay in this book, we are witnessing what might be called the "Judaization" of the Federation, at both the board and the staff levels. (This is a trend seen among national Jewish organizations as well.) Worried about the impact of assimilation, intermarriage, and diminishing population, late in July 2001 the Federation's Task Force on Jewish Day Schools decided to boost funding for area day schools, bringing funding for these institutions up to about $1,000 per pupil, a step toward equalizing funding to local day schools. Philadelphia is among the highest per capita providers for Jewish education in the United States.[44] Significantly, day-school education has expanded in area institutions such as Abrams Hebrew Academy, the Raymond and Ruth Perelman Jewish Day Schools, and Stern Hebrew High School. It is also expected that passage of Governor Tom Ridge's 2001 education reform package, providing significant tax write-offs to corporations for contributions made for religious and secular private schools, will further strengthen these institutions.[45]

A concerted effort has been made by Jewish leadership to develop a strong attachment to Israel among area youth. The Federation has created a "Passport to Israel" program that provides subsidies for youth trips to Israel. In 1998, the Federation spent an estimated $500,000 toward programs that develop Israeli experiences for youth.

In the past twenty-five years, there has been a burst of Jewish intellectual and cultural vigor locally that has not been seen since the early years of the twentieth century, when, as one of the authors wrote, Philadelphia was "the capital of Jewish America."[46] In 2001 the National Museum of American Jewish History, located in the Independence Hall area in historic Congregation Mikva Israel, celebrated its first quarter of a century. The museum, which is visited each year by thousands from all over the United States, has more than ten thousand artifacts in its collection depicting Jewish life in America. The facility offers education, exhibits, and programs that deal with American Jewish history and culture. At its quarter of a century celebration, it featured Senator Joseph Lieberman and his wife Hadassah as honorary chairs.

A revived Philadelphia Jewish Archives Center, sponsored initially by the Philadelphia Chapter of the American Jewish Committee and now the Federation, houses the records of the community's philanthropic, organizational, religious, and business endeavors. Jewish scholarship in the area has expanded. Jewish Studies programs exist at Drexel, Temple University, and the University of Pennsylvania. Through a gift from the Annenbergs, former Dropsie University, including its world-famous Judaica collection, has been merged with Jewish academic programming at the University of Pennsylvania in the Center for Judaic Studies, headed by the distinguished historian, David Ruderman.[47] The Center invites the leading Jewish scholars from around the world to come to the Center for a year and focus on a specific topic. It also has sought to bring some of this scholarship into the broader community.

In 1990 Temple University and the local chapter of the American Jewish Committee launched the Myer and Rosaline Feinstein Center for American Jewish History. The Center's major thrust has been to identify important vacuums in the study of Philadelphia and American Jewish history and arrange consortiums of Jewish scholars to fill them. Since its inception, the Center has sponsored the publication of a number of books and articles, including *When Philadelphia Was the Capital of Jewish America,* edited by Murray Friedman; *A Second Exodus: The American Movement to Free Soviet Jews,* edited by Friedman and Albert Chernin; a special issue of the professional journal, *American Jewish History,* "American Jewish Political Conservatism"; *Women and American Judaism: Historical Perspectives,* edited by Pamela S. Nadell and Jonathan D. Sarna; and *Passover Revisited: Philadelphia's Efforts to Aid Soviet Jews, 1963–1998,* by Andrew Harrison. The Center provides summer fellowships, a doctoral prize, and other grants to encourage younger scholars to enter the comparatively new field of the professional study of American Jewish history.

Norwegian historian Marcus Hansen has declared with great insight that what the fathers want to forget, the children seek to remember. Even as religiosity, save for the Orthodox, interest in Israel, organizations, and various causes that used to anchor identity and shape behavior have declined, there are countercurrents that appear to be growing. Jews, like other Americans, are looking for meaning in their lives. The American Jewish Committee's youth group, Bridges, is one example. The latter's programming indicates an emphasis on the religious and cultural tradition along with social activity. The wearing of the *kipah,* the traditional Jewish skullcap, is everywhere evident on campuses and elsewhere. Hillels are experiencing a revival, as evidenced by heavily attended holiday observances at the University of Pennsylvania and the popularity of its kosher kitchen. About a half dozen years ago, Orthodox students at Penn's Hillel started "Roots," a program that matches college students curious about Jewish texts with tutors. According to Rabbi Howard Alpert, executive director of Hillel of Greater Philadelphia, participation varies from twenty to sixty partners per year.[48]

It may be an indication of positive change underway that in the fall of 2001, philanthropist Sidney Kimmel, who had given substantial sums earlier for the Kimmel Center for the Performing Arts and other major secular charities, announced record-breaking gifts to the Jewish Federation of Greater Philadelphia and the Raymond and Ruth Perelman Jewish Day School. Each will receive $1 million a year, with the institutions getting $20 million each upon his death. (A day before the opening of the Kimmel Center, Kimmel, age 73, emotionally celebrated his bar mitzva at the Perelman Jewish Day School's synagogue in Wynnewood.[49]) Simultaneously, other Jewish donors who have been giving large sums to nonsectarian civic institutions in recent years were discussing with Jewish agencies the possibility of increased gifts. What we may be seeing is that the rush for broader civic approval by Jewish philanthropists in the post-war years and beyond is being overtaken by growing concerns about the Jewish future.

In their 2000 study, Steven M. Cohen and Arnold M. Eisen highlight the ambivalence that seems to characterize the Jewish community at the turn of the century. The "sovereign self," an ethos that weakens traditional religion, religious practice, and organizational life, continues to remain prominent. The labor of fashioning a Jewish self, however, remains significant to moderately affiliated American Jews, the authors add. "We can state with confidence that the quest for Jewish meaning is extremely important to our subjects, just as the search for meaning is important to contemporary Americans more generally. . . . Far from leaving faith behind in favor of secular national or communal loyalties, as many of the parents and grandparents did, the Jews we interviewed are dissatisfied with secular affiliations and are in search of personal spiritual meaning."[50]

Even the high rate of intermarriage, which alarmed the organized Jewish community when it was first reported in the National Jewish Population study in 1990, seems more complicated with the passage of time. Steve Bayme, director of the Jewish Communal Affairs Department of the American Jewish Committee, continues to view intermarriage as a disaster for the Jewish community. Others, like Brooklyn College sociologist Egon Mayer and Brown University sociologist Calvin Goldscheider, however, argue that intermarriage can be positive, particularly if the Jewish community reaches out and family and friends seek the conversion of the Christian partner. There are indications, nevertheless, that the children of mixed marriages are lost to the Jewish community unless conversion takes place.[51]

Here in the Philadelphia area, we are witnessing other signs of vitality, including the growth of collaborative efforts in Center City, Buxmont, and City Line Avenue, among synagogues and the organized Jewish community to battle against the erosion of Jewish identity. Casting aside institutional affinities, the seven congregations along Old York Road have set up and operate joint adult educational programs. These congregations also have been cooperating with Young Israel, an Orthodox body in the area, in creating an eruv. The Federation has been working with cluster groups to enhance their fund-raising capabilities. And, as has been indicated, the Federation has allocated increasing funds for Jewish education.

How can we make sense of these contradictory currents? What do they portend for Jewish life in the coming years? Pessimists argue that, freed from the crippling disabilities of the past and governed increasingly by the "sovereign self," the older traditions and forms are being cast aside and the future appears grim—that it is only in Israel and among the Orthodox that the maintenance of Jewish life can be assured. A number of students of Jewish life, however, are more positive, or at least more hopeful. Sociologists Calvin Goldscheider and Alan S. Zuckerman at Brown argue in *The Transformation of the Jews* that, in fact, the Jewish population in the United States is growing and that the intermarriage rate is not as high as has been usually reported. Moreover, the Jewish past in this country has not always been the "golden age" it has often been portrayed to be. From this vantage point, the Jewish community may be seen as less in decline than as transforming itself. The fact is that Jewish life has always been voluntary and must continue necessarily to remain so today.

Cohen and Eisen carry the argument a step further. Thoroughly aware of the threats and dangers, they report nevertheless that the moderately affiliated Jews they studied are "far from indifferent to Judaism and things Jewish." They "feel no need to express or enact their identity in regular activity. Judaism is rather an 'inner thing,' a point of origin, a feature of experience, an object of reflection." American Jews have opted for "a group identity that is characteristic of late modern religion, culture, and communal forms—and have also developed new patterns that seem to us best described as postmodern." "They express affection for and loyalty to the Jewish people. . . . They even exhibit a significant degree of belief in God, though the God they believe in differs from the one portrayed in the blessings they recite at home and the prayers they say in the synagogue." The tendency is toward privatization (as in celebration of Passover) and personalization. This form of "pick and choose Judaism," in short, is still loyal to the past and is struggling to find new ways of expression.[52] In any case, it is something, we would add, that can be built upon.

Philadelphia Jewry has played a proud role in helping to recast the Jewish community of

America in newer terms. At the turn of the century and at a time of large-scale immigration, such figures as Judge Mayer Sulzberger, Cyrus Adler, and Rabbi Sabato Morais, working with leadership in New York and elsewhere, created many of the institutional forms on which American Jewish life came to rest. If some of the emerging newer scholarship is correct and the Jewish community is in transition rather than in meltdown, the challenge beckons once again to join with others in the country to create the new Jewish community of the twenty-first century and beyond.

Fourth and Morris in South Philadelphia —
shopping for Passover, 1940

FROM OUTSIDERS TO INSIDERS?
Philadelphia Jewish Life, 1940–1985

Murray Friedman

Following army service in World War II, Marvin Comisky, a short, portly lawyer with an infectious grin, was practicing law with a Jewish law partner in the Suburban Station Building in the Center City section of Philadelphia. A brilliant law student (he would later serve as chancellor of the Philadelphia Bar Association), he found upon graduation from the University of Pennsylvania Law School in 1941 that while eighteen to twenty of his fellow students with lower class standing, none of them Jewish, had quickly found jobs in large, established law firms, he had difficulty getting placed. Comisky became friendly with a partner in one of these firms in his building who asked one day whether he would be interested in joining his firm. Told that he would, his friend checked into it, only to later report ruefully that he could not "sell the idea" of hiring a Jewish lawyer, however capable.[1]

Comisky's experience was typical of that faced by many talented and ambitious young Philadelphia Jews during the periods prior to and immediately following World War II. In his book, *Philadelphia Gentlemen,* University of Pennsylvania sociologist E. Digby Baltzell described the city in 1940 as divided into rigid parallel social systems.[2] Though relative insiders in the life of the community over a century earlier, Jews were now firmly locked out of the citadels of Anglo-Saxon power.[3] Anti-Semitism was at its height between 1930 and 1940. The patterns of exclusion were strong not only toward such brash newcomers from East European backgrounds as Comisky, but also toward more established figures who had fought their way into the system, such as real estate and department store tycoon Albert M. Greenfield. With a few exceptions, Jews found themselves excluded from the city's major status-conferring institutions. The prominent paper box manufacturer and music lover, Fredric R. Mann, who had helped secure a grant from City Council for the Philadelphia Orchestra, was dropped from its board after three seasons. "Fred's aggressiveness and outspoken ways offended the Board," a member was to tell the historian of the orchestra.[4] Elite Philadelphians were aghast (but could do little) when in 1936 Moses Annenberg, who had made a fortune in the billion-dollar-a-year racetrack gambling industry, purchased the staid, old *Philadelphia Inquirer,* the "Bible" of the city's more conservative elements since Andrew Jackson's time.[5]

If the upwardly mobile and "aggressive" East European Jews worried old, aristocratic Philadelphia families, members of the older and more assimilated German-Jewish group fared only a little better. A few found acceptance in the city's civic structures but were never permitted into any of the inner circles. Little had changed since 1900 when, as John Lukacs has written, there was less "opportunity to move into the city's elite, upper class than any other American (let alone European) town."[6] When Horace Stern, a founder of the distinguished Jewish law firm, Wolf, Block, Schorr and Solis-Cohen, was elected to the Pennsylvania Supreme Court in 1935—later going on to become chief justice—he could be seen at lunch each day, along with one of his colleagues, carrying his tray to a table at the Colonnade Cafeteria on Walnut Street rather than suffer embarrassment by going to the Union League, where Jews could come as guests but were not welcome as members.

The Philadelphia Jewish community had more or less stabilized at an estimated 245,000 people. It had grown by only about 10,000, or 4 percent, since 1924.[7] Contrasting it with New York

Left: Albert M. Greenfield in 1949.

Right: Horace Stern.

earlier in the century, Henry James declared it to be "the American city of the large type, that didn't bristle . . . couldn't and wouldn't ever."[8]

In its backwater ways, Philadelphia was more akin to Baltimore than to New York. If anti-Semitism was an ever-present and worrisome reality, the city during the war and the immediate post-war years was, nevertheless, a warm and secure world of neighborhoods. Comedian David Brenner, who grew up in West Philadelphia, would later describe it as the "largest, friendliest village in the world."[9] While some of the city wards in South Philadelphia and Strawberry Mansion still retained a considerable number of Jewish residents, the trend was away from this area to Logan and northern areas of the city. Two West Philadelphia sections, particularly Wynnefield, had gained a substantial Jewish population.[10] In these neighborhoods, a rich and vibrant Jewish life took hold. The South Philadelphia Hebrew All-Stars (SPHAS), one of the nation's best teams, recruited only Jewish players and performed regularly at the Saturday night "Basketball and Dance" at the Broadwood Hotel. As Ron Avery notes, many of Philadelphia's younger Jews first met here on basketball night and married.[11] Today older residents still recall with pleasure Passover in Strawberry Mansion, when all the grocery stores "devoted window space for holiday displays and clothing and shoe stores did a thriving business in outfitting the children with their new garments and footwear."[12]

The Marshall Street area located between 6th and 7th Streets on either side of Girard near Center City was a bustling market area similar to the Lower East Side in New York. Local Jewish families came here every day to purchase their daily needs from pushcarts or shops. Nearby communities of Poles, Lithuanians, Russians, and Hungarians found Marshall Street catering to them, too. The pickle barrels were never empty; the herrings dripped *schmaltz* (fat). The produce, halavah, and fresh-ground horseradish beckoned to the senses. Women came to try on the latest New York fashions in the local dress shops. A third-grade teacher recalls, "My mother bought fresh fish and floated it in the bathtub. Before Yom Kippur, she brought a live chicken home, twirled it about my head to *schlug kaporis* [transfer the sins]. Then we took the chicken back to be slaughtered."[13] These neighborhoods were a breeding ground for entertainers such as David Brenner, Joey Bishop, and Eddie Fisher, many of whom continue to come back to visit the old neighborhood.

Nostalgic memories, however, do not hide the pain and suffering experienced by poor Jews, little different, of course, than the hardships of Irish and WASP textile workers in Kensington. The harshness of their environment fueled a desperate need to rise and join the broader society. In his book, *Soft Pretzels and Mustard*, Brenner describes how growing up poor in West Philadelphia spurred him on. It came naturally, he said. His uncle had been one of the city's rabbis, his Aunt Esther was among the first women to graduate from the Philadelphia School of Pharmacy, and brother Melvin would become a distinguished sociology professor at the University of Wisconsin. "Four hundred years of Brenner poverty stops here," he vowed.

Jews in the immediate post-war years were a transitional generation whose greatest talent, perhaps, was the ability to synthesize the immigrant Jewish experience and the American urban culture in which they found themselves. One study of metropolitan Philadelphia found that between 1954 and 1958, 94 percent of Reform Jews, 78 percent of Conservative Jews, and even a small majority of Orthodox Jews had been born in the United States. Only a handful had not gone beyond the eighth grade by this time.[14] Religiosity, at least as measured by more traditional forms of observance, even among the Orthodox, was on the decline.

Religious discrimination was a serious problem, but in retrospect, it would now appear, it served as a hurdle to be overcome rather than as an insurmountable barrier. Studies conducted by the Jewish Community Relations Council and Fellowship Commission of graduating Jewish seniors who applied to medical schools in Philadelphia and elsewhere in the 1950s found that while Jews might not have gotten their first choice, a surprisingly large number found acceptance somewhere.[15] Their strong educational background and middle-class skills honed over the centuries, coupled with a society that was undergoing major economic expansion, made their rise all but inevitable.

Even before the Great Depression—and then in greater numbers after the war—many had become teachers in the city's public schools. Teaching was seen not only as a respectable career, but also as a means of indulging a liberal bent to improve society. Celia Pincus, who later became the first head of the Philadelphia Federation of Teachers, reminisced, "When I taught at Barrett Junior High School at 16th and Wharton during the depression the teachers fed hungry students. We'd say, 'All right, 15 cents per teacher feeds eight hungry kids for the day.'"[16] Some had advanced to middle-echelon administrative posts and beyond. A milestone was reached in 1957 when David Horowitz, a veteran educator, was named district superintendent of a heavily Protestant area.[17] As a result of their working-class background, a number of Jews had risen to head major trade unions: Joseph Schwartz, the Knit Goods Workers; Samuel Otto and later William Ross, International Ladies Garment Workers; Mike Harris, United Steelworkers; and, of course, "Cel" Pincus.

Locked out of the major banking, law, insurance, and industrial organizations, Jews flowed elsewhere. Some dreamed up opportunities not thought of by the older WASP business leadership. In the post-war expansion that featured the trek to the suburbs, Sam Cooke and George Friedland pioneered in the establishment of the Penn Fruit and Food Fair supermarket chains. Here, under one roof, they provided customers with a wide variety of services—at discount prices—becoming serious rivals and even overtaking the local A&P and Acme markets.[18] The newly established elec-

Eddie and Liz, May 12, 1959, the day after their Las Vegas nuptials in Temple Beth Shalom. Probably his second most famous moment.

William Ross, 1973, described himself as "tough-skinned."

Samuel Cooke, founder of Penn Fruit.

Governor Milton J. Shapp at a 1973 conference.

Left: Walter Annenberg in the late 1960s.

Right: J. David Stern, publisher of the *Philadelphia Review*, 1944.

tronics industry attracted Milton Shapp, who set up Jerrold Electronics, while Morris Kravitz founded Kravco, Inc., developer of a series of shopping centers in Philadelphia and nearby areas. Later, under its former attorney at Wolf–Block, Myles Tannenbaum, Kravco developed the vast King of Prussia Mall, said to be the largest in the world at that time.

In the soft goods field, Jews continued to remain figures of importance. Major area firms by the early 1960s included H. Daroff and Sons, L'Aiglon Dresses, Rosenau children's clothes, and Robert Bruce sportswear. Jews were important in the local cigar business (Bayuk, Consolidated); the liquor industry (Publicker, Jacquin, Kasser); entertainment (the Goldman, Shubert, Stanley, Milgram, Ellis, and Shapiro movie theater chains); and the industrial realty field (Frank Binswanger, Albert Grosser, Strouse-Greenberg). Local Jews had made significant inroads into the communications field. Issac and Leon Levy were major stockholders in CBS (run by another Philadelphian, William Paley), William and Harry Sylk owned radio station WPEN (as well as a network of drugstores), while William Banks and Max Leon controlled WHAT and WDAS, respectively.

Two Jewish businessmen, however, stood out among all the rest. Walter Annenberg became editor and publisher of the *Philadelphia Inquirer* in 1942 following the imprisonment of his father for income tax evasion. Through Triangle Publications, he came to preside over a vast communications empire that included the Philadelphia Daily News, radio stations WFIL-AM and FM, television station WFIL, the extraordinarily successful *TV Guide,* the monthly *Seventeen,* and many other holdings around the country. All told, one of his biographers writes, Annenberg "amassed a greater concentration of media in one city . . . than any other American communications mogul." Despite these achievements, he was initially dismissed and then shunned by the old Philadelphia elite, who abhorred his father's background and his (in their judgment) ruthless use of power.[19]

In local and national leadership, Albert M. Greenfield matched that of Annenberg. From financial disaster during the Great Depression, Greenfield and his Bankers Security Corporation came back and soon presided over a vast department store chain consisting of Lits and Snellenberg's here and stores in nineteen other states, including Bonwit Teller, Tiffany's, Franklin Simon, W. & J. Sloane, Maison Blanche in New Orleans, and B. Loewenstein's in Memphis. At one point, he owned seven of the nine hotels in Philadelphia, including the Bellevue Stratford, important sections of Society Hill, the Yellow Cab company, and many other financial interests. Through his support of J. David Stern's liberal Philadelphia *Record* and Presidents Roosevelt,

Truman, and Kennedy, he was a force in the local and national Democratic party, thereby estranging himself further from the staunch Republicans of the Protestant establishment.

In the period that followed the war, unlike many of their Italian and Polish neighbors, who tended to remain in their old neighborhoods, even when they attained greater affluence, Jews began to move to outlying sections of the city and suburbs.[20] In 1957, it is estimated that 48,300 lived in Olney–West Oak Lane, and 30,000 and 16,300, respectively, lived in the Wynnefield–Overbrook and Germantown–Chestnut Hill areas. Some 43,400 Jews were also living in the eastern and western suburbs of Abington, Cheltenham, and Lower Merion.[21] Before long, there would be few reminders of the early, large immigrant Jewish ghetto in South Philadelphia; even settlements in Strawberry Mansion and West Philadelphia were fast disappearing.

In the creation of the post-war suburbia, Jewish builders and developers played significant, if not dominant, roles. Fresh from his triumph on Long Island, where he constructed thousands of units of low-cost, mass-produced, and single-family housing, William J. Levitt began buying property in the early 1950s for a similar Levittown project in Bucks County. When he was done, some 17,311 homes were constructed here. In 1958, he built Levittown (now Willingboro), New Jersey, just across the Delaware River from Philadelphia. The typical buyer spent between $10,990 and $20,000 and obtained a house with picture windows, three or four bedrooms, an all-electric kitchen, garage, and a front and back yard. The homes were built in ready-made neighborhoods with streets curved in an attempt to eliminate the monotony of the houses' look-alike designs.[22] This and other developments spurred a significant movement of Jewish population across the river to New Jersey.

Simultaneously, Peter Binzen suggests in his essay that another kind of suburbia was taking shape within the city's borders—the Greater Northeast. Jews living here differed somewhat from those in suburban areas. They were, generally, not as well-to-do. In suburbia, Jews often tended to be dispersed among their Christian neighbors; in the Northeast, they constituted an identifiable Jewish community. As mentioned, in 1957, the Federation of Jewish Agencies estimated that some 48,300 Jews lived in the Near and Far Northeast. By 1984, a comprehensive study commissioned by the Federation estimated that almost 70,000 Jews lived there,[23] making it one of the largest Jewish communities in the United States—larger, for example, than the Jewish communities of Pittsburgh, St. Louis, and Atlanta. As a result, the area came to take on a Jewish ambiance, even though considerably more non-Jews resided there. Politicians were named Greenberg and Eilberg, and even streets like Knorr, Horrocks, and Levick "sounded vaguely semitic."[24]

Levittown homes and Northeast row and twin housing were often derided as "ticky tacky boxes" whose residents were said to live lockstep lives. The fact is, as Binzen writes, the homes there were good, sturdy structures that lasted, even if they were often architecturally unexciting. Moreover, the Kormans, Levitts, Tysons, Madways, and other Jewish builders who were taking America's working and lower middle classes out of congested areas of the city into the country, heretofore the special province of rural America and the country's wealthier classes, were democratizing the culture. Those who opposed them, Herbert Gans writes, often wanted to preserve America as a predominantly Protestant society in which *they* held political and cultural power.[25] Levitt made the point clearly: "Our philosophy says every person deserves a roof over his head, not a high-rise or an apartment, but a house for himself and his family on his own little piece of land." Blacks, it is true, were not yet welcome. This, however, was less because of the prejudices of these developers. Rather the social revolution they were effecting could not be completed in the face of white buyers unwillingly, as yet, to extend the American dream to others.

With the departure of Jews from older, and even newer, post–World War II areas of settlement, it was inevitable that most of the major congregations, including Rodeph Shalom (1959), Adath Jeshurun (1964) and Har Zion (1971), followed their congregants out of the city. (Rodeph Shalom retained its in-town temple at Broad and Mt. Vernon to serve its Center City constituency.) Germantown Jewish Centre (a synagogue despite its name), resisted this trend and sought to integrate its members with the surging black population that grew up all around it. Its rare success, Sydney Schwartz suggests in his essay, was due to the extraordinary efforts of its spiritual leader, Rabbi Elias Charry, the high proportion of academics and young professionals in the area, and, later, the use of innovative devices such as *Havurot* (less formal methods of worship), day care, and other services.

The post-war years saw the continued expansion of Conservative Judaism, which Philadelphia Jewry had helped to pioneer. It was the area's largest Jewish religious grouping. From some twenty-five synagogues in 1945, it grew to thirty-nine in 1955. A decade later, the number stood at forty-six.[26] Its success was due to the ability to provide rising and increasingly suburban-bound children of "Russian" Jews a framework within which they could be "behaviorally Americans while espousing an ideological commitment to tradition."[27] The influence of Har Zion on the growth of Conservative Judaism and Jewish education in Philadelphia, as well as on the national scene, was particularly significant, as Diane King, William Lakritz, and Saul Wachs note in their essay, because of a succession of brilliant and farsighted rabbis.

Reform Judaism, which had remained classically German, experienced growth as well. Rodeph Shalom and Keneseth Israel were joined in 1945 by a small congregation, Beth David, in Wynnefield, that appealed to "Russian" Jews and their children. By 1955 the number had grown to six temples; ten years later, it stood at eleven. Only the number of Orthodox congregations declined in the post-war years, and then only slightly by 1965. The Northeast accounted for the largest number. From only four in the Near Northeast in 1945, the figure had grown to twelve in 1965 and from none to nine in the area beyond Pennypack Park.[28]

In the second or third areas of settlement, where most Jews now lived, a multifaceted Jewish life took shape. "It was not unusual for someone who had little involvement in his or her local shul [synagogue] in the old neighborhood to become quite active in the congregation in the new area of settlement." In addition to worship, congregational activities included youth work, men's and women's groups, and other social activities. Jewish education was transformed from a communal enterprise lodged primarily in Talmud Torahs (afternoon and weekend schools) into a congregational function. In contrast with earlier periods of Jewish life, religion became increasingly child centered. While a fairly high proportion of parents were now affiliated with congregations, often because of the children, the synagogues were not, for the most part, inculcating a strong knowledge of Judaism.[29]

As a result, post-war Jewish religious life in Philadelphia and elsewhere came under attack as a form only of "symbolic identification." It managed, nevertheless, to inculcate some sense of Jewish identity and commitment to Jewish survival that could be built on in the coming years. What critics overlooked, Chaim Waxman writes, was the possibility of formal organizations being able to function in ways other than those intended by the people who erected or used them, especially when circumstances changed dramatically.[30]

The creation of Israel in 1948, the threat to its safety and security in succeeding years, and a delayed but powerful reaction to the Holocaust provided such stimuli. Jews in Philadelphia were confused and divided during World War II toward the Zionist movement. Caught up with their own adjustments to American life, liberal-Left ideologies, problems of anti-Semitism, and the war, they appear to have been more apathetic than even New York Jewry in raising their voices to protest the calamity happening to their brethren in Europe. Indeed, leading elements of the older Jewish elite, including D. Hays Solis-Cohen, Lessing Rosenwald, Rabbis Louis Wolsey of Rodeph Shalom and William Fineschriber of Keneseth Israel, and Morris Wolf played an active role in 1942 in the creation of and leadership of the American Council for Judaism (ACJ) to fight against the creation of a Jewish state. They feared Jews would be charged with "dual loyalty," and the already difficult position Jews faced in the community weakened further. Despite this, there was a strong Zionist movement in the city, led by Judge Louis E. Levinthal and others. Philadelphia became a major collection center for hand and automatic weapons shipped illegally to the Middle East in 1947 from a cache near Doylestown and such unlikely places as the basements of Rittenhouse Square apartments.

With the rise of Israel in the consciousness of Jews, resistance to the ACJ rapidly developed. (Rabbi Wolsey resigned as vice president of the national organization in 1946 because of what he described as the group's negativism.[31]) As the embattled, little Jewish state came to play a more central role in the life of the Jewish community, the role of Jewish philanthropy, particularly the Federation of Jewish Charities and Allied Jewish Appeal, took on growing importance. For much of its history, the focus of the Federation had been on assisting immigrants or refugees and the relief of the poor and incapacitated locally. Now it enlarged its role by helping to foster Jewish identity among the children of immigrants, who put greater distance between themselves and their ethnic roots. Philanthropy became the one common denominator of participation in the Jewish

community. Soliciting for contributions by the two agencies meant a sacrifice of time and energy by the solicitor and identification with Jewish communal needs. Also, for more successful members of the second generation, the fact that they still found themselves excluded from the larger social structure forced them to seek within the Jewish community the standing to which they felt their economic position entitled them. As Jewish philanthropy expanded, however, there were losses as well as gains. Subsequent years saw the rise of the wealthy, but not necessarily Jewishly informed, "big giver" to leadership roles. This was inevitable given the costs of running what were becoming multi-million-dollar structures, but it was less likely now that Philadelphia Jewry would see the likes of brilliant scholar-leaders like Judge Mayer Sulzberger, Cyrus Adler, and Rabbi Sabato Morais, who had earlier helped to fashion many of the communal institutions on which Jewish life in America rested.

The waning hostility between German and East European Jews, and the impending retirement of the executive heads of the Federation of Jewish Charities and Allied Jewish Appeal, led to their merger in 1956. A few months earlier, Donald B. Hurwitz came to Philadelphia from Cleveland, Ohio, to serve as executive head of the newly formed Federation of Jewish Agencies. Undergirding the augmented role of the Federation was the *Jewish Exponent,* an old and respected English-Jewish weekly purchased by the Federation and Allied in 1944. The *Exponent* that came to the home of Jewish contributors each Friday was to become a primary means of communication in the Jewish community. Communal sponsorship of the *Exponent* "cast it into a popular mode of rose colored (and middle class) respectability" rather than as a vehicle for probing deeply into the problems of the Jewish community, its historian, Maxwell Whiteman, suggested (interestingly enough, in the pages of the *Exponent* itself).[32] By the early 1960s, its circulation exceeded 52,000, with the number of readers estimated at 200,000. As a result of the *Exponent*'s extraordinary success, Federations in Newark, San Francisco, Omaha, Pittsburgh, and other cities soon followed suit by creating or purchasing their own newspapers. In 1976, the Federation purchased and began publishing the more "populist" *Jewish Times,* which emphasized news about the Northeast as well as general Jewish activities.

Concurrent with the increase in influence of the Federation, the growth of its local and national services, and the network of temples and synagogues, there had also developed a flourishing Jewish organizational life consisting of B'nai B'rith lodges and chapters, Hadassah, Brith Sholom, Zionist, Bonds for Israel, and other groups, as well as Jewish community relations bodies like the Anti-Defamation League, the American Jewish Committee, and the American Jewish Congress. To outsiders, this kaleidoscope of activity sometimes seemed frenetic and bewildering,

Cyrus Adler in 1937.

but the groups provided a rich array of services, opportunities for socialization, and group identification. Jewish life may have become "overorganized," but somehow it worked.

Caught up as they were in their upward climb in American life, Jews nevertheless threw themselves into a variety of liberal, social, and political causes. As Friedman and Beck report in their essay, through organizations such as the Philadelphia Fellowship Commission and Jewish Community Relations Council, local branches of national Jewish "defense" agencies, and individuals like Maurice B. Fagan (who headed both the Fellowship Commission and JCRC) and Morris Milgram (leader of the integrated housing movement), Jews were in the forefront of the battle against prejudice and discrimination and efforts to broaden civil liberties. Their identification with and passion for improving the condition of the disadvantaged and discriminated against had brought most Philadelphia Jews into the Democratic party and association with liberal-Left causes in the 1930s and 1940s.

This relationship with the political Left was to become a source of considerable controversy. As early as the mid-1930s, it had become clear that Local 192 of the heavily Jewish American Federation of Teachers in Philadelphia had come under Communist domination. This was fought by Celia Pincus and others who wanted the union to focus on bread-and-butter issues rather than ideological and political objectives. Early in 1941, this local along with others in three other cities was expelled from the AFT.[33] By the late 1940s, however, as the Cold War with the Soviet Union heated up, the Communist issue came forward more sharply. In 1948, the Smith Act was invoked against the Communist party in the United States, and two years later the loyalty-security issue reached a high point with the passage of the McCarran Act. In Pennsylvania, a loyalty act known as the Pechan Law was enacted and went into effect in 1952.

While the loyalty campaigns here and elsewhere were not directed against Jews as such, given their liberal-Left politics and activist roles in social improvement efforts, a number found themselves under heavy pressure. Except for New York City and Los Angeles (mainly Hollywood), Philadelphia received the most attention among all the large metropolitan areas during the McCarthy era. Ultimately, some seven cases reached the State Supreme Court, and one was argued before the U.S. Supreme Court.[34] The most celebrated episode, however, involved the arrest in May 1950 of Harry Gold, a chemist employed at a Philadelphia hospital, who was charged with transmitting wartime atomic bomb secrets to Russian agents. Later, Gold was named co-conspirator in the indictment returned by a federal jury in New York City against Ethel and Julius Rosenberg.

The Philadelphia schools became a special target during this time. As a result of investigations by the school board and hearings conducted by the House Un-American Activities Committee (HUAC) in the city in November 1953, some thirty-two teachers associated with the Philadelphia Teachers Union (formerly Local 192, AFT), of whom twenty-two were Jewish, were dismissed. In addition, there were investigations in the Welfare Department and Jefferson Medical College. Of the thirty-four social workers dismissed from the former, some twenty-six or twenty-seven were Jewish, as were all three of the physicians dropped from Jefferson.[35] The latter never told the physicians why they were fired, causing one historian to describe the episode as "the single most egregious violation of academic freedom that occurred during the McCarthy period."[36]

Jews in Philadelphia were thrown on the defensive during the Red Scares of the 1950s. The JCRC, according to Maurice B. Fagan, arranged for a Quaker attorney to defend the welfare workers.[37] In his essay, Paul Lyons shows how one Jewish organization, the American Jewish Congress, "cleaned house" by firing its executive director in 1950, even though it was never clearly established that the latter was a Communist or engaged in Communist-inspired activities. One effect of this effort, Lyons argues, was to force more militant or "progressive" elements of the organized Jewish community to lose interest in it as a vehicle for necessary social change. (This probably exaggerates the long-range impact of the McCarthy era; at the time and in subsequent years, Jews in Philadelphia continued to engage actively in a wide variety of reform activities in and out of their own organizations.)

The vast majority of Jews in Philadelphia, of course, were not Communists, although a high proportion of Philadelphia Communists were Jews.[38] The overwhelming number of leaders of mainstream organizations were never identified as such in local or McCarthy investigations. In fact, a few more assimilated, upper-class Jews took part in the effort to root out what they believed were "unreliable' or "disloyal" elements of local institutions. D. Hays Solis-Cohen, a partner at

Wolf, Block, Schorr and Solis-Cohen, chaired Jefferson's ad hoc committee looking into the charges against the several doctors. He was especially anxious that they "name names," and defended the dismissals as based on "standards for legal and moral conduct."[39] Leading communal figures, Leon Obermayer and Leo Weinrott, were members of the school board—the former its vice president—and were frequent spokespersons explaining its actions.[40] Chief Justice Horace Stern delivered an opinion of the Pennsylvania Supreme Court affirming the action of an Allegheny County court in the dismissal of a teacher for alleged past Communist affiliations.[41] For the most part, these upper-class Jews were conservative Republicans deeply worried about Communist influences in American life. A more penetrating reason, however, is suggested by Victor S. Navasky: Those who denounced children of immigrants felt they were consolidating their identification with the dominant society.[42] A number of older-stock Jews were nevertheless sharp critics of McCarthy-era tactics. (Morris Wolf's granddaughter writes that her mother refused to have anything to do with his law partner, Solis-Cohen, at social gatherings.[43])

The McCarthy witch-hunts comprised one of the shabbiest episodes in our history. Most of the teachers in Philadelphia who joined the Communist party had done so for idealistic reasons and were no longer associated with it by the time of the hearings. They were dismissed because they refused to answer questions of school officials and HUAC or for failure to "name names" of people they had once known as Communists. In 1960, some of the teachers were reinstated with back pay as a result of a decision of the State Supreme Court. The remainder were reinstated in 1967 with no back salary following a U.S. Supreme Court decision. However, only thirteen chose to come back.[44]

The few Jews here who still remained Communists were shocked even further in 1956 by the harsh Soviet response to the Hungarian uprisings and the revelations of Soviet premier Nikita Khrushchev about the crimes of Joseph Stalin. A full three-quarters of the American Communist party membership—people who had stuck it out through the worst of the McCarthy era—quit a year or so after 1956. Some Jews here even turned back to exploring their Jewish roots in the light of the revelations of Soviet anti-Semitism, according to Lyons.[45]

The havoc the Cold War and Red Scare played with the Left, however, had one consequence of perhaps broader significance to the Jewish community here—the formation of the Americans for Democratic Action. During the summer of 1946, many liberals became restless with the increasingly pro-Soviet foreign policy views of members of the Philadelphia Citizens Political Action Committee, the major vehicle of the wartime coalition of liberal and Left elements. In the fall, anti-Communist board members led by Philadelphia blue blood, John F. Lewis, Jr., and Johannes Hoeber, a refugee from Nazi Germany, set up the local ADA chapter,[46] which broadened the interaction of Jews with important elements of the WASP leadership class. Younger members of the latter had returned from the war loosened from narrow attachments by exposure to new experiences and people. The ADA now provided an opportunity to explore these relationships further. Jews active in the ADA included not only members of prominent upper-class Jewish families, such as those of Julius Rosenwald II, Jane Freedman, Edwin Wolf II, and Emily Sunstein, but a group of Jewish labor leaders, including Joseph Schwartz, business manager of the nine-thousand-member Knit Goods Workers Union; Harry Block, director of the Philadelphia United Electrical Workers; Harry Ferleger, the AFL representative to the Community Chest and executive director of ADA from 1948 to 1951; William Rafsky, research director of the American Federation of Hosiery Workers; and Leon Shull, who had been director of the Jewish Labor Committee from 1951 to 1964. Labor participation had a great deal to do with old-line Socialist opposition to Communism and the need to find a satisfactory liberal outlet.

In the process of working together, the Protestant elite gained access to the organizational and political skills Jews had honed over the years in philanthropic and trade union activity. The labor leaders also provided a constituency for political campaigns and filled tables at the ADA's annual Roosevelt Day fund-raising affairs. In turn, Jews from immigrant and working-class backgrounds were able to broaden their civic skills by interacting with business and civic leaders.[47] Jewish liberalism was not only a political posture that fit the ideological temperament of Jews, but, as Steven M. Cohen has noted, also a strategy of entry into modern society.[48] Largely missing from this coalition—which would become a major problem in succeeding years—were significant numbers of Roman Catholics and blacks.

Edwin Wolf, 2d, of the Library Company, March 1978.

Emily Sunstein, 1970.

The liberal ADA coalition came to play a critical role in the renaissance that Philadelphia entered with the election in 1951 of Joseph Clark as mayor and Richardson Dilworth as district attorney, both ADA members. Following World War II, the city remained, in Lincoln Steffens's earlier description, "corrupt and contented." The streets were deserted at night. Only a few decent residential streets remained around the fashionable Rittenhouse Square area. The remainder of the city was submerged in slums that surrounded the great universities and downtown hospitals. For years, the city's civic and business elite had tolerated these conditions along with the political corruption of the Republican machine ensconced in City Hall.

The impetus for change came from the "less parochial and contented members of the Philadelphia WASP business elite" that had helped to create the ADA and, later, the business-oriented Greater Philadelphia Movement.[49] At a time when television had not yet reached its current primacy, Annenberg's *Inquirer* broke with its 123-year-old Whig-Republican tradition to support the reform ticket of Joseph S. Clark, Jr., and Richardson Dilworth.

Under the new administration, the city began to "bristle." Mayor Clark, receptive to new ideas as never before, hired the best people "to help fight the battle for my mind," regardless of ethnic background. In the meritocracy he and, later, Dilworth (who succeeded him) encouraged, Jews were appointed to important posts. Abraham Freedman, a partner at Wolf–Block and active in the Fellowship Commission, was named city solicitor. Freedman suggested that Clark elevate his (Clark's) executive secretary, William Rafsky, to the newly created post of housing coordinator, a cabinet-level post. After Dilworth's election as mayor, Rafsky was made responsible for overall coordination of all developmental programs, including housing, slum clearance, industrial growth, and Center City development. Clark also named Fredric R. Mann as recreation commissioner, and, under Dilworth, Mann became city representative and director of commerce.

By the early 1950s, before urban renewal had become well established nationally, "the Philadelphia approach" had made the city a favorite of planners, architects, and housing reformers throughout the country. This combined rehabilitation of homes and small-scale clearance within single project areas. Innovative programs also were implemented in industrial development, and in port, university, and fiscal improvement. Wolf–Block, which began in the 1920s with most of the leading real estate and, later, entertainment businesses as clients, now came to represent many of the entities remolding the face of Philadelphia. Significantly, however, Jews who took leading roles in the city's development were no longer the descendants of nineteenth-century German-Jewish families, but the new knowledge technicians, men and women of East European backgrounds, such as "Abe" Freedman, Rafsky (who graduated from City College in New York), and Mr. Philadelphia himself, Albert M. Greenfield.

Greenfield was the one major economic power broker who had not become part of the city's revitalization under Clark, despite his enormous holdings both here and in other parts of the country. He had an exceptional knowledge of urban development, but as a result of his bitter earlier battle with "WASP-Republican bankers," he was not part of the city's exclusive power fraternity. Dilworth now appointed Greenfield head of the City Planning Commission, a move, it is said, initially opposed by Edmund Bacon, its executive head. Together, however, they formed a powerful team.

The two men set about to rehabilitate the old downtown Philadelphia area, which Greenfield knew intimately from childhood. Some believed his interest was linked to his holdings there; Greenfield felt, however, that if the big hotels and department stores went down, they would take with them the core of the city's tax base. It was necessary that people with higher incomes live near and use these facilities. The Georgian houses in Society Hill appeared to be the likeliest place to start bringing people back to Center City. Greenfield did not believe in house-by-house rehabilitation. "The reason nothing is moving and nobody has bought downtown," he said, "is because nobody has been given a guarantee that his investment will be protected and the climate of the whole area improved." The 1954 Federal Housing Act now made such a guarantee possible. Greenfield felt that one thousand acres southeast of Independence Hall—a quarter of Center City— had to be certified for urban renewal.

Dilworth backed this idea strongly. His initial official act as mayor was a directive to develop detailed plans for renewal of Washington Square in Society Hill. Bacon's role—indeed his vision—Jeanne R. Lowe has suggested, was vital, but the work of Greenfield, backed by Dilworth, was critical as well. The process of fitting together government and private enterprise was extraordinarily complex. Greenfield talked to major industrialists, bankers, merchants, and businessmen not simply in cold-cash terms, but also in terms of "this beloved city—this plot of one thousand acres that combines all that civilization has to offer."[50] He believed that a new, nonprofit corporation was necessary to ensure continuity between administrations, and the Old Philadelphia Development Corporation (OPDC) was formed in May 1956. Illustrative of the new ethnic as well as civic alliance, Harry Batten, one of the leading figures in the reform movement, suggested Greenfield as chairman of its nominating committee. OPDC was Philadelphia's unique creation, one that other cities would soon follow. Greenfield next brought to Philadelphia the architect of Pittsburgh's nationally famous Gateway Center downtown renewal, John P. Robin, to head OPDC. Robin applied his "free wheeling, do-it-now" style of action to the slow-moving Philadelphia timetable.

The renewal of Society Hill was an unabashed effort to bring back upper-income, elite taste setters to the city's urban heartland and reverse the movement to the suburbs, the first stage of a broader effort to revitalize the city as a place in which to live and work. This was criticized as pricing out of the area low-income groups, especially blacks. Nevertheless, by bringing back middle- and upper-middle-class elements, the reform movement went a long way to bringing back the city itself.[51]

A breach had been made by the ADA and the reform movement in the integration of Jews in the life of the community. Greenfield's successor at Bankers Securities in 1959, Gustave G. Amsterdam, who later headed the Greater Philadelphia Movement, was one of a very small number of Jews who were helping to legitimize Jewish businessmen in the top echelons of the Philadelphia economic community. However, the process was far from complete. Even among upper-class reform leaders, barriers to greater intimacy still remained. When one of the Jewish leaders active in the ADA was critical of the Philadelphia Art Alliance because it then barred blacks as members, John F. Lewis responded coolly, "It wasn't so long ago that Jews were allowed in."[52] Among many Jews who worked closely with him, the attitude of Joe Clark (who had now moved on to become a U.S. senator) to ethnic outsiders seemed aloof, even though Rafsky found him warm and friendly. Annenberg's biographer reports that Clark faulted Annenberg as a man who sought to infiltrate himself into the higher levels of Philadelphia society and referred to him and his father as "dirty kikom."[53]

At the close of the 1950s and early 1960s, Jews continued to remain essentially locked out of the central institutions of economic and social power in the community. A series of studies by the local chapter of the American Jewish Committee found that less than 1 percent of the managerial positions in major industrial organizations, insurance companies, and banks was held by Jews. McCready Huston reported that board memberships and presidencies of the museums, libraries, and higher civic institutions were still in the hands of the "right people." Jews were not acceptable as members in most of the Center City clubs, including the Union League and the Philadelphia and Rittenhouse clubs, and few were involved in major posts in large teaching hospitals and medical schools.

Perhaps the most egregious indication of second-class citizenship, however, was their continued absence from the city's large law firms. In 1962 fully half of these firms had no Jewish attorneys or, at best, one or two. Jewish lawyers were to be found mainly in several "mixed" firms; at Wolf–Block, the city's only large Jewish law office (which had a number of non-Jewish attorneys); or practicing as individuals or in limited partnerships. The barriers rankled because Jews were heavily drawn to the practice of law, an unusually prestigious profession in Philadelphia since colonial times. Moreover, these large offices tended to represent large-scale businesses in the city. In this respect, Philadelphia was far behind New York, where Wall Street law offices began hiring Jews immediately after World War II.[54]

The situation, however, was ripe for change. In the heightened civil rights atmosphere of the early 1960s, highlighted by marches led by the Reverend Martin Luther King, Jr., racial and religious barriers became increasingly incongruous. Jewish community relations agencies were bringing increased pressures to overcome discrimination. The American Jewish Committee in New York had commissioned several studies by scholars at leading academic institutions around the country to determine the dimensions of the problem of "executive suite" bias and how this could be overcome. As part of this effort, the Committee made a small grant to University of Pennsylvania sociologist E. Digby Baltzell. In 1964, Baltzell published his widely acclaimed and highly influential book, *The Protestant Establishment.* Baltzell reminded the Protestant elite (of which he was a member-academic) of the progressive role it had played in the past in bringing about orderly social change in society. He challenged members of his class to incorporate new and rising ethnic elements or remain a caste system interested only in preserving its power and privileges.

As these pressures mounted, friends and allies were found to challenge existing patterns of exclusion. The initial surveys of the Philadelphia AJC on barriers in banking and law carried introductions and appeals for change from Karl Bopp, chairman of the Federal Reserve Bank, and Jefferson B. Fordham, dean of the Law School at the University of Pennsylvania. The First Pennsylvania Banking and Trust Company (now First Pennsylvania Bank), then the city's largest bank, assigned a young executive vice president, John Bunting, Jr., to look into the matter. Bunting, who soon was named president, set about shaking up the structure of the bank and bringing in Jews. His speeches and interviews on the subject received wide attention. (In one widely reported address, he charged that the names on the front door of the "executive suite" in his bank read like a roll call at Hotchkiss.[55]) Somewhat less flamboyantly, companies like the Pennsylvania Railroad, Insurance Company of North America, and Scott Paper also began to move.[56] Stung by criticism for the exclusionary practices of the Union League, Samuel Fulton, its president, sought leaders of the Jewish community. At a meeting in the office of Morris Wolf, Fulton agreed that a number of leading Jews would be invited to become members.

Beginning in the mid-1960s and accelerating over the next decade, Jews began to find employment initially at entry and soon at middle-management levels of major businesses in the area. The most rapid changes, however, occurred in the legal profession. By 1964, an AJC survey reported "a certain amount of progress." Five years later, the number of Jews in large law offices had grown from thirty-five—mainly in "mixed" firms—to ninety-four, and now represented some 12 percent of the offices studied.[57] The following year, the local chapter of the AJC reported, "The problem we initially set out to explore a decade ago is on the way to solution." The Union League was the first to take in a small number of leading Republican Jews, including, initially, Leon Obermayer and Arlin M. Adams, attorneys in "mixed" firms. It was soon followed by the Racquet Club and even the more socially exclusive Rittenhouse and Philadelphia clubs.

Changes now occurring were a result not only of the more open atmosphere developing in the city, but also of more profound transformations occurring in the economy itself. The social arrangements of the 1940s and 1950s rested on manufacturing and a network of traditional businesses, such as commercial banking. With the passage of time, the manufacturing sector, particularly, declined, and the service and knowledge fields expanded rapidly. The University of Pennsylvania was soon to become the largest employer in Philadelphia. It was in these expanding areas that Jews had traditionally made their mark. In 1953, less than 10 percent of the Jews in Philadelphia were employed in manufacturing. The highest concentration was in wholesale and retail trades (38 percent) and the service fields (40 percent). In subsequent years, the proportion of Jews in manufacturing and the wholesale and retail sectors dropped further so that by 1983 they represented only 4 percent and 18 percent, respectively. By this time, service and miscellaneous areas accounted for 71 percent.[58] Large law offices expanded rapidly during this period, and by the 1980s the largest had as many as two and three hundred attorneys exclusive of support personnel.

These changes, as well as the increasingly competitive character of business and law, made it difficult to run large-scale organizations along blood lines. In the new "knowledge" society that was coming into existence, Jews found themselves increasingly sought after. (When Rawle and Henderson, the nation's oldest firm in continuous service, found Philadelphia's port business declining and its remaining clientele seeking broader service, it merged with another firm, half of whose attorneys were Jewish.[59]) It was not long before a number of Jews would become leading figures in these firms.

The period between the end of World War II and the mid-1960s has been called "the Golden Age" of American Jewry. From their East European immigrant origins, Jews had moved up rapidly and were beginning to find broader acceptance. A war against Nazism had been fought and won, and the United Nations was established to secure the peace. Alongside the decline in religious prejudice and discrimination, a civil rights revolution had gotten underway in which Jews had fully participated and which promised to give reality to the dream of a society open to all, announced by Reverend King at the historic March on Washington in 1963. There seemed to be no limits to the possibilities that lay ahead.

The high hopes engendered in the "the Golden Age," however, were to receive a series of severe jolts. In the summer of 1964, following an incident involving the police, racial rioting occurred in North Philadelphia and in several other cities. In subsequent summers, the disorders spread to other major cities across the land, ending only in 1968. As Friedman and Beck note in their essay, although it went largely unrecognized, Jews, along with blacks, were the chief victims of these disorders. Many Jewish businesses in North Philadelphia were wiped out or severely damaged. The growth of urban crime hit Jews in slum areas particularly hard. One study found that between 1968 and 1972, at least 22 Jewish merchants were killed in robberies, and 27 were shot or severely beaten in Philadelphia.[60]

The civil rights revolution in which Jews had joined so enthusiastically had by this time turned into a race revolution. New leaders like Stokely Carmichael, H. Rap Brown, and Malcolm X now emerged on a national level and shouted slogans such as "Black Power," derided integration, and utilized anti-Semitism as part of their anti-white rhetoric. Philadelphia, as Friedman and Beck suggest, may have provided a model for some of these younger men in Cecil Moore, the fiery head of the local NAACP chapter in the early 1960s who galvanized many younger blacks to challenge the oppressive system that exploited them but at the same time worried whites, moderate blacks, and especially Jews with his strident and often anti-Semitic utterances. In the following years, such issues as busing to achieve school desegregation and the use of racial quotas to open up greater opportunities for minorities and women would pull the two groups further apart, although efforts at cooperation continued.

The race revolution and other urban dislocations accelerated demographic changes already underway. Typical of the areas experiencing the greatest loss of Jews was Wynnefield–Overbrook. As David Varady shows, despite the optimism and dedicated efforts of the Wynnefield Residents Association, led by members of Har Zion and the local neighborhood division of JCRC between

Gustave G. Amsterdam, 1969.

1960 and 1970, the area went from all white to 51 percent black. The schools, once the highest ranking in the city, became overcrowded, and their quality along with property values declined. Neighborhood change in Wynnefield created, of course, greater opportunities for blacks moving up, but for Jews it spelled the end of a major center of Jewish life.

Mounting racial tensions tended to exacerbate class differences within the Jewish community. With the exception of Phoenix, Arizona, Philadelphia has the highest proportion of blue-collar workers of any city's Jewish community in the country. As more affluent Jews moved to more desirable sections of the city and suburbs, they left behind small, older, and often Orthodox populations. The tone of older and dissolving Jewish ghettos was demoralized, Samuel Z. Klausner and David P. Varady found in a 1969 study of Wynnefield. "It is not simply frustration . . . there is widespread conviction among residents . . . that the Jewish community there is declining, that the proportion of Blacks is increasing. . . . Everything seems harder and more difficult."

Anger was mounting also among many Jews living in the Northeast. Having abandoned the deteriorating neighborhoods of their childhood but "unable to jump to the golden ghettos of suburbia," many felt powerless as well. They were frustrated by rising rates of crime, the "threat" of busing poor black children into the schools, poor transportation, and other inadequate services. Some of their ire was directed against the "Jewish establishment" downtown. They felt that upper-class Jews did not provide sufficient services for them.[61] Philadelphia Jewry was experiencing many of the same class conflicts as had New York and other large metropolitan areas, where struggling working-class, white ethnics—"locals"—found themselves in conflicts with more affluent "cosmopolitans," who tended to be physically and emotionally more removed from urban problems. Significantly, a local chapter of the extremist Jewish Defense League was formed here in 1969, led by a rabbi in a small and fading Orthodox synagogue in Wynnefield and a school teacher in Northeast Philadelphia.[62]

A center of conflict involved the schools. Black parents were angry with the quality of education provided their children. Struggles also broke out between blacks and Jewish, Italian, and other white teachers and administrators seeking to move up in the education system. By this time, the reform movement had shifted from City Hall to the school administration building on the Parkway. Dilworth was now the head of the School Board. Dilworth and the Board selected Mark Shedd, a liberal educator and son of a minister, as school superintendent. Shedd saw the schools in need of sharp revamping. A memorandum signed by him soon came to light, noting that many of the current educators were second- or third-generation careerists who had archaic ideas about education and needed to be replaced. Although the memorandum was later retracted, Italian, Jewish, and other administrators from immigrant backgrounds felt under attack. In May, following budget cuts, just over a hundred administrators, many of them Jewish, were dropped, although some were later brought back. Shedd also began to move blacks up and created a parallel system of top-level staff from outside the system that the media quickly dubbed the "Harvard Mafia."[63]

Growing dissatisfaction of the "locals" with liberal "cosmopolitan" leadership and the race revolution now found political expression. When the ADA refused to support the Democratic candidate, Mayor James H. J. Tate, labor leader Joseph Schwartz resigned from the board. The following year, the ADA voted not to endorse Senator Hubert Humphrey as the Democratic candidate for president. The liberals "are out of touch with the people," William Ross, head of the Philadelphia Joint Dress Board of the ILGWU, declared.[64] The clearest expression, however, of middle-class rage was found in support given by Jews to hard-line police commissioner Frank L. Rizzo, who was elected mayor in 1971. As Dennis Clark notes in his essay, Jews unexpectedly split their vote 50-50 between him and his liberal Republican opponent, Thacher Longstreth. Four years later, the Jewish vote for Rizzo inched up to 53 percent.[65] Political conservatism for Jews, however, was an unnatural posture. When Rizzo sought to run for a third term by seeking to change the city charter, two out of three Jews voted against the charter change, in sharp contrast with white ethnic voters.

The most powerful force shaping growing Jewish anxieties and fears, however, was the situation in the Middle East. The Six Day War in 1967 "was like an electric charge that sparked up the synagogues, Jewish pride and solidarity," Rabbi Pinchos Chazin of Temple Sholom in Oxford Circle noted. Rallies were held all over the city, and volunteers for bond drives and behind-the-lines services for Israel appeared overnight. On the first day of the war, publisher Walter Annenberg, heretofore not known for a close association with the Jewish community, donated $1 million to the Israel drive, making it the largest single gift ever received.[66] When Egyptian and Syrian armies struck in surprise on Yom Kippur in 1973, the pattern of response was even greater. Five million dollars in Israel bonds were sold in the first week of the war. On the fourth day, Mayor Rizzo pledged to purchase $1 million in bonds out of city pension funds.[67]

The two wars completed the homogenization and "Zionization" of Jewish life. When it was merged with the Allied Jewish Appeal in 1956, only $4.4 million was raised by the Federation. By 1974, the figure had grown to $22 million.[68] Israel, to some degree, had begun to replace liberalism as the secular religion of the Jewish community. Ironically, as the broader society grew more egalitarian and seemed to be welcoming Jews, the latter were turning inward.

Other forces, however, were also affecting Jews. The development of new lifestyles and criticism of the institutional arrangements of society characteristic of the period attracted a number of young people. Sparked by a demonstration of Jewish students at the General Assembly of the Council of Jewish Federations in Boston in 1969, a Jewish youth movement emerged in Philadelphia that sought to transform Jewish life. Much of it centered around students at the Reconstructionist Rabbinical College, founded in 1968, and the Jewish Free University, initiated by a group of Jewish professors and students associated with the American Jewish Committee. They pushed for and soon received financial assistance from the Federation of Jewish Agencies for a Philadelphia Union of Jewish Students (PUJS), the student newspaper, *Hayom,* and a Jewish coffee house (*Makom*). The Federation also began to pour more resources into the Northeast. Faced with a series of new pressures, the Jewish "establishment" proved remarkably resilient. Concern for traditional liberal causes, however, continued to attract a number of Jews. Ned Wolf, a grandson of Morris Wolf and an attorney, came before the board of one Jewish organization to challenge it to focus more attention on the poor and disadvantaged in society. He went on to head the Public Interest Law Center of Philadelphia, which provided legal services to minorities and the poor.

Under the impact of the new social currents now flowing, many Jewish organizations began to move women into positions of greater responsibility.[69] By the early 1970s, three women were enrolled at the Reconstructionist Rabbinical College. An effort got underway to admit women to the Locust Club, the Center City eating facility of the Jewish business and civic leadership. Here the Jewish "establishment" moved considerably more slowly. It was not until 1983 that a woman attorney became the club's first female member.[70] Toward the end of the decade, Federation fundraising events at country clubs continued to be segregated.

In the 1970s, Jews consolidated the gains they had made during the previous decade. They found their way, increasingly, on the boards of civic organizations. By the 1980s, I. Jerome Stern, a past president of the Federation, headed the United Way of Southeastern Pennsylvania, and David Brenner, former managing partner of a major accounting firm, the Chamber of Commerce. In 1971, the University of Pennsylvania selected Martin Meyerson as its president, the first professing Jew to head a major university in the country. Some time later, he was invited to become a member of the prestigious Philadelphia Club. In addition, Marvin Wachman was named president of Temple University. Jews were now members of the professoriate at Penn, even in earlier resistant English and History departments.

Advances here were paralleled by growing leadership in politics on city and state levels, a sure sign of a group's coming of age. As Dennis Clark notes, individual Jews had been members of the state legislature and city council for many years and served as district attorneys here. In 1970, however, Milton Shapp became the first Jewish governor of Pennsylvania, and he was reelected four years later. In 1980, Arlen Specter became Pennsylvania's first Jewish U.S. senator. Jews came to play key roles in the administration of Frank L. Rizzo and, subsequently, that of William Green. They also served as important Democratic fund-raisers on a local and a national level.[71]

A number of Jews who had entered WASP law offices in the 1960s had moved up to become senior partners and leading members of these firms. By the 1980s, the Federation Allied Jewish Appeal drive had "captains" here as well as in other offices, a move that would have had some long-gone partners whirling in their graves. Several, like Harold Kohn and David Berger, founded their own highly successful law offices. Indeed, the period saw the rise of the "Jewish" law firm. In June, 1974, *Philadelphia Magazine* profiled the office in which Marvin Comisky was

Martin Meyerson as the new president of the University of Pennsylvania in September of 1970.

a leading figure—Blank, Rome, Comisky and McCauley—with some of the major businesses in the area that were its clients. Following a merger in 1984, it became the second largest law firm in the city. Wolf–Block under Howard Gittis remained a significant force, and its political clout was felt in both political parties.

By the early 1980s, however, the nature of Jewish business in Philadelphia had undergone change. Gone or mostly gone, except in suburban shopping centers, were the drugstores, bakeries, delicatessens, furniture stores, and other retail establishments that had been the underpinning of Jewish neighborhoods in the post–World War II period. A number of the major Jewish enterprises had also disappeared, including Botany (apparel) and Penn Fruit and Food Fair (supermarket chains). With Greenfield's retirement, his vast department store and hotel empire began to fall apart, no small factor in the decline in the city itself. In 1969, Walter Annenberg sold the Philadelphia *Inquirer* and *Daily News* to the out-of-town Knight–Ridder Newspapers, Inc. Jews continued to remain prominent in real estate (The Binswanger Co., Strouse Greenberg, and Richard I. Rubin & Co.) and the considerably diminished but still important garment industry (Charming Shoppes and Nipon). In the past 20 years, there has been an explosion of publicly owned business enterprises organized and run by a new breed of risk-taking Jewish businessmen mainly in the high technology, retailing, and health care fields. Nine of sixteen such firms, including U.S. Health Care, Burlington Coat Factory Warehouse, and Comcast, had Jewish CEOs in 1985, and all of these businesses were expanding at a time when the region's older and better known corporations were reducing their size and payrolls.[72] And for some reason, Jewish businessmen owned virtually all the sports teams in the area except for the Phillies baseball team.

The most significant Jewish enterprise was ARA Services, a service conglomerate founded by William S. Fishman in 1959. A $3.06 billion dollar business with 116,000 employees, it was larger than Campbell Soup and American Motors in 1984.[73] ARA, however, was the exception. Jewish businesses were small or medium size in comparison with such giants as SmithKline Beckman, the Philadelphia Savings Fund Society, and other companies in the area. Nevertheless, the Jewish community was seen as an important, even powerful force by the broader civic and business communities.

The 1980s was marked by the return of many young professionals, singles, and business people to newly restored town houses and apartments in Center City, as Bacon and Greenfield had projected earlier. This was now the "fastest expanding Jewish demographic area within the city," a Federation study reported in 1981. The 20,000 Jews who lived in the Center City–University City area along with others in different sections have played a key role in the rapidly expanding artistic and cultural life of the community.

Individual and younger Jews, many of them newcomers to the area, helped to shape and reshape the life of the community, Donald Harrison reports in his essay. Steven Poses, along with Jay Gubens of the Restaurant School, led a restaurant revival (the Frog most prominently) that attracted national attention. At age 29, David Schlessinger revolutionized the book-selling business by discounting books. By 1984, when he sold his business to Rite Aid, Encore Books in Center City had grown to eighteen stores in the city and surrounding area. *Philadelphia Magazine,* started in 1952 and published by D. Herbert Lipson, launched an entire generation of imitators in other cities, while Moe Septee, who arrived in Philadelphia in the early 1960s to take over the All-Star–Forum Series, introduced a number of musical and theatrical innovations, including an effort to serve black audiences by producing shows like *Bubbling Brown Sugar, Raisin in the Sun,* and an all-black *Guys and Dolls.*[74] When the "Queen of Broad Street," the Bellevue Stratford, was about to close as a result of the collapse of the Greenfield empire and the impact of the mysterious "legionnaires disease," Ronald Rubin of Richard I. Rubin & Company, bought the hotel and tastefully restored it. It was forced to close, however, in 1986. Jewish sports team owners, as Ron Avery notes here, had also turned Philadelphia into a "city of winners."

An older generation, however, was also active in what some were now calling the city's second renaissance. "Freddie" Mann capped his civic career by building a new symphonic music pavilion in Fairmount Park to replace the Robin Hood Dell, which he had created almost singlehandedly more than a generation earlier. (Appropriately, at age 80, he returned to the Board of the Philadelphia Orchestra as an emeritus member.[75]) Edwin Wolf II headed the prestigious Library Company of Philadelphia, founded by Benjamin Franklin, for more than thirty years. As it celebrated its 250th anniversary in 1981, he was told by a leading Philadelphia intellectual, "You know everyone hates it but you really are the elite." He stepped down in 1985.[76]

If Center City was the most exciting area in the city and an important focus of Jewish life in the 1980s, the Northeast is now the heartland. The bulk of the population lives north of Roosevelt Boulevard in the Far Northeast, the section contiguous to Bucks County. If one adds the northern suburbs in eastern Montgomery County and lower Bucks County, which, together with the Northeast, are sometimes referred to as the Greater Northeast, nearly half (45 percent) of Philadelphia's estimated 256,000 people living in Jewish homes reside there. (After reviewing the manner of calculating the figures in the Philadelphia Jewish Population Study, Dr. Eugene Ericksen suggests that there are between 250,000 and 300,000 Jews.) Some 60 to 70 percent of several new complexes built in Bucks County in the 1980s, it is believed, are inhabited by Jews. Philadelphia's Northeast is also where most of the six to seven thousand Soviet Jews who have recently come to the city have settled, one of the largest concentrations in the United States. The latter have not always been greeted with enthusiasm by other Jews, who found them "different" and wondered why they didn't go to Israel. Nonetheless, they were recipients of considerable communal resources. Unlike Center City's professionals, Northeast Jews tended to be an older population, a factor recognized by the Federation and other Jewish agencies that located here a group of services for the elderly, including the David G. Neuman Senior Center and several housing complexes for the elderly.[77] Also mixed throughout the various major areas of Jewish settlement in Philadelphia were an estimated eight to ten thousand Israelis.[78]

Other important Jewish areas in the 1980s include Northwest Philadelphia, encompassing West Oak Lane, Germantown, Mount Airy, and Chestnut Hill, where approximately 12,400 reside; the northern suburbs, including Cheltenham, Abington, and Moreland, with 22,000; Delaware County, with 27,000; and Merion-Wynnefield on the western edge of the city, where 28,000 live.[79]

The revival of Jewish identity that received sharp impetus during the Six-Day and Yom Kippur wars continued into the latter part of the 1970s and 1980s. *Kipot* (Jewish skull caps) were seen increasingly on campus and around town.[80] One in-depth study noted that even the area college and university professors, usually seen as indifferent, "maintain a sense of Jewish identity and attachment to the community."[81] In Germantown, Center City, Wynnewood, and other parts of the area, informal systems of Jewish learning and praying (*Havurot*) had sprung up inside and outside of synagogues. The groups were small but vigorous and appealed especially to young adults and professionals.[82]

Religious orthodoxy here was also undergoing a little noticed but significant revival. No longer locked into an immigrant and Yiddish-speaking world, many now were American born, highly educated, and enjoying a new-found affluence. There were four congregations in the western suburbs in the 1980s. An estimated fourth of the members of Lower Merion Synagogue had Ph.D.'s or M.D.'s. The old German-Russian wars had flared up for one final battle over the question of communal funding of Jewish education, but with the help of Edwin Wolf II, as King, Lakritz, and Wachs note in their essay, it was finally resolved in the affirmative, and schools like Akiba and Solomon Schecter now received significant financial assistance from the Federation. In addition Orthodox schools like Torah Academy and Beth Jacob receive Federation support along with noncongregational supplementary schools. Late in 1982, a small group of Jewish businessmen bought the building in Cheltenham at a sheriff's sale for Beth Jacob after the school had defaulted on its payments. A small but highly active Chasidic movement led by Rabbi Abraham Shemtov also exists mainly in the Northeast.

The good news, Lucy S. Dawidowicz has written, is that Jews have chosen "of their own volition to remain Jews and raise their children as Jews."[83] The bad news is that the Jewish population here was expected to decline to between 200,000 and 250,000 by the end of the twentieth century.[84] Assimilation was marching forward here as well as elsewhere, as evidenced by the dramatic growth in rates of intermarriage, low birthrates, and indifference to things Jewish, especially among the young. Organizational affiliation is very low in contrast to other cities of comparable size, and the number of Jews who designated religious preference other than the three main groups or none at all is the highest in the country. The 1983 Federation Allied Jewish Appeal/Israel Special Fund campaign raised a record total of $26 million, but as a *Jewish Exponent* editorial noted, this came from only 40 percent of the Jews living here.[85] The Jewish

Arlen Specter announcing his candidacy for the U.S. Senate at his East Falls home, 1976.

campus revival continued into the 1980s. However, as one knowledgeable local observer reported, it was "less potent now." Especially troubling to parents and Jewish communal leaders was
the attraction that various cult groups seemed to have for many younger Jews. In the spring of
1983, some three to four hundred could be found at Friday night services at Jews for Jesus Beth
Yeshua congregation in Overbrook Park.[86] Religious orthodoxy, it is true, was flourishing, but it
was still too small and isolated from the mainstream of Jewish life to make its impact felt more
widely. And the influx of Soviet and Israeli Jews was too few in numbers to be able to play the
invigorating role of earlier Jewish migrations.

By the mid-1980s, Jews had become a part of the broader society, some even said the
"power structure." In 1986, Ronald I. Rubin, Harvey Lamm, chairman of Subaru of America, and
George A. Ross of Goldman Sachs and Company were voted onto the board of the famous
Philadelphia Orchestra—the latter was preparing a report for future corporate giving—joining a
number of Jews elected earlier. But it was not at all clear how broader civic acceptance would now
affect Jewish communal life. Ideally, of course, Jews can and do function in both worlds, and this
is beneficial to both. However, there is only so much energy that can be taken away from businesses and professions. There was also the question of whether, in the long run, being on the board
of an old-age home or Jewish community center would remain as compelling as serving as a leader
of a prestigious civic or cultural organization.

It also was not entirely clear who ran Philadelphia anymore. In his famous book, Baltzell
had appealed to the Protestant establishment in 1964 to reassume its leadership role. In a little
noticed article a dozen years later, he reported that this was no longer possible. Many no longer
lived in the city. A considerable number of their children had "dropped out" or joined in much of
the aberrant social behavior and extreme political styles that characterized the period.[87] In addition,
a number of its leading business institutions, including the Pennsylvania and Reading Railroads,
Curtis Publishing Company, and Philadelphia *Bulletin,* had gone out of business. In some respects,
Philadelphia had become a branch-office town.

Simultaneous with the "decline of the WASP," the children of white ethnics and other
hitherto excluded groups were reaching out for economic and political power. The reform administrations of Clark and Dilworth were followed by those of James H. J. Tate, the city's first Irish-
Catholic, and Frank L. Rizzo, its first Italian-American mayors. In 1983, after the somewhat
bland term of William Green (Irish), W. Wilson Goode was elected its first black mayor. In short
order, the president of City Council, city managing director, school superintendent, and chief justice of the Pennsylvania Supreme Court were all black. With so many Jews having left the city,
Dennis Clark suggests in his essay, they would be less able to influence the future direction of
community life.

Despite the widespread discussion of the demise of the older Protestant leadership class,
there were indications that this picture has been somewhat overdrawn. Many, it is true, had retreated from public life, but only to dig in more deeply into the central economic structures they had
always dominated. Several analyses in the early 1980s indicated that while Jews could be found at
the entry and middle-management levels, there were none at almost half of the large industrial
organizations and only a handful in the major banks in 1984.[88] This gave some point to the observation of novelist Gore Vidal that "regardless of the considerable stir the newcomers have made in
the peripheral worlds of the universities, show biz and book-chat, [Jews] have made almost no
impact at all on the actual power structure of the country."[89]

Moreover, the small number of Jews employed in large-scale and more traditional businesses here tended to be those with few or no ties to the Jewish community. And even within the
now more integrated large WASP law firms, hard driving "workaholic" Jews were sometimes
viewed with mingled admiration and suspicion, particularly among some older partners who still
looked back nostalgically to the practice of law as a more leisurely and exclusive profession. There
were indications that some Jews, while enjoying greater affluence and acceptance, were still uneasy
in their new and more open environment.[90] "I firmly believe that we [Jews] are an endangered
species," Norman Braman, the new owner of the Philadelphia Eagles, who grew up in South
Philadelphia, and the son of a barber, declared in an interview with the *Jewish Exponent* in 1985.

As a result of a confluence of forces now, there is no mistaking the growing sense of anxiety among Philadelphia Jews, in spite of the many significant gains they have made. While recent

national surveys have charted the decline of prejudice and discrimination in this country against Jews, a high proportion of Jews refuse to believe this. The Federation's Population Study of Philadelphia found 32 percent of the sample hearing anti-Semitic remarks where they lived and worked, and 46 percent seeing hostile statements on television, on radio, and in the newspapers.[91] Their uneasiness was felt most sharply just prior to and following Israel's incursion into Lebanon in the summer of 1982, in the sharp response to editorials, feature articles, and cartoons in the Philadelphia *Inquirer,* as well as in national media of Israeli "genocide" and the questioning of Jewish loyalty to this country. From the special heights they had scaled since 1940, Philadelphia Jewry could congratulate themselves on how far they had come, but there was still some distance to go before they would feel fully at home in America.

Philadelphia JEWISH LIFE
1940–2000

Judy Geselowitz (left), Rabbi M. L. Barg, and Barbara Miedoff at the July 1947 Reyburn Plaza of the British seizure of the S.S. Exodus.

PHILADELPHIA JEWRY, THE HOLOCAUST, AND THE BIRTH OF THE JEWISH STATE

Section i. Philadelphia Jewry and the Holocaust

Philip Rosen · Robert Tabak · David Gross

*N*ow, more than forty years after the slaughter of six million Jews in Nazi-occupied Europe, the question of whether American Jewry did everything it could to rescue its European brethren is being hotly debated. Books and articles are being written, charges and countercharges are being hurled as American Jewry looks back at what it did or did not do to rescue those trapped in the grip of the Nazis.[1]

Jews in Philadelphia, like virtually all Jews in America, viewed the rise of Adolf Hitler and the Nazi Party with disgust and alarm. Their reaction to the increasingly disturbing events in Europe, however, varied according to their differing perceptions of the Jewish role in American society and their differing assessments of just what action was possible.

Prior to the outbreak of World War II, Philadelphia Jews responded in several ways to the growth of anti-Semitism in Nazi Germany. In the spring of 1933, a variety of Jewish and interdenominational protests against Nazi anti-Semitism took place in Philadelphia, the largest drawing 20,000 participants. These protests continued through 1934, though there was some disagreement as to their utility. Fear was also expressed that increased Jewish visibility would only increase local anti-Semitism.[2]

In addition to protests, Philadelphia Jews also participated in national attempts to organize a boycott of Nazi Germany. The first local call for a boycott came in an editorial in the *Jewish Exponent,* one of two Philadelphia Anglo-Jewish weekly newspapers in March 1933. By June, $50,000 had been raised to support the boycott. Several boycott rallies were held in the spring of 1934, none of them very large.[3]

There was a lull in local public anti-Nazi activity between 1934 and 1938, then activity picked up again, particularly after the events of *Kristallnacht,* November 9–10, 1938. The mass burnings of synagogues and the physical violence directed against the Jews of Germany and their property shocked many who had previously discounted reports of Nazi persecution. The widespread violence within Germany shattered all remaining hopes that Nazism would somehow moderate itself.

By mid-November, the number of public anti-Nazi activities rapidly increased. On November 14, the left-wing American League for Peace and Democracy picketed the German Consulate and called on City Council to pass an anti-Nazi resolution. Two days later, the mayor appealed for aid to German Jews. A number of churches joined in the condemnation of the Nazi persecution, and anti-Nazi rallies were again held in such neighborhoods as largely Jewish Wynnefield.[4]

In general, anti-Nazi boycott activity in Philadelphia seems to mirror the pattern of anti-Nazi political activity by Jewish and non-Jewish groups nationwide. The two high points of this

Arthur Bloch in 1952.

Rabbi William Finshriber in 1947.

Rabbi Bernard L. Leventhal, described as the dean of the American Orthodox Rabbinate.

activity were 1933–1934, after the Nazi seizure of power in Germany, and late 1938 following *Kristallnacht.* Boycott activity during the mid-thirties and from 1939 until American entry into World War II did not attract major attention in the Jewish or general press. But, generally speaking, the anti-Nazi boycott does not appear to have been a major organizational force in Philadelphia.

While the plight of the Jews of Germany—and, to some extent, the rest of Europe—attracted some attention and was a major focus for local fund-raising activity, efforts to actually resettle Jewish refugees in Philadelphia moved slowly. An early request to directly aid German refugees was made to an independent group, the Mastbaum Loan System, which had been founded in 1920 by members of Philadelphia's German-Jewish business and professional elite. The purpose of this group was to offer low-interest loans, particularly to help Jews (as well as others) establish or maintain small businesses.

The Society was asked, in conjunction with the National Coordinating Committee, the body helping German refugees in the United States, to help place six Jewish refugees in jobs. Meeting in 1934, the Mastbaum Loan System narrowly drew its institutional lines, concluding, "that [such action] definitely was not the province of the organization and was not acted upon." Similarly, proposals to establish a special loan fund specifically for German refugees were defeated in 1939. Only in March 1941, after the war in Europe had been raging for eighteen months, did the Mastbaum Loan System reach an agreement with the Allied Jewish Appeal to set aside $20,000 for loans for the purchase of steamship tickets. One-half of that sum was to be guaranteed by the Allied Jewish Appeal. In May, 1942, after months of resistance by the Mastbaum board, the idea of interest-free loans to refugees was finally accepted.[5]

This resistance and delay cannot be dismissed simply as another case of too little, too late. Nor was the Mastbaum Loan System a peripheral group; rather, it was an arm of Philadelphia's Jewish elite. Throughout the period in discussion, the Mastbaum board was headed by Arthur Bloch, a senior executive at Snellenberg's department store and president of the YM-YWHA. (Bloch later served as president of the Federation of Jewish Charities from 1943 to 1946.) The board was replete with such distinguished Philadelphia Jewish names as Gimbel, Lit, and Solis-Cohen. The reaction of the Society to the plight of Europe's Jews clearly shows the reluctance of the local Jewish elite to become directly involved with refugees.

The fear of anti-Semitism and anti-Jewish discrimination reached their peak in this period. Fear of exacerbation of anti-Semitism led to a reluctance to be overly involved with refugees. In 1942, the board of the Philadelphia Refugee Resettlement Committee, established in 1937 as the local branch of the National Refugee Service, unanimously endorsed a lobbying effort to get the immigration service to drop the "racial" category "Hebrew" from its statistics, in part because of the prominent play given to it by groups opposing Jewish immigration.[6]

Among those activities that could be considered a response to the rise of Nazism, the emergence of the Allied Jewish Appeal undoubtedly reached the largest number of people. Legally founded in June 1938, the AJA's constitutional purpose was "to establish and maintain an efficient organization for the purpose of collecting, dividing and distributing voluntary contributions and donations to such movements of exclusively or partly Jewish interest as are not provided for by the

Federation of Jewish Charities of Philadelphia." The FJC was almost exclusively concerned with local agencies; the AJA, therefore, was the conduit for aid to Palestine and other overseas Jewish communities.[7]

Mass participation in the Allied Jewish Appeal (the number of contributors rose from 9,042 in 1937 to 48,477 in 1939, and the amount pledged from $258,452 to $902,056) was in part an attempt by thousands of Jews not in leadership positions to positively affirm their Jewishness and participation in the Jewish people during a time of significant anti-Semitism in the United States and a major anti-Jewish onslaught in Europe.[8]

Even before the United States entered World War II, American Jews were more pro-Allies and pro-interventionist than the general population. In the early days of the war, Philadelphia Jews were prominent in sending aid to Britain. They sought, however, to focus these efforts under an interfaith banner. One local observer reported in the Jewish press that the Interfaith Section of British War Relief had actually been a Jewish section in all but name. This seeking of an interfaith cover again shows a Jewish reluctance to be openly viewed as pro-interventionist and a fear that Jews would be accused of seeking to involve the United States in a "Jewish war."[9]

Hitler's surprise invasion of the Soviet Union on June 22, 1941, reawakened a reservoir of sympathy for the Soviet Union, coupled with a pragmatic awareness that the course of battle on the Eastern Front meant life and death for hundreds of thousands of Jews.

Jewish aid to the Soviet Union can be tied to several motivations:

1. An actual endorsement of Communism—the International Workers Order, a Communist-led fraternal organization competing with the socialist Workmen's Circle, was relatively strong in Philadelphia;
2. A residual pool of goodwill, not absolutely uncritical, toward those who overthrew the czarist regime, which persecuted Jews; and
3. Identification with the large number of Jews who lived in the Soviet Union—a very large number, perhaps a majority, of Philadelphia Jews had relatives living within the pre-1939 boundaries of the Soviet Union, particularly in the Ukraine.[10]

Despite reservations about Communism, public opinion polls indicate that during the 1930s, American Jews had a more favorable opinion of the Soviet Union than did the general population. Particularly when pushed to choose Communism or fascism, American Jews overwhelmingly leaned toward the former, not necessarily from real conviction, but rather in a clear rejection of the intense anti-Semitism of Nazi Germany.[11]

Steps leading to the establishment of Russian War Relief nationally began in New York within weeks of the German invasion of the Soviet Union. By October 1941, a series of endorsements, chapter formation, and rallies were underway. (At the urging of the President's Commission on Overseas Aid, the organization later changed its name to the American Society for Russian Relief, Inc.—a number of other groups also changed their names to add the word *American*—but the group continued to be called Russian War Relief [RWR] by its own organizers and by the press.[12])

When the United States entered the war in December 1941, the Soviet Union became not only a hope for Jews threatened by the Nazis, but also an ally. Thus, a far wider base of support, Jewish and non-Jewish, could be enlisted for aid to Russia. Early in January 1942, prominent rabbis, including Israel Goldstein, and Zionist leaders Stephen S. Wise and Abba Hillel Silver endorsed RWR. Several Philadelphia labor leaders also endorsed the group, and its Jewish Council began operating in Philadelphia early in 1942.[13]

RWR's first major event in Philadelphia was a rally sponsored by the Jewish Council on Sunday, March 15. Yiddish writer Sholem Asch was the featured speaker and several prominent Zionist, religious, and communal leaders appeared on the program. Among them were Rabbi Bernard L. Levinthal, the community's senior Orthodox rabbi; Rabbi William Fineshriber, a leading Reform—and anti-Zionist—spokesman; John Frederick Lewis, Philadelphia chairman of RWR (not just its Jewish section); and Dr. Jacob Billikopf, former executive director of the Federation of Jewish Charities, who chaired the event. Rabbis Levinthal and Fineshriber served as honorary chairmen.[14]

The large-scale rally, repeated annually in March or April, was thus publicly led by well-respected communal and religious figures who had no leftist ties, certainly none to Communism.

March 10, 1943 "memorial pageant" in Madison Square Garden, attended by 34,000.

The rally was officially designated a conference, and each local Jewish organization was asked to send three to ten representatives. Widespread public support for RWR in the Jewish community continued throughout the war years.

The fact that Billikopf chaired the Jewish Council of Russian War Relief proved disturbing to Kurt Peiser, his successor as executive director of the Federation of Jewish Charities. Apparently concerned about the seeming Jewish-Communist link, Peiser wrote Billikopf a "Dear Billie" letter:

> For some time we have been very anxious not to have any of the specific war relief efforts divide themselves into Jewish, Catholic, and Protestant groups. This particular one in which you are participating has some implications about which I need not tell you because I know you are too familiar with them to indulge in explanations, implications which worry me a great deal.
>
> It is because of that particular worry that I wonder if you have given thought to the results of tying yourself as well as others into this picture in the development of a Jewish section of a Russian War Relief attempt.[15]

Samuel Fels, the prominent philanthropist whose name appeared as a sponsor of RWR's Philadelphia Jewish Council, apparently had not been consulted about the use of his name. He expressed his irritation to Dr. M. V. Leof, a leftist physician who headed the group's executive committee. Peiser had already spoken to Leof, reminding him that while Fels "is very much interested in the Russian War Relief movement, he is not interested in having his name attached to the Jewish fraternal end of it, and has asked me to so notify you."[16] Fels's distress was clearly tied to the idea of a Jewish Council and not to RWR itself.

Several observers found the role of the FJC leadership in the RWR effort clearly wanting. Writing to Peiser in the spring of 1942, Mrs. William (Henrietta) Steinberg said, "With the exception of Mr. Fels and a very few others, including those personally contacted by my father, I repeat, the record of the wealthy Philadelphia Jews with reference to the Russian War Relief is practically a disgrace."[17]

If the Jewish fund-raising elite was somewhat reluctant to aid the RWR, the leaders and membership of many Jewish religious and fraternal organizations were not. Many B'nai B'rith lodges, *Landsmanshaftn,* women's auxiliaries, sisterhoods, and other groups from Jewish neighborhoods were contributing by 1944 and 1945. Though money was, of course, needed, RWR collected in a different way than groups like the Red Cross or AJA. It collected literally tons of such items as used clothing, shoes, baby food, and household items. These collections provided a significant amount of direct material aid to Russian civilians.[18]

Russian War Relief was an important and visible presence in the Jewish community, as well as the city at large, from late 1941 until the organization closed nationally in the summer of 1946. Thousands of Philadelphia Jews contributed to RWR, many through a variety of religious and fraternal organizations.19 It is reasonable to estimate that at least one-quarter of the RWR's national income, aside from the National War Fund, came from Jews. In Philadelphia, the percentage raised from Jews was considerably higher. While the city lagged behind other large cities in per capita contributions to the United Jewish Appeal, the Jewish Council of RWR did better than average in Philadelphia. In 1944, it raised some 15 percent of its funds in Philadelphia, which had less than 7 percent of the U.S. Jewish population (290,000).[20]

Given the relative success of the AJA and Russian War Relief, it might be thought that any legitimate appeal to aid European Jewry would also succeed in Philadelphia. This, however, was not the case. The Emergency Committee for War-Torn Yeshivoth, formed by the Union of Orthodox Rabbis, and better known by its Hebrew name, *Va'ad ha- Hatzalah* (rescue committee), for example, was formed in November 1939 and, realizing that not all European Jews could be saved, concentrated on rescuing rabbis and yeshivah students and their families who had fled Poland. Its fund-raising efforts in Philadelphia were largely ineffective in comparison with results

in other cities. Few leading community figures outside the Orthodox segment of Philadelphia Jewry made contributions, and even those tended to be minimal.[21]

Several factors contributed to the Va'ad's failure in Philadelphia. The local Orthodox community was not strong. Although Rabbi Bernard Levinthal, head of the local Orthodox rabbinate, supported the Va'ad, this was not enough to guarantee success. The tradition of Jewish learning was also weak in Philadelphia, which had no adult yeshivoth, so that the Va'ad's goal of saving rabbis and Talmud scholars as a wellspring for future Judaism resonated less strongly in Philadelphia than elsewhere. Finally, the geographic origin of Philadelphia Jewry—largely Ukrainian and not Polish and Lithuanian, where most of the yeshivoth were located—again came into play, as it did in the success of RWR.

One of the questions that has occupied modern scholarship into the Holocaust period is that of "who knew what and when did they know it" regarding the Nazi plan for the "Final Solution to the Jewish Problem." The systematic Nazi extermination campaign began with the invasion of the Soviet Union in June 1941. Special murder squads called *Einsatzgruppen* followed hard on the heels of the invading German forces and, wherever possible, took the Jewish residents of newly occupied towns and villages into the forest and shot them in cold blood.[22]

From the invasion of the Soviet Union onward, both of Philadelphia's Anglo-Jewish weeklies, the *Jewish Exponent* and the *Jewish Times,* reported on the destruction of European Jewry in their news and their editorial columns. The *Times* and the *Exponent* were independent papers during the years 1941–1944. The *Times* had a circulation of 28,000 and the *Exponent,* 19,000. On May 5, 1944, the *Exponent* was purchased by the Allied Jewish Appeal. The *Times* was founded and run for English-speaking Eastern European Jews and their children. The *Exponent* was closer to the German-Jewish, older-stock elite. The *Times* had been explicitly pro-Zionist since it was founded in the 1920s. The *Exponent* was not anti-Zionist, but exhibited a more neutral stance until at least World War II.

Protest in front of Philadelphia's City Hall just prior to America's entry in the war.

Both papers drew on material supplied by the Jewish Telegraphic Agency, a daily news service, as well as Reuters, the Jewish Press Service, and information culled from the Yiddish press and general American newspapers and magazines. Both papers, therefore, had access to reports of escapees from Nazi Europe and its network of concentration and extermination camps. They also obtained material from observers of neutral nations, clandestine radio messages, documents from various European governments-in-exile, and reports from the staffs of international Jewish organizations based in London, Berne, and Ankara.[23]

Beginning with the Nazi invasion of the Soviet Union, both of Philadelphia's Anglo-Jewish weeklies increased their coverage of events in German-occupied Europe and gathered more information on anti-Jewish atrocities. In its Rosh Hashanah 1941 issue, the *Jewish Times* told of the "virtual extermination of the Jews in Croatia." It digested news reports from Moscow dealing with "experiments on Jewish youth to induce cholera" and ran a long article, entitled "The Most Terrible Year in Polish Jewry's History," which described death by famine, typhoid fever, and Nazi brutality.[24]

On October 31, the *Jewish Exponent* first used the term *extermination* to describe what was happening to Jews in Nazi-occupied Europe. The *Times* of that same date reported on "Jewish corpses in the Dneister in Nazi-occupied Ukraine" and told of the massacre of tens of thousands of Jews. In support of the Russian War Relief campaign, both papers featured stories on Russian efforts that resulted in the rescue of hundreds of thousands of Jews and on how "fighting Jews were standing side by side with other Russians against the Hitlerites." The papers also focused on the horrors the Nazis were inflicting on Gentiles as well as Jews.[25]

In April 1942, the *Times* reported that the Germans were employing poison gas to kill Jews in concentration camps. An editorial referred to ten thousand Dutch Jews gassed at Mauthausen in Austria. In May, the *Exponent* quoted Chaim Weizmann, head of the Jewish community of Palestine, as saying that 25 percent of Central European Jewry would be destroyed. Weizmann also expressed his concern that "the Allies were pigeon-holing the Jewish problem."[26] The paper also noted that, at a recent conference, major Jewish organizations—the American Jewish Committee, American Jewish Congress, Joint Distribution Committee, and Jewish Labor Committee—had been informed that the Jews in occupied Europe "were in danger of complete annihilation."[27]

The terrible threat of impending annihilation was made even clearer to Philadelphia Jewry in July 1942, when the *Exponent* carried a report from Dr. Ignacz Schwarzbard, a member of the Polish government-in-exile in London. Schwarzbard, who was privy to information collected by both the Jewish and Polish undergrounds in Poland, said that one million Jews had already died, and he warned, "All Jews are threatened with extinction! Only immediate reprisals would deter Hitler from carrying out his criminal activities."[28] On July 10, the *Jewish Times* also provided eye-witness accounts of the mass slaughter and editorially condemned the "conspiracy of silence, regarding the murder of the Jews, by the general press."[29]

The Philadelphia Jewish press, however, did not provide extensive coverage of a series of rallies around the country that were called to denounce Nazi atrocities in the summer of 1942. A major demonstration brought 22,000 people to New York's Madison Square Garden on July 21. The protest was co-sponsored by the American Jewish Congress, the Jewish Labor Committee, and B'nai B'rith. President Franklin D. Roosevelt sent a message stating that the "Nazis will not succeed in exterminating their victims any more than they will succeed in enslaving mankind."[30] In August, there were similar rallies in Boston, Cleveland, Los Angeles, and St. Paul. Neither Philadelphia Jewish weekly provided much coverage of these protests. They did not comment on the president's remarks, nor did they mention the fact that no such protest was held in Philadelphia.[31]

Both papers did report on the increase in the tempo of Nazi atrocities in the summer of 1942, which began the period of the greatest slaughter of Jews in occupied Europe. There were accounts of mass deportations from Holland, and the papers reported that deportations to "unknown destinations" meant a death sentence. The *Exponent* covered the suicide of Adam Chernikov, head of the Jewish Council of the Warsaw Ghetto. It attributed the suicide to the fact

that Chernikov "couldn't bear the suffering of the Jews."[32] Under the headline, "No Limit to the Barbarities," the *Exponent* reported on the removal of 280,000 Jews to camps in Poland and Russia and on the sterilization of Jewish children.[33] In August, the *Times* said that 700,000 Jews had been murdered in gas chambers in Poland.[34]

In September, the *Exponent* reported that the Germans were deporting Jews from occupied France to Poland.[35] As was often the case, *Exponent* editorials disclosed more information than the small news items scattered throughout the body of the paper. The editorial quoted an offer from Pierre Laval, premier of Vichy France: "Anyone wanting them [the Jews] may have them, America in particular." The editorial, however, did not go on to suggest bringing the French Jews to the United States, nor did it propose any other means of rescuing them. It did condemn the silence of the world and its apathy in the face of daily reports of the atrocities inflicted on the Jews of Europe. "Unfortunately," the editorial added, "Jewish leadership contributed to that feeling. They walk on tip toes." In seeking to explain the action of the Jewish leadership, it noted, "They fear anti-Semitism, fear the war will be called a Jewish war."[36]

By October, the *Exponent* had realized the ultimate fate of European Jewry. In a prophetic editorial on October 2, the paper stated that no more than one or one and a half million Jews would survive the war. The editorial scoffed at those Jewish organizations whose agendas "talked of post-war rehabilitation."[37]

In November, the *Exponent* condemned the failure of the Allies and the general press to focus on the terrible plight of the Jews under Hitler. "The first and most painful fact is that the system of the extermination of the Jews transcends in violence and scope the burden imposed on any other people in occupied Europe," the editorial said, correctly defining what has come to be called "the Holocaust." The only solution seen was a United Nations (then another term for the Allied powers) expression of punishment against anyone who murdered Jews.[38]

In November 1942, the facts about the Holocaust burst into the general press when Dr. Stephen Wise, the leading spokesman for the American Zionist Movement, released a report detailing the Nazi's "Final Solution to the Jewish Problem." The report had been given to Wise in August by the World Jewish Congress office in Switzerland, but the rabbi had been asked not to release it by Undersecretary of State Sumner Welles, who wanted time for the State Department to confirm the facts.[39]

The *Exponent* editorially thanked Wise for "utilizing the sounding board of Washington to make public the authenticated documents" and expressed its pleasure that the general press was finally "recognizing the vastness of the horror." Then, probably alluding to the paper's own earlier criticism, the editorial added, "There was an impression that American Jewish leadership had been cowed into silence about these infamies against humanity." Two weeks later, the *Exponent* again lashed out editorially against that leadership. Echoing Dr. Leon Kubowitski, a former Jewish labor leader in Belgium, the editor criticized American Jewry for its failure to save the lives of those who could have been rescued in satellite countries. The editorial quoted the exiled Kubowitski as deploring the "helpless resignation which seems to have gripped American Jewry."[40]

By the fall of 1942, those Philadelphia Jews who read either the *Jewish Exponent* or the *Jewish Times,* which certainly included the leadership of the Jewish community, had a great deal of information on the tragedy taking place in Europe. Nevertheless, this information was not necessarily believed. In a 1977 interview, Judge Lewis Levinthal, national president of the Zionist Organization of America from 1941 to 1943 and a major leader of Philadelphia Jewry, expressed a not atypical attitude. "It is incredible to me that these atrocities were taking place," he said. "I thought it was propaganda, exaggerated—and apparently a lot of others felt the same way." During those years, Levinthal said, he saw his mission as the Zionization of American Jewry. Levinthal's skepticism about the actual state of affairs in Nazi-occupied Europe might help to explain why the complex network of Philadelphia Jewish organizations—charitable, defense, Zionist, and religious—rarely focused on the ongoing destruction of their brethren in Europe.[41]

A précis of the sermons and guest speakers during 1941 and 1942 reveals that the synagogue platform was rarely used to inform congregants about events in Europe. In the Orthodox community, the smallest and least influential segment of Philadelphia, the European tragedy was discussed, but these talks were seldom publicized. One exception was an address by Isaiah Rubinstein, former chief rabbi of Vilna, at a meeting of the Mizrachi (religious Zionists).[42] The local Orthodox rabbinate observed August 12 as a fast day to memorialize the victims of Nazism, but the fast was unnoticed in the city's large Reform and Conservative congregations.[43]

This lack of attention to the events in Europe extended to Philadelphia's Jewish youth groups. Programs at the Young Men's and Young Women's Hebrew Associations centered on topics such as "The Jewish Youth Community" and "Jewish Youth at War." The Jewish Students' Association at Temple University heard Dr. Hayim Fineman, a professor at the college and a high-ranking Zionist with an international reputation, discuss "Jews After the War." AZA, the young men's group of B'nai B'rith, debated "Released Time for Religious Training," and the spring 1942 conclave of the Young People's League, the Conservative youth group, focused on "Design for Jewish Living."[44]

The *Landsmanshaftn,* the small organizations made up of Jews who came from the same town or area in Europe, however, showed more concern for those they had left behind. Rabbi Ephraim Yolles, the dean of Philadelphia's Orthodox rabbinate, was chairman of the Emergency Relief Committee for the Jews of Romania, an arm of the Romanian Beneficial Association, in 1942. A flow of food, religious articles, medicine, and clothing was directed to those Romanian Jews deported or interned. Similar packages were sent by EZRA, the overseas relief arm of the local Association of Polish Jews, headed by Helen Gartman. These packages were sent not only to those Polish Jews under Russian jurisdiction, but also, in defiance of the British blockade, to those in Nazi-occupied Poland. Other *Landsmanshaftn* sent packages to the 600,000 Polish Jews inside Asiatic Russia, many of them in Siberian labor camps. The Soviets permitted these packages to reach their destination. Frequently, these parcels were sent through Russian War Relief, particularly in the latter years of the war.[45]

Organizationally, the Zionist movement provided the cutting edge for Jewish political activism in Philadelphia. In order of size, the city's main Zionist organizations were the Zionist Organization of America, Hadassah, the American Jewish Congress, *Poale Zion* (Labor Zionists), and Mizrachi (Religious Zionists). The local Conservative movement, led by Rabbi Simon Greenberg of Har Zion Temple of Wynnefield, favored Zionism. So did many of the Orthodox, although they were uncomfortable with what they perceived as the irreligious ways of the movement's founders. Rabbi Bernard Levinthal of B'nai Abraham in South Philadelphia, the leading Orthodox rabbi in the city, was pro-Zionist. The city's Reform establishment, however, was generally anti-Zionist. The Zionists tended to be predominantly of Eastern European descent, while the anti-Zionists were mainly of German background.[46]

The Zionists generally looked for guidance to the Jewish Agency for Palestine, a body dominated by Labor Zionists and designated to represent Palestine's Jews by the British Mandatory authorities. Philadelphia's Zionists, like those elsewhere, saw free Jewish emigration to Palestine as the solution to the European Jewish problem. They did not explore the issue of how those Jews trapped in Nazi-controlled Europe were to get to Palestine.

Britain's Jewish policy was formulated in the "White Paper of 1939." Instead of encouraging the formation of a Jewish National Homeland, as promised in the 1917 Balfour Declaration and as charged through its League of Nations mandate, Britain closed Palestine to Jewish immigration and planned for an Arab state with a Jewish minority. The Jewish Agency, representing the vast majority of Palestinian Jewry, and the mainstream Zionist movement viewed the White Paper as a temporary lapse in British policy and remained convinced that it would be reversed in favor of the original Jewish homeland concept. This was also the position of mainstream Zionists in Philadelphia.[47]

In December 1941, however, a rival Zionist organization, the Committee for a Jewish Army, established a chapter in Philadelphia. CFJA was the brainchild of Hillel Kook, a Palestinian Jew (and nephew of Chief Rabbi Kook) who used the alias Peter Bergson. Bergson was a member of the Irgun, the underground army of the Zionist Revisionists who had split with the mainstream Zionists and favored the use of armed force to coerce Britain to relinquish Palestine. Bergson, who was convinced that Britain would reverse the White Paper policy only if forced to do so by the United States, thought that the establishment of a Jewish army to fight the Nazis would help create the climate for the end of the White Paper and the eventual creation of a Jewish state.[48]

The Philadelphia chapter of CFJA was headed by Alexander Wilf, a partner in a well-known carpet firm, who left the management of the family business to his brothers and worked full time for the new organization. The Bergson group also convinced J. David Stern, a prominent New Dealer and publisher of the Philadelphia *Record* and the *Camden Courier Post,* to support the idea. His papers, particularly the *Record,* gave the Jewish army idea a great deal of coverage from the fall of 1941 through 1942. The *Record* published twenty-one news items, editorials, and columns advocating the establishment of a Jewish army to help defend the Middle East from the advancing forces of Field Marshall Erwin Rommel's Afrika Korps.[49]

While the mainstream Zionists demanded that Palestinian Jews be given the right to defend themselves, they belittled Bergson's claim that the 200,000 stateless and Palestinian Jews could form an army. Despite the opposition of the mainstream Zionists and a membership of only a few hundred, the Philadelphia chapter of CFJA brought a number of national figures, such as U.S. Senators Guy Gillette and James Guffy, to Philadelphia to address Center City rallies in support of the Jewish army cause.[50]

On February 16, 1942, the national Committee for a Jewish Army placed a huge ad in the *New York Times.* Composed and signed by the popular Hollywood writer, Ben Hecht, the ad proclaimed: "For Sale to Humanity, 70,000 Jews. Guaranteed Human Beings at $50 a Piece." The ad referred to a *Times* story of an offer by the Romanians, made known in London, to transfer Jews transported to Transniestra in the Ukraine to any refuge designated by the Allies.[51]

Rabbi Stephen Wise immediately called the offer a hoax. The Exponent wrote an angry editorial denouncing the ad. Jack Richman, a local lawyer, Zionist activist, and chairman of the Executive Board of the Pennsylvania Division of the Committee for a Jewish Army, defended the ad, pointing out that the text clearly made no claim that the money raised would be used to save Jews, but publicized the opportunity to do so. "If it were possible to save one Jew," the *Exponent* replied, "the responsible leaders and agencies would do it."[52] Rabbi Wise was later to discover the offer was no hoax, but an opportunity killed by the State Department.

Another incident in February 1942 provided a focus for organized activities against Britain's White Paper policy. The *Struma,* a former Danish cattleboat outfitted in Romania for the rescue of Jews, had taken 767 Jewish refugees aboard at a Black Sea port. It sailed for Haifa even though the refugees had no immigration certificates for Palestine. The ship was stopped at Istanbul by Turkish authorities. The passengers pleaded with the British for immigration certificates, to no avail. In February, the *Struma* was finally towed from the harbor, where it exploded, and all but one of its passengers perished.[53]

This tragedy led to the proclamation of March 1942 as a month of mourning and protest by the Philadelphia Emergency Committee for Zionist Affairs, the umbrella political arm of the major Zionist organizations. A memorial service was held at Adath Jeshurun Congregation, and, in May, the local chapter of the Jewish National Fund established a forest in honor of the *Struma* victims. Both of these occasions were used to deplore British policy in Palestine, but not, according to reports published in both the Exponent and the *Times,* to focus on the plight of those Jews trapped in Europe.[54]

On May 10, 1942, representatives of the major Zionist organizations met at New York's Biltmore Hotel to establish policy. They advocated a clear goal for the movement—the establishment of a Jewish commonwealth in Palestine.[55] In a recent interview, Arnold Ginsberg, at one time a leading officer in the Zionist Organization of America, said, "A Jewish commonwealth or state meant Jewish control over immigration, which in turn meant a haven for the persecuted Jews of Europe."[56] This, in a nutshell, sums up the official Zionist strategy for dealing with the tragedy of European Jewry. Both the *Exponent* and the *Times* endorsed the Biltmore resolution and provided no forum for dissenting opinions.[57]

Throughout the rest of 1942, the Philadelphia Zionist establishment brought important figures in the movement, such as David Ben-Gurion and Louis Lipsky, a former ZOA president, to address local chapters about events relating to Palestine.[58]

On December 17, the Allies formally condemned Germany's genocidal program. In a joint declaration signed by eleven governments and issued simultaneously in Washington, London, and Moscow, the Allies pledged retribution against the Nazis and spelled out the Holocaust: "German authorities are now carrying into effect Hitler's oft-repeated intention to exterminate the Jewish people of Europe. . . . From all the occupied countries of Europe, Jews are being transported in conditions of appalling horror and brutality to Eastern Europe. In Poland, which has become the prin-

Rabbi Ephraim E. Yolles.

Rabbi Elias Charry.

Judge Louis Leventhal, in occupied Europe as Advisor to the Commander-in-Chief on Jewish Affairs.

cipal Nazi slaughterhouse, the ghettoes established by the Nazi invader are being systematically emptied of Jews. . . . None of those taken away are ever heard from again."[59]

Among the general press, from which most of Philadelphia Jewry probably received most of their news—including that on Jewish affairs—only the *Record* featured this statement. Its story, however, in the December 20, 1942, edition, was misleadingly headlined, "Nazis Kill 99 P.C. of Jugoslavia Jews." The details of the Allied declaration were found only in the body of the story. Both the *Exponent* and the *Times,* on the other hand, placed the story on their front pages.[60]

The only major organizational response to the Allied declaration was a meeting at the Benjamin Franklin Hotel to mourn and protest the Nazi killings. Under the auspices of the Jewish National Fund, a "*Nachlath* Philadelphia" (agricultural training settlement) was established to serve as a home for refugees in the post-war period.[61]

At the same time that Philadelphia Jewry received the full impact of the news of the Holocaust, a new national organization was formed that shifted the public discussion from the situation in Europe to the issue of Zionism versus anti-Zionism. The American Council for Judaism (ACJ, discussed elsewhere in this volume) was headquartered in Philadelphia. In response to the formation of this anti-Zionist group composed largely of members of the Reform German-Jewish elite, the mainstream Zionist organization filled the Anglo-Jewish press with arguments for the establishment of a Jewish commonwealth in Palestine in the opening months of 1943. The Zionist leadership sought to convince Philadelphia Jewry that creation of a Jewish state was the only answer to the problems raised by the Nazi destruction of European Jewry.[62]

While Zionist sentiment was widespread in Philadelphia Jewry before World War II, the news of Nazi victories increased Zionist organizational strength greatly. For the first time, virtually the entire organized Jewish community, except for a few small groups, such as the ACJ, endorsed the Zionist agenda of a Jewish commonwealth in Palestine. This Zionist response was clearly a reaction to the plight of European Jews, inadequate as it may have been in rescuing the victims of Nazi destruction.

Local Zionists spent their energy trying to refute the tenets set forth by the American Council for Judaism. The ad placed by members of the rabbinate of Philadelphia and immediate vicinity was revealing:

Hitler and his partners have decreed the extermination of the Jewish people. . . . No country has opened its doors to mass migration of Jewish people. Jews look to Palestine as their one haven of hope. Not only is Palestine a haven of hope, but a religious necessity. The survival of the Jewish people as a living religious movement is dependent on Palestine as a Jewish Commonwealth."[63]

The ad indicates that Philadelphia's rabbinate knew that a Holocaust was taking place. The signers were noted Philadelphia spiritual leaders crossing the Conservative movement and the Orthodox. They included Bernard Levinthal (Orthodox, B'nai Abraham), Simon Greenberg (Conservative, Har Zion), Elias Charry (Conservative, Germantown Jewish Centre), and Ephraim Yolles (Orthodox, Kerem Israel).

Their mentioning that Zionism was "a religious necessity . . . dependent on Palestine as a Jewish Commonwealth" was presumably directed at the American Council for Judaism's view that

Zionism was counterreligious, Judaism being merely a religion practiced by patriots from many national states. Throughout the period, 1942–1945, synagogue pulpits focused on creation of the Jewish Commonwealth to rescue the Jewish people.[64]

By the spring of 1943, the Allies had completed their defeat of the Axis powers in North Africa. The Philadelphia Jewish press kept its readers informed about the condition of North African Jewry before the Axis occupation, during, and after liberation.

Editorials condemned the failure of the Allies to restore Jewish citizenship, property, and political rights in Algeria and Morocco, but the local Jewish organizations did not pick up this protest. The Jewish press also noted that with North Africa and the Mediterranean largely in Allied control, it was possible to rescue Jews in occupied Europe by transporting them from Spain to North Africa. The editorials blamed inaction on the State Department's fear of "antagonizing the Arabs," and criticized Winston Churchill for rescuing 20,000 Poles by creating havens for them in East Africa while ignoring the Jews.[65]

Also in 1943, the Committee for a Jewish Army began to shift its focus from the Jewish army idea to that of rescue. In February, CFJA convened a two-day conference in Philadelphia to discuss possible means of rescuing Jews who remained trapped in Europe. The *Jewish Times* devoted a full page to conference coverage, noting the participation of local CFJA officers Alex Wilf, Jack Richman, and Maurice Rifkin. The paper also printed a long speech by U.S. Representative Francis Myers, the guest speaker, who pleaded with the Jewish community to tell him and his colleagues what to do. Ideas such as strategic bombing of concentration camps and railway hubs, in order to slow the Nazi extermination apparatus, were discussed.[66]

The Philadelphia conference was the forerunner of a larger conference held in New York in mid-July. At that meeting, Peter Bergson, who had founded CFJA, formed the "Emergency Conference to Save the Jewish People of Europe." Both Philadelphia Jewish papers covered the New York conference, the *Times* featuring it on its front page.[67]

Three mass events in the spring and summer of 1943 marked the apogee of efforts to inform and arouse Philadelphia Jewry about the events taking place in Europe. A "Stop Hitler" rally was held at the Academy of Music on April 9. The local chapters of the American Jewish Congress and other mainstream Zionist organizations, with the support of the local AFL and CIO, imported a program from New York that filled three thousand seats at the Academy of Music. The mayor and other local dignitaries in attendance heard pleas to President Roosevelt to stop the slaughter of European Jewry.[68]

Two weeks later, on April 22, the Committee for a Jewish Army brought the Ben Hecht–written pageant *We Will Never Die* to Convention Hall. For weeks before the show, paid advertisements appeared in both local Jewish weeklies. The ads did not feature CFJA's name; proceeds went to the "We Will Never Die Committee."[69] Nevertheless, there must have been a good deal of behind-the-scenes bickering between the Bergsonites and the mainstream Zionists, for a lead *Exponent* editorial on April 2 called for unity between CFJA and the ZOA and "an end to petty bickering."[70] Produced by Billy Rose, directed by Moss Hart, and scored by Kurt Weill, the pageant featured a cast of one thousand headed by a bevy of Hollywood stars, and attracted an audience of fifteen thousand. It concluded with the narrator saying, "No government speaks to bid that the murder of millions end. Those of us here tonight have a voice."[71]

During the summer, another ten thousand Philadelphians jammed the Arena to greet a Jewish delegation from the Soviet Union. They heard Solomon Michoels, chairman of the Joint Anti-Fascist Committee, tell them in Yiddish that four million of their co-religionists had already perished at the hands of the Nazis. (The rally opened with the singing of "The Star Spangled Banner," "The Internationale," and "Hatikvah.") With talks by government officials, heads of both Zionist and pro-Communist Jewish organizations, rabbis, and union leaders, this gathering was a symbol of the importance of Russian War Relief and ties to Soviet Jews for the Jewish community of Philadelphia.[72]

The summer also saw Philadelphia gear up for the founding of the American Jewish Conference, an umbrella organization that was to encompass sixty-four major Jewish groups and was designed to promote unity and provide a single voice for American Jewry. Even though it was organized in the midst of the greatest mass murder of Jews in history, the Conference's stated purpose was "to consider and recommend action on problems relating to the rights and status of Jews in the post-war world and upon all matters . . . of the Jewish people in respect to Palestine."[73] On

June 20, 1943, electors chosen from seven hundred Philadelphia organizations elected twenty-two delegates from a field of one hundred candidates. It is interesting to note that such well-known Federation figures as Morris Wolf, Leon Sunstein, Albert Lieberman, and Leo Heimerdinger withdrew from the ballot, and others, such as Samuel Daroff, Rabbi Max Klein, William Sylk, and Robert Bernstein, were defeated.[74]

The American Jewish Conference met in late August and, despite an unwritten agreement among its leaders not to go so far, adopted a pro-Jewish commonwealth resolution. This caused the (largely German-Jewish) American Jewish Committee and the (left-leaning, anti-Zionist) Jewish Labor Committee to withdraw in anger. The AJC charged the Conference organizers with "subordinating the rescue of European Jewry to the issue of a Jewish commonwealth." Neither the *Exponent* nor the *Times* made any effort to explain the position of the dissenters. Rabbi Bernard Levinthal, Philadelphia's unofficial Orthodox chief rabbi and a charter member of the American Jewish Committee since its founding in 1906, resigned to protest that organization's withdrawal from the Conference. In an open letter featured on the front page of the *Exponent,* he stated, "All Orthodox Jews are vigorously opposed to the stand taken by you."[75]

Reflecting its new emphasis on rescue, the Committee for a Jewish Army changed its name to the "Committee to Save the European Jews" in October. The new group sponsored a march on Washington to call attention to the need for rescue. Five hundred Orthodox rabbis, including

Samuel H. Daroff (in 1957).

Philadelphia's Bernard Levinthal and Ephraim Yolles, participated. The group sought to present a petition directly to the president, calling for activating the International Red Cross, the creation of havens in Allied-controlled territory, and the establishment of a presidential commission with full diplomatic powers solely for the purpose of rescuing Jews. Roosevelt, however, was advised that the group behind the petition was "not representative of the most thoughtful elements in Jewry," and the delegation was whisked off elsewhere. Levinthal managed to deliver the petition to Roosevelt's personal secretary Marvin McIntyre.[76]

Late in 1943, the Gillette-Rogers Bill took center stage. Sponsored by Senator Guy Gillette and Representative Will Rogers, Jr., both supporters of Peter Bergson, the bill called for the creation of temporary havens to which Jews could escape and the establishment of a rescue commission. The measure avoided the issue of opening Palestine to Jewish immigration so as not to offend the British. The *Times* and the *Exponent* gave the bill little publicity, but when Rogers came to Philadelphia, the *Times* came out in favor of the haven idea and suggested that European Jews should be part of a prisoner exchange plan with the Germans. On December 2, Rabbi Stephen Wise testified against the bill, saying he could not support it without an amendment favoring Jewish immigration to Palestine. An *Exponent* columnist echoed Wise's testimony, saying, "No plan makes sense without free immigration to Palestine." The mainstream Zionist organizations also failed to support the bill, in line with their emphasis on Palestine as a solution to the plight of European Jewry.[77]

Three major events in 1943 dramatically illustrated the Philadelphia Jewish leadership's tendency to take a back seat to New York. Under pressure from Jewish organizations pleading in Washington, and even more so in London, for the Allies to take some action to prevent the annihilation of European Jewry, Britain and the United States called a refugee conference in Bermuda on April 20. Recalling a similar conference at Evian, France, in 1938 that amounted to all talk and no action, neither the *Exponent* nor the *Times* expected much.[78]

The national Committee for a Jewish Army placed ads in the New York and Washington papers, calling the Bermuda Conference a "bitter mockery;" but the Philadelphia CFJA placed no ads. In spite of its own doubts about the Bermuda Conference, the *Jewish Times* attacked the CFJA ads, saying, "They resulted in even greater confusion." Proposals submitted to the Conference by the World Jewish Congress, the Jewish Agency for Palestine, and the United Jewish Emergency Committee, and an ad hoc group made up of several large Jewish organizations, were not given publicity in Philadelphia, nor did local organizations use them to stir up interest in the rescue issue.[79]

As the British and American conferees were meeting in Bermuda, young Jews in the Warsaw Ghetto took up arms against their would-be murderers. While the *New York Times* had been reporting on the situation in Warsaw all along, the *Jewish Exponent* and *Jewish Times* reports were spotty, brief, and unclear. Despite their poor news coverage, both papers editorially hailed the ghetto fighters—the *Exponent* calling them modern-day Macabbees and the *Times* suggesting that April 19, the day of the uprising, be proclaimed a new holiday, "Jewish Day."[80]

On May 11, Samuel Zygielbojm, a Jewish member of the Polish government-in-exile, committed suicide and left a farewell letter hoping that his act would help induce the Allies to mount rescue efforts. The *New York Times* published the full text of his letter; the Philadelphia Jewish papers published nothing. The New York rabbis declared May 3 a day of mourning for Jews in Europe; the Philadelphia rabbinate issued no such declaration. A New York rally honored those who fell in the ghetto fighting; Philadelphia Jews held no rally. One exception to Philadelphia's seeming apathy during this period was a September 25 commemoration of the Warsaw uprising by the Jewish Labor Committee.[81]

In the fall, the local Jewish papers ran stories noting that trouble was brewing for the small Jewish community of Denmark. The Nazis were pressing for the deportation of the Danish Jews. In October, both Philadelphia weeklies published the news of Sweden's offer of a haven, and, later, after a daring rescue of Denmark's Jews, both papers lavished praise on the people and kings of the two Scandinavian countries. In New York, emissaries from both countries were honored by the Emergency Committee to Save European Jewry and the Jewish Labor Committee; the Philadelphia chapters of these groups held no ceremonies. Nor was the rescue held up by organizations or editorialists as an example for others.[82] (Two Philadelphia members of the American League for a Free

Palestine, another Bergsonite group, explained later that their organization had limited funds and believed that activity in New York or Washington provided the greatest publicity. It is also possible that because most Jewish organizations were headquartered in New York, Philadelphia Jewry assumed a "let George do it" attitude.[83])

With the establishment of the War Refugee Board on January 22, 1944, rescue began to receive more attention. By early spring, however, the WRB had run out of money, and both Philadelphia Jewish papers began to question the president's sincerity in creating it.[84] Since the WRB received most of its budget, some $15 million, from the Joint Distribution Committee (JDC), which, in turn, received its funding from the United Jewish Appeal, Philadelphia Federation leaders used the Joint's need for money to help rescue Jews as a potent fundraising tool.[85] This campaign was given added impetus when the local Allied Jewish Appeal bought the previously independent *Jewish Exponent* on May 5. The *Exponent's* coverage of the plight of European Jewry was expanded, chiefly as a fulcrum to persuade readers to contribute to the AJA campaign, which helped fund the JDC.[86]

Probably the most important challenge facing the American Jewish community in 1944 was the fate of Hungary's 700,000 Jews, the largest remaining Jewish community in Nazi-occupied Europe. The local Jewish press followed events in Hungary with great concern, noting that in March, German advisers—SS and Gestapo operatives—swarmed across the border. Editorially, both Philadelphia papers stridently demanded the creation of temporary havens to save Hungarian Jewry. They called for the United States to treat Jewish refugees as prisoners of war, interning them within the borders of the United States. No local Jewish organization picked up on the idea. The papers also noted that Portuguese shipping had been used to transport Jews to safety, but there was no communal agitation to use such shipping to rescue Hungarian Jews.[87]

One local Jewish leader, Stanton Kratzok, later offered a reason: "We were afraid to suggest anything that would hamper the war effort. The War Department said that the first business

The staff of the Jewish World, Philadelphia's Yiddish newspaper, joined many others in Russian war relief (the headline of the paper held reads: "4,000 Allied Planes Bomb Nazi Territories/Russians Launch New Offensive for the First Time").

Dedication of Philadelphia's Monument to the Six Million Jewish Martyrs, April 26, 1964.

of this government was to win the war. We didn't want to defy the authorities who emphasized that all shipping was to be done for victory. We were afraid. People were saying that this was a Jewish war."[88]

When Admiral Horthy, the ruler of Hungary, offered to permit Hungarian Jews to emigrate if some country would accept them, there were no takers. The Germans then tightened the noose, and from May 15 to July 7, 437,000 Hungarian Jews were deported to Auschwitz. The *Exponent* ran a column by a well-known journalist, I. F. Stone, who charged that unless havens were created at once, the Allies must be considered accomplices in the extermination of Hungarian Jewry. A *Jewish Times* editorial on June 16, 1944, pleaded, "Now Time to Save." (Ads from all sorts of resorts in the Poconos, Catskills, and Atlantic City that surrounded the editorial give it, in retrospect, a sad poignancy.)[89]

But only one such haven was created. Nearly one thousand refugees were interned for the duration of the war at Fort Ontario, an old army camp in Oswego, New York. The *Exponent* gave Oswego front-page coverage, but the *Jewish Times,* now Philadelphia's only independent Jewish newspaper, considered it a "drop in the bucket, insulting," and grew impatient with the War Refugee Board. It called its activities "too slow in the face of planned destruction."[90]

The Jewish press also rejected other possibilities for rescue. When Joel Brand, a member of the Budapest Jewish Council, met with War Refugee Board member Ira Hirschman and revealed that he had been authorized by the Germans to negotiate a trade of Jewish lives for trucks, the *Exponent* dismissed his mission as a ruse, a transparent attempt to split the Western Allies and the Russians. This was essentially the same argument used by the British, who were seeking to avoid an increase in pressure for admitting Jews to Palestine.[91]

Palestine, however, continued to dominate local Jewish organizational activity. Britain's 1939 White Paper set a quota of 15,000 Jewish immigrants a year, up to a total of 75,000, ending March 31, 1944. As this deadline approached, agitation increased. In January, 1,200 local Zionists paid $100 a plate to hear Abba Hillel Silver denounce the British. In February, an ad hoc Anti-White Paper Committee drew 5,000 to a rally at the Academy of Music. Open immigration to Palestine for any Jew who managed to escape Hitler was an issue on which all segments of an otherwise divided Jewish community could agree.[92]

This concern for Palestine as *the* solution to the Jewish problem was reflected in the response to two pieces of legislation proposed in Congress. When Representative Samuel Dickstein of New York offered a measure calling for the immediate acceptance of refugees into the United States, where they could be granted temporary haven until six months after the war, the *Exponent* hailed the idea, but the Jewish organizations were conspicuously silent.[93] This was not the case with respect to another measure urging the opening of Palestine to immigration and the establishment of a Jewish Commonwealth. This bill, called Wright-Compton in the House and Taft-Wagner in the Senate, garnered major Jewish support. A Philadelphia letter-writing campaign generated ten thousand pieces of mail backing this legislation; full-page ads appeared; fifty Jewish youth organizations rallied; and the Jewish press lashed out against the anti-Zionists of the American Council for Judaism who testified against the bill, calling them "traitors and deserters." When it came to Zionism, Philadelphia Jews flexed their political muscle.[94]

The Palestine resolutions, however, were snuffed out when Army Chief of Staff General George C. Marshall testified before Congress that they would have adverse military effects on the Moslem world. The power of the "hurt-the-war-effort" argument was displayed when the Zionist Emergency Council then appealed to Congress to pass the resolutions "at an early moment consistent with the exigencies of the war effort," agreeing, in effect, with Marshall. While Revisionist-sponsored ads in the *New York Post* and the *New Republic* attacked Marshall, saying he had aligned "himself against the rescue of hundreds of thousands of torture-stricken people," the Philadelphia Jewish weeklies and local Jewish organizations carried no such criticism.[95]

Despite this setback, the year 1944 marked a dramatic leap in Zionist activity—a recruitment, publicity, and propaganda campaign that did not abate until the establishment of the Jewish State in 1948. The ZOA grew to eight thousand members. It sponsored Zionist Sabbaths, special speakers for neighborhood synagogues, and whole-page ads in the Jewish weeklies as well as ads on weekly radio programs. Walter Annenberg, publisher of the *Philadelphia Inquirer,* was influential in getting a pro-Jewish Common- wealth plank at the Republican National

Convention, and Judge Louis Levinthal rushed to the Democratic National Convention to strengthen its Palestine plank. The city's Jewish organizational clout focused on trying to establish a Jewish state.[96]

As the war wound down, both local Jewish papers began to publish accounts of the Russian liberation of several concentration camps. The *Exponent* carried a detailed eyewitness report on the liberation of Majdanek, and the War Refugee Board's statistics on Auschwitz revealing that some 1.8 million people had died there.[97] Yet, the dismissal of Herbert Pell, a member of the U.S. War Crimes Commission who had advocated strict punishment for Nazis involved in mass murder, was given scant coverage in Philadelphia, although it made the front pages of newspapers in New York and Washington. Pell had clashed with the State Department, which maintained that the Axis powers could not be held accountable under international law for crimes against their own nationals. An *Exponent* editorial passed off Pell's dismissal, saying, "The President doesn't always have his way."[98]

Despite the reports on the Russian liberation of the concentration camps, the real horror of the Holocaust probably did not sink in until American troops began to liberate the camps. When General Dwight Eisenhower invited the press corps editors, publishers, and movie makers to tour the camps, the horror finally struck home. When Americans, Jews and Gentiles, saw the pictures and films of the human skeletons in their striped uniforms, the piles of dead bodies, the bulldozers pushing corpses into mass graves, the endless piles of human hair, baby clothes, eyeglasses, they realized, most for the first time, what had happened. Nonetheless, Philadelphia's Jewish organizations did not use the death of Hitler or the final surrender of the Third Reich as occasions to memorialize millions of Jewish dead.[99]

What did provoke a mass reaction was the death of President Franklin Roosevelt in April 1945. A community memorial service was held at the Jewish Y (YM/YWHA), and AJA director Kurt Peiser eulogized the president. The *Exponent* printed Peiser's entire speech. That Friday and Saturday, the city's synagogues memorialized the dead president, and many synagogues held special Sunday memorial services. A few days later, Roosevelt was eulogized again at the Allied Jewish Appeal headquarters. Both the Jewish papers and the Jewish organizations refrained from mentioning FDR's failure to press for the rescue of Jews, his failure to urge the British to open Palestine, his failure to allow the United States to be used as a haven for refugees. So great was his standing in the Jewish community that it would take a quarter of a century for the questions about his wartime rescue role to begin to surface.

In retrospect, it appears that the Philadelphia Anglo-Jewish press played an ambivalent, but, on the whole, reasonably positive role. Both the *Jewish Exponent* and the *Jewish Times* reported on the major news of the Holocaust and even, at times, chastised the Jewish leadership for a perceived failure to act more vigorously.[100] The Jewish leadership—the rabbis, the Zionist leadership, the officers and staff of the Allied Jewish Appeal, the heads of other organizations—knew what was happening in Europe, yet they ignored many opportunities to educate their constituencies and the general public. They failed to generate mass support for a rescue effort, and when they did react, their manner was timid. There were no mass demonstrations, no marches on Washington, no hunger strikes, no work stoppages, no picketing, no synagogues draped in mourning black. This indecisiveness and apathy stood in sharp contrast to the energy and enthusiasm manifested simultaneously for Russian war relief, Zionism, and, of course, the war itself.

Why? The Philadelphia Jewish community, like the rest of American Jewry, was fearful and divided. Philadelphia Jews were divided into Germans and Russians, old settlers and new immigrants, wealthy and not, Zionist and anti-Zionist, religious and secular. All these divisions carried with them a history of internecine battling, a history that could not easily be overcome even in the face of unthinkable horror—so unthinkable that many Jews did not totally believe it themselves.

In addition, the period immediately preceding the war was a time of rising anti-Semitism. Father Coughlin was on the radio, and German-American Bundists marched in the streets.

America's Jews were not yet secure in their new homes. When the war began, Jews were super-sensitive to charges that they had dragged America into fighting to save the Jews.

These factors all hampered the organization of a concerted Jewish campaign in Philadelphia on behalf of the entrapped Jews of Europe. Philadelphia Jewry certainly wanted to do whatever could be done; it lacked the unity necessary to decide what had to be done, the sense of urgency necessary to implement their decisions, and the will to risk its tenuous position in this country in all-out effort.

EPILOGUE[101]

During the late 1940s and early 1950s, Holocaust survivors began arriving and settling in Philadelphia. In answer to their need for social contacts with those of similar experiences and the desire for Yiddish cultural activity, about 150 families joined together in 1953 to form the Organization of Jewish New Americans in Philadelphia. Many of these survivors wished to forget the Holocaust; they refrained from telling even their children about life under the Nazis. But there was a large number who wished to remember and memorialize their relatives and friends who perished. Each year from 1953 on, they met in hired halls and held a service in Yiddish, giving speeches and writing poetry about the terrible days during World War II. As the 1960s approached, the idea grew to erect a statue memorializing the Six Million.[102]

The Jewish New Americans raised money, held a variety of affairs, and solicited from wealthy Philadelphia Jews. When they had gathered about $60,000, they commissioned a Jewish sculptor, Nathan Rapoport, also a survivor, to carve out a monument. Working in Italy, Rapoport sculptured a marble base inscribed with the names of infamous concentration camps. The rest, in bronze, depicts a huge burning bush, an elderly Jew with his talit and Torah Scroll, the faces of a suffering mother and children, and, at the top, hands holding daggers of resistance. On the after-noon of April 26, 1964, near Passover, the time of the Warsaw Ghetto Uprising, and near the Holocaust Memorial Day, *Yom haShoah,* the statue was veiled at a dedication service, and the first community-wide Yizkor ceremony for the martyrs of the Holocaust was observed. It has since became a tradition in the city in late April to hold a Jewish memorial service commemorating the Jewish victims of Hitler's war.[103]

In the fall of 1966, representatives of nearly one hundred local Jewish organizations met under the auspices of the Jewish Community Relations Council and formed a citywide Memorial Committee for the Six Million Martyrs. It was the first such committee formed in any city in the world outside the State of Israel. The Committee is funded by the Federation of Jewish Agencies and contributions from community organizations. Under the prodding of the survivors, at last, the entire Jewish community of Philadelphia would take responsibility for institutional memorialization of the Six Million.

In 1970, the Association of New Americans organized and hosted the First National Assembly for delegations of Jewish Survivor organizations in the United States. The idea took hold in other places, including Jerusalem. In 1985, a World Gathering of Jewish Holocaust Survivors was held at Convention Hall, Philadelphia.

The Memorial Committee, seeking to get Christians more involved, joined with the Cardinal's Commission on Human Relations of the Archdiocese of Philadelphia and the Episcopal Diocese and the Philadelphia Board of Education to form a Coordinating Council on the Holocaust. In the fall of 1975, the Council organized the First International Conference on the Lesson of the Holocaust. Its workshops generated educational material sought by learning institutions. It is now an annual event, attracting educators from all over the world.[104]

In the winter of 1976, these groups and a number of educators from within the school district of Philadelphia testified before the Philadelphia Board of Education that Holocaust information be integrated within the secondary social studies program. The Board gave approval, and an official Holocaust Guide was produced and an inservice course for teachers was started.[105]

At Gratz College, under the leadership of Professor Nora Levin, a Holocaust Oral History Archive was begun. Since 1979, survivor testimony has been taken on sound tape. Documents, memorabilia, and Yad VaShem photographs have been acquired in addition to a library of two hundred tapes. In the Northeast section of the city, a survivor, Jacob Riz (now deceased), maintained a photographic and documentary museum, the Jewish Identity Center, operating largely from his basement. The museum, augmented by artifacts contributed by Arnold Shay, a survivor and holocaust documentarian, was housed at Gratz College.[106]

In 1980, a branch group from the Association of New Americans, called the Sons and Daughters of Holocaust Survivors, organized with a charter membership of two hundred families. They dedicated themselves to memorialize the Nazi victims and educate the community on the Holocaust. Their parent group, the New Americans, realizing their title was dated and identifying the thrust of their mission, changed their name to the Association of Jewish Holocaust Survivors.[107]

Decades after the greatest slaughter of Jews in history, led by survivors, the organized Jewish community has created institutions so that Philadelphia and its environs would never forget the Six Million.

2 SECTIONS

PUBLISHED EVERY FRIDAY SINCE 1887

2 SECTIONS

JEWISH EXPONENT

A Weekly Journal Devoted to the Interests of the Jewish People

Volume 118—No. 19   PHILADELPHIA, IYAR 19, 5708—MAY 28, 1948   One Dollar Per Annum

Pay Homage Sunday to Seven Jewish Heroes Of Revolutionary War

Revolutionary War markers will be placed on the graves of seven soldiers buried in the Mikveh Israel Cemetery, Spruce Street between 8th and 9th, by the Continental Chapter of the Sons of the American Revolution Sunday at 3 P. M.

The seven Revolutionary War soldiers are:

Major Benjamin Nones, who served on the staffs of General Washington, Lafayette, and Pulaski. Major Nones commanded a Jewish Legion of 400 soldiers. In 1779 he received a certificate for bravery and good conduct on the field of battle, including the Battle of Charleston and the Siege of Savannah. From 1791 to 1799 and from 1820 to 1822 he was President of Congregation Mikveh Israel.

Private Michael Gratz, who served in the Continental Army in Virginia. Private Gratz signed the Non-Importation Resolution in 1765, and was the father of Hyman Gratz, founder of Gratz College in this city, and Rebecca Gratz, immortalized as Rebecca in Sir Walter Scott's "Ivanhoe."

Private Aaron Levy, who served in the Northumberland County Militia. In 1786 he purchased a tract of land in Center County, Pennsylvania, which in 1786 he laid out and planned as the town of Aaronsburg, the first town in the country named after a Jew. During the Revolution he loaned a considerable sum of money to the Continental Congress, which was never fully repaid. He also furnished supplies
(Continued on Page 8)

Acting President Of Seminary

Rabbi Simon Greenberg, provost of the Jewish Theological Seminary of America, will be acting president of the Seminary for the academic year 1948-49. Doctor Louis Finkelstein, president of the Seminary, has been granted a leave of absence during that period to carry out further research in his rabbinic studies.

Dr. Greenberg

When he assumes his temporary post on September 1st, Doctor Greenberg will be continuing an academic association which began when he enrolled as a student with the class of 1919 at the Seminary's Teachers Institute. For 20 years Rabbi Greenberg was Rabbi of Har Zion Temple.

Impressive Ceremonies Mark Local Unfurling Of the Flag of Israel

With more than 10,000 persons thrilling to the spectacle, the flag of Israel was unfurled over Reyburn Plaza Tuesday afternoon, the first raising of the flag of Israel in Philadelphia.

The huge gathering cheered as the flag, bearing a blue Star of David on a white field, with two blue bars dividing the star, was raised.

A second flag of Israel was presented to Mayor Bernard Samuel, and it will be displayed in Independence Hall along with flags of other nations. The Mayor spoke briefly on tolerance in world affairs.

Judge Louis E. Levinthal declared that the circumstances of Israel's founding were similar to in Reyburn Plaza. It seems appropriate indeed that special ceremonies should mark this event in Philadelphia, the city which brought forth the Declaration of American Independence and also gave to us the flag which we as Americans all cherish. To all of you assembled for this occasion today, I wish to

---

Jews End Hunger Strike in DP Camp; Win Concessions

ROME, (JTA.)—A week-long hunger strike at the Scoula Cardona camp for displaced Jews, in Milan, and in several satellite camps in the area has been settled with assurances by the Italian Government and the International Refugee Organization that new refugees who cross the border from Austria and elsewhere will be admitted, it was announced here.

The I.R.O. has already begun distributing food in the camps and some of the DP's today started moving to the Senegalia Camp, near Ancona. The I.R.O. originally cut off DP rations when the Jews refused to move out of the Milan camps.

Displaced Jews in the camps of northern Italy viewed with suspicion the transfer order—latest of a series of moves by the Italian Government apparently aimed at clearing all of northern Italy of DP's, thus making it extremely difficult for new refugees to enter the country en route to Palestine. The refugees who occupy five major centers and some 35 small training centers refused to move pending a clear statement of intentions on the part of the Italian Government.

The Jews believed that the series of moves, which began with the evacuation of the inhabitants of a camp in Milan to the south because the authorities informed the I.R.O. that the center was needed for a police camp to guard against disturbances during the April 18 national elections, was inspired by the British or American Governments or both.

Dropsie Founder's Day June 2

Judge Horace Stern, Justice of the Pennsylvania Supreme Court, and Dr. Alexander Marx, Librarian and Professor of History at the Jewish Theological Seminary of America, will deliver the principal addresses at the fortieth anniversary Founder's Day celebration of The Dropsie College for Hebrew and Cognate

---

We 'Hold Key to Immigration Programme in Israel'
—*Golda Myerson*

Homeless Jews are now entering the new State of Israel at the rate of 15,000 a month and before the end of 1948 the total number of immigrants to Palestine will exceed 120,000 Mrs. Golda Myerson, Administrator of the Jewish section of Jerusalem and member of the Provisional Council of the State of Israel, now on a short visit to this country, last night told leaders of the 1948 campaign of the Allied Jewish Appeal.

Mrs. Myerson is guest speaker today (Friday) at the regular report luncheon at the Warwick Hotel.

Outlining plans for the greatest resettlement program in the history of the Jewish people, Mrs. Myerson called for immediate financial support to enable Israel to receive and settle the large number of new immigrants.

She reported that facilities of the Tel Aviv port are being expanded to accomodate the many ships that will be required for this mass transfer of refugees.

Mrs. Myerson

She also called for funds to make possible the establishment of 40 new agricultural settlements in the north and south of the New State to speed the absorption of the record number of new arrivals.

Mrs. Myerson declared that the 25,000 Jewish refugees now on Cyprus would be transferred to Palestine within the next two months.

American Jews "hold the key to the immigration program in Israel," she said as she emphasized that the $250,000,000 United Jewish Appeal, which in our city is included in the Allied Jewish Appeal, must be the source of the funds required for the mass exodus from the displaced persons centers to the new Jewish State.

As chief Jewish executive in the Holy City, Mrs. Myerson, who arrived in this country by plane earlier in the week, deplored the battle of Jerusalem. She charged

---

Italy Issues Israel Visas To 2 Americans

ROME (JTA) — Two Americans, Isler Solomon and his wife, this week received the first Hebrew-printed visas to Israel issued in this country. Signed by Arie Stern, Jewish Agency representative in Italy, the visas were inserted into the Solomon's American passports. They will leave shortly for Tel Aviv where Solomon will conduct several concerts.

Celebrations marking the establishment of Israel are continuing in various parts of Italy. The British consul in Bari celebrated the Israeli proclamation of statehood at a Jewish gathering there. Rabbi I. M. Levin, Minister without portfolio in the Israeli Cabinet, stopped off here en route to New York, becoming the first Israeli Minister to visit Italy.

Eleven planes believed to be en route to Israel were grounded by Italian officials after their papers were found not to be in order. They stopped at the Ciampinio airport near here. Other planes, whose papers were in order were allowed to proceed to their destination. Two or three planes, mostly from Western European countries, have passed through Rome daily en route to Israel since the British Mandate terminated.

IRO 'Explains' Ban On Migration Aid

Section ii. Four Fateful Years: Philadelphia's Jews and the Creation of the State of Israel

Philip Rosen

1945

At the end of the European war in May 1945, attention focused on the condition of the estimated 1.25 million Jews who survived Hitler's inferno. Their condition understandably was poor. Many Jews continued to live in concentration camps and prisons without proper food, clothes, sanitation, heat, or living space. The vast array of Jewish agencies, including the Joint Distribution Committee, had not stockpiled supplies in neutral and friendly countries, and the American Army was unprepared to help the unfortunates. Often, officers were ignorant of or indifferent to the plight of their new wards, or did nothing to help because of outright anti-Semitism. American Jewish army chaplains tried to step into the breach as best they could. They sent back pleas to the States for clothing, medicine, doctors, and health and social workers. There was no communitywide drive in Philadelphia to recruit these workers to aid overseas.[1]

There were individual elements, however, in the Philadelphia Jewish community that took direct action for their kindred overseas. The Orthodox community gathered lists of survivors and made their names and whereabouts available to local relatives in an attempt to bring the two parties together. They raised and distributed $300,000 in materials to "displaced persons"—those who could not or would not go back to their original home in Europe. The Orthodox raised money to establish religiously oriented orphanages to reclaim children raised among Christians in Europe. "Food for Jewish Children," a division of Agudas Israel (a worldwide union of Orthodox congregations) solicited money, employed young people as collectors, and sent kosher food overseas. Jennie Faggen, of the Strawberry Mansion section of the city, ran one such operation from her home.[2]

The Religious Zionists appealed to the community to send religious articles to survivors. It had three locations for such donations: 716 Pine, 4900 North 8th, and 3940 West Girard. Other segments had their own drives. Har Zion synagogue collected 40,000 pounds of clothing for survivors. The Philadelphia District of the American Federation of Polish Jews raised $100,000 for overseas aid. Rabbi Ephraim Yolles presided over the Rumanian Emergency Relief Committee from the Logan section, where they shipped religious items, food, and medicine. Hadassah, the Zionist organization for women, then 6,700 strong in the city, held a luncheon that raised $50,000. Rabbis Bernard Levinthal and Ephraim Yolles, both on the Presidium of the Vaad Hatzalah, the Orthodox rescue arm, affirmed that 1,200 packages a month would continue to be sent to rabbis and yeshiva students interned by the Soviet government during the war.[3]

Behind the scenes, the American Jewish Conference, an umbrella organization of sixty-four major Jewish organizations, was petitioning President Truman to act on behalf of Jewish survivors. They suggested attaching Jewish liaison officers to the military government to advise the army on the handling of Jews. Both General Eisenhower and President Truman rejected the idea. Secretary of the Treasury Henry Morgenthau suggested to the president that Earl Harrison, a Philadelphia lawyer, former U.S. Commissioner of Immigration, U.S. representative on the Intergovernmental Committee on Refugees, and, in 1945, dean of the University of Pennsylvania Law School, personally review the situation of Jews in the U.S. Army zone of occupation, and make a special report to the president.[4]

Louis Levinthal, Philadelphia jurist and a high official in the national Zionist Organization of America, hailed Harrison as one of the *chasidei umoth ha'olam,* the righteous among the gentile peoples. Harrison's report was released to the general press on September 29, 1945. In substance, he stated that, indeed, the condition of the Jewish survivors was disgraceful and that their suffering was unique. Jews needed to be recognized not merely as nationals of other countries, for due to the mass murder and anti-Semitism, most could not return to their former homes. Lastly,

Officers of the Jewish National Fund at their annual meeting, Bellevue Stratford Hotel, November 19, 1944. From left: Benjamin Shander, Samuel Kratzok (President), Nathan Edelstein, Dr. Solomon Stein.

because settlement in Palestine was a realistic solution, 100,000 Palestine certificates should be issued by the British so that the survivors could settle in the Holy Land.[5]

Both Jewish weeklies, the *Jewish Times* and the *Exponent,* hailed the report and picked up strongly on the recommended 100,000 Palestine certificates. There was little interest in Congressman Samuel Dickstein's (D, NY) bill to study and revise United States immigration laws so that more Jews could come to American shores.[6]

The British refused to budge from their position of barring Jews from Palestine. At first, the Irgun and Stern group attacked British military installations. Later in the year, the Haganah, the military arm of the Jewish Agency, joined in. They all promoted "illegal immigration," and the British bore down with their navy and armed forces. News of the open warfare between the British and the Yishuv (Jewish community in Palestine) came thick and fast. At year's end, a number of prominent Philadelphia figures went on personal missions to world leaders. Joseph Sharfsin, former Philadelphia city solicitor left by ship from New York to confer with Harold Laski, chairman of the British Labor Party, and Ernest Bevin of the Foreign Office. Sharfsin and his party of five were sponsored by the American League for a Free Palestine, the Peter Bergson Irgun-related group. Later, Sharfsin was joined by J. David Stern, the Philadelphia publisher of the *Record* and *Camden Courier,* allied with both the League and Bergson's Hebrew Committee of National Liberation. The substance of their deliberation was the proposal that the United Nations assume trusteeship over Palestine and that the UN supervise the immediate repatriation of Hebrews from Germany and Austria to Palestine.[7]

The talks were fruitless, and Stern and Sharfsin returned frustrated and disappointed. Stern, along with Chaim Weizmann, president of the Jewish Agency for Palestine, and Lessing Rosenwald, still presiding over the American Council for Judaism from Philadelphia, met with President Truman. The president expressed his opposition to a Jewish state, saying that a Palestinian state should be a democratic one, not associated with race, religion, or creed. He did not favor unlimited immigration to Palestine but "repatriation up to Palestine's absorptive capacity"—a term used by the British years before in the early Mandate to restrict Jewish immigration.[8]

1946

During the years 1941 to 1945, the Holocaust years, the *Exponent* ran low-key stories on the murders taking place in Europe. In 1946 the weekly, an organ of the Allied Jewish Appeal, publicized dramatically the plight of the survivors. Many photographs (some full-page) were published that showed the worst aspects of the Holocaust and the present poor conditions. Headlines and huge ads in a frequent supplement entitled "Survival" dramatized the plight of the victims of Hitler and the need to contribute to the Allied Appeal so that its agencies, principally the Joint Distribution Committee, could bring relief. The readers were given news about anti-Semitism in Europe; about the riot in Kielce, Poland; and the plight of Jews fleeing to American displaced-persons (DPs) camps.[9]

Philadelphia readers received only a glimmer of the idea that Jewish agencies were not doing enough about the conditions that 250,000 Jewish DPs lived under. The *Jewish Times* published letters from chaplains pointing out Joint's shortcomings. Rabbi Aaron Dector, officer of ZOA, working on the European scene, wrote how the chaplains and members of the Jewish Brigade, rather than Joint or UNRRA (UN aid organization), were helping Jews. He lashed out at the American Jewish community: "We are wallowing in wealth, and in a certain sense it is blood money." Both papers reported the dire need for social workers, doctors and health workers. The *Jewish Times* considered it pageone news when a young woman social worker volunteered to go overseas. The Allied Jewish Appeal, sensing that subscribers were balking because of the diversion of funds, promised that $5 million of the $6 million that was Philadelphia's share in a nationwide campaign for $100 million, would go for overseas relief.[10]

During the mass murder of Europe's Jews, there were few attempts to dramatize the tragedy to Jewish children in Philadelphia. Now, in 1946, Jewish schools participated in the Allied campaign to raise $6 million. Teachers received lesson plans and song sheets; they were encouraged to have children make posters, enter essay contests, and prepare special assemblies stressing the need to aid Allied in relieving the suffering of their fellow Jews. Students who won prizes attended a luncheon and pep rally at Bookbinder's Restaurant. On April 18, thousands of Jewish youth crowd-

ed into the Academy of Music at Broad and Locust to view a play, see a *March of Time* film on the DP camps, and hear, live on stage, a concert by Frank Sinatra.[11]

The idea of getting American Jews involved outside Allied was picked up by the JDC. Supplies for Overseas Survivors (SOS) was started by Joint and administered by Jewish women's organizations. Francis Bramnick, head of the Pennsylvania Ladies Auxiliary of the Jewish War Veterans, led the campaign to gather food, clothing, toys, medicine, and miscellaneous items. Food supplies constituted 54 percent; clothing, 28 percent; and miscellaneous supplies, 18 percent. Philadelphia, the city with the third largest Jewish population, came in third in the nationwide collection.[12]

The trial of the top Nazi leaders, which started in Nuremberg in October 1945, concluded in October 1946. The Philadelphia Jewish weeklies and organizations took very little interest in them. Unlike the *Palestine Post* of Jerusalem, which published reports of the testimony against Goering, Doenitz, Runstadt, and other criminals on the front page, the *Exponent* and *Times* reported and editorialized very little. The only war criminal on the minds of the Philadelphia leadership was the Grand Mufti of Jerusalem. The Mufti "escaped" from France via Egypt (controlled by the British) to Syria. The Jewish weeklies ran accounts of how the Mufti had advised Hitler on the murder of Jews. The Philadelphia Zionist Emergency Council, an umbrella organization that orchestrated political action in the city on behalf of the Yishuv, was convinced that the escape of the Mufti was "a British plot to trouble the waters of the Middle East, hatched by the desire to appease Arabs and protect [British] oil interests."[13]

Members of the Philadelphia Zionist Emergency Council and other organization picket the British Consulate on South 12th St., July 18, 1946.

Top leaders of the secrect Sonneborn "Institute." Left to right (seated) are William Sylk, drug store magnate and charter member of the Institute; Kurt Peiser, administrative head of both federation, Allied and Jewish Charities; Max Slepin, chairman of the "Material for Palestine, Inc." which clandestinely shipped arms; (standing) Samuel Daroff, clothing magnate and top officer in Allied; Lawrence Horowitz, ZOA head; unidentified member.

Zionist issues continued to take up the attention of Philadelphia Jewry in 1946. When the Anglo American Committee of Inquiry on Palestine gave its report, the Council seized on the recommendation it made for immediate 100,000 Palestine immigration certificates for Jewish DPs. Britain flatly rejected the Inquiry report. Foreign Minister Ernest Bevin made the provocative comment, "Why are American Jews pushing this idea? Because they do not want any more Jews in New York."[14]

The Bergson-related Palestine Emergency Fund and the Orthodox community, through the Yiddish daily *Morning Journal,* co-sponsored a pageant indicating British Palestine policy. Entitled "That We May Live," it filled Convention Hall and took the form of a trial.[15]

Meanwhile, the fighting intensified in Palestine. On Saturday, June 27, the British arrested over one thousand Jewish leaders—including leaders of the Jewish Agency who could no longer deny that its military arm, the Haganah, was fighting the British along with the Stern Group and Irgun. In July more hunts and arrests occurred in the Yishuv. The National Jewish War Veterans planned a March on Washington, DC, protesting British Palestine policy. Jacob Richman, representing the Philadelphia ZOA Council, supervised a small contingent of a few hundred that left from City Hall to join five thousand in the capital. Jack Gross, county adjutant, was clearly unhappy about Philadelphia's participation.[16]

In late July, the Irgun blew up the King David Hotel, site of British military offices in Jerusalem. The British retaliated by closing the Yishuv's self governing institutions and arresting members of the Jewish Agency, the very body elected by the Yishuv to represent it in dealing with the Mandate officials. The Agency began secret talks with the British regarding partition. By early August, the *Jewish Exponent* published partition plans, which looked very much like the lines drawn by the United Nations one year later. President Truman issued a Yom Kippur message urging partition. Arnold Ginsburg, local lawyer, Zionist activist, and columnist for the *Jewish Times,* was amazed that the Palestine branch of the Jewish Agency acted alone and had not sought any input from other Zionist groups. The *Exponent* gave full coverage to Rabbi Abba Hillel Silver's attack on Nachum Goldman, high agency officer, for negotiating the partition. The local American League for a Free Palestine protested the partition plan and the British unilateral move creating the new State of Jordan, once part of the League of Nations Mandate and set aside as the Jewish National Home. The ALFP urged a sympathetic Congressman Francis Myers to organize a congressional resolution against the move, but he found insufficient support.[17]

In the fall, the American Jewish Congress, with labor and veteran support, staged a huge parade and rally at Independence Hall that attracted 30,000 people. Their placards added a new grievance—British placement of so-called illegal refugees in concentration camps in Cyprus. The editorials in the *Jewish Times* could not understand why the official Zionist groups declined to participate and why notable leaders in the Zionist Emergency Council, the umbrella organization, were conspicuously absent.[18]

The Jewish National Fund, the land-redeeming organization, was active in 1946. It sponsored a pageant in November entitled "Out of the Depths." The theme of the Holocaust was used as a fulcrum to support immigration to Palestine. There were also programs to raise money for buying land in honor of Louis Levinthal, honorary president of the Zionist Organization of America. Over five thousand blue and white JNF collection boxes were placed throughout the city. Several Philadelphians, such as Samuel Kratzok, Abraham Silver, and Rabbi Chaim Barzel, rose to leadership in the national JNF.[19]

Ten days later, on July 30, ZEC pickets the offices of the British Consulate.

Lawrence Horowitz, head of the Zionist Emergency Council, addresses rally at Rayburn Plaza, July 20, 1947. The rally protested the boarding of the Exodus 47,

As the year ended, Zionists made all-out efforts to recruit members. Hundreds of workers flooded Jewish neighborhoods on "Palestine Days." But the Zionists were not united. The Haganah called off resistance, but the Irgun and Stern Group fought on in Palestine. The American Jewish Congress brought in Stephen Wise and Senator Claude Pepper to the Academy of Music to advocate UN Trusteeship over Palestine, a weakening of the position for a completely independent Jewish state. As the snow began to fall, the American League prepared to push the cause of military resistance against British occupation of the Yishuv.[20]

1947

In January 1947, the American League for a Free Palestine, the Bergson-founded, Irgun-related successor to the Jewish Army Committee, sponsored a play written by Ben Hecht entitled, *A Flag Is Born.* Kurt Weill arranged the music; Luther Adler directed it, and Marlon Brando played the lead role. It extolled violent resistance. The background showed tombstones of Europe and a young man's despair of ever reaching Palestine. The play ended with the line, "We promise to wrest our homeland out of British claws." Because Hecht and the League were part of the Irgun, the mainstream Jewish organizations opposed the play. The same internecine warfare that hampered rescue during the Holocaust years reared up again. Giant ads in both Jewish weeklies denounced the production. Picket lines formed around the Erlanger Theater, located at 20th and Market Streets. Nevertheless, the Ben Hecht drama had full houses for two weeks.[21]

The distress of 250,000 Jewish DPs living under poor conditions, their fate undecided, continued to be the concern of Philadelphia Jewry. Various personages went abroad to assay the plight of the survivors. Philadelphia Allied Jewish Appeal leaders Leonard Geis and Samuel Daroff made a tour of inspection in Europe. Lessing Rosenwald, Sears magnate, at the request of the United States War Department, toured Europe to give advice on economic recovery. Judge Louis Levinthal became advisor for European Jewish Affairs to the U.S. Military Governor, General Lucius Clay.[22]

The Allied Jewish Appeal of Philadelphia, made up of forty-seven agencies, fourteen of which were involved in overseas aid, was very concerned about the 1.2 million survivors. The United Nations Relief and Rehabilitation Agency was to be terminated on July 1. Allied, and particularly its major overseas relief constituent, the Joint Distribution Committee, needed funds. To bolster its campaign, Allied brought well-known Jewish and non-Jewish personalities to Philadelphia, including Herbert Lehman, former governor of New York; financier Edward

Rabbi Simon Greenberg, spiritual leader of Har Zion of Wynnefield and one of the city's most ardent and active Zionists, here greets Moshe Shertok (right) prior to mass meeting of Americans for Haganah at the Broadwood Hotel, December 18, 1947.

Warburg; and Henry Morgenthau. Entertainer Eddie Cantor was introduced by Walter Annenberg, publisher of the *Philadelphia Inquirer.* Eleanor Roosevelt and Supreme Court Justice Frank Murphy also came to urge support.[23]

Allied sponsored another rally for Jewish children in both the day and afternoon schools at the Academy of Music. The program featured Al Capp, the cartoonist and creator of "Li'l Abner." A chorus of children under the direction of Sholom Altman of Gratz College of Hebrew Studies sang, and the youngsters learned from various educators about the needs of Europe's Jews.[24]

Out on the streets, 2,500 volunteers from the women's division of Allied canvassed neighbors for funds. However, when the campaign was over, the goal of $10 million was not reached.[25]

Joint's direct aid program, Save Our Survivors, went into high gear. A full-page ad in the Jewish papers requested retailers and wholesale clothing merchants to volunteer "outdated" garments. Mrs. Harry Cohen led women in house-to-house canvasses. Public school children, after a three-day drive in March, collected 20 tons of clothes. By October, SOS had netted 500,000 pounds.[26]

Direct aid came from other sources. Hapoel HaMizrachi (Workers Religious Zionists) sent Passover goods to Europe. The Orthodox Vaad Hatzalah (overseas rescue arm) continued to gather funds for promoting the Jewish religion and came into conflict with Joint, which claimed this was a duplication of effort. Orthodox groups were particularly concerned about the placement of Jewish children in assimilating situations in Europe. JDC's primary concern was the children's physical survival.[27]

The Nazis continued to make news. While showing little interest in the Nuremberg Trials, the *Exponent* followed the Warsaw trial of Rudolph Hess, commandant of Auschwitz. Both papers were disturbed at the return of ex-Nazis to positions of power in the Soviet and Allied Zones of Occupation, and the failure to root out important Nazis in hiding. As in 1945 and 1946, both newspapers continued to carry news items over the failure to prosecute the Mufti of Jerusalem.[28]

Later in the year, the UN passedthe Genocide Convention by a vote of 38 to 9, which made all forms of race and ethnic murder an international crime. The *Exponent* favored the treaty, but questioned editorially, "Why did the 9 vote against the Convention?" The commentators failed to ask why the United States did not ratify this law against mass murder, or why the Philadelphia leadership did not place the treaty before the Jewish community as an issue.[29]

Henry Morgenthau, former secretary of the treasury under Franklin Roosevelt, in his diaries serialized by *Collier's,* indicted the U.S. State Department in duplicity and complicity in the genocide of the Jews of Europe. The articles revealed suppression of information on the Final Solution, deliberate stalling, and blocking of rescue plans and efforts. The revelations evoked little outrage in the Philadelphia Jewish establishment. The *Exponent's* tepid comment concerned Morgenthau's nobility for not making a profit from his diaries.[30]

The Stratton Bill, introduced in Congress in 1947 and supported by President Truman, called for the admittance of displaced persons at the rate of 100,000 a year for four years. There were 850,000 DPs in Europe, 25 percent of them Jewish. In Philadelphia, the interreligious, interethnic Citizens Committee on DPs, headed by Earl Harrison, favored the bill. David Galter, editor of the *Exponent,* praised Harrison and the Committee. At the YMHA, the National Council for Jewish Women heard immigration lawyer Abraham Orlow expound on the need to revise America's immigration laws. Both Lessing Rosenwald of the Council for Judaism and Horace Stern of the American Jewish Committee, reflecting their organizations' views, favored the Stratton Bill and opening America's doors. The *Jewish Times* carried a long piece by Albert M. Greenfield, noted Philadelphia business leader, explaining how during the years of 1940 through 1946, one million visas under the immigration law were not used, and how the Stratton Bill admitting 400,000 made sense. Despite this, the mainstream organizations did not campaign for the bill; the trust continued to be on Palestine as the place of refuge.[31]

The Jewish Agency had called off resistance late in 1946, but the Irgun and Stern Group escalated their rebellion. Judge Louis Levinthal, having been one of three Philadelphians at the World Jewish Congress in Basel in December, where the revolt was called "wrong political warfare," declared that "terror defeats Zionist hopes." Judge Horace Stern also condemned the "terror." In February, a debate took place between Jacob Snyder, head of ZOA's youth group, Masada, and Joseph Zitt, Philadelphia regional director of the American League for Free Palestine, on the issue "Should the ZOA Support Palestine Resistance?"[32]

The February 28, 1948 rally at the Academy of Music, at which Lawrence Horowitz called for an end to the U.S. arms embargo of Palestine. Others seated in the front row are (from left): Dr. Israel Goldstein (directly behind Horowitz); Mrs. Moses Epstein, national political chairman of Hadassah; Congressman Franklin P. Maloney; Rabbi Elias Charry; Dr. Nettie Edelkein (who sang the "Star Spangled Banner" and "Hatikvah"); Mrs. Rose Bender, director of ZOA; Mitchell Cohen, vice-president of Philadelphia ZOA.

In August, the American League for a Free Palestine distributed a movie entitled, *Last Night We Attacked*. The film, narrated by Quentin Reynolds, a well-known foreign correspondent, praised violence against British occupation troops in Palestine. The ALFP openly claimed its proceeds for the Irgun-related Psalestine Resistance Drive. During the month, Marlon Brando spoke in Center City, supporting the film.[33]

The mainstream Zionists were unhappy about funds going to maverick Irgun instead of to Haganah. As early as the summer of 1945, a secret meeting occurred in the New York home of Rudolph Sonneborn, millionaire entrepreneur. He and nineteen other wealthy and influential Jews heard Jewish Agency leader David Ben Gurion tell how America would not open its doors to Holocaust survivors, that Britain would have to be forced to give up the Mandate over Palestine, and that the Jews of the Yishuv would have to fight for an independent Jewish state. For this fight, the Haganah, the clandestine army of the Jewish Agency, needed money and supplies. There the "Sonneborn Institute" was created to raise funds and procure, warehouse, and ship vital goods to Haganah from America. William Sylk, owner of the Sunray Drug chain, was present at the charter meeting. Later, Lawrence Horowitz, ZOA leader, joined him. They attended frequent meetings of the "Institute" at the Hotel McAlpin in New York. These two men solicited their friends in the Philadelphia Zionist movement to help them.[34]

The violence in Palestine dominated the attention of Philadelphia Jewry. Dov Gruner, British World War II veteran and a member of the Jewish Brigade who joined the Irgun, was captured by British police while he participated in a raid on a British military compound. On January 24, 1947, he was sentenced to death by a military court. The American Jewish Conference urged the United States to intercede to avert execution. Francis Myers, U.S. senator from Pennsylvania, pleaded with the State Department to use its influence. The *Jewish Times* had interviewed Gruner's sister, who lived in Lancaster. Gruner was executed on April 16 for his revolutionary activities. Both Anglo-Jewish weeklies deplored the hanging. The ALFP called a mass memorial on April 29 at Independence Square. More than 2,500 persons listened to Paul O'Dwyer, brother of the mayor of New York and member of the Council of

American Irgunists. Peter Bergson also spoke, using the occasion to demand a *Hebrew* seat at the United Nations Assembly.[35]

Over five thousand Philadelphians sat in the beating, hot sun at City Hall's Reyburn Plaza on July 20 protesting British brutality in the *Exodus* incident. They were outraged by the British subduing the so-called illegal ship on the high seas near Palestine, engaging the 4,500 would-be immigrants, mainly survivors from Hitler's Europe, in a bloody battle and deporting them to Hamburg, Germany. The rally was sponsored by the Zionist Emergency Council, which brought out members of the ZOA, Hadassah, Mizrachi, Labor Zionists, and their youth affiliates. The young people were fresh from picketing the British consul the day before.[36]

In addition to focusing on the ship, *Exodus 47,* and the right to redeem Jewish survivors in a Jewish homeland, the program memorialized William Bernstein, an American killed in the boarding battle. One speaker, Lawrence Horowitz, the chairman of the Zionist Emergency Council, placed some blame on the United States "for not making its position clear in the United Nations." Horowitz had, as part of his Sonneborn group, used Haganah funds to repair and out-fit the vessel for passengers when the *Exodus* secretly slipped into a Philadelphia dock some months before.[37]

The summer saw the *Jewish Times,* under the editor-publisher Philip Klein, come out strongly for a boycott of British goods in the United States. Both Klein and his regular columnist, Arnold Ginsburg, pleaded with the Zionist leadership to support the move, or even answer the plea, but to no avail. Morton Kremer of Betar, the youth arm of the Irgun, tried to get stores to cooperate. Members of Philadelphia's ALFP sought the support of large and small Jewish businessmen. They wanted to focus particularly against Lever Brothers, a large British firm that made the then very popular Lux soap, but no support was found. Albert Liss, a staff member of the League then, sought a one-day symbolic boycott, but there was still no support. Lawrence Horowitz conjectured that this form of protest did not have appeal for local Jews. The mainstream Zionists did not go along with schemes developed by Irgun organizations against Great Britain. The *Times,* while not in the League camp, also opposed a three-quarter-billion-dollar loan to Britain by the United States, hoping to sway the former toward a more positive Palestine policy. The ZOA, American Jewish Congress, and Mizrachi did not openly join the opposition to the loan.[38]

The Jewish Community Relations Council (JCRC) set up a special committee in October, headed by Leon Obermayer, Philadelphia civic leader, to mute the vicious attacks hurled at each other by the Zionists and the strongly anti-Zionist American Council for Judaism. The latter was characterized as "traitors to Judaism," while the former were accused of being "unpatriotic Americans." The JCRC passed resolutions for both to desist but expressed no concern over the vituperative attacks by the Zionist Emergency Council against Irgun-related organizations. In the same edition of the *Jewish Times* in which the JCRC resolution was hailed editorially, a full-page ad condemned the American League for a Free Palestine, the Hebrew Committee for National Liberation, the Palestine Emergency Committee, the Palestine Resistance Fund, and the Palestine Freedom Drive.[39]

Dr. Chaim Weizmann (right), in Philadelphia just two days after the passage of the UN Partition Resolution, with Rabbi Greenberg and Lawrence Horowitz (standing).

On November 18, the *Times* carried a story under the heading, "Zionists Hear Rogers Flay British Policy." Will Rogers, Jr., a congressman closely associated with Bergson and the American League, pointed out how American war matériel was reaching the Arabs. Rose Bender criticized Phil Klein, *Times* editor, for using the word *Zionists* in reference to the League. The executive director of the Philadelphia ZOA would not accept Klein's good-natured explanation that a newspaper should not publish one group's opinion exclusively. Nevertheless, Bender canceled her subscription, so deep was the hatred of Irgun-affiliated organizations.[40]

The most dramatic event of the year was the United Nations resolution on the creation of a Jewish state on November 29. In February 1947, Britain turned the Palestine problem over to the UN. That international body established a special commission to investigate the problem (UNSCOP). In May, the Soviet Union expressed a friendly view toward the creation of a Jewish state, which went virtually unnoticed by the Anglo-Jewish press in Philadelphia, in spite of the fact that support by the Communist bloc was crucial to the passage of the UN partition resolution. The *Times* commented that it hoped that Russia would not tamper with the boundary lines proposed. Michael Egnal, former vice president of the Philadelphia Zionist Organization, suggested in an interview the reason for the Zionist reserve about Soviet support: "We Zionists asserted that a strong democratic Israel would be a bulwark against the expansion of the Soviet Union."[41]

Samuel Daroff (left) and Judge Harry Kalodner awaiting the premier showing of "My Father's House," a full-length English-language motion picture made in Palestine (March 27, 1948).

Lining up to sign petition urging President Truman to support the partition plan, City Hall, May 9, 1948.

Many Zionist organizations in the fall of 1946 were against partition; in the summer of 1947, there was a strange quiet as the professionals waited to see what would develop. With the UN resolution, the mainstream organizations fell in behind the Jewish Agency, agreeing to partition. Lawrence Horowitz recalled how ZOA persuaded Albert M. Greenfield to meet with President Truman to urge the president's full cooperation with the United Nations plan for separate Arab and Jewish states.[42]

Joseph Zitt, of the American League for a Free Palestine, declared that the partition was no solution for Holocaust survivors: "Restriction of Hebrew sovereignty to 13% of Palestine is wholly illogical and unjust." Zitt attributed the continued military revolt as responsible for putting the Palestine question on the UN agenda. At an ACJ convention, Lessing Rosenwald stated, "I can see nothing more lamentable than a petty Jewish state." The American Jewish Committee did not favor immediate statehood, but trusteeship by the United Nations. It also wanted immigration up to "absorptive capacity."[43]

A few days after the UN favorable vote on partition, Chaim Weizmann addressed an Allied Jewish Appeal luncheon. He assured those assembled that "our 60,000 boys can ward off any malefactors." On December 5, Friday evening, Conservative congregations dedicated their services to the UN decision to create a Jewish state, supplementing the Sabbath prayers with those of thanksgiving. The *Exponent* had little faith in the UN, editorializing, "The state will be brought about by the Jews now in Palestine."[44]

Fall saw many local indoor meetings and visiting leaders from the Yishuv stating that the British were behind the Arab unrest—but, they insisted the Haganah could cope with any Arab military action. Despite their assurances, the Philadelphia Jewish community had fears for their cousins in Palestine. To compound their worries, President Truman placed an embargo on all arms to the Middle East.[45]

Philadelphia's Jewish leadership responded by sending arms to the Yishuv clandestinely. The Sonneborn Institute contacted Abe Cramer, a coal broker from nearby Pottsville, Pennsylvania. He agreed to buy 30 tons of TNT from the Philadelphia office of the War Assets Administration (WAA) under the pretext that the TNT was for use in strip mining. Under the terms of the embargo, TNT could not be packed or sent to Palestine. That would have to be done secretly. Lawrence Alper, another member of the Institute, had strong wooden crates prefabricated at a Bronx warehouse and trucked to Camp Galil, a Labor Zionist recreation and youth training camp near Pipersville, Bucks County, about 20 miles from Philadelphia. A trucker with a permit to haul explosives took TNT tins from the WAA depot in Philadelphia to the camp. There they were packed fifty to a crate and bound with steel strapping and marked "Used Industrial Machinery from the Oved Trading Company to Haboreg Ltd. of Tel Aviv." A day later, on December 29, twenty-six crates, so marked, went to Pier F, Jersey City, then onto the SS Executor, which set sail January 3, 1948.[46]

Stanton Kratzok, a Zionist activist, and his father, Samuel, both attorneys, handled the legal work for the Labor Zionists and their youth group, *Habonim*. In an interview, Kratzok recalled, "Hardy boys loaded the TNT crates onto trucks, which made a dangerous ride to the dock through narrow, snowy roads. The boys and the truck drivers did not know what was in the crates. FBI agents visited me in January 1948, and told me about arms caches in Philadelphia and Camp Galil, but suggested by their conversation that they winked at them." The Kratzoks and the rest of Philadelphia's leadership were gravely concerned whether the Yishuv would have the wherewithal to meet Arab attacks certain to attend the creation of the Jewish state in 1948.[47]

1948

In contrast to Philadelphia Jewry's moderate response to the terrible plight of their kindred under the Nazis, the fear of the destruction of the Jewish community in Palestine stimulated the city's Jews to mass participation in 1948. Indeed, the situation looked critical and called for drastic measures. In addition to an American and British arms embargo, the two countries permitted no further emigration of Jews from Europe, depriving the Jewish defense forces of badly needed manpower. Arab irregulars from nearby Arab states and Mufti forces sought to wipe out the Yishuv. Local Jewish organizations and the weeklies dramatized the peril. Jacob Snyder, speaking to Masada, a Zionist youth organization, told how the British were arming the Arabs while disarming the Haganah. Max Slepin, a Philadelphia World War II hero, returned from Palestine, and described

JEWISH EXPONENT

The **Challenge**   SECTION 2

PHILADELPHIA, IYAR 5, 5708—MAY 14, 1948

SHALL THEY LIVE-OR SHALL THEY DIE?

DESPERATE HUMAN BEINGS are struggling to survive after a decade of confinement in Europe's camps.

DESPERATE HUMAN BEINGS are pleading for the chance to rebuild their lives in Palestine, the United States, and elsewhere.

DESPERATE HUMAN BEINGS — including thousands upon thousands of children — are praying for help!

Answer — by your gift to the Allied Jewish Appeal.
Answer — by your work in this campaign.
Answer **NOW** — There is not a moment to lose!

Below: Israeli flag raised, City Hall Plaza, May 18, 1948, by Mayor Bernard Samuel (left, holding staff) and Judge Louis Leventhal, Honorary National Chairman of ZOA. Adjusting the flag is William Sylk, chief figure in Americans for Haganah, and to Judge Levinthal's right is Hadassah officer Ann Sobatnik.

how Haganah youth were disarmed, then taken to hostile Arab quarters to be set upon by vicious killers. Dr. Israel Press, local head of Mizrachi, the religious Zionist organization, urged the area's synagogues to hold memorial services for a local Mizrachi pioneer murdered in a colony in the Holy Land. Unlike the effort during the Holocaust, every effort was made to dramatize the dangerous situation facing the Jews of Palestine.[48]

Nevertheless, Lessing Rosenwald, using *Collier's* magazine as a forum, denounced the partition plan as a means "of creating a ghetto." He predicted that once the British left, the Arabs would wipe out the Jews. But Rosenwald and the American Council for Judaism were losing influence. When the Jewish state was approved by the UN in November of 1947, Rabbi Louis Wolsey, one of the founders of the Council and its first president, called for the ACJ to dissolve and "support the present reality of the land of Israel with all our strength." Despite this, the Council, under Rosenwald, continued its anti-Zionist activities.[49]

Upset at Arab attacks and British obstruction of Yishuv defense, the Philadelphia Zionist Emergency Council brought 3,100 protesters to the Academy of Music on February 29. They demanded an end to the U.S. embargo and an international army to enforce the UN partition decision. While the editorials of the *Jewish Times* and *Exponent* favored the international army, Alex Wilf, speaking for the American League for a Free Palestine, believed that such an army, if it included Americans, would not be wise. Once an American was killed, anti-Semitism would ensue, and the Jewish state might be compromised.[50]

Jewish organizations brought prominent figures on the national scene to Philadelphia to deplore the situation in Palestine. They included Summer Welles, Herbert Lehmann, Senator Robert Wagner, Golda Meir, and Moshe Shertok.[51]

In March, Secretary of State George Marshall and President Truman called for a temporary trusteeship over Palestine. This new development was perceived as a betrayal of the partition plan by almost all of Philadelphia's Jewish organizations. Both Orthodox and Conservative rabbis called for April 8, 1948, as a day of intercession and prayer "for the attempt to nullify the decision of the United Nations." There then followed a flurry of activity to influence the chief executive. Christians joined with Jews in the Philadelphia ad hoc Committee to Save the Jewish State. It held over fourteen neighborhood protest meetings and sponsored a pilgrimage to Washington, DC, to demand recognition and implementation of the partition decision. Groups not seen before in these issues—such as the Jewish People's Order, the Ladies Garment Workers Union, and the Fur Workers Union—joined the march on Washington.[52]

On May 13, one day before the proclamation of the Jewish state by Ben Gurion, five thousand people withstood a rainstorm to hear Dr. Daniel Poling, Baptist Temple pastor, urge Truman to recognize the emerging state. The protesters had gathered 30,000 signatures to present to the president.[53]

Samuel Daroff, Judge Levinthal, and David Ben Gurion at the Liberty Bell.

Almost two weeks afterward, Judge Louis Levinthal handed Mayor Bernard Samuel a fresh blue and white flag to raise on City Hall's flagpole. Ten thousand moist-eyed Philadelphians gathered at City Hall to recognize the establishment of the third Jewish commonwealth after two millennia.[54]

During the years before World War II, in the 1920s, 1930s, and up to the United Nation's Partition Plan in 1947, most aid to the Yishuv was indirect, channeled through the Allied Jewish Appeal or long-established Zionist groups such as the Jewish National Fund. Now direct aid mushroomed. The Sonneborn Institute went into action. One of its fronts, "Land and Labor," operating in the city under the leadership of Samuel Kurland, ostensibly sought volunteers for agricultural work in Palestine. Using Jewish chaplains' records of Jewish war veterans, Philadelphia's veterans received letters and phone calls urging direct involvement in Israel's war for independence.[55]

Izzy Cohen, one such veteran, received such a telephone call in November 1947. He was asked to bring his discharge papers and birth certificate to the Bankers Security Building on Broad and Walnut Streets. The interviewer, an elderly American, made no reference to fighting, asking only whether Izzy wanted to help the Jewish Agency and refugees. No country was disclosed. Later, the small arms specialist received a call to go to the Hotel Breslin in New York for a physical. Izzy recalls seven other Philadelphians serving with him in the Haganah.[56]

Under the Auspices of the American League for a Free Palestine, which supported the underground struggle against the British, Menachem Begin, Commander of Irgun Z'vai Leumi, visited Philadelphia in December 1948 for the first time. He is shown here at the desk used by George Washington at Independence Hall. Shown with Begin (left to right) are Joseph Sharfsin, activist in ALFP, who at the time was the chairman of the Pennsylvania Utilities Commission; Maurice Rifkin, chairman of the Pennsylvania Division of ALFP; Martin McCullogh, curator of Independence Hall; Albert Liss, Regional Director of ALFP, who was responsible for arranging Mr. Begin's tour of Philadelphia; and Nathan Biederman, an executive with the League. After a whirlwind tour of the city including dinners and rallies, December 5 through 8, Begin left and the American League voted itself out of existence.

Leon Agriss, a Philadelphia student in the Hebrew University in 1948, remembers a handful of other Philadelphia volunteers in the MAHAL, as the international force of volunteers to fight in the Israel War of Independence were called. Harry Eisner, now head of the Association of American Veterans of Israel, estimated their number at less than twenty.[57]

In the spring, the American League for a Free Palestine campaigned for medical supplies, including penicillin and sulfur. It also created a nonprofit corporation called "Supplies for Palestine." Not to be outdone by an Irgun organization, Hadassah set up a blood donor program at its office, 1510 North American Building. B'nai B'rith Youth, active in war bonds and victory farming during the Holocaust, collected old army uniforms and aided Hadassah in soliciting blood donors. Sound trucks moved through neighborhoods, and door-to-door pledge cards were distributed. In May, the Galen Pharmaceutical Society, an established Jewish college and pharmacist group, in cooperation with leading drug concerns, dentists, and doctors, collected medical supplies and forwarded them to Haganah through Hadassah. The ALFP openly enlisted World War II veterans in a campaign that included a large Philadelphia *Evening Bulletin* ad. Albert Liss, who headed the ALFP campaign and now was director, said over half the registerees were gentile; he estimated the number of volunteers at fifty.[58]

Philadelphia delegation to the third National Economic Conference for Israel, at 30th Street Station, preparing to board train for Washington. Philadelphia's strong support for Israel has been both institutional and grassroots in the course of the past half-century.

In the summer, the Arab states attacked the new nation. In Philadelphia, as was the case in many American cities, house-to-house collections took place. Moshe Volk, a member of Betar, an Irgun-related youth arm, remembers collecting funds and supplies from Philadelphia's Strawberry Mansion and Logan sections. The contributors knew nothing of the difference between the Irgun and Haganah, nor did they care. The Labor Zionists struggled in vain, he recalls, to inform contributors by means of the Jewish newspapers against giving to the "unrepresentative, unauthorized, separatist group."[59]

A "friendship train" loaded with cases of food was unloaded and stored at 958 Franklin Street. In October, a ship heavy with 100,000 cases of food left Philadelphia for Israel. William Sylk, a charter member of the Sonneborn Institute, chaired the "Food for Israel" campaign that was to fill three warehouses. Men and Boy Scouts aided in the collections made in movie houses and synagogues. Ongoing campaigns at the time included "Tools for Israel," "Materials for Israel," and "Machinery for Israel." These were all part of the secret Sonneborn Institute, whose members solicited Philadelphia's businessmen to contribute their wares. Philadelphia's Jews, unlike during the period of the Holocaust, were marshaled at the grassroots level by their leadership through a variety of enterprises, aiding them to identify with the Jewish community of Palestine. ZOA membership, not incidentally, swelled to 15,000.[60]

On June 21, the Irgun and its American affiliates received what was to be a mortal blow. Ben Gurion ordered the Irgun ship *Altelena* fired upon in Tel Aviv harbor, an act that killed twelve crew members and seventy recruits aboard. The prime minister considered the docking of the ship an act of defiance of the new government's authority. Maurice Rifkin, travel agent and secretary of the Pennsylvania Division of the ALFP, denounced the new government for secretly negotiating parts of UN allotted territory under the Partition Plan with King Abdullah of Jordan. Members of Betar held a protest memorial service inside ZOA headquarters for those slain aboard the *Altalena*.[61]

As summer ended, the Bernadotte Plan, suggesting a reduction of the size of the new Jewish state, including the slicing off of the Negev, received the blessing of President Truman. UN mediator Count Folke Bernadotte's ideas to reduce territory in return for peace came just at the time when the Israeli Defense Forces were not only holding their own, but also counterattacking disorganized, retreating Arab armies. The Jewish weeklies put up a howl of protest for what seemed like another betrayal of the UN Partition Plan. Philadelphia Zionists mustered 7,500 at an open-air protest rally in early fall.[62] When mediator Bernadotte was assassinated, allegedly by dissident Stern Group members, the act was deplored by the Jewish press and mainstream organizations.[63]

The Israel Defense Forces' victory over the Arab invaders was complete by year's end. The latter, now that they were beaten, accepted the UN armistice terms for fear of losing more territory. Philadelphia ad hoc direct aid faded away. The virtually defunct American League for a Free Palestine made its last gasp in December, drawing a crowd to hear Menachem Begin speak in the city to answer detractors.[64] The ALFP had not only served as a conduit to the Irgun, but also acted as a goad, gadfly, and catalyst to the mainstream Zionists, prodding them into action.

With their raison d'être a reality, the various Zionist organizations began to quarrel about their role vis-à-vis the new state. Some wanted an ongoing political relationship with it; others saw support for its economic, scientific, and educational efforts as the proper course. Internecine rivalry exacerbated the situation. With the crisis at an end, Zionist membership melted away. The B'nai B'rith and the once highly Zionized American Jewish Congress turned toward liberal causes, particularly antidiscrimination.[65] However, the overwhelming majority of Philadelphia Jews was pro-Israel. Thousands who were once apathetic, neutral, or hostile to a Jewish homeland were now convinced of its necessity as a result of the Holocaust and DP experiences. Not having experienced the trauma of Nazi barbarism, and accustomed to American materialism and freedom, Philadelphia Jews, like the rest of American Jews, did not consider *aliyah* (emigrating to Israel). For Philadelphia Jewry, Israel was an insurance policy against extreme, violent anti-Semitism. The accomplishments of the pioneers in the Yishuv made them stand a little taller. Israel's military feats brought a new pride in the Jew that fights back. For the masses of Philadelphia Jewry, Israel would become an article of faith, and after 1948, support of the Jewish state emerged as a central pillar of Jewish activity.[66]

THE COUNCIL NEWS

Published by
THE AMERICAN COUNCIL FOR JUDAISM, INC.

*"Americans by
Nationality;
Jews
by Religion"*

VOL. 2: No. 5   MAY, 1948

ISRAEL IS A "FOREIGN STATE," COUNCIL SAYS

N. Y. CHAPTER ANNUAL MEETING ATTRACTS 1,000

The largest audience in the history of the New York chapter of The American Council for Judaism attended the annual meeting at Hunter College, May 11, and heard Dr. Israel Mattuck plead for a solution of the crisis facing the Jews of the world that would assure peace and immigration opportunities for Palestine and maintain the historic position of Jews in every land.

More than 1,000 members and guests heard speeches by Dr. Mattuck, rabbi of the Liberal Jewish Synagogue of London; Dr. Paul Hutchinson, editor of *The Christian Century*; Lessing J. Rosenwald, president of the Council, and messages from Dr. Virginia C. Gildersleeve, Governor Dewey, Representative James W. Wadsworth, and others.

Henry A. Loeb and Jacques Coleman, co-chairmen, headed a slate of chapter officers unanimously re-elected. Other officers are Mrs. Richard G. Conried, Arthur J. Goldsmith and Ralph Wolf, vice chairmen; Mrs. Joseph I. Saks, secretary, and Dr. Joseph J. Klein, treasurer. Thirty members were named to the Executive Committee.

Mr. Loeb presided at the meeting, which was arranged by a committee headed by Aaron W. Berg, Mrs. Conried, Mrs. Isaac Witkin, and the office staff of Executive Director Julius Grad.

Dr. Mattuck said that to make the Jews into a nation would affect adversely the position of the Jews in democratic countries where they have the full status of citizenship.

PHILADELPHIA'S MAYOR GREETS MATTUCK

Mayor Bernard Samuels, of Philadelphia (right), welcomes a visitor from abroad, Rabbi Israel Mattuck, at the annual meeting of the Philadelphia chapter at the Broadwood Hotel, May 12. Mrs. Kurt Blum, in center.

TEXT OF STATEMENT OF POLICY

Authorized by the Executive Committee, The American Council for Judaism
May 21, 1948

The State of Israel has been proclaimed and the United States has given de facto recognition to its provisional government. Time alone will determine the wisdom of these acts. We hope profoundly that our government through the United Nations will succeed in its efforts to end the conflict over Palestine and bring peace and security to all the people of the Middle East.

This is imperative to provide a secure haven in the State of Israel for Jewish displaced persons for whom the world has provided so little. It is of equal importance in view of the peril to 900,000 Jewish citizens of the several Arab countries and the insecurity of the Arab population in the State of Israel itself.

In the Proclamation of the State of Israel the Provisional

JEWS WHO ARE CITIZENS OF OTHER LANDS CAN HAVE NO RIGHTS OR OBLIGATIONS

Israel is a foreign state and can in no way represent those of Jewish faith of other nations, the American Council for Judaism declared in a statement of policy authorized by the Executive Committee at its monthly meeting, in New York May 18. The statement calling upon the provisional government of the new state in Palestine and the Zionist Movement to make clear the complete severance—political and national—of Jews who are citizens of other nations, was widely publicized by the press, radio and news magazines.

Informing both members and the public of the Council's future policy, the statement, (printed in full in this issue) was authorized by the Executive Committee in a five-hour session which attracted the largest attendance of the year.

The Committee also made plans for future action, authorizing the special committee headed by Ralph Wolf to consider any representations to the American government that may be required to protect the status of Americans of Jewish faith. The Committee also agreed with President Lessing J. Rosenwald's proposals that the Council engage in an intensified study of the whole problem of integration, which has been and remains, the long term program of the organization. In clarifying the relationship of American Jews to the state of Israel, it also was proposed that the Council again explore the opportunities for cooperative action with other Jewish organizations.

A short time after the proclamation of the Israeli provisional government of its independence on May 15, Mr. Rosenwald, issued a press statement declaring that "it must be clearly understood that the provisional government can be the government of its inhabitants and citizens only; and that it can have no claims upon the national attachments of those of Jewish faith who are citizens of other lands.

"The national loyalty and attachment of Americans of Jewish faith are to the United States, to this needed clarification and distinction, and the corollary of the balance of the Council's program of integration make the instrumentality of The American Council for Judaism a far greater need than ever before. . . ."

Mr. Rosenwald's press statement was issued by the Council's New York office after being telephoned from Lexington, Virginia, where he was addressing the International Relations Club of Washington and Lee University.

The text follows:

2

THE OPPOSITION TO ZIONISM
The American Council for Judaism
Under the Leadership of Rabbi Louis Wolsey
and Lessing Rosenwald

Thomas A. Kolsky

Philadelphia was the birthplace of the American Council for Judaism, the first and only American Jewish organization ever founded specifically for the purpose of fighting Zionism and opposing the establishment of a Jewish state in Palestine. Philadelphia provided the Council with its top leadership for thirteen years, from 1942 to 1955. The Council was the most formal expression of the anti-Zionist reaction of a number of rabbis and laypersons to the phenomenally rapid growth of Zionism in the United States in the early 1940s. The major ideological source of anti-Zionism was Reform Judaism, as it had evolved in America since the Civil War era.

Conceived in Germany, Reform Judaism was adopted as the dominant mode of religious expression by Jews who had come to America from central Europe before the latter third of the nineteenth century. In its Pittsburgh Platform of 1885, the Reform movement defined Judaism solely as a religion and rejected the idea that Jews constituted a nation. Optimistic, minimizing the significance of anti-Semitism, and expressing an almost religious love for America as the promised land, nineteenth-century Reform viewed Judaism as a religion with a universal message.[1]

It followed that Reform would reject political Zionism since its foundation by Herzl in 1897 and would firmly oppose any nationalist interpretation of the Balfour Declaration of 1917, which expressed favor for "the establishment in Palestine of a national home for the Jewish people." Two Philadelphians, Henry Berkowitz, the senior rabbi of Temple Rodeph Shalom, and Morris Jastrow, the son of Berkowitz's predecessor at Rodeph Shalom and a professor of Oriental Studies at the University of Pennsylvania, composed an anti-Zionist petition that San Francisco Congressman Julius Kahn submitted to the Paris Peace Conference in 1919 on behalf of almost three hundred prominent Jewish opponents of Zionism.[2]

Jewish anti-Zionism was weakened in the 1930s. During that decade, the Zionists benefited from the rapidly changing social composition of the Reform rabbinate and congregations as upwardly mobile East Europeans, who were predisposed to define themselves in more ethnic terms, joined the ranks of Reform and as the training of rabbis at Hebrew Union College was gradually becoming more traditional. Within the Central Conference of American Rabbis (CCAR), the professional organization of the Reform rabbinate and historically the stronghold of Reform anti-Zionism, Stephen S. Wise and Abba Hillel Silver worked diligently for many years to build up support for Zionism. Nevertheless, in 1935, following a stormy session, the CCAR adopted neutrality as its official position toward Zionism. Two years later, in 1937, the "Guiding Principles of Reform Judaism," or the Columbus Platform, replaced the Pittsburgh Platform as the statement of Reform principles. Passed by a majority of only one vote, the 1937 document declared that "Judaism is the soul of which Israel is the body" and that it was "the obligation" of all Jews to aid in the building up of Palestine "as a Jewish homeland by endeavoring to make it not only a haven of refuge for the oppressed but also a center of Jewish culture and spiritual life."[3]

The advent to power of Nazism in Germany, the rapid expansion of virulent anti-Semitism, and the precipitous global decline of liberalism, once the mainspring of Jewish emancipation and progress, contributed to undermining the position of Jewish anti-Zionists. Indeed, the growth of Zionism in the United States was directly related to the worsening conditions of Jews in Europe. Until 1941, before planning for the mass murder of Jews, the Nazis wished to rid themselves of Jews under their control, but by the late 1930s most of the areas of refuge had been closed to Jews. In the United States, in spite of strong expressions of sympathy for the victims of the Nazis, there was also vehement opposition to offering refuge to Jews by relaxing immigration restrictions, because of unemployment, nativism, and anti-Semitism. Even American Jews, perhaps fearful of anti-Semitism, generally failed to question the American immigration policy between 1938 and 1942. Instead, they tended to favor immigration into Palestine as the best solution for the Jewish refugee problem, which was also one of the major goals of the Zionists.[4]

When the British issued their May 17, 1939, White Paper, limiting Jewish immigration into Palestine to 75,000 persons over a period of five years, Jews lost one of their last areas of refuge. The fate of the Jews of Europe was finally sealed when the Second World War erupted in September 1939. At the end of 1941, following the German invasion of Russia, the vast majority of European Jews found themselves trapped under Nazi rule, confronting the most horrible catastrophe in their history.

From the beginning of the war, shifting the center of their political activities from Europe to the United States, the Zionists intensified their efforts to gain the support of American Jews, the general public, and the government for their cause. At their highly successful conference at the Biltmore Hotel in New York, held from May 9 to 11, 1942, American Zionists united and openly committed themselves to the goal of "a Jewish Commonwealth"—a Jewish state—in Palestine. On November 10, 1942, the Zionist Inner Actions Committee in Jerusalem approved the "Biltmore Program" as the official policy of the World Zionist Organization. Once united, American Zionists were determined to "Zionize," meaning, to convert to the Zionist cause, the entire American Jewish community. The incredibly rapid growth of Zionism in 1941 and 1942 alarmed its inveterate opponents.[5]

The conflict between Zionists and anti-Zionists burst into the open at the annual convention of the CCAR in Cincinnati in February 1942. Although officially silent on the Zionist issue since 1937, the CCAR had elected to its presidency in 1941 the Zionist Rabbi James G. Heller, who was presiding over the 1942 convention. The one organization that until the 1930s had been historically the bastion of American Jewish anti-Zionism had now come under the command of a Zionist.[6] In the afternoon of February 27, 1942, thirty-three rabbis introduced a resolution in favor of the formation of a "Jewish army" in Palestine: "Be it Resolved that the Central Conference of American Rabbis adds its voice to the demand that the Jewish population of Palestine be given the privilege of establishing a military force which will fight under its own banner on the side of the democracies, under allied command, to defend its own land and the Near East to the end that the victory of democracy may be hastened everywhere."[7]

Less than half of the 236 rabbis who had registered at the convention were present when the resolution came up for a vote. For the opponents of Zionism, the introduction of the Jewish army resolution signified a flagrant violation of the 1935 CCAR agreement to remain neutral on Zionism. Following a heated debate and an unsuccessful attempt by Rabbi Solomon Freehof to table the resolution and expunge the discussion of it from the minutes (45 to 51), the army resolution was adopted by a vote of 64 to 38. The opponents of Zionism were stunned.[8]

While the anti-Zionist rabbis were still recovering from this setback, Captain Lewis L. Strauss (later a rear admiral and, in the 1950s, the chairman of the Atomic Energy Commission) persuaded Dr. Samuel Goldenson, the rabbi of his own prestigious Temple Emanu-El in New York, to send a message to the British cabinet informing it that Jews held divergent views on the Jewish army issue. It was that Strauss suggestion that triggered the series of events leading eventually to the creation of an anti- Zionist organization.[9]

Goldenson's telegram to the British cabinet, signed by some sixty Reform rabbis, asserting that American Jewish opinion was sharply divided on the army matter, provoked a bitter Zionist reaction.[10] The dissidents, however, did not relent. One of them, Rabbi Morris S. Lazaron of Baltimore, although the brother-in-law of ardent Zionist Rabbi Abba Hillel Silver, had been one of

Dr. James G. Heller, described as a "tireless worker for a Commonwealth in Palestine."

the most outspoken anti-Zionists since the 1930s. He maintained close contact with the State Department and was particularly friendly with Undersecretary of State Sumner Welles. Professor William Yale, who was then in charge of planning for Palestine at the State Department, encouraged Goldenson's and Lazaron's opposition to the Zionists. "A thoroughly aroused American Jewry," Yale advised Lazaron in March 1942, "can best check the unbridled activities of the political Zionists." Undersecretary Welles, who was kept carefully informed by Lazaron about the thinking among American Jewish anti-Zionists and was grateful to him for rendering assistance to the State Department, revealed to the rabbi that both the British and American general staffs were opposed to the idea of creating a specifically Jewish army.[11]

Rabbi Louis Wolsey in 1953.

While the controversy aroused by the Goldenson telegram was still raging, Rabbi Louis Wolsey (1877–1953), senior rabbi at Congregation Rodeph Shalom in Philadelphia, assumed the leadership of the dissident Reform rabbis, who were not only resentful about the passage of the army resolution in Cincinnati, but also alarmed by what they perceived as the increasing retreat from classical Reform in the United States. Although partly responding to the suggestions of Lewis Strauss, Wolsey did not need much prodding, because he had been concerned about the growth of Zionism long before the 1942 Jewish army controversy.[12]

Since assuming the rabbinate at Temple Rodeph Shalom in 1925, the activist Wolsey had been a dynamic leader within the Reform movement. He presided over the CCAR (1925–1927), held the chancellorship of the Jewish Chautauqua Society (1925–1938), and participated in founding the World Union for Progressive Judaism in 1926. An excellent orator with a deep and resonant voice, prone to grand gesturing during his speeches and sermons, Wolsey was a dominant and overpowering figure in his congregation. A strong proponent of classical Reform, he was also a fierce foe of Zionism.[13]

Between 1940 and 1942, Wolsey attempted to establish in Philadelphia a magazine for the promotion and advancement of Reform Judaism. In that project Wolsey collaborated closely with William H. Fineshriber, senior rabbi at Reform Congregation Keneseth Israel. Although Wolsey did most of the work on the projected publication, *The Jewish Advance,* both he and Fineshriber were to be the editors in chief of the magazine. For the editorial board of *The Jewish Advance,* Wolsey and Fineshriber selected mostly non-Zionist and anti-Zionist rabbis. Significantly, the projected list of the contributors to the magazine named almost all the rabbis who in 1942 would become the founding fathers of the American Council for Judaism. Although the magazine venture failed, Wolsey and Fineshriber did learn to work together in matters beyond their congregational duties.[14]

The sophisticated, mild-mannered, and charming Rabbi Fineshriber came to Philadelphia from Memphis, Tennessee, in 1924. A captivating speaker, yet never robust, Fineshriber was a much less ambitious, less passionate, and a much more moderate man than Wolsey. He was, nevertheless, a highly principled person, who stood up to the Ku Klux Klan, lectured on evolution, and spoke in support of women's suffrage while in his rabbinical post in Memphis between 1911 and 1924. After settling in Philadelphia, Fineshriber continued to support a variety of liberal causes, including the liberalization of immigration laws, the American Civil Liberties Union, and numerous interfaith cooperative enterprises.[15]

Wolsey and Fineshriber began to prepare for an anti-Zionist offensive when they met on March 18, 1942, in Wolsey's office at Rodeph Shalom with Rabbis Eugene Sack, David Wice, Abraham Shusterman, and Samuel Sandmel. The sense of the meeting was that something had to be done about the army resolution in Cincinnati. The rabbis agreed to call for a conference in Atlantic City to discuss the situation within the Reform movement and thus end the "appeasement policy of a quarter of a century" toward the Zionists.[16]

From the very beginning, however, there were fears and doubts about the advisability of a meeting in Atlantic City. A number of dissident rabbis met on March 30 and April 6 to reach a final decision regarding Atlantic City. Despite some hesitation, expressed most vocally by Rabbis Jonah Wise and Samuel Goldenson, the rabbis decided to proceed and hold the meeting and even accepted the version of the invitation for the occasion that Rabbis Wise and Goldenson had prepared. On April 15, 1942, invitations to come to Atlantic City "for a meeting of non-Zionist Reform rabbis to discuss the problems that confront Judaism and Jews in the world emergency," signed by twenty-three rabbis, were sent out.[17]

First ACJ luncheon in Philadelphia, winter of 1945. On the left is Lester Hecht, and to his left Lionel Friedman; on the right is Theodore Rich, and to his right Elmer Berger; and in the center of the dais (from left) are Rabbi Fineshriber, Jane Blum, and Lessing Rosenwald.

The decision of the dissident rabbis, led by Wolsey, to go to Atlantic City not only sent a shock wave through the Reform rabbinate, but also almost immediately created serious tensions within Wolsey's camp. Rabbi David Wice (who later succeeded Wolsey at Rodeph Shalom) warned Wolsey that the tone of the paper assigned for presentation in Atlantic City by the elderly David Philipson, dean of the American Reform rabbinate, was too negative. The young and more militant Rabbi Elmer Berger, from Flint, Michigan, on the other hand, was greatly pleased. He was confident that, if adopted on a national scale, the anti-Zionist program would spread like wildfire.[18]

Rabbi James G. Heller, president of the CCAR, wanted desperately to prevent the Atlantic City meeting from taking place. The Zionists were angry and worried. The furious Stephen Wise confided to Heller that he was troubled over "Cardinal" Wolsey and his "bishops." Eager to fight the anti-Zionist dissidents and particularly indignant at Wolsey and Goldenson, but unsure of the weapons to be used against them, Wise, nevertheless, was certain that they deserved "moral decapitation" for having stuck out their heads. The more diplomatic Heller was much more concerned that a schism within the CCAR might occur under his administration. After several exchanges with the dissidents and through the help of the amiable Rabbi Solomon B. Freehof, Heller succeeded in arranging an informal meeting between Goldenson, Wolsey, Freehof, and himself in Pittsburgh on May 11, 1942.[19]

For a moment, it appeared that the conflict might be resolved through compromise. Wolsey reported that Heller proposed that if the Atlantic City meeting were canceled, he would be glad to call for a special meeting of the CCAR at which he would recommend the following:

1. the expunging of the Army Resolution from the minutes and record of the Conference;
2. the reviving of the 1935 contract and that "its policy of neutrality be made a permanent policy of the Conference";
3. the passing of a by-law which would put this action into immediate effect as an unchangeable rule of the Conference;
4. the committing of the Conference, as in the past, "to an economic and cultural reconstruction of Palestine, but not to any political or nationalistic activity, purpose, or interpretation."[20]

At the very time that the dissidents accepted Heller's offer by a vote of 17 to 2, a letter arrived from Heller denying that he had ever offered to expunge the army resolution. By May 20, when they realized that the army resolution would not be annulled, the rabbis resumed their preparations for the Atlantic City meeting. The decision was a victory for Elmer Berger, who had distrusted Heller all along.[21]

Under Wolsey's leadership, thirty-six rabbis assembled in Atlantic City on June 1, 1942, and conferred for two days. Among the rabbis who attended were six former presidents of the CCAR: Rabbis David Philipson, William Rosenau, Leo Franklin, Edward N. Calisch, Louis Wolsey, and Samuel H. Goldenson. Present also were Julian Morgenstern, president of Hebrew Union College; Isaac Landman, editor of the *Universal Jewish Encyclopedia;* Jonah Wise, the son of Isaac Mayer Wise; and, of course, Wolsey's right-hand men, Morris Lazaron and William Fineshriber.

In his keynote address to the Atlantic City conference, David Philipson, the oldest living Reform rabbi, the only surviving member of the first graduating class from Hebrew Union College, and one of the formulators of the 1885 Pittsburgh Platform, clearly declared that Reform Judaism and Zionism were incompatible. For Philipson, the difference between Reform and Zionism was simple: Reform Judaism was "spiritual," whereas Zionism was "political." "The outlook of Reform Judaism is the world, the outlook of Zionism is a corner in western Asia," maintained Philipson. Arguing that the army resolution was a breach of CCAR neutrality and asserting that "not to split the Conference, but to maintain the right of freedom of opinion" was the motivation for the Atlantic City gathering of the Wolsey group, Rabbi Philipson concluded that the ruthless activities of the nationalists could not be answered with silence.[22]

In his address, Rabbi Lazaron described the plight of European Jewry and told his colleagues about the six months he had lived in Nazi Germany. Although sympathetic toward the Jews in Palestine, Lazaron proclaimed that "we shall have nothing to do with an international Jewish nationalism which would organize Jews throughout the world behind an international political program to set up a Jewish state in Palestine." The very spirited discussion following Lazaron's speech indicated that there were serious differences in the group between those who stressed the necessity to revive Reform Judaism and those who primarily emphasized the need to oppose Zionism.[23]

One of the highlights of the Atlantic City meeting was a presentation by 34-year-old Rabbi Elmer Berger who described how he had organized the first anti-Zionist organization in America back home in Flint, Michigan. A turning point in Berger's career, his address before the group marked the beginning of his meteoric rise to the leadership of American Jewish anti-Zionism.[24]

Born in 1908 in Cleveland, Ohio, Berger attended the public schools in that city and was a member of Wolsey's Euclid Avenue Temple in Cleveland, the rabbi's pulpit prior to his coming to Philadelphia. Wolsey influenced Berger's decision to enter the rabbinate. After graduating from the Hebrew Union College and the University of Cincinnati, Berger held rabbinical posts in Pontiac (1932–1936) and in Flint, Michigan (1936–1943). He began his anti-Zionist activities in Flint when he became disturbed by the neglect of local Jewish needs and institutions while increasing amounts of money were being poured into Zionist enterprises. As his criticism of Zionism grew, he attracted a group of young members of his congregation, who persuaded him to form a discussion group on Jewish problems. From that group, the Flint Non-Zionist Committee eventually emerged. It was probably the first organized anti-Zionist group in the United States, and a model for Berger's future anti-Zionist work.[25]

Berger concluded the story of the Flint experience with a call for organizing laymen as soon as possible, warning that the failure to do so would be disastrous. "If we continue on as we have," Berger told the rabbis, "we shall fail in our responsibilities as leaders, not alone to Reform but to the whole historic past of our people and to the future of Israel as well."[26]

After an exhaustive discussion of the situation at Hebrew Union College, the rabbis finally turned to the formulation of a statement of principles. Again, as before the meeting, the dissidents were unable to form a consensus. Rabbis Wise, Goldenson, Morgenstern, and Wice wanted to be cautious. Wolsey, Philipson, Berger, and a few others sought a more aggressive approach. Consequently, for the sake of unity, the rabbis decided to withhold issuing a statement of principles until a carefully written statement had been drawn and approved by the majority of the rabbis who were sympathetic to the cause.[27]

By the middle of June, the Statement of Principles was ready and Rabbi Morris Lazaron assumed the chairmanship of a Lay-Rabbinical Committee, which was assigned the task of emulating the "Flint Plan" and gaining lay support for the rabbis. Wolsey and Lazaron were also beginning to hope that once enough rabbis joined their group, it could possibly grow into a national organization.[28] After a delay of some ten weeks, the Statement of Principles was published in August 1942. Prepared primarily by Rabbi Goldenson, who for about two months had opposed its publication, the manifesto was a compromise document, stressing that the meeting in Atlantic City was a response to "growing secularism"—a euphemism for Zionism—in American Jewish life. It called for devotion to Reform Judaism, which emphasized "the central prophetic principles of life and thought, principles through which alone Judaism and the Jew can hope to endure and bear witness to the universal God."[29]

The Zionists reacted to the "Statement of Principles by Non-Zionist Rabbis," as the dissident rabbis called their manifesto, with a torrent of vituperation and a number of hostile articles. In November 1942, a group of pro-Zionist rabbis managed to secure more than seven hundred signatures of rabbis representing the three branches of Judaism, for their own counterstatement, *Zionism: An Affirmation of Judaism.*[30]

During September and October 1942, Wolsey, Fineshriber, and Lazaron worked diligently on behalf of their cause. Yet, as late as October, Wolsey's group had only the meager sum of a little over $200 in its collective fund. Wolsey realized that only through the help of wealthy laymen would the group be able to obtain the kind of financial resources needed for implementing an effective program of opposition to Zionism. Lazaron, acting both as the statesman of the anti-Zionist group and as the chairman of its Lay-Rabbinical Committee, kept in close touch with Arthur Hays Sulzberger, James N. Rosenberg, Lewis L. Strauss, and other prominent lay opponents of Zionism.[31]

The first pledges of financial support for Wolsey and his colleagues came from Lazaron's staunchest supporter in Baltimore, Aaron Straus, and Berger's followers in Flint.[32] By October, Berger, who was increasingly unhappy in Flint and eager to leave the "ghetto" of Michigan, was calling for action. "I am ready to fight," he confessed to Wolsey, "and to stake everything I have on the fight," explaining that he could find no peace "as long as Reform rabbis are predominantly Zionists rather than religious men."[33]

On November 2, 1942, Wolsey summoned his colleagues to Philadelphia to discuss the formation of an organization. Goldenson came from New York, accompanied by Sidney Wallach, a public relations expert formerly employed by the American Jewish Committee. Wallach, who urged the rabbis to begin their campaign immediately, outlined a specific public relations program for them for combating Zionism. Again, as in previous meetings, the rabbis were divided into opposing factions. Nevertheless, they decided to create a position of an executive director for the "enterprise," to engage Wallach on a contingent basis to prepare a program, and to appoint a committee, headed by Lazaron, to formulate objectives for the organization they intended to form.

Many rabbis, however, felt most uncomfortable about Wallach. Rabbi Ephraim Frisch strongly objected to the very idea of a permanent connection with a public relations man, insisting that the group should remain pure in its methods of operation. He suggested that it would be much better to engage a young rabbi to serve as executive secretary and mentioned Elmer Berger as possibly the right person for the job. A majority agreed with Frisch's view, but the general discord among the rabbis continued throughout the entire meeting. Consequently, Wolsey felt the need to arrange for further discussions on the formation of the organization. Determined to see the movement go forward, Wolsey believed that no progress could be made until his group reached "a complete meeting of minds."[34]

On November 16, 1942, in New York, Rabbis Goldenson and Jonah Wise met several influential Jewish lay leaders, including Alan M. Stroock, William Rosenwald, Arthur Hays Sulzberger, Edward M. M. Warburg, Samuel Rosenman, and Paul Baerwald, who, according to Wise, "heartily commended the rabbinical group for its initiative and good sense." Since eleven days earlier Sulzberger had also publicly denounced the Zionists, Wolsey and his colleagues sincerely believed that there was substantial lay support for their position.[35]

Subsequently, at two meetings—in Philadelphia, on November 23, and in New York, on December 7—Wolsey's group decided to appoint Rabbi Elmer Berger to the position of executive director and accepted Lazaron's suggested name for their organization—the American Council for Judaism. At last an organization opposed to Zionism was formed.[36]

Virtually simultaneously with the creation of the Council, the rumors about the extermination of European Jewry were confirmed by the State Department. The public announcement by Rabbi Stephen Wise about the fate of the Jews of Europe, on November 24, 1942, in midst of the very formation of the Council, did not augur well for the new organization. Although the full extent of the catastrophe in Europe became known only after the war, the timing of the formation of the Council was inauspicious, because it rendered the organization extremely vulnerable to Zionist attacks.[37]

The final phase of Wolsey's provisional leadership of the Council, from December 1942 until April 1943, was far from easy for the old rabbi or the new organization. The Zionist press responded to the creation of the Council with enormous indignation. The December 1942 and January 1943 issues of *New Palestine, Congress Weekly, Jewish Frontier,* and the *Reconstructionist* all voiced contempt for the Council. In describing it, they resorted to using such wording as "a stab in the back," "conspiracy," "treachery," "treason," "internal enemies of the Jewish people."[38]

At this juncture, Rabbi Heller made one final abortive attempt to make peace with the Council. At a meeting on January 5, 1943, in Rabbi Lazaron's study in Baltimore, attended by representatives of the CCAR who were Zionists and members of the Council, Heller proposed to work for the passage of a CCAR bylaw of neutrality on Zionism in exchange for the dissolution of the Council. On January 18, a group of some twenty Council rabbis discussed thoroughly Heller's offer but decided to recommend to their followers not to disband the Council.[39] Despite Heller's continued pressure and warnings of a terrible storm gathering against the Council, Wolsey stood firm. On February 4, while assuring him that all the rabbis of the Council intended to remain in the CCAR and entertained no thoughts of schism, Wolsey rejected Heller's Baltimore offer.[40]

Early in 1943, however, the Council was already facing many serious problems. Extremely anxious about "keeping our men together," Wolsey was concerned about the growing rumors that the Council was disintegrating. Indeed, by February 1943, because of the pressure of world events, ideological differences, and professional considerations, many rabbis, including David Wice, Max Reichler, Abraham Shaw, Beryl Cohen, Abraham Shusterman, Julian Morgenstern, Sidney Tedesche, Jonah Wise, Max C. Currick, and William F. Rosenblum, had withdrawn from Wolsey's movement.[41]

On February 6, 1943, Rabbis Wolsey, Fineshriber, Goldenson, Lazaron, and Schachtel, hoping to gain support from the American Jewish Committee, met with Judge Joseph Proskauer, the newly elected president of the Committee. Admitting that theoretically he agreed with the Council, the judge asserted that his primary responsibility was to the Committee. Consequently, although unofficially encouraging Wolsey and his colleagues to continue in their work, Proskauer made it clear to them that the Committee could not and would not subsidize the Council.[42]

With the American Jewish Committee out of the picture, Wolsey and his followers realized that they were on their own. They immediately proceeded to look for other sources of support. Toward the end of March 1943, in Philadelphia, Rabbis Wolsey and Fineshriber together with Jerome Louchheim, a prominent Philadelphia contractor, and Morris Wolf, a distinguished attorney and senior partner at the prestigious Philadelphia law firm Wolf, Block, Shorr and Solis-Cohen, were exploring with Lessing J. Rosenwald the possibility of Rosenwald assuming the presidency of the Council.[43]

Lessing J. Rosenwald (1891–1979), the eldest son of Julius Rosenwald, was born in Chicago. After attending Cornell University, where he studied Chemistry from 1909 to 1911, he left the university without graduating and entered Sears, Roebuck and Company as a shipping clerk. Although the son of the company president, he was granted no special favors and was forced to rise in the ranks on the basis of his ability. He managed the first Sears eastern plant that opened in Philadelphia in 1920. After serving as executive vice president of Sears, he succeeded his father to the chairmanship of the board of the corporation in 1932, a position he held until 1939, when he resigned (in favor of General Robert E. Wood) and retired at the age of 48.[44]

Rosenwald was also a major philanthropist and an art collector. In Philadelphia, in addition to his involvement with many philanthropic and cultural works, he also presided over the Federation of Jewish Charities and was a director on the Board of Jefferson Medical College. Beginning with a single Scottish print purchased when he was only in his 20s, Rosenwald eventually became an internationally famous art collector. In 1943 he presented his collection of prints to the National Gallery of Art in Washington, DC, and a collection of illustrated books to the Library of Congress. For a brief period in 1940, he belonged to the America First Committee, but resigned when he discovered that it harbored anti-Semites.[45]

Lessing Rosenwald in 1968.

A member of Rabbi Fineshriber's Reform Congregation Keneseth Israel, Rosenwald, who was generally impatient with organized religion, deeply respected both Fineshriber and Morris Lazaron. Rejecting the idea that Jews are a race, a people, or a nationality, Rosenwald adhered to the view that Jews are a religious community. He believed that Jews in the United States should be differentiated from other Americans only in their religious affiliation.[46] Although not a scholar, the tenacious Rosenwald devoted much time and effort to the study of his collections of drawings and books. He brought the same kind of industriousness and perseverance into all endeavors, which he undertook seriously.[47]

On April 1, 1943, Rabbi Wolsey, Jerome Louchheim, and Morris Wolf visited Edith and Lessing Rosenwald. Wolsey told Rosenwald that his acceptance of the leadership of the Council "would change the whole history of American Judaism." Wolf argued that were the Zionists to fail to get Palestine, as was probable, "the Jews of the world would have nothing left with which to approach their world." After listening attentively to his visitors, Rosenwald promised to think the matter over seriously. Three days later, Rabbis Berger, Lazaron, and Reichert met with Rosenwald and also asked him to accept the presidency of the Council. Rosenwald agreed to accept the leadership of the Council, on the condition that the State Department would have no objections to such an organization. Expecting attacks from the Zionists, Rosenwald consulted his family about the implications of his acceptance of the Council presidency. After extensive deliberations, the family encouraged him to take on the challenge of leadership of the Council.[48]

Rabbi Morris Lazaron, who kept Undersecretary Sumner Welles informed about the internal developments within the Council and had even shown him statements prepared by the rabbis, visited Welles on April 6 and arranged for an interview with Welles for Rosenwald and himself for April 9. Sumner Welles' reaction was, apparently, favorable. "Mr. Welles told me," reminisced Rosenwald, "that the formation of an organization like the Council was not only something to which the government would not object, but that it was vitally necessary and it would be a distinct service which could be considered a high responsibility."[49]

While Rosenwald was pondering his final decision for approximately ten days and all were tensely awaiting his official response, Fineshriber and Goldenson succeeded in persuading Wolsey to agree to establish the headquarters of the Council in Philadelphia, where it remained until the summer of 1946.[50] Wolsey, unaware of the outcome of Rosenwald's conversation with Welles, and informed by Fineshriber that Rosenwald still had doubts about his own qualifications for the Council presidency, felt terribly pessimistic about the whole situation as late as the middle of April.[51] Consequently, when Wolsey learned on Passover eve 1943 that Rosenwald agreed to assume the leadership of the Council, he was ecstatic. "It made the festival," he wrote to Rosenwald in his congratulatory letter, "the most exciting spiritual experience I have had in a long, long time." Rosenwald replied that he would do his best, although he still felt "poorly qualified to undertake this type of work."[52]

On April 29, 1943, the leadership of the Council was transferred from Wolsey's provisional chairmanship to the presidency of Rosenwald during a day-long meeting at the Hotel Warwick in Philadelphia, attended by Rosenwald, Wolf, Louchheim, D. Hays Solis-Cohen, and Rabbis Wolsey, Lazaron, Fineshriber, Goldenson, Berger, Solomon Foster, Hyman Judah Schachtel, and William Rosenau. After officially electing Rosenwald to the presidency, the group chose Wolsey as one of its rabbinical vice presidents and Solis-Cohen as its treasurer, and formally named Berger executive secretary of the Council at an annual salary of $6,000. Rosenwald, who told the group that to become an effective organization, the Council would have to be guided by one responsible leader, appointed Rabbis Fineshriber and Schachtel to work with him on drafting a statement of principles for it. Supported by Solis-Cohen and Wolf, he also insisted that during its early organizational work, the Council should avoid publicity and ought not to engage in recriminations and name calling or in "needless conflicts with existing Jewish organizations in America." Thus, at the end of April 1943, the opponents of Zionism had an organization, a president, and money. At last, even Wolsey felt contented.[53]

Between May and August 1943, Rosenwald and Berger, now in control of the Council, devoted much of their energy to the establishment of the Council office at 1321 Arch Street in Philadelphia, to the formulation of the principles for the organization, to the preparation of Rosenwald's article for *Life* magazine (expressing the philosophy of the Council), and to the recruitment of members into the organization. The Council rabbis also were very busy defending the Council in June 1943, when it became a major subject of debate at the annual convention of the CCAR.[54]

By June, Wolsey was growing unhappy. Convinced that the Zionists were packing the CCAR convention, Wolsey was also impatient with the apparent inactivity of the Council. He strongly disagreed with Rosenwald's insistence on Council silence and avoidance of publicity. Resenting Rosenwald's instruction to "keep silent," Wolsey even volunteered to resign his vice presidency but was dissuaded from doing so by Fineshriber.[55]

The formulation of the Council platform was a lengthy and complex affair. The long and exhausting deliberations and haggling over the language of the document reflected conflicts of ideas and personalities among the rabbis and laymen engaged in its preparation. "There was a kind of tug-of-war between the laymen and the rabbis," recalled Berger. "The former were interested mainly in the social and political ramifications of Zionism, as they saw them. The latter were rather constant in their efforts to emphasize the theological and 'religious'."[56] The rabbis most active in the process were Berger, Schachtel, Fineshriber, Lazaron, Goldenson, Frisch, Jerome Rosenbloom, Wolsey, and Foster; the principal lay participants were Rosenwald, Louchheim, Wolf, Solis-Cohen, and Arthur Hays Sulzberger, publisher of the *New York Times*. Of all the laymen, Sulzberger proved most unpredictable. After convincing the Council to introduce several changes into its platform and creating the impression that he might accept a vice presidency of the Council, Sulzberger not only turned down the vice presidency, but also refused to join the organization.[57]

Before the final approval of the "Statement of the American Council for Judaism" by the Council as the official platform of the organization on July 7, 1943, Morris Lazaron sent a copy of the draft to Undersecretary of State Welles for his examination. "I have read the draft enclosed in your letter of 10 June very carefully indeed, and needless to say, with utmost interest," replied Welles to Lazaron, assuring him that "there is nothing in it with respect to the foreign relations of this country which would be in the slightest degree embarrassing."[58]

The publication of the "Statement of the American Council for Judaism" was postponed until the end of August 1943, from which time it became the platform of the Council during the entire period of its struggle against the creation of a Jewish state. The "Digest of Principles," which summarizes the "Statement," reads as follows:

We Believe That:

1. The basis of unity among Jews is Religion.
2. Jews consider themselves nationals of those countries in which they live and those lands their homelands.
3. The present tragic plight of our fellow Jews can be remedied only through ultimate victory for and a beneficient program of reconstruction and rehabilitation, for men of all faiths, undertaken by the United Nations.
4. The United Nations should attempt to provide the earliest feasible repatriation or resettlement under the best possible conditions of all uprooted victims of Axis aggression.
5. Numerous localities must be found throughout the world where resettlement can be effected under favorable auspices. Palestine, due to its splendid accomplishments, should continue to be ONE of the places where resettlement should be fostered.
6. Any hopeful future for Jews in Palestine depends upon the ultimate establishment of a democratic government there, in which Jews, Moslems and Christians shall be justly represented.

We Oppose:

7. The effort to establish a Jewish National State in Palestine or elsewhere, and its corollary, a Jewish Army, as a project that has been and will be deleterious to the welfare of Jews in Palestine and throughout the world.
8. All philosophies that stress the racialism, the nationalism and homelessness of the Jews as injurious to their interests.[59]

THE COUNCIL NEWS

MORE FUEL, MORE SPEED
by SKOLNIK

A Council News political cartoon, April 1947, in the same issue that editorialized on "the evil of the Jewish vote."

Thus, the Council committed itself to the position that Judaism was a religion, not a nationality, and to the creation of a democratic state in Palestine. Stressing the necessity for the normalization of Jewish life in Europe or wherever Jews lived, it emphatically rejected the founding of a specifically Jewish state in Palestine.[60]

Compared with the religiously expressed declaration of the dissident rabbis in August 1942, following their meeting in Atlantic City, the 1943 Council statement of principles was phrased in both less religious and much more militant political terms. The difference indicates that as it came under lay control, the Council changed into a primarily political organization committed to fight Zionism and only marginally concerned with purely religious matters.

Rosenwald wanted to work calmly on molding the Council into an effective organization and to avoid, if possible, unnecessary controversy. The Council platform, prepared discreetly, did not cause any problems until it was actually published late in August. In June, however, the Council did become a source of public controversy as a consequence of the publication of Rosenwald's article in *Life* magazine and the rather close attention the organization received at the 1943 annual convention of the CCAR.

In his article, "Reply to Zionism," using many of the arguments presented in the Council Statement, Rosenwald explained that many Americans of Jewish faith were opposed to the establishment of a national state in Palestine. The article outraged Zionists. The general Jewish reaction to the article was also mostly negative.[61]

The Council received a serious blow at the CCAR annual convention, held in New York, June 22–27, 1943. Rabbi Heller attacked the Council in his presidential message to the convention.[62] In afternoon and evening executive sessions on June 24, there was a "Great Debate" on the issue of the compatibility of Zionism and Reform Judaism. Rabbis Fineshriber and Hyman Schachtel read papers in which they asserted that Zionism and Reform Judaism were incompatible. Rabbis David Polish and Felix Levy defended the Zionist viewpoint.[63] The reading of the formal papers was followed by a heated discussion, described by Wolsey as "a scene of indescribable sordidness and bad manners and intolerance," climaxing in a highly emotional threat from Stephen S. Wise that, if the rabbis did not censure the Council, he would turn the CCAR into a "Zionist Conference of Rabbis." The indignant Wolsey, who remained silent during the convention, referred to the Zionists as fascists and dismissed their talk of "equality" in Palestine as a lie. "Wise," Wolsey wrote to Lazaron, "has revealed by his tyranny over the non-conformist what the Zionists would do to the Arabs."[64]

On June 25, the CCAR passed two resolutions that signified a major defeat for the Council. It approved by a voice vote a resolution that rejected the view that Reform and Zionism are incompatible. The Conference then passed, by a vote of 137 to 45, with 96 abstentions, a resolution urging the rabbinical members of the Council to "terminate" the organization.[65]

The beating inflicted on the Council at the convention of the CCAR, followed by the election of Abba Hillel Silver to the vice presidency of the organization, greatly pleased the Zionists, who vociferously urged the Council to disband. The Zionists even asserted that an organization for the purpose of combating Zionism was nothing less than *hillul hashem*—a desecration. They now portrayed organized anti-Zionism as both political and religious offenses: treason and blasphemy.[66]

Throughout the summer of 1943, as the Zionists were preparing for the American Jewish Conference, through which they expected to unify American Jewry behind their program, Rosenwald and Berger were working tirelessly to provide a solid organizational foundation and secure a respectable core of membership for the Council. They were helped by a number of the "founding rabbis" of the Council. Indeed, the most important Council centers emerged in cities where pro-Council rabbis occupied congregational positions. The assistance of the sympathetic rabbis was supplemented by the efforts of Rosenwald and his friends Wolf, Solis-Cohen, and Louchheim, as well as by those of other lay sympathizers throughout the country, who appealed to their friends and relatives to join the Council. This preliminary work, much of which was being carried out prior to the publication of the Council Statement, contributed to Berger's initial, relatively successful recruitment tours around the country during the summer and fall of 1943.[67]

Only after Berger had returned to Philadelphia from his tour to the South, the West, and the Southwest, where the Council seemed to enjoy substantial support, and following the decision to hire Sidney Wallach as the public relations consultant of the Council, was Rosenwald finally prepared to go public. Despite Arthur Hays Sulzberger's advice to the contrary and the hesitation of others, the American Council for Judaism released its Statement on August 30, 1943, the second day of the American Jewish Conference. Because the Zionists were using the Conference to mobilize American Jewish support for their program, their violent objections to the Council Statement, challenging the Zionist claims of Jewish unity regarding Palestine, were understandable.[68]

In response to an emotional speech by Rabbi Silver, the democratically elected American Jewish Conference, by a vote of 478 to 4, with 19 abstentions, adopted a "Declaration on Palestine" that essentially confirmed the Zionist Biltmore program. The Conference vote on Palestine was a decisive victory for the American Zionists, who could now claim that the vast majority of American Jews endorsed the Zionist program of a Jewish majority and a Jewish state in Palestine.[69]

The publication of the platform of the American Council for Judaism on the very same day that Rabbi Silver delivered his historical speech at the Conference immediately provoked sharp condemnation from the Zionists. The Conference itself passed a resolution repudiating the action of the Council as "unsportsmanlike and reprehensibly impertinent" and as an "attempt to sabotage the collective Jewish will to achieve a unified program."[70]

Ironically, the Council, the first Jewish organization created for the express purpose of opposing Zionism and the establishment of a Jewish state in Palestine, launched its public crusade against Jewish statehood at the very moment that the Zionists succeeded in winning over to their cause the preponderant majority of American Jews.

The national headquarters of the Council remained in Philadelphia until the summer of 1946, when it was moved to New York City. As of October 1943, the Council began to publish its official organ, the *Information Bulletin,* renamed *Council News* in the spring of 1947. The membership of the organization grew rapidly from some 2,500 by the end of 1943, to 5,300 in 1944, and 10,300 by the end of 1945. It leveled off at around 14,000 in 1948.[71]

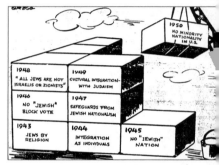

In April of 1950 the *Council News* editorial cartoon took on a more programmatic and historical approach.

During its five-year struggle against the creation of the Jewish state, the Council was guided by what Rosenwald called the "three musketeers," consisting of himself, Elmer Berger, and Sidney Wallach. Until the fall of 1943, when Undersecretary Welles resigned, Lazaron served as a kind of Council ambassador to the State Department because of his friendship with Welles. As of 1946, however, it was George L. Levison from San Francisco who assumed the role of the main Council contact with the Department. A close friend of Dean Acheson, Loy Henderson, and Kermit Roosevelt, Levison became an adviser to Rosenwald and Berger on foreign policy and Middle Eastern affairs. He was involved in all of the major Council policy decisions and participated in the formulation of all of its important documents from 1946 until the 1950s.[72]

The Council anti-Zionist campaign swung into high gear in February 1944, when Rosenwald and Rabbis Wolsey, Lazaron, and Fineshriber testified before the House Foreign Affairs Committee against House Resolutions 418 and 419, which called for free Jewish immigration into Palestine "so that the Jewish people may ultimately reconstitute Palestine as a free and democratic Jewish Commonwealth."[73]

The Council's testimony against the congressional resolutions enraged the Zionists, who lashed out against it mercilessly.[74] Particularly interesting, however, were the reactions to the Philadelphia Council leadership of Judge Louis E. Levinthal, the fellow Philadelphian and former president of the Zionist Organization of America, and of Stephen Wise. Levinthal attempted to approach Rosenwald amicably; Wise openly blasted Fineshriber and Wolsey in the press.

On March 18, 1944, Judge Levinthal sent Rosenwald a copy of Walter Clay Lowdermilk's book *Palestine, Land of Promise* with a personal, hand-written note:"In sending you, with my compliments, Dr. Lowdermilk's book 'Palestine, Land of Promise,' I am not doing so as 'a Greek bearing gifts' but as a Jew to fellow Jew. I know that you and I disagree on the subject of Zionism, but I am confident that if you visited Palestine and saw for yourself what the Jewish people have, despite all sorts of obstacles, managed to achieve, you would abandon your opposition and become a friend of our cause. Because it is impossible for you to go to Palestine now, I am bringing Palestine to you through the medium of this little book by an objective, scientific, non-Jewish observer."[75]

Unlike Levinthal, Stephen Wise made no attempt to be conciliatory toward Rabbis Wolsey and Fineshriber, and his attack on them stirred a controversy that did not easily subside. In his editorial, "The Philadelphia Rabbinate," in the March issue of *Opinion* magazine, Wise described

Judge Louis E. Levinthal in 1937.

Wolsey and Fineshriber as "pygmies who gravely misrepresent Jewish loyalties and Jewish ideals." Accusing the two of being "sinister" and "servants of the people who utterly betray their people," Wise compared them to the Norwegian traitor Quisling and asked indignantly whether there was "no way of ending the shame of Jewish Philadelphia."[76] In the central section of his editorial, the incensed Wise emotionally proclaimed:

> Is Philadelphia Jewry forever to remain corrupt and content? Philadelphia owes it to the honor of its one time giants to neutralize, if not displace, these dwarfs. They are a blot upon the landscape of a fair and even noble history. Honor demands of Philadelphia Jewry and the congregations which these men technically lead that it formally disown them. If these men knew what honor means, *Opinion* would say that honor demands that they have the decency not to denounce their people but to renounce their own treacherous leadership. The place for them is not within the pulpit of Israel but in some silent, if not penitential retreat wherein they will cease to be able, though perhaps willing, to defame their people, to defile their people's altars, and to blaspheme against the sacred dreams and passions and yearnings of Israel eternal.[77]

Despite many protests from prominent Philadelphians against Wise's derogatory comments about their city and the local rabbis, and allegations of breaching rabbinical ethics brought against him before the CCAR Arbitration Committee, Wise refused to retract his statement.[78] Only after more than a year of behind-the-scenes negotiations, a threat of censure by the CCAR Arbitration Committee, and Rabbi Heller's persistent appeals, did Wise give in.[79]

Neither Levinthal's rational approach to Rosenwald nor Wise's crude assault on Wolsey and Fineshriber succeeded in halting the Council's anti-Zionist activities. On September 25, 1944, Rosenwald wrote to Secretary of State Cordell Hull about the post-war status of Jews. He recommended that a policy of nondiscrimination be applied to the Jews after the war. Asking for the abolition of the 1939 British White Paper in Palestine, because of its unjust discrimination against the Jews, Rosenwald at the same time expressed his opposition to the establishment of a Jewish state.[80]

The Council did not soften its opposition to Zionism even when, at the end of the war, the full dimension of the European catastrophe became known. In late August 1945, Berger's book, *The Jewish Dilemma,* was published. Written by Berger in less than a year, during breaks from his extremely busy work schedule, the book, which summarized and explained the philosophy of the Council in simple language, became a major medium for advertising the anti-Zionist point of view of the organization.[81] On December 4, 1945, after prolonged and persistent efforts, Rosenwald met with President Harry Truman and presented to him a seven-point program, based on the philosophy of the Council, for "a fair and peaceful settlement" of the displaced Jews. He suggested that "a solution of the Palestine problem can become a token of our earnest resolve to deal with broad world problems before they reach crisis stage."[82]

The high point of Council activity was its response to the Anglo-American Committee of Inquiry in 1946. Rosenwald testified before the Committee in Washington, DC, on January 10, 1946, and submitted to it a memorandum expressing the views of the Council and numerous supporting documents. Specifically, Rosenwald asserted that the Council favored immigration for Jews without discrimination and favored political equality for them everywhere, but opposed the creation of a Jewish state in Palestine.[83]

Published on April 20, 1946, the report of the Anglo-American Committee of Inquiry called for the admission of 100,000 Jews into Palestine and recommended that Palestine become neither a Jewish nor an Arab state, pointing out that any measures to create an ethnic state would lead to serious conflict. The Council endorsed the Report of the Anglo-American Committee, which consisted of ten recommendations, "in its entirety and as an integrated whole."[84]

By the fall of 1946, Rosenwald and many individual Council members, without publicity, were actively promoting the relaxation of restrictions on immigration to the United States as a possible alternative to the Zionist program of a Jewish state. Rosenwald played a major role in organizing and financing the Citizens Committee on Displaced Persons (CCDP), which was formed for the express purpose of lobbying for the liberalization of American immigration laws. It was also Rosenwald who persuaded the Philadelphian Earl G. Harrison to assume the chairmanship of the CCDP.[85]

Earl Harrison, a former United States Commissioner of Immigration, and in 1947 dean of the University of Pennsylvania Law School, was well acquainted with the Jewish refugee problem. In 1945, after being sent by President Truman to report to him on the condition of the displaced persons in Europe, he recommended that 100,000 Jews be allowed to go to Palestine. Deeply impressed by Rosenwald's commitment and dedication to the cause of liberalizing immigration laws, Harrison in 1947 said about his fellow Philadelphian,

> "I have come to have unbounded admiration and respect for the way he had thrown himself into this work which represents, to my mind, one of the great causes of the day. In fact, such is my regard for him and what he has done that I have modified a hymn I sometimes sing: 'Praise God from Whom all Lessings flow.'"[86]

The attempt to liberalize American immigration laws to help Jews did not succeed. When the Displaced Persons Act of 1948 was eventually passed in June 1948, after all the intensive lobbying of the CCDP, it came a month after the creation of Israel and clearly discriminated against Jews.

When the Palestine problem reached the United Nations in February 1947, the Council continued its struggle against the Zionists in the international arena. Consequently, on June 4, 1947, it submitted a memorandum to the United Nations in which it reiterated its adamant ideological and practical opposition to the creation of a Jewish state. During the summer months, while the United Nations Special Committee on Palestine (UNSCOP) was examining the Palestine situation and preparing its recommendations for the General Assembly, the Council, through the services of Alfred M. Lilienthal, contacted many foreign United Nations delegations and informed them that there were Jews who opposed the formation of a Jewish state in Palestine.[87]

On November 29, 1947, the United Nations General Assembly voted to accept the recommendation of the majority of the UNSCOP to partition Palestine into an Arab state and a Jewish state. The efforts of the Council to prevent the formation of a Jewish state had failed.

When, on March 19, 1948, the State Department, in a policy reversal, intended to retreat from partition and suggested a temporary trusteeship for Palestine, the Council, still hoping to prevent the emergence of a Jewish state, quickly endorsed the move. But it was too late.

On May 14, 1948, Ben-Gurion proclaimed the independence of the State of Israel, and President Truman immediately granted it *de facto* recognition. A week later, the Council formally

1953 San Francisco conference of ACJ, (from left) Lessing Rosenwald, Hattie Sloss, Jane Blum, Elmer and Ruth Berger, George Levison.

accepted the reality of the existence of Israel but hastened to assert that it considered Israel to be a foreign state like any other foreign state and pledged itself to continue to oppose Jewish nationalism—meaning, Zionism—by continuing to work for the following objectives:

1. To make clear the sharp distinction between Judaism and Zionism and between Israelis (citizens of the State of Israel) and Jews who are citizens of other nations.
2. To insist that no Jew or organization of Jews speak for or represent all the Jews of America.
3. To deny the validity of any claim to the existence or control of a "Jewish" bloc vote in the United States.
4. To continue to work for increased immigration opportunities in the United States and elsewhere for displaced persons of all faiths and national derivations.[88]

Although the council's headquarters had been located in Philadelphia since 1943, its local chapter was not formed until the early spring of 1945, shortly after the first annual conference of the Council in January 1945, as a result of considerable instigation by Major Samuel Edelman. Major Edelman, a member of Rabbi Wolsey's congregation, was born in Russia and came to the United States at the age of 2. Educated at the Central High School, the University of Pennsylvania, and West Point, he entered the American Diplomatic and Consular Service in 1909 and served in Constantinople, Jerusalem, Aleppo, Beirut, and Damascus. During World War I, he was detailed for special intelligence duty in Switzerland. After retiring from the diplomatic service, Edelman worked as a public relations consultant in Philadelphia. Already in 1943 he considered the work of the Council as "a most sacred Crusade, which will affect our religion for generations to come."[89]

Although Edelman provided the initial impetus for local activity, the group that ultimately met on March 15, 1945, to form the Philadelphia chapter, elected Lionel Friedman, a prominent Philadelphia real estate broker and a former president of Rodeph Shalom, as its provisional chairman. By June 1945, the organization of the Philadelphia chapter was completed. The Executive Committee of the chapter then set out to expand the membership of the chapter by recruiting new members, mainly from Wolsey's Temple Rodeph Shalom and Fineshriber's Keneseth Israel Reform congregation, with the result that more than six hundred people had joined the Council in Philadelphia by the end of 1945.[90]

The most dedicated member of the Philadelphia chapter was, without doubt, Jane Blum, whose star began to rise in the Council after she had organized a highly successful luncheon on November 28, 1945, attended by some 350 guests. Blum, a tireless worker on the local scene and also active in the Council nationally until the 1950s, was educated at Oak Lane Country Day School and Goucher College, participated in numerous community affairs in Philadelphia, and presided over the Sisterhood of Keneseth Israel. A close friend and admirer of Rabbi Fineshriber, she joined the Council both because of her deep regard for Fineshriber and her conviction that Judaism was purely a religion. Throughout the years, others might have formally chaired the Philadelphia chapter, but Blum was usually the one in charge. Intimately involved with the national organization of the Council, she eventually became one of its regional vice presidents.[91]

In 1946, possibly the most active year for the Council in Philadelphia, Julius Grodinsky was elected chairman of the local chapter, a position he held until 1951. A native of Milwaukee, Wisconsin, Grodinsky was the son of a Lithuanian immigrant who had come to the United States in 1892. He was educated in Milwaukee public schools and graduated from the University of Pennsylvania, eventually joining the university's faculty in 1920. While chairman of the Philadelphia chapter, he was an associate professor of economics at the Wharton School of Finance and Commerce. Earlier, from 1926 to 1936, he had served as executive secretary of the Jewish Publication Society. Unlike most of the members of his chapter, and the Council in general, who were associated with Reform congregations, Grodinsky belonged to the Conservative Adath Jeshurun Synagogue in Philadelphia.[92]

Grodinsky's approach to the affairs of the Council was both moderate and youth-oriented. Arguing that without a humanitarian program the Council was vulnerable to the charge of selfishness and of exclusive preoccupation with preserving the comfort of its members, he continuously urged the Council to become involved in humanitarian work on behalf of Jews. Grodinsky, in cooperation with Stanley R. Sundheim, also was instrumental in founding a Council chapter at the University of Pennsylvania, one of the only two university chapters ever established by the Council in the United States (the other was formed at the University of Texas). The University of Pennsylvania chapter, jointly chaired from 1946 to 1947 by Herbert Fogel and Robert Loeb, remained in existence for a very brief period and acquired no more than twenty-seven members by May 1947.[93]

Due to the efforts of Stanley Sundheim, chairman of the Membership Committee, and to Jane Blum's tireless dedication to the cause, the Philadelphia chapter reached the peak of its membership—some one thousand—by the spring of 1947.[94] However, very rapidly, as the year progressed, both the local chapter and the Council nationally lost their momentum. During the period between the General Assembly vote on the partition of Palestine on November 29, 1947, and the creation of Israel in May 1948, the chapter experienced an ever-accelerating loss of membership, which, by the end of March 1948, declined to some 750.[95]

When Israel came into existence on May 14, 1948, the local chapter, already damaged by Zionist success, was also demoralized by the extensively publicized resignation from the Council of Rabbi Wolsey, one its most important founding fathers. Wolsey's gradual estrangement and eventual separation from the Council was one of the truly sad personal stories of the organization. An overly sensitive, strong-willed, and overpowering man, Wolsey did not take lightly his loss of power within an organization that he had helped to found and that he once led. Already in July 1943, Wolsey felt ignored by the decision makers of the Council. At the end of 1944, criticizing the "fascism" of the Council office in Philadelphia, he complained that Berger rarely bothered to see or consult him. Disturbed by what he thought were bad policies and poor management in the Council and deeply unhappy with his complete powerlessness in the organization, Wolsey finally resigned from its vice presidency at the end of 1945. In April 1946, arguing that its main goals were fulfilled by the creation of the Anglo-American Committee of Inquiry, Wolsey called on Rosenwald to dissolve the Council and informed Rosenwald that he wished to resign from it.[96]

This, however, was not Wolsey's final resignation. He remained a marginal member of the Council and continued to criticize Rosenwald and the policies of the "triumvirate" (Rosenwald, Berger, and Wallach) for snubbing rabbis and religion and his own constructive advice. Under Rosenwald's leadership, Wolsey claimed, the Council had become "a refuge for atheistic and un-Jewish Jews who joined because they looked upon the Council as an instrument for assimilation." Moreover, Wolsey also accused Grodinsky of being "a blatant anti-religionist" and asserted that Rosenwald's home had become "a gathering place for Jewish anti-Judaism."[97]

Wolsey sent his final resignation to the Council office on May 3, 1948. On May 15, in a speech before the Rodeph Shalom Men's Club (which was widely publicized by the Zionists), Wolsey explained how he had become disillusioned with the Council and called on the Council and the Zionist movement to dissolve "into a unity of world Jewry for the creation of a Jewish culture and a Jewish life in the land of Israel." He came to the conclusion that "in spite of all the mistakes on both sides, Palestine offers a great possibility of freedom, decency and dignity for our suffering people." Wolsey, therefore, urged all Jews to support it.[98]

At about the same time, Philip Klein, the publisher of the Philadelphia *Jewish Times,* called on Rosenwald to dissolve the Council because "the fight's all over" and "Israel is bigger than any of us." Replying that, for the Council, Israel was merely a foreign state and the United States the only homeland, Rosenwald asked Klein to render a great community service by upholding the rights of free speech and by demonstrating—to the Zionists and the anti-Zionists alike—respect for differing opinions. Rosenwald assured the publisher that the Council had no intention of disbanding.[99]

After the creation of Israel, Grodinsky and Jane Blum, chief leaders of the Philadelphia chapter, became increasingly concerned about the Council's future. Nationally, the Council lost membership but was determined to persist in its work of opposition to the "Zionization" of American Jews. Grodinsky, immediately following the emergence of Israel, recommended that the Council should

New State Creates Grave Responsibility for ACJ, Reichert and Lazaron Agree

The Council News asked two of the Council's most distinguished leaders—Rabbi Irving F. Reichert and Dr. Morris Lazaron—to express their opinions of the situation created by the proclamation of the State of Israel and its de facto government. They are especially qualified to speak because of the steadfastness with which they have championed Judaism and also because they have had unusual opportunities to discern the temper of the American people—Jew and non-Jew—during recent speaking tours. Dr. Lazaron made a coast-to-coast tour and Rabbi Reichert last week concluded a two-weeks' schedule of speeches in the East.

◆

by MORRIS S. LAZARON
Rabbi-Emeritus, Baltimore Hebrew Congregation

The declaration of a Zionist State and the United States' recognition of its *de facto* status does not change the basic issues in the Palestine question. If The American Council for Judaism were not in existence, it would have to be created to meet the graver possibilities that lie ahead for the millions of our brethren in this country and elsewhere who must perforce live outside Palestine.

Let us pray that the things many of us have feared—the destruction of much that has been buil‹ in Palestine; unnecessary loss of Christian, Moslem and life in a useless civil war;

by IRVING F. REICHERT
Rabbi-Emeritus, Temple Emanu-El, San Francisco

I returned to the Coast gratified with the enthusiastic reception accorded the principles of the ACJ in every college and community I visited. Everywhere I met with a growing realization that the principles for which the ACJ stands must prevail if Jews in America and other lands are to have any secure and hopeful future. While I discovered profound and legitimate concern for the welfare of Palestinean Jews, and an ardent desire to create emigration opportunities for the homeless Jews in Europe, two

LARGE TURNOUT AT CAPITAL FOR PEACE RALLY

WASHINGTON—A public rally in support of peace in Palestine "through truce and trusteeship" sponsored by the Washington chapter of The American Council for Judaism attracted more than 400 persons to. the Shoreham Hotel May 6.

Alfred M. Lilienthal, counsel to the chapter and GI representative at the San Francisco United Nations conference, presided and shared the platform with Rabbi Morris S. Lazaron, Baltimore; Irving F. Reichert, San Francisco, and Kermit Roosevelt, executive director of the Committee for Justice and Peace in the Holy Land.

WOL broadcast direct from the Shoreham the addresses of Dr. Lazaron and Rabbi Reichert from 9:30 to 10 p.m.

Rabbi Lazaron declared: "The time has come to let Arab and Zionist extremists know that they will incur NO support from the United States and that the moral conscience of the Jewish, Christian and Moslem world is not behind them.

"Let us strengthen the moderates so that they shall have the chance through truce, to reach honorably a just and democratic compromise in the land where they live side by side as neighbors. Such a compromise is still possible and necessary. It would

The Council News presents statements by two of its idealogues, Rabbis Lazaron and Reichert.

return to the religious orientation of its founders. He warned Berger that by subordinating the religious and ethical phase of the philosophy of the Council and emphasizing political considerations, the Council had lost and was losing support of a growing number of members and sympathizers.[100]

Jane Blum, on the other hand, informed Berger that she was "more for the American Council than I ever was—if that is possible." Berger replied that "now with the proclamation of a state of Israel, it was more important than ever to decide whether we are going to be known and act as Americans of Jewish faith or some kind of a national hyphenate known as Israel-Americans." Conceding that he was weary after five years of struggle, Berger confessed that "something irrepressible makes it impossible for me to let the thing go" and that his determination to continue to work with "this thing" was sustained by "the ever widening response that we are receiving from our Christian neighbors."[101]

In the fall of 1948, activity of the local Council was on the decline. Jane Blum criticized the national organization for not expressing itself vigorously. "We have a message," she complained to Berger, "why don't we shout it from the rooftops?" By December, as the situation in Philadelphia was deteriorating, Blum was urging Berger to come to Philadelphia to "set these strange people straight." If he could not come, she wanted him to send someone who would be able to respond to quick-thinking resentful people.[102]

In 1950 the membership of the Philadelphia chapter had decreased to 430. Several unsuccessful attempts were made to reawaken interest in Council activities at the University of Pennsylvania. The chapter considered subsidizing William Zukerman's *Jewish Newsletter*, a fiercely independent Jewish publication that was in constant financial difficulty and was being financed by contributions from sympathetic Council members. In October the executive committee of the chapter discussed the teaching of Hebrew at Central High School and agreed to inform the principal of the high school that there was a body of local Jewish opinion, including that of Sidney A. Farbish, the Jewish vice principal of the school, opposed to the study of modern Hebrew in a public school.[103]

When Harry Snellenburg, Jr., Rosenwald's son-in-law, was elected chairman in December 1951, only about 240 members, most of them inactive, had remained in the chapter. The situation did not improve in subsequent years, except for a brief interlude, which was essentially connected with the 1954 annual conference of the Council.[104]

In 1954 the Philadelphia chapter experienced a temporary revival of activity in preparation for the 1954 annual conference. The Executive Committee of the chapter met on January 14 at the home of the Blums, and on February 23 at Snellenburg's home, to prepare for the last conference under Rosenwald's presidency. The guest speaker at the 1954 conference was Henry A. Byroade, Assistant Secretary of State for Near Eastern, South Asian, and African Affairs, who spoke on the situation in the Middle East. Byroade suggested that the United States maintain friendship with both the Arab states and Israel, that the Arabs accept the existence of Israel, and that Israel become integrated into the Middle East and not view itself "as headquarters of worldwide groupings of peoples of a particular religious faith." Byroade's speech reflected the official Council position on the Middle East in 1954.[105]

In March 1955, Rosenwald retired from the presidency of the Council. Although Harry Snellenburg, Jr., became the first president of the American Council for Judaism Philanthropic Fund, established in 1955 with Solis-Cohen's assistance, Fineshriber remained a honorary vice president, and Jane Blum went on to become regional vice president, Rosenwald's relinquishment of the leadership of the Council brought to an end the era of the prominence of Philadelphia in the history of the Council.[106]

Philadelphia was not a typical Council center. At its peak, Council membership in Philadelphia amounted to less than one-half of 1 percent of the Jewish population in the city. The percentage of Jews who belonged to the Council was substantially higher in such cities as Little Rock, Shreveport, Nashville, Dallas, Cincinnati, New Orleans, Atlanta, and San Francisco. Indeed, the largest Council chapter during its early years was in San Francisco, with a Jewish population one-fifth the size of Philadelphia's. Thus, either San Francisco or one of the southern cities, where anti-Zionist sentiment among Jews was relatively more intense and widespread than in Philadelphia, would have been a more appropriate center to engender and guide a movement opposed to Zionism. Zionists were actually quite strong in Philadelphia. One of their leaders, Judge Levinthal, was the president of the ZOA from 1941 to 1943, which coincided almost precisely with the formative period of the Council. Consequently, there was little that particularly predisposed Philadelphia to lead the only American Jewish organized opposition to Zionism.

Why, then, was the Council formed in Philadelphia and directed from it for thirteen years? For the most plausible explanation, one must focus on the exceptional leadership of Rabbis Wolsey and Rosenwald. They fought for convictions in which they firmly believed, despite the immense pressures exerted on them by the Zionists and the general Jewish public. Without Wolsey's persistent and resolute leadership during its formative period, from 1942 to 1943, and Rosenwald's subsequent fierce and loyal commitment to it, the Council might either not have come into existence or have been crushed in its infancy.

On balance, Rosenwald played a more important role in the history of the Council than did Wolsey. Unlike the Rabbi, he never abandoned the organization. It is, therefore, ironic that Rosenwald, who was so disliked and ridiculed by American Zionists, enjoyed the respect of Prime Minister Ben-Gurion of Israel. In January 1957, at Ben-Gurion's behest, Lessing and Edith Rosenwald visited Israel and were the prime minister's personal guests. The Rosenwalds toured the country and were favorably impressed by the progress they saw there. Lessing Rosenwald, however, did not change his views on Zionism and made that clear to his host. The prime minister seemed to appreciate the integrity of the one-time leader of the major Jewish opposition to the creation of Israel. At the conclusion of the Rosenwalds' visit, Ben-Gurion presented to the former president of the American Council for Judaism a pictorial history of himself, in which he inscribed, "In recognition of deep sincerity and honesty in opposition and in friendship, (signed) Paula and David Ben-Gurion."[107]

The American Jewish Congress gained much support from Philadelphia's large Jewish population in the 1940s. Here, John Bernheimer surveys an AJ Congress display in the lobby of Congress Headquarters.

PHILADELPHIA JEWS AND RADICALISM
The American Jewish Congress Cleans House

Paul Lyons

On March 23, 1950, the assistant director of the American Jewish Congress, Isaac Toubin, arrived at the organization's Philadelphia offices at 1427 Walnut Street. According to leaders of the Philadelphia Council, they had already supplied Toubin with "information of an extremely grave nature [indicating] serious dereliction of duty and malfeasance" on the part of the local executive director John S. Bernheimer and his executive secretary Jerome Toobin.[1] Toubin interviewed both staff figures in the office of Nathan L. Edelstein, a national vice president and former Council president. Also participating were State Senator Maxwell Rosenfeld, the Council president, and Mrs. Estelle Price, president of the Women's Division. According to the Council's official account, Bernheimer and Jerome Toobin evaded or refused to answer questions, and often contradicted themselves, leading Isaac Toubin to immediately suspend them from office, deny them access to headquarters, and provide "that measures be taken to safeguard" Council records and files.[2] National Executive Director Dr. David Petegorsky met with Bernheimer at New York headquarters on March 27, whereupon the suspension was upheld. On March 31, Bernheimer and Jerome Toobin received letters from Petegorsky informing them that they were immediately dismissed from their respective offices.[3]

Some Council members, including several officers, disturbed by the dismissals, proceeded to organize an opposition against what they labeled a "star chamber proceeding." They challenged the "five hour grilling," during which stenographic notes were taken, for not making any specific charges nor providing opportunity for responses to accusations.[4] The dissidents argued that the closed hearing "had been carefully pre-arranged," as evidenced by the fact that the lock to Bernheimer's office was changed *during* the investigation. One secretary, Anna Kofsky, a dissident subsequently fired, stated in a court deposition that all office personnel, including secretaries, were "individually interrogated in the presence of a stenographer." She added, "While awaiting their turn to testify, they were forbidden to converse with one another." The dissidents, charging "defamation of character without trial," asked, "Is this the AJC of Dr. Stephen S. Wise?"[5]

Our purpose is to examine and analyze the context within which the aforementioned events occurred. The firing of John Bernheimer and subsequent actions taken against his supporters within the Philadelphia Council of the American Jewish Congress provide one with a means of understanding the decline of a Jewish left-wing in Philadelphia and, indeed, throughout the United States. The framework that must be established includes the historical development of American Jewish radicalism, the dynamics of the American Jewish Congress, and the particular organizational and political constellation of forces operating in Philadelphia.

The relationship between Jews and radicalism, astutely analyzed by Arthur Liebman,[6] is historical rather than inherent. In their emergence from the shtetls of Eastern Europe, a Jewish

Maurice B. Fagan in 1966, then director of the Fellowship Commission.

Rabbi Stephen S. Wise.

John S. Bernheimer in 1962, at the time chairman of the Anti-Defamation Committee of the B'nai B'rith Council of Greater Philadelphia.

working class established a Yiddish-socialist subculture, Irving Howe's "world of our fathers"—and mothers as well.[7] This subculture was spearheaded by a secularized Jewish intelligentsia who, in most instances, were reluctant to compromise their internationalist socialist visions with the glaring particularism of the Jewish masses. Nevertheless, in various ways, through diverse strategies—the Jewish Bund being the most sensitive to the needs of reconciling class with ethnicity—an alliance developed between a section of the Jewish intelligentsia and a part of the Jewish masses that was able to transplant itself from European to American soil in the latter years of the nineteenth and early years of the twentieth centuries.[8] As Werner Cohn notes, the newly American Jewish immigrant "was suddenly given the opportunity to theorize openly and to his heart's content."[9] A number of scholars, including Howe and Ronald Sanders, tell the story of the ways in which, at least on the lower East Side of New York City, this Yiddish-socialist movement achieved critical mass.[10]

Philadelphia, perennially in New York's shadow, never produced such a critical mass, although it shared similar dynamics. South Philadelphia, the home of 55,000 of 70,000 Jews in 1905, never produced socialist congressmen, state legislators, or local councilmen, nor did it generate cultural phenomena such as Abraham Cahan's *Forward.* But Philadelphia did develop a similar (albeit smaller) garment industry base, and generated the kinds of Jewish neighborhoods in South Philadelphia and then Strawberry Mansion, Parkside, and West Philadelphia within which it was quite normal to see both the social-democratic *Forward* and the Communist *Freiheit,* and to have parents, relatives, or neighbors who were passionately involved in the ideological disputes of the Yiddish-socialist subculture.[11]

The existence of a Yiddish-socialist subculture filled a partial leadership and ideological vacuum dependent on particular historical circumstances: the existence of a Jewish working class; the continuation of a populist Yiddish culture; the intraethnic conflicts between more affluent, Reformed, German Jews and immigrant Eastern European Jews; and the limited success of organized Judaism's ability to reestablish its organizational and moral authority over Americanized Jews.[12]

The inter-war years of 1918 to 1939 mark the transition from a more fluid Jewish working-class community strongly colored by radicalism to a more upwardly mobile, Americanized middle-class community beginning to build its own institutions. In Philadelphia, neighborhoods like Strawberry Mansion underwent similar processes, becoming 80 percent Jewish and 34 percent foreign born by 1929. By 1940, the area was already 43 percent white collar, with many of the most upwardly mobile already moving on to more middle-class neighborhoods in the Northwest or Northeast.[13] A clear Philadelphia difference is that the shift toward a predominant identification with the Democratic party lagged behind other urban Jewish concentrations. Not until the mid-thirties did Jewish voters shift decisively to the Democrats, and not until 1944 did they match the percentages in other Jewish concentrations.[14]

The inter-war trend marked the restoration in new forms under American conditions of the hegemony of rabbinate and business elite. Jewish philanthropy and charities federated, established national structures, and worked toward the reconciliation of old-money German and new-money Russian Jewish leadership. The growth of Conservative Judaism provided a satisfactory compromise for many Americanizing, upwardly mobile Jews stepping away from Old World Orthodoxy and yet uncomfortable with Reform Judaism.[15]

Such trends toward a distinctively Jewish embourgeoisement slowed, but did not halt, during the 1930s under the impact of both the Great Depression and the rising threat of fascist anti-Semitism. Surrounded by economic misery and social injustice, and fearful that their own hopes of upward mobility would be crushed, a small but potent percentage of Philadelphia Jews called on the Yiddish-socialist tradition that still lived within their increasingly second-generation urban neighborhoods. Most such Jews become New Deal Democrats. The Democratic party that Albert M. Greenfield welcomed to Philadelphia for its 1936 national convention was rapidly becoming home for the wealthy but socially ostracized children of immigrants such as Greenfield and John B. Kelly[16]; upwardly mobile Jews aware of the benefits of an activist government, including public employment; and, finally, working-class Jews pleased to discover a party supportive of the rights of organized labor.

It would be remiss not to note those Jewish activists who associated themselves with the Socialist party movement, including the major garment unions—ACWU and the ILGW—the Workmen's Circle, and the Jewish Labor Committee. Although Jewish social democrats played a very significant and yet to be analyzed role in Philadelphia social reform movements, by World War II, if not earlier, their political activities had moved away from radicalism toward a vigorously anti-Communist liberalism.

The Communist party was at the core of both American and Jewish-American radicalism between the Depression and the 1950s. The Party included two generations of Jewish radicals: The first and older was foreign born, Yiddish-speaking, and associated with the International Workers Order (IWO); the second consisted of the American-born, Depression generation. The IWO's Jewish lodges in Philadelphia contained perhaps eight hundred Party members in the late 1930s. These lodges, soon to be reorganized as the Jewish People's Fraternal Order (JPFO) of the IWO during the war, included a majority of non-Communists who joined for the insurance benefits. The JPFO suffered from a malaise similar to that of the social-democratic Workmen's Circle: the generational decline of the Jewish working-class and the declining interest in joining of an American-born, English-speaking, and upwardly mobile generation.[17] The JPFO did establish English-speaking lodges during the 1930s to attract younger people, but it remains clear that the order faced inexorable decline, exacerbated by government harassment, which finally wiped it out in the early 1950s.[18]

The second central factor that affected Jewish radicalism during the 1930s was the rise of fascism. Within the Jewish community, there was still significant fragmentation that hindered efforts to respond to the crisis.[19] The Communist party was not a part of such battles, both by choice and necessity. The established Jewish organizations refused to recognize the Party's Jewish institutions until the war years. Many Jewish organizations perceived Communists as oblivious to Jewish concerns and bitterly recalled the Party's anti-Zionist support for Palestinian Arab uprisings against Jewish settlers.[20] In fact, the Communist party's abstract universalism, which could support national liberation struggles in both the colonial world and in America's black belt, refused such legitimacy to Jews, at least until the 1940s. Therefore, whereas organizations such as Samuel Untermeyer's Anti-Fascist League organized boycotts of German products, Communists of Jewish background tended to group fascist assaults against Jews, trade unionists, Communists, Spanish Republicans, and Ethiopians within a common framework.[21]

Nevertheless, many young Jewish idealists found the Communists' anti-fascism compelling. The Popular Front, started by 1935, allowed such "non-Jewish Jews" to integrate both their internationalist visions of opposing fascism with their deeply rooted if ambivalently held ethnic identities.[22] Morris U. Schappes is undoubtedly correct that the Party never understood that internationalism is hyphenated, that is, that it joins nations together rather than eliminating their existence, even during the late 1930s when it allowed and then encouraged Jewish ethnic organization and emphases (e.g., Jewish media, support for Yiddish culture, and an emphasis on the particular evils of anti-Semitism).[23] Even at such seemingly supportive moments, the Party approached Jewish life instrumentally.

The Nazi-Soviet Pact destroyed much of the legitimacy that the Party had built during the Popular Front years as a genuinely anti-fascist champion and as an adversary of anti-Semitism. The Jewish community was not persuaded by the Party's criticisms of Western undermining of a Popular Front alliance of capitalist democracies with the Soviet Union and, understandably, was all the more contemptuous given the Communist conversion of what might be defended as necessity into a positive virtue.[24]

Yet the Communist party achieved a considerable retrieval of respectability within both the liberal and the Jewish communities during the war years. Membership soared, fronts and coalitions were rebuilt, such that in 1945, with hundreds of members returning from service, the Philadelphia district organization, as elsewhere, was moving toward its highest membership, if not its greatest influence. It is at this point that the general context and the conflicts within the American Jewish Congress begin to merge.

In the post-war years, the Communist party in the Philadelphia area had perhaps three thousand members, although with extraordinary turnover. Its strengths were still within the labor movement, including the local CIO Council, the Civil Rights Movement, and within the Jewish community. All of these strengths reveal the disproportionate Jewishness of the Party, although it is important to emphasize that most American, and Philadelphia, Jews were not Communists. The labor union presence included non-Jewish electrical and cannery workers, but derived much energy from disproportionately Jewish teachers, white-collar and public employment workers, fur and leather workers, painters, and retail clerks. The Communists never dominated the local labor movement, although they reached approximately one-third strength within the local CIO, and were soon crushed by the social democratically led area leadership in the aftermath of the Taft-Hartley Act.[25]

Nathan L. Edelstein, JCRC president, 1953.

Maxwell S. Rosenfeld in 1953.

Barrows Dunham in 1981.

Jewish Communists also played a key role within the American Veterans Committee, a post-war creation of what one former leader called "liberal gentry" who sought a progressive alternative to the mainstream and conservative veterans groups, including the Jewish War Veterans.[26]

The Party derived some strength from the success of its affiliated JPFO and American Jewish Labor Council (AJLC) in gaining membership in Jewish community life during the war years. In this period of Soviet-American alliance, with Communists participating in Russian War Relief and co-sponsoring the visits of Soviet representatives to Philadelphia, both the JPFO and the AJLC were admitted to the short-lived American Jewish Conference, the Philadelphia Jewish Community Relations Council, and the Philadelphia Council of the American Jewish Congress.[27] The Party encouraged Jewish Communists to participate in Jewish community affairs as their "mass work," with particular emphasis on fighting anti-Semitism and all forms of discrimination, engaging in efforts to ensure the de-Nazification of Germany, and joining the struggle for a Jewish homeland in Palestine.

The Party's post-war strategy, even with the removal of Earl Browder, remained within the Popular Front framework of seeking a Neo-New Deal coalition of Left and Center within the Democratic party, if possible, within the CIO, as well as within the liberal Jewish community. The emergence of the Cold War, which quickly began to split most of the liberal community off from the possibility of such a coalition, leading eventually to the Progressive Party debacle of 1948, marked the demise of this second Popular Front effort.[28] This failure played a central role in undermining, and finally destroying, the Communist presence within the Jewish community, most particularly within the American Jewish Congress.

In the post-war years, the Philadelphia Jewish community moved to consolidate efforts toward coordination that had built up in the inter-war years. Perhaps the most critical development was the emergence of the Jewish Community Relations Council (JCRC) under the leadership of Maurice Fagan. In the late 1930s, Fagan, with encouragement from such community leaders as Dr. Leon Solis-Cohen and Kurt Peiser, established an Anti-Defamation Council to represent all Jewish interests.[29] Fagan spearheaded what became the JCRC in 1943, a federation of seventeen Jewish organizations that matched similar developments in other cities. Such creations, which soon yielded a national federation of councils, was a measure of the ability of Jewish community leadership to transcend older organizational rivalries and, in particular, to produce a merger of older German and newer Russian, Eastern European elements. Fagan would play a central role in Jewish community affairs throughout the post-war era, including the establishment of the interfaith Fellowship Commission, in part, a reflection of the ability of a more cohesive Jewish community to confidently join with other religious and ethnic groups within the city.[30]

Of course, the Philadelphia Jewish community had not fully eliminated organizational rivalries. In the post-war years, the major targets of abuse were the anti-Zionist American Council on Judaism, dominated by Philadelphian Lessing Rosenwald, and the American Jewish Committee, still perceived by many as German-Jewish and insufficiently supportive of the struggle for a homeland in Palestine.[31]

Most significant was the renewed upward mobility among Jews during the post-war years, which intensified the secular trend, diverted by the Depression, toward middle-class and professional values. American Jews moved toward an American set of compromises that included suburban living among fellow Jews, affiliation with a more child or family-centered synagogue, and strong identification, including financial support, with the new state of Israel.[32] The older Yiddish-socialist subculture could not survive this constellation of forces, nor, as we shall see, could Communists and other radicals find effective ways of challenging it.

The *Jewish Exponent* provides a useful guide to the process by which financial support for what became Israel, through the Allied Jewish Appeal, helped to systematize a coalition of the rabbinate, the Jewish professionals working within the central agencies, and the suburbanized middle and upper class which dominated fund-raising efforts. The *Exponent*, which characteristically became an organ of the Federation of Jewish Charities and Allied Jewish Appeal during the war, became a vehicle of fund-raising drives. Nothing better communicates the transformation from "the world of our fathers" to a nonsocialist, comfortably middle-class Jewish community than scanning page after page, issue after issue of pictures of Jewish contributors, sitting at banquet tables, raising funds for Israel.

This was a triumph of Zionism, but not of Zionists, who suffered a fate comparable to that of the Left. The Jewish community became firmly pro-Israel but tended to eschew any significantly ideological positions that risked the comforts of secular, suburban life. Embourgeoisement limited the appeal of the two ideological lodestars: Zion and international socialism.[33]

Nevertheless, Jewish Communists and progressives, that is, non-Communists who were willing to work with Communists for liberal, social reform goals and for a more conciliatory foreign policy vis-à-vis the Soviet Union, remained active within the Jewish community in the post-war period. The most important focus of attention became the Philadelphia Council of the American Jewish Congress. The Congress, formed during World War I and revived in the early 1920s, was a pro-Zionist, Eastern European immigrant–based organization seeking to mobilize the broadest spectrum of the Jewish community behind its programs. It was headed by Dr. Stephen Wise, a figure of national stature with connections in liberal Democratic party circles. Although Wise maintained control of the Congress until his death in 1949, there was a powerful faction headed by Rabbi Abba Hillel Silver that pushed for a more consistently militant Zionist politics.[34]

During the 1940s, the Congress became a powerful force nationally and, within Philadelphia, the largest mass-based organization supporting Israel, fighting anti-Semitism, and aligning itself with a host of liberal programs consistent with the New Deal tradition.[35] Because it was the most liberal and grassroots Jewish organization, radicals of various stripes, including Communists and progressives, joined the Congress as their primary vehicle of ethnic identity and expression. In the post-war years, at least a half dozen Jewish communities, including Detroit, Los Angeles, and several boroughs in New York City, were headed by such radicals. In Philadelphia, the Council was always in the hands of a non-Communist, liberal group, but the radicals, mostly progressives but including Communists, established considerable strength in several chapters and within the Council staff.

Council leaders included the liberal Democratic party state senator Maxwell Rosenfeld and a group of civic-minded activists who not only played important roles in the Philadelphia Jewish community, but indeed became part of the city's liberal and Democratic party establishment, working within the Dilworth-Clark reform movement, the American Civil Liberties Union, the Fellowship Commission, and the city and state human relations councils.

The Congress engaged in sharp criticisms of less activist Jewish organizations, strongly supported efforts to service DPs in the aftermath of the Holocaust, criticized British resistance to Israeli statehood, waged battles to pressure the United States to maintain its commitments to the de-Nazification and against the re-Nazification of Germany, supported the rights of Jewish workers to obey the Jewish Sabbath without risking loss of employment, and engaged in a variety of activities in support of minorities, especially blacks. And, of course, the Congress enthusiastically threw itself into support for Israel in those critical early years of independence and war.[36]

From 1948 through 1950, the executive director of the Philadelphia Council of Congress was John Bernheimer, a local attorney from a prestigious family of German and Sephardic roots, who joined the staff in early 1948. Bernheimer had been deeply involved in Jewish community affairs for approximately ten years at that point, mostly with the Jewish "Y's," B'nai B'rith, and, with a special fervor and enthusiasm, as a member of the board of directors of the Jewish Welfare Board's Pinemere Camp, his special love.[37]

Bernheimer was a secular and progressive Jew, fervently supportive since the Depression of social reform, civil rights, and world peace; the Spanish Civil War had touched his social conscience. Whether Bernheimer was a Communist party member or not remains in dispute. Several of his lifelong friends deny the charge, suggesting that he was a genuine progressive, albeit sympathetic both to the Party's efforts and to the Soviet Union. Others, including some former associates, are convinced that he was indeed a Party member. Whatever the case may be, it is certain that Bernheimer was, at the least, what his enemies would call a "fellow-traveler," a progressive who worked closely with Communists in this period and who strongly opposed the increasingly hard-line foreign policy of the Truman Administration. Several knowledgeable veterans of the Party admit that Bernheimer occasionally met—in private—with district Party leaders to discuss policy. One strongly anti-Communist local activist, who still stressed that "Johnny was a nice guy," adds that when his daughter showed Bernheimer a copy of Orwell's *Animal Farm,* which she was reading, the stern response was that "this was not a book to read."

Most who knew Bernheimer describe him as a meticulous, demanding professional with lawyer-like foibles. Several found him excessively legalistic, verbally combative, and too aggressive. A few of his old friends spoke of his "ability to get people angry," his "incredible capacity to drive you nuts." Yet even among those who opposed him and actively worked for his dismissal, there are a surprising number who share the views of Bernheimer's supporters: that he was a warm, caring, and honorable man. As one of his friends noted, "John Bernheimer was not a saint; in fact, he could be a very difficult person in his need for perfection." But he perceived himself as fighting against the more conservative Jewish establishment.[38]

Bernheimer was a Congress enthusiast because he, like many other activists, believed it to be the most progressive and rank-and-file-oriented Jewish organization. One Bernheimer supporter, a non-Communist, calls the Congress of the late 1940s "the last citadel where liberals and progressives could work together." It was, without doubt, the most appropriate vehicle within which to construct a Popular Front strategy within the Jewish community.

Bernheimer did not control the Council during his tenure as executive director. He was supported by his assistant Jerome Toobin, several office personnel, and the Central Chapter, described by one of its former presidents as "the largest in the United States," including several hundred progressives, and, less dominantly, Germantown, Strawberry Mansion, and West Philadelphia chapters. One former Central Chapter leader admits that the progressives "took several provocative positions, sometimes just for the hell of it," suggesting that Party-oriented Congress members sometimes had small regard for the Congress other than as a vehicle for their own politics. On the other hand, several anti-Bernheimer leaders concur with the progressive self-description of being the catalysts, the agitators for practices consistent with Congress ideals. From this perspective, the progressive faction was an irritant, but, by constantly, sometimes dogmatically, demanding grassroots action, helped the organization remain as liberal as it proclaimed itself to be. The progressives prided themselves on their more rank-and-file approach, feeling that without their efforts, the Congress would dissolve into Jewish establishment moderation.

There is little evidence that there were substantial policy differences between the Bernheimer-led progressives and the Congress liberal leadership. The progressives seemed to have played a gadfly role, with differences centering on tactics, style, and context, at least before 1948. But, beginning in 1948, and then gathering steam in 1949, the Congress liberals began to perceive the progressives less as an annoyance and more as a positive and immediate danger to the organization and to the Jewish community in general.

The central point of departure was not attitudes toward Israel or concerning anti-Semitism or any particular Jewish concern, but rather the Cold War. As the Truman administration moved toward confronting Soviet policies in Eastern Europe and, increasingly, elsewhere around the globe, policies and practices developed to ensure a bipartisan consensus in support of the Truman Doctrine, a policy of containment, and the Marshall Plan. Those who sought a more conciliatory approach, soon led by Henry Wallace, both progressives and radicals, found themselves under assault from all sides: Truman's executive order establishing a new loyalty board, the Attorney General's list of allegedly subversive organizations, the Taft-Hartley Act's requirement of anti-Communist affidavits, the CIO purge of Communists, the extensive red-baiting of Wallace's Progressive party efforts, and the Smith Act indictments of Communist party leaders in 1948.[39] What would later, inaccurately, be called McCarthyism, a second Red Scare, began to make it clear that those opposed to American foreign policy objectives as defined in a bipartisan fashion by Truman and Arthur Vandenberg were at considerable risk.

Although the American Jewish Congress tended to remove itself from foreign policy issues not touching Israel or anti-Semitism, it did find itself affected by Cold War conflicts that pitted progressives against Truman liberals. Many Congress progressives worked actively in the Wallace campaign. As the Cold War deepened, progressives sought to influence the Congress toward a more conciliatory position, including opposition to the development of the H-bomb and support for the

Communist party–initiated Stockholm Peace Pledge.[40] From the vantage point of Congress leaders, the presence of a progressive, Communist party–influenced faction had become a liability.

The issue of Communism had long plagued the Jewish community. Reactionaries have tried to link Jews with radicalism as a part of their anti-Semitic arsenal. Concomitantly, many Jews mistrusted a universalistic Marxism that seemed to define anti-Semitism as epiphenomenal, and they suspected the motives of the secular and cosmopolitan Jewish radicals who seemed to approach the Jewish community instrumentally. Lastly, there were sufficient instances of questionable Communist policies—recall the 1929 Palestinian riots and the Nazi-Soviet Pact—to lead many non-Left Jews to eschew all associations with Communists.

The Philadelphia Jewish community shared in these concerns. As early as 1939, prior to the Nazi-Soviet Pact, Maurice Fagan of the Anti-Defamation League Council, later of the JCRC, addressed "The Communist Question" in a circulated memo, asking "how we may effectively restrain the activities of such Jewish organizations or individuals that profess a sincere belief in Communism." He indicated that avoidance was not a sufficient policy. JCRC files indicate that Communist meetings that touched on Jewish affairs were monitored.[41] During the period of the Pact, when Fagan condemned Party members as "Commu-Nazis," he wrote: "I believe it would be of considerable help to us to have all the names connected with the registration of the Communist Party in Pennsylvania and in Philadelphia. This information may be of considerable assistance in counteracting rumors concerning Jewish participation in Communism."[42]

Whatever caution Jewish community leaders showed in attacking Communists and their allies between 1941 and 1947 evaporated by the time of Truman's surprise victory over Thomas Dewey. The 1948 election indicated the relative weakness of the Communists and their progressive allies. The Party's relative strength in the trade union movement was rapidly vanishing, and a different kind of Popular Front, this time against Communism, was in full gear, directed by both liberal Democrats and conservative Republicans, each in their own fashion.

Thus, it is quite clear that by 1949 the national leadership of the American Jewish Congress, the Jewish organization most attractive to the Left, was ready, in the words of Will Maslow, "to purge the Communist divisions."[43] Some progressive Congress members claim that the death of Rabbi Wise allowed anti-Communist elements to sharply shift Congress policy away from an ideological ecumenism. Congress records indicate, to the contrary, that Wise was a shrewd and politic leader who was unlikely to have risked the existence of his lifelong creation in order to maintain a tenuous relationship with progressives.[44] In fact, the purge was carried out by a national leadership group that included both Wise's daughter, Justin Wise Polier, and her husband, Shad Polier. Although Rabbi Wise had been a Roosevelt man and, therefore, admired by many progressives, there is much evidence that he tended to eschew grassroots practices, becoming what Congress historian Morris Frommer calls a "*shtadlan* par excellence."[45]

In 1947 it was still possible for Congress staffer David Petegorsky to respond to charges of "Communist infiltration in Congress" by suggesting that progressive views are always labeled Communist and adding that only two of fifty Congress affiliates had been challenged as Communist.[46] By 1949, such an ecumenical response was riskier, and leaders like Petegorsky moved toward expelling left-wing Congress affiliates and purging all progressive councils, divisions, and chapters.

In the spring of 1949, shortly following Wise's death, national Congress leaders moved to expel the left-wing JPFO and AJLC, and to revoke the charter of a left-wing Metropolitan Detroit chapter. Despite Nathan Edelstein's contention that he, as chairman of the Hearing Committee, was "not concerned with the political ideology of anyone in Detroit," it is clear that procedural charges rested on an ideological base. The Detroiters had sponsored a Civil Rights Congress speaker, despite opposition from national and council leaders.[47]

The purge votes within both executive and administrative committees indicate that a progressive presence held into 1949. The JPFO and AJLC expulsions passed the executive committee 30 to 6 with two abstentions, but only 98 to 39 in the larger administrative committee. The Detroit revocation was upheld 83 to 40 by the administrative committee.[48] Such votes suggest that on the brink of the Philadelphia purge, the Congress included a progressive group able to attract one-quarter to one-third of the membership, at least as measured by their representatives. Indeed, as late as March 20, 1950, the Philadelphia Council discussed a motion requesting the Congress to institute an educational program at the chapter level on "the danger of the H-bomb to world peace" that, after a 19 to 19 vote, was only defeated by the chairman's vote.[49]

The Congress's biennial convention in New York City, November 9–13, 1949, confirmed the developing purge. The *Jewish Times* headlined "American Jewish Congress Cleans House," cheering the expulsion of "red-tinted groups": "As was repeatedly stated on the floor of the convention, there is no room in American Jewish life for Communism or Communists. Judaism and Communism are diametrical opposites."[50]

The progressives at the convention took "a terrible licking," including a minority from Philadelphia. The pro-administration Philadelphia delegation had already engaged in its own purge of the local JPFO and AJLC in the spring and had strongly defended the Detroit revocation at a tumultuous Council meeting.[51]

The actions at the biennial convention signaled to all Congress affiliates and councils that the elimination of all Communist and Progressive political practices had to follow at the risk of a widened house-cleaning. But Congress leaders quickly noted the necessity for further actions. As Isaac Toubin argued in a confidential report to the executive committee, "forces who attempted to subvert the American Jewish Congress had not ceased their efforts even after their defeat at the convention in the struggle around JPFO and the American Jewish Labor Council."[52] Toubin also noted "the very close relationship between the leftist dominated union and the dissident groups" and "a shocking fall-off of members in areas dominated by dissident elements." In referring to the further actions taken against New York, California, and Philadelphia groups, Toubin stressed that "the executive body . . . could no longer await individual reports of disloyalty, disruption and sabotage, but must deal with the situation comprehensively and with dispatch." After raising fears that the Communists meant to increase their grassroots efforts within the Congress, Toubin emphasized that "we cannot fight for democracy with totalitarian allies."[53]

The national Congress, as well as its Philadelphia Council, feared that left-wing activities against U.S. foreign policy would destroy the organization. One Philadelphia leader recalls progressive proposals that "would have embarrassed this country tremendously." Congress, fearful of being attacked from the anti-Semitic Right, joined the national consensus on the Cold War. As historian Morris Frommer suggests, "The hysteria which swept the United States, typified by Senator Joseph McCarthy, forced the Jewish Congress to adopt defensive measures."[54]

It is important to emphasize that anti-Communist liberals, like those heading the Congress, as well as others in such organizations as Americans for Democratic Action (ADA), began their internal purges well before Senator McCarthy started his meteoric rise. The Congress consistently opposed the excesses of the period—criticizing HUAC, opposing such repressive bills as Nixon-Mundt and McCarran—while continuing its liberal agenda for civil rights through its Commission on Law and Social Action (CLSA) and its Council on Community Inter-Relations (CCI). It was part of what Arthur Schlesinger, Jr., called "the vital center," perceiving itself as opposed to both right and left totalitarianisms.[55]

In arguing for constitutional amendments to eliminate left-wing membership, Toubin stated, "It is important . . . to note that decent democratic tactics are effective only when applied by or towards decent democratic people. They are of no use whatsoever in intellectual or organizational combat with those who lie or deceive. They are of no use whatsoever with those who are acting under instructions."[56]

Toubin spoke of naturalization procedures for Jewish immigrants being held up by membership in the Congress, of Treasury Department questioning of the Congress's tax-exempt status, concluding with "how catastrophic it would be for us to allow the irresponsible acts of a few to destroy the lifetime work of the many."[57] It seems that most of the Congress's liberal mainstream shared Toubin's justifications for a purge.

The outbreak of a hot war in Korea certainly made such self-protective assertions more understandable, albeit unfortunate. At an executive committee meeting just prior to the Bernheimer dismissal, another resolution on the H-bomb was rejected as "beyond the purview of the American Jewish Congress." Yet three months later, the committee reaffirmed its "unstinting support for our Government and the U.N. in meeting the challenge of aggression in Korea," adding, "We must . . . be on guard against those who use slogans of peace as a cover for acts of war. The so-called 'peace-petitions' now being circulated . . . have their source in that power which has planned and executed the breach of the peace in Korea."[58] Only criticisms of United States policy were ruled as extraneous to the Congress's affairs, or so it seems.

One may conclude with some confidence that Philadelphia and national Congress leaders directing the purges took less than kindly to a Barrows Dunham speech on "Thought Control" at the Germantown Jewish Center, sponsored by the Germantown Chapter, Women's Division of Congress. Philadelphia Congress leaders surely included the soon-to-be-fired Temple University philosophy professor in their precautions "to exclude Communists" from a January 1950 bus trip to Washington in support of a revived FEPC.[59]

The events of March 1950 in Philadelphia were simply one part of a Congress strategy established at the national level, itself part of a comprehensive drive, to exclude Communists and their progressive allies from all liberal organizations. Philadelphia Congress leaders, indeed, played significant roles in national Congress policy making. For example, Victor Blanc chaired the committee hearings concerning a Manhattan chapter, while Nathan Edelstein performed the same function with Metro Detroit. Key Philadelphia leaders attended virtually all of the national executive and administrative committee meetings in New York during this period. All local leaders, liberals, New Deal Democrats, anti-Communists, Cold War supporters, ACLU members, and integrationists, believed that the survival and integrity of the Congress depended on the removal of the slightest hint of radicalism from their organization. And, as Isaac Toubin had stressed, Communists and fellow-travelers could not be fought "with democratic tactics."

Why was John Bernheimer dismissed as Philadelphia Council executive director? In the termination letter sent to Bernheimer, Congress executive director David Petegorsky based charges of "irresponsibility and unfitness" on the following:

1. Secretly and improperly maintaining his law practice while working full-time for Congress
2. Taking a salary increase improperly
3. "Clandestinely" associating with and directing "those who sought to undermine the confidence of the members of Congress in its leadership, policies, and programs"[60]

Nathan Edelstein suggests that Bernheimer surreptitiously avoided carrying out Congress policies at odds with the Left and, in fact, destroyed records that would have demonstrated his use of Congress facilities for Communist party purposes.[61] No hard evidence remains that either proves or disproves such allegations. They are plausible, given the mounting tensions between mainstream and dissidents, but, in part, tempered by the fact that Bernheimer seems to have focused his attention on issues consistent with Congress policies—for example, anti-discrimination efforts, de-Nazification, and support for Israel. Although he supported Henry Wallace in the 1948 Progressive party campaign, Bernheimer did not take an active role. Furthermore, despite obvious loyalties, he did not fight to defeat the purge of both the JPFO and AJLC either locally or nationally.

On the other hand, Bernheimer's brother-in-law Sol Rottenberg was the head of JPFO and, as one mainstream leader argued, there was a fear that the Congress would suffer from "guilt by association." Moreover, Congress progressives did participate actively in the Wallace campaign, did resist various Cold War policies. And, as late as the spring of 1950, the Philadelphia progressive group included one of five Council vice presidents (Samuel H. Landy), the treasurer (Joseph E. Frankle), and the financial secretary (Albert M. Bershad); controlled the large Central Chapter; and had influence in at least three other chapters. In brief, they were a formidable, if minority, faction.

It is essential to emphasize that the progressive group was not monolithic and certainly not predominantly Communist. Most progressives were New Deal Democrats or independent radicals who worked with Communists for common goals, most particularly what today would be called "détente," and significant extensions of social reform. The progressives identified with the Congress precisely because it was the most left-of-center, rank-and-file Jewish organization. Most of them mistrusted what they perceived as the Jewish establishment of rabbinate, federation professionals, and affluent fund-raisers. They were strongly and unequivocally pro-Israel.

Most participants in the 1950 struggle, including the mainstream liberals, agree that the progressive group, while sometimes obnoxiously aggressive, pushed the organization toward more militant support of consensually accepted practices. The progressives pushed for demonstrations, rallies, mobilizations, and petitions. The liberal mainstream, for the most part, tended to prefer more diplomatic, less confrontational tactics. For example, national Congress leader Will Maslow, in criticizing progressive calls for greater militancy, argued that "picketing is the most irritating device to legislators of anything you can think of, because it is only coercive . . . if you start out by saying we must improve Congress as a mass organization, you will end up in disaster."[62]

The progressives argued, on the contrary, that if the Congress did not extend itself as a mass organization, it would simply replicate the practices of other, safer Jewish organizations—to them, a far worse disaster.

On April 10, Bernheimer brought suit to enjoin the Congress from dismissing him.[63] A week later, he met privately with Council leaders to seek a possible financial settlement of one year's salary compensation.[64] Meanwhile, according to Bernheimer's Bill in Equity, the transcripts of the March 31 interrogations, promised to Bernheimer, were not forthcoming but, instead, were being selectively leaked by Council leaders to justify the dismissals. Council leaders counter that at a negotiating session on April 19, the stenographic notes "were made available to Bernheimer and his counsel and read at length by them."[65]

At this point, several progressive leaders—Landy, Bershad, Frankle, and Maury Kolsky— circulated a pamphlet charging Congress leaders with improperly dismissing Bernheimer and Jerome Toobin, and they organized a protest meeting on April 26. The pamphlet, charging "star chamber proceedings," "defamation of character without trial," a "sham" hearing, infuriated Philadelphia Council leaders, who saw only "those whose interest in the American Jewish Congress is ulterior to its basic purposes" engaging in a "standard technique" of seeking to destroy the organization they could not capture or "pervert . . . to their own ends and purposes."[66] Leaders also blamed the progressive pamphleteers for "going public" through the courts and press and even charged that such agitation might impair the Allied Jewish Appeal campaign.[67]

Meanwhile, the court action proceeded. Rabbi Meyer Finkelstein of the Strawberry Mansion chapter and chairman of the World Affairs and Israel committees, sought to intervene in the suit on behalf of Bernheimer. Other progressives, including a fired secretary, submitted affidavits supportive of the suit.[68]

The protest meeting, at the Sylvania Hotel on April 26, lasted three hours. Congress local leaders charged that the protesters denied them the opportunity to address the assemblage. The Philadelphia Council had, during this tumultuous period, sent out a letter to membership defending its behavior and called for a general meeting on May 3 to address the controversy.[69]

Both sides perceived the righteousness of their own behavior and charged their respective adversary with bad faith and intentions. The liberal mainstream truly believed that only a "cleansed" Congress could survive and remain effective, and that Communists and their "dupes" only wished to use the organization for Party purposes. They felt that Bernheimer, who had been socially friendly with a number of mainstream leaders, had betrayed them through his secretive, dishonest behavior.

In fact, there were at least three parties to this struggle. The liberal mainstream, the Communist party radicals, and the progressives. The Communist group did, in fact, view the Congress instrumentally, as mass work for Jewish members seeking to implement Party positions. With few exceptions, Jewish Communists involved in the Jewish community were ambivalent about their Jewishness. The Party had moved toward significant support for Jewish organizational life beginning in the Popular Front era and then resuming and deepening during and after World War II.[70] Jewish Communists genuinely worked against anti-Semitism and enthusiastically supported the creation and then the very existence of Israel. Certainly they had helped to make the Congress a distinctively activist organization.

Yet Jewish Communists could remain both actively Jewish and Communist only so long as Soviet policy supported Israel's existence and appeared, at least, to oppose anti-Semitism. By the late 1940s, Soviet policies were beginning to shift, relations with Israel began to cool, and massive assaults took place against Yiddish culture that would culminate in Stalin's anti-Semitic and paranoiac charges of a Jewish doctors' plot.[71] When John Bernheimer was fired, strains were developing, most particularly over the Cold War, but, for the most part, not yet over Jewish or Israeli affairs. Within a few short years, as Israel moved toward alliance with the United States, and the Soviet Union began to make gestures toward the new nationalist governments of the Third World, including the Arab world, a Jewish Communist presence in the Congress would reach a breaking point.[72]

Liberal mainstream leaders and the membership of the Congress were not unjust in mistrusting Communist party loyalists, both for their manipulative behavior and for their primary allegiances. Moreover, the Congress realistically understood that without eliminating radicals it would face the same kinds of political assault and likely extinction faced by other progressive organizations. Nevertheless, the Congress did move to eliminate what was a declining influence with what can only be described as high-handed and undemocratic means. The American Jewish Congress, nationally and in Philadelphia, did not simply go along reluctantly with an emerging political repression; it acted ferociously.

For example, two former leaders of the Philadelphia Council admit that the FBI was in contact with their offices, with one of the previously mentioned figures serving as a liaison. The liaison official stated that "the FBI came to see me about" John Bernheimer and alleged Communist presence in the American Jewish Congress. He added that the Bureau provided "enough" information indicating that "Bernheimer was a confirmed Communist." Such liaison seems to go back to at least 1948. Another local leader, while confirming the existence of the liaison, suggests that it was neither the necessary nor sufficient cause of Bernheimer's dismissal. Yet it remains damaging to the Congress's integrity that contacts existed between organization leaders and the FBI to which general membership was not privy. Such contacts weaken the Congress's case against Bernheimer and the progressive dissidents, suggesting that specific charges against them were merely a ploy. At the very least, it may be said that Bernheimer was convicted before being tried.[73] Of equal importance, the Congress alienated a sizable number of members who had helped to make it the most democratic Jewish community force of its day.

On May 5, Bernheimer withdrew his suit, concluding that "the welfare of the Jewish community and the welfare of the American Jewish Congress within that community is more important than the welfare of an individual."[74] He denied any guilt to the various charges. Meanwhile, the actions set in motion by his dismissal continued.

Shad Polier was assigned to investigate the Philadelphia dissidents. He recommended that a hearing committee be established to review all the charges and hear all the appeals. On June 26, the national executive committee resolved that Polier conduct the inquiry. Dr. Horace Kallen, noted Columbia University professor of philosophy, agreed to chair the hearings, which were to be held November 28 and December 26, 1950, and January 7, 1951, in Philadelphia. On May 30, 1951, Kallen reported to the executive committee that those under investigation had refused to participate in the hearings. Kallen's hearing committee recommended that Bernheimer be expelled from the Congress, that three progressives be disqualified from office for three years, and that another five be disqualified for two years, and, finally, that the troublesome Central Chapter be placed under mainstream supervision. The recommendations passed unanimously.[75]

One must note that simultaneous with the Philadelphia events, the Congress was moving to purge its Southern California division for refusing to disaffiliate the JPFO, and moving to dissolve or purge divisions and chapters in Manhattan, Brooklyn, and Long Island. In fact, the progressive forces in these areas were significantly stronger than in Philadelphia, where pro-national administration forces always were in control.[76]

John Bernheimer, according to most sources, was not embittered by his dismissal and the train of events it generated. First of all, he had to address the very practical matter of making a living, resuming his law practice. Remarkably, he deepened his Jewish organizational activities as well. Bernheimer, a founder and "spirit" of the Beachcomber Swim Club, remained active with B'nai B'rith, the "Y" camps, and Pinemere Camp. Whether he was a Party member or not, he was perceived by many of his friends as "a genuine progressive," and engaged in both Jewish community affairs and progressive political activity—such as active opposition to American involvement in Vietnam—until illness and finally death overtook him in 1976.

Several progressive veterans of the Congress struggles in Philadelphia feel that Bernheimer actually let them down by dropping his lawsuit. One dissident recalls going to New York in the initial weeks after the dismissals seeking redress. David Petegorsky told them that they were being used. But the dissidents believed that the liberal mainstream leadership of the Congress was withholding information, acting in a dictatorial and manipulative manner, and indiscriminately branding all critics as either Communists or dupes of the Communists. The Congress progressives wanted to fight for a democratic organization; for that reason, they rallied to Bernheimer. But, in fact, they were caught between two forces at war, one of which possessed an overwhelming superiority in firepower. The Communist party retreated, faced with assaults from all sides. Its Jewish activities dwindled to the soon-to-be crushed JPFO and Party-related organs. It lacked the resources to wage a fight in Congress; its energies necessarily focused on mere survival, keeping its own members out of prison. When the Soviets later moved toward a fully anti-Israeli position, the links between Jews and the Communist party virtually ceased.

The year that Bernheimer was fired, the Rosenbergs were arrested. By 1953, when they were executed, there were no significant Jewish organizations in Philadelphia—or elsewhere— willing to question the severity of the sentences. Several of those who did, recall that a number of prominent Jewish leaders offered private support for their efforts, but were unwilling to take any public positions in fear of possible reprisals.

Jewish progressives and radicals continued to engage in political struggle through the fifties, but outside the organized Jewish community. The mainstream, predominantly liberal, can be proud of many of its accomplishments in antidiscrimination and civil rights work. But one cost of the purges of this second Red Scare was that the Jewish community, in becoming respectably liberal, had become intolerant of opposing voices—voices calling for a more activist approach to civil rights; voices more strenuously seeking to eliminate poverty; voices critical of American foreign policy; voices challenging the less than admirable aspects of the new suburban affluence; and voices troubled in their support for Israel.

The embourgeoisement of American Jews, the reconstruction of an establishment, the "Protestantization" of Judaism, all determined that the old Yiddish-socialist subculture and Depression-based Communist movement would decline.[77] But it remains unfortunate that when a portion of young Jews, touched by the Civil Rights Movement and opposition to the war in Vietnam, created a "new left," there was no place available to them within the organized Jewish community. The last such place had been the American Jewish Congress prior to its purge of progressive and radical voices in 1950–1951. "The world of our fathers" may still offer possibilities to the world of our children. If such is the case, one would hope that such worlds, such voices find recognition, if not agreement, within the organized Jewish community.

Congressman Joshua Eilburg addressing an Anti-Soviet rally in December
of 1970.

4

FROM PERIPHERY TO PROMINENCE
Jews in Philadelphia Politics, 1940–1985

Dennis Clark

To be a Jew in politics in the city of Philadelphia in the mid-twentieth century was to be engaged in a distinctive and enervating social experience. Jews were participating in urban politics in a competitive and interactive way that had been simply impossible even a generation earlier. As ambitious office seekers, as party wheelhorses, and as a voting bloc, Jews had moved from the margin of the city's politics to its center, in the very city where the American system had been invented.

The conditions making heightened participation of Jews in political affairs possible were as complex as the city itself. It was not solely their emergence from quasi-segregated immigrant communities that promoted this new political currency, though the residential redistribution of the group in newer areas of the city was certainly a factor that changed the orientation of Jews and the gentile perception of them. In addition, the experience of the Great Depression of the 1930s had provided a powerful political conditioning for Jewish radical activists and for those more moderate Jews who helped to form the New Deal coalition that altered so much domestic policy and government practice of the time. The highly emotional political bonding that occurred during World War II and involved all Americans in the war effort brought further strengthening of relationships between Jews and non-Jews. The growth of strong Jewish intergroup relations and fraternal organizations helped to define civic goals for Jews and also decreased the vulnerability of the group in the rough-and-tumble atmosphere of urban community jousting. Events overseas, the searing awareness of the Holocaust, the social mobility within American life, and the extraordinary episode of local government reform in Philadelphia itself after World War II all played a role in the new dispensation for Jews in the political life of the city.

The emergence of Jews from previous political constraints in the period that began with World War II was partly the result of their work in politics beginning in the years before World War I. The great immigration from Eastern Europe in the late nineteenth century and early twentieth century had pressed Jews indiscriminately into the turbulence of Philadelphia's life in greater numbers than ever before. By 1920 there were an estimated 200,000 Jews in the city, most of them tracing their origins to Eastern Europe.[1] Even though the Philadelphia Jewish population was regarded as historic and stable, and had been blessed with talented leadership, this did not mean that daily problems of immigrant and working-class Jews were diminished as they struggled to adjust to American life.[2] Many problems, such as the legalities of immigration, the need for jobs and housing, and ties to the dominant city Republican machine had to be dealt with through ward politics. Especially in the crowded South Philadelphia wards, immigrant Jews became part of the crude, corrupt, and often violent political infighting that characterized the electoral and patronage scrambles of the Republican regime.[3] By the 1930s this old tradition had moderated somewhat. When young Herbert Levin became a committeeman of the chronically underdog Democratic party in the Irish-dominated Fourth Ward in 1931, he was part of a grassroots pluralist spectrum in his ward that embraced Jews, Italians, Irish, and black voters. Longshoremen, hucksters, storekeepers, truck drivers, laborers, garment workers, and building trades members all jostled at the polls in a panorama of urban vote trading.[4]

This early ward-level political experience was repeated in an array of city neighborhoods where Jews had taken up residence, although the crowded South Philadelphia area was more intensely involved. Immigrants had settled before World War I in Kensington near Trenton Avenue, in West Philadelphia beyond 55th Street below Market Street, in Strawberry Mansion, and in a semi-rural area in Southwest Philadelphia near Island Road. In the far Northeast of the city in Mayfair, a congregation had established Temple Menorah in the 1920s, and in the same decade, Jews moved in substantial numbers to Wynnefield and Overbrook. In the 1930s Jews moved beyond the small orthodox enclave in Germantown and founded a large conservative congregation in Mount Airy. The older German-Jewish synagogues on North Broad Street and the historic Mikveh Israel congregation had been part of the city's social reform movements for decades, and an East European settlement around Franklin Street market mingled North Philadelphia Jews with Ukrainians, Lithuanians, Hungarians, and Germans.[5]

From this welter of ward politics, the city's Jews derived their primary fund of electoral knowledge. By the 1920s there were two city councilmen, over a dozen state representatives, and two state senators who where Jews. Common Pleas Court Number 2 was conceded to be the "Jewish Court," and assistant district attorneys, magistrates, and other local positions were held intermittently by Jews, though the picture generally was one of underrepresentation.[6]

Equally important to the future of the group's political fortunes was the shift from a predominantly Republican allegiance to the Democratic party, and the participation of Jews in the New Deal coalition that sponsored so many changes in the 1930s. Reformers such as Samuel S. Fels and Rabbi Joseph Krauskopf had been leading figures in the city in the Progressive era. Samuel Fels was a founder of the Committee of 70 and of the Fels Institute for Local and State Government, which would have a considerable influence for better government in Philadelphia and far beyond it in other cities. The Depression of the 1930s, however, gave reforms a mass appeal in the face of a crisis in economic and social life.[7] The migration of Jews to the Democrats, which had begun with their support for the presidential candidacy of Al Smith in 1928, rose to a flood in the 1930s. The affinity of Jews for others of immigrant background, the recognition that the common threat of prejudice against Irish Catholics and blacks also made Jews vulnerable, and the pressure of Depression conditions all added to the New Deal surge under Franklin D. Roosevelt. Jewish labor leaders, such as those in the Amalgamated Clothing Workers of America, worked diligently for the New Deal Democrats.[8] Radical and leftist Jews saw visions of a socialist transformation. Jews who were unemployed, bankrupt, and disillusioned flocked to the banners of Roosevelt, and read with delight the pro–New Deal editorials in David Stern's Philadelphia *Record,* the city's only

Samuel Fels in 1950.

Albert M. Greenfield.

Democratic newspaper. Still, they had to contend with the most crude kind of prejudice. In the 1935 mayoral contest, Republican S. Davis Wilson accused his Democrat opponent, John B. Kelly, of being the tool of "Jewish interests," but the real target was Kelly's backer, banker Albert M. Greenfield.[9] Thus, before World War II, Philadelphia Jews had already accumulated a history of practical political participation.

World War II brought to Philadelphia Jews a full quotient of suffering and dislocations of accustomed life as sons and fathers served in the armed forces, women took defense jobs, and shortages of all kinds plagued the home front. Most of the city's political affairs were in abeyance. The struggle to deal with housing shortages, production goals, and inadequate local control of events put politics into slow motion. The long discredited Republican rule of the city hung on, for younger aspirants to office had gone to war and civilian concerns were secondary to the war effort.

As Jews were dying in the battles in Europe and Asia, they were forging unbreakable bonds with their fellow servicemen and -women. This would mean a great deal in post-war politics. There were some ugly anti-Semitic incidents in the city even while the young were risking their lives in common jeopardy, but the overwhelming consciousness was one of patriotic amity.[10] Even more important for Jews was the gradual realization of the vast calamity overtaking European Jewry under Nazi tyranny. The Holocaust was to irrevocably and profoundly alter the worldview of every Jew. The identity of all Jews was enhanced and intensified by this momentous tragedy in an unprecedented way. The implications of this psychological shock for the conduct of local Jewish affairs were far-reaching.[11] This changed outlook, and a corresponding change in how gentiles viewed their Jewish neighbors, reached right down to the local level of community affairs and to personal relationships in the life of the city.

J. David Stern in 1947, arguing against CIO Guild in Washington following his sale of the *Record*.

The dramatic events attending the creation of the State of Israel also had political ramifications for the city's Jews that reached directly to the local community level. The mobilization of American Jews beyond the original core of committed Zionists was symbolized by a major national conference in 1943 that led to "a potent coalition of almost every significant group in the American Jewish community."[12] This mobilization overcame the anti-Zionist influence of the American Council for Judaism that had as its backers such prominent Philadelphians as Lessing Rosenwald and D. Hays Solis-Cohen. Indeed, as the war to establish Israel escalated, the endorsement of the Jewish state grew apace in avid enthusiasm. Zionism was "an authentic revolutionary movement," and as such, American Jews could take part in it with the keenest sentiments.[13] In the aftermath of the Holocaust, the birth of Israel was a "Jewish reassertion of manhood" after generations of political impotency.[14] The emotional, financial, and political commitment to Israel was amassed in a great catharsis of support, and this complex and sustained engagement that arose in the period after 1947 extensively affected Jewish participation in local politics in succeeding years.

Along with Jews all over the country, Philadelphia's Jewish population contributed toward the total of over $39 million for the Jewish National Fund in 1948.[15] This meant a great intensification of organizational activity, and this increase of activism had an impact on the political ties and dispositions of the city's Jews. It strengthened organization ties, expanded acquaintances, enhanced group consciousness, and gave the Jewish community a much more developed capacity to lobby and deal with politicians on behalf of Israel.[16]

There were certainly threatening challenges that reverberated on the local level. The anti-Communist furor that coincided with the onset of the Cold War with the Soviet Union produced sensational episodes of agitation that had a lurid potential for the revival of widespread anti-Semitism. The confession of a British atomic scientist that he was a Russian spy led to the apprehension and conviction of one Harry Gold, a research chemist at Philadelphia General Hospital. Gold's conviction as a spy for the Russians led in turn to the arrest and eventual execution of Julius and Ethel Rosenberg in 1953. These people of Jewish background tempted anti-Semites to revive their old conspiracy theories. Added to this was the histrionic malignancy of Senator Joseph McCarthy, whose anti-Red ranting pilloried some Jews and created a deep unease in Jewish liberal circles. The Philadelphia Communist party membership was very heavily composed of people, often enough anti-religious, who came from Jewish families.[17] The firing of public school teachers who were supposedly Communists symbolized the anti-Red crusading. Yet, these disturbing eddies of larger waves of national fear did not erode the confidence and community of interest Jews shared with non-Jews in the strenuous post-war decade.

Left: Marice Osser at City Hall Press conference, April 11, 1975.

Right: Herbert W. Salus, 1935.

The Jewish old hands at politics did not disappear in the post-war period. Many remained highly active. Although J. David Stern's power ended when his *Philadelphia Record* failed in 1947, Albert M. Greenfield was increasing his influence. Harry Kalodner (secretary to Governor George Earle), Dr. Leopold Jacobs, Manny Weinberg, Maurice Osser, Herbert Salus, Sr., Leon Sacks, and others, some of whom were former Republicans, began to foresee a new era for the Democratic party in the city. As Sandra Featherman has pointed out, the shift of Jews to the Democratic party that gradually took place was a popular movement with which political leaders had to scramble to catch up.[18]

After 1941 the federal government dramatically enlarged its role in American life, and this had notable political effects in urban areas. In Philadelphia, increased political benefits and patronage from the New Deal period onward added a new dimension to politics. Leon Sacks, elected to the U.S. Congress in 1937, was in a strategic position to direct federal benefits to his district. Those close to other Democrats, such as the Jewish colleagues of Congressman Michael J. Bradley or those close to Congressman William Barrett in South Philadelphia, were also able to bargain for favors, electoral nominations, and party positions. In this process a steady working relationship developed between Jews and the Irish Catholic politicians who dominated the Democratic party. As one long-time party worker noted, "The real control of the party was with the Irish, and the Jews recognized that fact and were expedient about it."[19]

The growth of the welfare state, the popular resentment against Communism and Russia, the strains of post-war readjustment, and the outbreak of the Korean conflict in 1950 all made for a turbulent public life that was far from the return to normalcy that the wartime generation had anticipated. The expansion of the city by the addition of vast suburban developments and the building up of largely vacant areas in the northeast section of the city lured Jews as well as others to new areas. Hyman Korman and A. P. Orleans were two Jewish builders who covered huge tracts with new, inexpensive housing in the city. Where the people went, politics followed, and as "Jewish neighborhoods" grew in the Oxford Circle and Mayfair areas, more Jews joined the ward committees.

Coincident with new housing opportunities was the surging expansion of the city's black population, which, after years of housing shortage, was finally penetrating previously all-white areas. Some of these areas were heavily Jewish, such as the old Franklin Street market area in North Philadelphia, the Victorian streets of Strawberry Mansion, and the row-house areas of Wynnefield. The greatly augmented black population of the city totaled 380,000 in 1950, and its growing mobility challenged the racial segregation that had controlled housing access in the past. Although the head of the Democratic delegation in the assembly of the Commonwealth of Pennsylvania, Philadelphian Charles Weiner, would fight vigorously to have the first Fair Housing statute adopted, other Jews did not view the swift movement of blacks to their neighborhood with equanimity. The departure of thousands of families, the disruption of accustomed social patterns, the out-migration of synagogues from old areas created a distressed reaction for a very large segment of the Jewish community.[20]

Far from producing overt forms of resentment and resistance against black social and economic goals, the black–Jewish tension stimulated an influential alliance of blacks with Jewish intergroup relations agencies in the 1950s. The National Association for the Advancement of Colored People and the Urban League were joined in many efforts to combat discrimination by the American Jewish Committee, the Jewish Community Relations Council, and the Anti-Defamation League of B'nai B'rith. Politicians vied with one another to join the Philadelphia Fellowship Commission—in which Jews provided most of the leadership—to have anti-bias laws enacted. Deputy City Solicitor Murray Shusterman wrote an antidiscrimination ordinance for the city, and Nathan Edelstein headed the city's Commission on Human Relations to ensure fair treatment in housing, employment, and public facilities. While neighborhood-level politicians experienced difficult times as the great racial transition proceeded, citywide politicians were able to increase their recognition and professions of principle as the racial issues unfolded. At the ward level, however, whole committees changed from white to black, and previously secure areas of Jewish voting power were transformed.[21]

These great changes in the orientation of Jews and in the life of the city took place during a singular episode of urban reform that came to be known as the "Philadelphia Renaissance." The new expectations of World War II veterans beginning civilian careers, the necessity to meet needs postponed by the war, and, most important, the spectacular corruption of the hoary Republican machine in the city created a unique opportunity for political change. Long-term Jewish politicians like Joseph Ominsky in Wynnefield sensed the trend and moved toward the Democratic party, but some, like Samuel Rosenberg, Director of Public Safety in the administration of Mayor Bernard Samuel, were unable to free themselves from the Republican debacle of the late 1940s. The Samuel administration was convulsed with indictments, thievery, scandals, and suicides accompanying exposures of extraordinary public abuses.[22]

As the Republican death wish exacted its toll, there arose a Democratic reform phalanx that was destined to alter the skyline and the public administration of the city in a way that would capture the imagination of the nation. A coalition of Irish Catholic Democratic politicians, downtown business leaders, a cadre of technical experts, and upper-class reformers took shape as socialite

Left: Jude Charles R. Weiner, 1970.

Middle: Joseph Ominsky, 1949.

Right: Judge Samuel H. Rosenberg, 1966.

Democrat Richardson Dilworth unsuccessfully ran for Mayor in 1947. The Democratic City Committee was reorganized under the prodigious Colonel James Finnegan. The Greater Philadelphia Movement of bankers and business heads was joined by labor activists in pressing for a new era in Philadelphia government. Part of this coalition was made up of Jews who were members of the liberal Americans for Democratic Action, the technical cadres of planners, finance specialists, and civil servants, and the activist lawyers who looked toward a full overhaul of the city's antique public institutions. Abraham L. Freedman, William Schnader, and notable Republicans like Nochem S. Winnet took part in a broad drive to draft and have adopted a new city charter to restructure local government. This charter was adopted in the primary election of 1951. When Joseph S. Clark was elected mayor that year, Richardson Dilworth was elected district attorney, bringing with him promising young Jewish attorneys like Samuel Dash, later to figure into the Watergate hearings as congressional counsel; Fredric R. Mann became recreation commissioner in the new administration; and familiar figures such as Maurice Osser, Harry Schwartz, Councilman Samuel Rose, and Harry Norwich all found places in the reform ranks. This was in part because in the voting for the adoption of the new city charter and for the Clark-Dilworth team, Jews heavily supported the reform. In the Olney–Oak Lane area where the Irish Charles Finley was allied with Jews, Wards 42, 49, and 50 went reform, as did Wards 53, 54, and 55 in the Oxford Circle area, Wards 24, 34, and 52 in Wynnefield, and Wards 46 and 60 in West Philadelphia. This represented the new residential concentrations of Jews, but within a decade all but the Oxford Circle section would be strongly subject to racial change.[23]

In subsequent political shifts within the Democratic reform elements in the 1950s, Jews remained wedded to liberal positions. Emily Ehly and Jewish ADA members joined old-line socialite Philadelphia converts to reform to oppose charter-wrecking schemes, to fight for expanded public housing, and to support the huge city-planning transformation of the Center City.

The ADA brought together upper-class Jews and activists from the labor movement such as Joe Schwartz, Bill Ross, and Willam Rafsky. Lenora Berson and Jane Freedman joined with socialite Ada Lewis and housing reformer Dorothy Schoell Montgomery to help create a brain trust that drafted legislation, lobbied for strong civil service controls, and expanded fair employment practices on behalf of minorities. The ADA was very heavily Jewish in membership, and it would not be possible to explain the reform period of the 1950s without comprehending its major role and its mingling of many talents.

Beyond this, the reform years effected several political advances for Jews in the city. The reform coalition further strengthened their ties to the class of "Philadelphia Gentlemen" whose Protestant dominance had marked the city's history.[24] When Nochem S. Winnet joined with Irish Catholic Democrat Francis Myers as co-chairman of the city charter drive, bonds were strengthened between Jews and the Irish politicians. The placement of figures like Abraham L. Freedman in the forefront of reform identified Jews with a new future for the city and gave them a distinguished prominence that was welcomed by the public at large. Further, the reform coalition brought Jews into a power status that had not existed before and ensured that their group would be truly important as a bloc in participating in the city's politics. The range of people of Jewish backgrounds related to the politics of the reform years is impressive. It included not only Natalie Sachs and William Rafsky, amazingly energetic assistants to the reform mayors, but also Harry Ferleger and Isador Lichstein, publicists and newspapermen, who paved the way for the reform by publishing a newsletter called "The Broom," with which they strove to sweep the Republican oligarchy out of City Hall.

Some of those promoting the Democratic reformers did so simply because their positions as powerful figures in the city required that they choose sides at the time of the political watershed. Albert M. Greenfield, financial backer of the Democrats and a real estate tycoon, continued his astute interest in politics. He was certainly a headstrong individual, and Manny Weinberg recalled meeting Democratic City Committee Chairman William J. Green after a session with Greenfield and listening to Green bemoan the fact that Greenfield wanted to dictate who the party could place on the ballot from top to bottom.[25] Similarly, Walter Annenberg, publisher of the *Philadelphia Inquirer*, also backed the reform administration, although he and his paper had always been staunchly Republican. Annenberg's reputation as an intolerant Conservative and a vindictive man, who used his newspaper to attack those from whom he felt personally estranged, alienated him from the reformers as such. His great wealth and partisan views set him apart from most Jewish politicians.[26]

William L. Rafsky, in 1965, Executive Vice President of the Old Philadelphia Development Corp., studying pre-developed Independence Mall.

Others supported the reform simply because they believed in its principles. Nochem S. Winnet, who had been a judge and head of a number of civic improvement groups, was a faithful Republican, but he supported the new city charter because he believed that Philadelphia desperately needed a new lease on life after decades of poor administration. When he worked to have a professional City Planning Commission established, and called on Mayor Bernard Samuel to push it, the Republican mayor had scoffed at the idea and asserted that he had hundreds of blueprints and plans stacked up in City Hall and nothing ever came of them. The need for concentrated professional planning could hardly have been more effectively confirmed.[27] There were dozens of Jewish professional people whose thinking mirrored Winnet's, including activists Leon Shull, Julius Rosenwald, Steve Remsen of the Jewish Labor Committee, and a broad spectrum of others who transcended the old ward politics.

For many Jews who had been in politics for a long while, the reform was more a practical opportunity than a conversion of the heart. Many were former Republicans who had changed their party affiliation. Joseph Ominsky of Wynnefield entered politics to keep the Republicans from fleecing Jewish shopkeepers like his father, who owned a butcher shop. Watching his chances carefully, he campaigned with Clark and Dilworth in 1949 and became coroner under the Democrats and later a state representative.[28] Herbert Fineman from the 52nd Ward in Wynnefield conducted a successful title insurance business with his brother. He worked diligently in the wards and was elected to the Pennsylvania legislature, where he became an extremely powerful leader of the Democratic representatives as Speaker of the House of Representatives from 1967 to 1971.

The opportunities now open to Jews were vividly illustrated by the electoral sallies of Arlen Specter. A Kansas-born attorney and a graduate of Yale Law School, he was associated with the old-line Philadelphia law firm of Dechert, Price and Rhoads. In 1965 Specter decided the Democratic party was too crowded for his ambitions and accepted the Republican nomination for district attorney. The Democrats, having lost party unity when James Finnegan and Congressman William Green died, were warring fiercely with Richardson Dilworth's successor, Mayor James H. J. Tate. Specter beat the Democrat incumbent James Crumlish. In 1967 Specter challenged Tate for the mayor's office, and the Republicans launched a major campaign for him. Tate, however, adeptly increased his support by highlighting his role in obtaining some state aid and free textbooks for Catholic schoolchildren and in reappointing Frank Rizzo as police commissioner. Specter lost the race but continued as district attorney until 1974. Specter's failure to become mayor was blamed by some Jews on his stated stand against any aid to Catholic schools and his opposition to the tough law-and-order role of Frank Rizzo, but Tate's control of the potent Democratic machinery and his gains in key Irish

Judge Nochem Winnet in his Walnut Street office, July 1978.

Left: Dr. Ada Haesler Lewis, 1965.

Right: Walter Annenberg in 1944.

wards in Kensington were considered by others to be the overriding factors in the race. After an interlude out of office, Specter ran for the U.S. Senate and was elected to that body in 1980.[29]

By the 1960s, sociologist Henry Klein calculated, in a study of the leadership of 199 Philadelphia organizations, that Jews held 19.7 percent of the top positions, certainly a changed condition from the days when Jews were absent and thoroughly excluded from many of those same groups.[30] Thus, the career of Arlen Specter symbolized the ascent of a new kind of Jewish "achiever," not a person especially successful in a profession or a business, but a public representative, a figure chosen by citizens of all backgrounds to manage public affairs, a person to be trusted with the common good.

Of great significance was the career of Milton Shapp, builder of a successful electronics business, who originally contested what he believed were abuses in the conduct of the Pennsylvania Railroad. Methodically, he set out to tour Pennsylvania from his base in Philadelphia. After many tough battles, he became the first Jewish governor of the state, despite the enmity of Walter Annenberg of the *Philadelphia Inquirer,* who allegedly castigated Shapp as a religious recusant for having changed his name from Shapiro. Shapp's election in 1970 was achieved on the basis of a platform promising fiscal control in Pennsylvania for a state government long plagued by inane budgetary wars. Shapp beat Republican Raymond J. Broderick by over half a million votes after fighting for the nomination for governor against the Democratic party organization. He was the first Pennsylvania governor to serve two successive terms, but his power declined as he tolerated more and more scandalous conduct by his appointees.[31]

The 1960s was a period of turbulence in all phases of social life, and politics was no exception. At the University of Massachusetts, two hundred young Jews celebrated Rosh Hashanah not in a synagogue, but by dancing and singing all night in a meadow, a shocking event for many Jews. The Vietnam war led to massive protests. President John F. Kennedy, Robert Kennedy, and Martin Luther King, Jr., were assassinated. The New Left radicals in Chicago in 1967 decried the 1967 Israeli war as "an imperialist Zionist war," and the whites in the radical ranks were heavily from Jewish families.[32] The national uproars had their counterparts in Philadelphia, and the most acutely unsettling events swirled around the rise of the Black Power Movement and the agitation of blacks for an expanded role in the life of the city.

After years of frustration and distress over unemployment, inadequate housing, and unfair treatment by the police, black resentment erupted in August 1964 in fierce riots focused on the Columbia Avenue area. After a weekend of riot, looting, and disorder, 2 people were dead, 329 were wounded, over 300 had been arrested, and property damage was estimated to be over $3 million. Philadelphia had joined a string of other U.S. cities where racial violence had broken out. One feature of the North Philadelphia riots was that the overwhelming majority of white businessmen

Left: As Philadelphia District Attorney, Arlen Specter argues for the death penalty before the State Legislature, July 1972.

Right: Governor Milton Shapp at the Warwick Hotel in 1971.

whose properties were looted and burned were Jewish. According to a study of the turmoil by the American Jewish Committee,[33] it was "as whites and as merchants and realtors rather than as Jews per se that they bore the brunt of the Negroes' attack. Anti-Semitism was not a primary factor in the rioting." For a great number of Jews, however, the toll on Jewish businesses appeared to be a clear example of a vast potential for disorder active within the black community. Such episodes would change the political orientation of Philadelphia's Jews from one of liberalism to one of conservative outlook. By 1967, when Police Commissioner Frank Rizzo rousted Black Panther adherents in raids in the middle of the night, the feeling against black protests and extremist groups was running high. Judge Leo Weinrott held the fourteen Panthers on $100,000 bail, and blacks fumed at the harsh Rizzo treatment that a broad range of whites supported.[34]

The diversion of large numbers of Jews from the liberal Democrat following was related to the emergence of Frank Rizzo as a key figure in the city's politics. Rizzo's tough stance as police commissioner, his repudiation of civil libertarian law enforcement views, and his apparent hard-line treatment of Black Power advocates made him the darling of Philadelphians who had been troubled for years by the onset of black mobility and assertiveness. Rizzo, "the toughest cop in America," was seen as a protector against crime and civil disorder. Jews, along with others, had been displaced from old neighborhoods and challenged politically by the advance of blacks. As an especially nonviolent group in the city, Jews felt keenly the threat of ghetto disorder and crime that they suffered disproportionately because of their isolated status as the remaining whites conducting businesses in black areas.[35] More affluent Jews who lived in places like Merion and Society Hill felt these pressures less, but lower-middle-class Jews who had moved from Strawberry Mansion and who perhaps still had relatives in business in North Philadelphia reacted with exasperation to the trends of the 1960s.

Senator-elect Arlen Specter and his wife, Joan, in Centre Square following his 1980 victory.

When Frank Rizzo ran for mayor against young liberal Democrat William Green, son of the congressman who had helped elect the reformers of the 1950s, heavily Jewish divisions voted 44.5 percent for Rizzo. While Green still got 55.5 percent of the votes in those divisions, this represented a big Jewish defection from previous patterns of strong liberal Democrat support, and was all the more notable because it was a defection in favor of Rizzo's antiliberal position. In the judgment of Lenora Berson, an experienced political activist in the city, this defection was symbolized by the adherence to Rizzo of men like Councilman Al Pearlman and Congressman Joshua Eilberg in the 54th Ward.[36]

In Northeast Philadelphia, the ward leadership under Eilberg gave Rizzo strong support in thirteen heavily Jewish divisions in the 54th Ward. South Philadelphia's Jews in the 39th Ward went for Rizzo two to one. West Philadelphia Jews split clearly along class lines, with middle-class and upper-income Jews voting largely for Green and lower-middle-class and wage-earning Jews voting for Rizzo. In the "silk stocking" areas of Center City and Northwest Philadelphia, Green won Jewish support handily. The split in this election between wage-earning Jews in row-house areas and professional and well-to-do Jews was clear evidence to the social strains brought about by urban tensions.

When Rizzo attempted to change the city charter in his second term to permit him to run for mayor a third time, Jews voted 69 percent to 31 percent in a special referendum against the Rizzo plan.[37] Opinion polls showed that Jews still favored many liberal causes, and they had reacted against Rizzo's rhetorical overkill. The personality of the tough-talking mayor itself was a factor. As the threat of civil disorder faded, as more astute black political leadership emerged in the person of such men as Congressman William H. Gray, Jr., and as Rizzo's imperious ways became irksome, Jews repudiated his attempt to set himself above the charter. The behavior of Jews confirmed an old political axiom: "You can push people too far."

It is appropriate to recall that after 1960, Jewish women assumed a new role in politics. At first as protesters against the Vietnam War and as supporters of Israel, Jewish women stepped beyond their traditional roles in congregation sisterhoods and civic organizations. Moving from activism to office seeking, they became candidates in growing numbers. Beatrice Chernock, a crusading school principal, became a Republican member of City Council. Several Jewish women were elected to the Common Pleas Court. Joan Specter was also elected to City Council, and faced the issues of school problems, taxes, and jobs that her constituents believed most important. Joan Specter (who happened to be the wife of Arlen Specter) saw Jewish women entering politics in

Joan Specter, from pies (1976)...   ...to politician's wife (November 1975)...   ...to City Councilwoman (September 1981).

about the same proportion as other women. Anti-Semitism was not an overt problem, but it could surface around issues related to Israel or church-state relations. Thus, while women were excluded from the all-male Locust Club, the city's sole downtown business club founded by Jews, until 1982, they had gained places in law firms, education, government, and politics. Women like Emily Sunstein and Lenora Berson, who had been ardent campaigners for the Americans for Democratic Action, had shown the way, and the feminist tradition-breakers of the 1970s broadened the political horizons for scores of Jewish women.[38]

Thus, the Jews of Philadelphia were indeed notable achievers in politics, just as they were "overachievers" in various professional and educational endeavors.[39] For them, group adherence and ethnic identity had paid off, as it had for other groups, in political participation and advancement. One scholar was able to document the fact that ethnic voting affinity in sixty heavily Jewish voting divisions in the city gave Jewish candidates nearly triple the support given candidates of other group identities. This behavior was consistent with grassroots political traditions of ethnic voting that augmented candidate vote totals by providing up to an eleven-fold advantage at the polls.[40]

Of course, the very ethnicity that represented one of the dynamics of political life created areas of conflict and disparity involving Jews. In neighborhoods that had experienced considerable racial change and in which Jews either shared power or retained leadership positions among a largely black constituency, Jews were vulnerable to interethnic antagonism. Along with whites of other backgrounds, they were criticized as retarding black political progress and maintaining dominance over urban political "plantations."[41] Anxiety over non-Jewish reactions to such events as the 1967 Israeli war or the Israeli invasion of Lebanon intermittently sent waves of concern through Jewish circles and inspired misgivings about the security of the status that had been won by the group.

With Jews having succeeded so markedly in occupational and social advancement, the proportion of Jews who shared the economic disabilities of very large numbers of blacks and others at the bottom of the income scale was relatively small. Hispanics and the trapped elements of the white working class who did not rise on the educational escalator had found themselves in the late 1970s in an outdated and collapsing economy in Philadelphia. Although the rhetoric of the New Left had faded, the decline of the city's industrial strength created a landscape of economic decay. The transfer of local jobs to cheaper labor markets overseas, the steady movement of plants out of the region, increased costs of living, inflation, deteriorating services, and a malaise of political deadlock at the national level combined to drain the city's morale and expectations.[42] Groups like ADA lost the power to command a strong Jewish presence. Jews were not usually in the welfare class, nor were they proportionately affected by the structural decline of blue-collar labor. Although city councilmen and activists such as David Cohen and Ed Schwartz championed neighborhood reconstruction, by the late 1970s they were fighting a lonely battle as intellectual Jews. The escape of Jews from areas of urban deterioration served to undercut to a certain extent their ability to lead in a city where black unemployment and blue-collar dislocation were grievous. Success was depriving Jews of political relevance to the city's severest problems.

In the 1970s Jews were thrust into the headlines in the way that Irish politicians had been in previous generations. They had much non-Jewish company in the exposés of corruption, but their prominence made their political downfalls particularly striking. Maurice Osser, a city commissioner, was convicted of receiving $200,000 in bribes to steer city contracts. City Councilman Isador Bellis was tried on charges that he took a bribe related to architectural work on the Philadelphia International Airport, and this led to his resignation from the Council. Herbert Fineman, the powerful Speaker of the Pennsylvania House of Representatives, was convicted of conspiracy to obtain gratuities for using his influence to have students admitted to medical and dental schools that received state support. Joshua Eilberg, an unusually effective congressman, was convicted of charges that he illegally aided a local hospital to obtain federal funds. Then, during the sensational national scandal called "Abscam," in which an informer for the Federal Bureau of Investigation masqueraded as an Arab sheik to bribe office-holders, George Schwartz, president of the City Council in Philadelphia, was photographed conferring about offers of money. He was convicted, and his office was filled by the first black ever to hold it.[43] The notable fact about these instances was that those involved were so experienced, so successful, and yet misconduct ruined their careers.

Lenora Bernstein on Penn Campus, 1977.

Several of those involved in these scandals were attorneys. Lawyers had become increasingly involved with politics as government expanded, and law firms had become powerful political influences in the city for mobilizing funds and support for campaigns. For a firm to have a man like Howard Gittis, advisor to Mayor William Green, or Isadore Shrager, long-time power in the Democratic City Committee, was to have a very significant resource for professional contacts. Jews had not been accepted readily into the legal profession. Elizabeth Pennell wrote before the first World War that the socialites who had inherited "the right of the law" had to fight for it with "the alien and the Jew." Although Bernard Siegal became the first Jewish chancellor of the bar association in 1952, discrimination continued for years and was attacked by the American Jewish Committee in the 1960s. By 1980 there were powerful law firms in the city composed mostly of Jews who fifty years earlier would have been summarily excluded from the concourse of the legal fraternity. The interface between law and politics was complex and continuous, and with Jews strongly represented in the legal profession, it provided one further field for political activity. The ethical questions involved symbolized the difficulties of relating the Jewish tradition and its values to the uncertainties of fast-moving political trends and events in a pluralist society.

The ultimate questions for Jewish political participation, however, might be seen as deriving from the moral content of Judaism. Granting that Jews should be preoccupied with their own group survival and interests, and granting a commitment to serve the common good in a complex society, the focus of thoughtful Jews was on what values they would bring to politics in coming decades. Jewish participation in American politics was the result of an evolution that began with the liberalization in the eighteenth century of Western democratic states. Jewish learning expanded beyond concentration on eternal problems and developed a body of pragmatic organizational and political criticism and social advocacy.[44] The old alienation from the political process was overcome, and Jews participated in recent years "openly, enthusiastically and brashly."[45] The context of this participation was secular and perilous. The early predominant liberalism was modified as more Jews assumed conservative views. Jews came to constitute a swing vote by 1980, when they gave substantial support to Ronald Reagan.[46] The ideological and ethical issues underlying this alteration in Jewish opinion were perhaps symptomatic of the general division of opinion in the electorate, which seemed baffled by the difficulties of an America challenged on all sides by changing values, eroding public confidence, and massive problems of social and economic adaptation.

It is frequently noted that Jews are a distinctively urban people. They are, but Jews were for most of Western history part of an urban environment that segregated them and curtailed their collaboration in the larger affairs of cities, whether this was in Northern, Southern, or Eastern Europe or in Mediterranean cities. In that ancient Philadelphia located in the arid land beyond the River Jordan, a city that was by turns Syriac, Greek, Roman, and Arab, Jews lived by sufferance through the ages. In modern America, this centuries-old pattern was dissolved. In cities such as Philadelphia on the Delaware, where the American Republic was conceived, democratic life summoned Jews out of doubt and reticence to full political advocacy.

David Cohen withdraws from 1971 mayoral primary and announces his support of William J. Green (looking on).

Rev. Martin Luther King visiting
Robert Klein, station manager of
WDAS, at the station in the early
1960s. From left, George Woods,
a WDAS community activist; Rev.
Ralph Abernathy, of the Southern
Christian Leadership Conference;
Klein, and Cecil Moore, president
of the Philadelphia Chapter of the
NAACP.

AN AMBIVALENT ALLIANCE
Blacks and Jews in Philadelphia, 1940–1985

Murray Friedman · Carolyn Beck

JEWS CAST DARK SHADOW ON JACKSON'S DREAM.[1] The column headline, running the width of a full page in the city's only major black newspaper, the Philadelphia *Tribune,* was an early reference to Jewish opposition to Jesse Jackson's campaign to win the 1984 Democratic presidential primary. His candidacy was one of a number of episodes that have created conflict in recent years between blacks and Jews.

Discussions of these collisions often contrast current strains with earlier cooperation, grounded in what has seemed to many a "natural" alliance that has always existed between the two groups, forged in the fires of racial and religious oppression experienced by both. Indeed, the years preceding the Black Power movement in the late 1960s are usually viewed as an era of good feeling and full cooperation that served the interests of blacks and Jews as well as the moral and egalitarian needs of a society that prided itself on seeking "liberty and justice for all."[2] The alliance began to break down, it is said further, as a result of the emergence of the Black Power movement, characterized by the use of anti-Semitism by some of its leaders, and the battle over racial quotas. In this view, the alliance has somehow gone awry.

The Philadelphia experience suggests, however, that the black-Jewish relationship has always been more complex. The idea of a "natural alliance" glosses over certain tensions that have been present in this relationship all along, or at least as long as these two groups have lived in significant numbers in proximity to one another.[3] The interaction between blacks and Jews was felt most immediately or directly in the neighborhoods. A prominent Jewish physician recalls that there was an uneasy truce between his parents, who ran a grocery store at 34th and Fairmont in West Philadelphia prior to World War II, and blacks living in that neighborhood. The daily scrapping for economic survival led to pilfering and hostile encounters over bills and extension of credit. Indeed, he recalls, it was not until his parents moved from the neighborhood that they began to view blacks with any degree of tolerance and understanding.[4]

The principal black newspaper, the *Tribune,* frequently reflected, as one study has noted, "the antiSemitic tendencies prevalent among Negroes." In April 1933, in an article that was not atypical, it attacked American Jews and others who protested against the atrocities of the Hitler regime while at the same time persecuting Negroes in America. "The Tribune," it wrote, "makes no attempt to justify the atrocities of Hitler, but it is simply pointing out that America is equally guilty in its persecution of the Negro." A columnist of that newspaper a few months later declared, "Being an American I am neither for nor against the Hitler government but strictly neutral, but when an American citizen makes the comparison between the German Jew and the Southern Negro, the German Jew has decidedly the better of it."[5]

A veteran black human relations and civic leader recollects, however, that at about the same time, blacks and Jews in Point Breeze in South Philadelphia sincerely and fundamentally understood one another. His teachers, his father's employer, and the candy store and delicatessen owners were all Jews who lived in the neighborhood. "These were Jews, not white Jews. They had not forgotten from whence they had been dug." They treated black youngsters with honest interest, from the store owner who scolded them for misbehavior, to the teachers who reminded them that

There have been many areas of sympathetic communication between the Black and Jewish communities in Philadelphia. One such has been in the religious sphere. Ceremonies and gatherings such as those shown here have occurred even when other relations between the two groups were strained. Shown here is the presentation of a Torah by Har Zion's Rabbi Wolpe (second from left) to Rudolph Windsor, spiritual leader of Adath Emeth Israel, and Rabbi Jeremiah Yisrael, of New York City.

they, like Jewish children, must remember that whatever they do reflects upon others of their group. The lesson he learned in his childhood was that every black should be responsible for every other black, just as every Jew is thought to be responsible for every other Jew.[6]

It seems likely that the experiences in Point Breeze and West Philadelphia were present in one form or another and in combination throughout the city where blacks and Jews lived and worked together side by side. The relations between the two groups were in the main peaceful and friendly earlier in the century. Jews along with Unitarians comprised most of the white leadership when the Philadelphia chapter of the NAACP was formed in 1911. As early as 1912, the Jewish philanthropist, Samuel Fels, began making annual contributions to the NAACP, sending $500 in 1916 to help in the campaign of opposition to the showing of the film, *The Birth of a Nation,* and two black women served on the predominantly Jewish ILGWU Philadelphia Local No. 15 executive board. During the Great Depression, Mary Fels responded to the challenge of William Rosenwald that three others join him in making a three-year gift to the organization.[7] The first neighborhoods blacks moved into after the war were Jewish. Jews were the group least prone to react to such movement with violence.

Proximity, however, did not necessarily lead to intimacy. Jews viewed blacks as culturally very different. Blacks coming up from the South after the Second World War were likely to think of Jews simply as other whites, unless some incident stirred anti-Jewish feeling.[8] Leaders of both groups utilized the general spirit of "live and let live" and cooperation as the occasion demanded. In 1939, the black leader Samuel L. Evans recalls, the Nazi-inspired German-American Bund was meeting at the Turngemeinde, a German-American Athletic Club at Broad and Columbia. The group paraded in front of the club with swastikas. Blacks and Jews joined forces, went to the facility, and broke up the meeting, and the Bund never returned to meet there.[9] In turn, blacks who had been rejected for membership by the plasterers' union on the eve of World War II came to Joseph Braginsky, head of the United Hebrew Trades, for counsel. As a result, blacks chartered their own plasterers' union through the United Hebrew Trades. Their leaders were trained through the labor education center that was operated by the Jewish organization in conjunction with the Workman's Circle.[10]

Growing awareness of the widespread prejudice and discrimination both groups faced, highlighted by World War II and the revelations concerning Hitler's death camps, generated broader interest in improving the climate of group relations in the city. This interest was reflected in the formation of the Fellowship Commission in 1941, the first American citywide human relations agency established on a private basis. The Commission, which consisted of a wide range of professional men and women, business leaders, clergy, labor leaders, and housewives, was created by Marjorie Penny and Maurice B. Fagan, the latter then head of the Anti-Defamation Council. (The Council became the Jewish Community Relations Council in 1944.[11]) The Commission's initial enrollment effort brought in four thousand members, which grew to seven thousand by 1954. Fagan served as executive head of both JCRC and the Fellowship Commission until 1960, when he retired from JCRC to serve exclusively as executive director of the Commission.[12] For all practical purposes, the two organizations were one.

The Fellowship Commission became "the really vital development in Philadelphia during the early part of the war" in the field of human rights, according to Clarence E. Pickett, the national secretary of the American Friends Service Committee, who served as chairman of the Commission for a number of years. It was not only the center of virtually all civil rights activity, but helped to give blacks closely associated with it, such as Reverend Luther Cunningham, Henry Nichols, and William Gray, Sr., a sense of broader support and experience in working as equals with other groups. Charles Bowser, Jr., who later ran for mayor, served as a part-time staff member directing the Committee on Community Tensions of the Fellowship Commission in the early 1960s.

In 1942, the NAACP, which received initial Fellowship Commission funding that permitted it to open an office, joined Fellowship House, the Anti-Defamation Council, the Philadelphia Council of Churches, and the Friends Committee on Race Relations as the Commission's fifth member. All of these groups were housed in the Fellowship Commission Building at 260 South 15th Street. Soon after, in 1944, the organization became involved in addressing the major concern of the NAACP at this time, upgrading black workers in jobs they had held for years.[13] The Fellowship Commission campaigned for the promotion of black platform and maintenance men to

Politics has often proven a meeting ground for blacks and Jews. Here (from left) William Rafsky, city redevelopment coordinator; John Clay, attorney for the citizens' Committee of University City; Paul D'Ortana, president of City Council; and Cecil Moore, at the signing of an agreement addressing the Citizens' Committee complaints, May 1963.

Instrumental in developing the civil rights agenda in Philadelphia have been the officers and professionals of the Jewish Community Relations Council of Greater Philadelphia. Here celebrating the JCRC's twentieth anniversary at the Warwick Hotel in October 1958 are (from left) Joseph Yaffe, JCRC president; Maurice Fagan, honoree; and Abraham L. Freedman, Federation president.

motormen by the Philadelphia Transportation Company, the predecessor of the Southeast Pennsylvania Transit Authority (SEPTA). The strike that broke out on August 1, 1944, tested the effectiveness of Fagan and his board of directors, which had urged white support for black PTC workers. As a result of the efforts of the Fellowship Commission and the strike, the Philadelphia NAACP chapter was able to solidify its position.[14]

Fagan also initiated wide-ranging and pioneering efforts in the field of intergroup relations. Following an acrimonious 1943 mayoralty election that featured attacks on the religious backgrounds of the candidates, Abraham L. Freedman, a Fellowship Commission board member, drafted a Fair Election Code, which was enacted by the city council in 1946, the first of its kind in the United States. In 1947, the Commission established a committee on community tensions that introduced the concept of religious dialogue as a means of alleviating intergroup strains. In 1953, the Commission organized the Citizens Council on Democratic Rights, which later became the Philadelphia branch of the American Civil Liberties Union.

The most significant work of the Fellowship Commission–JCRC, however, was drafting, then helping to push through City Council and the state legislature in Harrisburg, virtually the entire body of civil rights legislation that stands today as protection for citizens of all racial and religious backgrounds. Key figures, here, along with Fagan were Freedman, who later became a Judge of the U.S. Circuit Court of Appeals; Nathan Agran, who served for many years as general counsel; and Harry Rosenthal, the chief lobbyist for the Jewish Community Relations Council.

Following the demise of the national Fair Employment Practices Commission, a local ordinance was pushed through City Council by the Fellowship Commission in 1948. Until passage of the ordinance, only one city department store employed blacks in sales and clerical positions. Thereafter, the hiring of blacks became policy in all stores. Following up on this, the Fellowship Commission–JCRC set to work to obtain an FEP law on the state level. Five bills were introduced over the years, until legislation was enacted in 1955. Fellowship Commission leadership, including several blacks, Sadie T. M. Alexander, Tanner G. Duckrey, along with Freedman and Fagan, were also active in the City Charter movement, which was closely connected with the reform movement that swept Philadelphia in the late 1940s and early 1950s. A committee of the Charter Commission headed by Alexander called for the creation of a body to ensure guarantees of civil rights in the community's basic law with a Commission on Human Relations to enforce them. With the adoption of the city charter, Philadelphia became the first city in the United States to provide such guarantees.[15]

Perhaps the most far-reaching work of the Fellowship Commission–JCRC coalition was development of what was to become the Philadelphia Community College. Discrimination in education was a major motivation of the Fellowship Commission in drafting and working for enactment of the Pennsylvania Fair Educational Opportunities Law in 1961. But even more critical was the fact that the increasing cost of tuition and other social factors made it difficult for blacks and poor whites to attend college. The final and successful move for a local community college got underway, initially, as an attempt to emulate the free municipal college system established in New York City in 1847. Fagan, who became a central figure throughout, began his efforts here also as a "means of uniting the citizenry . . . to counterbalance the divisive effects" of racial and religious injustice.

In 1947 he organized the Citizens for Free College Facilities—later the Citizens for a Free City College—which soon gathered the support of 125 organizations. He prevailed on Leon J. Obermayer, the vice president of the Board of Education, who became the vice president of CPCC, to release Joseph L. Pollock, a teacher at Sayre Junior High School, to become its full time executive director from 1950 to 1951. Pollock operated out of the offices of the Fellowship Commission. The campaign was waged by many groups on a wide variety of fronts over a number of years, and Jews along with blacks and other civic leaders were at the forefront throughout. When the bill neared success but became bogged down in committee in 1963, Thomas D. McBride, the Commission president and chairman of Citizens Committee for a Free Community College formed in 1962; Louis Stein, president of Food Fair Stores; and Fagan flew to Harrisburg to encourage Governor William Scranton's intervention. The latter did so, and in 1963 the act authorizing a network of community colleges was passed and signed into law. Today, the Philadelphia Community College is the third largest in the United States.[16]

These broad-based efforts were of benefit to blacks and Jews as well as others. Nonetheless, the seeds of black-Jewish tension were sown in the midst of such activities. A number of blacks were sensitive to the intensity of the Fellowship Commission's work in combating anti-Semitism. There were rumblings early on that the Commission was, at heart, primarily concerned with protecting Jewish interests.[17] Fagan's dual role as head of both the JCRC and the Commission did reflect a need seen by Jewish leadership to have an outlet among liberal non-Jews for their own self-protection as well as the protection of all minorities. The initial study of discrimination in medical schools in the city, sponsored by the Commission and JCRC, for example, was of foremost concern to Jews.

In addition to charging that the Commission preferred to wrestle with Jewish issues, some blacks took exception to specific postures of the Commission. In particular, in 1951, the Commission was firm in its conviction that political candidates should be supported on the basis of merit, not because of their race or religion. A number of black leaders, including Charter Commission member Reverend Luther E. Cunningham, challenged that position by promoting black support for black candidates.[18] In the racially explosive 1960s and 1970s, this view would come to be the dominant one in the black community.

Despite such, as yet, minor strains, the efforts of the Commission, under Fagan's direction, were an important indication during the 1940s and 1950s of the Jewish commitment to black concerns and needs. Other support came from local branches of national organizations such as B'nai B'rith and its Anti-Defamation League, the American Jewish Congress, the American Jewish Committee, and other groups. Much of this aid came from the professional leadership and was not always endorsed at the grassroots level. Beatrice Harrison, who was associate director of the local ADL office at this time, recalls a postcard campaign of B'nai B'rith Women in 1945 on behalf of the Fair Employment Practices bill. As the cards were about to go out, the men's division of B'nai B'rith, according to Harrison, informed the group that they were "too far ahead of the times."[19]

Such foot dragging, however, was unusual. For the most part, Jewish support for civil rights measures was significant and wholehearted, and each new campaign generated increased backing. In the post–World War II years until the early 1960s, a series of bills was enacted at the city and state levels, making discrimination illegal not only in employment, but also in education and the rental and sale of housing. At the state level, the Pennsylvania Equal Rights Council, in which Jewish organizations were heavily involved, was the major sponsor of this legislation.

Jews were drawn to every phase of civil rights activity in the area. Under owner Dolly Banks Shapiro, WHAT was the first local radio station to have a full-time black announcer and black newscasters.[20] When in August 1957 the first black family purchased a home in Levittown in Bucks County—from a Jewish homeowner with the assistance of a Jewish friend—a move precipitating violence that attracted national attention, the director of the local Jewish Labor Committee, Steve Remson, moved in briefly with the family.[21] His predecessor, Leon Shull, the first director of the JLC, who later went on to become the executive head of Americans for Democratic Action in the city and nationally, had earlier held a press conference that led to the formation of the Negro Trade Union Leadership Council in 1958. Throughout the difficult 1960s and 1970s, the JLC and NTULC continued to work together closely on joint activities.[22]

The 1950s saw the launching of the integrated housing movement throughout the country led by Morris Milgram in Philadelphia. He had been secretary of the socialist Workers Defense League and had spent ten years in the rural South battling discrimination and exploitation of blacks. Milgram convinced his father-in-law, who was in the construction business, to approve his plans to build integrated housing in Philadelphia.[23] While not opposed to educational and other activities of the Jewish community on behalf of minority rights, Milgram felt they did not address the problem of segregated housing, which he viewed as the root cause of racial misunderstanding. Integration could only take place, he believed, when blacks and whites resided in the same neighborhoods and attended the same schools.[24]

In 1952, Milgram presented his plans for developing open-occupancy housing in Philadelphia to Frank Loescher, director of the city's Commission on Human Relations. He told the latter that he "would rather be a laborer and live in a slum than build housing for whites only."[25] In 1954, he opened Concord Park, a 50-acre tract in Bucks County, which soon received wide attention nationally and even abroad as the first planned, integrated community.[26] In 1955, he opened 9-acre Greenbelt Knoll in the Greater Northeast, and in subsequent years went on to open desegregated housing in various parts of the United States. The Pulitzer Prize–winning black playwright, Charles Fuller, grew up and still lives in Greenbelt Knoll.[27]

The leadership in this movement was primarily Jewish, in part because black leaders did not believe that the fight for segregated housing could be successful. Despite this, Milgram was able to get eight blacks to join his original group of sixty-five investors. His national organization, Modern Community Developers, formed in 1958, attracted increasing numbers of Jews. "My reputation doesn't scare Jews the way it does some others," he noted.[28] The decision of William J. Levitt, the largest builder in the East, who was initially resistant, to open his suburban Philadelphia property in New Jersey to minorities was an important step in furthering integrated housing here and around the country. Working through organizations like the Wynnefield Residents Association, Mount Airy Neighbors and JCRC neighborhood divisions, many Jews struggled to maintain integrated neighborhoods.

It is probably no exaggeration to suggest that the immediate, post–World War II years and well into the 1950s marked the "Jewish phase" of the civil rights movement. Jews not only were actively involved in civil rights activity, but also were often its leaders. Fagan stood as the embodiment and undisputed leader of efforts in Philadelphia. In 1959, Walter Gay, a black attorney associated with the Urban League, was elected president of the Pennsylvania Equal Rights Council, the coalition of groups responsible for pushing through much of the civil rights legislation enacted in Harrisburg. Throughout the 1950s and 1960s, however, the secretaries of PERC, and therefore custodians of the machinery of the organization, were the directors of the Anti-Defamation League and the American Jewish Committee in Philadelphia. With office staff, mimeograph machines, and other paraphernalia of organization, and backup from their national staff, they were the de facto leaders of the organization.

While these efforts appeared to be moving along smoothly, there were some signs of restlessness on the part of blacks at the dominant role played by Jews in Philadelphia. At an interracial dialogue held on November 17, 1961, sponsored by the Jewish Labor Committee and Negro Trade Union Leadership Council that dealt with black-Jewish relations, A. Leon Higgenbotham, Jr., a prominent black attorney and president of the local NAACP chapter, called for a full partnership in the effort to achieve equal opportunity. Jews "must absolutely discard paternalism. Because the Jews have been our best friends, don't be alarmed if we don't always listen to your counsel," he declared. In words that foreshadowed future and sharper frictions, he added, "our relationship must change." He called for greater financial commitment from Jews, asking that they publicly spend a portion of their profits for the improvement of the communities where their businesses are."

As the dialogue proceeded, Judge David Ullman, associated both with the Fellowship Commission and with the JCRC, reviewed the reasons for some strains and called for fostering friendlier ties. Jews were fully sympathetic to black demands for speeding up the movement toward equality, he said. "We are sympathetically aware," he added, "but with mixed feelings, of the relatively new Negro demands for a 'full share' of Negro business and for proportionate representation in the political and economic life of American society."[29] A Jewish leader present at the dialogue recalls that Jews were shocked by what Higgenbotham had stated so candidly.[30] A long-time black human rights leader summarized the impact of this forum in his evaluation of black-Jewish relations in the early 1960s: "A strain developed because Jews did not know how to share control and power."[31]

An episode early in 1963 illustrated even more sharply the growing black demand for self-direction. A major study was proposed for Philadelphia by the Ford Foundation on how city and other community resources could be mobilized to improve conditions of disadvantaged groups and

neighborhoods. The study was to be directed by a newly formed organization, the Philadelphia Council for Community Advancement (PCCA). Former District Attorney Samuel Dash, a Jew, who later achieved national prominence as chief counsel for the Senate Watergate Committee, was named study director. On January 12, Cecil Moore, a black attorney who had replaced Higgenbotham as head of the local NAACP (Higgenbotham was soon after appointed to a federal judgeship), demanded that Dash be replaced with a black. If he were not, Moore claimed that blacks would picket the project. He used the occasion of his attack also to protest the domination by the Fellowship Commission of black affairs. Five days later, the PCCA announced the appointment of a black, University of Pennsylvania scholar, Dr. Howard E. Mitchell, as associate director of the project, and enlargement of the board from fifteen to sixty, with a sizable number of blacks added. A number of black leaders, however, were worried about Moore's tactics. Fifteen prominent blacks issued a statement assailing Moore for his threats, which they felt presented a false and damaging image of blacks.[32]

As the civil rights movement now entered a more activist phase, involving marches, freedom rides, and sit-ins in the early 1960s, Jews continued to remain deeply involved as participants. The first sit-in[33] at the headquarters of Horn and Hardart restaurants in Philadelphia in 1962, was planned in the office of the Jewish Labor Committee. Through the many Jewish organizations and religious bodies in the area, Jews joined enthusiastically in the 1963 March on Washington. There they heard and applauded Reverend Martin Luther King, Jr.'s electrifying "I Have a Dream" speech. That summer was probably the high-water mark of black-Jewish cooperation in the city. Indeed, with the passage of the omnibus civil rights law the following year, it appeared that the goal both groups had sought for so long was well on the way toward realization. The strains that existed went either unrecognized or were pushed aside in the common effort at this time of high optimism and hope.

Beneath the surface, however, tensions were building. Blacks remained locked into the sweltering slums of North and West Philadelphia, where only a spark was necessary to set off an explosion. On Friday, August 28, 1964, the explosion occurred. Early that evening, police stopped an automobile, in which a husband and wife were quarreling, at 22nd and Columbia Avenue in the heart of a black neighborhood in North Philadelphia. Crowds gathered, and in the subsequent alter-

Columbia Avenue, heart of North Philadelphia, in 1964.

Same view after the riots of the summer of 1964.

cation, a major racial confrontation was underway. The Philadelphia rioting was one of a number of racial disorders that began that summer and spread in subsequent summers to Newark, Detroit, and other major cities, culminating in looting and violence in the Watts section of Los Angeles in 1968 following the murder of Dr. King. In Philadelphia, appeals to halt the rioting by city officials and black leaders like Judge Raymond Pace Alexander and even the fiery new head of the NAACP, Cecil Moore, had no effect. By Monday morning, when the rioting came to a halt, two people had been killed, 339 had been wounded, and 308 had been arrested. Some 726 stores and offices suffered damage estimated at $3 million.[34] The Philadelphia rioting was only one of a series that had wracked many American cities each summer, reaching a climax in 1968 with the murder of King.

The blue-ribbon Kerner Commission, appointed by President Lyndon Johnson to study the causes of the urban upheavals and bring in recommendations, reported in broad sociological strokes the underlying poverty and discrimination that fueled them. It called for a number of initiatives to overcome the tangle of pathologies that existed. Less understood, however, was that Jews, along with blacks, were the chief victims of the rioting. After German Jews began moving out in the 1920s, North Central Philadelphia became a major center for East European Jews during the Second World War. The Jews were to be replaced by blacks who had come up out of the South to work in labor-short factories. By 1960, a third of the city's black population of 535,000 lived in this area, occupying residences left vacant by Jews who had moved up and out.

Jews continued, nevertheless, to be deeply involved in the lives of black people. State Senator Charles Weiner represented the area in Harrisburg. As Democratic majority leader, he helped guide (along with Representative Herbert Fineman of West Philadelphia in the House) a number of the civil rights measures through the legislature. It is likely, according to Lenora E. Berson, that many, if not most, of the residents were treated by Jewish doctors, advised by Jewish lawyers, and served by Jewish teachers and social workers. The landlord and grocer were very probably Jewish,[35] and both radio stations that served predominantly black audiences—WHAT and WDAS—were owned and run by Jews.

Yet, anti-Semitism was not a primary factor in the racial disorders.[36] Nor were the merchants and landlords making inordinate profits despite the widespread image, even among Jews, of economic exploitation. The *Inquirer* reported a few years later in an article, "Many Landlords Abandon Solid Inner City Buildings,"[37] that housing was becoming unprofitable and a burden on landlords. Doing business in the ghetto involved higher costs as a result of the small scale of operations, pilferage, and the credit system often used in servicing the poor. A study of pricing patterns in Philadelphia, undertaken in November 1967 by Temple University and the Academy of Food Marketing of St. Joseph's College, found that, on the average, the market-basket cost for small inner-city stores was not higher than that for small stores in high-income areas.[38] Doing business in the slums had become increasingly difficult, and this was made no less so by the growth of serious crime. The essential problem that Jews working in the ghetto faced was that they had become surrogate targets, tangible representatives of the unreachable white establishment downtown. Both Jews and blacks were in the path of the urban storm that was now sweeping the land.

The racial disorders in North Philadelphia highlighted the fact that the civil rights revolution that Jews had joined so enthusiastically had taken a radical turn. New leaders emerged, such as Stokely Carmichael, Malcolm X, H. "Rap" Brown, and other militants, who articulated the grievances of slum-shocked blacks more forcefully than had Roy Wilkins, head of the NAACP, and

Left: The racial nature of the riots was underscored by many such signs in undamaged store windows in the midst of ransacked Jewish establishments.

Right: City commerce director Frederic R. Mann addressed a City Hall meeting of North Philadelphia merchants whose stores were looted.

even Dr. King on a national level and Judges Alexander and Higgenbotham locally. The new ghetto-based leaders were concerned increasingly with the cultural heritage of blacks and skeptical of cooperative ventures to foster integration. They called instead for Black Power and identified with the Third World and an increasingly anti-Israel ideology. While their major target was racism on the part of all whites, they frequently utilized anti-Semitism as part of their rhetoric and tactics. The new group was especially appealing to young blacks in the slums as well as increasing numbers now entering colleges and universities.

Indeed, Philadelphia provided an early model of this new leadership in Cecil Moore, the freshly installed head of the local NAACP. Known as "The Lion of North Philadelphia," Moore lived in the black ghetto and made his living as an attorney representing poor blacks. By championing their cause, he built a strong base for developing the Philadelphia NAACP into one of the most active, if not the strongest, in the nation during the mid-1960s. In a dramatic move, in 1965 he led young blacks in a series of marches around the walls of Girard College, a private institution in North Philadelphia, to protest the exclusion of orphaned black youths under the will of its founder, who made the facility available only to whites. When the courts admitted blacks in a case initiated earlier by the Fellowship Commission, Moore's standing rose sharply. Other demonstrations he staged were believed by many blacks to have opened up industry and government jobs.[39]

Moore understood instinctively the coming wave of black militancy and anticipated the cry of Black Power later voiced by Carmichael in 1966. "If the white community thinks I am difficult to deal with," he said, "you should see what is coming behind me."[40] "We're going to run the damn city," he declared in 1963, "now that we are going Catholic. We're already having all the babies."[41] While Moore was, and continues to be, a hero to a generation of mainly younger and grassroots blacks, his controversial and flamboyant tactics made more established black leaders, as well as Jews, uneasy.

The Columbia Avenue riots represented a violent outburst of black anger and frustration. Here, Stanley Branche (hand waving) addresses a rally at 17th and Columbia in June 1967. At his right is George Woods.

Jews were worried, especially, about his frequent and public use of anti-Semitism. Moore was the first of the new group of black leaders to consciously employ it even though he knew it would upset Jewish sensibilities. There was a hint of this in the controversy over Dash as 1963 began, and increasingly his remarks became more open and blatant. Shortly before the March on Washington, the *Pennsylvania Guardian,* an organ of the local Americans for Democratic Action chapter, published an interview with him in which he attacked "northern white liberals" as phonies and "people of a Semitic origin" who "exploit Negroes." Moore explained that his feeling was derived from his experience with Jewish landlords and tavern owners operating in heavily populated Negro areas and extended to Jews who worked in agencies where Negroes were employed or had a chance of employment. As for Jews working in civil rights, he declared, he knew of no one who was not a "goddam phony."[42]

The *Guardian* article received considerable attention in the local press, as well as in the *New York Times,* and led to the censure of Moore by the national NAACP organization.[43] The furor it created almost ended Philadelphia Jewish involvement in the March on Washington. It was only after an off-the-record meeting of black and Jewish leaders, initiated by Samuel L. Evans, organizer of the March in the city, and Murray Friedman, executive head of the American Jewish Committee, at the Bellevue Stratford that Moore made a conciliatory statement. The alliance was patched up in time for the full participation of both groups in the historic march.[44]

Moore continued, nevertheless, to attack Jews throughout the 1960s. At a court hearing in a suit in 1967 initiated by the Philadelphia school board, seeking an injunction to restrain Black Power demonstrations at public schools, Moore shouted at the Jewish special counsel for the board, "You're playing footsie with racial bigots! You and the rest of the Jews get out of my business."[45] Moore's fulminations against Jewish merchants during demonstrations he led on South Street were so vicious that Fagan, of the Fellowship Commission, arranged for Police Commissioner Frank Rizzo to record them for a possible complaint of questionable ethics before the Philadelphia Bar Association.[46]

Moore's anti-Semitism, however, was not deeply felt but usually an off-hand or casual part of his exaggerated rhetoric of leadership. He was always surprised when Jews were upset by it. At a private meeting with several Jewish leaders, he explained it was a political tactic to rally blacks rather than a reflection of his own personal feeling. He had to be visible, he said, in order to maintain his leadership.[47] His behavior was intertwined, nonetheless, with the broader need of newly emerging black leaders to distance themselves from liberals and Jewish leadership at a time of growing black pride and assertiveness.

Collision between blacks and Jews was now taking place against the background of national and even international events that reverberated in the community. The Six Day War that Israel fought in 1967 and the Yom Kippur War in 1973 brought to the fore for Jews memories of the Hitler Holocaust, stirring a new sense of group identity and growing anxieties about the fate of all Jews. Israel came to be seen as the "national liberation movement" of the Jewish people, standing alongside, if not displacing, political liberalism as the secular religion of American Jews. Simultaneously, the new militancy and Third World ideology taking shape among younger blacks began to link Jews in this country and in Israel with the problems that people of color faced throughout the world. Carmichael made the tie explicitly when he declared in 1968, "The same Zionists that exploit Arabs also exploit us in this country. This is a fact and it is not anti-Semitic. We have begun to see the evil of Zionism and we will fight to wipe it out wherever it exists, be it in the ghetto, in the United States or in the Middle East."[48]

The late 1960s and early 1970s also witnessed the development of several major collisions between blacks and Jews over community control of the schools in the Ocean Hill–Brownsville section of Brooklyn and a plan to introduce low-cost housing in heavily Jewish Forest Hills, Queens. These episodes produced anti-Jewish and anti-black statements in the nation's media. Indeed, so intense had the schools conflict and reaction become that the Anti-Defamation League reported in 1969, "Raw, undisguised anti-Semitism is at a crisis level in New York City . . . unchecked by public authority, it has been building for more than two years."[49]

Beyond the exaggerated rhetoric employed by Jewish and black leaders, a number of strains arose from situations in which the interests of members of both groups now came into direct conflict. In the historic process of ethnic succession that quietly plays so powerful a role in American life, blacks have tended to follow Jews in Philadelphia and elsewhere in residential neighborhoods and jobs, in education, social work, government employment, and other fields of work. Jews, for example, had entered public school education heavily in the 1930s and 1940s in Philadelphia. By the 1950s and 1960s, many had risen to principals, vice principals, and other administrative positions in the system, positions to which the newly emerging black middle class now aspired. Some 31 percent of the principals in the elementary schools, 54 percent in the junior high schools, and 27 percent in the senior high schools by this time were Jewish.[50] Jews also played prominent roles in the social welfare field in Philadelphia and in the State Capitol in Harrisburg. Journalists referred, not maliciously, to a "Jewish Mafia" as the dominant influence in welfare. What made the situation more complex was that the Jews were playing out their leadership roles at a time when an increasing number of clients for many of these services were black.

As the schools gained a black majority, a number of black leaders argued that there was a greater need for more black teachers and principals to serve as role models for students. Involved here was a mix of self-interest and the sincere belief that blacks would better understand the needs and problems of members of their own group. A small number of white and black school critics also argued that middle-class and largely Jewish educators had little interest in black children and, in fact, damaged their educational possibilities.[51] At the Department of Welfare in Harrisburg and its regional branch in Philadelphia, there was a running controversy between Jewish social welfare officials and black militants. The latter felt that the first priority was to raise cash grants to a level at which people can live decently. As professionally trained social workers, Jewish leaders were often partial to social services such as marriage counseling and teaching people how to budget.

As a result, there were growing pressures for the replacement of Jewish leadership at middle and upper levels in education and social welfare. Indeed, such replacement gradually occurred. Moreover, Jews at lower levels in governmental bureaucracies often came to feel that opportunities for them to rise were being closed off by the new black surge. By 1970, the state secretary of welfare and director of the Philadelphia regional office, both Jews, were replaced by blacks. The new secretary, Tom Georges, proceeded to replace the "Jewish Mafia" that had been in charge for so long.[52]

It was about this time, too, that the divisive issue of using racial quotas to broaden the involvement of minorities in American life came forward on national and local levels, especially in the fierce, competitive atmosphere for scarce positions in law and medical schools. Jews supported affirmative action programs, but they were deeply worried about quotas being used, as in previous years, to exclude them. Most blacks, on the other hand, saw quotas as a means of making up for their exclusion in the past.

As protest gave way to politics, neighborhood struggles began to be used for political control and as a means of attracting attention to more wide-ranging demands for increased opportunity. In this phase of their struggle, many blacks felt they no longer needed Jews and, indeed, believed Jews often stood in their way. In one highly publicized episode in West Philadelphia, State Representative Herbert Fineman was charged with hoarding power by taking over the position as head of the 52nd Ward Democratic Executive Committee when his brother resigned. An anti-Fineman committee of thirty blacks led by Edgar Cambell, argued that he discriminated against black students seeking scholarships and in his choices in elective and appointive positions.[53]

Although the new currents blowing in the black community often called for blacks to separate themselves increasingly from former Jewish allies in order to achieve greater self-reliance and the Jewish rank and file were becoming increasingly disinterested and sometimes hostile, the traditional Jewish civil rights orientation still allowed (perhaps even demanded) continuing attention to the black-Jewish alliance. In an effort to stimulate community involvement and ease tensions, Jules Cohen, who had succeeded Fagan as head of the JCRC, convened in August 1966 a meeting of Jewish merchants and real estate people from ghetto areas. The Lancaster Avenue project grew out of this meeting. The local businessmen's association sponsored a black junior executive program whereby black youths were paid $5 for a three-hour work period on Saturday afternoons and instructed in store operations. The association also sponsored a street beautification program. When those efforts were evaluated at a JCRC Neighborhood Division meeting, however, the tri-state director of the NAACP charged that the program had little meaning in the light of the excessively high prices that were still being charged by Jewish merchants. The clean-up campaign and painting of houses served only to make residents uncomfortable.[54]

Unperturbed, the JCRC continued its attempts to ameliorate the chronic tensions between Jewish merchants and residents. In 1969, associate director Nathan Agran developed a program to assist in the sale of businesses to blacks, a project that remained active until 1975, the peak period being between 1970 and 1972. The program recognized that most of the Jewish merchants operating in ghetto areas were elderly men and women whose children often had no interest in maintaining the precarious businesses there. It also fulfilled the Jewish sense of obligation to help create a black business class. The Jewish organization worked with the Small Business Administration's minority enterprise program, a federally funded project that guaranteed 90 percent of the loan for each business purchased. Through contact with black leaders and by neighborhood word of mouth, exchanges of forty-nine businesses in South, West, and North Philadelphia were arranged. The JCRC required that each seller be available for counsel to the purchaser for one year. The program was initially successful, in part because some 20 percent of the buyers were former employees of the seller. Follow-up studies by JCRC revealed, however, that while the short-term survival rate of two years was high, five years later, 50 percent of the buyers could not be located.[55] Despite the dedication of Agran, the program did not ease the tensions that had arisen between blacks and Jews. Some blacks dismissed it as an attempt by white (and Jewish) owners to unload dying enterprises rather than assisting blacks in the creation of a small business class.

Growing uneasiness about black-Jewish tensions and a sense that Jews must remain active in the battle for human rights prompted a flurry of activity in the Jewish community—the formation of committees, issuing of public statements, and discussions of programs on how to alleviate the causes of black distress. The Philadelphia Board of Rabbis urged temple and synagogue leaders in 1968 to take positive action and ask members to become involved in programs to improve educational opportunities for blacks, reduce discriminatory business practices, and support more adequate welfare legislation.[56] The local chapter of the American Jewish Committee set up a Negro-Jewish Relations Committee to make recommendations to the executive board on dealing with crisis situations. Working with Robert Klein, the station manager of WDAS, which had a large black audience, AJC leaders helped to obtain and assisted black gang and ex-gang members in rehabilitation of a house in South Philadelphia for out-of-school youngsters to use for educational and recreational programs.[57] The Committee leaders also helped to obtain a line of credit and provided counseling for a garment factory that employed gang youth in the basement of the Emanuel Baptist Church in North Philadelphia, a project developed by Reverend William Bentley, pastor of the church.[58]

One of the more unusual efforts to keep the black-Jewish alliance alive was the attempt of Klein, working with AJC leaders and Klein's close friend, black street activist Stanley Branche, to create a Jewish wing of the race revolution in Philadelphia. The wave of destruction during the North Philadelphia rioting worried upper-class Protestant business leaders who envisioned blacks next descending upon banks and department stores. No doubt there were also strong feelings that there was indeed a serious community problem they must help address. As a result, these white leaders joined with black neighborhood and activist groups headed by Branche in the formation of the Black Coalition in 1968. This was a forerunner of the Urban Coalition, which continues to function today. By July, the Black Coalition had put together $1 million in pledges from white business and industrial leaders to support various projects.[59]

Klein and Branche's attempt to build into this a Jewish component had elements of unwitting high comedy. Upper-class suburban and Center City Jewish leaders would meet surreptitiously with black militants, and with extremists such as Jeremiah X of the Black Muslims, and, presumably, ex-members of the Revolutionary Action Movement (RAM) like Jimmy Lester, who led the project in South Philadelphia, to plan a common black-Jewish strategy. Following one of these evening meetings, newspapers reported the next day that several RAM leaders present at the meeting were held for the Grand Jury under $25,000 bail for allegedly plotting to poison police officers with cyanide.[60] Discussions revolved around complaints of exploitation in the ghetto, establishing a series of educational centers for school dropouts, encouraging blacks to form their own businesses, and fostering mutual understanding between the two communities. Joint committees of blacks and Jews were appointed to look into these problems and recommend possible programs.

Whether useful could have come out of this effort is highly doubtful, given the nature of the times and the extraordinary mix of the people involved. Oddly enough and despite a process riddled with impossibilities, the ad hoc alliance worked smoothly enough for a while until more established blacks leaders loosely connected with the militants entered the discussions. (It is possible, of course, that this was how the scenario was meant to be played out.) As planning for the black-Jewish programs proceeded, Judge Robert N. C. Nix, Jr., and Judge Leon Higgenbotham began to take part in the discussions and added new demands to the arrangements worked out with Branche. Nix called for a formal relationship with Jewish agencies and asked for $1 million to be raised by the Jewish community for these programs, an amount Nix felt was not unreasonable, because Jews, he claimed, had made a great deal of money in the black ghetto. Although the Jewish leaders involved felt there was some interest in modest funding to be obtained from the Federation of Jewish Agencies, the request for such a large figure brought an end to this effort to build a formal black-Jewish Coalition with militants.[61]

The attempt to maintain ties between the two groups, however, was not entirely fruitless. In what may have been the only program of its kind in the country, the Federation, the major fund-raising and social-planning vehicle in the Jewish community, created at this time an Urban Affairs department to provide financial assistance to black self-help and neighborhood groups referred to them by Jewish and public agencies and black community resources. The decision was made to forego any publicity and to work quietly behind the scenes. Under the direction of Theodore Levine, a Jewish social worker, groups receiving aid included a day camp, preschool groups, residents' associations, welfare tenants, recreation, and gang- and drug-control groups. In addition to providing financial assistance, the Federation's Urban Affairs Department also offered business consultation, transportation, and legal services. Sixty black groups applied for funding. More than fifty received grants in seven black neighborhoods. These ranged from $50 to $2,500, with a median of $1,000.

A follow-up study indicated there was a noticeable absence of negative responses from both black and Jewish participants such as occurred in the JCRC business exchange and Lancaster Avenue project and the AJC's experiment in working with black militants. There was no perceived "grandstanding" and consequently no sentiment that the grants were demeaning. In general, participants looked forward to continuation of the Federation project.[62] The latter, however, was an unprecedented and unorthodox effort of an agency with essentially different functions: social planning and funding for the welfare and overseas needs of the Jewish community. After two years, the program was closed down. The Federation chose to withdraw rather than run the risk of failure, which might have inflamed the undercurrent of anti-Semitism in black neighborhoods.[63] Unlike the Quakers, Jews had not reached that sense of security and self-sufficiency at which they felt able to divert significant communal resources to alleviate the problems of the disadvantaged, although they continued to support government programs to achieve these goals.

An attempt also was made by the local AJC to help overcome what was seen as the isolation of the media from newly emerging Black Power and neighborhood groups. This move followed disturbances in the fall of 1967, when three thousand mainly black youths attending a Black Power rally in front of the school administration building were set upon by police and beaten with clubs. At the time, local newspapers and television came under criticism by blacks and others for their treatment of the incident. Working with an ad hoc Philadelphia Crisis Committee, the AJC arranged a meeting at a hotel in North Philadelphia of a number of important news executives, including William Dickinson, managing editor of the *Bulletin;* Philip B. Schaeffer, city editor of the *Inquirer;* and John Gillen, managing editor of the *Inquirer,* with representatives of CORE and the Area Wide Council of the Model Cities Program.[64] Thereafter, off-the-record meetings continued with little interruption from 1968 to 1970 under the sponsorship of the news executives themselves working with the North City Congress and the AJC. These were often highly emotional confrontations in which the news executives were accused by street-level blacks (with whom they normally would not come into contact) as indifferent and insensitive. At one point, a participant recalls, Dickinson, a hard-bitten newspaperman who had covered the surrender of Japan on the deck of the battleship *Missouri,* responded to the criticism with tears in his eyes. The meetings were held at a time when, with the exception of Orrin Evans, a general assignment reporter at the *Bulletin,* none of the local media employed blacks. It is likely that the temper of the times was already pushing news executives to consider employing black newspapermen and -women, but the meetings probably helped drive home this need more forcefully. Neighborhood blacks also gained direct contact with top-level news officials and learned from these meetings that they could pick up the phone and talk to important officials when they felt they had a problem.[65]

In attempting to lend assistance in a period of crisis and to keep the black-Jewish alliance going, Jewish leaders were aware they were walking a tightrope, attempting to honor their long-time commitments without intruding on the territory that was becoming increasingly defined as "for blacks only." In the final analysis, Jewish attempts to help blacks at this point had little impact on their situation. Supporting civil rights legislation and taking part in marches and demonstrations were relatively simple in contrast to issues such as the provision of educational and employment opportunities and the high rate of family disorganization that were now becoming the major obstacles to black involvement in the society as full and equal partners.

The collapse of the attempt to form the Black-Jewish Coalition and dissolution of the Federation's Urban Affairs Department in 1970 mark the last systematic effort to sustain the black-Jewish collaboration as such in Philadelphia. The process of black social and political maturation was now well underway, and Jews were no longer necessary to play the role of intermediaries with political, media, civic, and other elements of the white power structure. By this time, too, Jews were coming increasingly to focus on their own internal problems, most notably the safety and security of Israel. The flashpoints of black-Jewish conflicts had taken their toll. In the early 1960s, Jewish groups did not oppose the "Philadelphia Plan" of racial quotas for hiring construction workers, because few Jews were involved. But by the 1970s, the national bodies of a number of Jewish groups had filed briefs before the U.S. Supreme Court opposing blacks in the De Funis (law school) and Bakke (medical school) cases.[66] In the early 1980s, local branches of the Anti-Defamation

Unionism and labor relations have proven yet another area of rapport between Jews and blacks. Pictured here are the leaders of the Jewish Labor Committee and the Negro Trade Union Leadership Council meeting at the Weinstein Center in September 1974. From left (seated), James H. Jones, Council president; Phil Kluger, AFT guest speaker; Albert Alcovitz, JLC chairman; (standing), Joseph Schwartz, past JLC chairman; Lonnie Hughes, vice-president of NTULC; Alex Wollod, Philadelphia director, JLC; and Robert Robinson, NTULC executive vice-president.

Jefferson Fordham (right), president of the Fellowship Commission, and Maurice B. Fagan (center), executive director, receive City Council commendation on the Commission's twenty-fifth anniversary in October 1966 from City Councilman Marshal L. Shepard, Sr.

League, American Jewish Committee, and American Jewish Congress publicly supported a federal district court ruling, upheld by the U.S. Third Circuit Court of Appeals, that a racial transfer system for teachers to achieve greater desegregation in the Philadelphia schools was unconstitutional. The body of civil rights legislation they helped put on the books in the 1940s and 1950s guaranteeing racially neutral policies was now the basis upon which Jews fought against "reverse discrimination."

Politics remains the major arena where blacks and Jews have continued to cooperate in a significant if informal way. Jews were the only white group in the city that joined blacks in voting overwhelmingly against a change in the city charter in 1978, which would have permitted Frank Rizzo, widely seen as hostile to blacks, to run for a third term (as noted elsewhere in this volume). Five years later, Jews were particularly involved in the mayoral campaign and gave 50 percent more of their vote to Wilson Goode, the first black mayor of Philadelphia, than whites, generally. They have also generally supported Congressman William Gray, the only black congressman in Washington, DC, from Philadelphia. Clearly, however, the basis of the relationship of the two groups has changed significantly. Jews no longer serve as ward leaders and legislators from black areas of the city. Nor are they, for the most part, a major factor in the Goode administration. That Jews may not have adjusted fully to the growth of black power is evident in the fact that Goode, running on a Democratic ticket normally overwhelmingly supported by Jews, received only about a third of the Jewish vote; two-thirds went to his Republican and independent opponents.[67]

During the 1970s and early 1980s, black-Jewish cooperative efforts survived fitfully. JOINT, which began in 1961 with the classic exchange between Judge Ullman and Higgenbotham, continued to hold forums and informal "bull sessions" on issues of common concern in the labor movement. The Sholom Aleichem Club worked with the Black Economic Development Council and the Kensington Council on Black Affairs from 1970 to 1975. Other interfaith and interracial organizations, such as the Well-springs Ecumenical Renewal Associates, provided for a while an opportunity for blacks and Jews to engage in dialogue. In 1976, Jewish groups in Philadelphia rallied momentarily around the threatened national NAACP bankruptcy following a Mississippi court decision to fine the national organization. They responded with financial pledges that evoked memories of the enthusiasm of the early 1960s.[68] These efforts, however, were sporadic and were interspersed with moments of friction, particularly when Jews learned of anti-Jewish and anti-Israel sentiments voiced in the Philadelphia *Tribune* and on talk shows of the two local black-oriented radio stations.[69]

In 1979, the widening rift between blacks and Jews captured national attention once again with the resignation of the U.S. ambassador to the United Nations, Andrew Young, following his meeting with a leader of the Palestine Liberation Organization in New York. Some black leaders subsequently charged that Jews were responsible for forcing him out. The episode served as a catalyst for the gathering of Jewish and black leaders in April 1980 for a day and a half at Fellowship Farm in nearby Pottstown to clear the air. While the immediate cause was a national and international incident, the issues considered at the retreat included mutual black-Jewish misperceptions, the need to restore the partnership, black unemployment, and merit and affirmative action.[70] There were seventeen Jews and eleven blacks in attendance. While the former represented most of the Jewish organizations, blacks came mainly as individuals in response to the call of a few black leaders. It was clear that, for blacks, the issue of black-Jewish relations was not considered an urgent problem.[71] Growing black consciousness, especially among the black intelligentsia, has been reflected in a controversy that broke out in the fall of 1984 in the pages of the *Daily Pennsylvanian* at the University of Pennsylvania over the role of Jesse Jackson and Louis Farrakhan in the presidential election. One letter signed by several past presidents of the Black Student Union carried the headline, "Black Jewish Coalition Cannot Be."

While strains have increased between blacks and Jews, the situation in Philadelphia has remained calmer than in New York and perhaps other parts of the country. One reason for this is that a network of ties built up over the years continues to exist. They keep lines of communication open, even though the relations are no longer as strong as they once were. Congressman William Gray, now chairman of the House Budget Committee in Washington, is a significant "bridge" figure. In addition, there are currently no major provocative personalities in Philadelphia to inflame tensions further. Cecil Moore died in 1979, and Mayor Goode differs very sharply in personality and style from Mayor Ed Koch. The goodwill that continued to exist here in the 1980s was reflected in cooperation between the JCRC and Board of Rabbis and black clergy in raising money for Ethiopian relief; a trip sponsored by the American Jewish Committee, Congressman Gray, and prominent black leaders in the summer of 1985 for black and Jewish high school seniors to visit Africa and Israel; and the critical response of the Philadelphia *Tribune* to a series of anti-Jewish statements expressed on a local talk show hosted by Mary Mason.

The relative calm in Philadelphia reflects, also, the inward turning of both blacks and Jews. For blacks, the yearning for independence and self-reliance that has become their hallmark since the 1960s has, in part, superseded the earlier drive for integration. The situation is best summed up by the sale of the black-oriented radio station WDAS and the projected sale of WHAT-AM to black syndicates and the move from Wynnefield in 1984 of Reform Congregation Beth David. Thestation had attempted to adjust to the times by developing a black emphasis. It shifted to rhythm and blues music, and covered in detail the North Philadelphia riot, Moore's struggle to integrate Girard College, and the various confrontations between Rizzo and blacks. Klein had worked effectively behind the scenes to develop closer ties between blacks and Jews, and had won the respect of those who knew of his efforts. But by 1979, many influential blacks questioned whether a station owned by non-blacks could truly serve the needs of the black community.[72]

Like Klein, Rabbi Henry Cohen of Beth David had fought the good fight for neighborhood stabilization in Wynnefield throughout the difficult 1960s and 1970s. In a bold and controversial experiment, the congregation had admitted the community's black children to its nursery school, which had developed a bicultural curriculum, and had thrived for a decade until enrollment included so few Jews, that the temple was forced to discontinue its sponsorship. By 1984, it had purchased land and was preparing to move to the suburbs.[73]

Jewish concerns have been heightened more recently by Black Muslim leader Louis Farrakhan's vicious attacks on Jews and Israel, which attracted increasingly larger black audiences as he toured the country in 1985. Farrakhan visited Philadelphia several times, addressing crowds at the University of Pennsylvania, Temple University, and the Civic Center. At the last, early in his tour, a number of local black politicos shared the platform with him, and, for some reason, he seemed to be especially popular with the Penn Black Students' Union.

The new inward focus adopted by blacks and Jews has inevitably led them in divergent directions, magnifying the tensions that have always been present in their relationship. Given the differing black and Jewish perspectives that have guided the relationship in Philadelphia, it is a misnomer to label the traditional alliance as "natural." Rather, it might be more aptly characterized as ambivalent. Sherman Labovitz, who conducted interviews here in the early 1970s, reports there is no prevailing or consistent attitude toward blacks and black issues among Philadelphia Jews. Their views "may be racist, hostile . . . (and) patronizing" as well as "understanding or supportive." Sometimes, both views are combined.[74] Interviews with black leaders confirm that sharply conflicting attitudes toward Jews and Jewish concerns exist among blacks as well. This is not to denigrate what has been a genuinely felt sense of common destiny and need experienced by both groups and their leaders. This visceral feeling continues to be the main basis of hope for any future cooperation. The ambivalence, however, assures the perpetuation of this "special relationship" as a source of continuing controversy as well as mutual support.

Har Zion Temple at 54th Street and
Wynnefield Avenue, 1970.

WYNNEFIELD
Story of a Changing Neighborhood

David P. Varady

The settlement of Wynnefield by Europeans dates back to 1690 when Dr. Thomas Wynne, a colonial physician, built a farm in Upper Wynnefield. Up to 1890, the area remained largely rural, with a few scattered, rambling stone houses. However, at the time of the Centennial Exposition, development accelerated with the building of large single-family homes on large tracts of land in the upper hill section of the community. These were purchased by prosperous Protestant families. Elsewhere on the upper hill, more modest detached and semi-detached homes continued to be built prior to 1920.

Lower Wynnefield was subdivided and developed with row houses for single-family ownership during the 1920s and 1930s. Block after block was built about the same time at fairly high densities. Most of the families who purchased these houses were upwardly mobile Eastern European Jewish immigrants relocating from South Philadelphia. The more affluent Jewish families began to relocate to Upper Wynnefield. As the original Protestant families moved away, Wynnefield underwent its first ethnic change. A Catholic parish was developed during the 1920s, but the numbers of Catholics remained small. By the end of the 1920s, Wynnefield had all of the characteristics of a second-generation Jewish ghetto, such as Lawndale in Chicago.[1] Communal life centered around the many congregations in the community. Some of these included *shteblach,* which met in private homes. Social life was based on a variety of religious, social, and fraternal organizations. Fifty-fourth Street, a major thoroughfare, evolved into the major Jewish shopping street, with kosher butchers, bakeries, a bookstore, and similar establishments. Wynnefield also had the advantages of a suburban community with its proximity to Fairmount Park and accessibility to downtown Philadelphia by either commuter railroad or a combination of bus and elevated subway. However, Wynnefield's proximity to West Philadelphia also made it ripe for racial change.

After World War II, there was a relaxation of discriminatory housing practices aimed at Jews. Before the war, affluent Jews were unable to move into communities along the Main Line (a string of prestigious suburban communities along the Pennsylvania Railroad to the west of Philadelphia). Ironically, this is precisely what maintained the cohesiveness of the Wynnefield community. With the decline in such practices after the war, these affluent Jewish families were able to move away into nearby suburbs. In addition, there was a tendency for the children of these families to settle in one of the many other Jewish enclaves developing in other parts of the metropolitan area.

During the 1950s and 1960s, the boundaries of all three of Philadelphia's black ghettos expanded outward reflecting continued in-migration from the South, a high fertility rate in the black population and a desire among upwardly mobile blacks to improve their housing situation. West Philadelphia's black ghetto expanded out toward the city line, and toward Wynnefield. By 1960, sections of West Philadelphia immediately adjacent to Wynnefield were predominantly black.

During the 1960s, Jewish families did continue to move into the community, and as a whole, Wynnefield retained its predominantly Jewish character. However, the Jewish population was aging. Between 1940 and 1950 the proportion of the population aged 65 and over increased from 6 to 8 percent; from 1950 to 1960 it jumped to 13 percent. The aging of the population also increased the community's susceptibility to change. Much of the older Jewish population still resided in the semi-detached and attached row houses in the lower hill. It was obvious that during the 1960s many of these units occupied by the elderly would be put on the market as a result of deaths or retirement moves. It was only a matter of time before the community's all-white character would disappear.

RACIAL CHANGE ACCELERATES: WYNNEFIELD DURING THE 1960S AND 1970S

In 1963, the first black family moved into a home in Lower Wynnefield that had been made available by the Federal Housing Administration as a result of a foreclosure.[2] The succeeding black families tended to cluster in Lower Wynnefield but later purchased homes throughout the community. Black arrivals experienced little or no physical hostility from long-time white residents. This was in sharp contrast to the resistance they experienced in other communities, such as South Philadelphia. In fact, the perception that they would not be resisted undoubtedly was one reason why they chose to move into Wynnefield over other white ethnic areas. One of the first black residents recounted this observation: "When we moved here we were made welcome. I feel it worked for us because we moved into a Jewish enclave. . . . The Jews did not want to take on the role of an oppressor. Being an oppressed people themselves, they did not want that."[3]

The arrival of these first black families created among whites the fear that the community would undergo rapid racial change and it would experience declines in the quality of life. The Wynnefield Development Council (a coordinating body for religious and civic organizations) contacted the Jewish Community Relations Council to study these changes in order to deal with these concerns. The JCRC examined property transfers between 1963 and 1966 with respect to the racial characteristics of buyers and sellers. It also interviewed a small number of residents and workers in the community, such as school principals and police officials, to identify the impacts of racial change on the quality of life. The report documented the increase in blacks purchasing homes in the community; from 8 percent of the total in 1963 to 67 percent in the first five months of 1966. The rate of racial change was particularly rapid in Lower Wynnefield. In one twelve-block area where many black families had settled, there were no later property sales to white families.[4] As will be shown, racial change was due not only to a sharp decline in white in-migration, but also to a speedup in white out-migration.

The authors of the report asserted that the rapid rate of change in Lower Wynnefield was due to the modest prices of the homes, making them attractive to blacks from West Philadelphia seeking homes. They also alleged that real estate brokers induced many white families to sell in panic. The relative stability of the Upper Hill section, in contrast, was seen as attributable to the unusually attractive homes and streets. These higher priced homes were unusually good values for middle-income families but were still beyond the purchasing power of working-class black families. This point was borne out by later research.[5] The report concluded on an optimistic note: "Racial changes taking place in the area are not drastic, have not depreciated property values [and the] quality of public education, and have not in any way impaired the neighborhood."[6] The report's conclusions would prove to be unrealistically optimistic in terms of what actually happened in the community during the 1960s.

As has been the case in other racially changing communities, the local civic organization, the Wynnefield Residents Association, was the focus of efforts to achieve stable racial integration. The WRA was originally formed in 1957 around the issue of a proposed firehouse in the community, but only began to grow after black in-migration began. This was reflected in a sixfold increase in the income of the organization (from about $2,000 to about $12,000) between 1967 and 1974. Given the fact that growth was associated with the existence of racial change, it might seem surprising that racial stabilization was not listed as one of the goals of the organization. Instead, the WRA focused on improving the overall quality of life for all residents.[7]

The activities of the WRA have been typical of those of residents associations in changing communities in that it attempted to control real estate solicitation; worked with the Area Planner from the Philadelphia Planning Commission in preparing and updating the master plan for the community; participated through the Association's Zoning Committee in all actions relating to land use in the community; helped to organize security patrols for crime protection; published a biweekly newsletter; lobbied for improvements in city services and facilities; organized social and recreational activities; and organized block clubs throughout the community.

These stabilization efforts had little impact on the rate of racial change. Between 1960 and 1970 Wynnefield changed from all white to demographically biracial (51 percent black).[8] The rate of racial change was even greater in Lower Wynnefield, which was 70 percent black by 1970. Although Upper Wynnefield was still 85 percent white in 1970, the slow rate of change was due more to the attractive housing values than to any programs of the local residents association. Furthermore, the 85 percent figure probably exaggerates the amount of social integration that actually occurred. Many of the whites were elderly householders who lived in apartments. Their interaction with blacks in single-family housing was limited. In addition, a large proportion of the white families in Upper Wynnefield lived in Wynnefield Heights, an enclave of garden and high-rise apartments and newer attached homes, separated from the rest of the community by the Bala Country Club. It is fair to assume that whites in this neighborhood had relatively little contact with blacks in other sections of the community.

Because the federal census does not include questions on religion, it is not possible to measure changes in the religious composition of the population. The only source of information available, albeit for one point in time, is the Har Zion survey (to be discussed). As of 1969, Jews still constituted a majority (53 percent) of the population in Wynnefield.[9] Protestants, mostly black, constituted about a third (32 percent) and Catholics about a tenth (12 percent) of the total. The remainder were of other religions or specified none.

1800 block of 54th Street in the sixties.

In Wynnefield, as in other racially changing communities, succession involved the replacement of middle-aged and elderly whites by younger black families. As of 1979, the median age was eighteen years older for whites than for blacks (43 years of age as compared to 25). It should therefore not be surprising that between 1960 and 1970, the median age of the population dropped from 41 years to 37 years. The Har Zion telephone survey results show that black families were far more likely to be in the childbearing and childrearing stages of the life cycle, with a head of household under 41 years old and with at least one child (44 percent versus 13 percent). In contrast, whites were far more likely to be in the later stages of the family life cycle, with a head of household 41 years old or older and with no children (61 percent versus 20 percent).

This massive ethnic shift could have occurred without white panic moving. If whites stopped purchasing homes in the area, racial and religious turnover would still have occurred because all, or nearly all, of the homes made available in the course of normal turnover (e.g., job transfers, divorces) would have been bought by blacks.[10] In fact, however, there is evidence that white panic moving did occur. White Wynnefield residents had more rapid moving plans compared with Lower Merion residents when all other relevant background characteristics were controlled.[11] The most plausible explanation for the differences was the variation between the two communities in the extent of racial change. That Jews were moving in response to racial changes is shown by the fact that those in neighborhoods one-half or more black were far more likely to move than those in neighborhoods with fewer blacks.[12] Furthermore, nearly two-thirds of the Jewish respondents interviewed in the follow-up Har Zion survey cited the existence of racial change as a "very important" reason for moving from their 1969 Wynnefield location.[13] Apparently these families were concerned that if they remained, they would be part of an even smaller racial and cultural minority. A high proportion of those who moved cited concerns about personal safety, which was a real issue in the community.[14]

Contrary to what might be expected, integration attitudes had little bearing on the likelihood of moving. Those who were supportive of housing and educational integration—at least when whites constituted a majority—were just as likely to move as others if they lived in a predominantly black neighborhood or if their children attended a predominantly black school.

Although racial change was not associated with declines in the income and educational levels of the population, it was accompanied by a number of serious community problems, violent street crime being the most serious. During the early 1970s, the community sustained a series of muggings and stabbings of middle-aged and elderly women. Later, teenage gang violence became a serious problem. Established white residents were particularly likely to perceive street crime as a serious problem, because such crimes were a rarity in their daily community lives prior to the mid 1960s. Almost one-third of a sample of elderly residents interviewed as part of a communal survey financed by the Jewish Federation of Philadelphia, found the area "frightening."[15] Vandalism and other crime caused many store owners to go out of business. Police statistics, although fragmentary, highlight the severity of the crime problem. In 1973, there was a considerably greater number of homicides, rapes, and armed assaults committed in Wynnefield (49) than in Lower Merion Township (30), even though the population of the latter area was three times greater.[16]

A series of surveys of Lower Wynnefield residents, carried out as part of the U.S. Department of Housing and Urban Development's Urban Homesteading Demonstration (which included Wynnefield and thirty-nine other communities across the country), highlights the fact that blacks viewed street crime as less of a problem than did whites.[17] More than two-thirds of the respondents, almost all of whom were black, felt that street crime was not a serious problem, and more than three-fourths were satisfied with police protection. These assessments seem surprisingly favorable, given the other statistics on crime in the community that have been presented. The high levels of black satisfaction probably reflect the fact that their former neighborhood in West Philadelphia was even more violent. For these families, Wynnefield represented a significant improvement in their residential environment.

In Wynnefield, as in other racially changing communities, the racial change in the public schools occurred more rapidly than in the surrounding residential area. Overbrook High School, which served Wynnefield and a large section of West Philadelphia, had a black majority as early as 1961. The proportion of black students increased at a moderate rate after that point. On the other hand, the junior high school and two elementary schools serving Wynnefield (Beeber, Gompers,

The Samuel Gompers School in 1951.

and Mann) began to change in 1964, but the rate of change after that point was precipitous. By 1973, all four schools were at least 85 percent black.

The more rapid racial change in the schools than in the community underscores the fact that many of the remaining white families were middle aged and elderly whose children had left home. Those remaining white families with children adjusted to racial change by sending their children to private or parochial schools. The proportion of children attending private or parochial schools in the predominantly white Upper Hill section increased from 16 percent in 1960 to 33 percent in 1970. Unfortunately, there is no information available on the number of Jewish families that transferred their children from public to private schools, including Jewish day schools, in response to these racial shifts. The numbers must have been substantial.

The rapid racial change in the public schools undoubtedly made the area unattractive to middle-class white families. Overcrowding and declines in educational quality were seen as obstacles in attracting white families. All four schools serving the community were overcrowded, and in one, Mann, the problem was severe, with an overutilization rate of 134 percent. Results from the administration of the CAT test in 1974 highlighted the decline in quality of schools that earlier had ranked among the best in the city. In only one of the schools, Gompers Elementary, did a majority of the students score above the 50th percentile.

Not surprisingly, the replacement of a middle-aged and elderly white population by a younger black population led to an increase in residential overcrowding, defined as more than 1.0 person per room. This was particularly true in Lower Wynnefield, where the incidence of overcrowding increased from 1 percent to 4 percent during this ten-year period. It is unclear how serious this increase was to residents of the surrounding community. Data are unavailable to determine whether overcrowding led to increased "wear and tear" on the structures and, in turn, to housing deterioration.

Vacant homes were a more obviously serious problem for the community as a whole. The Office of Finance for the City of Philadelphia defined a vacant home as one that had been unoccupied for at least a year, regardless of its marketability or physical condition. As of spring 1974, there were a total of 116 vacant houses in the community. Although the lower part of census tract no. 119 in Lower Wynnefield contained the heaviest concentration, vacant units were dispersed throughout the community. The existence of this concentration led to the designation of Wynnefield as one of the U.S. Department of Housing and Urban Development's Urban Homesteading Demonstration neighborhoods.

Wynnefield is one of the areas where racial change lowered property values.[18] During the 1960s, the mean property value dropped by 17 percent, from $13,118 to $10,916, taking into account the decreased purchasing power of the dollar in 1970 as compared with 1960. In Lower Merion Township, on the other hand, average property values increased 7 percent, from $25,945 to $27,753. The depressed housing prices were not necessarily a bad thing. During the middle and late

1960s, the low housing values helped to attract many middle-class families, white and black, to Upper Wynnefield, who could not afford housing of comparable quality in nearby sections of Lower Merion Township. However, when these families tried to relocate, they experienced difficulty finding purchasers.[19] Often, they were only able to get back what they had paid, giving up appreciation and the cost of improvements.

Racial changes during the middle and late 1960s also had a profound impact on synagogues. Three congregations—Bnai Aaron, Beth Am, and Beth El—relocated. Beth David, a Reform congregation, decided to remain and to make part of its facility available to a black Baptist congregation. It also opened a bicultural nursery school for black and Jewish children.

The decisions of these four synagogues were made with little fanfare and on the basis of impressionistic information on demographic changes in the surrounding area. The 1970 census was not yet available. The decision on the future of Har Zion Temple, the largest Conservative congregation in Philadelphia and one of the largest in the United States, was quite different. It was made in conjunction with a large-scale study of the community and, in addition, was made under the scrutiny of local and national media attention (although this was not the intention of congregation leaders when the study was initiated).[20]

In 1969, the directors of Har Zion Temple retained the Center for Research on the Acts of Man at the University of Pennsylvania to study the synagogue and its surrounding community in order to assist congregational leaders in making a rational decision about the synagogue's future. The study was directed by Samuel Z. Klausner, Professor of Sociology (and a member of Har Zion), and myself, in the Department of City and Regional Planning at the University. The study had three aims: to estimate the 1969 religious and racial distribution of the population in the Wynnefield–Lower Merion area and to project the composition of the population ten years hence; to identify possible differences in the religious-cultural climate in the different parts of the study area; and to poll members of the congregation on their feelings toward different policy options, including the relocation of the synagogue facility. In the spring and summer of 1969, the Center completed a telephone survey of residents of the Wynnefield–Lower Merion area (Jews and non-Jews), a mailed survey of Jewish families in this area, and a mailed poll of Har Zion members (including those who lived outside of the Wynnefield–Lower Merion area).[21]

The study predicted that racial and religious changes over the next ten years (1969–1979) would be moderate and that, as a result, the center of the Jewish population would shift only slightly to the west.[22] This prediction proved to be overly optimistic. As of 1979, Protestants, mostly black, would comprise about half of the total population, while Jews would account for about two-fifths. The remaining one-tenth would be Catholics and those identifying with other religions or none.

Analysis revealed that the Jewish subcommunities of Wynnefield, southeast Lower Merion, and northwest Lower Merion were culturally and religiously distinct. Moving outward along this corridor of the metropolitan area, Jewish residents were more likely to choose an integrationist lifestyle, involving close Jewish-gentile social contacts, rather than a separatist one. This was reflected in greater support among Lower Merion residents for synagogue involvement in political and social action activities, as well as by more lenient attitudes toward intermarriage. On the other hand, Wynnefield residents scored higher on personal measures of Jewish commitment: knowledge and practice of Jewish rituals and support for Zionism. These findings implied that relocations to northwestern Lower Merion would lead to an "attenuation of Zionist commitment" and pressure for the synagogue to move in the direction of Reform Judaism.

Racial change in Wynnefield was leading to a breakdown in morale of Jewish residents. This was reflected, not surprisingly, in the items dealing with neighborhood change. A far higher proportion of the Wynnefield than the Lower Merion respondents expected the proportion of Jews in their neighborhood to decline along with declines in income and property values. What was surprising was the way the broken morale was shown by other survey items not dealing with neighborhood change. For example, a higher proportion of Wynnefield residents were dissatis-

Wynnefield is a neighborhood that has undergone many changes during the course of several decades. Pictured here is County Commissioner Morton Witkin (center), representing builders of Fairfield Apartments, addressing the zoning board at the City Hall hearing. Nochem Winnet, representing protesting neighbors, listens at left.

fied with goods in local department stores. Because Wynnefield residents shopped in the same department stores along City Line Avenue and in nearby sections of Lower Merion Township, these results reflected the fact that "life looked more difficult to Wynnefield than to Lower Merion residents."[23]

The results of the poll of members provided the Har Zion leadership with considerable latitude in choosing a future location. Similar proportions approved of a Radnor, Merion, or a Bala Cynwyd location or remaining at the current Wynnefield location. The report ended by advising that Har Zion not move from its current location in Wynnefield: "It remains nearest to the center of gravity of a large Jewish concentration in Wynnefield and southeast Lower Merion ."[24]

Klausner submitted the report to Har Zion Temple in February 1970. It was released through the University of Pennsylvania's news office in July 1970.[25] Summaries appeared in the two Philadelphia daily newspapers on July 27 and July 28.[26] In August, the congregation's president, in a letter to members, formally rejected the report's conclusions and indicated the congregation planned to relocate its facilities to the suburbs. It was felt desirable to build a school and an auditorium in the suburbs as soon as possible and to relocate the sanctuary at a later date. The rationale for the move was to bring the facilities, particularly the school, closer to existing and prospective members: "Of our entire membership of 1700 families, approximately 350 now reside in Wynnefield, with a relatively small percentage having children of school age. . . . Our mothers are complaining about driving their children into Wynnefield when they live in the suburbs. Many young people whose families have been associated with Har Zion for years have likewise expressed the hope that the Har Zion school will be located in the suburban area by the time that they are ready to enroll their children."[27]

The Planning Committee's proposal sparked a spirited debate. Some supported it, claiming the fear of crime made some families reluctant to send their children to the Temple school. In con-

Wynnefield is remembered by past residents as an area particularly conducive to Jewish religious life. Pictured here are two of the famous stained glass windows of the old Har Zion, 1952.

trast, a group of prominent members asserted that the crime problem was not serious enough to justify abandoning a physical plant that represented such a significant financial investment.[28]

Two years later, in December 1972, Har Zion's board of directors approved the purchase of a tract of land at Hagys Ford and Hollow Roads in Penn Valley. Before the Board's decision could be implemented, it was necessary that it be approved by the congregation membership. A group of members, including Daniel Elazar, Professor of Political Science at Temple University and an expert on the politics and sociology of local Jewish communities, and Chaim Potok, author, sent a letter to Har Zion members, urging them to attend the meeting and vote against the proposal.[29] The Board's decision was considered unwise because it would constitute a serious financial drain on the community, and it would threaten the congregational membership in the Wynnefield area. Klausner criticized the Board's decision because "it would represent the abandonment of the urban area by still another institution."[30] Given the available data, it is impossible to say whether this resistance was limited to a few intellectuals or whether it was more broadly based.

Har Zion's auditorium was filled with over one thousand families on January 7, 1973, for the special meeting. After a two-hour discussion period, the question was called and an overwhelming majority voted to support the board of director's decision. Following the vote, the president of the congregation attempted to heal the wounds caused by the vote. He stated, "First of all, as long as we remain at 54th Street and Radnor (a branch location) we will not diminish our efforts or our activities one iota. Our program in all its aspects will remain on the same high level. Secondly, Har Zion pledges to see to it that the religious needs of our members living in the Wynnefield area will be met even after the move is made."[31]

It is apparent that in carrying through the relocation decision, congregation leaders felt torn between their commitment to old members and the desire to attract new ones. The pledge to continue to meet the needs of Wynnefield members reflected this tension. Whether the congregation would be able to fulfill this pledge was another matter because of the potentially destabilizing impact of the relocation on the Wynnefield community. It must be noted that the closing of synagogues in other racially changing communities has been shown to have a severe psychological impact on the remaining Jewish residents, whether they attend services regularly or not.[32] The presence of these structures symbolizes the existence of a viable Jewish community. The closing of synagogues reminds residents of the demise of this community. It is impossible to say, with the available data, what impact Har Zion's relocation had on the morale of remaining Jewish residents. There is evidence that the actual relocation did not influence many household out-migration decisions. Relatively few of the Wynnefield Jewish residents who moved during the 1970s cited synagogue closings as very important in their decisions.[33] It is likely that these closings reinforced decisions that were already made.

WYNNEFIELD IN 1980: PROJECTIONS AND REALITIES

During the late 1960s and through the 1970s, newspaper articles echoed the hopes of Wynnefield residents that stable racial integration could be achieved.[34] There was a small surge of home purchases by young white families during the early 1970s that further reinforced these wishes. However, the exodus of whites continued during the middle and late 1970s. Whether this was due to panic selling or normal turnover is irrelevant. What is important is that nearly all of the homes that were put up for sale were purchased by blacks. Hopes for achieving an integrated community were dashed.

By 1980, Wynnefield was nearly three-fourths (74 percent) non-white. Only a tiny proportion of the non-white population was other than black, so it is valid to use *black* and *non-white* as interchangeable in this community. Lower Wynnefield was overwhelmingly (93 percent) black, while Upper Wynnefield still had a white majority (65 percent). Although no data are available on changes in the religious composition of the population, it is reasonable to assume that the rate of decline in the Jewish population paralleled that for the white population as a whole.

The fact that Upper Wynnefield had a white majority can be misleading. These figures probably overstate the amount of social integration that existed. One-half of the white households were nonfamily units, including students living in dormitories at St. Joseph's College and long-term patients in the Home for Incurables on Belmont Avenue. In addition, as stated earlier, a large proportion of the remaining white population lived in Wynnefield Heights, located in the northeast corner of the community. It is unlikely that whites in this neighborhood had much social contact with blacks in other sections of Wynnefield.

The potential for meaningful integration was also lessened by differences in demographic characteristics between whites and blacks, which made it less likely that they would share common interests. The out-migration of whites during the 1970s was selective from among younger and more affluent families. Differences in the age composition between whites and blacks that were apparent in 1970 persisted ten years later. A far higher proportion of whites than blacks were age 65 and older (34 percent versus 8 percent), whereas a far higher proportion of the black population consisted of children under age 16 (19 percent versus 7 percent). These differences in age were paralleled by differences in family type. Whereas the norm for blacks was a husband-wife unit with children present (40 percent), among whites the norm was a husband-wife unit without children (60 percent), typically middle-aged or elderly couples whose children had left home.

The decline in the number of Jewish families was accompanied by a diminished Jewish institutional presence in Wynnefield.[35] Only five of the eight synagogues that had been in the community in 1965 remained by the end of 1983, and one of them, Beth David, had made settlement on land and a school in suburban Gladwyne. Three were small Orthodox congregations: Young Israel, Lenas Hazedech, and Beth Tovim. A fourth was Temple Israel, a small Conservative congregation with a membership located mostly outside of Wynnefield.

The Reform congregation, Beth David, voted early in 1983 to relocate to Gladwynne. This followed a decision in 1977 to close its bicultural nursery school (which eventually became completely black), and a decision in 1980 to operate its religious school in the Solomon Schechter School building in Lower Merion. The decision to relocate was a painful but unavoidable one. The number of members living in Wynnefield had declined from 80 in 1967 to 3 in 1982. The decline in enrollment in the religious school was even more important in precipitating the move. Between 1980 and 1983, total school enrollment declined from 200 to 155, while enrollment in grades Kindergarten to 7 dropped from 145 to 95. Among the perceived reasons for the decline were the westward and northward movement of the Jewish population and fears among members concerning walking into and out of the synagogue on Wynnefield Avenue. Members felt that the congregation would fade away if it remained in Wynnefield and that this would serve no useful purpose.

The clock sculpture outside the Har Zion School.

Rabbi Cohen did not regret the congregation's 1967 decision to remain in Wynnefield and to work with the black community: "I . . . believe the effect that we had on people's lives was quite significant and beneficial and those effects—I would hope—still 'live on' even after the move."[36]

All four Jewish day schools that had been in Wynnefield had relocated by 1980: the Akiba Academy, the Solomon Schechter School, the Suburban Jewish Folkshul, and Torah Academy. The last move was noteworthy because this was an Orthodox school and many of the parents still lived in Wynnefield as of 1980.[37]

The only Jewish institution that was thriving was the Talmudical Yeshiva located on Drexel Road. The Yeshiva had approximately two hundred students who came from the entire East Coast and Canada.[38] Because most of the students lived in dormitories, and because they studied in such an intense, cloistered environment, spending fourteen or more hours a day in learning, the changing racial environment had little impact on the Yeshiva. Furthermore, it did not become involved actively in communitywide efforts to stabilize the area. Nevertheless, in 1983, it was "buying homes across the street for its rabbis and staff, adding a new *Bet Midrash* to its present facilities, and encouraging Orthodox families to buy in the area."[39] These efforts may help to maintain a viable Orthodox Jewish enclave in this one section of Wynnefield.

The fact that the Talmudical Yeshiva remained and thrived during the period of massive racial change should not be surprising. Case studies of racially changing Jewish communities have indicated that within these communities, the Orthodox subcommunities have been the most stable. This tendency is illustrated by the Lubavitch and Satmar Hasidic groups in the Crown Heights and Williamsburgh sections of Brooklyn, and by the Orthodox populations in West Rogers Park (Chicago) and in Cleveland Heights. An important reason for this stability is that these Orthodox communities have little social contact with their non-Jewish neighbors. This trend was also noted by results from the Har Zion survey: having a strict attitude toward intermarriage between Jews and gentiles contributed to remaining in the neighborhood when other personal characteristics were held constant.[40] Apparently, these householders exerted such strong social controls over their children that they were indifferent to changes in the population makeup of the surrounding area.

CONCLUSION

The Wynnefield story is a familiar one to those who have read other case studies of racially changing Jewish communities, or who have lived through the process. The factors that made other Jewish communities susceptible to change also made Wynnefield susceptible: an upwardly mobile population; a tendency for the children not to remain in the same community as their parents; a widely held image that Jewish communities do not physically resist black entry; a breakdown in discriminatory barriers facing Jews in the suburbs; and, most importantly, the proximity of the community to an expanding black ghetto.

In addition, the types of efforts of the organized Jewish community to promote stabilization, once black in-migration began, were also typical: working through the local residents association to improve the overall quality of life and working through the Jewish Community Relations Council to deal with rumors and fears, many of which proved to be well founded on the basis of later events. Furthermore, as in other communities, racial changes had a greater impact on community institutions (schools and synagogues) and community standards (street crime) than on the income and educational levels of the population.

Perhaps the most distinguishing feature of the history was the optimism about achieving a stable racially integrated community. This optimism was reflected in the Har Zion report as well as in newspaper and magazine articles about the community. This optimism reflected an awareness of the community's assets, its large attractive homes on tree shaded streets. It also reflected the desire of liberal Jews living in the community to be able to follow through on their beliefs about living in an integrated community. This hopefulness conflicted with the reality of the expanding black ghetto and the fact that little could be done at the local level to alter the forces of supply and demand directly affecting this community.

From the perspective of Philadelphia's Jewish community, neighborhood racial change in Wynnefield caused financial and other communal problems. It cost approximately $20 million to relocate Jewish institutions from Wynnefield during the 1960s and 1970s.[41] This amount was greater than the $17.8 million dollars raised by the Federation of Jewish Agencies of Greater Philadelphia in their 1980 drive. It was also impossible to recreate the type of Jewish environment that had existed in Wynnefield, a high Jewish density, yet with a diverse Jewish population that reinforced Jewish values and Jewish commitment.

The Wynnefield story for Jews is not over yet, because a small Orthodox community remains and middle-aged and elderly Jews are dispersed throughout Upper Wynnefield. Whether the quality of life will stabilize, so that this Jewish subcommunity is retained, or whether it will decline, leading to complete racial turnover, is an open question.

1948 photograph of the "Shomrim Society," led by Supt. of Police Guy Parsons down Castor Avenue to Temple Sholom on Roosevelt Blvd.

A Place to Live
The Jewish Builders of Northeast Philadelphia

Peter Binzen

When Hyman Korman, a rabbi's son, emigrated from Lithuania in 1903, Philadelphia was just beginning to "assume the sights and sounds of a modern metropolis."[1] Electric trolleys had been running since 1892, but the Market Street Subway-Elevated Line would not open until 1907. Horse-drawn wagons clattered along Broad Street, and neighbors drew water from three green pumps in Central Place. Policemen walked their beats, and lamplighters walked their rounds. Life was lived in the streets.

Korman was 21, and he spoke no English. He found himself in a city whose population was exploding. From 1.3 million people in 1900, it would grow to 1.7 million by 1915. Outside the central business district, however, Philadelphia was largely rural. Fewer than 500 automobiles were registered by its inhabitants in 1905, but the 1900 census had counted more than 4,000 dairy cows, 3,000 horses and 2,500 pigs on the city's farms.

Korman's uncles, who were industrial builders in Eastern Europe, had sent him to the United States to study railroading, which was then at its peak as a means of transportation for people and goods. Philadelphia was home for the mightiest railroad of all: the Pennsylvania. Hyman Korman never worked for the "Pennsy," nor did he make a career in the railroad industry. Like many Jewish immigrants, he found work in the field of women's apparel. What was more important, however, was that he found a wife and moved into his in-laws' farmhouse near what is now Oxford Circle.

There weren't many Jews living in that part of the city then—not many Christians, either. The Northeast was largely rural, cut off from the rest of the metropolis by Tacony and Frankford Creeks. Thomas Holme, William Penn's surveyor, had owned land there, and Benjamin Rush, physician-general of the Continental Armies and a signer of the Declaration of Independence, had been born in the Byberry section. But the Northeast was populated mainly by farmers who cherished their independence and who wanted to be left alone. Many of them opposed the Consolidation Act of 1854, which brought their farms into the city, and they resisted sending their children to city public schools.

There was a Quaker Meeting in the Northeast in William Penn's lifetime. The Episcopalians, Baptists, Methodists, Lutherans, and Roman Catholics established churches,[2] but Jews were unknown there for nearly two centuries. The nearest Jewish settlement at Tulip and Auburn Streets in Port Richmond, almost 2 miles below Frankford Creek, dates from about 1870. Max Whiteman, the historian, termed Port Richmond's William Street "the first exclusively Jewish street in Philadelphia,"[3] and Yehzekiel Bernstein, a Polish immigrant, its first settler. According to Whiteman, Bernstein's choice of the expanding industrial area of Richmond for his settlement was "not typical of the Jewish immigrants of other port cities who persisted in clustering close"[4] to the central business districts.

Certainly, Korman's in-laws' living on their farm near Oxford Circle was also atypical. And Korman himself did not fit the pattern of so many Jewish immigrants of this period, who had been forced from their homelands by poverty and pogroms and whose "fugitive status" helped give a unique character to their uprooting.[5]

Korman's sons were born on the farm, Max William in 1906 and Samuel in 1909, and as boys they did the chores. A newspaper account later said of Max, "The firm grip he displays proudly today (1962) resulted from years at the milking stool."[6]

Left: Hyman Korman in 1959.

Right: Samuel Korman in 1968.

According to Samuel Korman, his mother, Yetta, managed the farm while his father worked in town at the apparel trade. Then in 1914 there occurred an event that would alter the Northeast's rural character and change Hyman Korman's life. A 7-mile stretch of Northeast (now Roosevelt) Boulevard was opened to traffic. The new highway sliced "right through our farm," recalled Samuel Korman.

The effect of the highway construction was to raise land values in the Northeast and encourage rapid residential development.[7] Korman was well positioned to take advantage of this situation, and he did so. He was 35 years old, had lived in Philadelphia just fourteen years, and was still mastering English, but he saw more clearly than the natives what was about to happen. In 1917 he bought the Hamilton Farm at what is now Castor and Devereaux Avenues. The following year, he purchased the Dawson Farm half a dozen blocks away at Castor and Magee.

Meanwhile, another Jewish immigrant, Alfred P. Orleans, began making land purchases in the Northeast. Like Korman, Orleans was out of the conventional mold. He had come over from Russia at the age of 17 in 1906 intending to study medicine and return home to practice. He attended Central High School and Brown Preparatory School and passed entrance examinations for medical school. Instead of matriculating, however, he entered the real estate and insurance business. His son, Marvin, said his father was drawn to the Northeast by rumors concerning extension of the Market Street Subway-Elevated Line in 1919–1920. The rumors proved true. In November 1922, the Frankford Elevated opened at a cost of $15.6 million. It ran from Bridge Street and Frankford Avenue to Front and Arch Streets, thus vastly increasing the Northeast's accessibility to downtown Philadelphia.

Korman had been an investor in Orleans's real estate and insurance business, and at first they became partners in house building. Soon, however, they set up separate companies and groomed their sons to take over. In the decades that followed, they remained friendly competitors.

Hyman Korman's first houses were built on Oakley Street south of Levick and along Martin's Mill Road near the Cheltenham Township line in what is now Lawndale. The date is uncertain. According to one account, Korman founded his company in 1921. A second account said construction began in 1924. A third account, which was published in 1938, said that by that time Korman had already had "20 years of extensive building of single and twin homes in the Northeast."[8] That would mean he started in 1918. Whatever year Korman actually began, he entered the business with great enthusiasm, building new houses whenever his finances permitted.

For many years after they first began putting up houses in Northeast Philadelphia, the Jewish builders found the market limited to non-Jews. Although the city's Jewish population was increasing, its movement was to other parts of Philadelphia, not the Northeast. Sam Bass Warner noted that in the 1920s, the Kensington–lower Northeast area grew into a mill town of enormous proportions.[9] By 1930 its population had expanded to 479,000 people, and it claimed two thousand factories. "This was Philadelphia's workshop," said Warner, but the workshop, he noted, was strictly segregated.

"Unlike all other districts of Philadelphia," wrote Warner, "Russian Jews and Negroes in 1930 were notable for their relative absence. . . . The only Negroes lived in the decaying streets next to the downtown slum. . . . Jews were scarce throughout the entire district." There were no fair housing laws at that time. The Human Relations Commission did not exist. Most of the neighborhoods of Philadelphia were strictly segregated. Northeast Philadelphia had been originally populated by white Protestants primarily of German extraction, and it was from this group that Korman and Orleans first found customers for their houses. Marvin Orleans began working for his father as a "waterboy" in the summer of 1931. He was 12 years old, and A. P. Orleans was building houses on Rhawn Street just east of Bustleton Avenue. Hyman Korman was building half a dozen blocks away.

The nation was mired in the Great Depression, and the city's economy was near collapse. Somehow, the builders kept going. The Orleans family then lived at 4900 North 8th Street in Logan, and young Marvin Orleans attended Simon Gratz High School. "I came out on the bus after school and kept the model (house) open," he said.

Marvin Orleans in 1964.

Orleans said that, at that time, builders in the Temple Stadium area "ran restricted jobs," that is, refused to sell to Jews. Even the Jewish builders themselves were at first reluctant to sell to Jews. "As a kid in the models," he said, "I was told to warn any buyers coming in who happened to be Jewish that the rest of the neighborhood was all Gentile. Had they (Korman and Orleans) not been Jewish, I think they would have run their jobs restricted. They were not too crazy about selling to Jews for fear of what it would do to their market."

Not until the 1930s, he said, did Jewish families begin to move into the new houses of the Northeast. One of the first Jewish families to move in was that of Max William Korman. Berton Korman, Max's son and a grandson of Hyman, said his father built a single house at 1415 Brighton Street in 1931 and moved into it. Berton was born there in 1933 and grew up there. The Kormans were the only Jewish family on the block, he said, and he "used to get beat up regularly" going to and from Woodrow Wilson Junior High School.

Throughout the difficult years of the 1930s, house building continued in the Northeast. The pace was relatively slow but steady. Miles of sewer and water lines were installed as make-work for the unemployed. The builders were able to assemble land cheaply. "In the heart of the Depression," said Marvin Orleans, "my father bought land with sewers, curbs and water for $5 a front foot. The improvements alone were worth $15."

Hyman Korman's sales agent, starting late in the 1920s and continuing for perhaps thirty years, was Alex Burchuk, himself a Russian Jewish immigrant. Burchuk's son, Aaron, who took over the business after his father died, kept copies of sales brochures for Korman houses. One set of brochures advertised houses that Korman was selling in 1938 in the "Upper Northwood" section near Castor and Devereaux Avenues, four blocks north of Oxford Circle. This was the site of the old Hamilton Farm, Hyman Korman's first major acquisition in the Northeast.

The brochures promised: "Hyman Korman's air conditioned—insulated—oil burning homes. Built on lots 20 feet by 81.6 feet. Three large airy bedrooms. Two tiled bathrooms. Brick garage. All front walls stone 18 inches thick with wide front windowsills. Rock lath plastering throughout. Copper water lines and spouting throughout. Modern laundry in basement. Attractive, well-planned living room with built-in bookcases. Sunlit dining room. Modern spacious kitchen with breakfast room." The advertisement concluded: "A special note to the ladies . . . Closet space galore. Large clubroom in basement with open log burning fireplace." The price: $5,490.

Burchuk said Korman sold similar two-bedroom houses on Devereaux Avenue for $3,990. And as late as the early 1940s, he was selling houses on the 1400 block of Benner Street for $4,290. The new Federal Housing Administration helped the builders sell their houses by guaranteeing low-interest mortgages. By 1938, Korman was said to have sold more than four hundred houses in the Upper Northwood development and was opening a new unit of forty-two in the 6100 block of Belden Street between Devereaux and Benner. "The houses on Belden Street have been designed particularly for the working man with a limited income—averaging $25 a week," said a contemporary newspaper account.[10] It added that FHA approval made it possible for "the prospective owner to acquire a house at less than rental prices."

"Korman has his own code of wisdom when it comes to building," the article observed. "His success in this field has been the result of good judgment, coupled with the fact, he declares, that he was not and is not hampered in his undertakings by any partnerships or boards of directors. It is understood that his fortunate position of also being a 'cash buyer,' paying on delivery for his building materials, enables him to buy large quantities at favorable prices."

Aaron Burchuk said it was true that Hyman Korman and his son, Max, who succeeded him, cut through the bureaucratic red tape that strangles some business organizations. "I don't know many people who ever had a written contract with Max," Burchuk said. "We represented him exclusively on a verbal basis for many, many years." He termed Max a "tough, hard businessman but very fair," a "dynamic force," and a "very good administrator." He described Hyman Korman as "very bright and well respected." And he added, "His word was his bond."

Although both Korman and Orleans built hundreds of houses in Northeast Philadelphia before World War II, it was not really until after the war that the section's major development took place. Again, it was a case of the Jewish builders being in the right place at the right time. The war had left the city with a critical housing shortage. In 1950 over 70,000 dwellings lacked a bath or were dilapidated, and overcrowding affected a huge proportion of the inner-city housing supply.[11] The post-war baby boom exacerbated the shortage. Thousands of returned veterans needed homes of their own in which to raise their families. The federal government provided stipends to help underwrite the veterans' college education and then, through the Veterans Administration, guaranteed their house mortgages with virtually no money down and interest rates as low as 4 percent.

Thus began the vast democratization of the outer areas of American cities and their suburbs. On Long Island, William J. Levitt built and sold more than 18,000 single houses for the veterans. In 1952, he moved his operations to lower Bucks County, where, over six years, he built 17,311 houses. The base price was $10,000, and veterans could buy them for $100 down and $66 a month in carrying charges. Meanwhile, in Northeast Philadelphia, Korman, Orleans, and other Jewish builders also constructed thousands of houses during this period, providing working-class families opportunities for home ownership in a setting previously restricted to the middle class.

Most of the Jewish families that settled in Northeast Philadelphia in the years after World War II moved from other Jewish sections of the city. Many were the working-class children of Eastern European immigrants who had never before owned homes of their own. They were shopkeepers, salesmen, city employees, factory hands, clerks, and office workers. They were also lawyers, accountants, and school teachers. They drove trucks and operated delicatessens. Many policemen moved to the Northeast, and one long-time resident, Morton Solomon, later became president of his synagogue and the city's first Jewish police commissioner.

Left: Max W. Korman, in the early 1950s.

Right: Berton Korman in 1974.

Such men as Norman Denny, who developed the Robindale section near Poquessin Creek at Woodhaven Road in the far Northeast, and Samuel Korman considered the settlement of the area by Jews as inevitable and in character with traditional Jewish experience of movement and pioneering resettlement. Korman's own family experience certainly showed this.

As the Oxford Circle area filled up and the builders pushed farther out, a pattern developed. Roosevelt Boulevard came to be seen as a dividing line; some called it the "Gaza Strip." The east side of the Boulevard became heavily Roman Catholic. The largest concentration of Jewish families was on the west. As evidence of this demarcation, all of the Catholic high schools in Northeast Philadelphia were erected east of the Boulevard, while the two public high schools with the largest Jewish enrollments were on the west side. There continues to be endless speculation as to why the ethnic housing patterns developed as they did. Many cite the fact that Hyman Korman's farm was on the west side, and A. P. Orleans also started building there.

Ironically, though Korman and Orleans may have been the keys, and their building strategies catered to the older generations' ghetto mentality, they never felt such a need themselves. Korman built a house for his wife and himself at 4901 Oxford Avenue in predominantly Protestant Frankford, east of the Boulevard, and was living there at his death in 1970 at the age of 88.

When Marvin Orleans (who died in September 1986) was asked about the unwritten dividing line, he responded, "I would guess that was because of the start we had already made west of the Boulevard. The Jewish people felt more comfortable. I think it goes back to feeling comfortable."

Other observers cite the importance of Temple Sholom at Large Street and Roosevelt Boulevard near Oxford Circle. It was organized in 1939, and Hyman Korman was a founding member of the congregation. As house-hunting families motored out the Boulevard, their eyes were inevitably drawn to this impressive synagogue. It was a very visible symbol of the west side's Jewishness.

So swift was the Northeast's development that even those residents who were born after World War II and grew up there in the 1950s remember it now as a totally different kind of place. Fred Stein, who ran Philadelphia's Century IV celebration, is an example. Both of his parents were born and raised in Feltonville, near B Street and Roosevelt Boulevard. When Fred, the oldest of three children, was born in 1951, his family was living on Brighton Street near Oxford Circle. Fred lived there until he was married at the age of 23. The neighborhood was predominantly Jewish. The synagogue was Beth Emeth, and the elementary school was Solis-Cohen. He had fond memories of growing up on Brighton Street.

"The thing I enjoyed was being out on the street," he said. "Everything happened in the street. Cars were secondary. That's where we met and played boxball. No one was ever afraid. If we were out late our parents weren't concerned. If we wandered a couple of blocks they knew we were in the neighborhood. . . . We celebrated holidays. The parents on the block got along together. Being in a predominantly Jewish area, the non-Jew was minority. I never witnessed any tension but knew it could happen."

What Stein remembers as "Cottman Woods" is now the massive Roosevelt Mall shopping district. And in the part of the woods where he and his friends had a treehouse (at Cottman and Bustleton), there is now a Herman's sporting goods store.

Fred Stein does have one tragic recollection, and in a curious way, it bears on Roosevelt Boulevard as a line of demarcation. His best friend was a Catholic youth. One day when they were about 14, his friend went across the Boulevard to a commercial swimming pool that was then popular. He was knifed by another boy and killed. "This had a most profound effect on my life," Stein said. "After that, everybody was afraid to send their kids out. My parents echoed what was being said in many homes: 'Don't cross the Boulevard.'"

Stein's life as an adult has not been unlike that of many other Northeasterners. He stayed in the area but moved up. After getting married, he moved first to a duplex at Cottman and the Boulevard, half a dozen blocks from his parents. Then he and his wife bought a single house at Welsh and Verree Roads, between Bustleton and Burholme. Although he owns one-third of an acre on a cul-de-sac, he looks back with nostalgia at the old row house.

Such upward mobility in the Northeast is commonplace. Edward B. Rosenberg, a native of Atlantic City, lived in South Philadelphia while attending Central High School and Temple University. After getting his law degree at Temple, he lived in Logan for a few years, and then, in 1947, he moved to a row house at 1251 Kerper Street in Lawndale. The house had just been built by

William J. Levitt in 1974.

Morton B. Solomon on his appointment as Deputy Police Commissioner in 1966 (the Second Deputy Commissioner appointed then was Frank L. Rizzo).

Left: 4901 Oxford Avenue, site of Korman home.

Right: Edward B. Rosenberg in 1973.

A. P. Orleans. It had six rooms, a full basement, and sold for $11,200. Rosenberg stayed there for eight or ten years while he developed his law practice. Then he and his wife moved to a semi-detached new house at 1115 Brighton Street. It had three bathrooms. "That was a luxury," said Rosenberg. Even so, the house only cost about $13,500. In 1965, he and his wife made their third move, to a single house at 1201 Tyson Street. Here they raised their three sons, and in 1974, Rosenberg, a Northeast civic leader, was named to the Common Pleas Court of Philadelphia County. His property is about 75 feet by 100 feet. There are trees on the grounds, and he has a vegetable garden.

Of course, not all Northeast families aspire to move out of the old neighborhood. Benjamin S. Bennett, an accountant, and his wife, Ruth, moved into a sturdy stone house at 711 Tyson Avenue in 1951. The builder was Joseph Cutler Sons, and the price was $14,900. The neighborhood was nearly all farmland. Their two children attended Northeast High School. Bennett, who became a senior partner with Touche Ross, rode the Reading commuter trains to town from the Cheltenham station four blocks from his house. Mrs. Bennett became active in civic affairs and later served as a member of the Philadelphia Board of Education. She gave the Northeast its first representation on the school board.

In their block and a neighboring one were six physicians, six lawyers, and three dentists. The section remained a convenient, comfortable place for professionals.

When the 6600 block of Akron Street was developed in 1950, its 16-foot-wide stone-and-brick row houses were placed on sale for $8,750 each. They had three bedrooms and a bath, and buyers quickly filled them with small children. Years passed, and in November 1975, residents organized a block party to celebrate final payments on their twenty-five-year mortgages. Even after a quarter of a century, two-thirds of the original families were still living there.

Among the Akron Street "originals" were Jack and Roslyn Greenberg. He had grown up in Strawberry Mansion and she in the area of 6th and Clearfield Streets. They moved to Akron Street as newlyweds. "I woke up that first morning," Mrs. Greenberg recalled, "and I thought I was in paradise." With the exception of one family, her block of Akron Street was all Jewish. The synagogue was around the corner, and the elementary school was two blocks away. The mortgage was a manageable $75 a month. She and her husband had everything they needed and wanted. They raised their two children on Akron Street and loved it.

In 1983, Mrs. Greenberg spoke of how life has changed on Akron Street. And much of what she said may apply to the Northeast generally. The block was still heavily Jewish, but the residents were older. When somebody moved out, there were concerns over who would move in. The playground was in deplorable condition, and the Castor Avenue shopping district four blocks from her house wasn't what it was thirty years ago, either.

Crime was never a problem on Akron Street. Now the neighbors were concerned. "A month ago, I caught a kid trying to break into my house," said Mrs. Greenberg. "He heard me and he ran. This was in daylight. Ten o'clock in the morning. The brazen nerve. We had to put in a new door. Years ago, nobody locked. Now I'm busy locking everything. Everyone has better locks."

Mrs. Greenberg noted that most of Akron Street's residents were in their 50s and 60s. Most of the boys and girls who could be seen playing in the street were not the children, but the grandchildren of the original settlers. She was deeply concerned about what the future may hold for Akron Street. On the other hand, she had given no thought to moving.

The statistics that are available showed that there was reason for concern about the future of Akron Street and of the Northeast. The population was aging: the 1980 U.S. Census showed that men and women who were 60 years old and over comprised almost 19 percent of the Northeast's population. In ten years, the number of older people had jumped from just over 70,000 to 92,000—an increase of more than 30 percent. The *Jewish Times* referred to this phenomenon as "the graying of the Northeast."[12]

By contrast, the over-60 share of Bucks County's population of about 480,000 in 1980 was just over 10 percent of the total. And in many cases, of course, the younger people in Bucks County were the children of the Northeast's old-timers. In 1984 there were fourteen nursing homes with intermediate and skilled care services for the Northeast's aging population.

The Far Northeast was the only section of the city to register population growth in the decade of the 1970s. From Rhawn Street to the county line, the numbers increased from 181,894 in 1970 to 188,420 in 1980. This modest rise in population was more than offset, however, by a loss of more than 41,000 people in the area extending from Rhawn Street to Frankford Creek, which is the Northeast's lower boundary. As a result, the area's overall population fell under 420,000 from over 450,000 a decade earlier.

The section west of Roosevelt Boulevard registered the largest rise in non-white population to be found anywhere in the city. The increase exceeded 100 percent, but the numbers were small: 3,300 non-whites in a population of 180,000.

As the Northeast has gotten older, its school enrollments have shrunk. Nowhere was this more evident than at Northeast High School. The school was overcrowded the day it opened at Cottman Avenue and Algon Street in 1957. Double-shift rostering began in 1958 as class sizes jumped to unmanageable numbers. Al Zack started teaching at Northeast that fall. His memories were of a school with rigorous academic standards. Many of the parents were professionals and government workers. Zack believes that between 70 percent and 80 percent of Northeast's graduates in those early years went on to some form of post–high school education.

When Northeast High School's enrollment peaked at about 4,100 students in the early 1960s, the school was more than 90 percent Jewish. Then its enrollment began to fall off. In recent years, the declines have been sharp. In 1983 its enrollment was about 2,600, and about 30 percent of its students were black children attending Northeast High under the school district's desegregation program. "We are a beautifully desegregated Supreme Court school," said Zack, who was the vice principal. He said Northeast's current students came from "much lower economic levels" than did those of a generation ago. Fewer went to college. And Northeast High offered classes in English as a second language both to Asian immigrants and to increasing numbers of Jewish children from the Soviet Union who came to the United States in the recent wave of immigration. Zack indicated that the Asian children were, in general, very family oriented and education oriented, much like the Jewish immigrants from Eastern Europe eighty years ago. On the other hand, he said, many of the Russian youngsters encountered difficulties adjusting to life in a completely open society. The result has been numerous social problems.

There were widely publicized reports of a "criminal element"[13] emerging from the numbers of Soviet immigrants in northeast Philadelphia. How much substance there was to these accounts was unclear. But relative to crime in general, the Northeast's greatest problem was fear, according to Mary Furtig, an administrator with the Mayor's Commission on Services to the Aging. And much of the fear, she said was unfounded.

Of slightly more than 100,000 major crimes reported in Philadelphia in 1981, the Northeast accounted for 14,293. That was just under 15 percent of the total. Yet the Northeast had more than one-fourth of the city's population. Violent crimes were rare in northeast Philadelphia. "Murders don't happen for the most part on the Jewish side," reported Leon Brown, former editor of the Northeast *Jewish Times*. "Muggings are infrequent. I think people feel a lot safer in the Northeast than in other areas of the city."

Brown said burglaries were probably the most common felony in Northeast Philadelphia, and many of the break-ins were drug related. From time to time, certain neighborhoods faced minor crime problems, but there were no slums. In all of the Northeast, one did not see boarded-up stores or houses. For the most part, the properties were well maintained. Ethnic and community pride remained strong.

There is far more diversity in the Northeast than its critics will acknowledge. Nowhere else in Philadelphia is there a development quite like the one that Morris Milgram built on Longford Street near Holme Circle. Milgram, the son of an Orthodox Jew who emigrated from Russia in 1912, grew up on the Lower East Side of Manhattan. He involved himself in civil rights issues much of his life and worked for integrated housing for more than thirty-five years. On Longford Street, he built nineteen single houses in the contemporary style and created a small, racially integrated community. The purchasers of these houses, starting in 1955, were eleven white families and eight black families. Milgram, who lived there himself for many years, called it Greenbelt Knoll. Admittedly a tiny development, it was one of the few success stories in integrated housing.

In politics, the Northeast is heavily Democratic in registration but not infrequently elects Republican candidates. The section's voting patterns have been watched closely since 1971 when Frank L. Rizzo first ran for mayor. Until then, the so-called Jewish vote in Philadelphia was generally cast for candidates who pledged to help the disadvantaged and defend civil liberties. In 1971 law and order was a key issue, and former Police Commissioner Rizzo was the law-and-order candidate. He spoke to the concerns of the white working class, which felt threatened by liberal programs.

In the Democratic primary, Rizzo defeated William J. Green, who would later succeed him as mayor, and two other candidates, one white and one black. Rizzo's victory was widely attributed to strong support from Jewish voters. Newsweek reported that the former police chief had carried six of the city's eight "Jewish wards." Henry Cohen and Gary Sandrow, who analyzed the vote for the American Jewish Committee, disputed this finding. Although Rizzo carried all fourteen Northeast wards, Cohen and Sandrow's data suggested that "a majority of the Jews who voted in the Democratic primary voted against Rizzo."[14] They concluded that Green got 55 percent of the Jewish primary vote and Rizzo 42 percent. By contrast, they said that Rizzo captured 67 percent of the total white vote (including the Jewish vote) to Green's 31 percent.

In the predominantly Jewish wards, the vote split along class lines, with Rizzo getting 54.7 percent of the ballots in the lower-middle-class divisions but only 31.9 percent in upper-middle-class ones. The same split along class lines was found in predominantly Jewish divisions in Northeast Philadelphia. In the lower-middle-class 54th Ward, thirteen predominantly Jewish divisions gave Rizzo 53 percent of the vote to 44 percent for Green. But in the middle-class 58th Ward, Green got 56 percent of the vote from seven predominantly Jewish divisions to 41 percent for Rizzo. And six predominantly Jewish divisions in the 63rd Ward gave two-thirds of their votes to Green.

Rizzo won the general election with 53 percent of the total vote to 47 percent for Republican Thacher Longstreth. Cohen and Sandrow found the Northeast's Jewish voters again dividing along class lines. In the middle-class 63rd Ward, Longstreth carried the predominantly Jewish divisions by 60 to 40. But in the lower-middle class 54th Ward, the predominantly Jewish divisions swung to Rizzo by 58 percent to 42 percent. In the citywide balloting, Cohen and Sandrow concluded that although whites favored Rizzo by a margin of about 2 to 1, Jewish voters may have given a "slight edge" to Longstreth. They wrote,

> In view of these findings, the tendency of some to attribute Rizzo's victory to Jewish voters seems rather strange, until one considers the expectations which certain people, Jews and non-Jews alike, have of Jews. Blacks and white liberals have long counted on Jews to oppose political leaders and programs that seem to ignore the needs of the disadvantaged and to threaten fundamental liberties. Rightly or wrongly, Rizzo was thought to pose such a threat. Jewish voters did not rush to Rizzo as did more than two out of every three non-Jewish white voters in Philadelphia; they voted for and against him in approximately even numbers. But that was not good enough for those who had expected Jews—and Jews alone—to remain unaffected by the law-and-order issue.

When Rizzo ran successfully for reelection in 1975, an estimated 53 percent of Jewish voters supported him. Three years later, however, when the mayor sought a change in the Philadelphia City Charter that would have permitted him to run for a third term, Jewish Philadelphians voted against the change by 69 percent to 31 percent. In that vote, all classes of Jewish voters opposed the change. "It is probably no exaggeration to suggest," one observer noted later, "that Black and Jewish voters, along with some upper-class White Anglo-Saxon Protestants, defeated the Charter change and frustrated Rizzo's plan.[15] Rizzo lost the 1983 Democratic primary to W. Wilson Goode, who went on to win election that fall as Philadelphia's first black mayor. Sandra Featherman, who analyzed that year's voting for the American Jewish Committee, reported that in the city's predominantly Jewish divisions, Goode got about 30 percent of the primary vote against Rizzo and about 32 percent of the vote in the general election when he defeated Republican John Egan and independent Democrat Thomas Leonard.

In the Northeast's 53rd and 54th Wards, she found, Goode got about 32 percent of the "Jewish vote" in the general election but only about 13 percent of the "Italian vote" and 15 percent of the "Irish vote." Goode ran far stronger in the Northeast than had any previous black candidate for mayor. His promises to crack down on lawbreakers, his no-nonsense approach to city governance, and his independence of the Democratic party organization appeared to make a strong impression on the Northeast electorate.

As we have seen, Northeasterners' feelings of alienation have deep roots. That section has long believed that it owes nothing to either political party. Its farmers, it will be recalled, opposed the 1854 Consolidation Act that brought them into the city. In the 1950s Northeast groups opposed to housing sprawl threatened secession. And in 1983 Frank Salvatore, a Republican state assemblyman, sought to organize another secession movement. He charged that in viewing their city government and public school system, Northeast Philadelphians "too often feel unimportant and left out."

The secession movement never cohered, but Salvatore clearly spoke for many of his neighbors. In a 1971 study, Ruth Bennett and Jed Rakoff found that the Northeast's "most striking characteristic"[16] was its powerlessness. They saw the section's lack of "clout" as anomalous in that it was Philadelphia's largest community in terms of land area, population, and wealth. Its interests were suburban, but its politics were urban, Bennett and Rakoff said, and therefore it was "neither here nor there."

In the Bennett-Rakoff analysis, the typical Northeasterner was portrayed as feeling "poor and neglected" by comparison to suburbanites across the city line. But to other city dwellers, the Northeast's problems of education, transportation, zoning, recreation, and pollution seemed "comparatively trivial." Not only were Northeast Jews cut off from the city proper, said Bennett and Rakoff, they were also isolated from other, more affluent Jews in Center City and the suburbs.

"Their values are increasingly at variance with the Whig liberalism of better situated Jews," wrote Bennett and Rakoff, "not to mention the radicalism of the wealthier collegiate clique." And they added, "If the attitude of the Northeast Jews toward the Establishment Jew is tinged with trifle envy, the attitude of the Establishment Jew toward the Northeast Jew partakes not a little of aloofness, occasionally bordering on contempt."

Partly as a result of this estrangement, the Northeast Jew has not been well served by Jewish social services, Bennett and Rakoff said. "As in his relations with city government, he feels ignored, neglected, frustrated in his aspirations." Since Bennett and Rakoff completed their analysis, steps have been taken to improve relations between Establishment Jews and the Northeast's Jewish community.

A range of new facilities and social services has been provided by the Federation of Jewish Agencies of Greater Philadelphia and other organizations. Between 1972 and 1982, Federation Housing built 658 rent-subsidized apartment units for older adults in the Northeast. In 1975 Jewish Y's and Centers of Greater Philadelphia opened its Klein Branch at Red Lion and Jameson Roads. One of the largest and most complete community centers on the East Coast, it is used by more than 20,000 persons each year. With the opening of the Klein Branch, the David Neuman Center, formerly a neighborhood facility, was converted into a senior center.

In 1979 the Jewish Educational and Vocational Service opened a large vocational training facility at 1330 Rhawn Street in the Northeast. The A. P. Orleans Vocational Center offers training

The Klein Branch JYC.

in all trades, as well as classes in English as a second language for Russian and other immigrants and workshops for emotionally disturbed, physically handicapped, and mentally retarded persons.

The Samuel Paley Day Care Center, which opened in the Northeast in 1965, later added four branches and two extension programs. And the Jewish Family Service of Philadelphia offers walk-in service for elderly Northeast Jews at 6445 Castor Avenue.

In 1985, Northeast Philadelphia, in contrast to so many other parts of the city, was free of slums. Its schools were adequate and its housing serviceable. Some of its shopping districts were deteriorating, but its most critical need was probably housing for its aging population of over 91,000. The *Jewish Times* counted fourteen nursing homes, three government-subsidized senior citizen apartment complexes, and many personal care homes and boarding homes for the elderly. But it also reported that only two of the city's thirty-two senior centers were located in the Northeast, even though it had more older people than any other section of the city and was the only section to experience an increase in its elderly population in the 1970s.

It has now been over fifty years since the building of Northeast Philadelphia gained momentum. What is one to make of this remarkable section? It was developed at a time when low-cost, single-family housing was being mass produced in many metropolitan areas. And the social critics were virtually unanimous in their condemnation of the trend: "For literally nothing down," wrote John Keats, a former Philadelphian, in 1957, "you too can find a box of your own in one of the fresh-air slums we're building around the edges of American cities inhabited by people whose age, income, number of children, problems, habits, conversation, dress, possessions and perhaps even blood types are also precisely like yours. . . . They are developments conceived in error, nurtured by greed, corroding everything they touch. They . . . actually drive mad myriads of housewives shut up in them."[17]

While Levitt was the most obvious target, the developers of Northeast Philadelphia also drew criticism. In *Philadelphia: A 300-Year History,* Joseph S. Clark and Dennis Clark wrote that most of the Northeast's housing was unattractive, "inviting a slum of the future." "The exploitation of the Northeast in the period 1946–1968 is one of the great tragedies of modern Philadelphia," they charged. They also said that the market for its brand of "new cheap housing" was created by "white Jewish and Irish Philadelphians anxious to move away from the growing black population around center city."[18]

What happened in Philadelphia after World War II occurred in many other American cities. It was one of the most remarkable mass movements of population in U.S. history. The federal gov-

Looking northeast along Roosevelt Boulevard and Castor Avenue from Oxford Circle in the late twenties, there is clearly room for development and growth.

ernment encouraged it by building highways linking city and suburbs and by guaranteeing home mortgages in the new all-white sections while refusing them in black and integrated city neighborhoods. That the builders of new housing excluded blacks was surely a blot on their records. In a larger sense, however, it was a mark of the racism that then permeated all aspects of American life.

The Northeast's monotonous row housing has often been attacked but rarely by the people who live there. After declaring that there was "something basically obscene about row homes,"[19]

In the early thirties, houses were built in the Northeast that served as models for block after block of residential neighborhoods. These, on Elbridge Street, attempt to break the monotony of the rowhouse design.

writer Maury Levy, who grew up in the Northeast, said of it, "Despite a cookie-cutter housing, rotten transportation, overcrowded schools and spot zoning, the land, to its people, is still a little bit of heaven."

Herbert J. Gans, the sociologist, made a similar point about Willingboro, Levitt's New Jersey community: "It is easy to propose community improvements and even utopian communities that will make Levittown seem obsolete. Yet I should like to emphasize once more that whatever its imperfections, Levittown is a good place to live."[20]

In their 1971 analysis of Northeast Philadelphia, Ruth Bennett and Jed Rakoff wrote, "Since 1945 the Northeast has been filling up with Jews, Catholics and Protestants of German descent who wanted the amenities of suburbia but could not afford the price. Abandoning, at financial sacrifice, the deteriorated ethnic neighborhoods of their childhood—but unable to jump to the golden ghettos of suburbia—they compromised on the new little homes of the Northeast. . . . In recent years, however, many families who could afford to move elsewhere have elected to remain in the Northeast because they feel it convenient to live here. Though people refer to the Northeast often as a ghetto there is much more diversity here than in many suburbs."[21]

What is the future of Northeast Philadelphia? It has been losing population and probably will continue to do so. There has been no mass exodus, but Jewish families, one by one, have been moving to such suburbs as Melrose Park, Merion, Huntingdon Valley, and Pine Valley, New Jersey. Whereas Morrell Park was once heavily Jewish, "you couldn't get a minyan" there in the 1980s. Many observers correctly predicted that in the 1990s, the center of the Northeast's Jewish population would move from the Welsh Road area to lower Bucks County.

The outward movement of the Northeast's Jews may be inexorable, but it remains one of the nation's largest Jewish communities. A 1984 Federation of Jewish Agencies study[22] found that of 252,364 Jews in Philadelphia, Montgomery, Delaware, and Bucks counties, 70,000 were living in Northeast Philadelphia and another 46,000 in the nearby suburbs in eastern Montgomery County and lower Bucks. The Greater Northeast was the area leader in Jewish population, accounting for just over half of the city's total of 138,386.

While its problems are formidable, the Northeast has retained its basic stability. With the current emphasis on fuel efficiency, once-demeaned row houses are once again popular (but now they're called "town houses"), and Northeast Philadelphia has a huge stock of them. In time, the well-constructed, economically priced units built by Hyman Korman and Alfred P. Orleans may regain grudging respect. And if they do, the Jewish immigrants who played such a major role in the development of a large part of Philadelphia will enjoy posthumous vindication.

HOME AND HAVEN
Soviet Jewish Immigration to Philadelphia, 1972–1982

Nora Levin

Soviet Jews in the United States live scattered over the country in more than one hundred cities and towns, with most in large urban centers. More than half live in New York City. An exact count of the number in Philadelphia is not known, but the best estimate is 5,000 to 6,000, including 3,982 officially routed to Philadelphia by the United HIAS Service and 1,500 or so who have migrated from other cities.[1] Philadelphia is one of the more favored cities "because it has a large Jewish population and cultural attractions such as museums and musical activities and a reputed Old World atmosphere," as expressed by an émigré to one Jewish agency head. Undoubtedly, reunion with relatives already living here was also an influencing factor.

Many of the Jews who came to the United States during this period were third- and fourth-generation Soviet citizens and constituted the single, most highly educated ethnic group in the USSR, occupying prominent roles in technical fields, science, and culture. In 1979, the peak year of Soviet Jewish emigration (51,320), 1,369 came to Philadelphia. Of this number, 75 percent came from Kiev and Odessa, but other cities were also represented: 31 from Kharkov, 31 from Kishinev, 50 from Moscow, 41 from Lvov, 18 from Leningrad, 17 from Riga. Small numbers also came from Tashkent, Baku, Chernovtsy, and Belaya Tserkov. In terms of age groups, 217 were age 60 and over; 359, from 40 to 59; 380 from 20 to 39; and 327 from 1 to 19, with 181 up to 10 years of age. Occupationally, 163 were in professional-academic fields (engineers, doctors, economists, geologists, musicians, nurses); 468 in middle-level occupations (mechanics, bookkeepers, photographers, draftsmen, clerks); and 22 in unskilled positions.[2]

Generally speaking, the Soviet Jews who came to Philadelphia were very well-educated and highly acculturated into Russian/Soviet culture though not to Soviet society. Some came with a strong, positive sense of their Jewishness, but for most, Jewish identity was mainly a reaction to anti-Semitism. The entire experience of emigration, however, seemed to awaken an awareness of Jewish identity. Dr. Jerome Gilson of Baltimore Hebrew College pointed out, "It was only by asserting his Jewishness that [a Jew] could acquire the exit visa from the Soviet Government, and from the time he arrives in Vienna, he is given help because he is a Jew, and this help comes exclusively from Jews."[3] Suddenly, from being a disadvantage in the Soviet Union, Jewishness confers advantages. Attitudes seem to become more open to things Jewish. Observers have noted that many Russians buy Mogen Davids upon their arrival in Rome. Yet this very openness is soon overwhelmed by the first traumatic years of dealing with basic economic realities.

How much of a positive attitude toward Jewishness could be sustained during this period depended to a large extent on whether or not Jewish agency staffs, who had been primarily involved in the resettlement process, had themselves a strong sense of their Jewishness and transmit their commitment to the newcomers. In Philadelphia, as in other communities, the question of Jewish identity among Soviet Jews did not come to the fore until 1980, but early impressions confirmed the findings of other studies, namely, that most Soviet Jews came with a negative sense of their Jewishness and even a fear of it. Being Jewish was a handicap in the Soviet Union; it kept you out of many desirable places, robbed you of rightful recognition and promotion, and was fundamentally a handicap. No positive experiences surrounded Jewishness, and nothing in Soviet culture strengthened it. Quite the reverse. Contact with a caring Jewish agency might bring home a component of Jewish awareness, but this contact was itself at first surrounded by suspicion and mistrust. As Elizabeth Geggel, supervisor of the Soviet Resettlement Program of Jewish Family Service from 1975 to 1982, put it: "To force them into a Jewish identity without their understanding it is counterproductive."

Understandably, the primary adjustments in the first years were psychological, economic, and social, and the effectiveness of these adjustments was determined largely by the expectations, attitudes, and reactions of Soviet Jews, including relations with American Jews. For their part, American Jews, including communal staff, knew very little about the Soviet experiences of the immigrants; many believed they should have gone to Israel. Thee misunderstandings and mutual disappointments also involved vast cultural gaps that are hard to bridge.

Not only have these Jews from the former Soviet Union been officially denied access to Jewish traditions, sources, and contacts with other Jewries, but they have been overwhelmed by negative, disfigured images of Judaism, Zionism, Israel, and of themselves as Jews, fostered and inflamed by all the Soviet media, schools, press, literature, and official policy. It required enormous strength and will to feel proud to be a Jew in the Soviet Union, and few came with that pride. No other Jewish immigration has come to the United States so lacking in bonds with the Jewish past and with other Jews, so ignorant of Jewish history and tradition, and having so little to fill the substance of its Jewishness.

Initially and up to 1977, most Soviet newcomers came as conditional entrants, or, technically, refugees under old immigration laws. Between 1978 and 1980, they were accepted as parolees, that is, they were physically admitted to the United States conditionally and had to live here for two years before they became permanent residents, qualifying them to receive the prized "green cards."

A rally protesting Soviet anti-Semitism, Independence Square, March 29, 1965. The rally is being addressed by Philip M. Klutznik, flanked by Governor Raymond P. Shafer (left) and Mayor Tate.

This two-tier system involved the loss of two years from the naturalization requirement and caused a great deal of confusion and distress, which were largely resolved by the passage of the Refugee Act of 1980. Since that time, all immigrants have been admitted under a uniform code.[4]

Philadelphia HIAS and the Council Migration Service were the first Jewish agency contacts for the newcomers, with staff meeting them and putting them up in temporary housing. (In subsequent years, they were housed by relatives.) HIAS also acquainted them with their legal rights and obligations in the United States; helped in the naturalization process, the search for lost relatives, and reunification of families; and acted as a general counseling agency when an immigrant was reluctant to go elsewhere.[5]

When the first flow of immigrants came in the early seventies, some moved to the Logan neighborhood, as well as Oxford Circle, but the vast majority now live in the Greater Northeast, particularly in the area from 9000 to 12000 Bustleton Avenue, and both east and west of the street. Some apartment houses, such as the Diplomat, house many of the immigrants.

When the flow of immigration was high, HIAS held group welcoming receptions that many dozens, even hundreds of immigrants attended. A general orientation was given at such times by agency personnel and lay leaders, whose remarks were translated into Russian. *A Basic Handbook for Soviet Migrants* was also provided, containing basic facts about American society, education, health care, transportation, money, weights and measures, and Jewish organizations.[6]

From HIAS, newcomers moved along through a network of Jewish agencies: Jewish Family Service, reorganized in 1983 and renamed Jewish Family Children's Agency (JFCA); Jewish Employment and Vocational Service (JEVS); Federation Day Care Services for child care; and the Jewish Y's and Centers (JYC, now Jewish Community Centers), including the David G. Neuman Senior Center. The resettlement of Soviet immigrants was thus largely handled by professional social workers and counselors.

JFCA caseworkers had the primary responsibility for individual family adjustment, including the goal of self-support. In the course of interviews, social workers tried to explain the concept of a helping Jewish agency—a very difficult one to convey to the newcomers—and the availability of this help. Within a week of arrival, appointments were made with JEVS for language evaluation and assignment to appropriate English classes. JFCA also made appointments with the Department of Public Assistance to enable newcomers to apply for food stamps and medical assistance and with Einstein Medical Center in cases of known illnesses. Several newcomers had to be sent straight to the hospital. Monthly lists of new arrivals were sent to the JYC (Klein Branch) where they received one-year (later, six-month) memberships.

From 1976 to October 1978, one year's financial assistance through grants and loans was provided by the Federation of Jewish Agencies (FJA) through Jewish Family Service. After October 1978, the federal government agreed to help through a block grant agreement, with the government and the Federation each supplying 50 percent of the total amount for a half-year's support.[7] This grant was based on approximately $2000 per year per immigrant administered through various agencies. After December 1979, the term was reduced from six to three months, with increased emphasis on help from relatives.[8]

Soviet conditioning had created habits of thought and behavior worlds away from customary American patterns. Like other citizens of the former Soviet Union, Jews had been conditioned to expect all services and decisions to come from the government. While the dependence on authority is very strong, the need to deal with a faceless, oppressive, and often inconsistent regime created coping mechanisms such as evasiveness, vague responses to direct questions, distrust of most people, and sudden outbursts of anger and hostility. Sudden personal freedom was thus both thrilling and threatening. Autonomous, self-initiating activities and decisions and voluntary associations, so familiar and easy for American Jews, were strange and bewildering to Soviet Jews. An unregimented day-by-day life was frightening in the early weeks of resettlement, as was, and for many still is, the seeming chaos of a pluralistic society, democratic discussions, and a diverse organizational life.

In Philadelphia, as in other communities, interpretation of these strange phenomena and guidance in understanding them was given to various Jewish communal agencies involved in the resettlement process. Giving up their intense fantasies about America proved to be a major problem confronting newcomers. These expectations were much higher and in sharp contrast to those of previous immigrations. Soviet immigrants had almost no access to accurate information and discounted practically everything in the press and other media. Moreover, applying for permission to leave the Soviet Union was almost always accompanied by loss of work and stigmatization, making one an enemy of the country. It thus required courage to leave and a high level of expectation in order to undergo the many hardships connected with leaving.[9]

Newcomers also had illusions about what it meant to be an immigrant. Because of the worldwide publicity on behalf of Soviet Jewish emigration—the numerous newspaper stories, the rallies, the vigils before Soviet embassies, and adoption of *refuseniks* by Congressmen—they felt that they were uniquely wanted by the United States. Thus, they did not consider themselves refugees like Jews who fled from Hitler-Europe, but rather that they made a choice, involving some sacrifices, in emigrating and expected a reception commensurate with these expectations.[10] Such feelings were also reinforced by the privileged treatment accorded defectors to the USSR, including special housing and high-paying jobs. The collapse of these illusions on arrival in America was very painful and pushed some of the newcomers into severe depression.

In the early years especially, communication between Jewish agency staff and the immigrants was difficult. Very few staff had any substantial knowledge of Soviet life or Russian, while the immigrants, not having any experience of a voluntary counseling service, were suspicious and mistrustful and felt threatened. Benjamin Sprafkin, former executive director of Jewish Family Service in Philadelphia, acknowledged that "in the first few years of this resettlement experience we were preoccupied with learning to understand the Soviet Jewish family and its differences from earlier immigrant families that came in the 1930s and after World War II. This understanding we had to apply immediately while providing them with their basic needs. The specifics of the situation soon became clear to us: more than earlier immigrants, they needed help in coping with their unrealistic expectations of life in the United States. Further, they had to be made aware of the increased personal responsibility as it exists in a country with a non-authoritarian government."[11]

The counseling agency seemed threatening because it smacked of an official bureaucracy. Besides, Soviet Jews were used to concrete services, not people who "just talk." In order to overcome some of these apprehensions, Yiddish- and Russian-speaking social workers were used to interview and interpret procedures. At times, English-speaking newcomers also helped as translators. Regular counseling appointments were set during the time of community financial help, but generally the agency was little used after a family had become financially independent. Those who came back discussed family problems involving unemployment stress, role reversals, and family tensions.

Many stories reveal the rigidity of Soviet conditioning that complicates adjustment to America. For example, at one large suburban synagogue during Rosh Hashanah, Soviet Jews were aghast to see police standing by. "What! Police here in the United States, too?" they claimed. We also heard that a Soviet Jewish immigrant drove through a red light in his eagerness to show the police his identity card. At JEVS, counselors were asked how the American government could have invited Soviet Jews here and not provide jobs for them. A shoemaker asked why he wasn't being sent customers. A physician who could have worked with a famous cardiologist said that he couldn't study with him: "I have to study my books."[12]

To help newcomers through difficult adjustments and enable them to meet American Jews, an Adoptive Family Project was started in Philadelphia. Charlotte Bernstein, a board member of Jewish Family Service initiated the program in 1975 whereby a Soviet Jewish family was matched with an American Jewish family, with similar age levels, numbers of children, and occupations. The volunteers were trained by agency professional staff and worked closely with them. These American-Soviet family relationships were extremely helpful to the immigrants in finding apartments, making job contracts, shopping—the supermarkets were at first baffling—opening bank accounts, learning to send packages (a service that is handled by the post office in the Soviet Union), becoming familiar with public transportation, helping register children at school, recommending doctors, and answering questions about myriad problems of daily living. The program grew and eventually involved 250 American families. Both sets of families intervisited and some lasting relationships developed. In the early period, Rabbi Yaacov Rosenberg, then of Adath Jeshurun, and Rabbi Harold Romirowsky of the Oxford Circle Jewish Community Centre were especially active in encouraging this project in welcoming Soviet Jewish immigrants to their syn-

Left: Hanukah 1967 vigil outside
Independence Hall — holding torch is
Sydney C. Orloff, JCRC president.

Right: Rabbi J. Harold Romirowsky, 1970.

agogues, and in planning holiday programs, *sedarim,* and services for them. Dr. Leon Friedman, a volunteer for JFCA since 1976, an officer in B'nai B'rith, and fluent in Russian, also was very helpful in situations involving social and government agencies,[13] in arranging cultural events, and in encouraging self-help initiatives.

The Soviet authoritarian stance also exists within the Soviet Jewish family and, in collision with American values and practices, caused conflict and even breakdown. Children learn English more quickly and put parents' authority in jeopardy. If the wife finds work before her husband, his role may be diminished. Older parents may continue to be controlling, as they were in the Soviet Union, creating generational tensions and, at times, marital problems.[14] Problems also were created by our freer school system, as opposed to the strict discipline in the Soviet Union. Soviet parents were disturbed by the looseness in classrooms, the ease with which American children challenged teachers, and the absence of demanding, regular homework. They were also shocked by American sexual permissiveness, widespread crime, littered streets, graffiti, and what they termed "too much democracy."[15] These realities further strained the Soviet traditional family structure and added to the stress of adjustment.

Aged immigrants also underwent painful experiences, perhaps the most severe of any age group. These were the 50-, 60- and 70-year-olds who struggled and suffered in the Soviet Union through the early years of the Revolution, civil war, economic hardships, and the horrors of World War II. Just when they reached retirement age and received a pension that gave them independence and a certain equilibrium, they found themselves pressured into leaving the Soviet Union in order to enable their children to leave. Thus, they uprooted themselves unwillingly and found few compensations here, especially in the first few years.[16] Whereas in the Soviet Union it was common for three generations to live together in small quarters, in America it was not. Frictions were inflamed, and the former independence and respect enjoyed in the Soviet Union vanished. Older immigrants also found it very difficult to learn English, and many acutely missed their friends and the cultural attractions to which they had become accustomed. According to Iosif Shnayderman, a psychia-

Language is clearly a major obstacle the Russian immigrant confronts. Here, Helen Schneeberg conducts an English class for Russian Jews.

trist trained in the Soviet Union, who worked as a therapist at the offices of PATH (People Acting to Help), nearly half of the newcomers, especially the older ones, suffered from nervous disorders and depression due to the stress of resettlement, unemployment, and family problems. The drastic decline in emigration in more recent years caused a resurgence of depression among the longer settled as well, according to. Shnayderman.

This cultural yearning cannot easily be met in Northeast Philadelphia, and theater and symphony concerts, easily and cheaply accessible to Jews in Kiev, Odessa, Leningrad, and Moscow, were out of their financial reach. There was also an educational edge that Soviet Jews had over American Jews, which left some of them, at least initially, intellectually dissatisfied. In 1981 a comparison was made of twenty Soviet Jews and twenty others between ages 66 and 73 who attended the Neuman Center. Soviet Jews averaged twelve years of formal education, while the others averaged only nine years.

In contrast with the situation in the Soviet Union, where advancing age garnered respect and authority, the United States has a youth-oriented culture, in which everyone over 45 is considered as "older" and at some disadvantage. There was also the painful adjustment to the low American Supplementary Security Income (SSI) after having received a comfortable Soviet pension (at age 55 for women and age 62 for men).

It has been said that older Soviet Jews will never reap the benefits of America. They found it very difficult to learn English and generally could not find work except baby-sitting. They had a meager income from SSI—$300[17] per month for a single person and $450 per couple—and often had serious health problems: heart disease, circulatory problems, strokes, overweight, and gastrointestinal problems. Because extended medical care was needed, older Soviet Jews were reluctant to give up their medical assistance coverage by accepting a job that may not include medical insurance benefits.

Health care in the Soviet Union among the immigrants generally was neglected. They had no experience of preventive medicine and were reluctant to have medical checkups. Sprafkin noted, "Many women have had so many abortions that they have serious gynecological problems when they reach middle age. They need reassurance and help to get to the proper resources. A number of the men who were in World War II have health problems connected with injuries. Practically all are in need of dental and optical care." To help ease the problem of huge medical and dental costs, Jewish Family Service worked out a cooperative relationship with the Einstein Medical Center Family Practice Clinic, which agreed to see new immigrants even before they had their green cards. A Russian-speaking worker assisted both doctors and patients at the clinic. Einstein also set up a Russian/Yiddish Language Information Desk. Volunteers who spoke these languages were also available during clinic visits. They visited inpatients, interpreted for them, accompanied them for necessary medical procedures, and assisted staff by making phone calls to patients who missed or needed to reschedule appointments.[18]

Virtually every study and sampling of Soviet Jews who came to the United States agree that the most profound source of their initial distress lay in their inability to find work quickly and job declassment. In the Soviet Union, everyone worked, no one was unemployed, and no one ever had to search for a job. Work was provided by the State, and one often worked at the same job for life. Moreover, every job had a status-value and often a high-sounding title, of special significance to Jews, who had lost so much of their ego-strength because of mounting anti-Semitism in the Soviet Union and the closing off of many fields. Their job skills, however, were difficult to evaluate in American job-market terms. Moreover, many immigrants did not have salable skills in American terms. The concept of upward mobility was bewildering, and low, entry-level jobs were humiliating, especially for men. Professionally trained individuals, such as doctors, dentists, and nurses arrived with no understanding of our examination and licensing requirements and were hurt and resentful when they learn that they could not immediately step into positions on the level of their work in the Soviet Union. Moreover, job descriptions and connotations in the Soviet Union had little relevance in the United States. Many of the engineers especially were frustrated in this regard.

Newcomers were first given English language and job-skill evaluations. Some were so highly motivated, they sat in English classes three times a day. A number walked twenty to thirty blocks from home to classes to save bus fare; they "walked in Russia," they said. Those fortunate enough to obtain work quickly, even at low, entry-level jobs, adjusted best, it seems, even though the declassment was bitter for them. Often, in their eagerness to do well and make more money, they asked for overtime. For others, there was great bewilderment and disappointment. "You have my job," they told the job counselor, or, "I dreamt about my job in America," to which the counselor would have to say, "I don't have the job of your dreams, but a year from now we're going to laugh together."[19]

Beginning in October 1977, JEVS offered five training courses, at first funded by CETA, to unemployed, underemployed, or economically disadvantaged residents of Philadelphia, including Soviet newcomers. The courses were air-conditioning and refrigeration, electrical wiring, appliance repair and maintenance, heating and plumbing, clerical skills, and English as a second language. Later, courses in food service, machine shop skills, and building maintenance were added.

JEVS help and support was intensive, protective, and firm. Counselors often accompanied applicants to the workplace. Sample resumes were provided, and representative ads and job application forms were photocopied. Telephone inquiry calls to prospective employers were rehearsed and videotaped to provide a basis for evaluation, and newspaper job ads and abbreviations were studied. Paychecks and tax deductions were analyzed. The role of employment agencies was explained. An interesting self-inventory urged Soviet Jews to emphasize their positive traits and abilities. It was explained that if an employer asked someone to "come in Monday," it didn't necessarily mean he was hired. Emphasis was also placed on the importance of taking a first job—to gain experience, confidence, and practice in using English. Obviously, all of these experiences created great anxiety. Some Soviet Jews exploded with anger and frustration. They would ask for the job counselor's "superior" to make complaints or demands. Some found it hard to stay on the job eight hours a day and to start promptly at 8:00 or 9:00 a.m.[20] because of the somewhat casual atmosphere in many workplaces in the Soviet Union, but observers generally had the impression that newcomers here were ambitious and highly motivated.

Among those who were able to find work were bookkeepers, beauticians, and air-conditioning and heating technicians. Some who were particularly enterprising went into business for themselves, operating beauty parlors, fruit stores, and restaurants. But sports coaches, women linotype operators, economists, lawyers, teachers, Soviet-trained engineers, physicians, and city planners, among others, were virtually impossible to place in their fields and had to undergo retraining. As of the spring of 1983, only one of the fifteen to twenty physicians was practicing medicine.

Left: The Soviet Jewry Freedom Van at the Liberty Bell, April 1979.

Right: Russian immigrants find the foods, music, and camaraderie of their homeland in the Northeast's Stolichnoy Restaurant.

In the fall of 1976, Jewish Family Service conducted a limited study [21] to determine how the first one hundred Soviet Jewish families resettled in Philadelphia were faring. The period covered was September 1973 to January 1975. A questionnaire was devised that related to career and employment, housing, religious affiliation, education and culture, and adjustment. Fifty-eight families were contacted, and all but one person (who had died) were interviewed. The remaining forty-two could not be located, an "indication both that they are taking advantage of their freedom as well as expressing some mistrust of people who may wish to locate them." Ninety-one percent had male heads of households, 71 percent of whom were employed.

Twenty percent earned less than $5,000 per year; 33 percent from $5,000 to $9,999; 30 percent from $10,000 to $14,999; 6 percent from $15,000 to $19,999; and 11 percent, $20,000 or more. Most of those questioned regarding hoped-for family income in five years could not even guess at an answer. Thirty-eight percent of the heads of the household said that in five years they expected to do the same thing they were presently doing. These last two answers suggest that Soviet Jews had not comprehended the American process of upward mobility.

In answering a question contrasting their latest Soviet job with the present American job, forty-two people responded. Thirty-six percent said that their present job was better; 35 percent that it was lower; 19 percent said that there was no important difference. Seventy percent said they were satisfied with their career progress; 26 percent were not, and 4 percent were uncertain. Regarding housing, of the fifty-four who responded, 70 percent were renters, and 30 percent were property owners. A large percentage indicated that their present home had more space than their home in the Soviet Union, and many more conveniences, such as private kitchens and bathrooms, a private entrance, and laundry facilities. The average rental was $248.87 per month. Conspicuous consumption habits had become fixed very early, with many newcomers already owning televisions, automobiles, stereo record players, and air-conditioners.

Even if we discount some of these responses and see them as a desire to answer in a way that would please authorities, they showed an astonishing level of economic achievement. However, at the time, the country was not suffering from a recession. The survey, moreover, revealed little about the question of Jewish identity. Of the forty-three who answered the question, 77 percent had attended synagogue, and 33 percent said they had joined—an inconclusive response. This issue would be addressed later. A later survey also indicated a good rate of job placement after training, but at quite low rates. From October 1, 1978, to the end of 1982, 1,646 Soviet immigrants received employment counseling, job development, and job placement services. A cumulative total of 1,017 job placements were made.[22] It is estimated that 80 percent of all employable immigrants started working after one year, 26 percent of whom were working in their own field.[23] However, those holding low-entry jobs lost them in periods of recession. One agency counselor noted that they were "the last to be hired and the first fired."

In contrast to earlier immigrants, a self-help employment network among Soviet Jews was very slow to develop. Counselors noted that except for immediate family help, they were often secretive and competitive and didn't tell each other where they were working. Those who had "arrived" had been heard to say, "Don't send me any Russians." The habits created by the widespread underground economy in the Soviet Union lingered on and contributed to the unreported, secretive activity. Some beauticians and dentists, for example, operated from their homes.

Careful budgeting habits were difficult to instill among people accustomed to shortages and long queues. Some, in their excitement over material comforts, contracted for expensive apartments, bought large (used) automobiles, and took photographs of their new possessions, which they then proudly sent to the Soviet Union. In this desire to put their best foot forward and possibly arouse the envy of relatives and friends back home, they were not so different from Jews who came to the United States one hundred years earlier. America seems to provoke exaggeration. At the same time, many observers note that material benefits and opportunities here have inspired hard work and frugal habits.

Spurred by the large influx of immigrants in 1979 and the exposure to certain American Jewish models of self-help, eight Soviet Jewish immigrants decided to join together in October 1979 to help each other and other newcomers become "more successful, independent members of the American community." A sum of $13,480, in the form of a grant from the Refugee Resettlement Division of the U.S. Department of Health and Human Services, was given to the group, which called itself the Russian Immigrant Brotherhood (RIB) or, sometimes, the Soviet Newcomers Organization (SNO), for the period from January through October 1980. A community organization worker was assigned as a consultant to monitor their activities in a nondirective, advisory capacity. The group sold $1 membership cards and claimed a membership of five hundred very quickly. The founders formed into a "presidium," which was divided into such various committees as transportation, cultural activities, newspaper, and so on. The head of the group was Menasha Stelmakh, a poet and journalist in the Soviet Union, who was arrested and jailed four times for his writings before being expelled in 1975. The purpose of RIB, according to Stelmakh, was to "help Soviet Jews adjust to the differences in life-style they encounter in the United States." It's easy to

Russian immigrants bring with them a rich cultural heritage, which includes (among many other things) an exuberance in dancing, dining, and entertainment.

The Russian-Jewish community in America faces many of the problems experienced by the general population—such as elder care—but often does not have the resources to deal with them.

explain the difference, he observed. You just say, "It's another planet. . . . In the USSR, you need government papers just to get a new apartment. Here I move from New York to Philadelphia. I change cities and nobody says anything. I go; I come; it's my business. The whole thing is a different psychology."[24]

In her first report, the community worker noted that the group provided transportation for Jewish Family Service clients to the Einstein Medical Center and various offices; provided volunteer translators two full days each week to the Einstein Medical Center; distributed donations of clothing, furniture, and utensils to the Soviet newcomers; provided information regarding Section 8 housing; arranged three large Jewish holiday programs and a youth dance; printed and distributed a newsletter to five hundred Soviet Jewish families; organized a band; and began the organization of a sports team and day care center. The newsletter was typed in Russian and contained cartoons, photographs, news and sports events in Israel, current affairs, letters to the editor, and advice for adjusting to American life. In an editorial, Stelmakh himself spoke poignantly of the need to overcome self-isolation:

> Isolation—it is a dreadful crime! I can testify to this out of personal experience. . . . But these gloomy episodes are now far behind us. Yet, now, when we are in a free world, what a paradox it is, that many of us voluntarily lock ourselves in isolation chambers as in a private cloister. Of course, personal problems precede everything. And, in truth, much many-layered anxiety lies on our shoulders. We have to start our lives from scratch. For many of us, our life is autumnal. Our age is such that we cannot make long-ranging plans. Much of our waning strength we have left behind, through by no means easy toil, in our stepmotherland. And yet I remain a partisan of partnership, of the collective.

In numerous passages stressing the self-help concept, the paper used Hillel's maxim slightly revised: "If not We, who? If not now, when?"

Complications, however, arose over the roles of the community worker, and a leadership struggle resulted in the withdrawal of some members.[25] Efforts to organize a day care center and Soviet Jewish college youth also revealed the difficulties of developing immigrant initiative and arriving at a consensus because of previous conditioning, especially the absolute reliance on an external authority figure and bewilderment when it wasn't available.[26] The lack of advance funding also contributed to the decline of those efforts. One can point to numerous similar groping beginnings in the formation and collapse of *landsmanshaften,* Jewish unions, schools, literary societies, and Yiddish newspapers in the experience of earlier Jewish immigrant groups. What remained then, as now, was the spark of initiative that continues to find new challenges and channels of expression, as will be described.

Attitudes within the Philadelphia Jewish community were significant in the resettlement and acculturation processes. However, aside from the Adopt-A-Family Program, the specific professional tasks of Jewish communal agencies, and the occasional programs of a few organizations, the community as a whole lacked a coordinated approach and set of goals. The local Soviet Jewry Council was concerned solely with promoting the right of emigration to Israel, and the leadership generally had a negative view of Soviet Jews who immigrated to the U.S. Moreover, for several years, American Jews had been embroiled in the contentious arguments over so-called noshrim, or "dropouts," those Soviet Jews who go to countries other than Israel. The Council of Jewish Federations and a number of American Jewish organizations, including HIAS, favored the principle of freedom of choice for Soviet Jews, but the bias against those who come to the United States among Zionist organizations, Soviet Jewry councils, as well as American Jews generally is quite strong.[27] One articulate and politically acute Soviet Jewish journalist in Philadelphia perceived strong guilt feelings among Soviet Jews here because of these spoken and unspoken expectations among many American Jews.

In October 1979, at a "Professional and Lay Institute on Soviet Jewry," a communitywide focus on Soviet Jews on a limited scale emerged. At this all-day conference sponsored by the Klein Branch JYC in cooperation with numerous Jewish agencies in Philadelphia, the problems of resettlement, use of community resources in the process, and Soviet Jewish immigrant expectations and reactions were aired. For the first time publicly, a panel of Soviet Jews participated formally in a Jewish community project dealing with Soviet Jewry, and described their individual resettlement problems.

Agency staff members discussed Soviet family problems such as overanxiety over children, overdependence on children to interpret American life, depression among older immigrants and job-related adjustments. Various workshops addressed problems and entertained suggestions for more effective integration into American society. In one workshop, one local Jewish leader said, "We are and shall do everything possible to save them, but what are we saving them for?"—an allusion to the perceived absence or dilution of agency programs of Jewish content. A lively, sometimes heated discussion followed in which the question of Jewish identity of the immigrants and their absorption into the Jewish community was mooted. Counselors noted that participation in Jewish rituals and holiday celebrations and synagogue attendance had been encouraged, but that resettlement problems had to be addressed first.

The author suggested that the nonreligious Jewish organizations draw Soviet Jews into their activity and that a page in the *Jewish Exponent* be reserved for news about Soviet Jews in Russian. One Philadelphia Jewish agency executive declared that "all Jewish communal agencies must be Jewish" and must expose immigrants to the Jewish value system and to Jewish-content programming.

The institute undoubtedly made those who attended more aware of this community problem. More American Jewish–Soviet Jewish interaction did develop, but there still remained the problem of absorbing newcomers into a Jewish environment *after* they no longer needed the services of professional agencies. The most effective absorption in this regard occurred in the Neuman Senior Citizen Center of the JYC, directed by Judith Schwartz, where a natural social-cultural atmosphere exists and where Jewish-content programs have been developed informally for senior adults.

The Golden Slipper Club, B'nai B'rith, Lubavitcher Center, and the Jewish Identity League conducted *sedarim,* which several hundred newcomers attended. Rabbi Sol Isaacson conducted an Orthodox *shtibl* in the basement of his home, which drew about fifty older Soviet Jews. The Workmen's Circle and Association of Jewish New Americans also attracted some newcomers to their meetings. Some Soviet Jewish children attended Jewish schools, and synagogues conducted special holiday programs, especially at Hanukah and Purim, for Soviet Jews. The Klein Branch of the JYC granted free membership to Soviet Jews for one year, but much of the activity was recreational and sports-oriented.

By 1980 a perceptible shift in the role of social agencies took place, stimulated by discussions in many communities similar to the one in Philadelphia. These discussions revealed conflicting feelings toward Soviet Jews within the American Jewish community: anger at the demands and abrasiveness of some newcomers, resentment that they did not go to Israel, that too many community resources were being expended for questionable results, and expression of the ill-defined hopes and expectations of the American Jewish community regarding Soviet Jewish resettlement. Moreover, because Soviet Jews came into regular contact with many resettlement professionals and volunteers, *their* own sense of themselves as Jews had an important effect on the newcomers, and some were passive, neutral, or cool about their own commitment. The very great diverse forms of Jewishness in American also made it impossible to project an optimum or widely acceptable form of Jewishness for Soviet Jews to emulate.

A National Task Force on Jewish Identity, including communal professionals, rabbis, and educators, was set up by the CJF "to identify the central issues and concepts relating to the integration of Soviet Jewish immigrants into American Jewish communities . . . to determine programmatic implications . . . and provide the stimulus and the agenda" for communitywide planning and action.[28] Jewish identity programming replaced resettlement as a serious priority inasmuch as basic economic needs had been or were being met, and was to be integrated into maintenance as the chief tasks in the American Jewish absorption of immigrants. The central factors in the success of this process were to be a welcoming, positive community approach; as well as warmth among individual professionals and volunteers[29]; coordination among agencies; and immigrant-partnership in activities.

The question of with what and how Jews identify themselves as Jews was left to each community, but the general objectives included developing personal relations with American Jews, an active involvement in Jewish organizations and groups, and an understanding of modern Jewish life and thought. Interestingly, the Task Force report of November 1980 urged the professional not to "shy away from doing what he may have been educated to think as unthinkable, i.e., create and support programming that is clearly and unashamedly directive."[30]

The Soviet Jewry Council's Freedom Run, 1985.

Many Russian Jews coming to the United States have lived through wars, pogroms, revolution, persecution—and the virtually complete suppression of their religious rights. Pictured here, a Russian-Jewish immigrant stands before the Ark of a Northeast shul, preparing for the afternoon mincha service.

These guidelines, however, were and have been difficult to implement because of the immense cultural differences between American and Soviet Jews. In the Greater Northeast area of Philadelphia, there are few cultural institutions that offer programs familiar to urban Jews from the Soviet Union: museums, classical music, literary circles, university courses through which Jewish content programming might have been channeled. In 1980 Gratz College organized a subcommittee on Adult Educational Programming for Soviet Jewish Immigrants that drafted recommendations, but they failed to materialize. However, the question of Jewish identity was moving to the foreground in agency thinking.

In 1980 the Philadelphia FJA Task Force on Resettlement created a Sub-Committee on Acculturation and Jewish Identity "to forge links between American and Soviet Jews, to give expression to their sense of Jewishness and give impetus to more directive programming." All of the agencies involved in resettlement then intensified the Jewish components in their work. In their 1982 report, the Sub-Committee noted that "Soviet Jews . . . in Philadelphia . . . have shown an increasing interest in programs of Jewish acculturation and identification" evident in their "increasing participation in community-wide events such as the Israel Independence Day Celebration and their involvement in this FJA committee."[31] The committee emphasized that a number of projected programs were "initiated at the suggestion of Soviet Jews,"[32] of whom there were seventeen in a committee of forty.

During 1981, there were courses at the Neuman Center on introduction to the Bible, American Jewish history, and Jewish holidays. About sixty senior citizens completed the twenty-week sessions, for which a registration fee was charged. Interest and participation were high. The Jewish Campus Activities Board sponsored six children's holiday programs, which were held in various synagogues in the Northeast. Geared to children in grades 4 to 6, the programs explored the meaning and symbols of the holidays through storytelling, puppets, song, and dance. Some American Jewish children and college volunteers also participated. Many Soviet Jewish parents and grandparents attended, thus creating a shared Jewish family experience—the first for many.

Philadelphia HIAS developed a citizenship education program and used related Jewish content in the course, such as the history of the American Jewish community, development of its institutions, contributions of previous waves of Jewish immigration, and American and Jewish concepts of freedom, equality, and individual and group rights.

A program called UNICAL for Soviet Jewish children was started in 1981 at the Klein Branch of the JYC, which has been exploring Jewish themes through music, literature, and art. Soviet Jewish teachers, employed in non-teaching jobs initiated the idea of teaching classes to Soviet Jewish children on Sundays. These include Jewish history and customs, Russian language and literature, girls' gymnastics, a math club, and a soccer clinic. There were also plans for trips to places of Jewish interest, family retreats, or Shabbatonot, and Jewish Family Life Education programs.

In 1981, Rosh Hashanah and Yom Kippur services in Hebrew and Russian attracted several hundred Soviet Jews to the Neuman Center. This program was planned by the Philadelphia Board of Rabbis and involved a Russian-speaking American rabbinical student and a Soviet Jewish cantor chanting his first service in fifty years. Two Soviet Jewish teenagers, one of them a student at Akiba Hebrew Academy, read from the Torah and blew the shofar. The planning for these services directly involved Soviet Jews assisted by agency staff, and the services have been conducted each year.

Because most Soviet Jewish parents do not know how to conduct a seder but have expressed the need, several Passover workshops were held to help families move from being guests at a seder to celebrating Passover in their own homes. Most parents want their children to identify as Jews, but there had been no organized community effort to reach the children as a subgroup with particular needs and problems. Very few Soviet Jewish teenagers were involved in specifically Jewish programs, and relatively few children attended Jewish schools. A Gratz College survey revealed that as of the end of 1982 to early 1983, there were 21 children enrolled in Jewish nursery programs; 18 in primary school programs (5 to 7 years old); 38 in elementary departments (8 to 12); and 9 in high school and post–high school departments (13 and up).[33] Of the 86 children, 64 were in day-school programs, of whom 57 were in schools with a strong religious orientation.[34] Undoubtedly, an important Jewish experience in an informal setting has been that of day and overnight camping at the Y, and Lubavitcher camps for over 300 Soviet Jewish children.

Some Soviet Jewish college students had been involved in Hillel programs on campus, but most seemed too pressured by their studies and part-time jobs to attend functions. A number of teenagers went to the Klein Branch of the JYC for swimming, basketball, karate, and other physical activities. A few attended meetings of the Student Struggle for Soviet Jewry, but it was observed that a number of Soviet Jewish youths both at Philadelphia Community College and Temple University tended to bond together, speak Russian, and not mix with other students. This college-age group seemed to require more community attention and planning.

Meanwhile, Soviet Jews groped for their own inner-directed expressions. Subgroups formed to hear Russian writers; there were several exhibits by Soviet Jewish artists at the Klein Branch of the JYC; several journalists wrote and edited a Russian column each week in the Northeast *Jewish Times;* a number of concerts involving Yiddish dramatic artists and musicians from the Soviet Union drew eight hundred to one thousand newcomers. Dimitri Ganopolsky started a Russian radio program on Station WIBF-FM. By 1982, a twelve-page newspaper, *Novy Mir (New World),* was being published by and for the immigrant community under the professional editing of Josef Vincurov. The range of articles was unusually wide, covering world events, special articles dealing with Israel, a sports roundup, local news, and jokes. There were numerous ads and photographs. At first funded by a grant from the *Jewish Times* and the Association for the Protection of Jewish Immigrants, the paper is now a private undertaking.

In 1982, work was also started on a Babi Yar Memorial Book. The project was conceived by Shimon Kipnis, a Soviet Jewish writer who came to Philadelphia in 1979 and wanted a book to enshrine the names of Jews who were massacred at Babi Yar in 1941. The book was given impetus by the Yiddish Club of the Neuman Center, a trilingual editorial committee, and a grant from FJA. Funds were raised through contributions and at various concerts. The book, in Yiddish, Russian, and English, was published in 1983 and was acclaimed in many journals.

The large, fundamental question of relations between American and Soviet Jews was left hanging. However, in November 1981, the Philadelphia Jewish Community Relations Council developed the first known lay leadership seminar of its kind in the country: "Understanding Our Jewish Neighbors from the USSR," aimed at alleviating tensions and misunderstandings between American and Soviet Jews in the Northeast. There had been "growing awareness of negative feelings toward Russian immigrants among many Jews in Northeast Philadelphia," and community leaders realized that complaints had to be addressed.[35] Thirty lay leaders and nine agency sprofessionals participated. The Federation of Jewish Agencies of Greater Philadelphia initiated and financed the project.

The seminar involved three components: (1) eliciting the feelings, attitudes, and questions of participants regarding Soviet Jews; (2) providing factual information about the history of Soviet Jews, Soviet society, the emigration process, and services provided to immigrants; and (3) analysis of behavioral differences, the impact of the immigrant experience, and immigrant versus local community expectations.

As a result of lectures, workshops, written resources, and discussion groups involving Soviet Jews, a corps of well-informed speakers was developed to promote better understanding of Soviet Jewry. Twenty-three groups in the Northeast involving an audience of almost two thousand were reached during the year beginning January 1982, and eased some of the misunderstanding and tensions, as determined by various subsequent evaluations. The seminar report concluded that much of the tension "is the result of the difficulty in interpreting and understanding the cultural differences of Russian immigrants." Speakers developed at the seminar continue to speak to community groups.

Related to these tensions was an undercurrent (occasionally surfacing) perception that there were substantial criminal elements in the current immigration wave. Unsupported generalizations then flowed about the character of this immigration generally. Occasionally, there were newspaper and magazine articles containing undocumented material, slurs, and misleading innuendos.[36] These were very disturbing to the newcomers and aggravated the fear of KGB infiltration, which lasted a long time after arrival. Similar charges of criminality, shiftlessness, and antisocial habits were frequently made against Jews from Eastern Europe in the early 1900s.

Philadelphia Jewish leaders tried to allay fears that there might be an officially inspired conspiracy against them and pledged solidarity with Soviet Jews, but negative attitudes among

The plight of Russian Jewry has remained a deep concern of the Philadelphia Jewish community. Servicing the needs of Russian Jewish immigrants, however, has proven a challenging undertaking.

American Jews persisted, roughly comparable to the attitudes of settled German Jews toward East European Jews a century prior.

The two communities thus remain largely distant from each other. Philadelphia Jews, for example, are only dimly aware of the great wealth of musical and artistic talent within the immigrant community. Occasionally, creative activity by and awards of scholarships to Soviet Jewish children, who are high achievers, are described in the press. But the cultural gaps between the two Jewries remain great, and contact generally tends to be strained and infrequent.[37] Soviet Jewish news in the Anglo-Jewish press has dealt mostly with Jews struggling to leave the Soviet Union.

The fluidity of American Jewish life, the emotional power of Israel's views on Soviet Jewry, and the absence of a consensus on how or what to transmit in the way of Jewish culture to the immigrants has made the Jewish acculturation process somewhat problematical. The immigrants themselves have as yet made no specifically Jewish cultural impact, yet a number of surveys indicate that they want to be identified as Jews, not religiously, but in some not-yet-defined ethnic-national sense. They feel very strongly identified with the fate of Israel; some have already visited there; others wish they could live there. Some want their children to have a Jewish education; most want them to marry Jews. Many left the Soviet Union because of anti-Semitism and like America because they feel free of this incubus.[38] They want to be identified as "American Jews" or "Jews." Models for this identification, however, in view of the secular conditioning of Soviet Jews, are, for the most part, lacking. Except for the Jewish Y's and centers and the social service agencies specifically committed to helping Soviet Jews, the large Jewish national nonreligious organizations that might provide a comfortable cultural setting for Soviet Jews have not moved forward toward them, and, despite efforts to dispel ignorance and misunderstanding of their experiences, the local Jewish community, in the main, remains negative; most American Jews have little or no understanding of what Soviet Jews have lived through. They are often referred to as "Russians."

The availability of impressive structures of agency help does not comprehensively address the questions: What do we want from the immigrants, and what do they need and want from us? Addressing those questions "would necessarily lead to the question, 'What constitutes the Jewish identity of our communities?', a question we are generally too uncomfortable with to approach directly."[39] Soviet Jews will undoubtedly hammer out this definition for themselves, as have other waves of immigration. As to the frictions and tensions between the old and new Jewries, this pattern has also occurred in the past. A different orientation by Israel and a more general understanding of Soviet Jewish history would have helped ease the difficult adjustment process, but, like previous immigrations, Soviet Jews are survivors of a particular kind. They have struggled and will continue to struggle to find their place within American Jewry, to make their contributions and add one more component to the fluidity of American Jewish life. There is no reason to doubt that their impact will be felt in time. As with previous immigrants, some will assimilate, some will have only a diluted sense of Jewishness, but others will enrich Jewish culture in ways that will surprise us.[40]

Right: Har Zion main sanctuary. (In the foreground, the Soviet Jewry Freedom Forest.)

Below: Germantown Jewish Centre (photo taken May 21, 1954, day of first services).

Above: Adath Jeshurun, entrance.

Left: Adath Jeshurun, interior (a 1958 concert).

CHANGING STYLES OF
SYNAGOGUE LIFE
Conservative Judaism in Philadelphia

Sidney H. Schwartz

In the period immediately following World War II, Conservative Judaism clearly emerged as the largest branch in American Judaism. It currently has approximately 850 affiliated congregations nationwide compared with about 700 Reform affiliates. (There are no reliable figures for Orthodoxy.) In a survey of the Boston Jewish community in 1965, 44 percent of those surveyed identified themselves as Conservative, compared with 27 percent as Reform and 14 percent as Orthodox.[1] In smaller communities, like Providence, Rhode Island, an even higher percentage of Jews identified themselves as Conservative: 54 percent, compared with 21 percent for Reform and 20 percent for Orthodoxy.[2]

To a certain extent, the strength of each of the American religious movements in various parts of the United States reflects the history of their respective foundings. The Reform movement's first congregation was in South Carolina, and its major seminary, Hebrew Union College, was established in Cincinnati. As a result, the South and Midwest have been traditional strongholds of Reform Judaism. Orthodoxy, requiring a complex array of Jewish support institutions to supply the services associated with a traditional Jewish life—mikvah, Kosher butchers, yeshivot—found its early home in New York and has remained strongest there. Conservatism, by contrast, traces its founding to Philadelphia and continues to exhibit its greatest strength in the mid-Atlantic states and New England.[3]

The birth of Conservative Judaism in America can be dated from the appointment of Solomon Schechter as head of the Jewish Theological Seminary (JTS) in New York in 1902. While some historians[4] trace the roots of the movement back to Zechariah Frankel and the positive historical school in nineteenth-century Germany and to various earlier attempts to establish a traditional seminary in the United States, it was not until the arrival of Schechter that the Conservative movement began to take shape. Schechter assembled an impressive array of scholars—Louis Ginzberg in Talmud, Alexander Marx in history, Israel Friedlander in Bible, Mordecai Kaplan in homiletics—which immediately established the Seminary as the preeminent institution of Jewish learning in the United States at that time.

Schechter also founded the United Synagogue of America (USA) in 1913. Conceived as a union of traditional congregations, the twenty-two charter synagogues subscribed to a founding document that called for loyalty to Torah, observance of Sabbath and dietary laws, traditional liturgy in Hebrew, and the fostering of schools and homes, which would develop an appreciation for Jewish customs and traditions. Although the USA did not require specific practices beyond these general principles, it did exclude those congregations that allowed worship without covered heads or that used the Reform *Union Prayer Book,* which was mostly in English. As such, the USA was a traditional alternative to the already well established Reform, Union of American Hebrew Congregations, which in 1913 already boasted 179 congregations.[5]

After World War II, Conservative Judaism enjoyed its greatest growth. The second-generation children of immigrants had reached maturity. Thousands came back from the war, married, and moved out of the inner cities, where their parents had lived, to the suburbs. In these new communities, it was the Conservative synagogue that proved most suitable for membership. Impressive synagogue structures were built as signs that the Jews had "made it." The synagogue program was child oriented, suiting the needs of young families. Finally, the synagogue also became a community center where Jews could meet, learn, and socialize with other Jews, a need that continued to be felt even as Jews sought to integrate themselves into American life.

Even though the institution that gave birth to Conservative Judaism, the Jewish Theological Seminary (JTS), was always located in New York, many of the central figures in the establishment of Conservative Judaism in America were Philadelphians. Isaac Leeser (1806–1868) had been the *hazan* of Mikveh Israel and was crucial in upholding traditional Judaism during the mid-nineteenth century when Reform Judaism was much stronger in numbers. Sabato Morais (1823–1897) succeeded Leeser at Mikveh Israel and became the founding president of the Jewish Theological Seminary in 1886, even though it was in New York. Mayer Sulzberger (1834–1923) was a prominent judge in Philadelphia and one of the lay founders of JTS. His extensive Judaica library formed the nucleus of the Seminary library after his death. Finally, Cyrus Adler (1863–1940), the foremost Jewish communal leader of his time, was a Philadelphian who was instrumental in bringing Solomon Schechter to America to head up the Seminary in 1902. He then succeeded Schechter as president of the institution in 1915, even though he simultaneously carried the responsibility as head of several other national Jewish organizations and institutions.[6]

Yet the central role played by Philadelphia in the national Conservative movement goes beyond its historical roots in that city. In 1980 Philadelphia had more congregations affiliated with United Synagogue per capita than any other city in the United States, and it has consistently raised more money for the Seminary than other areas per capita. Two Philadelphia rabbis, Simon Greenberg and Yaakov Rosenberg, have been appointed to prominent national positions as vice chancellors of the Seminary.

Philadelphia itself has gained the reputation as "a Conservative city." From six Conservative congregations in 1920, there were twenty by 1940.[7] One survey[8] found that in 1965 there were fifty-one congregations that identified themselves as Conservative. Thirty-five of those were affiliated formally with United Synagogue. In comparison, there were twenty-three Orthodox congregations and eleven Reform. While total affiliation figures are not available, it is known that five-hundred-family congregations are not uncommon in Reform and Conservative synagogues; Orthodox groups tend to be far smaller. Daniel Elazar has suggested that the Baltimore-Philadelphia temper was shaped by the moderate traditionalism of Lord Calvert and William Penn. As such, it was ripe for a religious movement that reflected the same moderate, traditional tenor.[9]

The second factor contributing to the strength of Philadelphia Conservatism is less recognized but no less significant: In the early part of the twentieth century, there was far less geographical mobility than exists today. The tendency to stay close to family was even more pronounced among rabbinical students at JTS who, for the most part, came from Orthodox families. As a result, most of the early graduates of the Seminary tended to cluster around New York. Conservative congregations in the West had great difficulty attracting graduates of the Seminary to their pulpits. Well into the 1940s, officials of the Rabbinical Assembly (the rabbinical organization of Conservatism) tried to appeal to alumni's sense of responsibility in spreading the ideology of Conservative Judaism, in order to induce rabbis to move west. It was thus particularly true in the early years of the growth of Conservative Judaism that the very best rabbinical talent was to be found in the cities of the Northeast. Even in the post-war period, when mobility was less unusual, rabbis vied for the opportunity to take a pulpit near the center of Jewish life, which continued to be New York. One positive result of this was that Philadelphia always enjoyed the talents of some of the most dynamic rabbis in America. This had no small impact on the growth of the movement in the city.

To better trace the development of Conservative Judaism in Philadelphia, we shall look at three Conservative synagogues in different sections of the city, each with a character of its own—Adath Jeshurun, Har Zion Temple, and Germantown Jewish Centre.

ADATH JESHURUN[10]

Adath Jeshurun (AJ) is among the oldest Jewish congregations in America, though four synagogues predated its 1858 founding in historic Philadelphia—Mikveh Israel (1745), Rodeph Shalom (1802), Beth Israel (1840), and Keneseth Israel (1847). The first members were eager to establish a congregation to accommodate the thousands of Jewish refugees leaving Germany after the failure of the liberal revolution there in 1848. Besides providing religious services, for which the unordained S. B. Breidenbach was retained, the most pressing need of Jewish immigrants was for a Jewish cemetery. AJ provided this with a purchase of ground in the Frankford section of the city in 1861.

In those early years, AJ had a succession of locations. It first purchased Union Hall at Third and Brown Streets to use as a sanctuary in 1859. Six years later, the congregation was able to raise enough money to buy more suitable quarters at Newmarket and Noble Streets, a sanctuary that had been the former home of Reform congregation Keneseth Israel. AJ was also one of the few congregations in America to have an ordained rabbi, Dr. S. Nathans, a rarity for the time. In 1875, a merger with Adas Israel congregation made the purchase of the Juliana Street Synagogue from Rodeph Shalom possible. During these years, AJ introduced a choir and was the first synagogue in Philadelphia to hold late Friday evening services. In 1886 the congregation built the first synagogue structure it could call its own on a lot at Seventh and Columbia Avenue. Rabbi Elias Eppstein, who had been hired in 1883, began to deliver regular sermons at the evening service, which swelled attendance.

It was no coincidence that, just as the Eastern European immigration was beginning to change the ethnic and religious tenor of Philadelphia Jewry, AJ, being without a rabbi for six months in 1910, turned to the Jewish Theological Seminary for someone to lead the coming High Holy Day services. German had been used at services until 1896, and AJ was ideologically close to the Reform movement. At services they employed non-Jewish singers in the choir, many worshipped with uncovered heads, and they were considering a merger with the impressive Reform Temple, Rodeph Shalom. Max Klein was the rabbinical student who came to AJ, albeit reluctantly. Not only was he opposed to the congregation's breach of tradition, but he much preferred to spend the holidays with his family. Nevertheless, his professor, Israel Friedlander, prevailed upon Klein to accept the pulpit, a position that he was to hold for fifty years.

With Klein as rabbi, AJ came solidly into the fold of Conservative Judaism. He succeeded in requiring a strictly Jewish choir and covered heads at worship.[11] In 1913, when the Conservative, United Synagogue of America was established, AJ was one of the twenty-two founding congregations. Also significant was the move in 1911 to a new location at Broad and Diamond Streets, reflecting the general shift of Jewish populations from the older parts of Center City Philadelphia northward.

By the 1920s the congregation had grown to five hundred members with three hundred members and three hundred children in a Hebrew School program supervised by "Rabbey" Klein. With the addition of an auditorium in 1926, a Young People's Congregation was able to hold parallel services on the High Holy Days. The size and prosperity of AJ was able to carry the congregation through the financially difficult 1930s, but by the 1940s another major population shift was taking place. The movement to the suburbs was beginning to deplete AJ of its core members. Membership had peaked at about 750 families, but the trend of younger families was decidedly toward settling in the northern suburbs. To accommodate the needs of these families, AJ bought a property at York Road and Ainsley Avenue in Melrose Park to be used as a religious school, signaling the intention to eventually move the entire synagogue to the northern suburbs.

A most significant religious development took place in 1951 with the introduction of Max Klein's own prayer book, *Seder Avodah*. It was more liberal than the standard prayer book of United Synagogue and served to make AJ's service unique. Meanwhile, services continued to be

Rabbi Yaakov G. Rosenberg in a 1976 service at the Holocaust Memorial.

held at Broad and Diamond while the congregation purchased a number of properties in the suburbs and attempted to overcome various zoning problems to permit them to build a new synagogue. Since the initial move of the school to the suburbs in 1948, the membership had dropped from 750 to about 500 families. With hopes of reversing this membership decline, the congregation began construction of a new synagogue at York and Ashbourne Roads in Elkins Park in 1959. By this time, very few families lived in the North Philadelphia neighborhood served by the Broad and Diamond sanctuary. In fact, even though North Philadelphia was already doomed as a Jewish neighborhood, the 1948 purchase of land in the suburbs accelerated the Jewish exodus. Younger families with intense loyalties to AJ looked for homes in the northern suburbs where AJ had clearly signaled its future would be.

The end of the "urban" chapter of AJ's history was made even more complete with the retirement of Max Klein after fifty years of service and the hiring of Rabbi Yaakov Rosenberg in 1960. Rosenberg's youth, personal warmth, and charisma sparked a renewed vitality in the congregation. Although the new building, which opened in 1964, was only planned for nine hundred families, the congregation already exceeded that number under Rosenberg's tenure, which ended in 1978 when he was appointed to the Seminary as vice chancellor. Though Rosenberg introduced practices more traditional than those observed under Klein, AJ remained a liberal Conservative congregation with organ, choir, and its own prayer book. When Rosenberg left in 1978, Rabbi Seymour Rosenbloom was hired, and the congregation continued to grow to eleven hundred families.

HAR ZION TEMPLE[12]

Har Zion was founded in 1924 to serve the growing Jewish community of Wynnefield, in the western part of Philadelphia. The original members were all of Eastern European origin, so there was no tradition of German Reform Judaism to influence its development. Most of the members came from the adjacent communities of West Philadelphia and Strawberry Mansion. The former was served by Beth-El, a liberal Conservative congregation with an organ, while the latter was served by a more traditional Conservative congregation, B'nai Jeshurun. The move beyond those neighborhoods to Wynnefield already indicated a measure of prosperity, which was underscored by the raising of $30,000 from twenty-eight men at the organizing meeting in 1924 to build a temple at 54th and Wynnefield Avenue.

Founded as a Conservative congregation, the members naturally looked for a graduate of JTS to serve them as rabbi. Simon Greenberg, who had spent the previous year in Palestine and planned to devote his career to Jewish education, was coaxed into accepting the pulpit of Har Zion in 1925. Immediately, Greenberg began to shape the character of the synagogue—he insisted that the organ, which had been built into the new Temple, not be played at religious services. While few of the early members were strict observers of the Sabbath, they were staunchly anti-Reform. Most were European-born and spoke broken English, though Greenberg continued to preach in Yiddish on occasion. The promise of the community was already indicated by the fact that Har Zion grew to 250 families in its first year.

When Simon Greenberg left Har Zion in 1945 to become a vice chancellor at the Seminary, Wynnefield was already one of the most heavily populated Jewish neighborhoods in the United States, and Har Zion was virtually the only synagogue in the area. Har Zion's service continued to be traditional enough to satisfy the needs of more Orthodox worshippers, although, at one point, Ephraim Yolles, a leading Orthodox rabbi in the city, threatened to revoke the license of those *shochtim* (ritual slaughterers) who regularly attended the Conservative service. Beth David was a Reform Temple founded in 1942 in Wynnefield, but it remained quite small. In the ten years following World War II, Wynnefield became more than half Jewish, with a total Jewish population of 40,000.

With David Goldstein as the new, American-born rabbi, the congregation swelled to 1,800 families and 1,400 children in the Hebrew school. Adding to the attraction of Har Zion was the addition of a gym and a community center to its existing physical plant in 1952. The Temple's commitment to Jewish education went beyond its own school. Goldstein and lay leaders of Har Zion were instrumental in having Akiba Hebrew Academy, a Jewish all-day high school, housed at Har Zion from 1950 to 1958, until suitable quarters could be found in Merion. Subsequently, a Solomon

Schechter elementary day school was founded and first housed in Har Zion. The Poconos site of Ramah, the Conservative movement's summer camp, was also both bought and donated by Abe Birnbaum, a Har Zion member, in 1949. Not coincidentally, no other Conservative synagogue in America has produced more rabbis and Judaica scholars. Har Zion exemplified a commitment to Jewish scholarships by sponsoring a scholar-in-residence program that supported fellowships by Fritz Rothschild, Chaim Potok, and Nahum Sarna, while simultaneously exposing the membership to their erudition.

Ironically, even in the midst of Har Zion's most successful era—in terms of size of membership, school, and the extent of the programs offered—signs of decline were already apparent. The population of Wynnefield was aging through the 1950s, and younger families were buying starter homes in the suburbs where the public schools were considered to be better. Homes in Wynnefield coming onto the market were being bought by blacks, and families with children in the Hebrew school already were complaining about occasional unpleasant interracial incidents. West Philadelphia, a former Jewish neighborhood where many Har Zion members had once lived, was already a black neighborhood in 1955, and many Jews felt that Wynnefield's change to a black community was inevitable. In 1961, Har Zion purchased a tract of land in Radnor, northwest of the city, for use as a day camp. At that time, there were those, including members instrumental in the purchase, that foresaw the use of the Radnor property as a future site for Har Zion. Along those lines, regular services started to be held parallel to the main service at Radnor on a weekly basis in 1967, while a parallel Hebrew school was started in 1962 and enjoyed growing enrollment. Yet the conventional wisdom was that Wynnefield would continue to be a suitable congregational site for at least twenty-five years to come.

The Wynnefield site of Har Zion would not see twenty-five more years. By 1969, the year Gerald Wolpe replaced David Goldstein as rabbi, Har Zion's membership had dropped to one thousand families, and the school population even more precipitously to five hundred children. After an extended investigation and congregational discussion (to follow), the decision was reached to build an entirely new facility in Penn Valley. A $5 million building campaign was launched for property, building, and furnishings. That move was completed in 1974, and since that time, Har Zion has gradually built its membership up to 1,250 families.

GERMANTOWN JEWISH CENTRE[13]

Germantown is a unique neighborhood in the northwestern part of Philadelphia that served as a location for summer homes for many of the city's wealthier families through the nineteenth century. When many of the estates gave way to suburban residences in the twentieth century, Germantown became one of the more scenic areas in which to live within the city and a short commute to Center City. By the 1930s there were about five hundred Jewish families scattered through Germantown and the adjacent communities of Mount Airy and Chestnut Hill. Despite this, there was hardly any institutional Jewish presence in the area. Beth Israel of Strawberry Mansion ran a branch of its Hebrew school in the area to serve its members, and some of the area's older Jews were in the habit of renting quarters strictly for High Holy Day worship.

The younger, American-born Jewish residents were less interested in starting a synagogue than they were in starting a social and cultural organization. In fact, many who joined the Germantown "Fellowship" in 1936, whose moving spirit was Ed Polisher, were affiliated with synagogues in other parts of the city. Significantly, the Fellowship's first national affiliation was with the Jewish Welfare Board, the umbrella organization for community centers. The Fellowship offered courses on anything imaginable, taught by laypeople, and a concerted effort was made to attract Jewish families from across the widest possible spectrum. Many Jews, previously unaffiliated with any Jewish institution, took these classes, and the leadership took the initiative to rent a hall on the second floor of the Pelham Club at Emlen Street and Carpenter Lane.

Within a year, the group felt the need for a religious focus and the one-hundred-family Fellowship became the Germantown Jewish Centre (a point was made to use the anglicized spelling of *Centre*). Solomon Grayzel, on the faculty of Gratz College, served the congregation as a part-time rabbi for two years, and the Centre affiliated with United Synagogue of America. In

Rabbi Elias Charry in 1962.

1938 Judah Goldin became the Centre's first full-time rabbi. He served for two years, as did his successor, Leon Lang. Meanwhile, the congregation was sponsoring regular Friday evening and Sabbath morning services and a Hebrew school of eighty-five children. In addition, because of its origins as a cultural association, the Centre offered a broader range of activities than did most synagogues and was, consequently, able to retain members whose religious interests were weak but whose Jewish associational needs were strong.

In 1942 Elias Charry was brought from Indianapolis to serve as rabbi. The congregation was three hundred families strong, had two hundred children in the Hebrew school, and had clearly outgrown its quarters. The congregation resolved that a school building was a more urgent priority than a sanctuary, and a site was found at Lincoln Drive and Ellet Street. The new building opened in 1947, and soon both floors, fifteen classrooms in all, were being used to capacity. Rabbi Charry put great stress on education, Zionist activity, and also became deeply involved in civic affairs in the Germantown area. The congregation continued to grow, and an impressive sanctuary, modeled on the Mt. Sinai theme, was added to the school building in 1953. By 1960, the congregation had reached the peak of its growth with 650 families and 580 children in the Hebrew school.

During the 1960s, the Germantown area began to undergo the same kind of demographic transformation that was going on simultaneously in Wynnefield and that had already taken place in North Philadelphia. Faced with a declining membership, Charry and the synagogue leadership resolved not to flee the neighborhood. Cooperative efforts between the synagogue and the area Church Community Relations Council succeeded in making the Mount Airy section a model of an integrated community, and received national attention in the media. Charry and lay leader, Leon Magil, literally went door to door pleading with Jewish families not to abandon the neighborhood. Of course, even such concerted efforts could not prevent a sharp decrease in the size of Germantown's congregation. In the early 1970s, membership had dropped to 375 families and 85 children in the religious school.

Ironically, while the short-term costs in membership were obvious, the commitment to the semi-urban setting of Mount Airy also held unanticipated long-term dividends. In the 1970s, the trend of younger families moving to the suburbs began to reverse itself. The prices of suburban homes were starting to be out of reach for many young families, and the energy crisis made more people conscious of living closer to work locations in the city. Mount Airy, within the city limits yet removed from the bustle of the commercial and corporate center, became a prime beneficiary of young Jewish families looking for such living arrangements.

Many of these new families were a generation younger than the established membership of the Centre. A goodly number were a product of the counterculture movement of the 1960s and were now searching to deepen their Jewish connections. As might be imagined, their religious needs were not met by the service that had been established by the post-war, second-generation American Jews. The formality of a large service with rabbi, cantor, organ, and choir was rejected for a *havurah*-style service. The *havurah* phenomenon had started in 1968 in Boston with Havurat Shalom, a group of Jews who simply wanted to study and pray together without the embellishments of buildings and professional staffs. A similar type of *havurah* service began at the Germantown Jewish Centre in 1974, as an alternative to the regular service.

The Germantown Minyan, as it came to be known, attracted many young Jews who would never have joined a typical Conservative synagogue.[14] Interestingly, most were from out of town and were attracted to Mount Airy because of its reputation as an open, integrated neighborhood inside the city. In time, the Minyan itself, which was allowed to function autonomously within the confines of the Centre, developed its own reputation within the national Havurah community, and notable Jewish teachers like Zalman Schachter and Art Green were drawn to the group. As the Minyan grew from ten to over one hundred regular attendees, the synagogue leadership began resenting the fact that most were not contributing to the upkeep of the struggling congregation. It was Rabbi Charry who, more than anyone, guaranteed that the members of the Minyan would be welcome in the Centre, even though they had clearly developed a service that was competitive with his own. This policy continued to be in effect after Charry became the rabbi emeritus and was succeeded by Alex Shapiro (1972), Clifford Miller (1973), David Weiss (1974), and Sanford Hahn

(1978). By 1978 the synagogue and Minyan had reached an understanding, and about 75 percent of Minyan members were paying dues to the Centre, and facilities remained available to the Minyan at no charge. The congregation has also enjoyed a revitalization as a result of the influx of new families, and by 1980 its own membership has grown back to five hundred families.

THREE STYLES: COMPARISONS

Location and Constituency

Adath Jeshurun, Har Zion, and Germantown each represent Conservative synagogues in different sections of Philadelphia whose respective histories were shaped by the neighborhoods in which they found themselves. Quite apart from internal religious styles, each synagogue had to make major decisions about who their constituency was and how to best serve it. The most tantalizing question is whether synagogues follow their membership as they change their residential patterns, or whether members take their cues about a future residence from the indications that a synagogue is committed to move to a certain area or to stay in the same locale. All three synagogues seemed to exert a strong pull on families, as reflected in memberships that span two and three generations.[15] The fact is that one of the distinguishing characteristics of the Conservative synagogue is the desire to be a neighborhood synagogue.[16]

The three synagogues under study each had to make major decisions as to whether they would change locations and thereby change from being a "neighborhood synagogue" to a "commuting synagogue," though synagogues do not always change to successive categories. AJ had a series of neighborhood synagogues with schools at Juliana Street, Seventh and Columbia, and then at Broad and Diamond. This pattern of moving the synagogue so that it remains at the hub of the membership was unique to Conservative synagogues. Orthodox leadership in Philadelphia (Rabbi Bernard Levinthal being the best example in the pre-war period) was devoted mainly to the supervision of the local Kosher meat industry. Levinthal seemed quite content to allow Conservative synagogues to spring up in new neighborhoods, judging by his willingness to speak at their dedications.[17] Orthodox shuls tended to be of the "corner" variety—typified by a very local and loosely defined membership and modest facilities—and because there was no building or elaborate program of activities, when a neighborhood died, so did the shul.

The major Reform Temples of Philadelphia, Rodeph Shalom (RS) and Keneseth Israel (KI), exhibited almost the opposite phenomenon. Both developed large metropolitan temples with a stress on creating a stately, majestic edifice and service. While this met the needs of many members who were more interested in pointing to their temple with pride than in having it convenient to them, it bred a corporate mentality.[18] Instead of having new temples develop in new neighborhoods, Reform Jews wanted to continue their affiliation with one of the major temples in town, where membership carried a good deal of status. The sense that bigger was better even led to talk of a possible merger of Rodeph Shalom and Keneseth Israel, each with more than one thousand families in 1948. Although a merger did not take place, both KI and RS did act as the parent Reform congregations of Philadelphia, seeding new temples with their own money. KI's branch Sunday school in Oak Lane became Temple Judea in 1930, while both KI and RS underwrote a Reform group in Wynnefield until it could organize as Beth David in 1942.[19] Rodeph Shalom remained at its Broad and Mt. Vernon Streets site in North Philadelphia through 1980 while running a branch in Elkins Park. While KI did move from Logan to Elkins Park in 1955, following many of its members to the suburbs, neither RS nor KI can ever be said to have been neighborhood temples in the sense that most of their members lived in the immediately surrounding area. Their draw was always citywide.

The contrast between the Orthodox and Reform experiences, on the one hand, and the Conservative experience, on the other hand, as to location and attempts to serve its constituency is dramatic. AJ probably went through the least trauma in abandoning its neighborhood synagogue at Broad and Diamond, but it still was not an easy decision to leave North Philadelphia. Older members who lived in the vicinity of the synagogue, as well as within easy access to Center City and West Philadelphia, were opposed to the move to the northern suburbs, which was already indicated as early as 1948. Most significantly, Rabbi Klein was very attached to the Broad and Diamond building and wished to make it "the cathedral synagogue of Philadelphia." (He even lived in the building during the last few years before its closing in 1964.) Yet the movement out of the city was already paved by a Hebrew school and monthly services in Melrose Park immediately after the war. Loyal members of AJ bought homes near the future site of the synagogue in Elkins Park and in the surrounding communities of Abington, Jenkintown, Glenside, and Wyncote. These younger families formed the nucleus of a membership resurgence once AJ was fully relocated to Elkins Park.

Har Zion had greater difficulty resolving whether to stay or leave Wynnefield. This was due to a combination of factors that postponed the decision. Wynnefield was more densely populated with Jews than was North Philadelphia, and there was a greater sense of community because the boundaries were fairly well defined. As a result, well into the 1960s, Har Zion enjoyed larger attendance at services and events, giving the impression that the area would remain Jewishly viable. Also, because the physical plant was so immense and represented such a large expenditure of money, moving seemed more forbidding. Still, Har Zion's membership was declining through the 1960s. The existence of the Radnor branch, with a growing program of education and worship, serviced the membership already in the suburbs.

The board of Har Zion commissioned a major study of the demographics of the area in 1969 in order to make a more informed decision about a permanent move. The study was done by noted sociologist Samuel Klausner, and it has remained the center of controversy because its final recommendation—to stay in Wynnefield—was rejected.[20] The study did find a shift in the Jewish population to the northwest suburbs, but it did not deem it substantial enough to recommend a move of the synagogue.[21] The suburban population surveyed indicated that no high-density Jewish settlement comparable to Wynnefield would form (although it was found that, paradoxically, affiliation was higher in those locales where Jewish population density was lower.) Most important for a potential move was the finding that religious attitudes in the suburbs were significantly more liberal than in Wynnefield, which would suggest that the traditional character of Har Zion might be undermined in a new setting.[22] The study recommended that the program at the Temple's Radnor facility be expanded, while the Wynnefield program be regeared on a more modest scale to serve an aging and more racially integrated community.

Although the board rejected the study's recommendations, and the choice of a Penn Valley location was not the one favored by most of the members surveyed,[23] when a congregational vote was held on the question of moving, about 90 percent voted to leave Wynnefield. Fears about the racial balance in the neighborhood could not be calmed, and attendance at evening services and programs declined sharply through the 1960s. The decision to move to the suburbs, however, also served to abandon the remnant of a significant Jewish population in Wynnefield. While younger and more affluent families were moving to the suburbs, those members who had lived all their lives in the neighborhood and those who desired a traditional Conservative synagogue within walking distance of their homes (including several rabbis engaged in teaching who were members of Har Zion) would not follow Har Zion to its suburban location, where it would draw from the greater Main Line area.

Mention has already been made of Germantown Jewish Centre's refusal to abandon their neighborhood when faced with a situation similar to that of Wynnefield. To a certain extent, each synagogue had to decide how much its own presence in a deteriorating neighborhood could reverse what seemed an irreversible demographic trend. For a time, in the late 1950s, a group of men from Har Zion tried to buy every house coming on the market in Wynnefield to keep professionals in the area. In truth, this effort was no more effective than the door-to-door effort in Germantown during the same period. Germantown's decision not to move was based on a strong ethical commitment to an integrated community. Many of its members did not share that ideal sufficiently to remain in the neighborhood, and the Centre's membership consequently suffered. Yet the synagogue's decision helped stabilize the community. Additionally, it put the Centre in a position to serve a broader range of the population—elderly, singles, single parents—in the 1970s than at either of the suburban locations of AJ or Har Zion, where the memberships became primarily upper-middleclass families. Germantown thus chose to remain a neighborhood synagogue and proved that it could be viable, whereas AJ and Har Zion followed the more typical path of becoming commuting synagogues serving broad geographical areas.

It is interesting that even though the Conservative synagogue was, for a time, the classic neighborhood synagogue, it was more in the neighborhood than *of* it. That is to say, few congregations did much to reach out to non-Jews in the area or to mobilize any type of local social action. Thus, when the area began to change, the congregation had little emotional investment in it and had few qualms about moving. Germantown, which was active in community affairs before the neighborhood began to change, remained much more deeply committed to the area than was typical of most other Conservative congregations.

Worship Styles

In the early part of the twentieth century, style more than ideology separated Reform from Orthodox, and Conservative Jews from one another. The Orthodox service was typically the complete traditional liturgy and Torah reading in Hebrew. There was rarely any sermon, and on those occasions when one was given, it was delivered in Yiddish. Women would be seated in a segregated gallery, and there was neither uniformity in the pace of the service among worshippers, nor much emphasis on decorum. The Reform service was a reaction against Orthodox practice and borrowed heavily from the much-admired Protestant service. Decorum was paramount. Rabbis in long black robes stood in front of the congregation, leading the service. Organs and choirs dominated the performance-style service, and the musicians and singers not necessarily Jewish. The service was mostly in English (although German was used in the earlier period, even in America), and worshippers sat in family pews without *yarmulkes* or *talitot*. The liturgy was abbreviated, and the rabbi's sermon held a central place in the service. In the more radical Reform temples, like KI in Philadelphia, services were held on Sunday mornings.

When graduates of JTS began occupying pulpits around the country, they offered services that were fairly traditional, with the main departures from an Orthodox service being attention to decorum, a uniform prayer book, mixed seating, and an English sermon. This met the needs, particularly, of many Eastern European immigrants, who wanted an Americanized service but wanted to retain aspects of the tradition. Within these parameters, however, Conservative synagogues could differ widely.

Of the three synagogues studied, Har Zion clearly represents the most traditional worship service. From the time Simon Greenberg assumed the pulpit in 1924, there was a full service and full Torah reading and no organ music, although one had been built into the 54th street synagogue and one member continually agitated for its use. Because Greenberg did not want the service to be a performance, he insisted that the *hazan* face the ark and not the congregation. Still, there was always a professional choir to introduce new melodies and arrangements, although no non-Jews would be hired for it. While Har Zion offered a late Friday evening service, there always existed a service at sundown for more traditional members. Additionally, there has always been a daily minyan. At the main services, there would be an occasional English selection, but the bulk of the service was in Hebrew. Remarkably, there has been little change over the years in the worship format, largely owing to the presence of the much-respected Isaac Wohl, a very traditional cantor, who has been at Har Zion since 1945. Undoubtedly, the sermon at Har Zion has always been a major attraction, as all three rabbis—Greenberg, Goldstein, and Wolpe—were extremely powerful speakers.

Germantown Jewish Centre provided a more liberal service than Har Zion's, although when it introduced an organ at services in 1942 it had to overcome the resistance of some of the more traditional older members who were drawn to the Centre's broad cultural program. At that time only 15 to 20 percent of Conservative congregations nationwide allowed organ playing at services,[24] which put Germantown on the left wing of the movement's spectrum. When the choir was hired in the 1950s, no objection was expressed to the inclusion of non-Jews. Overall, the worship service at Germantown was a lesser factor in membership, and a much smaller percentage of the congregation attended services regularly than at Har Zion. Much of this can be attributed to the fact that Har Zion's membership began as largely European-born traditional Jews who were already familiar with the service—who knew how to *daven*. Germantown's American-born membership displayed more interest in other aspects of the Centre's program. Another factor may have been that Rabbis Greenberg and Goldstein were traditionalists who worked hard to keep Har Zion a primarily religious institution with a strong emphasis on worship. In contrast, Elias Charry was more liberal than most of his congregation, eager to challenge them to fulfill themselves Jewishly in areas other than worship.

The Germantown Minyan, on the other hand, was strictly a prayer community that provided a significant alternative to the main service. When it started in 1974, its members consciously rejected the performance-style service with organ, choir, rabbi, and cantor. In fact, the whole *havurah* phenomenon, of which the Minyan was part, can be seen as returning to a worship style that both Reform and Conservative Judaism rejected. While the service was clearly not Orthodox insofar as women were accorded full religious rights and certain prayers were changed, abbreviated, or omitted, and decorum was rejected as the bane of spontaneous, emotive prayer. Participants ran the service themselves, and the responsibility for leading a discussion on the Torah reading rotated. Children could be seen playing on the floor in the middle of the classroom set up in a circle that formed the "congregation." Dress was considerably less formal than in the regular service, and it would not be uncommon for someone to begin playing a tambourine in the midst of the singing of a prayer in this fully participatory worship experience.

In truth, the Minyan cannot really be considered part of the Conservative movement. Its founders rejected almost everything Conservative synagogues had come to represent, especially the tendency to allow the rabbi to rule every facet of synagogue life autocratically. Yet the members of the Minyan were mostly raised in Conservative synagogues, and their worship style was learned in the movement's youth and camp organizations, USY and Ramah. Furthermore, the Minyan would have been hard pressed to find a congenial home in an Orthodox synagogue, which would have seen them as too heterodox, or a Reform Temple, which would have found the traditional-counterculture Minyan blend positively alien. Although Minyan members brazenly told the Centre that it needed them more than they needed it, one senses that they were pleased that they could find a home in a synagogue rather than in someone's house. Ironically, it was the democracy and openness at Germantown that allowed the Minyan to get established and flourish. That same pluralistic spirit prevailed within the Minyan when, in 1978, the group became so large and diverse that new *minyanim* were being run simultaneously, each with a different style and blend of tradition.

The worship style at AJ was clearly the most unique for a Conservative congregation; it also was the one that underwent the most changes. Unlike Har Zion's Eastern European founders or Germantown's American-born founders, AJ was influenced by a strong German flavor and its flirtation with Reform in its early years. While Rabbi Klein insisted on covered heads at worship and the use of only Jewish singers in the choir as conditions of his employment in 1911, the service still bore a close resemblance to the two Reform temples in the vicinity, Rodeph Shalom and Keneseth Israel, with which it competed for potential members. The use of the liberal Jastrow prayer book required Klein to insert certain standard Hebrew prayers himself. The organ was still played by a non-Jew; the Torah portion was read, not chanted; and the haftarah was read in English. The Hebrew of the Friday night service was transliterated, and English was still more prevalent than Hebrew as the language of prayer.

The tone of the service was set by Rabbi Klein. His stress on decorum and pageantry led many to describe the service as "awe-inspiring" and "poetry in motion." Klein even had the number of steps from his lectern to the ark counted off and rehearsed. Those ascending the *bimah* donned silk hats in the German tradition. Klein also wrote his own prayer book, *Seder Avodah,* which was adopted in 1950. The book was more liberal than the standard Silverman prayer book sanctioned by United Synagogue and bore an ideological resemblance to Mordecai Kaplan's Reconstructionist *Sabbath Prayer Book,* which was burned by Orthodox rabbis when it was issued in 1945. *Seder Avodah* changed traditional passages that referred to Israel as the chosen people, dropped the references to the reestablishment of the sacrificial service, and retranslated prayers that implied God's supernatural power to heal the sick or resurrect the dead. Many congregants took great pride in the uniqueness of Klein's service and in the fact that he produced a prayer book exclusively for AJ.

When Yaakov Rosenberg assumed the pulpit in 1960, the change in style was dramatic. His style was loose and *hamish* (folksy) in contrast to Klein's stiff formality. Rosenberg's impassioned sermons were peppered with Yiddishisms, which would have scandalized Klein, whose generation was intent on creating a fully "American" service. The language of prayer became predominantly Hebrew, and *talitot* and *kipot,* instead of hats, became standard. The Torah and *haftarah* portions were now chanted, and the full seven *aliyot* were called instead of two or three. More congregational singing was introduced—especially by Cantor Charles Davidson, who came to AJ in 1966—although the organ, choir, and prayer book were retained. On the whole, the younger membership was receptive to Rosenberg's "informalizing" of the service and the move toward a more traditional style that now included a daily morning *minyan.*

Interestingly, even this shift to the right was not enough to meet the needs of a group of members that sought an informal, full participatory service along the lines of the Germantown Minyan. In 1976 the Havurah Alternative Service began to be held on *shabbat* mornings at AJ parallel to the main service. The forty to fifty members tended to be those in the congregation who were more knowledgeable in Jewish tradition and personally observant. The AJ Havurah was older and more family oriented than its Germantown counterpart, and found its members more within the congregation than from the outside. For that reason, there was less controversy about financial obligations of participants toward the synagogue and use of facilities.

Though the *havurah* service has hardly become an option for the masses, its influence is heavily felt in services that are trying to shift away from stiff formality and what can be called the high-church mode of worship service, in which emphasis is placed on performance over participation. Younger Jews who have no agenda of trying to acculturate, as did their parents and grandparents, are less interested in a dignified service that is consistent with its American setting than they are in a service that is authentic and able to meet their spiritual needs.

Liberalization and the Role of Women

Conservative Judaism has always prided itself on being the movement most capable of bringing Judaism into step with the values and circumstances of modern life while remaining true to Jewish tradition. In fact, through the scholarship at the Seminary, the point was stressed that Judaism has always undergone change and that Conservatism was best equipped to sponsor such prudent change in the twentieth century, thus making it worthy of its claim to be the authentic heir to traditional Judaism. Orthodoxy was viewed as too resistant to any changes, while Reform was seen as having made too many.[25]

Through the liberal interpretation of *halacha* (Jewish law) by the Law Committee of the Rabbinical Assembly, Conservatism sanctioned many changes in Jewish life, particularly in the synagogue. The best example of such changes in *halacha* comes in the realm of granting equal status to women in the synagogue. Traditional law relegated the women to a segregated seating section and denied them any public role. Virtually all Conservative synagogues began with allowing seating of men and women together, but not until the post-war period were other issues raised.

The RA Law Committee first discussed and approved the principle of allowing women to ascend the *bimah* for an *aliyah* to the Torah in 1949, but the specific circumstances under which it could be allowed were not detailed.[26] Moreover, even after the Law Committee rendered a decision, it was up to the rabbi in each congregation to act as the *mara d'atra,* the sole arbiter, in deciding whether institute the change. Over the next few years, this issue was discussed within the Conservative movement, and a full responsum was produced, providing a ceremony parallel to the *bar mitzvah* for girls. Mordecai Kaplan, representing the most liberal position in the Conservative movement, had already introduced the *bat mitzvah* ceremony in 1922 at his Manhattan congregation, the Society for the Advancement of Judaism, but the practice had not been generally accepted.[27]

Max Klein first introduced a *bat mitzvah* ceremony for girls at AJ in 1952, although the girls who opted for it did no more than lead a few prayers. Har Zion introduced the ceremony later in the 1950s for girls whose parents requested it from Rabbi Goldstein. He allowed the few girls who expressed an interest to come up in a group a few times a year and lead parts of the service and chant a Biblical portion. Germantown was by far the most liberal congregation on the issue: *bat mitzvah* ceremonies took place individually and on shabbat morning, the same as for boys, starting in 1954. It was not until much later—1964 for AJ and 1971 for Har Zion—that girls in those congregations were accorded the same recognition upon attaining religious maturity as boys.

Rabbi Gerald I. Wolpe in 1973, now retired.   Rabbie Seymour Rosenbloom of Adath Jeshurun.

The introduction of *bat mitzvah* did not imply general permission for women to take *aliyot*. While Germantown granted women equal status across the board in 1954, AJ and Har Zion took longer. When AJ gave final approval for *aliyot* in 1973 and Har Zion in 1979, the resolutions passed with easy majorities due to strong positions voiced in favor by Rabbis Rosenberg and Wolpe, respectively. (Until that time, girls called to the *bimah* for their *bat mitzvah* had to have their fathers recite the blessings for them, or they read from the Torah with no blessing at all.) All three synagogues, however, found that the passage of a resolution did not create instant equality. Each congregation had to make the psychological adjustment to seeing women on the *bimah*. Many women never received the Hebrew training that gradually became standard for girls through the 1950s and 1960s, and therefore did not have the ability to take advantage of the rights accorded them. Because the decision on *aliyot* was left to each congregation, liberalization was subject to many internal factors. In 1967 only 23 percent of Conservative rabbis were prepared to offer women *aliyot*,[28] but by 1975 that number had increased to 50 percent.[29]

The RA Law Committee ruled in 1973 that women should be counted in the *minyan,* the quorum of ten that was traditionally required for public worship.[30] Germantown was far ahead of the Conservative movement on this issue, permitting it also in the same 1954 decision that permitted *bat mitzvah*. AJ approved this innovation immediately in 1973, while Har Zion did so in 1977.

The last area of liberalization left in the realm of women's status was to allow women to serve as *shlichat tzibbur,* leader of the congregation in prayer. This was a much harder issue for Conservative Judaism to resolve because there seems to be little ambiguity in the traditional *halacha* that might allow for a liberal ruling. The implication of such a decision would allow women to function both as rabbis and cantors. Neither AJ nor Har Zion seemed prepared to move on this issue in advance of the national movement, but Germantown had already hired a female cantor in 1980, and women had been leading services on occasion since 1976. Interestingly, both *havurot* functioning in Germantown and AJ, while more traditional in many aspects of the service, never had reservations about allowing women to lead in worship.

The liberalization that has taken place in the Conservative movement nationally has served to put much more distance between it and Orthodoxy than was the case early in the twentieth century, simply reflecting the general secularization that has increased with each successive generation of American Jews. It is clear from our three synagogues, however, that the Conservative rabbi is given great latitude in shaping the public ritual practice of the synagogue by the laity.

In Conservative congregations, decisions regarding religious matters are not participated in by laypeople. While laity run the day-to-day affairs of the synagogue, the rabbi is ceded the privilege and right to be the primary arbiter of religious issues. Both Rabbis Wolpe and Rosenberg, at Har Zion and AJ, respectively, used public discussion and committee and board votes to help raise consciousnesses on the *minyan* and *aliyot* decisions and to prepare members for a major change in public worship. But it is also clear that they had the right, in the eyes of their congregants, to move unilaterally on those issues. Germantown always had a more democratic spirit, one that was fostered by the founders but unquestionably supported by Rabbi Charry. When the issue of women's equality was raised, far earlier than in most other Conservative congregations, there was hardly a problem, for both congregants and rabbi were extremely liberal.

Clearly, both Germantown and AJ stand on the left wing of the Conservative movement. But the most radical transformation has taken place at Har Zion. Under Rabbis Greenberg and Goldstein, Har Zion was one of the most right-wing Conservative congregations in the country. Yet, in the 1970s, it has adopted the gamut of liberal changes that have hardly become universal in the Conservative movement, even in the 1980s. Two reasons may be forwarded. First, because Har Zion had the most autocratic tradition in terms of ceding power to its rabbis, just as Greenberg and Goldstein could prevent liberalization, Rabbi Wolpe has been able to pioneer it with little opposition, even given the congregation's strong traditional roots. Second, the move to Penn Valley served to strip the congregation of its most observant, right-wing members, who would only belong to a synagogue they could walk to on *shabbat*. The Klausner study predicted what has, in fact, happened. The low-density suburbs have resulted in a weakening of traditional practice and attitudes, thus setting the stage for the synagogue's liberalization. This same phenomenon, however, provides a major challenge to all Conservative synagogues serving suburban populations that would like to stem the tide away from religious observance.

Other Factors in Philadelphia Conservative Judaism

Education

In addition to the Conservative synagogue's ability to be a neighborhood institution and the attraction of its traditional, yet modern, pattern of worship for Jews of Eastern European origin, a prime source of its strength was education. Each of the Conservative synagogues under study offered religious schools for children that were prime sources of growth. In the early part of the century, most immigrants had their children educated in Talmud Torahs that met five days per week but whose instruction was somewhat uneven. Reform temples offered one-day-per-week programs that were not very intensive. When Conservative synagogues began offering two-day, and then standard three-day-per-week Hebrew schools in the post-war period in Jewish neighborhoods, many parents joined the congregation for that reason alone. The Board of Jewish Education, created by all the Conservative congregations in Philadelphia in 1937, ensured high-quality instruction.[31]

Affiliation

Some Conservative rabbis believed that the attraction of the movement lay in its ideology and program. That seems only partially true, and it certainly was a secondary factor to laypeople who wanted to establish synagogues in their neighborhood, and who found the style of Conservative worship most in keeping with their Jewish and American sensibilities. It also seems apparent that the intensity of commitment to Conservatism, per se, has slackened considerably with the generations. Many lay leaders report negative experiences in dealing with the movement's national organizations, and few feel that their synagogue's denominational label is a source of their strength. More prevalent among lay leaders is a strong sense of loyalty and identification with their own congregations. Each has a sense that they belong to a unique group with a special character all its own. As a result, laypeople are more willing to give of their time and money to local, congregational efforts rather than to the national body.

Rabbi Sanford H. Hahn of Germantown Jewish Centre, now retired.

Har Zion is a case in point. Not only was the congregation the leading contributor to the Seminary for twenty-one years, with annual gifts in excess of $50,000, but it also built the Seminary's Israel branch, Neve Schechter, and many of its laypeople assumed leadership in Conservatism national organizations. However, with the move to Penn Valley, all resources were turned inward, and Har Zion has not regained the leadership role it once played in the movement. Another reason for this is that the local Federation, with its ability to generate much publicity and prestige, has co-opted most of the talented congregational leaders in the city. There also is the general phenomenon that congregational leaders since the 1960s have come increasingly from the ranks of professionals and middle-management, in contrast to the self-made businessmen of the pre-war period. The consequent change from aggressive, "think-big" leadership to lower profile lay leaders has robbed national Conservatism of vital strength.[32]

Rabbinic Authority

One constant has been the power of rabbis to shape the character of their synagogues. We have pointed this out in the realm of ritual, but the rabbi's influence has also extended to other realms of congregational activity. The fact that all the rabbis discussed at Har Zion, AJ, and Germantown were avid Zionists made their congregations strong supporters and fund-raisers for the State of Israel. In contrast, the support of Rabbis William Fineshriber (KI) and Louis Wolsey (RS) in the 1940s for the non-Zionist, American Council for Judaism made their respective Reform congregations lukewarm in their support for Israel for some time. Examples abound of interests of rabbis being reflected in subsequent emphases of congregational activity in the same areas: David Goldstein and Har Zion in day-school education and Zionism; Elias Charry and Germantown in adult education, interfaith work, and social action; Yaakov Rosenberg and AJ in Jewish community relations and Soviet Jewry; and Gerald Wolpe and Har Zion in Soviet Jewry and Federation work. Undoubtedly, the ability of rabbis to shape their congregations will continue.

PROSPECTS

It is ironic that in discussing prospects for the future of Conservative Judaism, some of its historic strengths no longer seem to be working in its favor. The transition from neighborhood to commuting synagogue makes the Conservative synagogue no more convenient or accessible than Reform Temples. The move toward more traditional worship patterns in Reform Temples makes it seem less radical and alien to Jews who would once never have considered joining Reform over Conservative congregations. Finally, even with liberalization, the policies of the Conservative movement seem increasingly out of step with the Conservative laity. While Conservatism advocates observance of *shabbat* and *kashrut,* a survey conducted of the membership of Har Zion before the move to Penn Valley showed that only 52 percent lit candles on Friday night and only 41 percent purchased Kosher meat.[33] There is every reason to believe that those figures would be even lower since the congregation relocated to the suburbs. Although neither rabbis nor the national movement is in a position to coerce observance or to sanction a congregation, questions are raised concerning the credibility of a movement that exhibits such a gap between theory and practice.

Though Conservative congregations are clearly stronger than the Conservative movement, their viability is at the mercy of emerging trends. If the *havurah* phenomenon at Germantown and AJ indicate a trend, then the message being sent to synagogues by Conservative Judaism's most knowledgeable and committed offspring is this: Decentralize or die. There exists disenchantment, not only with the cathedral-like service, but also with what is perceived as the large, hierarchical, cold institution with the rabbi as the autocrat who has lost touch with human needs. The establishment of the Reconstructionist Rabbinical College in 1968 in Philadelphia, devoted to training rabbis to serve *havurah*-type, small synagogues; the growth of the *havurah* movement nationwide through the 1970s; and the growing trend of young professionals swelling the ranks of Young Israel–type Orthodox synagogues seem to herald a pattern that most Conservative synagogues do not currently fit.

Conservative synagogues may fill the needs of the majority of American Jews who are middle class, suburban, and still in family units, but the era of suburban growth has subsided, money is more scarce for large building projects, and there are emerging more alternative lifestyles in the Jewish community. Higher mobility will result in fewer congregational memberships that pass down over the generations. Distance from family will probably demand that the synagogue become more of a surrogate fellowship for caring and belonging and less of a status institution to a generation secure in its identity. Jews with no memories of religious parents or grandparents are becoming more typical, and their search for roots will be met less by nostalgia than by the willingness of institutions to experiment and innovate in meaningful Jewish ways. If Conservative synagogues begin to adjust themselves to meet these needs, they may yet survive the post-suburban phase of American Jewish life.

Gratz College.

A GENERATION OF LEARNING
Jewish Education in Philadelphia, 1940–1980

Diane A. King · William B. Lakritz · Saul P. Wachs

A complete network of supplementary Jewish schools existed in Philadelphia at the start of the 1940s, ranging in intensity from the Yeshivot (talmudical academies), which offered up to seventeen hours a week of classes, to Sunday schools sponsored by individual congregations and by the Hebrew Sunday School Society.[1] Each system was a distinct entity; coordination and cooperation were uncommon between the groups. The community had recognized the need for an agency to eliminate waste and duplication as far back as the twenties,[2] but while many could agree on the utility and desirability of coordination for the sake of efficiency, there was little consensus over how and by whom such coordination should be introduced.

Traditions of autonomy and decentralization are very strong in American life and even more so in the Jewish community. The struggle to overcome the isolation of each discrete educational unit and to reach reasonable levels of cooperation that would bring unity but not uniformity represent one of the key chapters in the story of Jewish education in Philadelphia during the period since 1940.

To grasp the fierceness of the struggle and its longevity, one must understand the ideological frame for the process. One of the major issues that had exercised Jewish educational theorists and practitioners since the early decades of the twentieth century was the question of who should sponsor and administer Jewish schools. Two broad ideologies competed in this area. One asserted that Jewish education was, properly, a community concern, while the other saw the individual congregations or groupings of congregations sharing elements of a common ideology as the proper sponsorship. Much more was at stake than a battle for "turf." Each group had a different vision of Jewish education and thus different answers to questions such as: Are the goals of Jewish education primarily Hebraic-cultural or religious? Is the Jewish school best served when it is a unit in a larger congregational entity or when it serves no cause but the fulfillment of its own educational ends? Are student loyalties best directed primarily to a Rabbi and a congregation or to the Jewish community and the Jewish people (*Klal Yisrael*)? Can communal schools develop strong, passionate, and long-lasting commitments among the young?[3]

As long as the vast majority of congregations offered minimal programs (i.e., Sunday schools), the choice for parents was often clear. If they wanted intensive text-centered Hebraic education, they would probably choose communal schools like the Associated Talmud Torahs or the Yeshivot (later, these merged into the United Hebrew Schools and Yeshivos). If they were satisfied with a more modest program (as was generally the case where girls were concerned), then a congregational school seemed more attractive (though, of course, the community offered this type of education as well through the Hebrew Sunday School Society).

However, in the post–World War II era, congregations, particularly Conservative congregations, began to intensify their programs in keeping with the rising standards of the United Synagogue Commission on Jewish Education, and the result was a blurring of distinctions and intensified competition for the same students (primarily male, but increasingly female). The struggle for coordination of Jewish education in Philadelphia was waged on at least three fronts: elementary education, central agencies, and secondary schools.

ELEMENTARY EDUCATION

The period from 1940 to 1980 was marked by a steep decline in the number of students attending communal or noncongregational supplementary schools. In 1942–1943 more than 7,600 students representing a majority of the 14,000 students enrolled in Jewish schools studies in communal schools. By 1961–1962 this figure had dropped by two-thirds and represented about 10 percent of the total of 22,500. In 1982–1983 fewer than 1,300 students remained in the communal system, and well over half of these were attending the one-day classes of the Hebrew Sunday School Society.

The major supplementary Hebrew school system, the United Hebrew Schools and Yeshivos, was reduced at the end of the period under study to three schools with a population of about 360. Its hours were now reduced from a previous high of ten (in the Talmud Torahs) and seventeen (in the Yeshivos) to six, and had a clientele that included many with no synagogue affiliation.

The fall of this structure in Philadelphia and many other cities was attributable to many causes. First, there was a rapid movement of Jews to newer neighborhoods in the city and to the suburbs that followed the close of the Second World War. In that setting, without the comfortable signs of ethnicity (e.g., Jewish stores, restaurants, etc.), many who had taken their Jewish identity for granted felt a need to express that identity through affiliation. Synagogues, particularly Conservative synagogues, were transplanted from older neighborhoods or started as new institutions.[4] These synagogues became favored gathering places for Jews. It was not unusual for someone who had had little or no involvement in his or her local *shul* in the old neighborhood to become quite active in the congregation in the new area of settlement.

Another factor was the emerging definition of the Jew as a member of a religious group, a definition that seemed best suited to his or her self-image as a member of the middle class in American society. Third-generation American Jews who felt secure in America sought to identify themselves as Jews, and this self-identification was essentially religious in nature.[5] Jews liked the idea of being considered one-third of the spiritual heritage of America. They did not see themselves as an (immigrant) ethnic enclave but rather as full-fledged Americans who attended a different "house of worship" on their Sabbath from their fellow Americans. In addition, many parents found it both appropriate and convenient that all members of the family, adults and children, express their Jewishness in the same building—the synagogue.

Finally, in Philadelphia, the process of the congregationalization of elementary Jewish education was accelerated by the use of political clout. Religious groups working through the Council for Jewish Education were able to prevent communal schools from competing effectively in the newer neighborhoods of the city and in those suburbs that were within the ambit of the Allied Jewish Appeal. Thus, for many reasons, synagogue-based Jewish education won an almost complete victory in the arena of elementary Jewish education.

COORDINATION AND CENTRALIZATION

In 1910, the Bureau of Jewish Education of the Jewish community of New York was founded, the first central agency for Jewish education in the United States. At that time, Jewish education was in a deplorable state in New York City. Teachers were generally men who had failed at some other business or profession. They lacked training in pedagogy and were not always deeply learned in Jewish studies. Those who did have strong qualifications for their work were treated as shabbily as the least professional among the teachers. Yearly contracts were rare, salaries were very low, and teachers worked without any professional benefits or protection.[6]

The Bureau of Jewish Education was organized as part of the abortive effort to create a *Kehillah,* or unified community, in New York City, such as had once existed in Europe. While the *Kehillah* experiment lasted only seven years, the Bureau survived its sponsor. Among its activities were the creation of an association of principals of Jewish schools, a group for laity interested in Jewish education, creation of texts for Jewish schools, organization of model schools, development of licensing examinations for teachers and principals, and the dispensing of community funds to schools that met certain standards. This institution (which survived into the period under study) set a model for the sister bureaus that were created in almost every large city in the country.

The need for such a coordinating and consultative agency for Jewish education in Philadelphia was grasped by the community leadership, but the questions of ideology and autonomy were sufficient to arouse opposition to the creation of a central agency of the type just described. The first effort, in 1927, produced a study group called the Council of Jewish Education, which considered some of the problems facing Jewish schools.

A decade later there was renewed effort to create a Bureau of Jewish Education. At that time, the leading communal educator was Ben Rosen, director of the Associated Talmud Torahs. A recognized educator with a strong personality, he advocated the idea of a central committee that would bring together congregational and communal schools for deliberation on matters of common concern and would also provide aid, supervision, and improvement for all schools in the community. This call for the replacement of the existing Council on Jewish Education with a broadly based body that not only would think about the problems of Jewish education, but also would also seek to do something about them, was sufficient to galvanize the forces for whom such a call represented a masked effort to gain administrative control over all forms of Jewish education in the community.

In May and June of 1937, shortly after the appearance of a major article by Rosen, advocating the creation of a Bureau,[7] two leading Conservative rabbis—Max D. Klein, spiritual leader of the Congregation Adath Jeshurun, and Julius H. Greenstone of Gratz College—organized the response of the religious forces. Both Dr. Greenstone and Rabbi Klein were convinced that such a Bureau "would lead to a diminution of the religious influences, fearing the emphasis would tend to be on purely Hebraic rather than religious studies. They foresaw that the personal contacts between the rabbis and the pupils would be diminished and that eventually, the community would take over the educational facilities of the city."[8]

The sense of urgency was so great that in less than eight weeks this fear, together with the desire to improve and coordinate the schools of the Conservative ideology, led to a response. Fully five years before another call for a central agency was made citywide, the Board of Jewish Education of the United Synagogue of America, Philadelphia Branch, was established. The BJE offered several of the services and fulfilled several of the functions that were associated with the work of "Bureaus of Jewish Education" in other cities. In the process, it acted as a counterweight to efforts to centralize the coordination of Jewish education in Philadelphia in a communal agency.

In regard to its purpose, the BJE could point to many accomplishments. It developed and gradually raised standards among its affiliated schools (which at one point reached thirty-eight in number). One can appreciate the general state of such standards in congregational schools by knowing that in the first set of such standards, a student was required to have attended a religious school for at least one year prior to bar mitzvah and two years prior to confirmation. This standard was gradually raised until 1958, when the BJE adopted the national (Conservative) standard for bar mitzvah (promulgated in 1947), requiring an 8-year-old ceiling for one-day-a-week education. By 1960, bar and bat mitzvah on a Sabbath morning in a Conservative synagogue was limited to those who had studied at least five years in three-day-a-week classes, while confirmation was celebrated by those who had continued on a three-day-a-week basis for at least three years following the bar or bat mitzvah ceremony.

The BJE also facilitated the use of curricula and materials produced by the national commission on education of the United Synagogue. It produced texts and materials for the local schools, and some of these were utilized elsewhere in the country. It also prepared a curriculum leading to admission to Gratz College.

The period of greatest strength for the BJE was during the sixties. In 1961–1962, for example, more than thirteen thousand students attended BJE schools, constituting 70 percent of the congregational school enrollment and a numerical majority of all those attending Jewish schools in the community. In later years, the number declined both as part of the general decline in school enrollments and relative to the enrollment in Reform religious schools.

The BJE supported the establishment of Camp Ramah in the Poconos, a major educational institution developed cooperatively between the Philadelphia branch of the United Synagogue and the Jewish Theological Seminary of America. It also established a network of secondary schools, and it played a role in the establishment of the Solomon Schechter Day School. Particularly during the tenure (1953–1973) of Dr. William B. Lakritz as Educational Director, the BJE played an important role in raising standards in Conservative congregational schools. Its aspirations were to make of the congregational school the peer, in quality, of the best of the communal schools of the past. Although the functioning of the BJE contributed to slowing the development of a central agency, the idea and need persisted, leading to the eventual establishment of such an agency.

Ben Rosen left the community in the middle 1940s, to assume a national role in Jewish education, before any action could be taken on his proposal to establish a central agency for Jewish education in Philadelphia. In 1943, after a major survey of Jewish education in the city by Leo L. Honor and Morris Leibman, the community acted to implement this idea, which was also a recommendation of the survey.

While the proposal envisaged a central agency of the type that was found in other major cities, what actually emerged was something quite different: a federated system of education, consisting of representatives of various school systems, both those financed by the Allied Jewish Appeal (communal) and those which received no funding (congregational).[9] While all of the representatives were prepared to cooperate in organizing interschool assemblies, music festivals, and the like, under the sponsorship of the Council, they were ambivalent, if not actually hostile, to the idea of the Council providing consultation and guidance in educational matters.

The BJE was unwilling to accept such consultation; the Reform schools were initially interested but gradually withdrew from this relationship. The smaller Orthodox schools, most of which were located in the older neighborhoods, did take advantage of the expertise of the Council's staff.

A study of the Council in 1955–1956 by the AJA recommended its continuance, with the important change that the Council should now assume responsibility for the direct operation of the two major communal systems: the United Hebrew Schools and Yeshivos and the Hebrew Sunday School Society. The response of the two systems was extremely negative, and they lobbied successfully through the AJA against implementation of the recommendation.

The Allied Committee resumed its deliberations the following year. The amended plan, proposed and adopted, spelled the demise of the Philadelphia Council on Jewish Education.[10] The major provisions required that the Council on Jewish Education be dissolved, and that Gratz

Left: Rabbi David A. Goldstein, 1968.

Middle: Sol Satinsky in 1951.

Right: Dr. Leo Honor in 1947.

College should develop consultative services to replace those of the Council. The planning function of the Council was to be lodged with the Federation[11] Committee on Jewish Education. The newly reconstituted Gratz College was to serve as a consultative arm for that committee.

According to Dr. Abraham Cannes, director of the Council on Jewish Education, one of the major causes of the dissolution of the Council was that it lacked authority and finances to make and implement major decisions on Jewish education.[12] Ezekiel Pearlman, who was executive assistant of the Allied Jewish Appeal at the time this decision was made, pointed to the structure as the key reason for the dissolution. The Council, by its definition, was made up of the counting of noses (400 children = 1 voice on the Council).[13] Therefore, there were about eight communal voices as opposed to twenty-seven congregational voices. There was no way the community schools could be well served under those conditions. The congregational schools, coming into their own at this time, used their strength to the detriment of the development of community schools.

The major problem was the question of whether the communal school system had the right—or even the obligation—to open new schools in newly developed neighborhoods where congregational schools were established. Because communal schools received the financial assistance of central community sources, they were subject to guidelines that stated that no school could open with fewer than one hundred pupils, and no school could remain open with fewer than fifty pupils. Congregational schools received no such financial assistance and, therefore, were not subject to the same guidelines. By insisting on rigid adherence to the guidelines, the Council hampered the growth of the communal schools while, at the same time, allowing the congregational schools the freedom to flourish. The Federation eventually lost confidence in the Council[14] and created in its stead the Division of Community Services of Gratz College, which would offer the community, upon request, the essential educational services previously offered by the Council.

By transferring the essential functions of the defunct Council on Jewish Education to Gratz College, the Federation of Jewish Agencies provided a fresh start for the idea of a central agency. Gratz had greater acceptability in the eyes of the community than the Council ever had.

The merger took place in 1959, with Dr. Elazar Goelman, newly appointed dean of the college, assuming the directorship of the Division of Community Services, as the central agency was called. The Division provided consultation for Conservative schools in cooperation with the BJE, allowing ideological integrity along with Central Agency coordination. Similar arrangements were developed for Reform, Traditional, and Communal schools.

The Division, in time, came to include, in addition to instructional consultation, five resource departments: Music, Audio-Visual, Art, Educational Games and Activities Center, and the Chomsky Educational Resource Center.[15] The community also was served in the areas of adult education and public relations and recruitment for all schools (The Jewish Education "Hot-Line"). The Division sponsored a Board of License for Teachers and Principals that was nationally recognized, an educational cabinet that brought directors of all systems together, and conferences for teachers and administrators.

Viewed from this list, the DCS was a true central agency. But there were problems as well. For Conservative schools, consultation arrangements called for consultants to be responsible both to the Division and to the BJE. This sometimes led to overlap and tension. Funds were not allocated for day-school consultation, thus minimizing the relationship between the central agency and the most developed schools in the community.[16] Because the supplementary schools underwent decline in the late 1960s and afterward, more and more of the faculties tended to be paraprofessionals—in some cases, teenagers taught—who were far less motivated to seek help than the professionals who, in earlier years, had staffed the same educational institutions. Conversely, their principals were more motivated to seek help.

The issues of communal versus congregational ideology were reflected in the modest use of the facilities and staff talents of the DCS by sectors of the Orthodox community. Where, in the past, schools associated with the (Traditional) Rabbinical Association did not hesitate to turn to Gratz, or to the Council on Jewish Education before it, the newer groups that greatly increased the presence of Orthodoxy in Greater Philadelphia were far more reluctant to associate themselves with the Division, for all of the pedagogical expertise of its staff.

GRATZ COLLEGE

The changes that affected the Jewish community and its Jewish educational institutions did not leave Gratz College untouched.[17] While Gratz could boast of being the oldest college of Jewish studies in the western hemisphere (having opened its doors in 1897), it had fallen behind many of the institutions in the *Iggud Batei Midrash Lemorim* (National Association of Hebrew Teachers Colleges). Students were admitted as young as 15 years of age, academic standards were not sufficiently high, course offerings were limited, no academic degrees were granted (graduates receiving a Hebrew Teachers Diploma), and the program of teacher preparation was quite limited in scope. With that, the college was blessed with a strong, if tiny, faculty and attracted some outstanding students, many of whom went on to serve the local and national Jewish community as rabbis, teachers, principals of Jewish schools, communal servants, and active laity.

As a result of the Honor-Leibman study of Jewish education in Philadelphia, undertaken in 1943, which called attention to a number of Gratz's strengths and weaknesses, a number of steps were taken to bring a college into line with the schools in the *Iggud*.[18] Under the administrations of Dr. Honor, who served as acting dean in 1945, and Dr. Azriel Eisenberg (1946–1951), faculty was added, curriculum was intensified and enriched, and a "Post-Graduate" department was added that enabled students to work beyond the level of a Hebrew Teacher's Diploma toward an undergraduate degree. The "Normal Department," which trained teachers for Sunday schools, was intensified, and an extension department was opened to offer courses for teachers in service and to laity. In addition, during the forties and fifties, Gratz's elementary School of Observation and Practice under the leadership of Elsie Chomsky flourished as an independent Community school.

The Self-Study of Jewish Education carried out by the AJA in 1951 affirmed Gratz's role as "the key institution in the system of Jewish education in Philadelphia," but recommended, among other things, the appointment of a full-time dean, new facilities for the college, and further intensification of the teacher preparation program and other academic programs. These recommendations became the basis for future efforts by the college to grow and develop.

The first Bachelor of Hebrew Literature degree was awarded in 1952, a high school department offering intensive Hebraic preparatory work for the college was established, and the minimum age for collegiate admissions moved to 18 years of age. With these developments, Gratz was accepted into the *Iggud*.

In 1959, Dr. Elazar Goelman was appointed as the first full-time Dean of the College.[19] During his term (1959–1973), Gratz opened the Isaac Mayer Wise department, which prepared high school students to teach in Reform religious schools, and, with an enabling grant from the Netzky foundation, also established the Samuel Netzky Adult Institute of Jewish Studies, which provided college-level extension courses throughout the city. During his tenure, Gratz, which had earlier been housed at Broad and York Streets and afterward from 1953 to 1962 was the guest of Congregation Rodeph Shalom, acquired in 1962, with the help of FJA, its own building at Tenth and Tabor Road on land owned by the Albert Einstein Medical Center. In 1967, the college was accredited by the Middle States Association of Colleges and Secondary Schools. Gratz was now, by anyone's definition, a bona fide college.

However, the period under study brought its share of problems to Gratz as well as other Jewish institutions of learning. College enrollment rose and fell with that of the overall Jewish school enrollment, reaching a peak in the 1960s. There were many reasons for this. First, there was a general drop in Jewish population during the latter part of the period under study. Then, too, more and more of the Jewish high school students, including Gratz's own Hebrew High School students, its most natural recruiting ground, left town for collegiate studies. Of those who remained, some, particularly among those who were accustomed to having secular and Jewish studies in one school setting, preferred to study Judaism as part of their secular studies.

The location of the college in Logan—an ethnically changing area experiencing increased vandalism—seemed unattractive to potential students. Finally, the communal nature of the institution, the ideological and religious heterogeneity of its faculty and student body, deterred many within the Orthodox community from taking advantage of its academic programs.

The college responded to these challenges with new programs under the leadership of Dr. Daniel Isaacman, president of the college. As its traditional pool of students (those who had received an intensively Hebraic elementary and secondary education) decreased, it established a Bachelor of Arts degree in Jewish Studies. For those whose decision to serve the Jewish community professionally had come during the undergraduate years or later, it established graduate programs in Jewish music, Jewish education, and Jewish studies. It established a certification program for Judaica librarians (1984), the first in America. It opened branch programs using other Jewish schools and agency buildings. It enriched and expanded its professional training program through an intensified practicum developed in cooperation with the day schools and a select group of supplementary schools in the area. This allowed those preparing for the teaching profession to practice under the eye of master teachers in the best schools in the community.

The college further demonstrated strong commitment to education as a field of study by establishing, in cooperation with the Myer and Rosaline B. Feinstein Endowment Fund, a chair (its first) in that field (1984). The chair was named in memory of Rosaline B. Feinstein, an outstanding communal leader and a benefactor of the college.[20] With the graduate programs growing, greater emphasis was placed on research than had been true in the past. The library expanded its holdings extensively (the music portion being one of the most important collections in the hemisphere), and a Holocaust survivor study was launched under the direction of noted historian and faculty member Nora Levin.

During the period under study, the College dramatically expanded its adult education offerings through the Samuel Netzky Adult Institute, offering high-level continuing Jewish education. These courses eventually were offered in various locations in the community and on the main campus.

At the end of the period under study, the profile of the college had changed considerably. From a small school, limited to full-time students of high school and early college age, it grew to an academic institution with a multifaceted program, with an increasing number of graduate and older undergraduate students pursuing personal and professional goals. Plans were underfoot to seek a new location, and with the inauguration of a new president, Dr. Gary S. Schiff,[21] the college seemed poised to respond to the changing realities that had affected Jewish life in the second half of the twentieth century.

DROPSIE COLLEGE

For much of its early history, Dropsie College served as the primary school on the continent for the education of scholars of Judaica and Near Eastern Studies. By the mid-1950s, as more and more colleges and universities opened undergraduate and graduate programs in Jewish studies, the college began to experience a steady decline in enrollment, particularly among Jewish students.

The veritable explosion of Jewish studies, particularly during the 1960s and 1970s, brought many outstanding scholars of Judaic studies to the Philadelphia area to teach in such programs. (Among many, the names of Judah Goldin, Jeffrey Tigay, and Arthur Green of Penn; Norbert Samuelson of Temple; and Samuel T. Lachs of Bryn Mawr may be mentioned.) Indeed, alumni of Dropsie were among those whose very programs appealed to students who might otherwise have attended the venerable institution. In addition, the location of the college in a declining neighborhood and the illness of its long-time president, Abraham A. Neuman, took their toll.

The Dropsie College building on North Broad Street.

Continuing financial difficulties, very liberal retirement policies that limited the ability of the college to introduce "fresh blood" into its faculty, and a negative image that stemmed from the idiosyncratic views of its most famous scholar, Solomon Zeitlin, toward the Dead Sea Scrolls (his dating of the Scrolls being much later than the consensus dating of the intertestamental period) also harmed the college.

Abraham Katsch acted as president from 1967 to 1976. During his tenure, the college added programs and changed its name briefly to Dropsie University. The school of education, opened in 1948, closed its doors in 1974 amidst some controversy.

In 1981, David Goldenberg, an alumnus and former dean, was appointed president. Shortly thereafter, on November 9, 1981, a fire (later determined to be arson) caused over $800,000 in damages, particularly to the famed library. Under the leadership of Dr. Goldenberg, the *Jewish Quarterly Review,* edited by the faculty of the college, recovered from the controversies of the Dead Sea Scrolls and was able to continue its historic role as a serious journal for Jewish scholarship.

In 1984, the college moved to the buildings of Temple Adath Israel in Merion. Having rejected, throughout the years, offers of merger or absorption by Temple University, the University of Pennsylvania, Gratz, and Bryn Mawr, the college soon found itself unable to continue its work.

A major gift by Walter Annenberg was the basis for a decision in 1985 to transform the college into a research institution. The Moses Aaron Dropsie Institute for Advanced Research in Judaic and Near Eastern Studies, patterned after the Institute for Advanced Study at Princeton, is scheduled to move into new quarters in the Independence Hall area. Its first director is to be Bernard Lewis of the Princeton Center, a world famous scholar of Judaeo-Arabic History. By 1986 Dropsie College stood poised to begin a new era in its institutional life.

REFORM RELIGIOUS EDUCATION

In Philadelphia, the proportion of Reform congregations in the first half of the twentieth century was particularly small, despite the presence of several outstanding rabbis.[22] In 1947, for example, Reform Judaism was espoused in three congregations, Temple Judea, the first congregation to be Reform in affiliation from its inception, and two very large congregations, Rodeph Shalom and Keneseth Israel.

Because these congregations offered one-day-a-week education and the number of students was not large relative to the entire student population (e.g., 1,300 children in 1942–1943), there was little competition between the leaders of the movement and the communal forces. No Reform counterpart to the BJE was developed, but there was some coordination among the congregations. As Rabbi David H. Wice, spiritual leader of Rodelph Shalom during this period, put it, "individual congregations are zealous for their autonomy."[23] This zealousness placed severe limitations on the ability of a central group to mandate changes in congregational standards as had been done by the BJE.

A Council of Reform Synagogues had been organized in 1942–1943 that, in addition to serving as the local agency for the Union of American Hebrew Congregations, had sponsored an *Institute of Jewish Studies* for Sunday school graduates of UAHC congregations and older adults. Most of the students proved to be of the latter group. In 1943 the rabbis indicated an interest in improving teacher training for the schools of their congregations. They did not see Gratz College as an appropriate setting because the spirit of the institution did not seem to them to conform to the Reform point of view.[24] Eventually, in 1969, after several years of persistent independent effort, the movement, which since 1947 had established a branch of the UAHC in the region, developed, in cooperation with Gratz College, a secondary education program with a teacher-training component as a subdivision of the college. In this program (named for Isaac Mayer Wise), high school students devoted one evening a week to the study of Jewish content and pedagogy at the college and another day in continued study and paraprofessional teaching experiences at Reform Temples. Though the program was ostensibly a cooperative effort, the UAHC insisted on total autonomous control of curriculum and independent classes. Eventually, all local Reform congregational schools but one required a second day of weekly instruction for *all* pupils in grades 4 or 5 to 7. Confirmation was conducted at the end of the tenth grade.

Regionalization was also reflected in the activities of the Principals' Council of the Reform religious schools; in the operation of the Hebrew Honor Society, which they helped to establish and which certified members through Hebrew language examinations (taken by more and more students each year); and in the publication of an annual educational pamphlet, *Kinnereth,* as well as an annual pedagogical conference for teachers at Gratz College.

In the years following World War II, Reform Judaism changed radically. After the Holocaust and the rise of the State of Israel, extreme rejection of tradition was less common in the movement than had been true in the past. There was a general readiness to give greater emphasis to ceremonies and rituals and to stress ethnicity, traditional behaviors, and modern Israeli language and culture. Bar and bat mitzvah ceremonies, for example, became common among Reform youth, and, as noted previously, this led to an increase in the number of hours and days each week that became the norm for Reform Jewish education. Reform summer camps, like Harlam in the Poconos, provided Jewish educational experiences that helped to strengthen the highly successful teenage programs for Reform youth.

Moreover, Reform congregations were often at the forefront of social concerns, which appealed to basic Jewish sensibilities. All of this narrowed the gap between the respective public images of Reform Judaism and Conservative Judaism to the point at which more and more Jews of East European background did not hesitate to affiliate themselves with Reform congregations.

For a long time, Philadelphia was a "Conservative" city. There were more Conservative congregations and members relative to the general Jewish population than in any other city in the country. As noted, at the start of this period, Reform Judaism was limited to three congregations, two of which were quite large. By the end of the period, the balance had changed dramatically. In 1942–1943, the approximately 1,300 students enrolled in Reform religious schools had represented 20 percent of all congregational school students. By 1982–1983, the 3,500 students represented 46 percent of the figure, the same percentage as were enrolled in Conservative supplementary schools (though there were several hundred other students enrolled in Conservative day schools). The number of area congregations had grown to fifteen.

SECONDARY EDUCATION

As noted earlier, during the period under study, Gratz College made the transition from a hybrid high school–college status to that of a true college. In the process, an intensified preparatory track was developed in the form of a five-year high school program that was strongly Hebraic in flavor and curriculum.

In 1959, during the presidency of Dr. M. David Hoffman, the BJE opened the Cyrus Adler school, the first of three regional secondary units that were cooperatively planned with the participating congregations but under the direct sponsorship and administrative control of the BJE. Adler served congregations in the Northwest section of the city. Julius Greenstone High School, which opened in 1960, and Main Line–Wynnefield Regional Hebrew High School (later renamed for M. David Hoffman), which followed in 1961–1962, served congregations in the Northeast section and the Western section (with adjoining suburbs), respectively. Unlike the Gratz Hebrew High School, these schools were "comprehensive," that is, they offered several tracks to cater to students with differing backgrounds and degrees of readiness to study advanced Hebrew texts and language. It was intended that graduation would take place after the tenth grade, and then students would continue in the last two years of either the Hebrew High School Department or the Normal Department at Gratz.

In a major agreement, the BJE and Gratz[25] cooperated to obtain funding from the FJA for the regional schools and for a high school consultant at the DCS. A joint personnel committee of the DCS and the BJE was responsible for selecting teachers and principals for the regional schools, and a standard curriculum was worked out that would relate to the curriculum of Gratz College Hebrew High School.

Although this arrangement worked well for many years, particularly when enrollments were high at the BJE schools,[26] tensions developed as enrollments in the three schools began to slide. As the numbers of students in the feeder Conservative elementary schools declined, fewer students applied to the BJE schools. During the seventies, curricular innovations in the spirit of the sixties led to greater emphasis in those schools on effective dimensions of learning and less stress on Hebrew language and textual study (in Hebrew or in the vernacular). Students whose parents favored a more essentialist approach to learning began to enroll their children in the Gratz High School rather than at the local BJE school. Tensions were created between the two agencies. Fewer and fewer BJE graduates chose to continue their studies at Gratz High School. Fewer seemed able to pass the entrance examination. The (non-Hebraic) Normal Department felt the loss most keenly because it depended almost entirely on BJE graduates for enrollment in its eleventh- and twelfth-grade programs. Finally, the Normal Department collapsed, the few candidates for its program being integrated into the Gratz Hebrew High School.

Toward the end of the period under study, a few congregations approached Gratz with the idea of housing branches of the Gratz High School on their premises. In some cases, this would have meant a withdrawal by that congregation from the BJE regional school system. The BJE fought this idea vigorously, claiming an invasion of "turf," and a *kulturkampf* that would lead to the deletion of the religious component in secondary education in the Conservative movement. At the close of the period under study, this complex matter still awaited resolution.

Rabbi Elias Charry at Torah dedication at Akiba Academy.

Enrollment for Jewish supplementary schools in Philadelphia and elsewhere peaked in the early sixties. Congregational school enrollment had risen steadily (over 85 percent) between 1951 and 1962, and overall enrollment had risen 55 percent. Then began a steady decline in enrollment caused largely, but not solely, by a falling birthrate in the Jewish community. Other factors included an increased tendency of people to leave the area; increased willingness of young parents to forego synagogue membership and Jewish education for their children; increased number of intermarried couples who avoided problems of split loyalties by eschewing religious affiliation; an increase in the number of two-profession households, single-parent households, and other untraditional household arrangements that made it inconvenient or difficult for a parent to transport children to the Jewish school; and a general loss of commitment to ethnicity and religion, both of which were seen by some as anachronistic in an age in which the stress was increasingly on universal ideals. To all of these may be added some dissatisfaction with the quality and achievements of supplementary schools.

The notion that a Jewish child requires some form of Jewish education was no longer considered a given in the Jewish community. But the same set of factors that caused many to keep their children away from any Jewish education caused others to seek a different kind of Jewish education for their children. Troubled by what they saw as a serious weakening of Jewish identity, and continuing problems in supplementary schools, they began to create and support new forms of maximal Jewish education. Thus, the Jewish day school came to Philadelphia.

ORTHODOX JEWISH SCHOOLS[27]

Although Jewish day schools were created by all the religious groups in the United States Jewish community, the overwhelming majority and the earliest of the schools created during the period under study were established by and for Orthodox Jews. At the start of this period, Orthodoxy was a weak and disorganized group in the city. Its constituency was very largely working class, foreign born, lacking in secular education and wealth, and with almost no influence as a movement on community policy. The supplementary schools conducted in Orthodox congregations were often small, poorly organized, and located in neighborhoods with declining Jewish populations.

Another type of congregation was nominally Orthodox. Here, the rabbi was usually ordained at Yeshiva University and considered himself to be a "Modern Orthodox Jew,"[28] while the congregation he served in many ways (including, at times, seating for worship) resembled a Conservative congregation.[29] These rabbis generally belonged to the Rabbinical Council, and the schools associated with their congregations were known as Rabbinical Council schools. While there were a number of such schools at the beginning of the period under study, by the end of that period, only two such schools remained, one of which, Shaare Shamayim, participated in the BJE secondary school in Northeast Philadelphia.

During the sixties and seventies, the community experienced an influx of Orthodox Jews from other communities. These included many professionals and graduate students (some of whom remained in the community after graduation). Favored areas of location for these groups were Northeast Philadelphia, Wynnefield, Overbrook Park, and the western suburbs, particularly in the Bala Cynwyd and Wynnewood areas. Unlike older generations, whose personal lifestyles did not always cohere with the demands of Orthodoxy, the movement with which they affiliated, these Jews were fully *Halakhic* (committed to Jewish law). For them, the only kind of Jewish education that was acceptable was the day school or the Yeshivah. Thus, in the course of fewer than forty years (the first day schools were created in the middle of the forties), and with accelerated tempo since the sixties, Orthodox institutions of learning together with Orthodox synagogues sprang up to serve this new constituency.

Between 1946 and 1980, no fewer than seven schools opened their doors in the community.[30] In this, Philadelphia was typical of the Jewish communities of North America. According to Alvin Schiff, the "Era of Great Expansion" began in 1940.[31] At the onset of this period, there were thirty-five Yeshivot in six communities, with an approximate enrollment of 7,700. Toward the end of this period, every community in the United States with five thousand or more Jews had at least one day school, and the student population of these 545 schools had reached 92,000, representing about one-quarter of the total enrollment in Jewish schools.[32]

Many explanations have been offered for the rapid growth of Jewish day schools. These include the intense commitment of Orthodox lay leaders and educators, demographic changes in urban communities, questionable quality of public school education, dissatisfaction with Jewish supplementary schools, the post–World War II immigration of Hasidic Jews, the active commitment and strong advocacy of day schools by the Conservative movement,[33] the emergence of significant support for day schools among leaders in the Reform movement,[34] and a growing concern by communal leaders for Jewish survival and the quality of Jewish life. Other factors include the impact of the Holocaust and the destruction of the great centers of Jewish learning in Europe, which engendered a desire to create sources of scholarship and leadership on this continent.[35] There was an awareness among Protestant and some Jewish groups that the spirit of scientific naturalism that animated many public schools constituted a threat to the development of religious commitment. Also, a factor was the desire to emulate the development of a vibrant Hebrew culture to be found in Israel.[36]

Each school was unique in its history, ideology, structure, and placement on the communal-ethnic-congregational-religious continuum. The Akiba Hebrew Academy (founded in 1946) was communal in ideology, one of a handful of secondary Jewish day schools in the country espousing a multi-ideological approach to Jewish education. Its faculty and student body were drawn, by design, from every group in Jewish life.

The Talmudical Yeshiva (1952), Torah Academy (1964), Beth Jacob (1946), and Solomon Schechter (1956) were religious in ideology (all but the last being Orthodox) and not connected to a particular congregation.

In Schechter's case, much of the initiative came from Rabbi David Goldstein and leaders of Har Zion Temple, but, from the beginning, there was consensus that the entire movement in the community had to support, and offer some degree of sponsorship for, the school. The Talmudical Yeshiva, modeled after the famed Bet Midrash Gavohah of Lakewood, New Jersey, sought financial support from the larger community but, for a long time, maintained a stance of aloofness from it. This was modified in the latter part of the period under study as the Yeshivah forged stronger links with the Jews of Philadelphia. Forman Hebrew Day School (1973) and the Hebrew Academy of the Northeast (1982) were each housed in a synagogue but constituted independent entities.[37] In 1985, Forman merged with the Northeast branch of the Solomon Schechter Day School. Finally, the (short-lived) day school at Temple Adath Israel (1971) was conceived from its beginnings as a totally integrated part of the congregation and its educational program.

With all of these differences, there were commonalties as well. Each school was established to be a "real" school, that is, a serious, self-respecting place of learning that would evoke, and probably require, significant commitments of time, energy, and money from those connected with it. While, in theory, the same might have been true of supplementary schools, in reality few of them evoked the kind of loyalty and commitment of resources that is associated with a primary institution of learning.

Another point to be noted is the small number of day schools relative to the size of the Jewish population. Baltimore and Cleveland, with much smaller Jewish populations, had as many day schools as did Philadelphia. Whether this was best explained as a reflection of the weakness of Orthodoxy for much of the period under study or the wide dispersal of the Jewish community within the metropolitan area or some other reason was unclear. Whatever the reason, nationwide the percentage of day-school students among the total Jewish school enrollment at the end of the period under study was about one-third; but in Greater Philadelphia, however, only about 10 percent of the Jewish schools' population was to be found in day schools.

Another significant aspect of the day-school story in Philadelphia was the unusual degree of support for Orthodox institutions that came from within the Conservative movement. Perhaps because Orthodoxy lacked the resources to support its own institutions for many years, individuals who identified themselves with the Conservative movement provided much of the financial backing for Orthodox day schools. In this connection, the role of Har Zion Temple was unique. From its beginnings, Rabbi Simon Greenberg had projected the image of that congregation as a "Staat-Shul," a synagogue that took its responsibilities to the larger community very seriously.[38] With strong support from Rabbi Greenberg and, particularly, from his successor, Rabbi David Goldstein, men like Hyman Bomze, Abe Birenbaum, Abner Schreiber, Sol Satinsky, Herman Landau, and Nathan Pearlstein helped to establish and support Orthodox schools as well as those of Conservative and communal ideologies.[39]

Finally, the issue of day schools ignited more passion in the community than any other single issue having to do with Jewish education during the period under study. By 1980 the day schools of Philadelphia were, in the main, well-established and well-accepted components of the educational system of the community. But this was not always so. The process of acceptance and support was gradual and fitful. It is to that story that we now turn our attention.

FJA AND THE FUNDING OF AKIBA

The evolution of communal attitudes toward Jewish day schools is, perhaps, best captured in the story of the funding of the Akiba Hebrew Academy by the Allied Jewish Appeal (later, the Federation Allied Jewish Appeal or the Federation of Jewish Agencies of Greater Philadelphia). Akiba was opened in 1946, and with most of the other day schools that opened after it, funding was an immediate and serious problem. The correspondence of Martin Feld, first president of the school, reveals his ongoing strenuous efforts (including substantial use of his personal resources) to meet the budget of the school.[40]

Sometime during the first years of the school's existence, an approach was made to the Allied Jewish Appeal, then responsible for dispensing monies to the cultural and educational   institutions of the Jewish community. Given the climate of the time, it was deemed advisable to develop a vehicle for indirect funding of the school. The strategy called for the conclusion of a "working relationship" between Akiba and the United Hebrew Schools and Yeshivos, a system of communally funded and sponsored supplementary schools. The approach was approved by a subcommittee of the AJA Committee on Education, the Committee on Education,[41] and finally, by the AJA Board of Directors. By this arrangement, a portion of the UHSY allocation would be "passed through" to Akiba.

The need for indirect funding reflected strong feelings, pro and con, that existed in the Jewish community with regard to day schools. The very announcement of plans to open Akiba sparked a vigorous debate in the pages of the Jewish Exponent between Professor Julius Grodinsky,

Gratz College
NORMAL DEPARTMENT

Class of 1969

R. WALLACH · R. GERSHENFELD · P. PERKINS · S. POLLACK · M. YOUNG · I. LEVINSON · S. YONDORF · C. GERSHKOW · S. ROSEN · H. LITWACK · S. LEVIN

M. BARTASH · C. BERG

P. MELLON · DR. S. LACHS · DR. L. SPOTTS · DR. W. CHOMSKY CHAIRMAN of FACULTY · DR. E. GOELMAN DEAN · MR. D. ISAACMAN REGISTRAR · DR. S. KURLAND · MR. J. YENISH LIBRARIAN · K. MILLER

V. LIPSHUTZ · S. COLE · MR. S. ALTMAN · RABBI N. REISNER · MR. A. COHEN · RABBI M. SCULT · B. HABER · H. GABRIEL

S. GEVER · M. NIGUS · R. MILLER · L. IVKER · S. HOFFMAN · S. CARROLL

S. SABUL · J. PANITCH · A. TABAK · E. FREEDMAN · K. AARON · B. TABAK · I. GASTON · R. RUBIN · C. STUDENT · M. SOLOMON · S. SUKOL

president of the Philadelphia chapter of the American Council for Judaism, and Dr. Simon Greenberg, Rabbi of Har Zion Temple and founder of the school.[42] For Grodinsky, the issues included the impact of such a school on the American public school, "The Keystone of American Democracy," and the need to provide students with "a thorough training in the principles of democratic ideals of civic responsibilities." "This," asserted Grodinsky, "can be carried out only through the public school system . . . The parochial school cannot function effectively in teaching democratic ideals when the children are removed from contact with other American children who are members of other religious faiths."[43] When Greenberg countered with the argument that other religious groups, such as the Roman Catholics, Society of Friends, and others, had conducted schools for many years without destroying the public school system, Grodinsky retorted that Jewish day schools are different because they advocate the establishment of a Jewish state.

At least some of these arguments, and others as well, were voiced or felt by many Jewish leaders in Philadelphia and throughout the nation. In fact, a decade later, when, as part of a national study of Jewish education, community leaders were asked to express their personal feelings about day-school education, fully 75 percent of those responding registered opposition to such schools on principle or practice.[44] These attitudes were still very much alive when, after three years of indirect funding, Akiba turned to the AJA with a request that it receive direct funding. The AJA established a special committee, chaired by Edwin Wolf II to consider this volatile issue.[45] The committee met for a year. In reviewing the minutes of the meeting, one sees the extent to which AJA tried to avoid setting off an explosion in the community with regard to Akiba.

> Rabbi [David] Wice [of Rodeph Shalom] . . . stated that we cannot close our eyes to the fact that a number of people have strong negative feelings on Akiba and have real feelings as to the validity of any communal support for it.[46]
>
> Mr. [Edward] Polisher felt that AJA had been side-stepping any real resolution on the matter of Akiba for a number of years and it is time that we made up our minds as to where we stand on it. Mr. Wolf added that previously AJA committees in relating to this question tried to solve it in such a way so as not to antagonize even the few.

Two reports were drafted, one reflecting the majority view that Akiba should be funded and one reflecting Rabbi Wice's view that its request ought to be denied.[47] The AJA accepted the majority view, and, beginning with the 1953–1954 campaign, the school received funds to support its *Jewish Studies* program.[48]

At this time, Beth Jacob School, also founded in 1946, was making unsuccessful efforts to receive AJA funds.[49] These efforts continued until 1957, when the president of the newly merged Federation of Jewish Charities–Allied Jewish Appeal, Judge Abraham L. Freedman, and the chairman of the Committee on Inclusions, Jacob G. Gutman, recommended that a special committee on All-Day Schools be established to study the issue and to make recommendations.

Because the issue was one of the first to be faced by the newly merged units of FJA and because passions ran very high on the issue, it was judged to be very important that the chairman of the special committee be someone of great prestige and unusual sensitivity. In what was called a "brilliant decision,"[50] Judge Freedman chose one of the vice presidents of FAJA, Edwin Wolf II, to fill this post. Wolf's previous involvement in the deliberations of the AJA with regard to the question of direct funding for Akiba and his personal background equipped him with a profound understanding of the views of all concerned.

Scion of a distinguished family of German Jews, he grew up in a home that was strongly anti-Zionist.[51] But Wolf was different. A scholar and thinker, he had belonged to the Palestine Society, an informal discussion group that numbered among its members such men as Louis Leventhal, Samuel Daroff, and William Sylk. Wolf's family background, his personal prestige, his position in the Federation, and his understanding of the issues involved made him an admirable choice to lead the deliberations that represented the first real test of the workability of the merger of the older German-Jewish group and the rising leaders of East European background.[52]

The committee met from September 1957 to December of that year. A split vote developed on the following resolution: "All Day schools have a recognized position in Jewish education. From a philosophic point of view, therefore, All Day schools should be included in the framework of FJA communal support for Jewish education."[53]

This resolution was passed by the committee and, subsequently, by the standing Committee on Jewish Education and the overall Planning and Budgeting Committee, all without unanimity.[54] The Executive Committee rejected the resolution as drafted and revised it as follows: "Cognizant of its responsibility for the support and encouragement of the Jewish education and in view of the position of All Day schools in American Jewish life, Federation recognizes the right of these schools to its support for the sectarian aspects of their work. At the same time, Federation does not recognize the right to communal support directly or indirectly for the secular aspects of these schools."[55]

The resolution, together with the original resolution and a minority report opposing any support for Jewish Day schools that emanated from the original committee, were presented at a meeting of the Board of Trustees of FJA on June 26, 1950. One participant later said that it was the fullest debate that he had ever witnessed at an open meeting of the Board of Trustees of the Federation.[56]

The president, Abraham L. Freedman, announced that he had received a number of letters and telephone calls from people unable to attend but with strong opinions on the topic. He explained that the Federation could not accept votes in absentia or by proxy. According to one participant, Edwin Wolf's presentation was powerful and effective.[57] The minutes record a spirited debate. Among those opposing any support were D. Hays Solis-Cohen, a member of Congregation

Left: Dr. Daniel Isaacman, 1966.

Right: Rabbi Arthur Green in 1970. Rabbi Green has become a moving force at the Reconstructionist Rabbinical College in Wyncote.

Mikveh Israel, an observant Jew, and leader in the American Council for Judaism. Solis-Cohen argued that the community should support only the teaching of Hebrew as a "tongue of prayer." Furthermore, he argued, Jewish day schools would be a "threat to our concept of American citizenship." He called for the support of only those areas of Jewish activity that "serve specific religious needs."[58] Rabbis David Goldstein and Max Klein, of Congregations Har Zion and Adath Jeshurun, respectively, supported the resolution. Both stressed the need for programs that would supply the community with scholars and teachers. Earl Gratz opposed the proposal on the grounds that it would divide the community. The arguments of the minority report of the original committee expressed many of the traditional arguments against day schools: that they were "ghettoizing forces," that they would usurp the rightful roles of home and synagogue in "making the children better Jews." While granting the right of such schools to exist, the report concluded its arguments by stating, "Let those who want such schools pay for them!"[59]

After extensive debate, a vote was taken on the resolution as revised by the executive committee. The resolution was adopted by a vote of 41 to 28.[60] This resolution, which limited communal aid to the "sectarian" aspects of the day school, remained on the books of the Federation as a bedrock of policy. It was referred to frequently in discussions on day-school matters. It also was cited outside of the community for its clarity.[61] While, in later years, it proved impossible to implement strictly as capital needs for day schools arose (it being somewhat difficult to decide what percentage of a roof was "sectarian"), it did provide a theoretical basis for consensus on communal support for day schools. Most important, because the focus of the debate was the issue of support for day schools in general, the door was now open for consideration of the needs of schools other than Akiba (Beth Jacob immediately, other schools as they arose). The Federation had reached a milestone; it had voiced a commitment (never again to be publicly questioned) to support day-school education.[62]

The Federation's role as a funder of day schools inevitably led it to take an ever increasingly active interest in the schools. Already in 1951, the study of Akiba and Beth Jacob was included as part of the *Philadelphia Self-Study of Jewish Education,* and the recommendations of that study had included a call for the support of the Jewish Studies programs of the day schools of Philadelphia.[63]

In 1964, the Federation undertook a study of Akiba and Beth Jacob. Solomon Schechter, which was a candidate for beneficiary status, was invited to participate in the study and did so. The representatives of Beth Jacob found difficulty with the procedures and personnel (lay and profession-

Rabbi Abraham Shem Tov of Lubavitch and Beth Jacob.

al) involved in the study and withdrew for a while, delaying the process for a year.[64] Other key decisions regarding day schools included the acceptance of the Solomon Schechter Day School in 1964 and the Torah Academy of Greater Philadelphia in 1970 as beneficiaries of FAJA and the continued refusal to provide funds to support the Philadelphia Talmudical Yeshiva, based on its self-definition as a "national" institution and the small number of students coming from the Philadelphia area.[65]

In 1971, the Federation, through its Committee on Jewish Education, organized a subcommittee to assess the role that the FJA had played in the past, in regard to Jewish education and to plan ahead for its future role. The report of that committee, issued in 1973, charged with determining educational priorities, was popularly known as the Rockower Report after its chairman, Jacob R. (Jack) Rockower. A communal leader active in the Reform community, Rockower had demonstrated deep commitments to improving the quality of Jewish education.

The Rockower Report examined Jewish education as a whole within the entire community. Among other findings, it took note of the growth of the day schools and of their distinctive contributions to the community, stating that day-school graduates appeared to have a greater commitment to Jewish values and lifestyles.[66] The committee recommended that the Federation continue its financial support for day schools, including assistance in capital fund-raising efforts; and that encouragement should be provided for new day schools, be they communal or ideological affiliates of Conservative, Orthodox, or Reform Judaism.[67] Finally, the committee recommended that efforts be undertaken to encourage more continuity of study among day-school graduates. In its final ranking of priorities, the committee listed day-school education as third in importance, after teacher training and secondary education.[68]

The community, through its planning and funding agency, had changed its attitude toward day schools fundamentally during the period from 1940 to 1980. From a stance of ambivalence, indifference, or hostility, it grew to tolerate, then accept, these schools as valid and legitimate expressions of the desire by some Jews to improve the quality of Jewish life at home and in the community. In this evolution, Philadelphia mirrored what was happening throughout the country. The continued expansion of the day-school movement was one of the bright spots in Jewish education during the period under consideration. By 1980, about one-third of all students in Jewish schools nationally were studying in day schools. Notice must be taken, however, of problems that remained to be solved, among them problems of professional staff availability and competence, adequate educational materials for Jewish studies, funding for consultation services, and parent education.[69] Yet, there was great progress. Almost all of the schools were housed in good or excellent facilities. By 1980, increased Federation funding to four schools represented about 25 percent of their total budget. Truly, the period of 1940–1980 was a time of dramatic growth and consolidation for the day schools of Greater Philadelphia. The community came to recognize the contributions of the day schools and was prepared to support their continued development as an investment in the future.[70]

RECENT DEVELOPMENTS

The Jewish educational scene not only has grown in size, but also has become more variegated in form. Taking its lead from the alternative education movement that has arisen during the past two decades, Jewish education has found ways of serving wider populations with newer programs. One such phenomenon is the *Havurah* (fellowship, *Havurot,* plural), which offers opportunities for worship, study, and celebration in a setting participants believe is more intimate, personal, and spiritually meaningful than what is found in larger synagogues.

Begun as a Jewish manifestation of the counterculture of the 1960s (though with roots in ancient Judaism), the Havurah flourished in university areas (e.g., Encino, California, and Somerville, Massachusetts) and appealed to young families who generally eschewed the formality and social accoutrements of large synagogues. In the Philadelphia area, several such Havurot have been founded—among the most important being the Germantown Jewish Center Havurot; the Havurah at Adath Jeshurun; the Center City Havurah, formerly housed at the Broad Street Y, now at Beth Zion-Beth Israel; the "Library Minyan" at Beth Hillel-Beth El in Wynnewood; and "Haminyan," housed in the Kaiserman Y on City Line. These groups, though representing a small segment of the Jewish population, represent intense and energetic affirmations of Jewish identity, and have opened up new vistas of Jewish education in the area.[71]

Another new form of Jewish education was developed through and by the Federation of Jewish Agencies for young leaders and potential leaders in the community. Known as The Young Leadership Council and guided by the Department of Leadership Development of the Federation, the group provided formal and informal lectures and study sessions for people between the ages of 21 and 40. Many of these sessions attracted hundreds of participants. Topics included anti-Semitism, Israel, definitions of Jewishness, intergroup relations, and Jewish tradition. Participants tended to be young, middle-class, Center City professionals and business people. Programs also included a social component that was important, particularly for the singles who made up the vast majority of the group.[72]

One of the most exciting developments to affect Jewish education in Greater Philadelphia took place in 1985 when the Mandell Educational Campus was established on a 30-acre site in Melrose Park. Formerly the site of the Melrose Academy, the campus offered a unique opportunity for cooperative effort by Jewish educational institutions offering service to preschoolers, children, teens, and adults. Named after Samuel P. and Ida Mandell, the campus was purchased by Joel Weisbein, Marcel Groen, and Steven D. Rudman and was supported by Dr. Morton S., Ronald B., Seymour G., and Dr. Gerald A. Mandell, and Judith Delfiner, children of the Mandells.

The institutions committed to moving onto the campus include Gratz College, the Gratz College Hebrew High School, a branch of Federation Day Care Services, and the Forman Center of the Solomon Schechter Day School. In addition there is a strong possibility that a branch of the Akiba Hebrew Academy or a new Junior High Jewish Day School would be added to the campus later on.

Many of the trends occurred in other cities as well. What made Philadelphia different? First was the absence for much of this period of a large, well-organized, and united Orthodox community. The community (one of the largest in the world) was unable, for years, to support a single kosher restaurant when such a facility was available in much smaller towns. Second, the large area encompassed by the community meant that there was no natural center, no neighborhood in which its central institutions could be placed as an address for the Jewish community. There was no *Yiddishe Gass* like Harvard Street in Brookline (Boston), or Park Heights Avenue in Baltimore, or Devon Avenue in Chicago.

Lacking this ambiance, which in many communities was tied to Orthodoxy, it was the Conservative Jews of Philadelphia, particularly those of Har Zion Temple, who became the key supporters of intensive Jewish education—the Yeshivot and the day schools, particularly those started prior to the 1960s. By 1980, conditions had changed in this regard. A newly revitalized Orthodox community was developing in the Northeast and Western sectors of the community. Two kosher restaurants were functioning in the Center City area. Interest in day-school education, while less than in other cities, was growing. The community still tolerated many small, underfunded supplementary schools, educationally nonviable units, maintained for fear that without them the congregations sponsoring the schools would not survive. The community was faced with an increasing problem of recruiting and retaining qualified teachers in Jewish schools, a problem it shared with many other communities.[73]

One special characteristic of the period under study was the ongoing struggle between communal and congregational agencies to cooperate without surrendering autonomy. This struggle had both ideological and political dimensions. At the end of the period, it had not been resolved except on the supplementary elementary school level, where congregational schools (of very mixed quality) achieved an almost total victory in the struggle for dominance.

The community still faced the question of how it could "lever up" the quality of its schools without violating the norms of school autonomy. In Los Angeles, Miami, and other cities, this problem had been solved by having the central agency allocate funds directly to individual schools *that met professional standards of quality*. With no such "carrot" to offer, the central agency could do little to affect individual schools but rely on goodwill and a common commitment to education.

With all of this, there was reason for some optimism where Jewish education was concerned. The rhetoric of support in Philadelphia and elsewhere was greater than ever before in American history. It seemed likely that more care, more resources, and an even better quality of leadership would be placed at the service of this cause than had been true in the past. By the 1980s, it seemed that the Greater Philadelphia Jewish community had come at last to recognize the inextricable link between the quality of Jewish education and the quality of Jewish life.[74]

"The big story of 5717," read the
Jewish Times caption, "was the merger
of the Allied Jewish Appeal and the
Federation of Jewish Charities…"
Leaders in the historic move were
(from left, seated) Myer Feinstein,
AJA president; Abraham L. Freedman,
president of the Federation of Jewish
Agencies; and Bernard L. Frankel, FJC
president; (standing) Donald B.
Hurwitz, executive director of AJA, FJC,
and now of the new Federation;
Bernard G. Segal, past president of AJA;
Leon C. Sunstein, past president of
AJA and chairman of the Consolidation
Committees; and Samuel A. Goldberg,
past president of the FJC and chairman
of Committee on New Agency Bylaws,
September 7, 1956.

THE JEWISH FEDERATION OF GREATER PHILADELPHIA:
A Quarter Century of Change

Ernest M. Kahn

As the United States celebrated its bicentennial, the Federation of Jewish Agencies of Greater Philadelphia (FJA) faced a critical juncture. New issues were troubling the nation and the Federation's leaders: the confrontations of urban crisis, racial discord, and the Vietnam War; precarious Federation finances; Jewish population movement to suburbia; increasing intermarriage; and the early stages of the women's movement.

Amidst these pressures, the Federation's longtime chief professional, Donald Hurwitz, decided to retire. A search committee was formed and selected Robert P. Forman to take over from Hurwitz. The handover would be gradual. Hurwitz, a congenial and easy-going leader who served the Federation for some twenty years, planned to ease out of the job slowly. However, when Hurwitz was diagnosed with cancer, Forman was expedited to the scene.

Trained at the Jewish federations of San Francisco, Miami, and New York, Forman came with a reputation as a hard-working, dedicated, and knowledgeable professional devoted to his family and his work. He was aware of the need for change at the Philadelphia Federation from his very first interview about the position. The extent to which that feeling was shared by the volunteer leadership of FJA remained to be determined.

Forman's mandate, however, was clear. The Articles of Incorporation of the Federation of Jewish Charities of Philadelphia, incorporated on April 8, 1901, state, "The object of the Association is to provide an efficient and practical mode of collecting voluntary contributions from the Israelites of Philadelphia, and to devote the sums so collected to the support and maintenance of Jewish Charitable Organizations of said City, and to such other charitable purposes, as may be provided for in the By-Laws, to the end that each institution may the more effectively carry on its charitable work by being relieved of the necessity to make separate appeals and collections.[1]

Since 1901, and continuing until almost the end of the century, it has been the collective view of Philadelphia's Jewish communal leadership that raising money for charitable causes was its principal task and its biggest problem. Money and its distribution are at the very core of the Federation and its purposes, but the implementation of its mission has been subject to trends and issues far removed from the efficient collection of charitable contributions.

In 1976 the bulk of the Federation's funds came from an annual campaign of the Federation Allied Jewish Appeal (FAJA). Limited support came from the income of the Federation's small endowment and a thrift shop. In addition, the Federation benefited substantially from the annual United Way campaign, which provided funds for both the Federation and some ten social service agencies that were members of both the Federation and the United Way. In 1975 the United Way allocation for these agencies was $2,607,500. The Federation was assigned the task of allocating funds to each agency that held such dual membership, a task that continues to this day.

Two categories of agencies were eligible for Federation funding. The first, constituent agencies (some of which originally formed the Federation), provided human services, community services, and Jewish education in the Philadelphia area and were entitled to participate in the governance of the Federation. The second, beneficiary agencies, usually national in scope, received Federation support for their work in exchange for a commitment not to raise funds in Philadelphia. In rare instances, small grants were provided for nonmember agencies.

Before 1976 the greatest concern of Federation member agencies had been the extent to which the Federation's campaign would provide funding for them. Agencies were dependent on the FAJA campaign because they had given up their right to raise funds on their own. But by 1975 the funding of human services in the United States had undergone significant changes. A post–World War II federal government's vision of providing support for basic human needs had gained in popularity, resulting in large federal programs to create senior adult housing, day care, supplementary training for the disabled, foster care, and similar programs. The human service agencies of the Philadelphia Jewish community, along with voluntary organizations of other religious groups and those under nonsectarian auspices, became heavily involved in offering publicly mandated services under government contracts that precluded compulsory participation of clients in religious practices.

The impact on the planning and allocations efforts of the Federation was immediate. Federal funds enabled Jewish human service agencies (and those under other auspices) to meet the needs of substantial numbers of clients without requiring further Federation funding. The result was a decrease in the agencies' dependence on the Federation. Of course, the expansion of federal programs occurred slowly over many years, so Jewish agencies continued to depend on Federation funds for activities not covered by government grants. But soon, government funding began to cause tension within the Federation's family of agencies, especially between those for whom only FAJA campaign funds were available and those with access to government and United Way resources in addition to Federation funds. Several agencies worked creatively to secure financing and still meet the sectarian needs of their clients. For example, Joseph Taylor, executive of the Association for Jewish Children (later merged with Jewish Family Service), formed a consortium with Catholic and Protestant child welfare agencies based on the need to serve children of all denominations. In this way, all three groups became eligible for public funds.

While the nondiscrimination requirements of government grants enabled agencies to serve non-Jews as well as Jews, they also raised concerns at the Federation and its agencies about the future of sectarian agencies in such a political climate. As federal funding swelled, so did its rules and accountability mechanisms. And, in very short order, the Federation was contending with federal regulations with different priorities, frequently limiting the opportunity for and impact of Federation planning activities. Forman decided the time was right to reevaluate the Federation's planning and allocation efforts.

In the mid-1970s, the Federation was still operating as it had in 1956 when the Federation of Jewish Charities merged with the Allied Jewish Appeal (AJA) to form the Federation of Jewish Agencies (FJA). Under this structure, Charles Miller headed planning, and Ezekiel Perlman directed allocations. Both were senior, seasoned professionals, respected for their expertise and strong leadership. However, the complexities of running two separate departments with different fiscal years resulted in more time devoted to allocations, which left little time for planning. A task force, chaired by Arlin Adams, a judge of the U.S. Court of Appeals, reviewed both departments and recommended the establishment of a single, integrated department under one director. The timing was fortuitous because both Miller and Perlman were eligible for and interested in retirement, and following an extended search, I became director of the merged department in mid-1978.

The Federation's new planning and allocations structure annually involved some three hundred different members of the Jewish community in planning and allocations. Most committee members served with great diligence, but the complexity of the system was difficult to manage. Moreover, substantial contributors to the Federation as well as active fund-raisers were rarely involved in the deliberations that had previously involved them.

Early in the 1980s, the Philadelphia Federation agreed to participate in a national project of the United Jewish Appeal (UJA) that intended to improve fund raising by using methods of more successful communities. The UJA proposed that the FJA reduce the size of its 240-member board and rotate those members. The already large size of the board precluded serious deliberations, but the possibility of a required rotation caused great consternation. I recall meeting one of the leading board members on a street corner in Center City. The board member shared his objections so loudly that a policeman approached to inquire about the "trouble" and advised us that any physical altercation would result in our arrest.

The 1980s were difficult times for Federation volunteers. Agencies advocated for their clients' needs, but how should the Federation prioritize those needs? What was known about the quality, efficiency, or effectiveness of a particular program? How were Federation volunteers (many of whom had been or still were active at various member agencies of the Federation) to set aside their experiences and commitments in order to make "communal" decisions? Should the Federation help with immediate needs or address itself to laying the foundation for long-term solutions? And there never was enough money.

Intersecting at times with volunteers' concerns were issues of Federation-Agency Relations. Basic responsibility for this aspect of the Federation's activities was assigned to the Department of Allocations and Planning (DAP) in the plan for the merger of planning and allocations approved in 1979. However, agencies often attempted to sidestep DAP and work through other Federation influences to move their agendas forward. In the early years of a newly merged department, functioning essentially under new rules, the avoidance of new patterns of communications and relations could be viewed as old habits dying hard. After all, many of these relationships had previously proved effective. Such "end runs" were usually attempted when the DAP would not agree to particular actions requested by an agency. A "higher authority" was thought likely to be more productive than the appeals process provided in the DAP plan.

As Federation leadership became more familiar with DAP procedures, such "end runs" became less frequent. In retrospect, the agencies were correct in continuing to view the Federation and the DAP as a political system, but they failed to see that political interventions could rarely advance incomplete or inadequate proposals.

Agency executives were inherently conflicted. Their leadership expected them to represent their particular agency's interests. Yet the Federation's leadership saw them as key officials of a communitywide service system and urged them to address issues from a communal perspective. Increasingly, agencies questioned the importance of their Federation affiliation versus their membership in service area consortia, groups of agencies funded by government, foundations, and national service organizations. All too often, discussions centered on fiscal issues, exacerbated by the inability of the Federation to allocate the substantial increases sought by agencies endeavoring to meet new and continuing communal needs. Frustrations created by dependence on Federation funds surfaced, as did the frustration of larger agencies that felt unduly constrained by Federation limitations on their fund raising.

Expectations for agency accountability and resulting requirements for fiscal and program reports were an ongoing source of contention between the agencies and the Federation. For many agencies, these reports represented additional work on top of the requirements of governmental and accrediting bodies. The Federation attempted to be responsive to such concerns but was both slow and late in doing so. The idea that all funding required accountability was difficult to digest for some volunteers and professionals used to the Federation's earlier procedures.

Federation efforts to save costs or increase operational efficiency by combining support services with its agencies often foundered due to the reluctance of agencies to participate. Some objected because they received similar services from consortia in which they participated, while others sought to guard their independence.

Into this scene stepped Irv Kun. Employed by the Federation during the 1980s and 1990s, Kun was a civil engineer who dealt with physical plant issues and related insurance. He was widely praised by the agencies as "the best thing Federation ever did for us." Efforts to link marketing or computerization in a similar manner ran aground. Recent years, however, have seen increased cooperation in writing grants and soliciting endowments. In fact, the Federation's "Business Vision 2000 Implementation" plan, adopted in 1999, called for significant expansion of such technical assistance.[2]

In that plan, the Federation stressed the need to improve its relations with both donors and agencies, suggesting that both have too long been taken for granted. Steps to change this attitude and provide alternative ways of dealing with both groups are included in the "Business Vision 2000 Implementation" plan.[3]

Clearly, the Federation attaches great importance to its relations with its agencies. Witness also the report of its Strategic Planning Committee (SPC), adopted by the Federation's Board of

Trustees in July 1990. That report notes, "The succeeding section on 'Federation/Agency Relations' is included in this report because it was the strongly held view of the SPC that agency relations are so integral to the work of Federation that they warrant inclusion in a report on Federation's internal operations."[4]

In the day-to-day struggle to serve the multiple needs of a large, diverse, and widespread community, attention is frequently centered on the differences in opinions and practices within the community and its institutions. On the other hand, an opportunity to review the record of the Philadelphia Jewish community reveals that the contending parties often struggled toward a common good: a community of values, of affirmative Jewish identification, of caring and concern, and of service to their fellow citizens. In doing so, the community's conflicts have reflected a philosophical contradiction: the authority of tradition (in the sense of policies and procedures, if not of theology) versus the freedom to create (new institutions, services, and methodologies). Fortunately, both the agencies and the Federation have strong commitments to upholding tradition as well as encouraging creativity.

As Philadelphia's Jewish Federation struggled to meet new demands and expectations, it also began to identify a multitude of societal trends and changing needs. By the mid-1970s, suburban development saw sizable, stable towns emerge where once there had been farms, forests, or small, historic villages. Large numbers of Jews were among the residents of these towns, and at least some of these Jewish suburbanites set out to meet their Jewish needs and interests. Contrary to tradition, a cemetery was not the first institution established. After all, these were young Jewish suburbanites, and death was far from their minds. Instead, Jewish religious schools and synagogues sprang up everywhere. Convenience of access was crucial for these suburbanites.

Over the years, these synagogues developed subgroups like sisterhoods and youth groups, similar to those of synagogues in urban settings. As the communities matured, many also saw the establishment of chapters of national Jewish organizations. For other Jewish communal services, however, the suburbanites depended on the Jewish agencies in Philadelphia.

Jewish communal development in various sectors of the Philadelphia metropolitan area differed substantially. Shortly after World War II and until about 1970, Jewish population movement from the core of the city had an alternative to movement beyond the city limits: the greater Northeast. This area became a magnet for large numbers of Jews, particularly those seeking reasonable housing. This population was responsible for the fact that the 1984 Jewish population study of the five-county Philadelphia area found the majority of Jews still living within the city limits—something no longer true even at that time for most large American Jewish communities.

The substantial Jewish population in Northeast Philadelphia was clearly within the service area of the Federation and its agencies. Many services and programs were developed for this population, and almost all continue to this day. Among these was the Feinstein Campus, opened in 1975. It provided adjacent facilities for the Klein Branch of the JCCs, Federation Day Care Services, and the Rieder House of Federation Housing.

Many viewed the Northeast as needing human services but unable to make significant financial contributions to Federation fund raising. That view prevailed through much of the last quarter century but changed during the 1990s when the need for community building came to the fore. The area was the point of initial settlement for most Soviet Jews who came to the Philadelphia area. By the mid-1990s, significant numbers of native-born as well as immigrant Jews were moving from the Northeast to adjacent suburban counties.

Almost the converse prevailed in the "near suburbs" of the Main Line (to the west of the city) and those immediately due north of the city. Substantial numbers of Jews seeped into these long-established townships shortly after the end of World War II, joining small numbers of Jews already there. Prior and new residents were often already known to the Federation, so for purposes of fund raising, the Federation treated these two suburban areas as part of the city. Indeed, many of the residents were solicited annually through generic Federation divisions. This population was not perceived as needing communal services, because they had the economic means to secure needed supports.

Economic needs were no longer the sole concern of many Jewish communities. Jewish education was increasingly seen as important to Jewish identity, creativity, and continuity. Witness the Jewish renaissance of the 1990s and the even earlier development of Federation-supported day schools that began to function in both of these "near suburban" communities. Federation-owned campuses, aggregating facilities for several agencies, opened in both areas. The Saligman campus on City Line and Haverford Avenues provided facilities for the Kaiserman branch of the JCCs and the Stern branch of the Perelman Jewish Day School. The Mandell Education Campus in Elkins Park (acquired in 1984) provided space for the relocation of Gratz College, a branch of the Jewish Family and Children's Service (JFCS) and the Gutman Center of Federation Day Care Services (FDCS). It also housed the Forman Branch of the Perelman Jewish Day School (PJDS), which added a second branch on the campus when it inaugurated its first Middle School in the fall of 2001, the Auerbach Central Agency for Jewish Education (ACAJE), and a summer day camp of the JCCs.

In the further reaches of the four Pennsylvania counties surrounding Philadelphia, a very different pattern emerged. In each of these areas, there were annual fund-raising campaigns for Israel, encouraged and assisted by the United Jewish Appeal (UJA), which sought to secure support from so-called unorganized communities. Frequently, but not always, such campaigns were based at local synagogues. However, the first of the suburban campaigns to develop ties with the Philadelphia Federation was the Buxmont Jewish Appeal (BJA), started by a group of men in central Bucks and Montgomery counties after first raising money for Israel during the 1973 Yom Kippur War. Over the course of a decade, initial contacts intensified, and the BJA eventually became the first suburban region of the Federation. A synagogue in Norristown, Pennsylvania, called the "Jewish Community Center," also conducted an annual UJA campaign. In relocating to Blue Bell, Pennsylvania, the synagogue merged its UJA efforts into the BJA and thus into Federation's FAJA.

In Chester and Delaware counties, the UJA campaigns were conducted by consortia of local synagogues that, following the example of Buxmont, negotiated separate agreements with the Federation. The Delaware UJA campaign had included subsidies for the schools of each congregation—a practice continued in the pact with the Federation. For the Philadelphia Federation, long supportive of communal and day schools, it marked its first direct assistance to congregational schools.

Very different circumstances prevailed in Bucks County, where a local federation had been established. It proved unable to meet the needs of a growing community. In a series of convoluted moves, it merged with the Jewish Federation of Mercer County, New Jersey (Trenton), but later abandoned the merger over the objections of its partner. These and other factors precluded the new Bucks federation from achieving its aims. Two leading Bucks County rabbis, later joined by several key lay leaders, then asked the Philadelphia Federation to provide service in Bucks. After extended and complex negotiations with the Mercer County Federation, the Philadelphia Jewish Federation and its agencies began to phase in services in the mid-1980s.

With the initiation of service in Bucks County, the Greater Philadelphia Federation assumed responsibility for Jewish community services in a five-county area of Southeastern Pennsylvania. According to the 1996–1997 Jewish population study of that area, 59 percent of the Jews in the area were living in the four suburban counties. The Jewish Federation of Greater Philadelphia had, in the course of twenty years, experienced a major reorientation based on the movement of its population. Initially, Federation leadership approached the suburbs in the hope of gaining and recouping lost campaign contributions. Over the course of the same twenty years, it realized that both communal and individual needs for service were unavoidable. Amidst much stress and strain, the development of the suburban regions and of various agency services has been a notable success story.

As the Philadelphia Federation focused on the suburbs, a number of other population groups began advocating for their particular needs. Some of these groups had not done so previously within the Jewish community. Among these were people with physical and/or mental disabilities, single parents, the gay/lesbian/bisexual community, the poor, the elderly, and other, smaller segments of the Jewish population. Among the smaller advocacy groups, for example, were elderly parents concerned about middle-aged children who suffered from various disabilities and the care they would receive when these elderly parents could no longer provide care for them.

In recent years, the Federation has made grants to a number of advocacy groups, including Tikvah (mentally ill), OROT (children with special learning needs), J/CHAI (housing for the developmentally disabled), the Jewish Relief Agency (JRA), and others. Its allocations to JFCS include designated funds for HIV/AIDS Support Services and Gam Yachad (socialization of young adults with developmental disabilities).

One of the largest groups to impact the Philadelphia Jewish community was Soviet Jewish immigrants. From the beginning of advocacy for Soviet Jewry in the 1960s, Philadelphia rapidly achieved a reputation as a center for such activities. Its proximity to New York was very attractive to new arrivals, and later, the large number of fellow immigrants already in the area added to that appeal. Altogether, Federation estimates that some 30,000 Jews from the former Soviet Union came to the Philadelphia area between 1975 and 2000.[6]

In September 1976, the Federation's Executive Committee discussed, for the first time, the financial implications of Soviet Jewish resettlement in the community. Given all the basic human needs of these immigrants, including—in most cases—learning a new language, it was an undertaking involving considerable financial, human, physical, and political resources. With the exception of some of the elderly, most of these immigrants were not familiar with a democratic, open society or the fundamental tenets and beliefs of Judaism.

By the mid-1980s, thousands of Soviet immigrants had established firm roots in the Philadelphia area and its suburbs. Those who arrived a few years after the collapse of the Soviet Union in 1991 brought with them a new set of problems, having lived in an "open" society whose values were not always those cherished in America.

The Federation and its agencies were besieged with requests for funding and services. Most of the resettlement programs were financed through a creative mix of federal, state, and Jewish communal resources that, in turn, were accountable to various government agencies and the national Jewish community. It was difficult for the Federation and the agencies to adjust to this surge in caseloads, serve new interest groups, cope with finding staff skilled to do so, and at the same time fend off public reservations about some of the programs. After all, they still had obligations to prior and continuing clients.

Jewish education agencies had their hands full, too, dealing with the integration of immigrant children and more requests for special education. For many years, the Philadelphia Federation was in one of the first three ranks for annual education allocations; however, Jewish day-school enrollments were low and static, and those of supplementary schools were slowly declining in the 1970s and 1980s. These trends have slowly reversed since 1990. The purchase of the land and buildings for the Mandell Education Campus and its dedication on November 2, 1986, marked a new step in local Jewish education. The new Mandell facility was the first community campus in the country specifically dedicated to Jewish education.

Until about 1990, Federation constituent schools struggled with continuous financial problems. They were unable to address deteriorating physical facilities, pay their teachers adequately, or update educational resources. This picture began to change in the early 1990s, as results of the 1990 National Jewish Population Study (NJPS) highlighted sharply escalating intermarriage rates, particularly in the most recently married cohort. The Greater Philadelphia Federation, along with many others, was deeply troubled, but felt that it could not develop effective interventions on this issue. However, as concepts of Jewish identity and continuity emerged as potentially effective responses to intermarriage, as well as to others engaged in spiritual search, Jewish education was viewed as a primary instrument for their attainment. Although it ranked high in national comparisons of allocations for Jewish education, the Philadelphia Federation began to increase resources available for Jewish education still further, particularly those for new and innovative approaches. Among these were a Congregational School Initiative, a Jewish Continuity Initiative, Jewish Culture Grants, increased grants for Jewish Educators Training, and a Community Teen Initiative. Starting in 2001, a new Day Schools Task Force has also been launched.

In the second half of the 1990s, the Federation suggested that "community building" was an essential instrument for maintaining Jewish continuity. Its planning, financial, human, and technical assistance resources were employed to bridge denominational and other differences between Jewish institutions. It particularly sought to foster closer relations between synagogues and Jewish organizations on the one hand and the Federation and its constituent agencies on the other. Strong emphasis was given to collaborative projects.

The plans for community building also include ongoing efforts to reach unaffiliated Jews and emphasis on providing multiple points of entry into the Jewish community. In the context of its community development plans, the Federation has also been struggling with a number of societal trends that impact such efforts: the changing nature of philanthropy, the decline of voluntarism, readiness of volunteers for short-term projects but not extended committee processes, and the lack of communal cohesion, at least partially due to the geographic spread of the population.

In 1984 and again in 1997, the Federation conducted extensive Jewish population studies of the five-county Philadelphia area. The studies, both published, served to provide a framework for the Federation's planning and related activities.[7] The 1997 study, as did its predecessor, documented the scope and size of the three population groups with which the Federation has been most concerned: the Jewish poor, the elderly, and single parents. Most recently, the Federation has reactivated a Task Force on Jewish Poverty to deal further with the needs of that population.

In 1996–1997, 12 percent of Jewish households in the study area had incomes under $15,000. This involved 6,800 households with 15,200 individual members living below federal poverty guidelines. Another 40,000 Jews were estimated to live in households above the poverty line, but with annual incomes of less than $25,000.

At the same time, some 20 percent of Jewish households (including 22 percent of the Jewish population, or an estimated 44,700 individuals) comprised people over age 65. Almost one-quarter of the Jewish elderly lived in households with annual incomes of less than $15,000. Forty percent of the elderly lived in households with annual incomes less than $25,000. The elderly constituted approximately 66 percent of the Jewish poverty population. The Philadelphia-area population also included some 3,300 Jewish single-parent families, 40 percent of whom were in the low-income group.

Such research produced a number of unanticipated reactions. In 1984, for example, the Federation had to assign and publicize a special phone number because Jews in the community were concerned that such a study would produce lists of Jews that could be used in the future by anti-Semitic public authorities. Because the Federation was making numerical estimates based on a limited number of interviews, such concerns were readily allayed.

An altogether different concern arose at the conclusion of the 1984 study in connection with the public release of the results. The Federation's officers worried about releasing much of the data, particularly those figures dealing with annual incomes and, more specifically, with the large number of people in the highest income category. The issue was debated at length until I. Jerome Stern, a thoughtful and judicious former president of the Federation, suggested that if the group refused to release high-income data, it stood to reason they also could not release Jewish poverty data. This percentage was much larger than the affluent percentage and would have been of great importance for fund-raising efforts. The Federation released the data.

In any discussion of the work of the Philadelphia Jewish community, one cannot speak only of its local activities. Of particular importance is the Federation's relationship with Israel. The Federation supported the *Yishuv* (Jewish community) in Palestine prior to the founding of the State of Israel and has done so without interruption since the momentous event in 1948. It has been an emotional experience, ranging from great joy to deep anxiety and even despair. But it has been characterized consistently by a demonstrated readiness to act on behalf of Israel.

The Federation's principal support has been through fund raising on Israel's behalf in the annual FAJA campaign. While annual support is subject to varying circumstances and requests, the most recent FAJA allocation (for fiscal year 2001–2002) was for $9,160,000. The specific amounts allocated each year by large American Jewish communities, including Philadelphia, are based on a complex formula they developed with the Committee on Overseas Needs Assessment and Distribution (ONAD) of the United Jewish Communities (UJC), the umbrella organization of the North American federations. The allocation goes largely to the Jewish Agency for Israel (JAFI), which supports the settlement of new *olim* (immigrants), social services, and cultural programs in Israel. Through a series of complex agreements, the $9,160,000 also includes Philadelphia's share of the support of three other national communal agencies. They are the American Jewish Joint Distribution Committee (AJJDC), which provides support for overseas Jewish communities other than in Israel; the ORT Federation (for vocational training of new immigrants); and the New York Association for New Americans (NYANA), which assists the large number of Jewish immigrants in New York.

Money from the Federation's campaign, however, is by no means the only support it provides for Israel. During the 1990s, there was a growing interest among North American federations, particularly those in the larger communities, to make their own decisions concerning the utilization of funds allocated for Israel. This stance developed from a perceived inability—because of political and bureaucratic attitudes—to influence the decisions of the Jewish Agency for Israel. JAFI has made numerous changes in its operations during the past decade, but the desire of donors to have some control over their contributions continues unabated.

Philadelphia's federation has been more restrained on this issue. This is probably due to opportunities Philadelphia has had for impact at JAFI through its own lay leaders (like Bennett Aaron and Miriam Schneirov) who serve on its Board and—to a lesser degree—a philosophy that decisions for Israeli institutions should be made by the people living there. However, most recently, the Greater Philadelphia Federation has begun to make some direct grants to overseas agencies outside of JAFI and AJJDC channels.

The Philadelphia federation is also proud of its participation in all of the national supplementary campaigns for Israel. "Operation Exodus" witnessed the migration to and absorption of one and a half million Soviet Jews in Israel. In 1984, "Operation Moses" rescued 20,000 Ethiopian Jews from refugee camps in the Sudan. "Operation Solomon" airlifted 14,400 Ethiopian Jews from Addis Ababa airport to Israel within thirty hours. "Project Renewal" embodied the physical and social rehabilitation of neglected Israeli neighborhoods by twinning them with Diaspora communities. Philadelphia supported projects in Ramat Hashikma, Tel Giborim, and Maalot. "Partnership 2000" assists the development of two communities in the Negev: the town of Netivot and the surrounding region of S'dot Negev. This project, marked by intensive collaboration between Philadelphia Jewry and the Israeli communities, began in 1997 and continues today. An Israel Emergency Fund (IEF) initiated after the second intifada in September 2000, had raised more than $10 million by the summer of 2002.

The Federation also shows its support by funding Philadelphians who seek to participate in programs in Israel. These include the local Israel Programs Center/Community Shaliach, the Aliyah Initiatives, and at least six different programs for high school and college youths. In 1999–2000, support for these programs amounted to $440,500.

Additional financial support for Israel comes through the Federation Endowments Corporation (FEC) through designations made by the holders of trusts and other instruments within that program. The Federation has also supported Israel through nonfinancial programs and has done so since before the founding of the state. It has taken Federation supporters for educational visits in Israel, created opportunities for learning experiences in the Philadelphia area, and encouraged citizen action on Israel-related issues. It has assisted the local Consulate General of Israel on various issues, covered Israeli developments in the *Jewish Exponent,* and celebrated Israel's fiftieth anniversary with several events, including a joint concert of the Philadelphia Orchestra and the Israel Philharmonic.

Under the Federation's auspices, literally thousands of people, including agency professionals, Soviet immigrants, FAJA contributor groups, local opinion makers, clergy, public officials, and the young and old, have had opportunities to visit and learn about Israel. These "missions" programs took as many as one thousand people to Israel at one time in 1989. For some, the first stop is Europe, enabling participants to experience some of the trauma of the Holocaust, as well as life in Israel. Many of these missions became vitally important fund-raising opportunities.

The Federation has been raising money for its agencies, Israel, and other Jewish causes for one hundred years. While its leaders and FAJA solicitors are proud of their achievements, they are still troubled by the knowledge that "it's not enough to meet the needs." Philadelphia has been troubled by such concerns over at least the past fifty years.[8] In the past twenty-five years, crises in Israel or Jewish migration, especially from the Soviet Union, have has the biggest impact in increasing contributions to the Federation.

A review of the results of the Federation's annual FAJA campaign will show that in 1975 it raised $18,269,000. These results do not include the Federation's income from its annual United Way allocation, special campaigns, or endowment income. A careful examination will show a decrease of almost $1.5 million from 1975 to 1976. This drop started in 1974 after record contributions poured in as a result of the 1973 Yom Kippur War. With two rather minor exceptions, FAJA contributions show steady increases from 1976 until 1989 and 1990, when the campaign produced $30 million each year. After falling into the $25 million to $29 million range during the 1990s, at least partially due to several executive transitions, the Federation anticipated that the campaign results would once again rise to over $30 million in 2001.

This achievement gains in significance when the number of contributors is compared with the dollars raised. As one example, in 1985 FAJA raised $27,415,000 from 43,996 contributors. In 2000, it raised $28,040,592 from only 31,372 contributors. Beyond the declining population base (documented by its own studies), the Federation has been exploring other reasons for this drop in participation and possible remedies.

The pervasive concern during the 1970s and 1980s was that the Federation was not providing adequate funding for its agencies. When Forman took the helm in 1976, he aimed for steady growth by making key changes in FAJA staff, establishing new relationships, and letting the new campaign director, Al Gilens, train his staff and learn the ropes. The resulting increase of FAJA campaign dollars during this period demonstrates the validity of Forman's approach. New instruments for fund raising—for example, Super Sunday; missions to Israel, Washington, DC, and locally; event sponsorships; and others—were developed.

An entire new process and structure for campaign clearance was also put in place in an effort to ensure the priority of the FAJA campaign and to avoid competition between other agency fund raising. At the same time, there developed an awareness by Federation leadership that the FAJA campaign alone could not produce sufficient income. Other income streams would need to be developed, but Forman was seriously concerned about the extent to which a tradition-bound community was ready to accept change.

An initial step was taken in 1985 when FJA president Bennett L. Aaron appointed a Committee on Long Range Strategic Planning, chaired by Bernard Fishman. That committee selected the following from among issues of critical importance to the Federation:

• Developing a new Federation mission statement
• Defining the Federation's geographic boundaries
• Long-range development of the Federation's financial resources

While this work was in progress, but unrelated to it, the Federation experienced a little-known incident that was to become perhaps its finest hour. During the 1973 Yom Kippur War, Philadelphians, like Jews in other communities, made large pledges amidst fears of the moment. Later on, after Israel had won the war, federations around the country and the UJA nationally found that many of the large pledges were not collectible. The UJA agreed to negotiate settlements with the local federations, substantially reducing the amounts owed. Philadelphia's unpaid pledges to the UJA from the 1973 campaign amounted to some $7 million.

The Federation's representatives were offered a dramatic reduction in their debt and an extended payment plan. Yet when the Executive Committee heard the proposal and discussed it, some of its members were appalled. They explained that UJA and JAFI had accepted these pledges in good faith in a time or war and crisis and made expenditures based on anticipated payments. The Committee therefore decided that it had a moral obligation to make full payments and turned down the offer.

Meanwhile, the Committee on Long Range Strategic Planning was making its own recommendations. Miriam Schneirov became the Federation's first woman president during 1987–1988 and proceeded to appoint the entire Executive Committee of the Federation as its Strategic Planning Committee. Schneirov had sound knowledge and conviction about the merits of planning, coupled with a sense of urgency about changes at the Federation. Under her leadership, the Federation addressed the changing environment and produced six "white papers" on demography, economic trends, employment, Jewish identity, organizational (Federation) concerns, and philanthropy.[9]

Stemming in part from the paper on philanthropy, the Federation began to conceptualize a different FAJA campaign. Among ideas advanced were those of donor recognition, multiyear campaign solicitations, ongoing donor relations reaching beyond fund raising, new accountability mechanisms, and others. Particularly appealing was the concept of Financial Resource Development (FRD), which involved assignment of an account executive for substantial donors. This staff person was to deal not only with an FAJA gift, but also with endowments, special campaigns, the donor's participation in Federation activities and committees, and wider Jewish interests. The single most troublesome proposal was the suggested adoption of some version of designated giving. If donors could now designate how monies were spent, it could undercut the entire notion of communal decision making.

When United Way moved in this direction, the Federation's concerns were heightened by reports from several communities about significant difficulties created by such donor designations. A donor's wishes could entirely change an allocation. This was, of course, troublesome for non-profit organizations subject to such expectations, and many sought to construct mechanisms that could accommodate both donors' wishes and communal priorities.

Many agencies across the country struggled with this issue, but it held a particular threat for the Philadelphia Federation. Other agencies were endeavoring to retain their contributors. The Federation was trying to recruit new ones. As the Federation debated the matter, it began to hear reports about some major philanthropists who stopped making gifts to federated organizations and had begun their own fund distribution processes.

Complaints about inadequacies of the FAJA campaign made their way onto the agenda of the new Strategic Planning Committee. Chaired by the late Isaac L. Auerbach, this was the first Federation planning group with an appropriately encompassing strategic focus, adequate funding, an experienced consultant and a chair who, as an incisive entrepreneur, had himself used strategic methods. The report of that group set forth a number of concerns, principles, and recommendations. It called for the implementation of a comprehensive FRD plan and a previously approved name change for the Federation. These and other recommendations were approved by the Board on July 5, 1990.

The change in name has, over the years, had a significant reinterpretation. It was recommended initially in order bring Philadelphia in line with communal practice throughout North America and to make it easier for people to contact the Federation. Both the prior "Federation of Jewish Agencies" and the current "Jewish Federation" concluded their name with "of Greater Philadelphia." However, in recent years, it is the closing phrase to which importance is assigned: For the majority of Jews now living outside the city limits, it is confirmation that they are truly a part of the community. Moreover, the Federation works hard to convey that sense in many iterations. Still further, it conveys to the synagogues and other Jewish organizations a message that they are full partners in the "community building" that is now the focus of Federation.

By mid-1990, Federation leaders and professional colleagues began to notice that their chief executive, Robert Forman, seemed unwell. A man of prodigious energy, he now seemed exhausted early in the day, a symptom increasingly evident as the year wore on. Many in the Jewish community speculated as to the cause, but no explanation was provided. By the fall of 1990, numerous volunteer leaders and Federation professionals developed informal channels for the pursuit of their work in the face of their executive's illness. In November 1990, Forman gathered his remaining strength and made a trip to the annual General Assembly (G.A.) of the Council of Jewish Federations (CJF) in San Francisco. Those in Philadelphia who realized the seriousness of his illness—whatever its formal diagnosis—viewed this as Forman's farewell visit. His colleagues from other communities were traumatized when they saw him. During that conference, Miriam Schneirov and Ted Seidenberg, as the outgoing and incoming presidents of the Federation, met with me, as the associate executive of the Federation, to discuss and ensure the continued functioning of Federation.

Robert Forman passed away on January 13, 1991, and the first action of the Gulf War—an air attack on Baghdad—took place on the day of his funeral. By that time, Ted Seidenberg had asked me to assume responsibilities as the Federation's acting executive vice president. All other members of the executive staff were asked to remain in their positions.

Forman's death created a lack of continuity in Federation leadership. He was succeeded by several executives, who, for a variety of reasons, moved on. During and after these transitions, there was speculation whether the experience of a strong executive at the head of the Federation might have created a reluctance to repeat the experience. Nothing negates that question more convincingly than the esteem in which Forman is still held in Philadelphia more than ten years after his death. He is still admired for his sensitive development and nurturing of volunteer leadership. It is, however, quite correct to suggest that, in providing strong leadership and influence, Forman was a prototype of current Federation executives in large communities throughout the country.

Forman's early training as a social worker was evident in the degree of freedom he gave to each president with whom he worked. He was not bashful in setting expectations and limits but was pleased and encouraging about the presidents' initiatives—unless they conflicted with his sense of what was best for the Federation. His first two presidents, I. Jerome Stern and Ronald Rubin, were of inestimable value in teaching Forman who was who in the life of Philadelphia's Jewish and general communities. While Stern brought particular insights concerning the continued relevance of local traditions to Forman's attention, Rubin was able to introduce him to the proverbial movers and shakers. Rubin also proved to be a highly valued counselor as Forman struggled to understand Federation finances.

Edward Rosen, who next assumed presidential responsibilities, had previously helped Forman rejuvenate planning and allocations activities. As president, he not only worked to promote a better understanding of the Federation's need for substantial growth of its endowment, but also helped in defining that effort as the new Federation Endowments Corporation (FEC). Rosen gave practical and conceptual leadership to a new—at least for Philadelphia—vision of volunteer training and placement, and even volunteer career paths. Additionally, he envisioned an integrated approach to volunteer service at the Federation's agencies as well at the Federation itself. Unlike many Federation presidents who became president after serving as FAJA campaign chair, Rosen became campaign chair after having been president.

Bennett L. Aaron, on the other hand, came to the presidency largely because of his superb leadership in the role of campaign chair. He also brought to the presidency wider experience than many of his predecessors, having been a synagogue president, head of a B'nai B'rith lodge, and president of a day school. Aaron was one of those Philadelphians who recognized early on the historic significance of the Soviet Jewry movement. Accordingly, he and Forman, together with their wives, spent his first days as president in Moscow visiting refuseniks.

Having established Soviet Jewry as one goal, he set the acquisition of the Mandell Education Campus as his other, especially after initial efforts to do so did not receive much support. Some fifteen years after completing his term as Federation president, Aaron continues his Jewish communal work in leading roles with the UJC after having held positions with the UJA. He also continues to serve on the Board of JAFI.

Following Aaron, Miriam Schneirov assumed the presidency in 1987. If ever there was a case of a Federation president whose time had come, "Mimi" Schneirov was it. There was widespread sentiment within the Federation that she had earned the position by dint of long, diligent, and very effective work in all spheres of the Federation's activities. During her watch, the Federation provided leadership and staff support for the "March on Washington" for Soviet Jewry, in which at least 12,000 Philadelphians made the trip to Washington in 140 buses, untold numbers of private cars and railroad seats, at least one corporate plane, and one helicopter. Issues concerning Israel repeatedly required attention during her term in office, especially when the first intifada broke out. Debates about a peace process for Israel deteriorated repeatedly into communal discord, and the *Jewish Exponent,* the Federation's weekly paper, become the object of bitter contentions between opposing points of view.

Schneirov was not afraid to confront conflict, and the word *dayenu* was not in her vocabulary. She moved forward with a full-scale strategic planning process, even in the face of contrary advice from key leaders and initial objections from Robert Forman. A plan emerged and was approved by the Federation's Board in July 1990, only a few months before her term ended.

The implementation of the strategic plan was left to her successor, Ted Seidenberg, who—just weeks after assuming the presidency of the Federation—led a mission to Israel to express support for a people on the verge of Iraqi attack. When the mission returned to Kennedy Airport in New York early on a Monday morning, he was informed that Robert Forman had died on Sunday evening. Seidenberg immediately took decisive steps making interim arrangements and communicating with the Federation's constituencies. An old campaigner, Seidenberg also realized the urgent need to maintain the progress of the FAJA campaign. He relished early success when two $1 million gifts were secured in 1990 and achieved, together with the Exodus campaign, income of over $30 million. His keen insights and strong convictions were critical in the transition period.

Seidenberg was succeeded by Alan Casnoff, a president convinced that changes being discussed at the Federation were too little, too late and who encouraged suburban leaders and contributors to develop their regions in their own fashion. Faced with substantial givers (and some not so substantial givers) clamoring to make decisions about the use of their contributions, Casnoff pushed the developers of the FRD concept to create viable options for designated giving. He also raised doubts about "allocations to agencies where problems are never resolved."[10] In a role of "leader as gadfly," Casnoff reopened an old, unresolved issue. Was the Federation engaged in social service or in social justice? It was a discussion worth having, but some feared it could encourage lack of concern for the poor. In the end, given the Jewish ethical tradition, the answer to the question had to be "both."

Casnoff sought to open the Federation's doors to those who wanted to contribute the work of their hands. The results were the "mitzvah projects" like food pantries for the poor and cleanups of abandoned cemeteries. He initiated action on a long-discussed move by the Federation to more functional quarters, a move he envisioned not only as cost saving, but also as symbolic of changes at the Federation. He also took the initial steps to recruit Howard Charish, who was head of the federation of MetroWest, New Jersey (Newark area), as Philadelphia's next executive. As a seasoned big-city executive, Charish understood the need for change in the fund raising, governance, and programs of the Federation in greater Philadelphia. Several of his efforts to do so were, however, stillborn for various reasons.

The purchase and move to a new Federation building, known as "Jewish Community Services Building" at 2100 Arch Street, came to a successful conclusion under the Federation's next president, Michael Belman. Belman was on good terms with all sectors of the community, and his term can be characterized as one of consolidation. He and the new executive vice president, Howard Charish, poured their energy into a new planning process. "Business Vision 2000"—or BV 2000, as it was commonly called—sought to focus planning on the Federation's internal operational issues and on the coming millennium—an activity much in vogue in the entire country.

Rarely had the Federation seen as much enthusiasm as it did for its next president, Joseph Smukler. Smukler was of an older generation, but his commitment to infusing new people, groups, and procedures into Federation activities was welcomed by leaders of every age, albeit with concerns by some about the impact of a "populist" approach on fund raising.

Former presidents had served three one-year terms, but Smukler set a two-year limit for himself. During his tenure, Howard Charish asked that, for personal and family reasons, his contract not be renewed. On completion of his term, Dr. Sol Daiches, the Federation's vice president for community services, became the interim president (that title now being assigned to the chief professional officer, while the chief volunteer officer was designated Chair of the Board.)[11]

The Federation set out, once again, to find a new executive. A search began, this time staffed (at Smukler's request) by me and supported by an international search firm. After diligent work by the search committee, the position was offered to Dr. Harold Goldman, at the time the executive director of the Jewish Family and Children's Service of Philadelphia. Goldman's appointment was praised for many reasons—his personal integrity, his professional vision, his ability in managing a nonprofit organizations and fund raising, and his knowledge of the issues animating the Federation's leadership.

Goldman looked forward to learning the ropes at the Federation, but given a second intifada embroiling the state of Israel, he never had that luxury. He was able, however, to begin to structure his job and staff in such a manner that even with several unavoidable trips to Israel, he could begin to think through, often together with Smukler, a long-range vision and a collaborative approach to the changes that needed to be made.

In structuring a long-range perspective, these Federation leaders were able to consider a phenomenal achievement of the Federation as one of the factors. In February 1983, the Federation Endowments Corporation (FEC) had various assets amounting to $33 million. At the end of 2001, the FEC's assets amounted to $159,602,000. This aggregate amount included both restricted and unrestricted funds as well as donor-advised funds. This, of course, means that the Federation does not have full control over the disposition of many of these resources. In many cases, only the income from these endowments is available.

One of the first steps in the direction was the selection of the next chair of the board, Andrea Adelman, who was viewed as a fine and well-deserved choice. She has begun to lead the Greater Philadelphia Federation, during its hundredth anniversary year, to a UJC General Assembly in Philadelphia in November 2002 (the first since 1976), and beyond.

If the fourth quarter of the Federation's first century can be dated from our Bicentennial on July 4, 1976, then September 11, 2001—the date of the terrorist attacks on New York and Washington, D.C.—can be viewed as its ending. Since then, it has been commonplace to suggest that America and our world have changed. What we cannot yet perceive is into what they have changed.

The multifaceted needs the Federation has addressed for a hundred years may change, as may the structure for governance and/or service delivery. But the needs will not disappear or be easily resolved. It is therefore particularly significant that the Federation has recorded important achievements since that tragic date:

- For the first time since 1989, the FAJA campaign is estimated to have raised more than $30 million (in 2001).
- The Federation received the largest single gift since its founding. Philanthropist and entrepreneur Sidney Kimmel made a commitment to include a $20 million endowment gift in his will. In addition, he pledged an annual gift of $1 million in his lifetime for the FAJA campaign and made similar pledges for the endowment and annual funds of the Perelman Jewish Day School.
- The Federation raised over $1 million for its September 11 Relief Fund and shared the money in equal amounts with similar funds of the UJC and the United Way.

Almost two years ago, Graham S. Finney, a careful analyst of the greater Philadelphia community, wrote, "Across the board, old service delivery patterns are disintegrating and new connections are being forged as the public, private and non-profit sectors attempt to position themselves for future success."[12]

In a volatile, uncertain environment, the future can, at best, be barely perceived. But a Federation that has valuable and substantial human, financial, and physical resources; serious commitments to values and traditions; as well as an impressive record of success, can be expected to play an important role in helping to shape that future for the Jewish community of greater Philadelphia and all of its fellow citizens.

David Zinkoff, inimitable "Voice of
the Sixer" for many years, surrounded
by memorabilia, 1981.

FROM A TO "ZINK"
Philadelphia Jews in Sports

Ron Avery

For reasons not easily understood, American Jews have embraced sports with wild enthusiasm. They have become avid (or is the word *rabid*?) fans and have built their own golf courses, tennis clubs and Y's—even after the barriers of exclusion to American social club society was breached. Jews are team owners, managers, coaches, promoters, sports writers, and participants in the full range of athletic endeavor—from bull fighting to Ping-Pong—in numbers far above their percentage of the population. This has been especially true in Philadelphia, where the mark Jews have made on the sports scene has been nothing short of profound.

This new-found passion for physical contests may lie partly in the desire to shed the old stereotype of the Jew as physically inept, and partly in the drive for acceptance in Gentile America.[1] What better way to become a "real American" than to wear a baseball uniform? There is an inherent democracy in sports. Goldstein's curveball has no idea of its Hebraic origins, and if it hops better than Johnson's, then let him pitch! Sports has been a well-traveled highway to recognition and prestige in America; it offered an escape route from the "ghetto" when the word referred to a place where immigrant Jews lived, just as it offers opportunities to young blacks today.

In a city as sports crazy as Philadelphia, it was inevitable that Jews would distinguish themselves in all manner of sport, including four all-American football players, two world boxing champs, an all-Jewish basketball team that was considered one of the best of its era, nearly a dozen Olympians, and countless high school and college coaches and athletes. In addition, a large proportion of Philadelphia team owners have been Jewish. By the mid-1980s, in fact, Jewish owners could count the (football) Eagles, the (basketball) 76ers, the (hockey) Flyers, and the (football) Stars (of the United States Football League) among their teams.

Any examination of the Jewish involvement in and contribution to sports in Philadelphia must begin with the sport of basketball. There was a time, in fact, when basketball could be called a "Jewish game." Its birth in the 1890s coincided with the arrival of the great waves of immigration from Eastern Europe. There was no WASP establishment already in control of the game; the game has always had a blue-collar appeal and image.

Basketball was ideally suited to crowded city neighborhoods: All one needed to play was a hoop and a utility pole.[2] It was also ideal for slum settlement houses. The constant pace of the game allowed tough neighborhood kids to work out their aggressions. Edwin "Hughie" Black, the last surviving member of the original 1918 South Philadelphia Hebrew Association team (the SPHAs) recalled, "Everyone in South Philly played basketball. We played day and night in the settlement houses and on the street."[3] Dave Dabrow, a founder of the Jewish Basketball League, and basketball coach at South Philadelphia High School for twenty years, recalled that he started playing the game in 1910 at Star Gardens Playground at 6th and Lombard, where one could play indoors or outdoors, virtually around the clock. According to Dabrow, a Jewish youth team was formed as early as 1902 at the Young Woman's League near 4th and Bainbridge. (One of those early stars later

Left: Edwin I. (Hughie) Black points to himself in photo of the original SPHAs basketball team, in 1981.

Right: Eddie "The Mogul" Gottlieb, 1980.

Gag photo of Wilt Chamberlain signing contract with the Warriors, using Eddie Gottlieb as desk – May 13, 1959.

gained fame in the ring as Battling Levinsky.) In 1912, a committee met in a cigar store at 10th and Wolf in South Philly to form a Jewish basketball league (and were reportedly tossed out of the store for making too much noise.) The league disbanded during World War I, but reformed in 1922 and played without interruption for the next 54 years.[4]

The level of performance and competition in the Jewish League was high, the highest level of amateur sports in the city, Dabrow claims. Competition for a spot on one of the five teams was fierce. The League was the spawning ground for many outstanding college players, and practically a "farm team" for the professional SPHAs. The teams reflected the pattern of Jewish settlement in the various neighborhoods: West Philly, Wynnefield, Germantown, Oxford Circle. The League's reputation was so high that occasionally non-Jews tried to join the teams. (Generally, only Jews were accepted on the teams, but an exception was made for one youngster named Tom Gibbons, who later became the city's police commissioner.)

Weekly double-headers were played at the YMYWCA at Broad and Pine, first on Tuesday evenings and later on Sundays. During the 1930s, the games were followed by dancing, and as many as 1,500 attended. The League always closed its season with a lavish awards banquet,[5] at which some sixty trophies were awarded. (The premier award was a 6-foot-high, 110-pound cup known as the Spike Shandelman Championship Trophy—named after the trophy's maker—for winning the League title three consecutive years. There were regular games between the best teams in the city's Catholic League and the best in the Jewish League.

By the mid-1960s, it seemed that the city's Jewish youth had lost its passionate interest in basketball. Though the admission charge to Jewish League games was dropped, rarely did the games draw more than fifty spectators. Joe Goldenberg, former Temple University player and coach at West Philadelphia High School, played in the Jewish League for some fifteen years, even after leaving college. "It was my ambition to play on the same team as my son, but people just lost interest," Goldenberg said.[6] Though the League folded in 1976, it is anything but dead. Its alumni association, begun in 1938, is still strong, drawing over three hundred to its annual banquets.

While the Jewish League involved several thousand players over its long history, it was a single remarkable team that was Jewish Philadelphia's greatest contribution to the world of basketball, the SPHAs, an all-Jewish pro team. The history of the game shows hundreds of professional teams in dozens of leagues until the founding of the National Basketball League in 1948.

The SPHAs grew out of the desire of several Southern High players to continue in the game. They received the backing of an organization called the South Philadelphia Hebrew Association.

They kept its name long after the association with the organization was broken. Their jerseys sported the Star of David and the Hebrew letters samach, pey, hey, and aleph. Looking at the world of basketball in the 1920s, sports historian Ted Vincent wrote, "Basketball's three best teams were the (all-black) Renaissance, the (New York) Celtics and the SPHAs."[7] No history of the game fails to mention the contribution of the SPHAs and its near-legendary manager-coach-owner, Eddie "the Mogul" Gottlieb. The first SPHAs team was composed of Gottlieb, Black, brothers Harry and Chickie Passon, Mark "Mockie" Bunnin, Lou Schneiderman, and Charlie Newman, the tall man at 5'10".

They played a rough, physical game inside a chicken-wire cage for $3 to $5 a game. They dribbled with two hands, and pushed opponents into the cage the way a hockey player checks an opposing player. They traveled the eastern half of the nation as a "barnstorming team" and eventually played in three different leagues. The record shows the SPHAs won three championships in the Philadelphia League, three in the Eastern League, and seven championships during fourteen years in the American League, the highest level of professionalism at the time.[8]

They were the pride and joy of every sports-conscious Philadelphia Jew. Regular Saturday night home games at the Broadwood Hotel became the social hub of the Jewish singles scene. A game was a social event that always ended in a dance, and nearly every game was sold out, even during World War II. After a quick change of clothes, player Gil Fitch became the band leader. "He made a very pungent orchestra leader," recalled Dave Zinkoff, the voice of the SPHAs and later of the Warriors and the 76ers. It is safe to say that scores of Philadelphia Jews met their future spouses at an SPHAs game and dance.

There was an obvious psychological element present in every SPHAs game. It was Jew versus gentile; them against us. "Half the fans would come to see the Jews killed. The other half were Jews who came to see our boys win," said Hughie Black.

Anti-Semitism was always a factor when the SPHAs played away from the safe confines of the Broadwood. One of the more famous incidents occurred when player Harry Litwak was attacked by a mob in a game at Union City, New Jersey, and was struck in the head with a Coke bottle. His teammates came to Litwak's rescue. Litwak went to the hospital, but the SPHAs returned at halftime with a police escort to finish the game. A fan once jabbed SPHAs star Joel "Shikey" Gotthoffer in the thigh with a lit cigar. Sometimes the players had to dodge objects thrown from the balcony.[9] To make ends meet during the Depression, SPHAs players often played simultaneously on other teams, especially in the coal region, where they were considered "star imports."

Left: Dave Dabrow.

Right: Harry Litwack on the Temple bench in February of 1956.

Dolph Schayes, at one time the NBA's all-time leading scorer, in 1960.

Gottlieb was "Mister Basketball" in Philadelphia. He is a member of the Basketball Hall of Fame and is one of the three Philadelphians in the International Jewish Sports Hall of Fame in Israel. He devoted his entire life to basketball and the promotion of other sports in the city. At one time, he fielded a semi-pro SPHAs baseball team. He was one of the founders of the present-day National Basketball Association (NBA) and first owner of the Philadelphia Warriors, which numbered several former SPHAs on its roster. He coached the team to a championship in its first year of play. Gottlieb died in 1979 at age 81. The *Inquirer's* Frank Dolson wrote of him, "Eddie Gottlieb remained youthful to the very end. . . . He bridged the old days of pro basketball with the new. He was the one constant, the one breath of fresh air in a constantly changing world."[10] Gottlieb sold the SPHAs in 1947, but they continued to play into the early 1950s, often traveling with the Harlem Globetrotters. One of the later SPHAs was South Philadelphia's Herman "Reds" Klotz, who became owner of the Washington Generals, the Globetrotters' perennial opponent. Still dribbling onto the court in his 60s, Klotz claims he is the oldest basketball player in the world.

The Jewish presence in basketball was strong into the early 1950s. Almost half of the names on a roster of the 1947 Eastern League were Jewish. It soon became apparent, however, that the "Jewish game" was becoming a "black game." Whereas Jewish names appeared twenty-four times in the 1930s among All-American college selections and fourteen times in the 1940s, only one Jew made All-American during the decade of the 1970s, Ernie Grunfeld.[11]

Former SPHAs Harry Litwak, another Philadelphian in the Jewish Hall of Fame, was one of this city's great basketball coaches. Litwak played for Temple University, became an assistant coach after graduation, and was the head coach for twenty years. He retired in 1973 as the basketball coach with the greatest number of victories in the school's history. Litwak coached many outstanding Jewish players at Temple University. Of special note are West Philly's Nelson Bobb, who later played for the Warriors, and Southern's Eddie Lerner. They played together at Temple in the late 1940s. Both set scoring records, and both have been named to Temple's Sports Hall of Fame. Sportswriters nicknamed the pair "the scoring twins."[12] Temple's finest years under Litwak came in the mid-1950s with such black stars as Hal Greer and Guy Rodgers. However, three local Jews, Joe Goldenberg, Over brook's Mel Brodsky, and Southern's Barry Goldstein, helped make Temple number three in the nation in 1956 and again in 1958.

When the Warriors left Philadelphia for San Francisco in 1963, a new team, the 76ers, came to town under Jewish owners Irv Kosloff and Ike Richman. The 76ers' first coach was Adolph "Dolph" Schayes, perhaps the greatest Jewish basketball star of the post-war era. Schayes stayed on in the city for three years, leading the Sixers to a division championship in its third year. A

second Jewish coach, Roy Rubin of Long Island, was brought in for the 1972–1973 season when the Sixers fell into a slump. Rubin was fired after a record of four wins and forty-six losses.[13] The only Jewish player to make the Sixers lineup was Penn's Dave Wohl, who was half Jewish and played under Rubin for one season.

While Philadelphia Jews have made their most important imprint in basketball, boxing ranks as a close second. Boxing's history reflects the changing ethnic composition of the urban poor. The Irish predominated in the early years, followed by the Jews in the 1920s and 1930s, followed by Italian fighters, then blacks; more recently there has been an influx of Hispanics into the sport.[14] Jews seemed to dominate the lighter divisions from World War I to 1940. The obvious attraction of boxing is what appears to be large financial rewards for a few minutes of action and danger in the ring. A more important motivating factor is the desire for recognition and prestige. A man may spend only a few years in the prize ring, but for the rest of his life he is remembered and respected as a boxer.

Philadelphia has always been a major "fight town." There was a time when a dozen fight clubs flourished in the city, and a fan could see a boxing card every night of the week. It had the gyms, the managers, trainers, and promoters. If one man can be credited with keeping boxing alive and healthy in Philadelphia, even when the sport hit a low ebb in the late fifties and early sixties, it would be a South Philadelphia Jew, Herman "Muggsy" Taylor, the dean of American fight promoters, who died in 1980 at age 93.

Promoter Herman Taylor poses between Joe Louis and Harold Johnson at the Christian St. YMCA, December 13, 1948, on the eve of the bouts fought at Convention Hall the following day.

Scores of Philadelphia Jews took a crack at boxing as a career, and two rose to become world champions. Battling Levinsky (born Barney Liebowitz) held the light-heavyweight crown from 1916 to 1920. Durable little Benny Bass was world featherweight champion for a brief period in 1927–1928. Bass later held the junior lightweight championship for three years.[15] Levinsky was born in West Philly in 1891. He fought all the greats of the era, including Jack Dempsey, Gene Tunney, Harry Greb, and Georges Carpentier. Levinsky once fought three times in a single day. During one forty-week period, he had forty-one bouts. Levinsky died in 1949, still living in West Philadelphia and not much richer than the day he started boxing. But he is considered a ring great whose name is in Boxing's Hall of Fame and the Jewish Sports Hall of Fame.

Harry Blitman in the 1920s. He beat
Tony Canzoneri in a memorable
non-title fight in Shibe Park in 1928.
Other Jewish boxers who gained
notoriety were Al Gordon, a South
Philadelphia featherweight who
fought Benny Bass to a draw in
1930; Frankie Bradley (who changed
his name from Bloch), who twice
beat bantamweight champion in a
career that began in 1911; Jackie
Lesser, a flyweight who made the
1920 Olympic team (but was later
disqualified) and who, during World
War I, was Army flyweight champion;
Murray Friedlander, who fought over
100 featherweight bouts in the late
twenties and early thirties before he
lost his sight; and Charlie Micklin
(who fought under the name Charlie
Nevins), who won the city and state
Golden Gloves flyweight titles during
the Depression era.

Bass's amazing career stretched from 1919 to 1940. Contrary to the record book, Bass estimated that he fought more than four hundred bouts.[16] Pound-for-pound, Bass was certainly the toughest Jew that ever walked the streets of Philadelphia. His battle for the featherweight title in 1926 against Red Chapman of Boston stands as one of the most savage and dramatic fights in ring history.

Chapman (whose real name was Morris Kaplan) and Bass met in Philadelphia's Municipal Stadium to fight for the title vacated by another Jew, Louis "Kid" Kaplan. It was a bloodbath fought in front of 30,000 screaming fans. Both were badly battered and bleeding when they came out for the ninth round and simultaneously landed haymaker rights. Both fell to the canvas. It looked like a double-knockout, and the referee started counting over both men. Both men beat the count, however, and Bass took the decision and the title. Writing about the fight twenty years later, author Harold Ribalow recalled, "What is remarkable about the Bass-Chapman fight is that the violence was so strong, the animalism so great that the bout stands as a classic of savagery all these years. And two slightly built Jewish fighters were the battlers involved."[17] Bass was a ladies' man, a drinker, a saloon singer who lost or squandered much of the cash he made in the ring. But he was loved by his Jewish fans and respected as a great by the boxing fraternity.[18]

Philadelphia's Lew Tendler would surely have been the world lightweight champion in 1920 if Benny Leonard had already been holding the title. Tendler's fifteen-year boxing career started when he was a fatherless teenager. He fought 169 professional fights, including two losing title bouts against Leonard, probably the greatest Jewish boxer of all time. Tendler became well known as a restaurant owner in Philadelphia and Atlantic City. He died in 1970. He was called "the best southpaw boxer of all time" and "the best fighter to never hold a title."[19]

"Irish" Abie Kauffman earned his nickname after beating a highly regarded opponent from a neighborhood church. The local priest and fight promoter were so impressed, they gave Kauffman a pair of boxing trunks. One side was kelly green with a harp. The other side was blue and contained the Mogen David. He turned professional in Baltimore about 1934 and fought into the mid-1940s as a featherweight. He figures he had about 150 fights but never kept an accurate record. "I fought at least once or twice a month," Kauffman recalled. "You'd get about $200 for an eight-rounder. My largest purse was $1,000 against Tony Rios in San Antonio." Kauffman fought such greats as Willie Pep (three times), Lenny Mancini, and lightweight champion Ike Williams. "I was a bleeder," he said. "I got stopped many times on cuts. But after awhile the referees would get to know me. They'd let me bleed from the first to the 10th round. The fans like blood, you know." Kauffman talked about the mutual respect and great camaraderie among boxers. He never heard an anti-Semitic slur from an opponent; the fans were a different story. "Especially at the Cambria (a famous boxing arena in Kensington), you'd hear 'kill the Jew' and this and that. It just makes you fight harder to spite them." By the mid-1940s, just about all of Philadelphia's fighting Jews had hung up their gloves. Middleweight Marvin Edelman stormed into the scene about 1950 with a thirty-fight win streak. Like many Jewish athletes, Edelman was a lone Jew, isolated in a gentile neighborhood. He was brought up in the mostly Irish Fairmount section where his father was a bar owner. "I was chubby," he said. "All the kids were calling me a fat Jew bastard. I fought every kid on the street, and I won most of the time." To lose weight, he became a boxer.

To a great extent, the cornerstone of boxing in Philadelphia for almost seventy years was the remarkable promoter Herman "Muggsy" Taylor. Muggsy promoted his first fight card in 1912 with $400 in borrowed money. He had learned the game from promoter Jack McGuigan, who took the fatherless boy under his wing when Taylor was only 13. With Tex Rickard, Taylor co-promoted the first Dempsey-Tunney fight in 1926 at Municipal Stadium. The fight drew 120,757 paying customers, which is still the record. He was matchmaker and promoter for practically every championship fight ever held in Pennsylvania. He had a sterling reputation for honesty and always paying the fighters first. Taylor kept boxing alive and healthy in Philadelphia during its bleak days. He was still the biggest and best fight promoter in the city in his 80s.[20]

In 1969, a 22-year-old Temple University student named J. Russell Peltz scraped together $5,000 and became the nation's youngest fight promoter. This meant that two Philadelphia Jews may have been the youngest and oldest boxing promoters in the world.[21]

Left: Dave Smukler in 1935.

Below: Saul Rogovin.

Lou "Zingy" Sandrow, June 1932.

Unlike boxing and basketball, the national pastime, baseball, has not seen a sizable number of Jewish players. About fifty to sixty Jews have played in the major leagues. A few, like Hank Greenberg and Sandy Koufax, have been bona fide stars. Two Philadelphia-born Jews who made it to the big leagues are almost forgotten names. Infielder Eddie "Itzy" Feinberg played sixteen games as a Phillie in 1938 and 1939. Harry Shuman, a pitcher, played part of 1942 and 1943 with the Pittsburgh Pirates and part of 1944 in a Phillies uniform. Shuman had pitched for Temple University and had climbed the ranks in the minor leagues. However, he candidly admits that the manpower drain created by World War II was the most important factor in his rise to the majors, where he was a relief pitcher.[22]

In the years before television, scores of semi-pro teams drew sizable crowds and great interest in and around Philadelphia. A handful of Jews achieved relative fame on the city's sandlots. The best might have been Lou "Zingy" Sandrow, a third baseman who swung a wicked bat from the mid 1920s into the early 1940s. Sandrow's son, Elwood, has preserved a thick stack of newspaper clippings to prove that a now-forgotten name was once a common one on the city's sports pages. Zingy could always be counted on for a double, and one time he hit three homers in one game. Zingy even got three hits off the great Satchel Paige in a game played at 44th and Parkside Avenue in West Philly.

Henry "Henny" Fogel, another great Jewish sandlot player, remembers Sandrow as "the best 'bad' ball hitter around." Sandrow grew up in the Nicetown section, practically the only Jew in the neighborhood, and Fogel was practically the only Jew in his section of Kensington. Both men saw baseball as a way to prove themselves and win acceptance. Often they were the lone Jews on their teams. Fogel said anti-Semitic abuse was common. "We held our own. We didn't let them get away with anything," he said.[23]

Fogel was a left-handed pitcher who played for many sandlot teams in the 1930s and 1940s. When he played for the Philadelphia Italians, Fogel was jokingly called "Henny Fogeletti." Fogel said he usually played three times a week and can remember pitching both games of a double-header for the Italians.

It might be said that the Philadelphia Jew who went further in baseball is Max Patkin, "the clown prince of baseball." Patkin was a West Philly boy with the dreams and the potential of becoming a major league pitcher. He played on a farm team of the Chicago White Sox in 1940 and then served in the Navy during World War II, where he mostly played baseball. Following the war, he was again pitching for a semi-pro team in Wilkes-Barre, when his arm gave out. But Max had another talent. He was naturally funny and admittedly funny looking. He had also become a proficient jitterbug and "eccentric" dancer.[24] There were at the time several baseball comedy acts, Al Schacht's the most famous. Patkin inherited Schacht's title of "crown of prince of all baseball clowns." More than thirty-five years later, Patkin was still at it. Most of his performances were given at minor league games in small towns across the country, and he performed before millions of fans.

In addition to locals Feinberg and Shuman, it appears that only three additional Jews wore the Phillies uniform. Pitcher Saul Rogovin of New York was the last to play on the team in 1955. He had been with Baltimore, Chicago, and Detroit and ended his career with the Phillies. It was jokingly said that Rogovin had three pitches "slow, slower and stop."[25]

Atlanta-born Erskin Mayer wore the Phillies uniform from 1912 to 1918 and helped contribute to the team's 1915 Pennant with twenty-one wins that season.[26] Wisconsin native Morris "Morrie" Arnovich came up through the Phillies farm system and played with the team from 1936 through 1940. Arnovich was an outfielder and a very dependable hitter, whose lifetime major

Left: Randy Grossman ("The Rabbi") in 1979.

Right: Richie Richman, outstanding Villanova athlete, excelled in baseball, football, and basketball (while posting a 3.42 index) in the mid-1960s.

Steven Cohen in 1969.

Fred Turoff at Temple meet, January 1969.

league batting average was .280. His best season was with the Phillies in 1939 when he hit .324.[27]

Looking further back, one finds the name Lipman "Lip" Pike (1845–1893) of New York, who has the distinction of being the first baseball player on record to be paid a regular salary while engaged by the Athletic Club of Philadelphia in 1866. Lip was an all-time great who hit six homers—five in succession in Philadelphia on July 16, 1866.[28]

Football, like baseball, has not attracted large numbers of Jewish players. However, Philadelphia has produced some outstanding Jewish gridders. Victor Frank, a Philadelphian who played guard and center at the University of Pennsylvania (1918–1920), was a second-string All-American in 1918. Frank was also on Penn's crew and the lacrosse teams.[29]

Power-driving fullback Dave Smukler grew up in the small town of Gloversville, New York, but he made a name for himself in Philadelphia at Temple University and with the Eagles. An *Inquirer* sportswriter in 1936 called Smukler "the greatest football player in Temple's history."[30] He played offense and defense and was a key factor in the Owls' undefeated 1934 season, which ended in a trip to the Sugar Bowl. Smukler was a first-string All-American that year. He played three seasons with the Eagles and was traded to the Detroit Lions in 1940 but never showed up. Smukler decided to join the Army instead. He played briefly after World War II for the Los Angeles Rams and did a bit of college coaching.

Olney High School's Bernard Lemonick was a first-string All-American defensive back for the University of Pennsylvania in 1950. Lemonick, who combined brains and brawn, was All-Ivy, All-East, All-Pennsylvania and played in the 1950 East-West Game. Penn coach George Munger once told a sportswriter, "[Lemonick] has the fastest reaction and greatest speed of any lineman we have ever had. In fact, of any lineman I have ever seen."[31] And Lemonick played the game both ways—offense and defense.

No Jewish player has gone further in football than Haverford High School's Randy Grossman, the only Jew who can say he has played in four Super Bowls. A tight-end with gifted hands, Grossman was a third-string All-American pick at Temple. During his college years (1971–1974), Grossman caught eighty-nine passes for 1,505 yards.[32] The Pittsburgh Steelers decided to take a chance with Grossman in 1974 and signed him as a free agent. Grossman not only made the team, but went to the Super Bowl in his first year and held his spot on the Steelers until 1981. Those were great years for the Steelers, and while Grossman was never a star, he turned out to be a very reliable player. In the 1975 Super Bowl game against Dallas, Grossman (nicknamed "the rabbi" by his teammates) scored the first Pittsburgh touchdown.

Smukler and tackle Sid Youngelman appear to be the only Jews who ever made the Eagles. Youngelman played from 1956 to 1958. However, Sid Gilman helped coach the team from 1979 to 1982, and Marv Levy was an assistant coach during the years 1968 to 1970.

Two fine quarterbacks in the early 1960s were Temple's Mark Lichtenfeld and Villanova's Richie Richman. Richman was an all-around athlete who was signed as a first baseman by the Phillies and played two years in their Bakersfield, California, farm team. But he was also an outstanding basketball player in high school and college. He was part of, perhaps, the finest city high school basketball team of all time—the Overbrook squad that included Wally Jones, Wayne Hightower, Walt Hazard, and Ralph Heywood.

One day in 1962, Richman shared quarterback duties against Oregon State in the Liberty Bowl, and that same day played for Villanova's basketball squad at the Palestra. Richman not only played professional baseball, he was with the Philadelphia Bulldogs of the Continental Football League in the late 1960s.[33]

In some sports, reaching the professional level is the height of achievement, but the pinnacle of success for others is becoming an Olympian. Jewish Philadelphians have been over several U.S. Olympic teams, and one distinguished himself by competing in three Olympiads. That honor goes to David Micahnik, now head fencing coach at the University of Pennsylvania. Micahnik competed in epee competition at the 1960, 1964, and 1968 Games. American fencers rarely win medals in international meets, and Micahnik was eliminated in the second round of competition each time out. (Interestingly, fencing is the Olympic sport in which Jews have shined brightest. Between 1896 and 1980, Jews took an incredible eighty-four medals in fencing—forty-three gold, twenty-four silver, and seventeen bronze. All were Europeans, representing Austria, Hungary, France, Belgium, Great Britain, and the USSR.)[34]

Micahnik, a native of Wilkes-Barre, was an All-Ivy fencer at Penn. After graduating, he became the U.S. national champion in epee (a medium-weight sword). He competed in two Maccabiah Games in 1965 and 1968, taking home a total of four gold, two silver, and a bronze medal. He remained at Penn as an assistant coach and was appointed head coach in 1974 with the retirement of Penn's great fencing master Lajos Csiszor.

Another Philadelphia Jew who went to more than one Olympiad was a colorful boxer who changed his name from Willie Ostreicher to Willie Clark. He went to the 1920 Olympics in Antwerp as America's welterweight, but won no medals.[35] By 1924, Clark had filled out to a light-heavyweight and went to his second Olympics in Paris, where he broke his wrist in the semi-finals after scoring two knockouts. Clark never turned professional, but he trained and managed several good Philadelphia fighters. He taught boxing at Princeton University for three years. Then for many years he was athletic director at the Broadwood Health Club. He was a physical fitness fanatic with an Adonis physique and was a well-known professional wrestling referee. (At age 57, the hearty Clark became a hero by rescuing two women who nearly drowned in the ocean off Miami Beach.)[36]

Another local Jew in the 1920 Antwerp Olympics was wrestler Samuel N. Gerson, who took home a silver medal. Gerson was a collegiate champion at the University of Pennsylvania and a whiz at chess. In 1954 Gerson formed an organization of former American Olympians, which he expanded in 1960 into an international association.[37]

Perhaps, the most unique Olympic experience of any Philadelphia Jew belongs to David Mayor, America's heavyweight weightlifter in the 1936 games in Berlin. He was one of four Jews on the American team. Hitler had tried to exclude blacks and Jews from the games, but relented when America and other nations threatened a boycott.

"Several (Jewish) organizations contacted me and asked me not to compete," Mayor recalled. "I asked them, what purpose would it serve. Who would it benefit? I wasn't going to bypass that opportunity. I felt I was representing the United States and that was my only attitude."[38] Mayor said he felt little tension at the games, although in a tour of the city he was shocked to see businesses with the German word *Jude* (Jew) painted on the walls.

Hillel Levinson, April 1960.

Jack Emas in 1962. Among the nation's best handball players of the late 1940s, Emas was a five-time Middle Atlantic AAU champion. Other outstanding Philadelphian athletes include Dr. Harry Fields, who was an outstanding professional wrestler (while attending medical school!); Sylvia Wene, the top woman bowler of the 1950s (who once defeated Dick Weber in a bowling match held aboard an airplane); Alan Sussell, outstanding amateur golfer and member of the 1969 American Golf Team at the Maccabiah Games; George Eiferman, Philadelphia's answer to Charles Atlas, named Mr. America in 1948; Al Berger, the city's 1938 weightlifting champion, who at one time held the world's record for the reverse-curl and operated a well-known gym, first in Center City, and later in Ardmore.

Mayor did not fare well in the competition. He had just turned 20 and had been lifting for a little over two years. He was entirely self-taught. Two years after the Olympics, however, Mayor reached his prime and set national records.

Weightlifting has been Mayor's life's work. He has been a longtime public relations representative for the York Barbell Company, a weightlifting coach, and national official in weightlifting and body-building competitions. He coached America's 1961 Maccabiah lifters, who took every gold medal. He is in the Weightlifting Hall of Fame.

The only local Jewish athlete to take home a gold medal from the Olympics stands at the opposite physical extreme from big, brawny David Mayor. Five-foot-one, 105-pound Allen Rosenberg was the coach of the Vesper Boat Club, which brought home a gold medal from the 1964 games in Tokyo. Until Rosenberg's arrival on Boat House Row, crew was easily the most blue-blooded, least Jewish sport in the city.[39] A Central High School and Temple graduate, Rosenberg is both a pharmacist and lawyer. In 1954 he became friendly with John B. Kelly, Jr., and started hanging around the Vesper club. He was bright and had the small size and competitive spirit necessary for an excellent coxswain—the man who steers and cheers the crew on to the finish line. Rosenberg became an expert in the sport and soon became the club's coach. He was also rowing coach at St. Joseph's College, the first Jewish athletic coach at the Catholic school. He coached an American team that took all the gold medals in the 1961 Maccabiah. Rosenberg was called on again in 1976 to coach U.S. rowers at the Montreal Olympics.

Irving "Moon" Mondschein, who has coached track at Penn since 1965, was National Decathlon champion in 1944, 1946, and 1948. The Brooklyn native came in seventh in the 1948 Olympic Games in London (the winner was Bob Mathias). He coached America at the 1950 Maccabiah games, and stayed on in Israel to coach its 1952 Olympic track squad.[40] Mondschein's two sons, Mark and Brian, were both outstanding pole vaulters at Haverford High School. Brian went on to become one of the nation's leading decathlon competitors in the late 1970s and early 1980s.

Left: Walter Blum in 1972.

Right: Jerry Wolman.

(From left) Dan Tabas, Jack Wolgin, Leonard Tose and Sylvan Cohen after unsuccessful bid for Eagles in December 1963.

Harold Katz, former owner of the 76'ers.

Rosenberg's breakthrough into the gentile world of rowing was duplicated in yachting by a Philadelphia lawyer, Donald S. Cohan, who took bronze in the 1972 Olympic Games. Cohan was the first Jew to break into the highest levels of world yachting competition and the only Jew to win a Olympic medal in yachting. Cohan has raced in six different categories of the sport and won his medal in the Dragon Class. He has made the Olympic finals on five different occasions, and has represented the United States in twelve World Championships.

Jewish gymnasts have shone almost as brightly as fencers in Olympic competition. West Philadelphia High School's Steve Cohen had a brilliant career at Penn State in the mid-1960s. He was the number one collegiate gymnast in the country in 1967. He went to the world championships in 1966 and was selected for the U.S. Olympic squad that went to Mexico City in 1968. Going to the Olympics that year put an extra strain on Cohen because he was also in his first year of medical school. Cohen was seen reading medical books when not competing at the Olympics.[41]

Two other outstanding Jewish gymnasts of the 1960s were Mark Cohn and Fred Turoff, who now coaches the Owls. Cohn went to the Pan American Games and was all-around champion at the 1965 and 1969 Maccabiah. Turoff went to the World championships in 1970.

Hillel Levinson holds the title of Philadelphia's fastest Jew. Levinson became well known as city managing director under Mayor Frank Rizzo, but he had already made a name for himself as a top sprinter at Central High School and Temple University in the 1950s. When Levinson went out for baseball at Central, the track coach spotted him and convinced the student that his future lay in track. By his senior year, Levinson was the fastest high school runner in the city and had won an athletic scholarship to Temple. At Temple he broke school records in the 100- and 200-yard sprints, was Middle Atlantic Conference Champion, and was undefeated in his junior and senior years. Levinson stopped running when he entered law school, by then only a few tenths of a second off world-class Olympic caliber.[42]

Another political figure who first made his mark in sports was former city councilman Isadore Bellis, one of the finest amateur tennis and Ping-Pong players in the nation during the late 1930s and 1940s. Bellis was a Strawberry Mansion boy who learned his tennis in Fairmount Park

and was the perennial winner of a citywide park tournament. He won the National Boys Tennis Championship in 1935 at age 15 and was a member of the Junior Davis Cup Team. He won the Middle States tennis title five years in a row (1937 through 1941).

At the University of Pennsylvania, Bellis was captain of the school's tennis squad, which went undefeated for two years, but Ping-Pong was his first love. Bellis considered himself among the top three table tennis players in the nation and proved just how good he was in 1938 when he defeated the reigning world champ, Hungarian Victor Barna.

The Delaware Valley even had a great Jewish jockey in the person of Brooklyn-born Walter Blum, who lived for many years in Cherry Hill. Blum's racing career stretched from 1953 to 1975. Blum rode 4,384 winners during his career, among the highest totals in American history. He rode in four Kentucky Derbies, and won the Belmont Stakes in 1971 riding a 35 to 1 shot named Pass Catcher.

Of course, the city never produced a Jewish star in ice hockey. But there was a memorable Jewish player on the Flyers during the team's first two seasons, 1968 and 1969. At age 39, after twenty years of play in the minor leagues, Larry Zeidel convinced the new team to give him an opportunity to play in the big time. He did it by mailing a $150 promotional package about himself to every team in the National Hockey League.[43]

Zeidel was a rugged, brawling defenseman with a face full of scar tissue and more than 2,500 minutes spent in the penalty box in the minors. Zeidel became a cause celebre after a stick-swinging brawl with the Boston Bruins in Toronto. Zeidel, backed by several witnesses, claimed the Bruins were hurling anti-Semitic remarks at the only Jewish player in the NHL. There was an investigation by the league, and Zeidel was vindicated.[44]

It would seem that the heyday of Jewish athletes has passed. The 1930s appear to have been the peak years for Jewish participation in sports in the city. Perhaps it was the harsh poverty of the Depression years that made so many Jewish boys dream of fame and fortune in baseball, basketball, and boxing. The neighborhoods that produced so many Jewish athletes are no longer Jewish. Blacks and Hispanics now fill the playgrounds of South and West Philly where Jews once shot hoops.

The level of play and the level of competition in all sports has risen. There now seem to be many more secure and realistic routes to success and acceptance. Few, if any, Jewish, middle-class suburban youths dream of a career in professional basketball or the prize ring.

Today the Jewish role in professional sports is increasingly that of team owner and sports promoter. A special breed of men has emerged on the sports scene, whose names are as well known

as the athletes whose salaries they pay: Leonard Tose; Harold Katz; Norman Braman; Ed Snider; Jerry Wolman; Myles Tanenbaum; Irv Kosloff; J. Russell Peltz, the boxing promoter; and horse racing's Herb Barness.

As a group, the Jewish team owners are intriguing and seem to share many similarities. They are hard-driving, mostly self-made, rugged men who have often overcome adversity. Many seem to be frustrated athletes. It is sometimes said of them that they couldn't make the team, so they bought the team. There is at least a grain of truth in the comment. Tose was a high school football player who tried to make the team at Notre Dame. Former Sixers owner Kosloff played basketball at South Philadelphia High School. Katz made Olney High's basketball squad through sheer determination. Peltz took boxing lessons as a puny Main Line youngster. Stars owner Tanenbaum was a benchwarmer at Central High School.

If one seeks a bit of the limelight, owning a sports team is certain to attract attention. Tose was hardly known outside the business world before he purchased the Eagles in 1969. As *Philadelphia* magazine pointed out three years later, Leonard Tose received more publicity in the Philadelphia newspapers—not all of it favorable—in three years than any local figure except the mayor.[45] The Jewish team owners have been worthy of much the attention: they have been colorful, interesting, and often controversial, and they have been winners. Snider created a new ice hockey team and within a few short years had a Stanley Cup winner and a great financial success. Katz's willingness to spend large sums of money purchased the stars that turned the 76ers into a championship team. Tose took the Eagles to the Super Bowl. Tanenbaum's Stars played for the title in the first year of the new football league and brought home another championship to the city in its second year. Peltz has been a major force in maintaining Philadelphia as a great fight town. Wolman was the man chiefly responsible for building the Spectrum. Barness, a soft-spoken real estate developer from Bucks County, built Keystone Race Track.

Whatever motivating factors brought all of these Jews into professional sports, there is little doubt that the public and the city have been the better for it.[46]

Fredric R. Mann on the grounds of
the Mann Music Center, 1978.

Jews and the Cultural Revival of Philadelphia

Don Harrison

Friday afternoons still belong to the Old Families. Just as their mothers and grandmothers did before them, the dowagers and post-debutantes enter the Academy of Music for the Philadelphia Orchestra's Friday concerts, using seats passed down from generation to generation.

But the Philadelphia Orchestra's Saturday night concerts attract a different audience. It is predominantly Jewish, and many in the audience are the same people who frequent the city's museums and theaters and art galleries. It is an adage in the cultural community that "Jewish dentists" and their wives are the indispensable patrons of the city's arts.

Jewish artists and performers are not a new phenomenon. They were common even before Jews gained acceptance in American society. Jewish "tummlers" were the heart of vaudeville. Yiddish theater played a vital role in the lives of immigrants. Jewish boys in the poorest tenements took violin lessons; their sisters learned piano. Jews have always been in American audiences, but only in recent years have they been joining the once exclusive boards that run the cultural institutions and dominate the arts.

At one time, Jewish representation on these boards, if it existed at all, was confined to a few of the city's old aristocratic Jewish families who were such dominant figures that their role in the cultural establishment was unchallengeable. Today, it is unthinkable that any Philadelphia artistic or cultural or reforming enterprise would be without Jewish participation—at all levels. The barriers to Jewish participation have fallen as part of the general democratization of culture in America, but an equally important explanation is money. In keeping with Jewry's traditions of philanthropy and respect for culture, some Jewish Philadelphians have invested astonishing sums in the arts.

Walter Annenberg,[1] for example, made the Annenberg Center at the University of Pennsylvania a major cultural force. He rescued All Star Forum from oblivion, when—as owner/publisher of the *Philadelphia Inquirer* and the *Daily News*—he tied All Star Forum to *Inquirer* Charities. A pioneer in Philadelphia television, he secured the city's first TV franchise for his station, WFIL, helped in converting WHYY from an "educational" station to the city's Public Broadcasting System outlet (transferring space in WFIL's old studios at 46th and Market Streets into a studio for Channel 12), and created *TV Guide,* which he developed into America's largest-circulation magazine and a major force in the nation's broadcasting.

Annenberg and his wife, Lee, have also been active in the Art Museum and other Philadelphia cultural institutions. Their own art holdings constitute one of the world's most highly regarded private collections.

Jewish philanthropy is also reflected in the names of the Sidney Kimmel Regional Center for the Performing Arts, the Fredric R. Mann Music Center in Fairmount Park, where the Philadelphia Orchestra's Robin Hood Dell Concerts are presented every summer; the Franklin Institute's Samuel Fels Planetarium; the Art Museum's Samuel Fleisher Memorial.

Money, however, is not the whole story. According to the late Edwin Wolf II, longtime librarian of the venerable Library Company of Philadelphia, a private institution founded by Benjamin Franklin, many of the Delaware Valley's wealthiest Jews are still not accepted in the cultural establishment.

The Annenbergs in their London Home in 1973.

Wolf, whose family has been in the forefront of Philadelphia communal and cultural activities for generations, said expansion of the Jewish role in Philadelphia arts and culture was preceded by dramatic social changes on the college campuses, in the political arena, and in organized charity. Until after World War II, Wolf recalled, not many Jews were on college faculties. At the University of Pennsylvania, not only were Jewish faculty members a rarity, but Jewish students were a very small minority. Today, the Ivy League university has a heavy Jewish enrollment; a large percentage of staff and faculty members are Jewish; and the university has had two Jewish presidents, Martin Meyerson and the incumbent, Judith Rodin. (During the same period, Temple University—with much more of a tradition of Jewish participation—also has had a Jewish president, Marvin Wachman).

This campus revolution thrust Jews into the city's scholarly and cultural life as never before, and in growing numbers. It also brought together Jews and Old Family Philadelphians, in many cases, for the first time.

Simultaneously, a political revolution was taking place in Philadelphia. After World War II, a new Democratic coalition, headed by blue bloods Joseph S. Clark and Richardson Dilworth, overthrew the long-entrenched Republican machine with a team composed of Old Family aristocrats, labor unionists, and Jewish liberals. People whose contacts had previously been limited, at best, were now working together in politics.

Organized charity had always been parochial, each group in society "looking after its own." When the Federation of Jewish Charities (now the Federation of Jewish Agencies) joined the Community Chest (later United Fund, now United Way), not only was the justifiably admired Jewish charity structure integrated into the city's philanthropic network, but communal leaders hitherto confined to milieus of narrower dimensions came into contact with others, and a new path of acceptance was opened.

Thrown together in business, politics, charity, and academia, Jewish and non-Jewish movers and shakers lost much of their mutual apprehension. It was inevitable that this would extend to the cultural scene. The city's cultural enterprise, particularly the fund-raising, was tied up with social activities—many of the society balls, for example—and these remained the last bastions of exclusivity. (One observer insists that even today, at elegant social events raising funds for the Philadelphia Art Museum, many participants are segregated, perhaps voluntarily, at what are referred to—unofficially, of course—as "Jewish tables."[2])

Annenberg Hall, Temple University Center for Performing Arts and Communications.

Annenberg School of Communications, Graduate School of University of Pennsylvania.

Fredric R. Mann in his Suburban Station Building office, 1979. His cigar, his international patronism of the arts, and his outspoken ebullience have become Philadelphia landmarks.

Fredric R. and Sylvia Mann receiving award from Dr. Chevalier Jackson, president of the Philadelphia Grand Opera Company, 1959.

Edwin Wolf, 2d, in the stacks of the Library Company in 1957, shortly after the publication of his and Maxwell Whiteman's early history of the Jews of Philadelphia.

In the "popular arts," the gap was never that apparent, if it existed at all. In nightclubs, comedy, pop music, the movies, and broadcasting, there were no barriers to speak of. Jews, in fact, have represented most of Philadelphia's impresarios, promoters, press agents, ticket sellers, and talent scouts. Most of the city's past movie theater moguls were Jewish—such as William Goldman, the Budco chain's Schlanger family, and the Eric chain's Shapiros.

William Paley and the Levy brothers, Isaac and Leon, were broadcasting pioneers in Philadelphia and nationally, and Walter Annenberg brought television to Philadelphia when his WFIL became the city's first broadcasting company licensed for television. William Goldman and Philip Klein played key roles in the emergence of public television. Radio history was made by independents like Max Leon (WDAS) and William and Dolly Banks (WHAT). Many of the city's radio and TV personalities have been Jewish; at one time in the early 1980s, the main news anchor on each of the city's three network stations was Jewish. The long-time manager of KYW News Radio is Roy Shapiro. Of Jewish performers who have reached national prominence, singers Eddie Fisher and Kitty Kallen, comics Joey Bishop and David Brenner, and actor Jack Klugman are native Philadelphians.

One man who bridged the worlds of fine arts and popular arts was the late Moe Septee.[3] Septee was manager of Philadelphia's All Star Forum concert series, which brings symphony orchestras, recital artists, and ballet companies to the Academy of Music and other stages. Septee revived the Philly Pops orchestra; he ran the New Locust Theater before it was razed for a parking garage; and he produced several shows that went on to Broadway.

Although Septee concentrated here on classical music and legitimate theater, it was the Beatles who brought Septee to Philadelphia for the first time. On the British group's first tour of the United States, impresarios were invited to draw lots for chances to represent them in different cities on the tour. Septee, then working in Newark, New Jersey, drew Philadelphia. That was in 1962. Five years later, when Emma Feldman, longtime manager of All Star Forum, died, the board searched for a successor. Septee, a protégé of famed New York impresario Sol Hurok (a former Philadelphian), was invited. He accepted the invitation at the urging of auto tycoon Vic Potamkin, Fredric R. Mann, and Philip Klein.

In his Philadelphia tenure, Septee lent his expertise to Robin Hood Dell Concerts in their early seasons at what is now the Mann Music Center. He was also a pioneer in musical theater with black themes and predominantly black casts, producing hits like *Bubblin' Brown Sugar, Don't Bother Me, I Can't Cope, Raisin,* and an all-black *Guys and Dolls.*

Some observers estimated that Philadelphia classical music and legitimate theater audiences are "well over 50 percent Jewish." *Commentary* magazine music critic Samuel Lipman wrote, "Music has long seemed a Jewish interest, a Jewish art, and a Jewish business.... The place of Jews in American song and show music is a matter of documentation [and] in serious music ....

Claude Schlanger, 1973.

Jews are by far the largest ethnic grouping...at the level of stars and supporting players alike.... If, for many Jews, music has served as a vehicle of assimilation into the wider culture, it has also served at the same time as a vehicle for the preservation of a distinctively Jewish identity and even, sometimes against their own best efforts, as a vehicle for Jewish survival."[4]

Philadelphia is a world center of classical music, thanks largely to the Philadelphia Orchestra. The Orchestra has always had a sizable percentage of Jewish artists, and was conducted for two decades by the world-renowned Eugene Ormandy, a Hungarian-born Jew. But the dominant force in Philadelphia classical music over the years was cardboard box tycoon Fredric R. Mann. Outspoken and abrasive, Mann astounded the unsuspecting with his musical sensitivity (he had been a promising pianist in his youth) and was an intimate of many of the world's music immortals. Mann had been the guiding light behind Philadelphia's Robin Hood Dell Concerts, a summer music-under-the-stars series, which he rescued from disaster and nurtured to its present unique status.[5]

A former Philadelphia city representative and onetime U.S. ambassador to Barbados, Mann was a member of the boards of the Philadelphia and New York Philharmonic orchestras, Carnegie Hall, opera and ballet companies, and music schools. He may be the only individual with two major concert halls named for him—in Philadelphia's Fairmount Park, where the Robin Hood Dell concerts are held, and in Tel Aviv (he and his wife, Sylvia, were founders of the Israel Philharmonic).

The Robin Hood Dell series began in 1931 in an open-air amphitheater in Fairmount Park, near 33rd and Dauphin Streets, when the Strawberry Mansion neighborhood was predominantly Jewish. In 1948, beset by financial crisis, it was forced to shut down in midsummer—musicians

William Goldman with the cast of "The Goldbergs" at a ribbon-cutting ceremony for his new theatre on Chestnut west of Broad, 1950.

Philip Klein (second from right) at a meeting with President Truman in 1949, celebrating 100 years of the Anglo-Jewish Press.

unpaid and patrons left with useless tickets for which they had already paid. Mann, who had resigned from the Dell board two years earlier (in protest against its fiscal policies, he said in an interview for this chapter), was asked by the city to return as Dell president and resurrect the program.

Mann purged the staff, convinced the musicians to waive back pay, gave refunds to ticketholders, held off creditors, and sold City Council on what would be known nationwide as the "Philadelphia Plan," which called for free general admission to all concerts. Costs were underwritten by contributions from private citizens who became "Friends of the Dell" (receiving reserved seats and parking privileges), matched by an allocation from the city.

The following summer, with Mann as unpaid president, Robin Hood Dell reopened. In 1976, the concerts were relocated to a new, partly covered amphitheater across Fairmount Park, near 52nd Street and Parkside Avenue. Mann sold the city on the need for the new "Dell," supervised its planning and construction, and reportedly sank some of his personal fortune into the costs of creating it. Three years later, it was renamed the Mann Music Center.

Jews have played a key role in Philadelphia music institutions for years. Some of the nation's foremost musicians received their training at the Settlement Music School, founded for immigrants' children and overseen for many years by board chairman Henry Gerstley and director Sol Schoenbach.[6]

The faculty at Philadelphia's renowned Curtis Institute of Music has included Jewish musicians (often Philadelphia Orchestra members), and many of its most illustrious alumni (including Leonard Bernstein and Philadelphian Susan Starr) have been Jewish. Two of America's most prestigious classical composers are Jewish Philadelphians and former colleagues on the University of Pennsylvania faculty. They are George Rochberg, a Curtis Institute alumnus and former teacher whose work is performed by the world's major orchestras, and Richard Wernick, who was associated with the Philadelphia Orchestra as former Maestro Riccardo Muti's advisor on contemporary music.

Jack Klugman, once a waiter at Bookbinder's, before his 1968 appearance in "The Sudden and Accidental Re-Education of Horse Johnson."

Eddie Fisher in a 1955 publicity photo. The caption read "Eddie repeats what he did as a youngster, ride the famous bronze goat in Rittenhouse Square."

Joey Bishop on the Cystic Fibrosis Float in the 1976 Thanksgiving Day Parade Down the Ben Franklin Parkway.

Increasing Jewish interest in opera is reflected on the board of the Opera Company of Philadelphia—itself an outgrowth of a merger of two smaller and once-competing companies, one founded and headed by the late Max Leon, a candy manufacturer who owned Radio Station WDAS and once led (and conducted) an orchestra called the Philadelphia Pops.

Ballet in Philadelphia, to a great extent, is the story of one Jewish woman's extraordinary accomplishment. This was acknowledged on June 6, 1984, when ballet superstar Peter Martins, the company's artistic advisor, speaking from the Academy of Music stage after the Pennsylvania Ballet's twentieth anniversary celebration, announced, "Without Barbara Weisberger, there wouldn't have been a Pennsylvania Ballet; anyone who cares about ballet is indebted to her."[7] In a dispute with the board, Weisberger had severed ties two years earlier with the Philadelphia-based ensemble she had created almost single-handedly, directing and nurturing it over eighteen years into what *Inquirer* music critic Daniel Webster once called "probably the premier company outside New York."

A onetime ballet prodigy and protégée of George Balanchine, Weisberger, wife of a Wilkes-Barre business executive and mother of two young children, set out to start a ballet school and "maybe a company" in Philadelphia, where dance had never quite caught on. Working with Stella Moore's Philadelphia Dance Alliance and the Philadelphia Lyric Opera, she set up Pennsylvania Ballet, operating it for years on a shoestring, until Ford Foundation funds gave it the fiscal push it needed.

Prosperity always eluded the company, even while it was growing in popularity and critical esteem. In January 1982, after a series of payless paydays, curtailed performances, and other problems, the company temporarily suspended operations. In an ensuing reorganization, Weisberger clashed with the board, and left. The company survived the crisis, and apparently was restored to solvency, but without the woman who, in Peter Martins' words, had "made it all possible."

Left top: David Brenner began his career as a producer for KYW-TV. Here he talks to inmates at Pennsylvania State Penitentiary during the filming of a public service program, 1966.

Right top: David Brenner visits West Philadelphia, his old neighborhood, during a 1975 appearance.

Left: Emma Feldman in 1965.

Right: Moe Septee, in his Locust Street office, 1974.

Just as Barbara Weisberger created a Philadelphia cultural tradition, the late Phil Klein preserved one.[8] In 1969 the Walnut Street Theater, the oldest in continuous operation in the English-speaking world, was about to shut down. Built to house a circus, it had featured plays, concerts, recitals, dance, films, and lectures. Edwin Forrest had played the Walnut, as had Dame Judith Anderson, Helen Hayes, and the Marx Brothers.

Left: Sol Schoenbach, 1981.

Right: Gene and George Rochberg in 1978.

Left: Dr. Mac Leon in 1973.

Right: Barbara Weisberger in 1978.

A nonprofit charitable Walnut Street Theater Corporation was set up to rescue the theater. Its president was Philip Klein, an advertising executive, educator, and philanthropist. A self-proclaimed maverick in the Philadelphia Jewish community, Klein published the weekly *Jewish Times* (with his wife Esther) in competition with the *Exponent*, organ of the Federation of Jewish Agencies.

Klein was a past president of the All Star Forum series, a board member of the Philadelphia Orchestra, and a leader in the Philadelphia Art Alliance. But he turned most of his efforts to restoring the Walnut as an all-purpose performing arts facility. Largely with funds Klein secured from the Haas Community Fund, he personally oversaw the theater's almost four-year-long $4 million reconstruction project, and remained active in the corporation until his death in 1982.

Jews played key roles in Philadelphia theater through its glory years. Two once-thriving theaters, since razed, were named for Jews—the Erlanger and the Mastbaum. Another razed theater, the Locust, was operated by Moe Septee. The Shubert (also named for a Jew) is now the Merriam, owned by the University of the Arts. People's Light and Theater Company in Malvern is called "Danny's Theater" by many who work there, because its producing director, Danny Fruchter, guided it from its humble origins in an old grist mill to its present status as one of the nation's largest nonprofit professional theaters.[9]

Many professional theater and dance productions have been presented at the Annenberg Center of the University of Pennsylvania. This $5.7 million performing arts center was the gift of Walter Annenberg, who already had established the Annenberg School of Communications at the University.[10]

A show business success story began in Philadelphia when Valley Forge Music Fair was launched by Lee Guber, Sheldon Gross, and radio personality Edward (Frank Ford) Felbin. This developed into Music Fair Enterprises Inc., headed by Guber and Gross, and, at one time, one of the nation's major theatrical producing companies.

Guber gravitated into theater through a club known as the Rendezvous, in the old Hotel Senator, on Walnut Street near 7th. He bought the property from Irving Wolf, who was moving on

Left: Danny Fruchter.

Right: Shelly Gross (left) and Lee Gruber onstage at the Valley Forge Music Fair, which (with Frank Ford) they founded.

Edward ("Frank Ford") Felbin.

John Taxin of the Old Original Bookbinder's.

Steve Poses of The Commissary, 1981.

to Atlantic City, where he would operate the famous 500 Club (Wolf is often credited in show business circles with bringing together Dean Martin and Jerry Lewis). Under Guber, the Rendezvous became the city's trendiest showplace of the 1950s, featuring jazz greats such as Sidney Bechet and Muggsy Spanier, folk music pioneers such as Burl Ives and Josh White, Sr., and the popular hometown comic Ronnie Graham.

Guber eventually sold the property, and the hotel was torn down. Turning to new ventures, he, Gross, and Felbin opened Valley Forge Music Fair, the first of several such non-urban playhouses (including the Camden County Music Fair). The Music Fairs are no longer operating, but Music Fair Enterprises is producing plays for Broadway and touring companies.

Like the Rendezvous, most of the clubs that used to dominate Philadelphia's live entertainment scene were Jewish owned or operated, some having evolved from Prohibition-era speakeasies. At one time, there were many of these clubs—the Latin Casino, Pep's, Benny the Bum's, the Embassy Club, the Celebrity Room, Little Rathskeller—but only one, the Latin Casino, survived World War II. It moved across the river into New Jersey, where years later it, too, went out of business.

Contributing to the demise of this entertainment form were such factors as competition from TV, migration to the suburbs, fear of street crime after dark, mid-city parking and traffic problems, and the escalating costs of a "night out" because of higher ticket, food, and travel prices. In the late sixties, the pendulum started swinging back. When affluent young people began moving into Society Hill and other "gentrified" Center City areas, they brought a new sophistication, more disposable income, and additional leisure time.

Only a few Center City restaurants of quality had been in continuous operation before World War II, most of them Jewish owned, but with the revival of Center City came the Philadelphia Restaurant Renaissance, an explosion of imaginative, attractive, and prosperous new dining places, offering a wide variety of quality cuisine. After taking hold in Center City, it spread into the neighborhoods and the suburbs, attracting national attention and spurring a revival of the city's dormant tourist industry.

Jews were at the heart of the city's Restaurant Renaissance. The Restaurant School, whose alumni opened many of the metropolitan area's quality dining places, was started by Jay Guben and his father, Gilbert, a onetime pharmacist who entered the restaurant business in his 1960s, and was associated with many of the city's finest newer restaurants.[11] Steve Poses's offbeat quality restaurants (including Frog, The Commissary, and others) became models for many establishments throughout the nation.[12] The Spivak brothers, Herbert and Allen, were in the restaurant and entertainment businesses. With a young Philadelphia-born New York theatrical agent, Larry Magid, they operated the Electric Factory, a rock music club at 22nd and Arch. It became so popular that the 2,500-seat showplace was not large enough to handle the crowds, especially when some of the major up-and-coming acts of the sixties and seventies were featured.[13] Magid and the Spivaks began booking these acts into the Spectrum, the Civic Center, the Academy of Music, and the Tower Theater in Upper Darby.

The club itself eventually closed down (it has since been resurrected at a different site), and Electric Factory Concerts Inc. became primarily a booking enterprise, handling acts ranging from Sinatra to the Sex Pistols, in Philadelphia and in other major cities. Under Magid's leadership, it became a major booker of live entertainment in Philadelphia, and one of the biggest and most influential in the nation. So powerful had this operation become that it was repeatedly challenged in court—unsuccessfully—by other promoters seeking a piece of the big-city action.

Until the Electric Factory—and the counterparts it inspired in other cities—restructured the world of popular music, radio disc jockeys with large followings among young audiences were determining what was "in," but, Magid has said, they had "no investment in talent," and much as they may have been influencing taste, they were primarily responsive.

Radio, despite a brief decline when television first became accessible to mass audiences, remains a vibrant force in popular culture. In Philadelphia and elsewhere, many of its key figures have been Jewish. Two Philadelphia brothers, Isaac and Leon Levy, gave up careers in law and dentistry, respectively, to establish WCAU, and with Philadelphia cigar manufacturer William Paley, parlayed the Columbia Broadcasting System (CBS) into one of the nation's three major networks.[14]

Left: Herbie Spivack in 1968.

Larry Magid (center) and Allen Spivak (right), founders of the Electric Company and the molders of Philadelphia (and, by example, American) rock music.

Left: Dolly Banks in 1976.

Right: Marian Locks of the Locks'
Gallery, 1978.

Two of the city's most successful stations with appeal to black audiences were developed by Jews: WHAT, by William and Dolly Banks, and WDAS, by Max M. Leon and his son-in-law, Robert Klein.[15] Leon was a candy manufacturer with cultural interests. A violinist and band leader, he started, conducted, and bankrolled the original Philadelphia Pops Orchestra; was president of the Philadelphia Civic Grand Opera Company for twelve years; and was then general manager, for three years, of the Opera Company of Philadelphia, formed from the merger of the Civic Grand and the Lyric Opera. Leon purchased WDAS in 1950 and sold it in 1979, reportedly for twelve times his initial investment.

For years, the Inquirer Company owned WFIL, the American Broadcasting Company's Philadelphia outlet. *Inquirer* publisher Walter Annenberg owned the station, and it was Annenberg's foresight that made WFIL one of America's first commercial television stations.[16] Recognizing TV's awesome potential, Annenberg overruled his Triangle Company's top executives, who were convinced that television was too risky and that the return on the investment would take too long. Annenberg sent a two-cent postcard to the Federal Communications Commission, announcing his intention to build Philadelphia's first television station, WFIL.

The station prospered, and at least two of Annenberg's personal ideas proved to be innovations with lasting impact in the fledgling field. One was a dance program for teenagers, "Bandstand," which developed into an immensely popular and influential national network show, "American Bandstand." Televised from Philadelphia, with Dick Clark as master of ceremonies, it had a tremendous effect not only on the popular music of the day, but also on American teenage fashions and mores.

The other Annenberg innovation was "University of the Air," a pioneering program in educational television, a concept close to Annenberg's heart. Philadelphia already had an "educational" channel, the Wilmington-based WHYY (Channel 12). When Annenberg moved WFIL to its new studios on City Line, he turned over the station's former headquarters at 46th and Market Streets to WHYY radio and TV. (The station, now part of the Public Broadcasting System, has since moved to 6th and Race Streets.)

One of the key figures in the early years of "educational TV" was movie tycoon William Goldman. As a member of the Philadelphia Board of Education, Goldman had helped settle a dispute between radio station WHYY and the educational television channel (then channel 35), which had been started with matching funds from the city and school district. Goldman forced a revamping of the station's board, reversing what was considered a loose and directionless operation. He increased local representation on the board and became its chairman.[17]

William Goldman had been in the movie business since 1911, when he converted the nickelodeon he was operating into one of St. Louis's first movie palaces, then expanded the operation into a chain, which he merged in 1925 with movie houses owned by Spyros Skouras. Two years later, the Stanley Company (forerunner of Stanley-Warner) bought them out, assigned Skouras to national operations in Hollywood (where he became a movie production giant), and asked Goldman to manage its two hundred movie houses in Pennsylvania, New Jersey, and Delaware.

Six years later, Goldman resigned and went into business for himself, eventually acquiring two hundred movie houses throughout Greater Philadelphia. An eleven-year legal battle with his old bosses at Stanley-Warner over distribution was settled out of court in 1954. The Nickelodeon at Philadelphia's Franklin Institute Science Museum, which Goldman donated, is a replica of the one Goldman operated in St. Louis five decades earlier.

Goldman's successor as Stanley-Warner zone manager was Ted Schlanger, a former film salesman for Universal. Schlanger's son, Claude, was president of the sprawling Budco chain, which, ironically, included all of the old Goldman theaters. Unlike other chains, which begin in mid-city areas and expand into the suburbs, Budco (inspired by Claude Schlanger's boyhood nickname, "Buddy") began with the County Theater in Doylestown, where Claude Schlanger lived. He was operating a dozen theaters in the suburbs before crossing the city line. Not until 1972, when Schlanger bought out the Goldman chain, did Budco move into center city.[18]

Budco's major competition was the Sameric chain, named for Samuel Shapiro and a grandson, Eric, who died in 1971 at the age of 15. Samuel Shapiro was in the real estate and development business, and one of his specialties was constructing motion picture theaters for film production companies. In the 1940s and 1950s, he and a son, Merton, also built and operated some drive-ins, but not until the late 1950s—when the government ordered motion picture producers to divest themselves of theater interests—did the father and son start Sameric. When the elder Shapiro died in 1977, there were ninety Sameric theaters. Sameric was one of the innovators in multiple-screen theaters in the Philadelphia area.[19] (During the conversion process, a sign would be posted that read, "Closed. We're Having Twins.")

One by one, the garish old movie palaces of the past have vanished, along with other vestiges of an era of opulence that had embarrassed the post-war generation because of their gaudiness. Not until the seventies did a counterreaction occur, with an emphasis on preserving some of the structures of that turn-of-the-century period, many of the world's finest in Philadelphia.

In the forefront of theater restoration was Philadelphia architect Hyman Myers, who, according to one newspaper account, "rescued more endangered buildings than most knights of the Round Table did damsels in distress." It was Myers who oversaw restoration of the Pennsylvania Academy of the Fine Arts building, designed by Frank Furness, the Academy of Music, and the Bellevue Stratford Hotel, now the Park Hyatt at the Bellvue.[20] Myers founded Studio Four, the preservation wing of the Vitetta Group, a Philadelphia architecture and engineering firm. In addition to presiding over restorations, he had to "sell" preservation projects to reluctant officials. It was Myers who convinced then-Mayor William Green to restore Conversation Hall in Philadelphia's City Hall; he did it by punching a hole in the wall to show the mayor the original chandelier, hanging intact between two later-added walls. At the Academy of the Fine Arts, Myers had the ceiling restored to reveal a spectacular dome, decorated with the stars of the firmament, and had the plywood ripped off the building's extravagantly sculptured pillars.

Myers is in the grand tradition of Philadelphia architects whose influence has been felt far beyond the metropolitan area (his restoration projects have been hailed in many cities). Perhaps the major figure in American architecture during a good part of the twentieth century was Philadelphia's Louis I. Kahn, called by *Inquirer* architecture writer Thomas Hine, "one of the most charismatic figures in 20th century architecture." A trailblazer in basic form, he influenced generations that followed.[21]

Kahn's buildings are found all over the world. Perhaps the best example in the Philadelphia area is the Richards Laboratories at 38th Street and Hamilton Walk on the campus of the University of Pennsylvania, where Kahn studied and taught. Almost as famous as Kahn's completed buildings are some of his plans for projects that never materialized, including one for Mikveh Israel syna-

Louis I. Kahn (left, with Sol Hurok and Chaim Potok) and the plans for the Mikveh Israel Synagogue, at the American Jewish Cultural Festival, May 1970. Though the designs have become world-famous, another plan —one that accommodated the American Jewish History Musuem— was adopted.

gogue on Independence Mall, where another plan was eventually used. Kahn's drawings attract disciples and admirers to the Louis Kahn Archives at the University of Pennsylvania. They remind the *Inquirer's* Hine of people "coming into a church, making a pilgrimage."

Philadelphia has been a center for the fine arts for decades, but only in more recent years have Jews become a major force in the region's visual arts establishment. Historically, Jewish interest in the visual arts lagged behind Jewish involvement in music and the performing arts. Some art historians attributed this to the prevalence of pagan and Christian iconography through centuries of painting and sculpture. Whatever the reason, Jews are prominent in Philadelphia's art world, as artists, collectors, curators, art historians, museum administrators, dealers, and taste-setters.

Marian Locks, who founded a prestigious Center City gallery, is credited with a key role in turning Philadelphia's "gallery" scene around, by encouraging local young artists and showcasing their work, instead of exhibiting the more established, "safer" artists from New York.[22]

Helen Drutt is credited with single-handedly spurring a crafts revolution in Philadelphia. As director of a gallery of her own and former gallery director at Moore College of Art, she has been a major figure in the growing acceptance of the crafts as art.[23]

Janet Kardon, who helped found the Institute of Contemporary Art at the University of Pennsylvania, is a major collector of contemporary American work. She follows in a growing tradition of prominent Jewish collectors of art in Philadelphia, going back to the late Lessing Rosenwald, who specialized in Old Masters prints. Others include Vivian and the late Meyer Potamkin, whose interest in pre–World War American art helped establish a national trend; Muriel Wolgin and Jack Wolgin; and Walter and Lee Annenberg, whose collections in their Wynnewood and Palm Springs mansions are world renowned.

It was Annenberg, incidentally, who played a key role in making it possible for the public to see what may be one of the world's most extraordinary private collections—at the Barnes Foundation in Merion, just a few blocks from the Philadelphia City Line.[24]

The edifice that combines Mikveh Israel Synagogue and the American Jewish History Museum.

David Schlessinger, founder of Encore Books.

Joseph Fox (right) and his son Michael in front of their Sansom St. store. Philadelphia has a distinguished history of bookselling, with some Jewish-owned establishments (such as Sessler's on Walnut St.) achieving national repute. The Fox Bookshop, though a cramped basement store, carries on this tradition.

The eccentric Dr. Albert C. Barnes, who had made a fortune by inventing the antiseptic Argyrol, had amassed an astonishing collection of painting and objets d'art, including hundreds of Renoirs, Matisses, Picassos, Seurats, and Rousseaus. But he allowed very few visitors, and actually barred art critics and connoisseurs. His will, establishing the Barnes Foundation, barred all but a small group of students from seeing the collection.

After Barnes was killed in an auto accident in 1951, Annenberg's Philadelphia Inquirer launched a campaign to force the opening of the tax-free institution for public access to the gallery. It took years of *Inquirer* publicity-generated pressure and legal action in the Pennsylvania courts before the beleaguered foundation finally agreed in 1961 to broaden its admission policy and to open its doors (with restrictions) to the public.

Philadelphia's more orthodox art institutions, until the mid-1980s, were dominated—professionally, as well as socially—by old established WASP families. Jews now have more than token representation on the boards of institutions such as the Philadelphia Museum of Art and the Pennsylvania Academy of the Fine Arts.

Jews also are no longer a rarity on museum staffs. Nessa Forman, who was a critic for the now-defunct Philadelphia *Bulletin,* recalled that only one or two other Jews were in her graduate school class when she majored in art history in 1968 at the University of Pennsylvania. Today, there are Jewish art historians and curators at most art museums, and Jews on the faculties of the city's art schools and colleges.

Other Philadelphia museums also reflect the growing Jewish presence in the city's cultural life. The Museum of American Jewish History opened during the Bicentennial year of 1976. Located in the historic district, it is housed at Mikveh Israel, America's second oldest Jewish congregation, and its collection includes many items from the synagogue's archives pertaining to Philadelphia Jewry as far back as the colonial era.[25]

Joel N. Bloom was director of the Franklin Institute Science Museum and Fels Planetarium, after eleven years as a researcher and head of the Institute's systems science department.[26]

The JPS executive board often represented the cream of Jewish intellectual life. Pictured here is the 1960 board: (from left, standing) Solomon Grayzel, Louis Leventhal, J. Solis-Cohen, Jr., Bernard Frankel, and Jerome Shestack; (seated) Myer Feinstein, Edwin Worl, 2d, Sol Satinsky, Horace Stern, executive director Lesser Zussman.

Disseminating Jewish books to Jewish communities throughout the United States and worldwide has been the mission of JPS for a nearly a century. Picture here, at a JPS 1955 members meeting, is a book display overseen by Beatrice Diamond, membership secretary.

Because it is an old city, Philadelphia is a treasure-house of antiques, and interest in antiques runs high here. The section of Pine Street known as "Antique Row" includes several stores that have been owned by the same Jewish families for generations, often tracing back to an immigrant entrepreneur's second-hand store. In most cases, the business has gone from father to son, but at least one boasts a different sequence. M. Finkel & Daughter, at 10th and Pine Streets, is run by Morris Finkel, who worked for his father, and his daughter, Amy, whose expertise in antique quilts is such that she lectures on the subject at museums and universities.[27]

Books have always attracted collectors, and Philadelphia is rich in bibliophiles. As the people of The Book, Jews have been in love with the written word throughout the millennia, and Jewish Philadelphians have been no exception.

The oldest library of any kind in the nation is the Library Company of Philadelphia, which was headed for thirty-two years by Edwin Wolf II before he retired in 1984. Founded by Benjamin Franklin, the Library Company was an Old Philadelphia establishment that "opened up," Wolf said, like most scholarly organizations, including the Bibliographical Society of America and the Grolier Club (both of which Wolf headed) and such venerable Philadelphia institutions as the Pennsylvania Historical Society, the Athenaeum, and the American Philosophical Society,.

For years, Philadelphia's premier bookstore was Sessler's on Walnut Street between 12th and 13th, an establishment with appeal to traditionalists who enjoyed browsing through its used-book and print collections. But in a city once rich with privately owned and fanatically patronized bookstores, the business has changed. It is now dominated by mass-merchandising and discount-price chains. The Philadelphia-based Encore Books was an American business success story of classic dimensions.[29] Encore Books was founded in 1973 by a University of Pennsylvania sophomore, David Schlessinger. It eventually became a chain with gross sales in the multimillions. Schlessinger launched this empire in a discount bookstore in Center City with $1,000 he had saved from gifts, part-time jobs, investments, and loans from relatives. His formula was to sell in quantities large enough to keep the prices down, at easy-to-reach stores with low overhead, using energetic promotion techniques.

Book publishing in Philadelphia was once a thriving industry, but most of the publishing houses have been absorbed into conglomerates headquartered elsewhere. Not so the Jewish Publication Society (JPS).[29] Founded in 1888 by representatives of the nation's Jewish organizations to publish, in English, books, sermons, and lectures relating to Judaism, JPS has been in Philadelphia ever since. Its first editor was Henrietta Szold, who later founded Hadassah, and subsequent editors have included such major literary figures as Judaic scholar Solomon Grayzel and novelist Chaim Potok.

Left: Irvin J. Borowsky of North American Publishing, 1971.

Right: D. Herbert Lipson of *Philadelphia* Magazine, 1970.

Below: Philadelphia spawned a number of big-band orchestras, probably the most famous being Lester Lanin's, which has played at several functions of British royalty. Pictured here is orchestra leader Abe Neff, a Philadelphia favorite, entertaining Israeli sailors at the Broad St. YMHA, May 1981.

Philadelphia Jews have been energetically involved in amateur theatrical production since before the turn of the century. Few national companies can match the dedication and polish of the Neighborhood Players. Pictured here is the Neighborhood Players' Theatre at 22nd and Walnut (in the Sidney Hillman Center) during the 1960 production of "The Drunkard."

Jewish Publication Society board member Irvin Borowsky was president of North American Publishing Company, at 401 North Broad Street, which publishes slick trade and industrial magazines. In the annals of magazine publishing, however, Borowsky has an even more lasting claim to fame.

He and his brother, the late Arthur Borowsky, were publishing a television program guide in the late 1940s in conjunction with local Philco distributors, who paid half the costs and provided lists of TV owners from which the brothers could solicit subscribers. The magazine was starting to grow and attract advertisers when it attracted Walter Annenberg's attention.[30]

Intrigued by the Borowsky brothers' publication and similar ones in other cities, Annenberg conceived the idea of a national magazine, with a general section published at his Triangle plant in Philadelphia and shipped to cities all around the country, where it would be bound around local TV listings. One by one, Annenberg bought out local TV publications (the Borowskys sold for a reported $1 million), and built *TV Guide* into its present market-commanding position. Publishing out of its own plant in Radnor, Delaware County, *TV Guide* is America's largest-circulation magazine.

Philadelphia no longer is the magazine publishing center it was when Curtis Publishing Company, among others, was thriving here. But in one phase of magazine publishing, Philadelphia has led the way—the local city magazine.

Philadelphia magazine is generally acknowledged to be the most successful (and possibly the best) publication of its kind in the nation. An outgrowth of what began as a Chamber of Commerce newsletter, *Philadelphia* magazine has perfected a blend of glass-slick trendiness, investigative reporting, and a trademark sauciness that is attractive to a large and financially upward-bound readership, which, in turn, has attracted abundant and upscale advertising.

Presiding over the magazine's glory years was publisher D. Herbert Lipson, who inherited the business from his father. Its longtime editor was Alan Halpern, who is usually credited with having developed the magazine's successful formula.

Philadelphia magazine has many imitators in cities all over the nation. Two of them are published by Lipson: *Boston* magazine, which he founded in 1971, and *Manhattan, Inc.,* which was launched in September 1984. Influenced by Philadelphia's style is *Inside,* the quarterly magazine published by the Federation of Jewish Agencies, in conjunction with the weekly *Jewish Exponent.* Slick, sophisticated, and upscale in appeal, *Inside* neatly offsets the alleged parochialism some criticize in the *Exponent.*

Left: Dan Rottenberg of the *Welcomat.*

Right: Edwin Guthman of the *Inquirer.*

Parochial or not, the *Exponent* cannot be underestimated as an influence on Philadelphia's Jewish community. Not only does it reach almost every Jewish home in the metropolitan area, surveys indicate that it is read thoroughly by a surprising percentage of its subscribers, and Philadelphia's business community agrees that it is an extraordinarily productive advertising medium.

In Philadelphia's mainstream journalism, Jews have been playing a role since Annenberg's *Inquirer* and J. David Stern's *Record* were thundering at each other across Broad Street. Many of the top editors, reporters, columnists, and critics on the city's newspapers—past and present—have been Jewish.

In the wake of a series of newspaper collapses, the "only game in town" is Philadelphia Newspapers Inc., a Knight-Ridder chain subsidiary, which publishes the city's two remaining daily newspapers, the *Inquirer* and the *Daily News*. There is nothing like a dominant Jewish influence on either newspaper, but Jews are integrated at all levels, including at the top. Both have or have had Jewish editors.

Although the number of metropolitan daily newspapers has declined, weeklies and small suburban dailies prosper. Perhaps the most talked-about mainstream weekly is the *Welcomat,* edited by Dan Rottenberg, which circulates in Center City among a devoted following of young professionals who have been "gentrifying" once-blighted areas like Society Hill and Fairmount.

There is heavy Jewish representation in this segment of Philadelphia, from the affluent in the huge condominiums on the Parkway to the avant garde, who have helped turn South Street from an East Side strip of second-hand stores into a Philadelphia version of Soho and Greenwich Village, a bizarre mix of offbeat restaurants and clubs, art galleries and bookstores, chic boutiques and pricey schlock shops. It wouldn't be surprising if some of today's South Street entrepreneurs are working on the same sites where their grandparents sold "schmatas" to fellow immigrants.

The story of Jewish involvement and leadership in the cultural life of Philadelphia mirrors the gradual but determined efforts of the Jewish community to gain acceptance into the society at large. To the degree that they have been successful—and by all accounts, that degree has been very high—it seems likely that such participation and leadership will increase (perhaps into areas of culture that are specifically Jewish) in the years to come.[34]

THE ONCE AND FUTURE CITY
One Jewish Philadelphian's Odyssey

Dan Rottenberg

It was the worst of times. The "putrid corpse of liberty," as Mussolini called it, had already been buried in Italy, Germany, Spain, Austria, Czechoslovakia, Poland, Norway, Denmark, Belgium, and the Netherlands. France, cradle of the Rights of Man, had decided after six weeks of fighting that the Rights of Man were not worth defending. Hitler's empire extended from Spitzbergen to the Sahara and from the Atlantic to the outskirts of Moscow. Imperial Japan's domain stretched from the East Indies to the Aleutian Islands of Alaska. Millions of innocent men, women, and children had already been herded into concentration camps. The last, best hope of democracy—the U.S. armed forces—had been caught flat-footed at Pearl Harbor and driven in humiliation from the Philippines.

On the day I was born—June 10th, 1942—the German army opened a new front with an attack on the Russian army near Kharkov. That same day, in retaliation for the assassination of the deputy Gestapo chief Reinhard Heydrich two weeks earlier, the Nazis demolished the entire town of Lidice, Czechoslovakia. The men of Lidice were executed, the women sent to concentration camps, the children entrusted to what German officials called "appropriate educational institutions," and all the buildings were leveled.

It was not the most auspicious moment to enter the world, but, of course, nobody consulted me. And in retrospect, among the billions of people who have walked the earth since its creation, I belonged to a tiny group whose lives have been uniquely blessed, for two reasons that we had nothing to do with: First, more than a century ago, our Old World ancestors demonstrated the courage and foresight to pull up their roots and transplant themselves to an unknown land across the Atlantic; and second, more than two centuries ago (and just a few blocks from my present home), a group of total strangers (to us) displayed the courage and foresight to commit their lives, their fortunes, and their sacred honor to an unproved concept of human governance—democracy and freedom. In a world afflicted by wasted human potential, we lucky few have enjoyed the opportunity to shape our individual destinies as well as our communities to an extent unknown to nearly all peoples, past or present.

Much has been written about the historical forces that, in the course of four thousand years, dispersed the Jewish people from the Middle East to Europe and then to America. As one effect of these migrations, Philadelphia became the world's fifth-largest Jewish metropolis—in Jewish population today only by New York, Los Angeles, Tel Aviv, and Jerusalem. Why did so many of us wind up in Philadelphia? And why do we stay even now, when we enjoy the option of a Jewish homeland in Israel as well as the material means to move wherever we please? The peculiar tapestry woven from the strands of my personal experiences as a Jew, a journalist and a Philadelphian may offer some insight.

Begin with my medieval ancestor, the German rabbi Meir of Rothenburg, who in the thirteenth century was said to exercise quasi-legal authority among the Jews of central Europe—not through any official position (he didn't even have a congregation), but solely by virtue of his scholarship. Five hundred years before John Locke and Thomas Jefferson, this remarkable thinker contended that under the principles of Jewish public law, man is absolutely free, the legitimacy of government is derived solely from the free and uncoerced consent of the governed, and the legislative power of the majority is limited only to certain areas and cannot encroach upon the individual's private and inalienable rights.

Had Meir lived in a more receptive society, he might have prompted the Renaissance or the Enlightenment. Instead, he became a pawn in a political squabble between the Holy Roman Emperor and the Hapsburg dukes. He was held for ransom in prison for the last seven years of his life and is remembered today mostly for his martyrdom. Half a millennium would pass before Meir's ideas would bear fruit in the Declaration of Independence and the U.S. Constitution.

Meir's distant descendant, my great-great-grandfather, Marcus Rottenberg, was an educated, multilingual man of 35 when he arrived in America from Hungary in 1862. The United States was then in the midst of a bloody and traumatic civil war, but Marcus—whose people had, after all, suffered persecution for centuries—viewed America from a different perspective. To Marcus, it was that rare place where, finally, he would not be judged by his background but was free to rise or fall on his own individual merit.

Marcus settled in Cleveland and found a job there. After a few years he had saved enough to send steamboat tickets to his wife, Esther, in Hungary, so she and their children could join him. But Esther—unwilling to give up her familiar world for her husband's strange new land—refused to make the journey. So three years after his arrival—just after Lincoln's assassination—Marcus Rottenberg returned to Hungary.

He never saw America again, but he never forgot it. Once back in Hungary, he built himself an American-style cottage. He distributed American silver dollars to his children and grandchildren and encouraged them to move to America, and, ultimately, most of them did.

His son Herman, my great-grandfather, was perhaps the first of the nonconformist Rottenbergs. In a Hungarian village populated mostly by Galician Hasidic Jews, Herman alone cut his hair short, wore Western business suits, read a German (rather than Yiddish) newspaper, and practiced a rational (as opposed to mystical) brand of Judaism. Despite these differences (or perhaps because of them), Herman's Hasidic neighbors chose him as their community judge as well as their liaison with the Austro-Hungarian crown.

After his four eldest children had moved to America, Herman followed them to New York in 1902 with his wife and his remaining four children, the youngest of whom—my grandfather, Marc—was then 8. As a youth, this Marc was a devout and eager student of Torah, but at 17 he rebelled after his father died suddenly of pneumonia at the age of 58. "If God makes decisions of that kind," Marc concluded, as he told me years later, "then there's something wrong with God."

For months Marc refused to attend synagogue, despite his mother's anguished pleas. But after a while it occurred to Marc that the Torah couldn't have survived for thousands of years unless it possessed some value. So he began to examine the Torah to see if it might be susceptible to some fresh interpretation.

Ultimately, Marc found that the Torah worked very well for him if, in each place where the word *God* appeared, he substituted the word *ideal*—that is, that the term *God* represents not some supernatural heavenly force, but the ideals to which men and women aspire. This, of course, was the essence of the Reconstructionist creed later expounded in the 1920s by Rabbi Mordecai Kaplan: the notion that Judaism is not so much a religion as a civilization that has been constantly "reconstructed" over thousands of years through a trial-and-error process conducted by thinking individuals. Just as Meir of Rothenburg was an Enlightenment man long before the Enlightenment, so my grandfather Marc Rottenberg in effect was a Reconstructionist in spirit long before the birth of Reconstructionism.

After moving from Brooklyn to Manhattan in 1941, Marc attended a Shabbat service at Rabbi Kaplan's Society for the Advancement of Judaism and heard Kaplan tell the congregation, "Now, you know that Moses wasn't up in heaven for 40 days and 40 nights. It isn't humanly possible. And you know that the Torah was not given to the Jews on Mount Sinai. The Torah was given by Ezra, seven or eight hundred years later." Marc was astonished to hear the very thoughts he had long harbored but had never dared to express. "This is home," he told himself. "This is where I belong."

To me, the lesson of Rabbi Meir of Rothenburg and my grandfather alike is that—Thomas Carlyle notwithstanding—great ideas do not begin as a minority of one. They often occur simultaneously to many people in isolation. But the ideas perish unless a community connects such people, reinforcing their beliefs and emboldening them to convert their thoughts into actions. (Behind the Jewish requirement of a *minyan* for prayer lies the insight that a community of worshippers is greater than the sum of its parts.) But some communities perform this function better than others.

Philadelphia, to cite one such example, was not merely the birthplace of modern democracy; it was also the only major city in the world founded and profoundly influenced by that most tolerant and egalitarian religious sect, the Quakers. As such, it became a haven for Europeans fleeing oppression as far back as the French Huguenots in the seventeenth century. It was the only North American center of the Enlightenment, that great eighteenth-century awakening that ushered in modern political culture. (The historian Robert Darnton has identified eleven sources of the Enlightenment: ten European cities and Philadelphia.) The ideas of Meir of Rothenburg and Mordecai Kaplan alike found a home here. But Philadelphia's blessings were unknown to my grandfather and his forebears. That discovery would be left to me.

My family's first exposure to Philadelphia occurred in January of 1933, when my father, upon graduating from Boys High School in Brooklyn, found that only one college on the East Coast would accept him in the middle of the school year: the University of Pennsylvania. He enrolled at Penn for that reason. As a further consequence, a generation later, when the time came for me—a lifelong New Yorker—to choose a college, my passionate (and not entirely rational) attachment to my dad's alma mater dictated that I would go there, too. At Penn I met and married a native Philadelphian. After graduating in 1964, we spent eight years in the Midwest before returning to Philadelphia in 1972. We've lived here ever since.

In this respect, at least, my story is typical of this city in our times. Overwhelmingly, new arrivals move to Philadelphia for one of three reasons: Either they attended school here, or they married a Philadelphian, or their company transferred them here. Only after arriving in Philadelphia do they notice the unique charms of a city capable of harboring world-class achievement without sacrificing its small-town intimacy. Only after living here for a while can you appreciate how this character translates into a remarkably effective marketplace for ideas and for business. In my case, a simple lunch-hour stroll through Center City on any given day usually becomes a goldmine of serendipitous encounters with people who represent either potential jobs or assignments, potential subjects for articles, potential sources of information, or potential friends.

As a Jewish arrival in Philadelphia, my case was typical in other respects as well. Like most modern American Jews, my Jewishness manifested itself not so much religiously as culturally. In Philadelphia, I instinctively melted into that great Jewish nucleus of audiences and patrons who support and nurture everything from the Orchestra and the Art Museum to theater and dance troupes to the city's restaurants and upscale food purveyors, even if we rarely set foot in a synagogue except on the High Holy Days. (As the protagonist of the film *My Favorite Year* put it: "Jews know two things: suffering, and where to find great Chinese food." Or as a Catholic clarinetist once remarked to me, "Thank God for the Jews—they're the only ones who still hire live musicians at weddings.")

In effect, we are (for better or worse) Jews communing with other Jews mostly through secular institutions. Yet, in the process, these institutions inadvertently assume a Jewish coloration because, paradoxically, Jews of my generation and younger tend to be more overtly assertive about our Jewishness among gentiles. We are living proof of "Hansen's Law," as articulated by the sociologist Marcus Hansen: "What the son wishes to forget, the grandson wishes to remember." My insecure immigrant ancestors, eager to be accepted as Americans, bent over backward to conceal their European pasts. (My maternal grandfather, brought to America from Russia as an infant, insisted to his dying day that he had been born in New York.) But Jews of the post-war baby boomer generation, secure in our American identity, have been eager to discover and assert our roots before the traces of our European backgrounds are lost to posterity forever.

Thus, as a 15-year-old attending my grandmother's funeral in 1958, I found myself copying names and dates from relatives' tombstones at the family plot in a Queens cemetery. That simple exercise launched my lifelong hobby of tracing my ancestors. And when, years later in Philadelphia, I despaired of finding a guidebook geared specifically to Jewish ancestor-hunting, I decided to write my own. The result, in 1977, was *Finding Our Fathers,* the first English-language guide to Jewish genealogy.

For me, genealogy became the portal to whatever Jewish consciousness I possessed. Yet, in those days, tracing ancestors was a lonely hobby, devoid of community: By definition, Jewish genealogy seemed to involve communing with dead Jews, not live ones. But that definition changed in the years after *Finding Our Fathers* first appeared, as the Jewish genealogy movement exploded into a cottage industry of organizations, publications, books, Internet chat rooms, and database services. Jewish genealogists who had once labored in isolation now shared information and even socialized with each other over the Internet, at conventions, and at meetings of groups like the Jewish Genealogy Society of Philadelphia. Thanks to the unseen incubating presence of the larger Jewish community, in effect a "Jewish genealogy community" evolved where none had previously existed.

Similarly, without really trying, in Philadelphia I did indeed discover a compatible religious community to complement my secular ones. As a young man in the Midwest, I had despaired of finding a congregation like Mordecai Kaplan's Society for the Advancement of Judaism anywhere outside New York. To my surprise, on my return to Philadelphia in 1972, I learned that the Reconstructionist Rabbinical College—America's first major, new rabbinical school in generations—had opened its doors in 1968, not in Kaplan's New York, but on Philadelphia's North Broad Street, near Temple University. Its first president was Ira Eisenstein, Kaplan's son-in-law, who had led the SAJ when I was a boy. Why were he and his college in Philadelphia? As Rabbi Eisenstein explained it to me, to succeed, the college needed three things: a flourishing local Jewish community; access to other universities where students could study simultaneously; and reasonable housing costs. Only Philadelphia satisfied all three requirements.

Eisenstein, in turn, directed me to the newly created Society Hill Synagogue, where a young rabbi named Ivan Caine was challenging his congregants (as indeed he would continue to do for thirty-three years) to engage their brains in the service of a moral and Jewish approach to the advancement of civilization. Here was a community of confident, intelligent adults, capable of exchanging conflicting viewpoints without feeling threatened by them. Like my grandfather when he first heard Mordecai Kaplan, I found myself thinking, "I'm home."

Like many American Jews, especially in my generation, I was endowed with an individualistic streak that caused me to question conventional wisdom and to strive to create new genres and institutions as opposed to accepting existing ones. Indeed, this characteristic may have steered me toward journalism in the first place. (As the Chicago writer George Murray once observed, much of the manpower for America's urban newspapers in the first half of the twentieth century came from two otherwise dissimilar ethnic groups: the Irish and the Jews. These two groups may not have had much in common, but they did share common histories of oppression, a philosophical bent, and a fondness for the written word.)

Even before my return to Philadelphia in 1972, I sensed that this city might be a good place for a journalist like me to practice his craft: close enough to New York and Washington to feel the world's pulse, but sufficiently distant to retain one's perspective. During a visit to Philadelphia in 1967, when I was a 25-year-old small-town Indiana newspaper editor, I showed up unannounced at the *Inquirer* and asked to see Andrew Khinoy, the *Inquirer's* veteran assistant managing editor, whose daughter-in-law was a friend of my wife's. I explained that I wanted to write the *Inquirer's* Section B feature column—a slot then occupied by the famous Joe McGinniss. McGinniss was good, I acknowledged, but I was better—as I assumed the samples I thrust before Andy would clearly demonstrate.

Andy gently explained that thousands of other journalists also wanted that column; that no matter how good I was, they couldn't just kick McGinniss out; and besides, Andy was on deadline at that moment. What a na'f I must have seemed to Andy's grizzled eyes! Yet eleven years later I did indeed start writing a column for the *Inquirer* (on the op-ed page) that continued for eighteen years. What did not occur to me then were the subliminal ways in which Philadelphia's Jewish influences would shape my subsequent career.

During the late 1960s and early 1970s, I was a reporter and editor in Chicago—a heady time and place for a journalist, thanks to Mayor Richard J. Daley and his political machine, Hugh Hefner and his *Playboy* empire, the 1968 Democratic convention riots, the Chicago Seven conspiracy trial, and the police murder of sleeping Black Panthers. America's great public preoccupations of those times—the Civil Rights revolution and the Vietnam War—were being played out against an equally significant backdrop: For the first time, television had replaced newspapers as Americans' preferred vehicle for connecting with the world.

Whatever the deficiencies of newspapers as information sources, at the very least the act of forming words and sentences out of abstract symbols required mental exercise. Watching pictures on a TV screen, on the other hand, required no mental exertion whatever. Americans were growing addicted to this seductive but shallow medium, in the process impairing their capacity to think analytically or independently. American political life would instead become (as Arthur Miller later observed), "profoundly governed by the modes of theater, from tragedy to vaudeville to farce."

The solution, it seemed to me, was to rekindle Americans' appetite for the written word. But how?

My inspiration in those days came not from my Chicago colleagues, but from the monthly arrival in my mail of *Philadelphia* magazine. From the mid-60s onward, under the leadership of its editor, Alan Halpern, and its publisher, D. Herbert Lipson, this former Chamber of Commerce promotional organ had evolved into a courageous, irreverent, trend-setting magazine whose writers brought style and wit to every subject, no matter how mundane. There was nothing like it anywhere in the country, including New York (it subsequently provided the model for New York magazine). Although *Philadelphia* magazine's small staff represented a diverse range of ethnic backgrounds, Philadelphia's establishment perceived it (astutely) as a gadfly voice of Jewish outsiders in contrast to the cautious status quo protectiveness of the *Bulletin* and *Inquirer.*

The difference between *Philadelphia* and other publications in those days was roughly the difference between a movie and a lecture. Instead of reporting the dry facts about urban prostitution or suburban burglaries, *Philadelphia* writers portrayed the night's work of a fictitious "composite" prostitute and a "composite" burglar, based on real people. They wrote not as objective journalists, but as passionate humans sharing their excitement about their subjects.

This was the dawn of what came to be known as "the new journalism." At that time, you bought *Philadelphia* magazine not to read specific stories or writers, but for the general expectation that anything you read in any issue would surprise, delight, shock, or fascinate you. In this manner, *Philadelphia* magazine introduced its readers to a broad range of weighty subjects—education, transportation, poverty, city planning—that wouldn't otherwise have interested them. Yet, until the mid-70s, *Philadelphia* offered no graphic design to speak of, no color, no splashy layouts, really nothing to please the eye. The magazine then was a testament to the sheer delight of the written word.

It was the chance to work there—as well as the pull of family ties—that brought me back to Philadelphia in 1972. On my return, I discovered that *Philadelphia* magazine was not the only local publication undergoing a remarkable turnaround. The *Inquirer*, after thirty-three years under Walter Annenberg's heavy hand, had been sold to the Knight chain and was about to be transformed from one of America's most despised newspapers into America's most honored newspaper, winning seventeen Pulitzer Prizes over the next eighteen years. Yet, strangely, once I was ensconced in Philadelphia, I drew my inspiration not so much from local journalists as from another Jewish-influenced secular community: Philadelphia's restaurateurs.

About a year after my return, Philadelphia's downtown area blossomed with a wonderful and (for a city that had never been known for its cuisine) inexplicable "restaurant renaissance." The reason for it, I theorized, was that the end of the Vietnam War had released the creative energies of a whole generation of youthful antiwar protesters. Experimenting with restaurants was an ideal counterculture activity for such socials activists, and Philadelphia—with its combination of sophisticated population and low property costs—was the ideal incubator for such experiments. At Center City restaurants like Frog and The Commissary, a former social worker named Steve Poses was using *nouvelle cuisine* as a tool to bring diverse people together. At La Terrasse on the Penn campus, a former VISTA volunteer and communal entrepreneur named Judy Wicks was creating an informal left/liberal salon. Armies of freshly divorced 30-somethings searching unhappily for love in singles bars found a nonthreatening, nondegrading environment at the "salad bars" popping up around town.

One of the driving forces behind that 1970s' dining renaissance was a former druggist named Gil Guben, who spent the last seven years of his life launching and reviving innovative restaurants in Center City—among them, Friday Saturday Sunday, Morgan's, Maxwell's Prime, Bogart's, Les Amis, and The Restaurant School. Guben was no empire builder: Once he put a restaurant on its feet, he usually moved on to open another new restaurant. In the process, he taught Philadelphians that dining out could be fun, and that there's more than one way to operate a restaurant.

As I observed Guben's late-life career, it occurred to me that I'd like to do for the printed word what Gil was doing for restaurants—that is, create a variety of local publications. In the process, readers would discover that there's more than one way to run a newspaper. They might even discover that written communication can be more fun than watching TV.

Center City Philadelphia had provided the ideal "incubator space" for innovative restaurants, just as Philadelphia was the ideal incubator space for the Reconstructionist Rabbinical College. In that case, I reasoned, why couldn't Center City also provide an incubator space for ideas?

What sort of ideas? I didn't know. I only knew that a stodgy city that was once the butt of W. C. Fields jokes was suddenly being celebrated for its trend-setting magazine, its Pulitzer Prize–winning morning newspaper, and its world-class restaurant scene. To me, Philadelphia seemed to be fulfilling Mordecai Kaplan's interpretation of the fundamental message delivered by Moses on Mount Sinai: The way things are is not the way things have to be. Individually and collectively, we humans possess the power to break the bonds of the past and transform the world.

I found my vehicle in 1981 when I met Susan Levin Seiderman, who had recently inherited control of the *Welcomat,* a free weekly newspaper distributed in Center City since 1971. Susan was eager to transform her late father's conventional and rather pedestrian paper into a local equivalent of New York's *Village Voice.* Her reasoning was refreshingly unpretentious: "If I have to *read* this paper,' she said, "I want it to be interesting." Attracted by her offer of near-total freedom, I came on board as editor. "You can do whatever you want with the paper," my new boss told me, "as long as you don't bore me."

Faced with such a delicious challenge, I inventoried the *Welcomat's* available resources. I had only one full-time assistant and a free-lance budget that allowed me to pay no more than $40 for articles. On the other hand, I had a community overflowing with affluent, educated, articulate, opinionated people—many of whom, I speculated, would come out of the woodwork and write for me if given a good outlet and a good audience. I had a relatively intimate circulation of 31,500, through which people could speak their minds without the self-consciousness of appearing before a mass audience. I had a free-circulation paper, which meant I needn't worry about marketing my product, concocting splashy cover stories, or hyping the articles; writers could speak in a conversational tone, just as if they were gathering with friends in a living room. And I had a weekly publishing schedule—frequent enough to maintain a dialogue between editor and readers, infrequent enough to permit thoughtful reflection between editions.

In short, the resources at my disposal, though puny by most editors' standards, were actually considerable. Even the meagerness of my budget turned out, in retrospect, to be a valuable resource. It altered the relationship between this editor and his writers, placing me at their mercy instead of vice versa. Lacking the enticement of big bucks, I had to find other ways to compensate writers—which I did by offering them, among other things, great freedom, instant gratification, a responsive audience, an absence of red tape, and an editor who was always happy to see them (no small concern, if you've ever been a free-lance writer). Instead of assigning stories—which is tough to do at $35 a crack—I simply asked readers and writers to submit unsolicited pieces on subjects *they* cared about.

The response exceeded my wildest hopes. A nurse wrote about the psychological pressures on doctors she worked with. Three readers argued in print about the quality of life in Communist East Germany. A suburbanite criticized gay leaders for failing to perceive AIDS as a moral issue, and gay activists responded. A Jewish woman expressed the frustrations of her search for a synagogue that didn't equate Judaism with unquestioning support for Israel. A Common Pleas Court judge, Lisa Richette, reported enthusiastically on her visit to Nicaragua, then ruled by Sandinistas. A black man who operated a housekeeping service shared his innermost thoughts about the things he found in white people's homes. A black woman described how it feels to work in a glitzy downtown office building and return home to the ghetto each night. What editor could assign stories like these?

The loyalty and affection of the *Welcomat's* readers translated into a potent advertising audience, with the result that the *Welcomat* became, in effect, a small-scale reflection of the twentieth-century Jewish experience in Philadelphia: In the course of my twelve years at the *Welcomat,* this ostensible "outsider" publication grew into the largest secular weekly in Philadelphia, not to mention one of the nation's first profitable "alternative" publications. *Advertising Age* called it "a vanguard for the future of big-city publishing," adding, ":Small weeklies like the *Welcomat* may be the wave of the future."

But, in fact, the *Welcomat's* "forum" format was not replicable anywhere but in downtown Philadelphia. Few other cities in the world offered Center City's unique combination of numbers, affluence, educational levels, stability, security, and tolerance—the combination that creates the necessary environment for experimentation with new ideas. Center City's heavily Jewish character was, I suspect, a critical factor in that environment.

In time, as these things inevitably go, the *Welcomat* became the victim of its own success. Its circulation and revenue growth attracted a buyer more interested in its commercial prospects than in its editorial innovations. In short order, this rambunctious, iconoclastic paper was corporatized into a generic (albeit more profitable) alternative newspaper with a quintessentially generic name: *Philadelphia Weekly.* But what initially struck me and my Welcomat colleagues as a tragic turn of events was in fact part of the natural process through which people and institutions shed their skins, leaving the seeds they planted to be harvested by others in ways we can't imagine.

Who could have predicted, when I wrote *Finding Our Fathers* in 1977, that a peripheral hobby like genealogy would one day become—thanks to photocopiers, computers, the Internet, and the collapse of the Soviet bloc—a major Jewish cultural phenomenon and, at least to some Jewish leaders, the last best hope of reconnecting Jews to Judaism? Similarly, the *Welcomat* may have represented a fresh and vibrant forum for written communication when I started there in 1981; but who in 1981 could have anticipated the profusion of written forums offered today by the Internet? As Henry Ward Beecher put it in the nineteenth century, "The blossom cannot tell what becomes of its fragrance, and no man can tell what becomes of his influence."

Like most of Gil Guben's restaurants, the *Welcomat* was gone by 1995, but Philadelphia's role as a cultural incubator remained. In the years that followed (and in what I like to think of as the best tradition of Gil Guben), my eclectic experiments included *Seven Arts*, a monthly arts magazine; *Philadelphia Forum,* a highbrow Center City weekly; and *Family Business*, an international quarterly based in Philadelphia. At the least, these publications represented exercises in the

Reconstructionist process of trial and error; at best, they planted seeds that may yet sprout in forms I can't imagine. And if I never create a successful publication for Philadelphia's thinking classes—well, as the Talmud reminds me daily from my bulletin board, "It is not upon thee to finish the work; neither art thou free to desist from it."

The secular Jewish life that I and others like me have pursued in Philadelphia and a handful of similar cities represents a break that our ancestors would have found inconceivable. From the time of Abraham until the late twentieth century, our culture was essentially defensive: It assumed that Jews would relate to the rest of the world as underdogs and, consequently, would voluntarily keep to their own narrow group even when they weren't being segregated in Jewish ghettos. I, on the other hand, live in a metropolis where any citizen so disposed enjoys not only relative security, but the opportunity to rub elbows with talent and genius. As my own experience suggests, many of these movers and shakers happen to be Jews themselves. The authors of the Torah or the Talmud would be astounded by the notion that gentiles might freely (and even routinely) choose Jews as their governors, U.S. senators, mayors, district attorneys, or heads of major local universities, as Philadelphians have done. Philadelphia has offered Jews the rare opportunity to fulfill their potential as individuals, and, in the process, Philadelphia's Jews have elevated the city's vision of its own potential.

In effect, as we enter the Third Millennium of the Common Era, we Philadelphia Jews are engaged in one of global Judaism's two remarkable experiments. The first, in Israel, seeks to determine whether Jews, after two thousand years of statelessness, can exercise political power collectively without being corrupted by it, as the rulers of every other state have been. The second, in Diaspora communities like Philadelphia, tests whether Jews, having sustained the Ten Commandments and the Golden Rule among ourselves for three thousand years, can now work alongside our former tormentors—most notably Christians and Muslims—to apply those principles to the development of compassionate societies beyond our own immediate Jewish circle. Both experiments are important, but I personally feel more sanguine about the latter challenge than the former.

To be a Jew is to understand, perhaps more keenly than other people, that in a fallible human world, guaranteed security is a delusion. Our Jerusalem, I think many of us are discovering, is not so much a geographic location as a set of principles with which to build humane communities wherever we happen to find ourselves. To the extent that any of us, Jew or gentile, can be assured of life, liberty, and the pursuit of happiness, that assurance rests on our willingness to work at sustaining those freedoms daily—not just for ourselves, but for all individuals, regardless of background.

Until recently, ethnic or theocratic states represented necessary steps along the road to such a goal. The Jewish state of Israel serves the immediate needs of all Jews who at any given moment lack a viable alternative elsewhere. Israel's forceful presence over the past half-century, I suspect, has also bolstered the confidence and assertiveness of Diaspora Jews in places like Philadelphia. But the model for the future, I would argue, is the secular, tolerant, democratic ideal proposed by (among various assorted thinkers) Genghis Khan, Meir of Rothenburg, and the Quakers who founded Philadelphia—the same model nurtured by the diverse peoples who run Philadelphia in remarkable harmony today.

The world of a thousand years ago accepted tyranny, slavery, and cruelty as necessary evils (the best anyone could hope for was enlightened despotism). Today's world is characterized by the growing global embrace of democracy and freedom (resisted, to be sure, with increasing desperation by tyrants and terrorists). The next millennium may well witness the end of violence and coercion altogether, and possibly even government as we know it, due to the alignment of four otherwise unrelated factors: Gandhian tactics, which will further demonstrate the utility of passive resistance as the best practical means to achieve one's ends; the Internet, through which information will replace force as the primary means of organizing people; psychology, which will further unlock the secrets of the human mind; and biotechnology, which will extend human life spans to centuries, thus producing a far more mature world population.

We won't live to see it, of course. But if and when it happens, swaggering, rambunctious cities will be out, and mature, civilized cities like Philadelphia will be in vogue once again. The city that nurtured the greatest achievement of the Second Millennium c.e.—democracy—could engender the greatest achievement of the Third Millennium as well.

It is no small thing to be a descendant of Abraham living in the shadow of Independence Hall. It is not unreasonable for even an incurable optimist like me to suggest that the best days of both Judaism and Philadelphia lie ahead, and that thanks to the convergence of these two historic forces, the best days of the planet itself may yet lie ahead as well.

Notes

INTRODUCTION TO THE NEW EDITION: THE EIGHTIES TO A NEW CENTURY

Acknowledgment: The authors express appreciation to Sol Daiches, vice president of community services of the Jewish Federation of Greater Philadelphia, for his helpful suggestions with regard to the manuscript and keeping us from making errors.

1. See, for example, Tom W. Smith, *Anti-Semitism in Contemporary America,* American Jewish Committee, 1994.
2. There are several country clubs in suburban areas that have few, if any, Jews. Jewish civic leadership, however, has little interest in breaking down barriers here, as they once did with regard to Center City clubs. Significantly, in terms of the growing integration of Jews in the community, the Locust Club, created by upper-class Jews early in the twentieth century in response to barriers in gentile clubs, closed its doors in the 1990s.
3. Gerald Gamm, *Urban Exodus: Why the Jews Left Boston and the Catholics Stayed,* (Cambridge: Harvard University Press, 1999).
4. *Philadelphia Inquirer,* January 25, 1998; Inside, Fall l996, pp. 74, 76–77; National Museum of American Jewish History Newsletter, vol. 9, no. 2, Summer 2000.
5. Interview with Sol Daiches, September 28, 2000.
6. Jewish Population Study 1996–1997, pp. 4–10.
7. *Philadelphia Inquirer,* March 12 and December 1, 2001.
8. As quoted in the *Jewish Exponent,* June 4, 1998.
9. Jewish Population Study 1996–1997, pp. 4–10.
10. *Philadelphia Inquirer,* February 24, 2001.
11. Steve Feldman, "Saving the Northeast: A Community Ponders the Future," *Jewish Exponent,* November 16, 2000.
12. *New York Times,* January 16, 1997; *Jewish Exponent,* December 14, 2000.
13. Samuel Z. Klausner, *Succeeding in Corporate America, The Experience of Jewish M.B.A.s,* The American Jewish Committee, September 1988.
14. *Philadelphia Inquirer,* April 3, 1997; April 24, 1998; and May 2, 2001.
15. *New York Times,* July 16, 2001.
16. *Philadelphia Inquirer,* November 25, 1997; December 2, 1997; June 14, 2000; *Jewish Exponent,* July 26, 2001.
17. *Philadelphia* magazine, March 1995, pp. 29–32, 34–38.
18. Kathryn Levy Feldman, "Golden Girl," *Inside,* Summer 1999, pp. 55, 70.
19. As quoted in *Forward,* February 2, 2001.
20. Ibid.
21. Jewish Population Study, pp. iv, 12–13, 19.
22. Arlen Specter, *Passion for Truth* (New York: William Morrow–HarperCollins, 2000), pp. 422–427.
23. Steven N. Cohen and Arnold M. Eisen, *The Jew Within: Self, Family, and Community in America* (Bloomington: Indiana University Press, 2000), p. 143.
24. Ibid., pp. 2, 91–92.
25. Mayer, *Believing, Behaving, Belonging: Jewish Identity and Affiliation in Greater Philadelphia,* Special Report No. 3, 1998, pp. 1, 9–13; *Jewish Exponent,* August 5, 1999; July 15, l999; September 9, 1999.
26. Ibid., *Believing,* p. 31. 1996–1997 Jewish Population Study of Greater Philadelphia.
27. Ibid., p. 188.
28. Ibid., pp. 31–33; *Jewish Exponent,* March 29, 2001.
29. Tobin, Jewish Population Study, pp. iv, 17, 22–23.
30. Murray Friedman, "Are Jews Moving to the Right?" *Commentary,* April 2000, pp. 50–52.
31. Henry Cohen and Gary Sandrow, *Philadelphia Chooses a Mayor,* 1971, The American Jewish Committee, 1972, p. 21.
32. Sandra Featherman, *Jews, Blacks and Urban Politics in the 1980s: The Case of Philadelphia,* October 1988, p. iii.
33. Sandra Featherman and John Featherman, *Race and Politics at the Millennium. The 1999 Mayoralty Race in Philadelphia,* American Jewish Committee, February 2000, pp. 3–26.
34. Brian Mono, "Did Young Jews Stray from Dems?" *Jewish Exponent,* November 16, 2000.
35. Andrew Harrison, "Passover Revisited: Philadelphia," in *Efforts to Aid Soviet Jews, 1963–1998* (Madison: Fairleigh Dickinson University Press, 2001).

36. *Jewish Exponent,* April 7, 1995; November 28, 1996; and November 30, 2000.

37. *Philadelphia Inquirer,* September 10, 2000.

38. *Jewish Exponent,* February 1, 2001.

39. Ibid.

40. Ibid., December 28, 2000.

41. January 4, 2001. See also Zlati Meyer, "Kosher Restaurants Thriving, Expanding," *Philadelphia Inquirer,* March 19, 2001.

42. *Philadelphia Inquirer,* March 19, 2001.

43. Interview with Sol Daiches, November 30, 2001.

44. Ibid.

45. *Jewish Exponent,* August 9, 2001.

46. Murray Friedman, *When Philadelphia Was the Capital of Jewish America* (Philadelphia: Balch Institute Press and Associated University Presses, 1993).

47. *Jewish Exponent,* November 28, 1996.

48. *Jewish Exponent,* March 22, 2001.

49. *Philadelphia Inquirer,* November 8 and December 14, 2001.

50. Cohen and Eisen, *The Jew Within,* p. 8.

51. See the discussion in Peter Y. Medding, Gary A. Tobin, Sylvia Barack Fishman, and Mordechai Rimor, "Jewish Identity in Conversionary and Mixed Marriages," The American Jewish Committee, 1992, pp. 2–4; and Egon Mayer, *Children of Intermarriage: A Study in Patterns of Identification and Family Life* (Philadelphia: American Jewish Committee, 1989), p. 43.

52. Cohen and Eisen, *The Jew Within,* pp. 183, 185, 191, and 195.

INTRODUCTION: FROM OUTSIDERS TO INSIDERS?

Acknowledgment: I would like to express appreciation here to Carolyn Beck, who served as my research assistant in the preparation of this essay and was particularly helpful in organizing some of the materials relating to the exclusion from and later broader acceptance of Jews in key areas of community life.

1. Interview with Marvin Comisky, September 7, 1983; Comisky to Friedman, November 21, 1984.

2. Glencoe, Ill.: The Free Press, 1958.

3. Murray Friedman, ed., *Philadelphia Jewish Life, 1830–1940* (Philadelphia: Institute for the Study of Human Issues, 1983), p. 24.

4. Edward Arian, *Bach, Beethoven and Bureaucracy* (Birmingham: University of Alabama Press, 1971), p. 64.

5. John Cooney, *The Annenbergs: The Salvaging of a Tainted Dynasty* (New York: Simon and Schuster, 1982), p. 102.

6. *Philadelphia Patricians and Philistines 1900–1950* (New York: Farrar, Straus, Giroux, 1981), p. 19.

7. Julian L. Griefer, *Neighborhood Center, Adjustment of a Culture Group in America,* doctoral dissertation in School of Education of New York University, 1948, p. 130. Max Whiteman estimates the Jewish population in 1940 as 293,000. *Human Rights and Civil Rights: A History of the First Twenty-five Years of the Philadelphia Fellowship Commission,* 1969, unpublished, American Jewish Committee files, Philadelphia, p. 11.

8. Leon Edel, ed., *The American Scene* (Bloomington: Indiana University Press, 1968), p. 275.

9. *Philadelphia Inquirer,* March 2, 1983.

10. Griefer, *Neighborhood Center,* p. 130.

11. See also Ted Vincent, *Mudville's Revenge: The Rise and Fall of American Sport* (New York: Seaview Books, 1983), p. 249.

12. Manfried Mauskopf, "Death of a Neighborhood," *Jewish Exponent,* undated, Philadelphia Jewish Archives Center.

13. *Jewish Times,* March 31, 1983.

14. Jack Porter, "Differentiating the Features of Orthodox, Conservative and Reform Jewish Groups in Metropolitan, Philadelphia," *Jewish Social Studies,* vol. 25, no. 3, July 1963, p. 189.

15. Sixty-one percent of Jewish students and 69 percent of Protestants were admitted. *A Five Year Study of the Selection of Medical Students,* 1957, p. 11.

16. *Philadelphia Inquirer,* November 29, 1982.

17. Daniel J. Elazar and Murray Friedman, *Moving Up* (New York: Institute on Pluralism and Group Identity of the American Jewish Committee, 1976), p. 29.

18. James Cooke, "How Penn Fruit Checked Out," *Philadelphia* magazine, July 1977, pp. 113–205.

19. Cooney, *The Annenbergs,* pp. 9, 14.

20. Caroline Golab, *Immigrant Destinations* (Philadelphia: Temple University Press, 1977), p. 165.

21. Map of Estimated Jewish Population of Philadelphia and Suburbs as of January 1957, in "Analysis of Movement of Jewish Families in Philadelphia in 1967," Federation of Jewish Agencies.

22. *Philadelphia Inquirer,* November 14, 1982; Herbert J. Gans, *The Levittowners* (New York: Vintage Books, 1967), pp. 3–4.

23. William L. Yancey and Ira Goldstein, *The Jewish Population of the Greater Philadelphia Area,* Institute for Public Policy Studies, Social Science Data Library, Temple University, November 15, 1984, p. 74.

24. Bruce Buschel, "The Promised Land," *Philadelphia* magazine, February 1977, pp. 85–117.

25. Gans, *The Levittowners,* p. 424.

26. Robert Tabak, "[Geographical] Movement of Synagogues in Philadelphia: 1945–1965, Development of a Methodology," July 1978, Philadelphia Jewish Archives Center.

27. Chaim I. Waxman, *American Jews in Transition* (Philadelphia: Temple University Press, 1983), p. 66.

28. Tabak, pp. 3, 11.

29. Lucy S. Dawidowicz, "A Century of Jewish History, 1881–1981: The View from America," *American Jewish Year Book,* 1982, vol. 82, American Jewish Committee and Jewish Publication Society of America, pp. 79–80.

30. Waxman, *American Jews in Transition,* p. 86.

31. Samuel Halpern, *The Political World of American Zionism* (Detroit: Wayne State University Press, 1961), pp. 283, 290.

32. June 8, 1962.

33. Philip A. Steinberg, "Communism, Education, and Academic Freedom: Philadelphia, A Case Study," doctoral dissertation, Temple University, March, 1978, pp. 78–94.

34. Steinberg, p. 305.

35. Interviews with Maurice B. Fagan, December 20, 1983, and Fred Zimring, December 23, 1984; Steinberg, "Communism, Education, and Academic Freedom," p. 4.

36. Ellen W. Schrecker, typescript of manuscript on loyalty programs and higher education, chapter 9, p. 8.

37. Interview, December 20, 1983.

38. Paul Lyons, *Philadelphia Communists,* 1936–1956, manuscript page proofs, pp. 1–3.

39. Schrecker, chapter 60, p. 11.

40. Steinberg, pp. 175, 187, 311–312.

41. Steinberg, pp. 162, 164, 235.

42. *Naming Names* (New York: Penguin Books, 1981), p. 322.

43. Schrecker, footnote 7, chapter 60.

44. Steinberg, pp. 2, 308.

45. Lyons, *Philadelphia Communists,* p. 245.

46. Harold Libros, *Organizational Integrity: A Case Study of the Philadelphia Chapter of the Americans for Democratic Action,* doctoral dissertation submitted to the Temple University Graduate Board, 1970, p. 75.

47. Libros, p. 106.

48. *American Modernity & Jewish Identity* (New York: Tavistock Publications, 1983), pp. 136–137.

49. Jeanne R. Lowe, *Cities in a Race with Time* (New York: Random House, 1967), p. 324.

50. Kirk R. Petshek, *The Challenge of Urban Reform: Policies & Programs in Philadelphia* (Philadelphia: Temple University Press, 1973), pp. 96–98; Lowe, pp. 341, 345.

51. Jonathan Barnett and Nory Miller, "Edmund Bacon: A Retrospect," Planning, 1983, pp. 4–11.

52. Interview with confidential source.

53. Cooney, pp. 161, 254.

54. *Jews and Large Law Firms in Philadelphia,* A Report of the Philadelphia Chapter of the American Jewish Committee, May 18, 1964; Baltzell, *Philadelphia Gentlemen,* p. 38; Gaeton Fonzi, "The Philadelphia Lawyer," *Greater Philadelphia Magazine,* April, 1962, p. 46.

55. Annual Meeting, Philadelphia Chapter, American Jewish Committee, October 26, 1966, AJC files.

56. Edwin Kiester, Jr., *The Case of the Missing Executive* (New York: The American Jewish Committee, Institute of Human Relations, 1968), p. 3.

57. Robert A. Leon and Murray Friedman, "The Relationship of Jews to Large Law Firms in Philadelphia," 1969, AJC files.

58. Allied Jewish Appeal: Tentative Goals and Quotas, Trade Council, 1953 Campaign; Federation of Jewish Agencies of Greater Philadelphia, Federation Allied Jewish Appeal Campaign; Numerical Division List, 1983, Philadelphia Jewish Archives Center.

59. Vickie Quade, "1783 Rawle & Henderson 1983, Two Centuries of Success," *ABA Journal,* May 1983, pp. 590–596.

60. Murray Friedman, in Peter I. Rose, Stanley Rothman, and William J. Wilson, eds., *Through Different Eyes* (New York: Oxford University Press, 1973), p. 155.

61. Jed Rakoff and Ruth Bennett, "The Northeast, Its Jews and the American Jewish Committee," Summary Report, January 1971, AJC files.

62. *Jewish Times,* September 11, 1969.

63. Elazar and Friedman, *Moving Up,* pp. 34–37.

64. Libros, *Case Study of Philadelphia Chapter, Americans for Democratic Action,* p. 268.

65. The 1978 "Vote White" Charter Campaign in Philadelphia, Sandra Featherman and William L. Rosenberg, *Jews, Blacks and Ethnics* (New York: American Jewish Committee, 1979), p. 13.

66. *Jewish Exponent,* June 4, 1982.

67. *Jewish Exponent,* September 16, 1983.

68. Donald B. Hurwitz, "1956–1976, 75 Years of Continuity and Change, Our Philadelphia Community in Perspective," a Supplement of the *Jewish Exponent,* March 12, 1976, pp. 42, 92.

69. Rela Monson, *Bringing Women In,* AJC, Philadelphia Chapter, 1977.

70. *Jewish Exponent,* May 13, 1983.

71. Jack Smith, "Walter Mondale's Money Man," *Philadelphia Inquirer Magazine,* July 29, 1984, pp. 15–25.

72. *Philadelphia Inquirer,* August 18, 1985.

73. *Philadelphia Inquirer,* January 16, 1984.

74. *Philadelphia Inquirer,* October 30, 1983.

75. Stephen Fried, "The Music Mann at 80," *Philadelphia* magazine, July 1983, p. 152.

76. *Philadelphia Inquirer,* October 18, 1981.

77. *Jewish Times,* July 15, 1982.

78. Howard S. Shapiro, "Exodus into Guilt," *Today, Inquirer Magazine,* June 6, 1982, p. 28.

79. Yancey and Goldstein, *Jewish Population of Greater Philadelphia Area,* p. 74.

80. Joel Paul, "Reflections on Twelve Years of Campus Service," Jewish Campus Activities Board, p. 3.

81. Albert G. Crawford and Rela Geffen Monson, "Academy and Community: A Study of the Jewish Identity and Involvement of Professors" (New York: AJC Institute of Human Relations, 1980).

82. *Philadelphia Inquirer,* September 18, 1983.

83. "A Century of Jewish History, 1881–1981: The View From America," *American Jewish Year Book 1982,* AJC and JPS, p. 98.

84. Yancey and Goldstein, *Jewish Population of Greater Philadelphia Area,* p. 41.

85. June 10, 1983.

86. "Jewish Community Relations Council Fact Sheet," May 29, 1984.

87. "The Protestant Establishment Revisited," *American Scholar,* Autumn 1976, pp. 499–518.

88. Leonard E. Grossman and Michael Steinig, "Jewish Involvement in Top Corporate Management in Philadelphia," 1984, American Jewish Committee files.

89. "Real Class," essay review of Louis Auchincloss's *A Writer's Capital* and *The Partners, New York Review of Books,* July 18, 1974, pp. 10–15; see also Kit Konolige, "The Persistence of WASP's," *Philadelphia* magazine, November 1976, pp. 125–245.

90. This observation is based on a wealth of anecdotal information in my files. A typical one is the observation of a Jewish attorney in a previously large WASP firm who blurted out in one conversation that if the Nazis were to take over in this country, he was not certain that even one of his partners would hide him and his family. That such an eventuality would even arise in his mind is significant.

91. Page 316.

Chapter 1i PHILADELPHIA JEWRY AND THE HOLOCAUST

1. The recent literature on American Jews and the Holocaust is extensive and at times polemical. See David Wyman, *The Abandonment of the Jews* (New York: Pantheon, 1984); "Indicting American Jews" by Lucy Dawidowicz in *Commentary,* June 1983, and the lengthy exchanges of letters following, particularly September 1983; Henry L. Feingold articles, including "Indicting American Jewry: Matching Power and Responsibility," *Reconstructionist,* March 1984, which argues that except in organized fundraising, the Jewish community was too weak and divided to do much; Yehuda Bauer, "The Holocaust and American Jewry" in his *The Holocaust in Historical Perspective* (Seattle: University of Washington Press, 1978); Haskel Lookstein's *Were We Our Brothers' Keepers?* (New York: Hartmore Publishing, 1985), a study of the American Jewish press and the Holocaust based on his earlier dissertation; and Alex Grobman's "American Jewry's Initial Response to World War II" (Hebrew, English summary) in *Studies in the History of Zionism Presented to Israel Goldstein,* Yehuda Bauer, ed. (Jerusalem, 1976). Also forthcoming are two books, *American Jewry During the Holocaust: A Report Sponsored by the American Jewish Commission on the Holocaust,* edited by Seymour M. Finger, and *Their Brothers' Keepers: American Jewry and the Holocaust,* written by Finger (both to

be published by Holmes and Meier, New York). Except for some reference in Lookstein, all of the published works deal with national rather than local developments.

2. "20,000 Jews Here March in Protest Against Hitlerism," *Philadelphia Public Ledger,* May 11, 1933, p. 1.

3. Moshe R. Gottlieb, *American Anti-Nazi Resistance 1933–1941* (New York: KTAV, 1982), is the standard work on national boycott groups. He does not discuss local boycott efforts. For Philadelphia, see *Public Ledger,* April 14, 1933, p. 4; June 5, 1933, p. 2.

4. *Philadelphia Jewish World,* November 25, 1938; *Public Ledger,* November 14, 1938, p. 1; November 16, 1938; November 17, 1938, p. 4.

5. Mastbaum Loan System, 47th Board Meeting, November 15, 1934, in Jewish Family Service records, Philadelphia Jewish Archives Center (PJAC). Suggestion of Samuel Fels, 56th board meeting, January 24, 1939. Jacob Billikopf, past executive director of the Federation of Jewish Charities explained that other groups were helping refugees; no special funds were set aside. See also the regular meeting of January 29, 1941; special meeting of March 19, 1941; regular meetings of March 31, 1941, and May 10, 1942.

6. Beck to Kurt Peiser, executive director of the Federation of Jewish Charities (FJC) April 10, 1942. In FJA papers, "Refugee Resettlement Committee," Box 0093.

7. It is noteworthy that the local AJA actually began functioning in 1937, even without a formal legal charter, preceding the formation of the national UJA in 1938. In Philadelphia, as in a number of other cities, the need for cooperation was seen on the local level while national organizations were feuding. For brief histories of the national UJA (without adequate attention to local developments), see Marc Raphael, *United Jewish Appeal,* Brown Judaic Studies, no. 34 (Chico, CA: Scholars Press, 1982); Abraham Karp, *To Give Life: The UJA in the Community,* 1981; Yehuda Bauer, *My Brother's Keeper: A History of the American Jewish Joint Distribution Committee, 1929–1939* (Philadelphia: Jewish Publication Society, 1974); and Philip Rosen, "German Jews vs. Russian Jews in Philadelphia Philanthropy," in *Jewish Life in Philadelphia, 1830–1940* (Philadelphia: ISHI, 1984).

8. For a longer treatment of the formation of the AJA, see Robert Tabak's forthcoming dissertation, "The Transformation of Jewish Identity: The Philadelphia Experience 1920–1945," Philadelphia, Temple University.

9. National statistics on Jewish and other groups' attitudes as seen in polls is discussed in John O. Diggins, *Mussolini and Fascism: The View from America* (Princeton: Princeton University Press, 1972), pp. 336–337. Quotation on British war relief in *Jewish Exponent,* September 11, 1942, p. 38.

10. For material on Jews and Communism, see Zosa Szajkowski's four volumes on *Jews, War and Communism* (last two volumes published privately); Melech Epstein's volume on *The Jews and Communism* (1959); Arthur Leibman, *Jews and the Left* (1979). Certainly a majority and probably on the order of two-thirds of the Eastern European Jewish immigrants in Philadelphia came from the Ukraine. See Tabak, "Transformation of Jewish Identity." There was also the important general American impulse to aid any allies fighting Nazi Germany.

11. See Diggins, *Mussolini and Fascism.*

12. See, for example, *New York Times,* October 1, 21, 27, and 28, 1941, for endorsements. There has been virtually no research on Russian War Relief in general. Maurice Isserman's history of American Communism during World War II, *Which Side Were You On?* (Middletown: University of Illinois Press, 1982), gives brief mention to Russian War Relief: "In the fall of 1941 the Communists set up Russian War Relief . . ." (p. 111). Of course, most RWR supporters and many of its officers were not Communists. A collection of RWR public documents, such as press releases and newsletters is at the New York Public Library (American Association for Russian Relief collection). Some materials on Jewish activities are at the Jewish Labor Bund Archives in New York (Charles Zimmerman papers). Additional materials on the Jewish Council are at the Yeshiva University archives.

13. RWR in New York Public Library collection, "News Bulletin for Local Committees," January 15, 1942.

14. March 1942, JC-RWR rally for some six hundred delegates, "We Call Upon You" flyer from Council of Jewish Fraternal and Benevolent Organizations affiliated with Russian War Relief of Philadelphia (February 1942, FJA Box 0093). See also the description of the meeting and the Jewish Council's beginnings in Malamut, *Philadelphier Yidishe Anshtaltn un Zayre Fiher,* 1942, pp. 207–209.

15. Letter from Peiser to Billikopf, February 19, 1942, Peiser Papers, FJA collection, Box 0093, PJAC.

16. Peiser to Leof, March 3, 1942, Box 0093, FJA collection. See also copy of letter from Billikopf to Leof, March 7, 1942, in the same file.

17. Letter to Peiser, May 14, 1942; reply by Peiser May 21; her response of May 23: "when and if you decide to do something . . . please notify me." Box 0093, FJA Collection.

18. Programs from annual meetings for 1944 and 1945 (including lists of contributing local organizations) are in the papers of the Mazirer and Vicinity Relief Committee (a Philadelphia *Landsmanshaft*), at the American Jewish Archives, Cincinnati. National statistics, *Voluntary Relief During World War II,* President's War Relief Control Board (Washington, DC: Government Printing Office, 1946), show

RWR as one of the largest charities (in 1943–1944, one-fourth to one-fifth of all private overseas aid), collecting over half of all goods ("in kind" contributions).

19. It is difficult to estimate exactly how large the Jewish support for RWR was in Philadelphia. The Jewish membership in the group's citywide board was carefully limited. Nonetheless, it seems clear that while many local groups from churches to avowedly Communist organizations supported RWR, Jewish energy, money, and goods played a disproportionate role. Only the Jewish Council of RWR maintained an ongoing presence in Philadelphia. Incidental references in RWR newsletters mentioning Philadelphia include a disproportionate number of Jewish individuals and organizations with many Jewish members (such as clothing manufacturers and clothing workers).

20. "Russia and American Jews" editorial in *Jewish Exponent,* September 4, 1942, said that Jews were doing more than their proportional share for Russian War Relief. Exact financial breakdowns are not available, but in 1944, for example, the Philadelphia Jewish Council goal was $300,000 worth of goods and money out of a national Jewish goal of $2 million (*Jewish Times,* March 24, 1944, p. 15, and RWR Inter-Committee Memo, May 1944, at New York Public Library). The national Jewish goal was later increased by $500,000 due to the "heavy response," although only about a tenth of the additional goal was actually raised. There seems little doubt that Philadelphia Jews met their goal; for example, $100,000 was pledged at one testimonial dinner for Dr. M. V. Leof late in that year (RWR Intercommittee memo, December 1944). None of these figures include the many contributions made by Jewish manufacturers, unions, store owners, and individuals to nondenominational RWR drives. In 1944, RWR collected over $14 million in kind and cash nationally, in addition to receiving $8 million in cash from the National War Fund. While it is difficult to compare RWR's combination of cash, clothing, food, and other in-kind contributions with the cash sought by the Allied Jewish Appeal, the latter raised $1.69 million in Philadelphia in 1944. A major contributing factor in this high level of contributions to the RWR was the high percentage of Ukrainian Jews in Philadelphia. Thus, despite the involvement of a number of active Communists in the RWR, the bulk of the interest and concern of the Philadelphia Jewish community was based on Jewish concerns, and not on support for the politics of the Soviet Union.

21. See "Rescue Priority and Fund Raising Issues During the Holocaust: A Case Study of the Va'ad ha-Hatzalah and the Joint: 1939–1941," by Ephraim Zuroff, *American Jewish History,* March 1979, pp. 305–326; financial sources in FJA collection, Galter papers, Box 0038, and Sherman papers, Box 0104. In 1944, for example, the local AJA increased the allocation to the Va'ad ha-Hatzalah to $10,000 despite a request for $25,000. The Va'ad received considerably more from federations in other cities, such as Chicago and Detroit. For the lack of success in direct appeals in Philadelphia, see Bernard L. Levinthal papers, PJAC. (In 1941, they raised only $3,145 in direct contributions here.)

22. General works include Wyman, *Abandonment of the Jews;* Monty Penkower, *The Jews Were Expendable* (University of Illinois Press, 1983); Martin Gilbert, *Auschwitz and the Allies* (New York: Holt, Rinehart, and Winston, 1981); and Walter Lacqueur, *The Terrible Secret* (Boston: Little, Brown, 1980). (Deborah Lipstadt's book on the American secular press, *Beyond Belief: The American Press and the Coming of the Holocaust, 1933–1945* (New York: Free Press, 1985), appeared as this chapter was going to press.) Sources dealing with specific Jewish community knowledge include Lookstein, the most thorough work, and Alex Grobman, "When Did They Know? The American Jewish Press and the Holocaust, September 1, 1939 to December 17, 1942," *American Jewish History,* March 1979, pp. 327–352; and "The Warsaw Ghetto Uprising and the American Jewish Press," *Wiener Library Bulletin,* vol. 29 (1976), pp. 53–61; Yehuda Bauer, "When Did They Know?" *Midstream,* April 1968; and Lucy S. Dawidowicz, "American Jews and the Holocaust," *New York Times Magazine,* April 18, 1982.

23. Conversation with Carl Goodman, *Exponent* staff, Summer 1982, Philadelphia. Our study focuses on the two weekly English-language newspapers. An examination of the Yiddish dailies would also be of interest. However, the independent Yiddish daily *Jewish World/Yidishe Velt,* which included an English section, ceased publication in 1942. Philadelphia editions of several New York Yiddish dailies, including the *Forward, Der Tog (The Day),* and the *Morgen-Zhournal (Jewish Morning Journal),* continued to appear and include local as well as national and international news. However, their editorial policies were based on their New York namesakes, which have been extensively studied in Haskel Lookstein's book.

24. *Jewish Times,* September 19, 1941.

25. *Jewish Exponent,* October 21, 1941; *Jewish Times,* July 17, 24, and September 11, 1942; *Jewish Exponent,* March 20 and April 27, 1942. Dr. Julius Greenstone was editor of the *Exponent* in 1941.

26. *Jewish Times,* April 26, 1942. (A. C. Biber was editor and publisher of the *Jewish Times* in 1942.)

27. *Jewish Exponent,* May 22, 1942.

28. *Jewish Exponent,* July 3, 1942.

29. *Jewish Times,* July 10, 1942.

30. *New York Times,* July 22, 1942.

31. *Jewish Times,* July 24, 1942; *Jewish Exponent,* July 24, 1942; Grobman, "When Did They Know?"

32. *Jewish Exponent,* August 21, 1942.

33. *Jewish Exponent,* August 14, 1942.

34. *Jewish Times,* August 28, 1942.

35. *Jewish Exponent,* September 25, 1942.

36. *Jewish Exponent,* September 18, 25, 1942. In an interview with Professor Nora Levin, Summer 1983, Gratz College, Philadelphia, author of the book The Holocaust and activist in the Labor Zionist organization during the war years, she emphasized how Philadelphia Jews feared anti-Semitism, and were generally timid toward gentiles regarding Jewish matters.

37. *Jewish Exponent,* October 2, 1942.

38. *Jewish Exponent,* November 6, 1942. (Felix Gerson and Norman Ginsburg were publishers of the *Exponent,* and Milton J. Feldman was the paper's managing editor in 1942.)

39. Discussed in Arthur Morse, *While Six Million Died* (New York: Hart, 1968), pp. 79–80; Rabbi Stephen Wise, *Challenging Years* (New York, Putnam, 1949), pp. 272–279.

40. *Jewish Exponent,* November 20, December 4, 1942.

41. Melvin Urofsky, *We Are One: American Jewry and Israel* (Garden City, NY: Doubleday, 1978) p. 41.

42. *Jewish Times,* February 20, 1942.

43. *Jewish Times,* July 10 and 24, and August 7, 1942.

44. *Jewish Times,* March 27, April 24, 1942; *Jewish Exponent,* May 22, 1942.

45. Interview with Rabbi E. Yolles, Philadelphia, Summer 1983, *Jewish Times,* June 19, July 31, 1942. Efraim Zuroff, "Rescue Priority," *American Jewish History,* vol. 48, no. 3, March 1979, pp. 305–326 *passim.*

46. *Jewish Exponent,* November 7, 1941, "Interviews in Philadelphia," Summer 1982, with Stanton Kratzok, former head of Brith Sholom Lodge; Michael Egnal, president of ZOA in 1945; and Lawrence Horowitz a former president of ZOA during the post-war period. Russian Jewry and German Jewry are discussed in Philip Rosen's work cited here.

47. *Jewish Exponent,* October 31, 1941. See J. Bower Bell, *Terror Out of Zion* (New York: St. Martin's Press, 1977) p. 112.

48. Sarah E. Peck, "The Campaign for an American Response to the Nazi Holocaust 1943–1945," in *Journal of Contemporary History,* 1980, pp. 367–400. The most important archival source is the Palestine Statehood Group collection at Yale University Library. It includes a brief history of the Pennsylvania section (Philadelphia) of the Jewish Army committee by Alexander Wilf, dated 17 June 1943. In it, the author reports three thousand local members. This may mean the number of endorsers of the Jewish Army idea, rather than active or paying members of the committee. See, also, the interview with Ellen Wilf, sister of Alex Wilf, head of the Philadelphia Chapter, Committee for a Jewish Army, Summer 1982, Philadelphia, in Samuel Katz, *Days of Fire* (Jerusalem: Steimatzky, 1968), pp. 66–69; Yitshaq Ben Ami, *Years of Wrath, Days of Glory* (New York: Robert Speller, 1982), pp. 250–251, 370–374.

49. "Test Case for Democracy" pamphlet by American League for Free Palestine, New York, 1943; anthology of articles in newspapers on the need for a Jewish Army; interview with Ben Ami, Summer 1982, Philadelphia, in Ben Ami, *Years,* pp. 370–374.

50. *Jewish Times,* January 16, 23, 1942; *Jewish Exponent,* January 23, April 10, 1942.

51. *New York Times,* February 16, 1982.

52. *Jewish Exponent,* February 26, March 5, 1942; interview with Jack Richman, chairman of the local and state (PA) Committee for a Jewish Army, also an officer in the Philadelphia ZOA; Wise, pp. 277–278; Ben Ami, p. 372. Rabbi Wise confirmed the truth of the Rumanian offer in March; he tried to act upon it, but never retracted his denunciation of the Committee for a Jewish Army.

53. See Philip Rosen, "Death in the Bosporus," *American Zionist,* vol. 70, November-December 1979, pp. 10–14.

54. *Jewish Times,* March 13, 1942; *Jewish Exponent,* March 20, 27, and April 25, 1942.

55. *Jewish Exponent,* May 15, 1942; Urofsky, pp. 1–13.

56. Interview with Arnold Ginsburg, Summer 1982, Philadelphia.

57. *Jewish Exponent,* October 23, 1942; *Jewish Times,* October 23, 1942.

58. *Jewish Exponent,* December 25, 1942.

59. *Jewish Times,* December 25, 1942; *Jewish Exponent,* December 25, 1942.

60. *Record,* December 25, 1942, p. 1.

61. *Jewish Exponent,* December 4, 18, 1942.

62. *Jewish Times,* December 25, 1942; *Jewish Exponent,* January 29, 1943.

63. *Jewish Times,* April 9, 1943.

64. Lawrence Horowitz, of the executive committee of the Zionist Emergency Council during those years, insisted this was the only answer. Interview, Summer 1982, Philadelphia.

65. *Jewish Exponent,* February 5, April 16, 1943.

66. *Jewish Times,* February 12, 1943; *Jewish Exponent,* February 5, 1943.

67. *Jewish Exponent,* June 30, 1943; *Jewish Times,* June 30, July 23, 1943; Ben Ami, p. 293.

68. *Jewish Times,* April 2, 1943; *Jewish Exponent,* April 2, 1943. Sam Merlin, formerly with the Jewish Army Committee, was convinced the "Stop Hitler Rally" was prompted by plans for the Ben Hecht pageant, *Commentary* letter, September 1972, p. 12.

69. *Jewish Exponent,* April 9, 1943.

70. *Jewish Exponent,* April 9, 1943. For hostility of the mainstream Zionists toward the Bergsonites, see Ben Hecht, *Child of the Century* (New York: Signet, 1954), pp. 519–522; Katz, pp. 66–69; Ben Ami, pp. 323–327; Wyman, pp. 345–347.

71. *Jewish Times,* April 16, 1943; *Jewish Exponent,* April 30, 1943; Hecht, pp. 520–521, Ben Ami, pp. 285–286.

72. *Jewish Exponent,* April 27, July 16, August 20, 1943; background on Solomon Michael's trip to the United States is found in *Jewish Currents,* July-August, 1984, p. 31.

73. *Jewish Exponent,* April 16, 1943; *Jewish Times,* May 19, 1943; Urofsky, pp. 23–30; Wyman, pp. 162–166.

74. *Jewish Times,* June 18, 25, 1943.

75. *Jewish Exponent,* November 5, 26, 1943. On Rabbi Levinthal, see Rosen, "German Jews."

76. *Jewish Times,* October 10, 1943; *Jewish Exponent,* November 26, 1943. The *Times* had this march ex post facto on page 8; the *Exponent* on page 21 as part of a column. Both papers carried no ads or feature stories to arouse Philadelphia Jews. Interview with Rabbi E. Yolles, Philadelphia, Summer 1983; Wyman, p. 152; Lookstein, pp. 164–166.

77. *Jewish Exponent,* September 3, 1943; *Jewish Times,* October 15, 1943. Telephone interview with Peter Bergson, Tel Aviv, Israel, May 1983. Bergson believes that had Congress passed the measure, it would have appropriated millions for it; Wyman, pp. 193–208; *Report of the Interim Committee of the American Jewish Conference,* November 1944, p. 14; also Lookstein, p. 175.

78. *Jewish Exponent,* April 23, 1943; *Jewish Times,* April 23, 1943. Background to conference in Morse, pp. 52–62, and Wyman, pp. 104–123.

79. *New York Times,* May 4, 1943; *Jewish Times,* May 21, 1943; Wyman, pp. 110–111, 120.

80. *New York Times,* April 22, 23 and May 5, 7, 24, 1943; *Jewish Exponent,* May 21, June 6, 1943.

81. *New York Times,* May 2, 3, 22 and June 4, 1943; *Jewish Exponent,* June 9, 1943; *Jewish Times,* June 11, 1943.

82. *Jewish Times,* October 8, 1943; *New York Times,* November 4, 1983; Wyman, pp. 153–154. One exception was a Brith Sholom award to King Gustaf of Sweden in February 1944, held in Philadelphia.

83. Interview with Albert Liss and Leon Eisenstadt, Summer 1983, Philadelphia. Both men were active with Bergson's American League for a Free Palestine, established in Philadelphia, November 1943.

84. *Jewish Times,* February 25, 1944; *Jewish Exponent,* March 3, 1944.

85. *Jewish Exponent,* February 4, 1944; Wyman, *Abandonment of the Jews,* pp. 213–214.

86. *Jewish Exponent,* May 12, September 15, October 6, 1944. Kurt Peiser, Executive Director of the Allied Jewish Appeal, the fund raiser for the Joint Distribution Committee, bewailed the lack of giving to the Appeal by Philadelphia Jews and the scarcity of funds in the Joint to do rescue work, in *Jewish Exponent,* October 6, 1944.

87. *Jewish Exponent,* April 28, August 11, 1944; *Jewish Times,* May 12, June 9, July 21, 1944.

88. Stranton Kratzok interview.

89. *Jewish Exponent,* March 3, July 21, August 4, 1944; *Jewish Times,* March 31, 1944.

90. *Jewish Exponent,* August 11, 1944; *Jewish Times,* June 9, August 11, 1944.

91. *Jewish Exponent,* July 21, 1944. See Gilbert, pp. 227–230.

92. *Jewish Exponent,* January 5, February 8, February 27, March 3, 1944.

93. *Jewish Exponent,* April 28, 1944.

94. *Jewish Exponent,* February 18, March 3, 1944; *Jewish Times,* February 25, March 24, 1944.

95. *Jewish Times,* March 17, 1944; Wyman, pp. 172–173, 253–254; Joseph B. Schechman, *The United States and the Jewish State Movement* (New York: Thomas Yoselof, 1966), p. 76.

96. *Jewish Times,* March 3, 10, 17, 1944; *Jewish Exponent,* October 3, 1944, and February 9, 1945. Wyman, pp. 172–173, tells of the decision to move for a Jewish state rather than rescue; Urofsky, pp. 32–33, points out that during Holocaust period, Zionists "unleashed their greatest organizational and propaganda drive."

97. *Jewish Exponent,* December 8, 29, 1944.

98. *Jewish Exponent,* February 2, April 16, 1945; *Jewish Times,* September 7, 1945; Morse, pp. 375–380; Wyman, pp. 257–260.

99. *Philadelphia Inquirer,* April 16, 1945; *Evening Bulletin,* April 16, 1945; *Jewish Times,* April 18, 29 and May 9, 16, 1945; *Jewish Exponent,* April 18, May 9, 16, 1945.

100. *Jewish Exponent,* April 18, 20, 1945; *Jewish Times,* April 20, December 14, 1945.

101. Written by Philip Rosen.

102. Interview with Harry Bass, President of the Association of Jewish Holocaust Survivors of Philadelphia, May 1986; also, interview with Abram Shnaper, past officer, archivist for the Association, chairman of Monument Committee, May 1986, Philadelphia.

103. Abram Shnaper, "The Monument," in *The Story of Philadelphia's Monument to the Six Million Jewish Martyrs,* printed privately by Memorial Committee for Six Million Jewish Martyrs, Philadelphia, 1984, pp. 4–6; Mina Kalter, "Twenty Years of the Monument," and Samuel Feige, "A Dream Realized," in Bulletin no. 28 of the Association of Jewish Holocaust Survivors (AJHS), Philadelphia, privately printed, 1984, pp. 3–6.

104. Franklin Littell, "The Philadelphia Story," printed in Bulletin no. 23 (1979), AJHS, pp. 8–9. Dr. Littell, a Temple University religion professor, formed his own organization, the National Institute on the Holocaust. Each year since 1975 he has organized scholarly conferences at which celebrated writers present papers on various aspects of the Holocaust. The name of the organization was changed recently to the Anne Frank Institute.

105. Harold Kessler, "Why Teach the Holocaust?", Bulletin no. 25 (1981), pp. 3–4. Many teachers within the Philadelphia school system demanded that Holocaust studies be a part of the curriculum.

106. Nora Levin, "For the Sake of History," Bulletin no. 27 (1983), pp. 4–5. Yaakov Riz, "The Holocaust G-d and Israel," Bulletin no. 25 (1981).

107. Ad by Sons and Daughters of Holocaust Survivors, Bulletin no. 28 (1984), p. 13. Mark Cuker, "A Message from the Second Generation," Bulletin no. 29 (1985), p. 3.

Chapter 1ii FOUR FATEFUL YEARS

1. Alex Grobman, *The American Jewish Chaplains and the Remnants of European Jewry, 1944–1948* (Unpublished Ph.D. Dissertation, Hebrew University, 1981), pp. 103–105, 221–223, 243; *Jewish Times* (hereafter, JT) 7-27-45; *Jewish Exponent* (hereafter, JE) 7-20-45, 7-27-45, 8-24-45.

2. JE 7-24-45; JT 9-14-47, 11-2-45.

3. Rabbi Ephraim Yolles interview, Philadelphia, July 1982. Rabbi Yolles, who took over the unofficial mantel of Rabbi Bernard Levinthal as "Dean of Orthodox Rabbis" in Philadelphia, was an officer in Agudas Israel, the worldwide Orthodox organization; the Vaad HaHatzala, Orthodox rescue arm; president of the Rumanian Beneficial Association; and a member of the Committee for a Jewish Army, friendly to the Revisionists-Zionists. JT 5-4-45, 9-14-47.

4. *The Record* (October 1945), a magazine published by the American Jewish Conference, an umbrella group of mainstream Jewish organizations. JE 10-5-45.

5. Melvin Urofsky, *We Are One* (New York: Doubleday, 1978), p. 105. JE 4-6-45, 10-5-45.

6. JE 11-5-45; JT 11-5-45.

7. Yitshaq Ben Ami, *Years of Wrath, Days of Glory* (New York: Robert Speller, 1982), p. 124; JE 11-23-45, 12-7-45.

8. JE 12-7-45.

9. JT 4-19-45; JE 4-5-46, 2-21-47.

10. JE 5-31-46; JT 5-31-46; JE 3-1-46, 5-17-45; JT 8-9-46, 9-20-46.

11. JE 4-5-46.

12. *Save Our Survivors Bulletin,* May 1947; JT 6-14-46, 9-13-46.

13. *Palestine* Post 10-19-45, 12-16-45, 2-19-46, 3-10-46, 7-17-46; JE 7-27-45, 8-17-45, 10-4-46; Bartley C. Crum, *Behind the Silken Curtain* (New York: Simon and Schuster, 1947), pp. 108–114.

14. Robert Silverberg, *If I Forget Thee O'Jerusalem* (New York: Morrow, 1970), pp. 309, 318, 305–309. JT 6-21-46. Martin Gilbert, Exile and Return (Philadelphia: Lippincott, 1978), pp. 284–288.

15. JE 5-17-4; JT 6-3-46; JE 6-21-46.

16. JT 7-19-46.

17. Michael Cohen, "Truman, the Holocaust and the Establishment of Israel," *Jerusalem Quarterly* (Spring 1982), pp. 82–83, 88–89; JT 10-25-46; JE 11-1-46; JT 9-5-47. Abram Sachar, *The Redemption of the Unwanted* (New York: St. Martin's Press, 1983), pp. 211–212. JT 8-22-46; JE 8-22-46.

18. JT 11-8-46, 8-9-46.

19. JT 6-28-46; JE 6-28-46; JT 9-13-46, 10-4-46.

20. Samuel Katz, *Days of Fire* (Jerusalem: Steimatzky, 1968), pp. 92–93; the mysterious withdrawal of support against British policy in Palestine by the mainstream Zionists might be due to the Jewish Agency's calling off of resistance in August and a tacit understanding or acceptance by the British of the Jewish Agency's partition plan. Before, both the Revisionists and the Agency wanted the whole

Mandate allotted by the Balfour Declaration and League of Nations for a Jewish Homeland. JT 11-15-46, 11-29-46; JE 11-29-46.

21. JT 1-31-47, 2-7-47, 2-14-47; Ben Ami, *Years of Wrath,* pp. 383–384.
22. JE 8-8-47; JT 8-8-47, 6-6-47.
23. JT 5-2-47; JE 5-2-47; JT 5-9-47; JE 5-9-47.
24. JT 4-4-47. Julian Grodinsky, then head of the Philadelphia chapter of the American Council for Judaism, believed Allied's allocation of funds to Zionist causes was responsible for the shortfall.
25. JT 8-1-47; the United Jewish Appeal, of which Philadelphia's Allied Jewish Appeal was a local arm, gave almost 35 percent of collected funds to Zionist organizations (1943). Silverman, *If I Forget,* p. 233.
26. JE 10-24-47; JT 10-31-47; JE 1-9-48.
27. Efraim Zuroff, "Rescue Priority and Fundraising," *American Jewish History,* March 1979, p. 172; JT 7-24-45, 9-14-47, 11-2-45.
28. JE 7-27-45, 10-4-46, 11-28-47.
29. JE 11-28-47.
30. Henry Morganthau, "Refugee Run-Around," *Collier's,* November 1, 1947, pp. 22, 23, 62ff; JE 10-31-47.
31. JE 3-4-47, 5-23-47, 7-11-47, 7-25-47; JT 9-12-47, 8-8-47.
32. JE 12-13-46, JT 8-8-47; Ben Ami, *Years of Wrath,* p. 385; Urofsky, *We Are One,* pp. 117–120.
33. Leon Eisenstat interview, Philadelphia, July 1982; Eisenstat was an officer in the local chapter of the American League for a Free Palestine. Albert Liss interview, July 1982; Liss was campaign director and officer in the local chapter of the League at the time. Ellen Wilf interview, July 1982; Wilf, sister of Alexander Wilf, who headed the local Committee for a Jewish Army and League, was active in New York and Hollywood, contacting Ben Hecht and Peter Bergson; Ben Ami, *Years of Wrath,* pp. 383–384.
34. Lawrence Horowitz interview, Philadelphia, July 1982, 1986. Horowitz served as local chairman of the Zionist Emergency Council and president of the local ZOA during the post-war period. Urofsky, *We Are One,* pp. 154–159; Abram Sachar, *Redemption of the Unwanted* (New York: St. Martin's Press, 1983), pp. 247–250.
35. Katz, *Days of Fire,* pp. 132–137; JE 3-22-46, 5-2-47.
36. J. Bowyer Bell, *Terror Out of Zion* (New York: St. Martin's Press, 1977), pp. 229–234. JT 7-30-47; JE 7-30-47; JT 8-6-47; JE 8-13-47.
37. Horowitz interviews; JT 7-23-47.
38. Interview with Morton Kremer, Philadelphia, June 1982; Al Liss interview; Horowitz interviews; JT 9-5-47, 9-12-47, 8-22-47. Philip Klein took over as editor and publisher of the *Jewish Times* in May 1946 and followed an independent, sometimes maverick policy vis-à-vis the Jewish establishment.
39. JT 10-10-47; JE 10-24-47; JT 10-24-47.
40. JT 10-24-47, 11-7-47.
41. Michael Egnal interview, Philadelphia, August 1982. Egnal was vice president, later (1948) president of the local ZOA; JT 10-17-47, 12-5-47; JE 12-5-47. Howard Sachar, *A History of Israel* (New York: Knopf, 1979), pp. 283–286.
42. Horowitz interview.
43. JE 5-9-47, 6-6-47; JT 12-12-47, 12-19-47.
44. JE 12-5-47; JT 12-5-47.
45. Sachar, *A History of Israel,* p. 301; JE 12-26-47; JT 12-26-47.
46. Leonard Slater, *The Pledge* (New York: Simon and Schuster, 1970), pp. 155–156. Urofsky, *We Are One,* pp. 158–159.
47. Stanton Kratzok interview, Philadelphia, August, 1982. Kratzok, like his father, Sam, was former president of the Brith Sholom Lodge, a Philadelphia lawyer, and a Zionist activist.
48. JT 1-23-48, 3-5-48.
49. The March 5, 1948 article in *Collier's* was described in JT 3-5-48. JE 5-21-48; JT 7-16-48; Urofsky, *We Are One,* p. 72.
50. JT 2-27-48, 3-26-48; JE 5-21-48.
51. JT 2-27-48; JE 2-27-48; JT 3-26-48; JE 3-26-48; Sachar, *A History of Israel,* pp. 302–320.
52. JT 4-16-48, 5-2-48; JE 5-2-48; JT 5-16-48; JE 5-16-48.
53. JT 5-7-48, 5-14-48.
54. JE 5-21-48; JT 5-21-48.
55. Gunter David, "From Here to Israel," Philadelphia *Bulletin,* May 14, 1978. Stanley Hoffman interview, June 1983; Hoffman was a bombardier in the U.S. Air Force who received a call to serve.
56. Izzy Cohen interview, Philadelphia, July 1982; Cohen, a local manufacturer, fought in the MAHAL for two years.
57. Harry Eisner interview by phone, New York, July 1982; Eisner fought in the MAHAL and was the presi-

dent of the former Volunteers for Israel group at the time of the interview. Leon Agriss interview, Philadelphia, July 1982. Agriss fought in the MAHAL during the period from 1947 to 1948.

58. Interview with Bernard Stern, Philadelphia, July, 1982. Stern was active in the American Veterans Committee, which worked closely with the Zionists after World War II. Albert Liss interview. JT 5-2-48, 4-16-48, 5-21-48.

59. Moshe Volk interview, Lower Bucks County, June 1982.

60. Stern interview; Horowitz interview; JT 6-18-48, 6-25-48; JE 6-25-48; JT 7-30-48.

61. Ben Ami, *Years of Wrath,* pp. 449–522; Bell, *Terror Out of Zion,* pp. 400–414; JT 7-2-48, 7-9-48; JE 7-9-48, 9-17-48.

62. Bell, *Terror Out of Zion,* pp. 330–340; JT 7-2-48, 7-9-48, 9-17-48.

63. JT 9-24-48; JE 9-24-48.

64. JT 11-26-48, 12-3-48; Ben Ami, *Years of Wrath,* p. 572. The Begin reception was the ALFP's last activity. The Irgun was no more, dissolved into the regular Israel army forces.

65. Jacob Richman interview, Philadelphia, July 1982; Richman chaired the local Committee for a Jewish Army, later switched to the ZOA, where he was an officer during the post-war years. Horowitz and Agriss interviews; that the American Jewish Congress move toward liberal causes was evident in their ads for membership, which appealed for members to join the fight against discrimination, JT 12-19-47.

66. Melvin Urofsky, "American Zionism after the State," *American Jewish History,* vol. 69, September 1979, pp. 84–85.

Chapter 2 THE OPPOSITION TO ZIONISM

1. David Philipson, *The Reform Movement in Judaism* (New York: Macmillan, 1931), p. 356.

2. Elmer Berger, Memoirs of an Anti-Zionist Jew (Beirut: Institute for Palestine Studies, 1978), p. 2; Charles Israel Goldblatt, "The Impact of the Balfour Declaration in America," *American Jewish Historical Quarterly* 57 (June 1968), pp. 460–484; also Naomi W. Cohen, "The Reaction of Reform Judaism in America to Political Zionism (1897–1922)," *Publications of the American Jewish Historical Society* 40 (July 1951), pp. 361–394; *New York Times,* March 5, 1919, p. 7; Max Berkowitz, *The Beloved Rabbi* (New York: Macmillan, 1932), p. 92.

3. Abraham J. Karp, "Reaction to Zionism and the State of Israel in the American Jewish Religious Community," *Jewish Journal of Sociology* 8 (December 1966), pp. 150–174; Barry Chazan, "Palestine in American Jewish Education in the Pre-State Period," *Jewish Social Studies* 42 (Summer-Fall 1980), pp. 229–248; Howard R. Greenstein, *Turning Point: Zionism and Reform Judaism* (Chico, CA: Scholars Press, 1981), pp. 117–121; *CCAR Yearbook* 45 (1935), pp. 102–103 and *CCAR Yearbook* 47 (1937), pp. 98–99.

4. Yehuda Bauer, "Genocide: Was It the Nazis' Original Plan?" *Annals of the American Academy of Political and Social Science* 450 (July 1980), pp. 40–43; David S. Wyman, *Paper Walls: America and the Refugee Crisis, 1938–1941* (Amherst: University of Massachusetts Press, 1968), pp. 210–213, 3–23; David Brody, "American Jewry, The Refugees and Immigration Restriction (1932–1942)," *Publications of the American Jewish Historical Society* 45 (June 1956), pp. 219–247.

5. Melvin I. Urofsky, *We Are One!* (New York: Anchor Books/Doubleday, 1978), pp. 11–13; "Declaration," *New Palestine,* May 15, 1942, p. 6; Naomi Cohen, *American Jews and the Zionist Idea* (New York: KTAV Publishing House, 1975), pp. 60–61.

6. Berger, *Memoirs,* p. 6; also "Rabbi James G. Heller Offers a Program for American Jewry," Philadelphia *Jewish Exponent,* July 4, 1941, pp. 1, 5.

7. *CCAR Yearbook* 52 (1942), pp. 169–170.

8. Interview with Rabbi Jacob R. Marcus, Cincinnati, July 13, 1980; interview with Rabbi Malcolm H. Stern, Elkins Park, Pennsylvania, May 26, 1982; Berger, *Memoirs,* p. 7; Rabbi Solomon B. Freehof to author, August 12, 1982; Rabbi Sidney L. Regner to author, June 10, 1982; Greenstein, *Turning Point,* pp. 33–38; Samuel Halperin, *The Political World of American Zionism* (Detroit: Wayne State University Press, 1961), p. 80.

9. Interview with Rabbi Elmer Berger, New York, May 6, 1980; Berger, *Memoirs,* p. 8; "Lewis Strauss," *New York Times,* January 22, 1974, pp. 1, 64; *Encyclopaedia Judaica,* s.v. "Strauss Lewis," Louis Wolsey to Lewis Strauss, April 28, 1942, Box 1/6, Louis Wolsey Papers, American Jewish Archives, Cincinnati—hereafter cited as LWP.

10. Samuel H. Goldenson to colleagues, March 13, 1942, Box 20/1, Morris S. Lazaron Papers, American Jewish Archives, Cincinnati—hereafter cited as MSLP; "Statement by 63 Rabbis," Philadelphia *Jewish Exponent,* March 20, 1942, p. 1; "American Protest-Rabbiner," *New Palestine,* March 27, 1942, pp. 4–5.

11. William Yale to Lazaron, March 24, 1942, Box 20/1, MSLP; Philip J. Baram, *The Department of State in*

the Middle East (Philadelphia: University of Pennsylvania Press, 1978), pp. 83–86; Welles to Lazaron, March 31, 1942, Box 20/1, MSLP; Welles to Lazaron, April 22, 1942, September 23, 1942, and October 23, 1942, MSLP.

12. Louis Wolsey to Lewis L. Strauss, April 28, 1942, Box 1/6, LWP; Berger interview; Berger, *Memoirs,* p. 8.

13. *Universal Jewish Encyclopedia,* s.v. "Wolsey Louis"; James G. Heller, "Louis Wolsey," *CCAR Yearbook* 63 (1953), pp. 232–234; *New York Times,* March 5, 1953, p. 27; interview with Malcolm H. Stern, interview with Edwin Wolf, II, Philadelphia, July 28, 1982.

14. Undated letter by Wolsey, ca. January 1940; Wolsey to Fineshriber, February 29, 1940; Julian Morgenstern to Wolsey and Fineshriber, March 28, 1940; Solomon Freehof to Wolsey, March 26, 1940; Maurice Eisendrath to Wolsey, March 27, 1940, C/1; Prospectus of the *Jewish Advance* and "The Advance's Platform," C/4, "Reform Advance," 1940–1942, Rabbi William H. Fineshriber Records, Archives of Reform Congregation Keneseth Israel, Elkins Park—hereafter cited as WHFR.

15. Interview with Jane Blum, Philadelphia, August 17, 1983; Julian Feibelman, "William Fineshriber," *CCAR Yearbook* 78 (1968), pp. 161–162; J. Jacobson, *The Man Who Walked Humbly with God* (privately printed, 1950); "Fineshriber, William H.," *National Cyclopedia of American Biography,* vol. 54 (Clifton, NJ: James T. White, 1973), pp. 103–104.

16. Wolsey to Goldenson, March 18, 1942, and March 19, 1942, Box 1/4, LWP.

17. Rosenau to Wolsey, March 23, 1942, and Goldenson to Wolsey, March 23, 1942, Box 1/4, LWP; Minutes of the Meeting of the Rabbis, March 30, 1942, Box 2/1, American Council for Judaism Collection, American Jewish Archives, Cincinnati—hereafter cited as ACJC; also Box 4/8, LWP; Minutes of the Meeting of the Rabbis at Hotel Warwick, Philadelphia, April 6, 1942, Box 2/1, ACJC; also in Box 4/8, LWP; Wolsey to Rabbi Irving F. Reichert, April 15, 1942, Box 1/5, LWP; the twenty-three rabbis to Rabbi Herman Snyder, April 15, 1942, Box 2/1, ACJC.

18. David Wice to Wolsey, April 22, 1942, and Berger to Wolsey, April 23, 1942, Box 1/6, LWP.

19. Stephen S. Wise to Heller, April 28, 1942, and Heller to Wise, May 8, 1942, Box 99/ACJ, Stephen S. Wise Papers, American Jewish Historical Society, Waltham—hereafter cited as SSWP; Freehof to Wolsey, May 6, 1942, Box 1/7, LWP.

20. Goldenson and Wolsey to the twenty-four rabbis, May 12, 1942, Box 2/1, ACJC.

21. Heller to Lazaron, May 15, 1942, Box 1/8, LWP; Wolsey to Berger, May 20, 1942, Box 1/8 LWP; the twenty-four rabbis to Heller, May 21, 1942, Box 1/1, ACJC.

22. David Philipson, "The Message of Reform Judaism to American Israel and World Jewry," Atlantic City, June 1, 1942, Box 4/10, LWP.

23. Morris Lazaron, "Jewish Post-War Problems," Atlantic City, June 1, 1942, Box 1/1, ACJC.

24. Elmer Berger, *The Flint Plan* (Committee on Lay-Rabbinical Cooperation, 1942). Berger, *Memoirs,* pp. 4–5; Berger to author, June 10, 1982.

25. Background information sheet on Elmer Berger, Box 29/Berger, 1941, 1943–1945, ACJP; interview with Berger; Berger to author, June 10, 1982; Berger, Memoirs, p. 5.

26. Berger, *The Flint Plan,* pp. 18–19.

27. Minutes of Atlantic City Meeting of Non-Zionist Rabbis, Atlantic City, June 1–2, pp. 98–142, 167–210, Box 4/9, LWP; Leo M. Franklin, "The Reform Movement and Hebrew Union College," Atlantic City, June 1, 1942, Box 4/10, LWP.

28. Wolsey to Rosenau, June 11, 1942, Box 2/1, LWP; Lazaron to Neville Laski, June 26, 1942, Box 20/1, MSLP; Wolsey to Berger, June 10, 1942, Box 1/10, LWP.

29. "Statement of Principles by Non-Zionist Rabbis," in Berger, *The Flint Plan.*

30. *Zionism: An Affirmation of Judaism* (New York, November 1942), Box-American Council for Judaism, Jacob R. Marcus Papers, Cincinnati; "733 Rabbis Rap Opponents of Zionism," Philadelphia *Jewish Exponent,* November 20, 1942, pp. 1, 8.

31. Lazaron to Arthur Hays Sulzberger, August 26, 1942, Box 2/3 LWP; Sulzberger to Lazaron, September 17, 1942, Box 21/6; James N. Rosenberg to Lazaron, October 8, 1942; and Lewis L. Strauss to Lazaron, November 9, 1942, Box 20/1, all in MSLP.

32. Wolsey to David Lefkowitz, September 7, 1942, Box 2/4, LWP.

33. Berger to Wolsey, October 16, 1942, Box 2/5, LWP; Leo M. Franklin to Wolsey, September 17, 1942, and Wolsey to Franklin, September 30, 1942, Box 2/4; Berger to Wolsey, October 7, 1942; Wolsey to Berger, October 13, 1942; and Berger to Wolsey, October 16, 1942, Box 2/5, all in LWP.

34. Minutes of Lay-Rabbinical Chapter Committee Meeting, Philadelphia, November 2, 1942, Box 2/1, LWP; Frisch to Goldenson, November 4, 1942; Goldenson to Lazaron, November 5, 1942; Wolsey to Lazaron, November 8, 1942; and Wolsey to members of Committee on Lay-Rabbinical Cooperation, November 16, 1942, Box 2/6, LWP.

35. Jonah Wise to Wolsey, November 18, 1942, Box 2/7, LWP; *Congress Weekly,* November 13, 1942, pp. 3–4.

36. Confidential Minutes of the Meeting of the Eastern Contingent of Non-Zionist Rabbis, Philadelphia,

November 23, 1942, Box 2/1, ACJC; telegram, Berger to Wolsey, November 23, 1942, and Wolsey to Berger, November 23, 1942, Box 2/7, LWP; Minutes, Meeting of the Provisional Committee for the Formation of the American Council for Judaism, New York, December 7, 1942; and Minutes, Lay-Rabbinical Session of the Provisional Committee for the Formation of the American Council for Judaism, New York, December 7, 1942, Box 2/1, ACJC.

37. "Himmler Program Kills Polish Jews," and "Wise Gets Confirmation," *New York Times,* November 25, 1942, p. 10; "Slain Polish Jews Put at a Million," *New York Times,* November 26, 1942, p. 16; Urofsky, *We Are One!,* pp. 40–42; Walter Laqueur, *Terrible Secret* (Boston: Little, Brown, 1980), pp. 77–93.

38. "The Conspiracy Against Zionism," *Congress Weekly,* December 18, 1942, pp. 2, 11, 12; Shlomo Grodzensky, "United Front Against Zionism," *Jewish Frontier,* January 1943, pp. 8–10; "Anti-Zionist 'Religion'," *Reconstructionist,* December 25, 1942, pp. 3–4; "A Stab in the Back," *New Palestine,* December 18, 1942, p. 5; "They Sharpened the Dagger," *New Palestine,* January 8, 1943, p. 5.

39. Heller to Wolsey, January 4, 1943, and January 11, 1943, Box 3/1, LWP; Confidential Minutes of Meeting of Members of CCAR, Baltimore, January 5, 1943, Box 2/1, ACJC; Proceedings of the American Council for Judaism at the Community House of the Central Synagogue, New York, January 18, 1943, Box 2/1, ACJC; confidential letter, Wolsey to the ninety-five rabbinical members of the ACJ, January 25, 1943, Box 3/2, LWP.

40. Heller to Wolsey, January 28, 1943, and Wolsey to Heller, February 4, 1943, Box 3/3, LWP.

41. Wolsey to Berger, February 12, 1943, Box 3/3, LWP.

42. Wolsey to Berger, February 8, 1943, and Lazaron to Wolsey, Box 3/3, LWP.

43. Wolsey to Berger, March 25, 1943, and March 30, 1943, Box 3/5, LWP.

44. *Universal Jewish Encyclopedia,* s.v. "Rosenwald, Lessing Julius"; "Lessing Rosenwald," *New York Times,* June 26, 1979, Section 3, p. 12; "Rosenwald, Lessing J.," in *Current Biography,* 1947 (New York: H. H. Wilson, 1947), pp. 551–554.

45. Ibid.

46. "Questionnaire Relating to the Present Status and Prospects for Better Integration of Jews in American Life," late December 1945, written comments by Lessing J. Rosenwald, Berger 1945, American Council for Judaism Papers, M80–405 (Rosenwald's unprocessed papers), State Historical Society of Wisconsin, Madison—hereafter cited as ACJP-R.

47. Interview with Berger, May 6, 1980; telephone conversation with Clarence Coleman, September 28, 1982; interview with Jane Blum; interview with Edwin Wolf, II; Moses Lasky to author, July 9, 1982.

48. Wolsey to Lazaron, April 1, 1943, Box 3/6, LWP; Fineshriber to Julian Feibelman, April 5, 1943, D-4, WHFR; Lessing J. Rosenwald, "Talk Given before the New York Chapter of the ACJ," November 8, 1965, Ready Reference 1965, ACJP-R; pp. 11–12; Berger, *Memoirs,* p. 10; Lazaron to Wolsey, April 6, 1943, Box 3/6, LWP.

49. Lazaron to Goldenson, April 6, 1943, Box 3/6, LWP; Rosenwald, "Talk," p. 12; Berger, *Memoirs,* pp. 11–12; interview with Berger, May 6, 1980; Berger to author, June 22, 1982.

50. Wolsey to Goldenson, April 14, 1943, Box 3/6, LWP.

51. Wolsey to Lazaron, April 16, 1943, Box 3/6, LWP.

52. Wolsey to Rosenwald, April 21, 1943, and Rosenwald to Wolsey, April 22, 1943, Box 3/6, LWP.

53. Minutes, American Council for Judaism, Philadelphia, April 29, 1943, Box 2/1, ACJC; Wolsey to Lazaron, April 30, 1943, Box 3/6, LWP.

54. Minutes, Board of Directors of ACJ, Philadelphia, May 12, 1943, ACJ Office, New York—hereafter cited as ACJ-NY; Elmer Berger, "Report to the Executive Committee of the American Council for Judaism, Inc., March 9, 1944, Council Committee Meetings and Reports, ACJP-R.

55. Wolsey to Edgar Aub, May 27, 1943, Box 128/Wolsey, 1943, ACJP; Wolsey to Berger, June 2, 1943, and Wolsey to Irving Reichert, June 3, 1943, Box 3/7, LWP.

56. Berger, "Report," March 9, 1944; Berger, *Memoirs,* p. 12; Berger to author, June 22, 1982.

57. Minutes, ACJ Meeting, Philadelphia, May 12, 1943. ACJ-NY; Berger to Rosenwald, June 1, 1943, Box 106/Rosenwald, 1943, ACJP; Sulzberger to Rosenwald, May 24, 1943, and June 7, 1943, Statement, ACJP - R; Berger, *Memoirs,* p. 13; Berger to author, June 22, 1982.

58. Sumner Welles to Lazaron, June 11, 1943; Statement, ACJPR; Minutes, Board of Directors of ACJ, Philadelphia, July 7, 1943, ACJ-NY.

59. "Digest of Principles," *Information Bulletin,* December 15, 1943, p. 4; for the full statement, see *Information Bulletin,* October 15, 1943, pp. 3–4, and the *New York Times,* August 31, 1943, p. 4; also comments by Berger, *Memoirs,* p. 12; interview with Berger, May 6, 1980.

60. Berger, *Memoirs,* p. 12; interview with Berger, May 6, 1980.

61. Rosenwald, "Reply to Zionism," *Life,* June 28, 1943, p. 11; James G. Heller to Henry Luce, June 30, 1943, Box 75/*Life* article, 1943, ACJP; Rosenwald's Analysis of comments by readers, Comments on *Life* Article, ACJP-R; "Rosenwald First," *New Palestine,* July 16, 1943, pp. 3–4.

62. James G. Heller, "The President's Message to the Fifty-Fourth Annual Convention of the Central Conference of American Rabbis," *CCAR Yearbook* 53 (1943), pp. 183–189.

63. *Are Zionism and Reform Judaism Incompatible?* (New York: CCAR, 1943).

64. Wolsey to Lazaron, June 26, 1943, Box 22, MSLP.

65. *CCAR Yearbook* 53 (1943), pp. 92–93; "Rabbis Seek Unity on Homeland Plan," *New York Times,* June 26, 1943, p. 9; *CCAR Yearbook* 53 (1943), pp. 93–94; "Rabbis Seek Unity on Homeland Plan," *New York Times,* June 26, 1943, p. 9.

66. "Reform Judaism and Zionism," *Jewish Frontier,* July 1943, p. 6; "Is the Shouting Over?," *New Palestine,* July 16, 1943, p. 4.

67. Interview with Berger, May 6, 1980; Berger to author, June 10, 1982; identical note to rabbis and laymen, July 8, 1943. Box 124/Trips, 1943, ACJP.

68. Rosenwald, "Talk," November 8, 1965, p. 15; Berger, "Report," March 9, 1944, p. 3; Berger to author, July 25, 1982; Berger to Wolsey, September 9, 1943, Box 3/8, LWP; "New Jewish Group Appeals to Allies," *New York Times,* August 31, 1943, p. 4.

69. Halperin, *The Political World of American Zionism,* p. 248; Nahum Goldmann, *The Autobiography of Nahum Goldmann* (New York: Holt, Rinehart and Winston, 1969), p. 113; *New Palestine,* September 10, 1943, p. 4.

70. "Jewish Conferees Assail Rival Plan," *New York Times,* September 1, 1943, p. 12; James G. Heller, "Treachery to Israel," *New Palestine,* September 10, 1943, pp. 9–10; Alexander S. Kohanski, ed., *The American Jewish Conference* (New York: American Jewish Conference, 1944), pp. 286–290; "The Voice of American Jewry," *New Palestine,* September 10, 1943, p. 10.

71. Elmer Berger, Executive Director's Reports to American Council for Judaism Annual Conferences, January 13, 1945, January 19, 1946, February 12–13, 1947, January 17–19, 1948, April 22, 1949, Box 44, ACJP (M71-77), unprocessed.

72. George L. Levison to author, June 8, 1982, and extensive use of Levison's personal files; Berger to author, June 10, 1982; Dean Rusk to author, June 2, 1982 (he insists that the ACJ played no decisive role in formation of American policy).

73. U.S. Congress, House, Committee on Foreign Affairs, *Hearing on H.R. 418 and H.R. 419, Resolutions Relative to the Jewish National Home in Palestine,* 78th Cong., 2d sess. (Washington, DC: Government Printing Office, 1944), pp. 120–124, 197–200, 327–331, 347–350; Berger, *Memoirs,* p. 22; Berger to author, July 25, 1982.

74. "Foes in League," *New Palestine,* March 3, 1944, pp. 274–275; "End of A Dream," *Congress Weekly,* March 3, 1944, pp. 3–4; "Ebb and Tide," *Congress Weekly,* March 24, 1944, pp. 3–4; David Polish, "Against Four Million," *New Palestine,* July 14, 1944, pp. 458–459.

75. Louis E. Levinthal to Rosenwald, March 18, 1944, Other Correspondence, ACJP-R.

76. Stephen S. Wise, "The Philadelphia Rabbinate," *Opinion* 14 (March 1944), p. 47.

77. Ibid.

78. Stephen S. Wise to Ginsburg, March 13, 1944; Bernard L. Frankel to Wise (Counsel of Rodeph Shalom asking for retraction), April 27, 1944, and Wise to Frankel, May 11, 1944; Lester S. Hecht to Wise, May 24, 1944; Joseph G. Shapiro to Wise, May 27, 1944, and Wise to Shapiro, May 31, 1944; Simon Greenberg to Wise, November 10, 1944, and Wise to Greenberg, November 16, 1944; Emil Leipziger to Wise, December 8, 1944, all in Box 99/ACJ, 1918-1948, SSWP; Wise to Leipziger, December 18, 1944, and January 24, 1945, Box 7/8, SSWC.

79. Leipziger to Fineshriber, April 9, 1945, D/10, WHFR; James G. Heller to Wise, May 21, 1945, Box 99/ACJ, SSWP; a copy of Wise's retraction was enclosed in a letter by Leipziger to Fineshriber, July 2, 1945, D/11, WHFR.

80. Rosenwald to Hull, September 25, 1944; Hull to Rosenwald, October 14, 1944, Hull Correspondence, ACJP-R.

81. Elmer Berger, *The Jewish Dilemma* (New York: Devin-Adair, 1945); Berger to author, July 25, 1982.

82. *Information Bulletin,* December 15, 1945, pp. 1–2.

83. Lessing J. Rosenwald, "Memorandum to the AngloAmerican Commission of Inquiry," ACJP-R; text of Rosenwald's statement before the Committee on behalf of the ACJ, *Information Bulletin,* January 15, 1946, pp. 1–4.

84. The *Anglo-American Committee on Inquiry* (New York: American Council for Judaism, 1946); Berger, *Memoirs,* pp. 22–24; *Information Bulletin,* May 15, 1946, pp. 1–6; Berger to author, July 25, 1982.

85. Leonard Dinnerstein, *America and the Survivors of the Holocaust* (New York: Columbia University Press, 1982), pp. 117–136; Berger to author, July 25, 1982; Berger to Levison, December 18, 1946, Box 74/Levison, 1946, ACJP; Minutes, ACJ Executive Committee Meetings, New York, November 21, 1946, pp. 2–3; December 17, 1946, pp. 2–3, January 21, 1947, pp. 4–5, all in ACJ-NY; "Citizens Committee for DPs," *Information Bulletin,* January 15, 1947, p. 1.

86. Earl G. Harrison, "Address," Philadelphia, February 12, 1947, p. 5, Box 2/2, ACJC.

87. "Memorandum on Aspects of the Problem of Palestine," June 4, 1947, George L. Levison Papers; confidential letters from Alfred M. Lilienthal to Berger, July 16, July 30, August 11, August 19, and August 26, 1947, Box 75/Lilienthal, ACJP.

88. "Text of Statement of Policy," *Council News* 2 (May 1948), p. 1.

89. Edelman to Rosenwald, August 21, 1943, ACJP-R.

90. Minutes of the Organizational Meeting of the Philadelphia Chapter of the American Council for Judaism, March 15, 1945, Box 94/Philadelphia, 1945, ACJP.

91. Interview with Jane Blum, Philadelphia, August 17, 1983, and numerous telephone conversations with Blum between 1981 and 1984; interview with Edwin Wolf, II. Telephone conversation with Stanley R. Sundheim, January 10, 1984; informal discussion with Edith G. Rosenwald, February 7, 1980.

92. "Grodinsky, Julius," in *National Cyclopedia of American Biography,* vol. 49 (New York: James T. White, 1966), pp. 138–139; "Dr. Grodinsky," *Council News* 1(June 1947), p. 3.

93. Grodinsky to Miller, May 9, 1947; "Report of Campus Organization Committee," May 12, 1947, Box 97/Philadelphia, University of Pennsylvania, 1945–1950, ACJP; Council News 1 (June 1947), p. 1; Minutes, Hillel Council Meeting, November 11, 1946, Box 94/Philadelphia, 1946, October-December, ACJP.

94. Grodinsky to Berger, January 24, 1947, Box 95/Philadelphia, 1947, January-June, ACJP; Berger to Annual meeting, April 30, 1947, Box 95/Philadelphia, 1947, January-June, ACJP.

95. Grodinsky to Berger, March 9, 1948, March 29, 1948; Grodinsky to Nathan Lowenstein, April 26, 1948; Grodinsky to Sigmund Miller, April 5, 1948, Box 95/Philadelphia, 1948, January-June, ACJP.

96. Interviews with Rabbi Malcolm H. Stern, Edwin Wolf, II, and Jane Blum; Wolsey to Leo Franklin, July 9, 1943, Box 3/8; Wolsey to Irving Reichert, December 8 and 22, 1944, Box 4/4; Wolsey to Elizabeth Stern, December 26, 1944, Box 4/4; Wolsey to Rosenwald, November 29, 1945, Box 4/5; Wolsey to Rosenwald, April 2, 1946, Box 4/6, LWP.

97. Wolsey to Schachtel, December 16, 1946, and Wolsey to "Gentlemen," May 3, 1948, Box 4/6, LWP; Berger to author, October 24, 1982.

98. Louis Wolsey, "Why I Withdrew from the American Council for Judaism," in Louis Wolsey, *Sermons and Addresses* (Philadelphia: Congregation Rodeph Shalom, 1950), pp. 12–16; "'Support Land of Israel' Is Rabbi Wolsey's Plea," Philadelphia *Jewish Exponent,* May 21, 1948, pp. 1, 9.

99. Philip Klein to Lessing Rosenwald (an undated, open letter); Rosenwald to Klein, May 26, 1948, Box 107/Rosenwald, 1948, ACJP.

100. Grodinsky to Berger, May 21, 1948; May 25, 1948; June 4, 1948, Box 95/Philadelphia, 1948, January-June, ACJP.

101. Jane Blum to Berger, June 1, 1948; Berger to Blum, June 2, 1948, Box 95/Philadelphia, 1948, January-June, ACJP.

102. Blum to Berger, November 11, 1948, and December 15, 1948, Box 95/Philadelphia, 1948, July-December, ACJP.

103. Minutes, Executive Committee Meeting, Philadelphia Chapter of A.C.J., September 19, 1951, Box 96/Philadelphia, 1951, September-December, ACJP; *Council News* 4 (June 1950), p. 8; Minutes, Executive Committee, Philadelphia Chapter of the A.C.J., June 13, 1950, Box 96/Philadelphia, 1950, ACJP; Minutes, Executive Committee, Philadelphia Chapter of the A.C.J. October 19, 1950, Box 96/Philadelphia, 1950, ACJP.

104. *Council News* 5 (December 1951), pp. 29–30; Minutes, Executive Committee, Philadelphia Chapter of the A.C.J., December 17, 1951, Box 96/Philadelphia, 1951, September-December, ACJP; Minutes, Executive Committee, Philadelphia Chapter of A.C.J., December 9, 1952, Box 97/Philadelphia, 1952, May-December ACJP.

105. "Israel Is Warned of Soviet Threat," *New York Times,* May 2, 1954, p. 30; State Department Release, No. 223, May 1, 1954, passim; see also Council News 8 (June 1954), pp. 1–19.

106. Harry Snellenburg, Jr., "The Council's Philanthropic Fund Gets Its Charter," *Council News* 9 (July 1955), pp. 3, 12.

107. Confidential summary of notes on Lessing and Edith Rosenwald's comments on their trip to Israel, February 10, 1957, RG 7, FDA-1, American Jewish Committee Record Center and Archives, New York: Interview with Edith Rosenwald, February 7, 1980.

Chapter 3 PHILADELPHIA JEWS AND RADICALISM

1. Letter to general membership, April 21, 1950, from American Jewish Congress Officers, Exhibit "B," John S. Bernheimer vs. American Jewish Congress, Inc., Court of Common Pleas #5, March Term 1950, No. 3035.

2. Ibid.

3. Both letters in American Jewish Congress, 1-77, Box 7, Executive Committee Minutes 1950–1969 (1972) Reports, American Jewish History Society files.

4. Pamphlet, "Is This the AJC of Dr. Stephen S. Wise?", in the author's possession.

5. Ibid.

6. *Jews and the Left* (New York: John Wiley & Sons, 1979).

7. *The World of Our Fathers* (New York: Harcourt Brace Jovanovich, 1976).

8. Liebman, *Jews and the Left,* pp. 7–11, 26–33.

9. "The politics of American Jews," in Marshall Sklare, ed., *The Jews: Social Patterns of an American Group* (New York: Free Press, 1958), p. 621.

10. *The Downtown Jews—Portraits of an Immigrant Generation* (New York: Harper & Row, 1969).

11. See my own account, *Philadelphia Communists, 1936–1956* (Philadelphia: Temple University Press, 1982), pp. 32–33.

12. Liebman, *Jews and the Left,* pp. 32–33.

13. Meredith Savery, "Instability and Uniformity: Residential Patterns in Two Philadelphia Neighborhoods, 1880–1970," in William W. Cutler III and Howard Gillette, Jr., eds., *The Divided Metropolis—Social and Spatial Dimensions of Philadelphia, 1800–1975* (Westport, CT: Greenwood Press, 1980), pp. 193–226.

14. Sandra Featherman, "Jewish Politics in Philadelphia; 1920–1940," in Murray Friedman, ed., *Philadelphia Jewish Life, 1830–1940* (Philadelphia: Institute for the Study of Human Issues, 1983), p. 14.

15. Jerome E. Carlin and Saul H. Mendlowitz, "The American Rabbi: A Religious Specialist Responds to Loss of Authority," in Sklare, ed., *The Jews,* p. 302.

16. Conrad Weiler, *Philadelphia—Neighborhood, Authority, and the Urban Crisis* (New York: Praeger, 1974), p. 158.

17. Howe, *World of Our Fathers,* pp. 357–359; Liebman, *Jews and the Left,* pp. 285–325.

18. Ibid., p. 312.

19. Morris Frommer, *The American Jewish Congress—A History, 1914–1950,* vol. 1, Ph.D. Thesis, Ohio State University, 1978, pp. 510–512.

20. Liebman, *Jews and the Left,* p. 503.

21. Frommer, *American Jewish Congress,* chapter 7; Isaac Newstadt-Noy, *The Unending Task: Efforts to Unite American Jewry from the American Congress to the American Jewish Conference,* Ph.D. Thesis, Brandeis University, 1976, p. 80.

22. See Isaac Deutcher, *The Non-Jewish Jew and Other Essays* (New York: Hill & Wang, 1968), pp. 25–41.

23. "The Jewish Question and the Left: Old and New" (New York: *Jewish Currents* Reprint, 1970), pp. 13–14.

24. Liebman, *Jews and the Left,* pp. 508–509; *Jewish Exponent,* September 1, 1939, editorial, "Pity the Poor Communists," p. 4.

25. Lyons, *Philadelphia Communists,* passim; Joseph Starobin, *American Communism in Crisis, 1943–1957* (Berkeley: University of California Press, 1972), p. 114.

26. Interview, Bernard Stern, July 20, 1982. Stern, who served as editor of the *Citizen Vet,* was most helpful in his recollections and memorabilia concerning the AVC.

27. Melech Epstein, *Jewish Labor in the U.S.A.—An Industrial, Political, and Cultural History of the Jewish Labor Movement, 1882–1974,* vol. 1 (New York: KTAV Publishing House, 1969), p. 124; Neustadt-Noy, *Unending Task,* pp. 147–148, 215, 248–263, 336.

28. Norman D. Markowitz, *The Rise and Fall of the People's Century* (New York: Free Press, 1973).

29. Jewish Community Relations Council, Jewish Archives, T28, Miscellaneous 1939–1945 (H.R. files), "Community Relations in Philadelphia During the Years 1937–47," mimeo, n.d.

30. Ibid.; E. Digby Baltzell, "The Development of a Jewish Upper Class in Philadelphia: 1782–1940," in Sklare, ed., *The Jews,* pp. 274, 284.

31. Such criticisms appeared regularly in both the *Jewish Exponent* and the *Jewish Times* in the post-war years (e.g., October 22, 1948).

32. Nathan Glazer, "The American Jew and the Attainment of Middle-class Rank: Some Trends and Explanations," and Hubert Gans, "The Origin and Growth of a Jewish Community in the Suburbs: A Study of the Jews of Park Forest," in Sklare, ed., *The Jews,* pp. 138–146, 205–248; also, Daniel Elazar, *Community and Polity: The Organizational Dynamics of American Jewry* (Philadelphia: Jewish Publication Society of America, 1976), p. 3.

33. Liebman, *Jews and the Left,* p. 417; Elazar, *Community and Polity,* pp. 21, 200.

34. Neustadt-Noy, *The Unending Task,* p. 138; Frommer, *American Jewish Congress,* p. 184.

35. Ibid., pp. 521–524, 540–541.

36. *Jewish Exponent,* October 27, 1949; January 13, 1950; *Jewish Times,* July 22, 1949. Also, see American Jewish Congress files, 1-77, Box 7, Administrative Committee, minutes, 1934–1959 Reports, May 13, May 14, 1950, American Jewish Historical Society.

37. *Jewish Exponent,* December 26, 1947, p. 3; interview with Mrs. John Bernheimer, October 22, 1982, who was most helpful in providing materials concerning her late husband.

38. Over a dozen participants in the local Congress provided me with insight into John Bernheimer's life and personality; I thank them all. Of particular value was the tape of Bernheimer's memorial service, graciously provided by his wife, Lotte.

39. David Caute, *The Great Fear* (New York: Simon & Shuster, 1978).

40. American Jewish Congress, 1-77, Box 7, March 15, 1950, p. 4; May 4, 1950, p. 2; Philadelphia Council, American Jewish Congress, Board of Directors meeting, minutes, March 20, 1950, in author's possession.

41. JCRC files, T28, Miscellaneous 1939–1945 (H.R. files), "The Communist Question," July 12, 1939; memo from "j. l." to "m. b. f.", August 29, 1940.

42. Ibid., letter to Martin Witkin, June 24, 1940; letter to George Huxter, August 28, 1939.

43. Telephone interview, November 15, 1982.

44. Frommer, *American Jewish Congress,* passim.

45. Ibid., p. 456.

46. American Jewish Congress, 1-77, Administrative Committee meeting, minutes, January 19, 1947, pp. 3–4.

47. Ibid., Administrative Committee meeting, minutes, June 7, 1949, pp. 4–5; September 8, 1949, pp. 2–5.

48. Ibid.

49. Board of Directors meeting, minutes, in author's possession.

50. *Jewish Times,* October 14 and November 18, 1949.

51. Ibid.

52. American Jewish Congress, 1-77, Box 7, July 20, 1950, p. 2.

53. Ibid.

54. Frommer, *American Jewish Congress,* p. 525.

55. Ibid., pp. 525–526; *The Vital Center* (Boston: Little, Brown, 1948).

56. American Jewish Congress, 1-77, Box 7, Administrative Committee meeting, minutes, November 19, 1950, Report to the Officers of Congress, July 19, 1950.

57. Ibid., p. 9.

58. Ibid., Executive Committee minutes, March 15, 1950, p. 4; May 4, 1950, p. 2.

59. *Jewish Times,* December 30, 1949, January 13, 1950.

60. American Jewish Congress, 1-77, Box 7, letter from Petegorsky to Bernheimer, March 31, 1950.

61. Interview, December 7, 1982.

62. American Jewish Congress, 1-77, Box 119, panel discussion, "Safeguarding American Democracy," November 10, 1949, pp. 68–69, microfilm.

63. Court of Common Pleas #5, petition for Temporary Restraining Order.

64. Ibid., Exhibit "B", letter to general membership, April 21, 1950.

65. Ibid.

66. Pamphlet, "Is This the AJC of Dr. Stephen S. Wise?"

67. Court of Common Pleas #5, Exhibit "B".

68. Ibid., pp. 3, 10–14; *Jewish Times,* April 21, 1950, p. 1.

69. *Jewish Times,* April 28, 1950, p. 1.

70. Liebman, *Jews and the Left,* pp. 428–429, 504–514.

71. John Donovan, ed., *U.S. and Soviet Policy in the Middle East, 1945–56* (New York: Facts on File, 1972), pp. 121, 126, 175.

72. Ibid., pp. 152–159.

73. Interviews. The author has been unable to either confirm or disconfirm these statements through a Freedom of Information request of FBI materials concerning the Philadelphia Council of the American Jewish Congress.

74. *Jewish Times,* May 5, 1950, p. 1.

75. American Jewish Congress, 1-77, Box 7, Executive Committee meeting, minutes, October 14, 1950, p. 2; March 27, 1951, p. 2; April 30, 1951, p. 3.

76. Ibid., p. 4.

77. Liebman, *Jews and the Left,* pp. 160–168; Elazar, *Community and Polity,* pp. 3, 21, 33, 92.

Chapter 4 **FROM PERIPHERY TO PROMINENCE**

1. *Jewish Exponent* (Philadelphia), October 29, 1920.

2. Daniel J. Elazar, *Community and Polity: The Organizational Dynamics of American Jewry* (Philadelphia: Jewish Publication Society of America, 1976), p. 240.

3. Abe Feinsinger lived as a youth in the Fifth Ward in South Philadelphia, known as the "Bloody Fifth," and remembered constant combat between political factions prior to World War I. Interview of Abe Feinsinger with Dennis Clark, October 2, 1982, Philadelphia.

4. Interview of Hon. Herbert Levin with Dennis Clark, January 12, 1983, Philadelphia.

5. These neighborhood dispositions are based on research into synagogue locations by Allen Meyers during his studies at Gratz College in 1981–1982. He traced the establishment of over four hundred synagogues in the city over its entire history.

6. Sandra Featherman, "Main Stream, Side Stream: Jewish Politics in Philadelphia from 1920 to 1940," in Murray Friedman, ed., *Jewish Life in Philadelphia, 1830–1940* (Philadelphia: Institute for the Study of Civic Values, 1983), pp. 276–289.

7. Dale E. Phalen, *Samuel Fels of Philadelphia* (Philadelphia: Samuel S. Fels Fund, 1969), pp. 24–26, 70–74.

8. Elden LaMar, *The Clothing Workers in Philadelphia: A History of Their Struggles for Union and Security* (Philadelphia: Amalgamated Clothing Workers of America, 1940), p. 118.

9. John P. Rossi, "The Kelly-Wilson Mayoralty Election of 1935," *The Pennsylvania Magazine of History and Biography,* vol. 107, no. 2 (April 1983), p. 187.

10. At Olney High School in 1943, a conflict between Jews and non-Jews on the school's football team led to fights among students and anti-Semitic agitation. Interview of Judge Isador Kranzel with Dennis Clark, June 3, 1983, Philadelphia.

11. Brett Hawkins, *Politics and Urban Policies* (New York: Bobbs-Merrill, 1971), p. 57.

12. Samuel Halperin, *The Political World of American Zionism* (Detroit: Wayne State University Press, 1961), p. 316.

13. Jay Y. Gonen, *A Psychohistory of Zionism* (New York: Mason-Charter, 1975), p. 61.

14. Ibid., p. 346.

15. *Reports of Twenty-third Zionist Congress at Jerusalem* (Jerusalem: The Zionist Organization and the Jewish Agency of Palestine, 1951), p. 768. Halperin gives higher figures: Halperin, *The Political World of American Zionism,* Appendix IV.

16. *Jewish Exponent* (Philadelphia), December 1, 1950, and June 18, 1954, and continuous examples in other issues. This newspaper carried a weekly column of Washington news largely devoted to issues concerning Israel. See also Hal Lehrman, "The U.S. and Israel," *Commentary,* vol. 23, no. 3 (May 1957), pp. 201–214; Arthur Hertzberg, "Israel and American Jewry," *Commentary,* vol. 44, no. 2 (August 1967), p. 69, asserts polls showed that 99 percent of U.S. Jews supported Israel.

17. Paul Lyons, *Philadelphia Communists, 1936–1956* (Philadelphia: Temple University Press, 1982), p. 71.

18. Featherman, "Main Stream, Side Stream: Jewish Politics in Philadelphia from 1920 to 1940," in Murray Friedman, ed., *Jewish Life in Philadelphia, 1830–1940,* pp. 276–289.

19. Interview of Hon. Herbert Levin with Dennis Clark, January 12, 1983, Philadelphia.

20. The heavily Jewish Strawberry Mansion area, for instance, experienced a great population change in the 1950s. Congressman Earl Chudoff, elected in 1949, found his Jewish constituency almost gone by 1958. Meredith Savery, "Instability and Uniformity: Residential Patterns in Two Philadelphia Neighborhoods, 1880–1970," in William W. Cutler III and Howard Gillette, Jr., eds., *The Divided Metropolis: Social and Spatial Dimensions of Philadelphia, 1800–1975* (Westport, CT: Greenwood Press, 1980), p. 217. Dennis J. Clark, *The Ghetto Game* (New York: Sheed and Ward, 1962), pp. 120–125.

21. Peter O. Muller, Kenneth C. Meyer, and Roman Cybriwsky, *Philadelphia: A Study of Conflicts and Social Cleavages* (Cambridge, MA: Ballinger, 1976), pp. 19–22.

22. Joseph S. Clark, Jr., and Dennis J. Clark, "Rally and Relapse, 1946–1968," in Russell F. Weigley, ed., *Philadelphia: A 300-Year History* (New York: W. W. Norton, 1982), pp. 649–657.

23. Ibid., pp. 657. Dennis J. Clark, "The Urban Ordeal," Research Paper No. 1, Philadelphia: Past, Present and Future Project, University of Pennsylvania, Philadelphia, 1982.

24. Joseph D. Crumlish, *A City Finds Itself: The Philadelphia Home Rule Charter Movement* (Detroit: Wayne State University Press, 1959), appendix. Within the reform cadres were City Representative S. Harry Galfand and City Councilmen George Schwartz of Wynnefield–Overbrook, David Cohen of Logan–Oak Lane, David Silver of Oxford Circle, and Edward Cantor, At Large—*1970 Bulletin Almanac* (Philadelphia: Evening Bulletin, 1970). Harold Libros, *Hard Core Liberals* (Cambridge, MA: Schenkman, 1975), passim, shows the ADA board as 39 percent Jewish in 1949, but membership was more heavily Jewish overall.

25. Interview of Allen Weinberg with Dennis Clark, March 16, 1983, Philadelphia.

26. *Philadelphia Inquirer,* September 28, 1982, review of John Cooney, *The Annenbergs* (New York: Simon and Schuster, 1982).

27. Nochem S. Winnet, "The Public Life of Nochem S. Winnet," Phillips Collection, Urban Archives, Temple University, Philadelphia, pp. 25–29.

28. Interview of Joseph Ominsky with Charles Hordy of Station WHYY, October 7, 1982, Philadelphia.

29. Weigley, *Philadelphia: A 300-Year History,* pp. 662–663.

30. Henry Klein, "The Network of Community Leadership," Ph.D. dissertation, Sociology, Temple University, 1964, pp. 81–82.

31. *Philadelphia Inquirer,* January 28, 1973.

32. William L. O'Neill, *Coming Apart: An Informal History of America in the 1960's* (New York: Quadrangle Books, 1971), pp. 186, 255, 288.

33. Lenora E. Berson, *Case Study of a Riot* (New York: Institute for Human Relations Press, The American Jewish Committee, 1966), p. 46.

34. Clark and Clark, "Rally and Relapse," in Weigley, *Philadelphia: A 300-Year History,* pp. 666–667.

35. Berson, *Case Study of a Riot,* p. 46.

36. Henry Cohen and Gary Sandrow, *Philadelphia Chooses a Mayor* (New York and Philadelphia: The American Jewish Committee, 1972), pp. 8–16. Interview of Dennis Clark with Lenora Berson, July 15, 1982, Philadelphia. Milton Himmelfarb, "Jewish Class Conflict," in Murray Friedman, ed., *Overcoming Middle Class Rage* (Philadelphia: Westminster Press, 1971), pp. 204–205.

37. Sandra Featherman, *Jews, Blacks and Ethnics: The 1978 "Vote White" Charter Campaign in Philadelphia* (New York, The American Jewish Committee, 1979), pp. 11–23.

38. Interview of Councilwoman Joan Specter with Dennis Clark, June 30, 1982.

39. David C. McClelland, *The Achieving Society* (Princeton, NJ: Van Nostrand, 1961), p. 29.

40. Sandra Featherman, "Ethnicity and Ethnic Candidates: Vote Advantages in Local Elections," *Polity,* vol. 15, no. 3 (Spring 1983), pp. 397–415.

41. Chuck Stone, "Philadelphia's 6 Plantation Wards," Philadelphia *Daily News,* May 11, 1982.

42. Jobs in Philadelphia declined from 938,600 in 1969 to 775,700 in 1981. "Philadelphia Employment Trends, 1980," U.S. Department of Labor, Bureau of Labor Statistics, Regional Report 140, 1981, tables 4 and 5.

43. Interview of Dennis Clark with Fred Voight, Executive Director, Committee of 70, Philadelphia, June 23, 1983.

44. Lawrence H. Fuchs, "Jews and the Presidential Vote," in Lawrence H. Fuchs, ed., *American Ethnic Politics* (New York: Harper and Row, 1968), pp. 68–73; William S. Berlin, *On the Edge of Politics: The Roots of Jewish Political Thought in America* (Westport, CT: Greenwood Press, 1978), pp. 12, 156–157.

45. Stephen D. Isaacs, *The Jews in American Politics* (Garden City, NY: Doubleday, 1974), p. 267.

46. *Jewish Exponent* (Philadelphia), November 14, 1980. This divergence of opinion is not unusual. There were earlier divisions that belied simplistic views of a "Jewish vote." See Ben Halpern, "The Roots of Jewish Liberalism," *American Jewish Historical Quarterly,* 66 (1976), pp. 190–214.

Chapter 5 AN AMBIVALENT ALLIANCE

1. December 16, 1983.

2. See Earl Raab, "Blacks and Jews Asunder?" *Midstream,* November 1979, for an elaboration of this perspective, including attention to the fundamental tensions in the alliance. See also David G. Singer, "An Uneasy Alliance: Jews and Blacks in the United States, 1945–1953," *Contemporary Jewry,* 1978, for an examination of the tensions inherent in the alliance. The contrasting assumption of a natural alliance is most frequently found in appeals for black-Jewish cooperation, such as Alvin F. Poussaint, "Blacks and Jews: An Appeal for Unity," *Ebony,* July 1974, and John Jacob, "Revitalization of the BlackJewish Alliance," *Moment,* July-August 1983, pp. 48–52.

3. In interpreting the relationship, the authors stress the role of Jewish organizations and black organizations, because that is the focus of the available historical materials. We hope this essay will stimulate oral history research to illuminate the changes in the relationship as they were played out between "grass-roots" blacks and Jews living in Philadelphia's neighborhoods.

4. Interview with Dr. Howard Pollack, October 23, 1983.

5. Lunabell Wedlock, "The Reaction of Negro Publications and Organizations to German Anti-Semitism," Howard University Studies in the Social Sciences, the Graduate School, Howard University, Washington, DC, 1942, pp. 84, 146.

6. Interview with Rev. Henry Nichols, August 2, 1983.

7. Charles F. Kellogg, *NAACP* (Baltimore, 1967), p. 125; Dale Phalen, *Samuel Fels of Philadelphia* (Philadelphia, 1969), p. 24; David Levening Lewis, "Shortcuts to the Mainstream: Afro-American and Jewish Notables in the 1920's and 1930's," in Joseph R. Washington, Jr., *Jews in Black Perspectives: A Dialogue* (Rutherford, NJ, 1984), p. 94; Hasia R. Diner, *In the Almost Promised Land: American Jews and Blacks 1915–1935* (Westport, CT, 1977), p. 220.

8. Interview with Henry Aaron Rubin, November 30, 1983.

9. Interview with Samuel L. Evans, August 2, 1983.

10. Interview with Benjamin Stahl, August 10, 1983.

11. Maxwell Whiteman, *Human Rights and Civil Rights: A History of the First Twenty-five Years of the Philadelphia Fellowship Commission* (unpublished, AJC Files, 1969), introduction.

12. Whiteman, p. 48; Murray Friedman, ed., *Philadelphia Jewish Life: 1830–1940* (Philadelphia, 1983), p. 20.

13. Clarence E. Pickett, *For More Than Bread* (Boston, 1953), p. 375. Interview with Maurice B. Fagan, March 5, 1985.
14. Whiteman, pp. 24, 36, 38.
15. Whiteman, pp. 42–64.
16. Allen Thomas Bonnell, *Community College of Philadelphia: A Chronicle of the Years 1964–1984* (Philadelphia, 1984), pp. 14, 57–58.
17. Whiteman, p. 57.
18. Whiteman, p. 71.
19. Interview with Beatrice Harrison, July 26, 1983.
20. Philadelphia *Tribune,* September 13, 1985.
21. David Sawyer Memo to Lucky Dawidowicz, American Jewish Committee Files, July 27, 1958.
22. Interview with Ben Stahl, August 10, 1983.
23. David Diamond, "Remnants of a Dream," *Today Magazine, Philadelphia Inquirer,* March 21, 1982, p. 12.
24. Morris Milgram, *Bulletin: Fund for an Open Society,* May 1983.
25. Morris Milgram, *Good Neighborhood: The Challenge of Open Housing* (New York, 1979), pp. 15, 20.
26. Diamond, p. 12.
27. *Philadelphia Inquirer,* April 13, 1982.
28. Interview with Morris Milgram, July 22, 1983.
29. Statements by A. Leon Higginbotham, Jr., and David L. Ullman at "Meeting Convened by the Philadelphia Negro Trade Union Leadership Council and the Jewish Labor Committee to Consider Negro-Jewish Relationships," American Jewish Committee Files, November 17, 1961.
30. Interview with Benjamin Stahl.
31. Interview with Rev. Henry Nichols.
32. Philadelphia *Evening Bulletin,* January 13, 1963; January 17, 1963; *Philadelphia Inquirer,* January 22, 1963.
33. Interview with Benjamin Stahl.
34. Lenora E. Berson, *Case Study of a Riot: The Philadelphia Story* (New York, 1966), pp. 16–30, 40.
35. Berson, p. 46.
36. Berson, p. 46.
37. *Philadelphia Inquirer,* November 2, 1970.
38. *Survey of Jewish Businessmen Operating in Selected Inner City Areas of Philadelphia* (Philadelphia, Center for Community Studies of Temple University and the Jewish Community Relations Council of Greater Philadelphia, n.d.). For further discussion of this issue, see Murray Friedman, "The Jews," in Peter I. Rose et al., *Through Different Eyes* (New York, 1973), pp. 151–152; Berson, p. 45.
39. Jules Cohen, "Build or Burn," American Jewish Committee Files, 1968. The Fellowship Commission had originally filed a complaint before the Philadelphia Commission on Human Relations and brought together seven attorneys of the Commission's office, leading to the suit.
40. Interview with Robert Klein, July 12, 1983.
41. *New York Times,* August 15, 1963.
42. *Pennsylvania Guardian,* June 7, 1963.
43. *Philadelphia Inquirer,* June 21, 1963; *New York Times,* August 15, 1963.
44. Murray Friedman Letter to Morris Milgram, American Jewish Committee files, October 29, 1963.
45. Robert G. Weisbord and Arthur Stein, *Bittersweet Encounter* (Westport, CT, 1970), p. 144.
46. Interview with Maurice B. Fagan, March 5, 1985.
47. Murray Friedman Memo to Will Katz, American Jewish Committee Files, August 7, 1967.
48. "Black Panther Party: A Review Factsheet," American Jewish Committee Files, November 19, 1970.
49. Friedman, in Rose et al., p. 148.
50. Daniel Elazar and Murray Friedman, *Moving Up: Ethnic Succession in America with a Case History from the Philadelphia School System* (New York, 1976), p. 28.
51. See Jonathon Kozol, *Death at an Early Age* (New York, 1967).
52. Philadelphia *Evening Bulletin,* November 10, 1971; Lawrence Rutter, "Let Georges Do It," *Philadelphia* magazine, January 1970, pp. 156–161; Murray Friedman memo to Charles Kahn, Jr., et al., American Jewish Committee Files, December 10, 1969.
53. *Tribune,* May 11, 1965.
54. Jules Cohen, "Build or Burn," pp. 5–7.
55. Interview with Burt Siegel, November 3, 1983.
56. *Tribune,* January 9, 1968.
57. Murray Friedman memo to Will Katz, American Jewish Committee Files, September 25, 1967.
58. *Tribune,* June 21, 1975.
59. *Philadelphia Inquirer,* June 28, 1968; *Philadelphia Evening Bulletin,* July 28, 1968.
60. *Philadelphia Inquirer,* October 10, 1967.

61. Murray Friedman Memo to Isaiah Terman, American Jewish Committee Files, July 17, 1968.
62. Sherman Labovitz, "A Study of the Reaction of Recipients of Assistance from the Urban Affairs Department of the Federation of Jewish Agencies" (Unpublished Manuscript, August 25, 1970).
63. Interview with Theodore Levine, July 25, 1983.

Chapter 6 WYNNEFIELD

1. See Louis Wirth, *The Ghetto,* Phoenix Books (Chicago: University of Chicago Press, 1928, 1956).
2. Census data indicate that Wynnefield was 4 percent non-white as of 1960. However, all of the black families lived in a neighborhood south of Lancaster Avenue, separated from the rest of the community by railroad tracks and not considered part of Wynnefield.
3. Clifton O. Lee, "Integration Success: Wynnefield Survives, Prospers as a Community in Which Races Exist Together," *Philadelphia Bulletin,* December 9, 1979.
4. Jewish Community Relations Council of Greater Philadelphia, *Survey of Racial Changes in the Wynnefield Area of Philadelphia* (Philadelphia: JCRC, undated).
5. David P. Varady, *Ethnic Minorities in Urban Areas: A Case Study of Racially Changing Communities* (Boston: Martinus Nijhoff, 1979), pp. 78, 97–98.
6. Jewish Community Relations Council, *Survey of Racial Changes,* p. 10.
7. *Newsletter* (Wynnefield Residents Association), November 1969, p. 3. Later racial issues were confronted directly by the WRA, a fact that was brought to the attention of the author in a letter from Dr. Seymour Mandelbaum (undated). Avoidance of racial issues is typical of residents associations in racially changing communities. A similar pattern occurred with the South Shore Commission (Chicago); see Harvey Molotch, *Managed Integration: Dilemmas of Doing Good in the City* (Berkeley: University of California Press, 1972).
8. Unless otherwise indicated, the results presented in this essay are from the 1960, 1970, and 1980 censuses.
9. The Har Zion survey results appear to understate the rate of racial change when they are compared with the 1970 census results. This could be due to the fact that the reverse telephone directory used for the Har Zion study was about six months out of date. As a result, some of the white families listed in the directory moved by the time of the survey. Conversely, recent black in-migrants were underrepresented.
10. This is what occurred in the South Shore community in Chicago; see Molotch, *Managed Integration,* pp. 148–173.
11. Varady, *Ethnic Minorities,* p. 73.
12. Ibid., p. 96.
13. Ibid., p. 107.
14. Ibid., pp. 107–108. Many of the Wynnefield families who moved in response to crime relocated to the high-rise apartments in Upper Wynnefield. Apparently, the security features of these buildings shielded residents from the crime problem in the surrounding area. Other researchers have noted the tendency for whites to continue to move into rental apartments despite the existence of racial change. Such residents are less likely than owners to be concerned about long-term declines in property values; see Chester Rapkin and William Grigsby, *The Demand for Housing in Racially Changing Areas* (Berkeley: University of California Press, 1960).
15. *Jewish Exponent,* December 22, 1972.
16. The disparities were not as great with respect to crimes affecting property only. For example, there were roughly two and a half times as many burglaries in Lower Merion as in Wynnefield in 1973 (617 versus 245).
17. For a more detailed description of the Urban Homesteading Demonstration evaluation, see Carla I. Pedone, Patricia M. Remch, and Karl E. Case, *The Urban Homesteading Program: An Assessment of its Impact on Demonstration Neighborhoods 1977–1979* (Cambridge, MA: Urban Systems, Research and Engineering Inc., 1980).
18. There is no necessary relationship between price changes and the existence of racial change. The magnitude of change is a function of such variables as the level and nature of black housing demand and the number and types of dwelling units that are available; see Charles Abrams, "The Housing Problem and the Negro," *Daedalus,* vol. 95, no. 1 (Winter 1966), pp. 64–76.
19. Donald Janson, "Racial Change Slashes Values and Produces Bargains," *New York Times,* January 21, 1973 (Real Estate Section).
20. *Newsweek,* "A Suburb That Struck a Truce," November 15, 1971, p. 63.
21. For additional details on these surveys, see Varady, *Ethnic Minorities,* p. 8.
22. Samuel Z. Klausner and David P. Varady, "Synagogues without Ghettos" (Unpublished technical report, Philadelphia: Center for Research on the Acts of Man, 1970).

23. Ibid., p. 117.
24. Ibid., p. 193.
25. Later, Klausner justified the decision on the basis of the impact of the relocation on the surrounding community; see Joe Adcock, "Wynnefield's Har Zion Plans Move to the Suburbs," Philadelphia *Bulletin,* August 7, 1983.
26. Philadelphia *Bulletin,* "Wynnefield Exodus is Slowed," July 27, 1970; and *Philadelphia Inquirer,* "Study Advises Against Move of Synagogue," July 28, 1970.
27. Letter to Har Zion members from Bernard Fishman titled, "A Statement about Har Zion's Present and Future Plans," August 1970.
28. Joe Adcock, "Some Oppose Har Zion Move to the Suburbs," Philadelphia *Bulletin,* August 11, 1983.
29. Letter to friends of Har Zion Temple from Daniel J. Elazar et al., January 2, 1979.
30. Kathy Begley, "Large Conservative Synagogue Leaving City for the Suburbs," *Philadelphia Inquirer,* December 17, 1972.
31. *Har Zion Bulletin,* February 1973.
32. Yona Ginsberg, *Jews in a Changing Neighborhood: The Study of Mattapan* (New York: Free Press, 1975).
33. Varady, *Ethnic Minorities,* p. 106.
34. *Jewish Exponent,* "Wynnefield Is a Neighborhood That Is 'Making It'," June 6, 1969; and Lee, "Integration Success."
35. This section draws heavily from Janice Goldstein, *Jewish Neighborhoods in Transition* (New York: American Jewish Committee, 1980).
36. Letter from Rabbi Henry Cohen, Beth David Reform Congregation, September 16, 1983.
37. It was possible to maintain a surprisingly high density of Jewish institutions after the relocation of these facilities from Wynnefield. Akiba Academy and Solomon Schechter Day School relocated a short distance across the city line to what amounted to a Jewish cultural park on Old Lancaster Avenue. In addition to these schools, the "park" contained Adath Israel Synagogue, a large Conservative congregation, and Lower Merion Synagogue (Orthodox). Similarly, Torah Academy made a relatively short move and had a *mikveh* at its new location.
38. Ian Blynn, "In the King's House," Friday (*Jewish Exponent*), June 24, 1983.
39. Goldstein, *Jewish Neighborhoods,* p. 29.
40. Varady, *Ethnic Minorities,* p. 98.
41. Goldstein, *Jewish Neighborhoods,* p. 29.

Chapter 7 A PLACE TO LIVE

1. Lloyd M. Abernethy, "Progressivism 1905–1919," in Russell M. Weigley, ed., *Philadelphia: A 300-Year History* (New York: W. W. Norton, 1982), p. 524.
2. This background is drawn from *Old Northeast Philadelphia County, 1608–1854* (Pied Typer Press, Northeast High School, 1969).
3. Maxwell Whiteman, "Philadelphia's Jewish Neighborhoods," in Allen F. Davis and Mark H. Haller, eds., *The Peoples of Philadelphia* (Philadelphia: Temple University Press, 1973), pp. 233–234.
4. Ibid., p. 234.
5. Caroline Golab, "The Immigrant and the City: Poles, Italians, and Jews in Philadelphia, 1870–1920," in Davis and Haller, eds., *The Peoples of Philadelphia,* p. 221.
6. *Jewish Exponent,* June 1, 1962, p. 19.
7. Abernethy, in Russell M. Weigley, ed., *Philadelphia: A 300-Year History,* p. 525.
8. Philadelphia *Record,* December 11, 1938, p. 24.
9. Sam Bass Warner, *The Private City* (Philadelphia: University of Pennsylvania Press, 1968), pp. 178–179.
10. Philadelphia *Record,* December 11, 1938, p. 24.
11. Joseph S. Clark and Dennis J. Clark, "Rally and Relapse 1946–1968," in Russell M. Weigley, ed., *Philadelphia: A 300-Year History,* p. 669.
12. *Northeast Jewish Times,* July 8, 1983, p. 1.
13. *Philadelphia Inquirer,* April 24, 1983, p. 1.
14. Henry Cohen and Gary Sandrow, "Philadelphia Chooses A Mayor," 1971, p. 8. Published by American Jewish Committee, 1972.
15. Murray Friedman in introduction to *Jews, Blacks and Ethnics, the 1978 "Vote White" Charter Campaign in Philadelphia,* by Sandra Featherman and William L. Rosenberg (New York: American Jewish Committee, 1979), p. vi.
16. Jed Rakoff and Ruth Bennett, "The Northeast, Its Jews and the American Jewish Committee: Summary Report," 1971, p. I.17. John Keats, *The Crack in the Picture Window* (Boston: Houghton Mifflin, 1957), pp. xi, xii.

18. Clark and Clark, in Russell M. Weigley, ed., *Philadelphia: A 300-Year History,* p. 699.

19. Maury Levy, "And On the Seventh Day, When the Lord Rested, Man Made the Northeast," *Philadelphia* magazine, November 1970, p. 89.

20. Herbert J. Gans, *The Levittowners* (New York: Pantheon Books, 1967), p. 432.

21. Rakoff and Bennett, "The Northeast," p. 2.

22. William L. Yancey and Ira Goldstein, "The Jewish Population of the Greater Philadelphia Area," published by Federation of Jewish Agencies of Greater Philadelphia.

Chapter 8 HOME AND HAVEN

1. Annual statistics of immigration to Philadelphia, obtained from Philadelphis HIAS and Migration Council, are as follows:

1972	85	1977	289	1981	346
1974	212	1978	514	1982	58
1975	281	1979	1369		
1976	234	1980	594	TOTAL:	3982

2. Figures developed by author from monthly intake figures for 1979, kept by Elizabeth Geggel, for Supervisor, Russian Resettlement Program, Jewish Family Service of Philadelphia, from 1975 to 1982.

3. Quoted in Simcha R. Goldberg, "Jewish Acculturation and the Soviet Immigrant," Presented at Annual Meeting of Conference of Jewish Communal Workers, Denver, May 26, 1980. In Rome, however, Christian missionary groups have also been active in extending help.

4. Under the new law, a refugee who qualifies for asylum is someone outside his country of origin who is unable or unwilling to return because of a "well-founded fear of persecution on account of race, religion, nationality, membership in a particular social group, or political opinion." Apropos this point, Benjamin Sprafkin, former executive director of Jewish Family Service, has commented, "By accepting Soviet Jews who wish to come to the United States, American Jewish agencies have been instruments in having the U.S. Government pass comprehensive refugee legislation. As a result of this, not only has the number of admissible refugees substantially increased, but the government has, in addition to this legislation, accepted a high degree of financial responsibility." This is a reference to the block grant formula discussed below.

5. The warmth extended by HIAS staff and board members at the initial receptions of groups of Soviet immigrants and in subsequent individual contacts by phone or person has made HIAS one of the most trusted and well liked of the agencies among people who have a strong distrust and suspicion of all bureaucracy. As of September 1982, HIAS helped three hundred Soviet Jews become citizens. (Interview with John R. Fishel, September 1982.) The vast majority want to become citizens quickly, in contrast with other immigrants. As of this writing, over three thousand have become citizens.

6. David Harris, *Handbook for Soviet Migrants* (New York: HIAS, 1976). Translated into Russian by Marina Rappoport.

7. During the first three months, funds for rent (except the one-month rent deposit, which was given as a loan) and food were provided as a grant. Grants ranged from $215.27 for two persons to $344.95 for five persons. (From "Orientation Guide," Jewish Family Service, supplied by Sylvia Thomas.) The Council of Jewish Federations was the prime contractor that arranged U.S. government block grants and their allocation to local communities. Locally, the Soviet Resettlement Task Force of the Philadelphia Federation of Jewish Agencies allocated portions of this sum to the social agencies involved in the resettlement process. In 1979, for example, local HIAS was granted $80,625 to manage the vast increase in the number of Soviet Jews seeking assistance. This sum, among other things, permitted the agency to hire a Russian-speaking case worker and supervisor. At the time, the Resettlement Budget Subcommittee stressed the importance of increased participation by local Soviet families in the resettlement of newcomers. (Minutes, HIAS Board of Directors Meeting, December 20, 1979.) Twelve thousand dollars was contributed to the Federation by Soviet Jews in 1979.

8. Ibid.

9. Interview with Elizabeth Geggel, November 3, 1982.

10. Ibid.

11. Benjamin R. Sprafkin, "Resettlement of Jewish Families in Israel and in the Diaspora," presented at the International Conference of Jewish Communal Service, Jerusalem, August 24, 1981.

12. Interview with Louise Yermish, Employment Counselor, JEVS, November 4, 1982.

13. Dr. Friedman was particularly concerned about the plight of the 120 or so Jewish veterans who served in the Soviet army during World War II, who were stripped of all their pension ben-

efits and documents when they left the Soviet Union. Many were physically disabled, as well as poor and too old or ill to work. Dr. Friedman interpreted federal and state laws for them and intervened in obtaining social security and disability benefits, free medical care, food stamps, and low-income Section 8 housing. (They have, however, not been able to obtain the special veterans benefits given Polish and Czech veterans of World War II who fought against the Nazis, probably because of anti-Soviet feeling in this country and the lobbying efforts of the American Legion and the Disabled War Veterans. Nevertheless, former State Senator James Lloyd introduced a resolution acknowledging their wartime achievements, which was passed.)

14. Sprafkin, "Resettlement of Jewish Families." These problems were also noted in an interview with Sylvia Thomas, case worker in the Resettlement Division of Jewish Family Service, October 7, 1982.

15. In a questionnaire in Russian developed by the author in 1983 and distributed to forty-five newcomers at random, in response to the question, "What do you dislike about America?" fifteen wrote "crime" and five, "too much freedom."

16. In the questionnaire cited in note 15, seventeen newcomers were over age 60, of whom fifteen said they had come to be with children and grandchildren. Mrs. Thomas confirmed the reality of these dilemmas and traumas for older immigrants. Many are forced to live meagerly on SSI grants and baby-sitting fees. The Neuman Center is an indispensable refuge for them.

17. Raised to $336.70 in 1981.

18. Memo from Helen Bloom, Director of Volunteers, Einstein Medical Center, March 1980.

19. Quoted by Louise Yermish.

20. Details provided by Louise Yermish.

21. Shelley D. Harrison, "A Report on Survey of First 100 Soviets Resettled in Philadelphia," May 1977.

22. Wage levels were as follows:

Hourly Entry Wage Rate	Number of Different Placements
Under $2.90	12
$2.90–3.99	301
$4.00–5.99	370
$6.00–7.99	134
$8.00 and over	71
Self-employed	1
Unknown	128
Total	1,017

These figures do not reflect referrals and assistance by relatives and friends. Letter from Eleanor Hewitt, Director of Training and Placement, JEVS, March 21, 1983.

23. *The Soviet Jews' Adjustment to the United States,* by Rita J. and Julian L. Simon, published by the Council of Jewish Federations in April 1982, includes data based on interviews with seven hundred Soviet Jewish immigrant families, fifty from Philadelphia. The interviews were conducted in the spring of 1981. Their composite tables show a similarly rapid movement into a job: "Within 1 1/2 or 2 years, the immigrants as a group have achieved as high a level of labor-force participation as they will reach. . . . We see that within six months after entry, 60 percent of the males and 34 percent of the females had found a job; within a year, 78 percent of the males and 56 percent of the females had found a job" (p. 20).

24. Quoted in I. J. Blynn, "For Soviet Jews in the United States; Welcome to Another Planet," *Jewish Exponent,* March 14, 1980.

25. Ronald E. Myers, "An Evaluation of a Demonstration Program in the Organization of a Refugee Population," 1980, pp. 18, 23–24.

26. See "Summary Report," by Cecily Rose Itkoff, in *Organization of Refugee Population Self-Help Groups for Soviet Jewish Emigres,* vol. 6, 1979, Council of Jewish Federations, for an analysis of the expectations, confusions, "ineffable importance of power and prestige," and inner group conflicts that these projects exposed.

27. See, for example, "The Soviet 'Dropouts': A Discussion of the Issues," by Karen Rubinstein, *Issue Analysis,* no. 16, American Zionist Federation, December, 1979; "The Noshrim: A Jewish Tragedy," *The American Zionist,* February-March 1980, pp. 6–12; "Russian Emigrants and Jewish Policy," *Moment,* April 1977, pp. 59–62; "Culture Shock: From Russia to Philadelphia," by Gloria Hayes Kremer, *Inside,* Fall 1980, p. 51.

28. "Integrating Soviet Jewish Emigres: The Continuing Agenda for the American Jewish Community," in *Report of the Task Force on Jewish Identity,* Council of Jewish Federations, New York, November 12, 1980, pp. 1–2.

29. Elizabeth Geggel pointed out that staff "friendliness and warmth was what confused some of our clients. They had us equated with their government agencies, where they were treated in a rough manner. Being too friendly made some of them suspicious. . . . They could not figure us out."

30. "Integrating Soviet Jewish Emigres," p. 6.

31. FJA Task Force on Resettlement. "Report of Sub-committee on Acculturation and Jewish Identity," June 1982.

32. The programs noted are described in ibid.

33. Statistics provided by Dr. William Lakritz, then Director of Educational Priorities, Gratz College. A significant warning regarding possible future conflict between the tradition-oriented day school and the essentially secular Soviet Jewish home was sounded by Dr. Daniel Isaacman, late President of Gratz College: "Since Russian families are appreciative of the value of learning and are emotionally moved by the efforts of teachers and others to make them part of the Day School community, nevertheless, the wide gap between the Day School, which is generally Traditional in its approach, and the home, which is basically secular in its philosophy, results in a significant number of dropouts from Day School education by Russian children. For example, in Baltimore, where a few years ago some 60 percent of the children of Soviet immigrants attended Traditional Day Schools, the figure has dropped to 39 percent." Letter from Dr. Isaacman to Rosalie Alexander (Planning Associate of JFA), July 25, 1980: In this letter, Dr. Isaacman also urged that the Gratz College Division of Community Services, as the education arm of FJA, be centrally involved in coordinating educational services for Soviet Jewish children. To date, this suggestion has not been taken up.

34. This represented a very small percentage of the estimated eight hundred to nine hundred Soviet Jewish children under age 16 in Philadelphia.

35. "Understanding Our Jewish Neighbors from the USSR: A Training Seminar for Jewish Lay Leadership and Special Speakers Bureau Program," Jewish Community Relations Council of Greater Philadelphia, November 1981.

36. Particularly disturbing to the newcomers were articles in the *Philadelphia Inquirer* (April 24, 1983) on the first page and *Philadelphia* magazine (May 1983), which alleged that the criminals had roots in an Odessa-based international criminal conspiracy, named Malina.

37. In the questionnaire distributed by the author, twenty-two newcomers said they had little or no contact with American Jews. Twenty-one did, many of whom mentioned the Neuman Center. An important effort toward drawing groups together was the exhibit ("Culture Shock") of paintings and photographs interpreting Soviet Jewish immigration and life in America, sponsored by the Museum of American Jewish History and the Balch Institute in Philadelphia, beginning October 16, 1983. This was followed in December by a special tour and reception for Soviet Jewish newcomers. This program was described as "part of a process initiated by the JCRC Northeast Division to help integrate the American and Soviet Jewish communities. We have been extremely pleased by the positive response to this program, with over 50 Soviet Jews expected to join about 30 members of the JCRC Northeast Division." Letter from Abby L. Stamelman, Director of Community Services, JCRC, December 12, 1983.

38. In the questionnaire distributed by the author, eighteen indicated that they left the USSR because of anti-Semitism. Forty-three expressed deep interest in Israel and special concern for its security and continued existence. In a study by Zvi Gitelman, "'I Didn't Collect Baseball Cards': Soviet Immigrant Resettlement in the United States," presented at Touro College Conference on Immigration, New York City, November 19, 1981, when asked how they would like to be identified, nearly 75 percent of the respondents answered "American Jews" or "Jews," and 24 percent, simply "American" (p. 18). In The Soviet Jews' Adjustment to the United States (cited earlier), for 57 percent of the nine hundred respondents, being Jewish is "very important"; for 28 percent it is "somewhat important" (p. 64).

39. Simcha R. Goldberg, "Soviet Jewish Integration: A Study Report," presented to the Subcommittee on Jewish Integration of the Soviet Jewish Resettlement Program Committee, Council of Jewish Federations, April 10, 1981, p. 9.

40. Part of this study appeared in *Soviet Jewish Affairs* (London), vol. 14, no. 3, 1984.

Chapter 9 CHANGING STYLES OF SYNAGOGUE LIFE

1. Axelrod, Fowler, and Gurin, *A Community Survey for Long Range Planning* (Boston: The Combined Jewish Philanthropies of Greater Boston, 1967), p. 119.

2. S. Goldstein and C. Goldscheider, Jewish Americans (Englewood Cliffs, NJ: Prentice Hall, 1968), p. 177.

3. Daniel Elazar, *Community and Polity* (Philadelphia: JPS, 1976), pp. 121–124.

4. Moshe Davis, *The Emergence of Conservative Judaism* (Philadelphia: JPS, 1963).

5. *American Jewish Yearbook,* 1912–1913 (Philadelphia: JPS, 1912), p. 242.

6. Davis, *The Emergence of Conservative Judaism,* pp. 311–328.

7. Mortimer J. Cohen, "Two Decades of Conservative Judaism in Philadelphia," *Jewish Exponent,* September 8, 1939, p. 1.

8. Robert Tabak, "Geographical Movements of Synagogues in Philadelphia: 1945–1965," in the Philadelphia Jewish Archive Center, p. 3.

9. Elazar, *Community and Polity.*

10. The outline of this history was excerpted from two congregation-sponsored histories: "Dedication Book: Congregation Adath Jeshurun, 1858–1967," Marion Shore and Charlotte Bernstein, eds.; and "A History of Adath Jeshurun," Marion Bernstein in *1979 Service of Re-Dedication.* Also interviews with Rabbis Yaakov Rosenberg and Seymour Rosenbloom; and AJ laypeople Charlotte Bernstein, I. Jerome Stern, Elliot Kane, Gladys and Marshall Berstein, Francis Mann, Steve Davidoff, and Adele Cohen—all in late 1982.

11. Adath Jeshurun, "Minutes of the Board," March 30, 1911.

12. The outline of this history comes from a brief survey in Har Zion's *25th Anniversary Volume* and interviews with Rabbis Simon Greenberg (in Jerusalem), David Goldstein, and Gerald Wolpe—all in mid-1982.

13. This history relied on an essay in a 1954 synagogue-sponsored anniversary book, *From Dream to Reality,* entitled "The Story of the Germantown Jewish Centre," by Leo Dushoff, as well as interviews with the following laypeople: Ed Polisher, Miriam Gafni, Harold Laden, Leonard Rosenthal, Leon Magil, Baruch Bricklin, Diana Stern, Annette Temin, Don and Hilda Dorfman, and Gerda Lakritz (October 14, 1982).

14. Information on the Germantown Minyan came from an interview with Bob and Kate Zimring, Baruch Bricklin, Stan Wolf, Bill Beck, and Miriam Gafni (October 28, 1982).

15. Caution must be urged in this observation, as there are no collected data to substantiate it. This phenomenon was observed primarily in members interviewed, all of whom tended to be from the families most deeply involved over the years.

16. The prevailing theory of demography and synagogue patterns is offered by Marshall Sklare, *Conservative Judaism* (New York: Schocken, 1955, 1972), p. 47. But for the purposes of this study, we found the model presented in Robert Tabak, "Geographical Movements," p. 6, more useful. Sklare's model (based on research done in the Chicago area) sees Conservatism thriving only in the so-called third area of American Jewish settlement: affluent suburbia, following settlement in the inner-city slum and the middle-class adjacent areas. This model is clearly not applicable to Philadelphia: first, because one would be hard pressed to find many features common to Wynnefield, Germantown, and Elkins Park; and second, all three of the synagogues here studied (though to varying degrees) thrived within a densely populated Jewish area, or in a second area of settlement. Tabak's model emphasizes the transition in function and organization and makes demographics a secondary factor in characterizing a synagogue. Thus, in terms of historical development, first comes the "corner synagogue," serving a purely worship function; then a "neighborhood synagogue," serving wider social and communal functions, but to a constituency in the same neighborhood; and finally, a "community synagogue," serving the dispersed, low-density suburbs, but meeting the needs of affiliation and social cohesion.

17. Robert Tabak, "Orthodox Jewry in Transition: Philadelphia, 1920–1940" (Philadelphia: American Jewish Committee, 1982), manuscript, p. 23.

18. This observation was made by David Wice, rabbi of Rodeph Shalom from 1947 to the present (interviewed October 1982).

19. *Reform Congregation Keneseth Israel: Its First 100 Years, 1847–1947* (Philadelphia: 1950), pp. 45–51.

20. Samuel Klausner and David Varady, Synagogues Without Ghettos (Philadelphia: Center for Research on the Acts of Man, University of Pennsylvania, 1970). Sam Klausner phone interview, December 30, 1982.

21. Ibid., p. 197.

22. Ibid., pp. 94–98.

23. Ibid., p. 159.

24. Morris Goodblatt, "Synagogue Ritual Survey," Proceedings of the Rabbinical Assembly, 1948, p. 108.

25. See Riv-Ellen Prell, "The Dilemma of Women's Equality in the History of Reform Judaism," *Judaism,* vol. 30, no. 4, Fall 1981, pp. 418–426.

26. Committee of Jewish Law and Standards, Minutes, February 21, 1949. RA Law Archives (JTS, New York).

27. Aaron Blumenthal, "An Aliyah for Women," Proceedings of the Rabbinical Assembly, 1955, pp. 168–181.

28. Aaron Blumenthal, "Hilchot Ishut Questionnaire," November, 1967, RA Law Archives (JTS, New York).

29. D. Elazar and R. Monson, "Women in the Synagogue Today," *Midstream,* vol. 27, no. 4, April 1981, p. 25.

30. Committee of Jewish Law and Standards minutes, October 29, 1973. RA Law Archives (JTS, New York).

31. Interview with Dr. William Lakritz, Gratz College, May 21, 1982. See the article on Jewish education in this volume for more extensive treatment.

32. Interview with Burton Shanker, Director of Philadelphia Region United Synagogue, December 1982.

33. Sklare, *Conservative Judaism*, p. 274.

Chapter 10 A GENERATION OF LEARNING

1. For prior background, see Diane A. King, "Jewish Education in Philadelphia," in Murray Friedman, ed., *Jewish Life in Philadelphia* (Philadelphia: ISHI, 1983), pp. 235–252.

2. *Report of the Committee of Fifteen on Jewish Education,* November 4, 1926, published in the *Jewish Exponent,* April 29, 1927.

3. For one view, see Simon Greenberg, "The Prayerbook in Elementary Jewish School Curriculum," *Jewish Education,* January-March, 1938, pp. 28–34. For other views, see "The Jewish Community School," *Jewish Education,* vol. 35, no. 2 (Winter 1965), pp. 67–95. For a description of the various school systems, see King, "Jewish Education in Philadelphia," p. 244ff. Also see note 8 here.

4. See Marshall Sklare, *Conservative Judaism,* Rev. Ed. (New York: Schocken, 1972), particularly chapter 3.

5. See Will Herberg, *Protestant-Catholic-Jew* (Garden City, NY: Doubleday, 1955), p. 200ff.

6. See Nathaniel A. Entin, "The Founding of the Jewish Education Committee," in *Gratz College Annual of Jewish Studies,* vol. V, Isidore David Passow and Samuel T. Lachs, eds. (Philadelphia: Gratz College, 1976), pp. 93–110, especially p. 96f and citations listed there.

7. Ben Rosen, "Jewish Education in Philadelphia—1936," in *Jewish Education,* vol. 9, no. 2 (April-June 1937), p. 66. The entire article is a goldmine of information on the character of Jewish education in Philadelphia at that time.

8. Solomon Grayzel, "Reflections," in the Philadelphia Board of Jewish Education of the Philadelphia Branch of the United Synagogue of America *Program Book for Chassidic Song Festival of 1977,* p. 37.

9. International Workers' Order (or "Shalom Aleikhem") Schools were excluded from the Council because of their overtly Marxist, antireligious orientation.

10. Abraham P. Cannes, "The Philadelphia Council on Jewish Education," *Jewish Education,* vol. 35, no. 2 (Winter, 1960), p. 19f.

11. It was at this time that the Federation of Jewish Agencies was created out of a merger between the Allied Jewish Appeal and the Federation of Jewish Charities.

12. Cannes, "The Philadelphia Council on Jewish Education," p. 27f.

13. In 1953, the board of directors consisted of thirty-six members. In 1951, congregational school population was 10,500 (and rising), while that of communal schools was about 3,500 (and declining). At the ratio of one voice to four hundred pupils, the representatives of the former had twenty-seven votes and those of the latter, only eight.

14. Interview with Ezekiel Pearlman, July 27, 1983.

15. The last of these was named in memory of William and Elsie Chomsky, famed educators who had taught at the College for many years.

16. Throughout the continent, it was standard for a bureau in a large or middle-size city to assign at least one consultant to work with these schools and their special needs. A small grant for these purposes was given to DCS in 1983.

17. For the earlier history of the College, see King, "Jewish Education in Philadelphia," pp. 245, 338n.71; Diane A. King, "A History of Gratz College, 1893–1928" (Ph.D. Thesis, Dropsie University, Philadelphia, 1979). Also, Mitchell E. Panzer, "Gratz College," in Isadore David Passow and Samuel Tobias Lachs, eds., *Gratz College Anniversary Volume* (Philadelphia: Gratz College, 1971), pp. 1–14.

18. Leo L. Honor and Morris Leibman, *Jewish Education in Philadelphia: A Survey* (Philadelphia: 1943). p. 20ff.

19. In 1951, Dr. William Chomsky, distinguished scholar educator and a member of the Gratz College faculty, was appointed Chairman of the Faculty, in which capacity he served until retirement in 1969. Day-to-day administration was carried out by Itzhak Sankowsky from 1945 to 1951, and by Dr. Daniel Isaacman from 1951 to 1973, when he succeeded Dr. Goelman as president of the College.

20. The initial occupant of the chair was Dr. Saul. P. Wachs, an alumnus of the College.

21. Dr. Schiff assumed the presidency in August 1983, following by a year the untimely death of Dr. Daniel Isaacman. For that year, Dr. E. Goelman was called from Israel to serve as acting president.

22. See *Jewish Life in Philadelphia 1830–1940,* Murray Friedman, ed., chapter 10.

23. Interview with Dr. David H. Wice, October 1983.

24. Several Reform rabbis did play active roles in supporting the college. See Mitchell E. Panzer, "Gratz College," p. 13.

25. Don Dorfman and Daniel C. Cohen were presidents of the BJE and Gratz College, respectively.

26. Beginning with an enrollment of one hundred students in 1959, the BJE system at its peak in 1967–1968 taught 885 students. In 1982–1983 that figure had fallen to 352 students.

27. For the early history of Orthodoxy in Philadelphia, see Murray Friedman, ed., *Jewish Life in Philadelphia 1830–1940,* chapter 3.

28. Modern Orthodox Jews combined university education and a basic validation of secular culture with commitment to Halakhah. Sectarian or right-wing Orthodox Jews minimized their contacts with the non-halakhic world, frequently eschewing a collegiate education and tending to live in self-segregated enclaves. This latter group included hasidim and graduates of many American yeshivot, Yeshiva University and the Hebrew Theological College of Chicago being noteworthy exceptions.

29. In many cities, such congregations were called "Traditional" rather than Orthodox.

30. In 1851, the Hebrew Education Society opened a day school in Philadelphia, which it operated for almost thirty years. No new schools were started until 1946.

31. Alvin I. Schiff, *The Jewish Day School in America* (New York: Jewish Education Press, 1966), p. 48.

32. Alvin I. Schiff, "Jewish Day Schools in North America," *Pedagogic Reporter,* vol. 29, no. 1 (Fall 1977), p. 2.

33. Ibid. By the end of the period under study, there were more than sixty Conservative day schools in North America. The Solomon Schechter Day School Association was organized in 1964. Two area rabbis who contributed greatly to the day school movement from its inception were Rabbi Pinchos J. Chazin of Temple Shalom, who worked tirelessly on behalf of the Schechter School; and Rabbi Elias Charry, who was a moving force in the founding of Akiba.

34. Ten Reform day schools had opened by 1985. In 1969, the Commission on Jewish Education of the UAHC had passed a resolution supporting Day Schools as "an attractive option." See Daniel B. Syme, "The Reform Day School: Its History and Future Prospects," *Pedagogic Reporter,* vol. 29, no. 1 (Fall 1977), p. 15. Also, Michael Zeldin, "No Longer Waiting in the Wings: Reform Jewish Day Schools Poised to Take Off," *Reform Judaism* (Spring 1986). It is noteworthy that one of the earliest advocates of day-school education in the United States was Isaac Mayer Wise, who founded such a school in Cincinnati in 1849.

35. See Judah Pilch, "From the Early Forties to the Mid-Sixties," in Judah Pilch, ed., *The History of Jewish Education in the United States* (New York: American Association for Jewish Education, 1969), p. 140f.

36. See, for example, Jack J. Cohen, "New Trends in Jewish Education," in Judah Pilch, ed., *The History of Jewish Education in the United States,* p. 210f; and Marvin Fox, "The Case of the Day School," in Judah Pilch and Meir Ben Horin, eds., *Judaism and the Jewish School* (New York: American Association for Jewish Education, 1966), p. 209f.

37. Forman's relationships to Beth Shalom were very close. Rabbi Aaron Landes was instrumental in establishing the school, and he, Cantor Tilman, and other staff members contributed time to the school. But Forman was open to the community and had its own board of directors.

38. Interview with Rabbi David Goldstein, May 25, 1983.

39. Har Zion's contributions to Jewish life were of unusual magnitude. Aside from the large number of rabbis, educators, professors of Jewish studies, and communal leaders who were educated there, the congregation took the lead in establishing Akiba, Schechter, Camp Ramah in the Poconos, and many other educational ventures that strengthened the community. For some years, the congregation maintained a special fund to provide scholarships for young people from other congregations who needed financial aid to attend Camp Ramah. Rabbi Goldstein's leadership in education was recognized through the granting of honorary degrees by Gratz College and Dropsie College. The congregation also was blessed with highly professional leadership of its religious schools, a tradition begun by its founding rabbi, Simon Greenberg, and his successors, Rabbis Goldstein and Wolpe, and such educational directors as Oscar Davinsky, Hyman Pomerantz, Elazar Goelman, Samuel Sussman, and (current) Sara Cohen.

40. Letters of Martin Feld, Philadelphia Jewish Archives. Feld's commitment was limitless. Akiba lore includes a story in which he met with a representative of the IRS to discuss some problems facing the school and emerged from the meeting with a pledge.

41. The former committee was headed by Leon Sunstein, the latter by Edward N. Polisher. *See Report of the Sub-Committee of the Committee on Jewish Education,* AJA, January 11, 1949.

42. "The Jewish Day School: An Exchange of Correspondence," *Jewish Exponent,* November 8 and November 15, 1946 (reprint).

43. Ibid., p. 6.

44. Alexander M. Dushkin and Uriah Z. Engelman, "Jewish Education in the United States," in *Report of the Commission for the Study of Jewish Education in the United States,* Vol. I (New York: American Association for Jewish Education, 1959), p. 28ff.

45. The committee also included Rabbi Max D. Klein of Congregation Adath Jeshurun, Rabbi David H. Wice of Congregation Rodeph Shalom, Rabbi Bertram W. Korn of Reform Congregation Keneseth Israel, Nathan I. Miller, and Edward N. Polisher. The staff person assigned to this key committee was Ezekiel

Pearlman, a newcomer to the city, who was to play a major role in mediating the Federation's relationships with the Jewish educational institutions of the community.

46. Rabbi Wice explained his view as based on a concern that the proliferation of private schools would, ultimately, contribute to the destruction of the public school system. In addition, he was concerned that an inability of the Jewish community to maintain day schools would lead, ultimately, to a quest for public funds and a break in the wall between church and state. Interview with Rabbi David H. Wice, October 6, 1983.

47. Report of the AJA Board Committee on Akiba Academy, April 23, 1953.

48. Gail Gaisin Glicksman has suggested that Akiba was the "least attractive" type of Jewish private school that could have been designed to meet the approval of the community leadership of the time. It was presented as elitist (and therefore not intended to attract large numbers of students away from the public school), progressive, communal (not parochial), and designed to prepare a cadre of leaders for the Jewish community of the future. Moreover, a possible link to Gratz College (whereby Akiba would serve as a laboratory school for the training of Jewish teachers studying at the college) was projected. See Gail Gaisin Glicksman, "Making the Day School Palatable to American Jewish Taste: A Case Study in Decision Making," paper presented to the Eastern Sociological Society and the Association for the Sociological Study of Jewry, March 6, 1983 (unpublished), p. 10. The authors express appreciation to Ms. Glicksman for having furnished useful materials on the topic. While not dismissing any of these factors, a number of those interviewed who participated in or had knowledge of the process stressed the fact that many of the advocates of Akiba (e.g., Sol Satinsky, Judge Louis Levinthal, Joseph Kohn) were highly respected communal leaders—members of the "Our Crowd" of AJA. Their support was deemed crucial to winning over the AJA leadership to provide community funding for the new school.

49. See Minutes, Inclusions Committee, AJA, February 22, 1955. On a comparison of Beth Jacob and Akiba, see Glicksman's study, p. 10. The comparison is based on Glicksman's categories.

50. Interview with Ezekiel Pearlman, October 11, 1982.

51. His father, Morris Wolf, a founder of what was to become the largest Jewish law firm in the city, was a member of the American Council for Judaism. Other members of the family shared the same view of Jewish life. Founding president of AJA, the father offered to pay ACJ dues for the son while the latter was in the U.S. Army, an offer that was firmly refused! Interview with Edwin Wolf II, October 4, 1983.

52. In addition to Wolf, the other members of the committee who actually participated were Albert M. Bershad, Maurice G. Cohn, Bernard L. Frankel, Joseph Kohn, A. Leo Levin, Frank L. Newberger, and Morris Satinsky. All views were represented in this group. One key member was A. Leo Levin, perhaps the first actively Orthodox leader to reach the higher levels of Federation leadership. A national figure of great stature in the legal profession, his active involvement in the work of Beth Jacob helped win support for that school. Three others served on the committee but did not attend meetings. (Memo from Ezekiel Pearlman to Donald B. Hurwitz, June 23, 1958, FJA Archives.)

53. Ibid.

54. The vote in the original committee was 6 to 3 in favor of the resolution. In the standing committee, it was 23 to 3 favoring the resolution. Donalad B. Hurwitz, Memorandum to the Board of Trustees, FJA, May 19, 1958.

55. This revision represented a continuation of the policy that had been in force since the earliest funding of Akiba by AJA. During the earliest stage of (indirect) funding, the amount of money given by AJA to the United Hebrew Schools and yeshivos and then "passed through" to Akiba, was based on the number of hours in the Akiba program devoted to Jewish studies. According to Ezekiel Pearlman, Judge Freedman was the guiding force behind the revision.

56. Interview with Edwin Wolf II, October 4, 1983.

57. Interview with Rabbi David Goldstein, May 25, 1983. Unfortunately, these comments were unrecorded in the minutes.

58. Minutes of the Board of Trustees, FJA, June 26, 1958, p. 6, FJA Archives.

59. Bernard Frankel, *Minority Report of the Committee on All Day Schools,* submitted January 9, 1958.

60. After the vote, Edwin Wolf called for a rescinding of the revised resolution in favor of the original one. This was defeated by the close margin of 28 in favor to 31 opposed.

61. Cf. Alvin I. Schiff, *The Jewish Day School in America,* p. 223f.

62. The next step was to develop criteria for the inclusion of day schools. These related to the communal character of the institution, acceptable standards of administrative and fiscal controls, housing, tuition, educational quality, and governance. See "Criteria on Standards for All Day Schools," Jewish Education Committee and Committee on Planning and Budgeting, FJA, April 22, 1959.

63. *Philadelphia Self-Study of Jewish Education* (Philadelphia: Council on Jewish Education, 1951), pp. 34–37, 145–159.

64. The school insisted that it have the right to approve or disapprove the choices of those who would partic-

ipate in the professional aspects of the evaluation. For a summary of FJA's view of the controversy, see "Federation of Jewish Agencies Study Committee on All Day Schools, Chronology and Summary of Beth Jacob's Activities," May 1964. The committee was chaired by Mitchell E. Panzer.

65. This policy, which limited support of national cultural and religious groups to the Jewish Publication Society, Dropsie College, the Synagogue Council of America, and the Jewish Educational Service of North America (formerly known as the American Association for Jewish Education), was longstanding. See, for example, Minutes of the Inclusions Committee, FJA, December 3, 1970. The policy was set aside in 1983.

66. FJA *Report of the Committee on Educational Priorities,* June, 1973, p. 9.

67. Ibid. Attempts to start a Reform day school in Philadelphia in the early 1970s yielded a proposal, but the idea, spearheaded by Jacob (Jack) Rockower, Milton Creamer, and Albert Farber aroused little enthusiasm and more apathy and opposition. See Gabriel Cohen, *A Proposal for the Establishment of "a New Day School" by the Union of American Hebrew Congregations of Greater Philadelphia,* 1972 (mimeographed). According to Ezekiel Pearlman, prominent lay and rabbinic leaders in the community opposed the concept (interview, October 1982). In 1984, the Greater Philadelphia Region of the Central Conference of American Rabbis voted "by an over-whelming majority . . . in favour of the creation of a Reform Jewish Day School in the Philadelphia Area." *Jewish Exponent,* September 7, 1984.

68. FJA *Report of the Committee on Educational Priorities,* June, 1973, p. 9.

69. Given the heterogeneity of non-Orthodox school populations and the fact that parents felt very much "at home" in the schools, there was an almost limitless supply of issues and problems that might stir up a controversy. Thus, the question of what place, if any, worship and the study of synagogue skills should have at Akiba created considerable dispute involving parents, students, faculty, and Boards of Education and Trustees members at the end of the period under study. In another area, discontent among faculty with working conditions at the school led to the formation of a faculty association that later affiliated with the American Federation of Teachers. Akiba suffered three strikes between 1975 and 1980. Schechter teachers also affiliated with AFT, increasing the possibility of a strike.

70. One of the great contributions of day schools was their ability to attract some of the most talented and professional teachers and administrators in the field of Jewish education. At the end of the period under study, Philadelphia and its suburbs were blessed with several outstanding educators serving as educational heads and teachers in its day schools.

71. See Daniel J. Elazar and Rela Geffen Monson, "The Synagogue Havurah—An Experiment in Restoring Adult Fellowship to the Jewish Community," *Jewish Journal of Sociology,* vol. 21, no. 1 (June 1979). On the history of the Havurah, see Jacob Neusner, *Contemporary Judaic Fellowship in Theory and Practice* (New York: KTAV Publishing, 1972). For a thorough analysis of the Havurah movement, see Bernard Reisman, *The Chavurah: A Contemporary Jewish Experience* (New York: Union of American Hebrew Congregations, 1977). For a more recent study of Synagogue-based Havurot, see Gerald B. Bubis, Harry Wasserman, and Alan Lert, *Synagogue Havurot* (Washington, DC: The Centre for Jewish Community Studies and Hebrew Union College–Jewish Institute of Religion, 1981).

72. Interview with Elliot Karp, October 1984. According to Karp, for many of the singles, this group was a "synagogue."

73. For more information on this, see Saul P. Wachs, *The Jewish Teacher* (New York: American Jewish Committee, 1984). This reasoning was spurious to a large extent. Conservative congregations in Minneapolis and Detroit, to use two examples, were highly successful without direct control over schools. Their effectiveness and attractiveness were based on worship services, youth groups, adult education programs, social action efforts, and other activities.

74. The authors wish to express their appreciation to all of those who were interviewed, and to Richard Siper, Burt Kaplan, and Dr. Ernest Kahn of the staff of the Federation of Jewish Agencies, the staff of the Philadelphia Jewish Archives, and Anna Glassman for their help in making available materials that were utilized in the preparation of this chapter.

Chapter 11 THE JEWISH FEDERATION OF GREATER PHILADELPHIA

1. From the official, signed copy of the Articles of Incorporation hanging in the offices of the Jewish Federation of Greater Philadelphia.

2. Jewish Federation of Greater Philadelphia, Business Vision 2000 Implementation Report and Recommendations, June 15, 1999, 1 Tammuz 5759, p. 19.

3. Ibid., pp. 15–24.

4. Federation of Jewish Agencies of Greater Philadelphia, Report of the Strategic Planning Committee, July 30, 1990, p. vii.

5. Federation of Jewish Agencies of Greater Philadelphia, Minutes of the Meeting of the Cabinet, September 8, 1977.

6. Conversation with Joy Goldstein, Director of Planning and Allocations, Jewish Federation of Greater Philadelphia, January 15, 2002.

7. Federation of Jewish Agencies of Greater Philadelphia Population Study Committee, "The Jewish Population of the Greater Philadelphia Area," by William L. Yancey and Ira Goldstein, Institute for Public Policy Studies, Social Science Data Library, Temple University, November 15, 1984; and Jewish Federation of Greater Philadelphia, Jewish Population Study of Greater Philadelphia 1996–1997, Summary Report by Ukeles Associates, Inc.

8. Federation of Jewish Agencies of Greater Philadelphia, Report of the Strategic Planning Committee, July 30, 1990, p. 50. In addition, the minutes of the Executive Committee of the Federation are replete with the expression of similar concerns.

9. Ibid., p. 69.

10. Conversation between the author and Alan Casnoff, Philadelphia, August 22, 2001.

11. Jewish Federation of Greater Philadelphia, Business Vision 2000 Implementation, Report and Recommendations, p. 28.

12. Graham Finney, "The Final Report of the Managing Change (Devolution) Project of the 21st Century League" (Philadelphia: The 21st Century League, April 1999), p. iii.

Chapter 12 FROM A TO "ZINK"

1. James Yaffe, *The American Jews* (New York, 1968), p. 67.

2. Ted Vincent, *Mudville's Revenge* (New York, 1981), pp. 225–239.

3. *Jewish Exponent,* June 25, 1982, pp. 48–49.

4. Interviews with Dave Dabrow, May and June 1984, and written history of Jewish Basketball League provided by Dabrow.

5. *Jewish Exponent,* February 12, 1960, p. 43.

6. Interview with Joe Goldenberg, May 10, 1984.

7. Vincent, *Mudville's Revenge,* p. 253.

8. *Jewish Exponent,* June 25, 1982.

9. Frank Dolson, *The Philadelphia Story* (South Bend, IN, 1981), p. 31.

10. Ibid., p. 35.

11. Roster of Eastern Basketball League 1947, in the *Philadelphia Inquirer* Library.

12. *Inquirer,* November 30, 1948.

13. Dolson, *The Philadelphia Story,* p. 95.

14. S. Kirson Weinberg and Henry Arond, "The Occupational Culture of the Boxer," *American Journal of Sociology* (March 1952), p. 460.

15. *Jewish Exponent,* January 8, 1982, pp. 44–45.

16. *The Encyclopedia of Sports,* by Frank G. Menke, shows Bass with a career total of 197 fights.

17. Harold Ribalow, *The Jew in American Sport* (New York, 1965), pp. 136–140.

18. *Inquirer,* October 29, 1932, and author's interview with Charles Micklin, a friend of Benny Bass.

19. *New York Times,* November 7, 1976; Jewish Exponent, January 8, 1982.

20. Philadelphia *Daily News,* April 17, 1967.

21. *Inquirer, Today Magazine,* May 7, 1978.

22. Author's interview with Harry Shuman, July 13, 1984.

23. Interview with Henry Fogel, May 26, 1984.

24. *Inquirer Sunday Magazine,* December 13, 1953.

25. *Jewish Exponent,* July 29, 1955.

26. Richard Siegel and Carl Rheins, *The Jewish Almanac* (New York, 1980), p. 80.

27. *Inquirer,* July 23, 1959.

28. Siegel and Rheins, *The Jewish Almanac,* p. 74.

29. *Inquirer,* April 26, 1942.

30. *Inquirer,* March 22, 1936.

31. *Inquirer,* November 23, 1950.

32. Robert Slater, *Great Jews in Sport* (Middle Village, NY, 1983).

33. Philadelphia *Bulletin,* August 25, 1981.

34. Siegel and Rheins, *The Jewish Almanac,* pp. 84–88.

35. Philadelphia *Evening Ledger,* October 17, 1941.

36. Philadelphia *Bulletin,* December 10, 1957.

37. *Inquirer,* August 14, 1960.
38. Author's interview with David Mayor, June 27, 1984.
39. *Jewish Exponent,* October 2, 1964.
40. Author's interview with Irving Mondschein, June 12, 1984.
41. Philadelphia *Daily News,* October 23, 1968.
42. Author's interview with Hillel Levinson, July 6, 1984.
43. Philadelphia *Bulletin,* February 17, 1968.
44. *Inquirer,* March 14, 1969.
45. *Philadelphia* magazine, November 1972, "The Loneliness of the Short-Distance Trucker."
46. Information concerning owners and Jewish athletes was provided by Hal Freeman, a former sportswriter and former associate of Jerry Wolman; Sy Roseman, sportswriter and public relations; and William Steelman, long-time Philadelphia official with U.S. Committee Sports for Israel.

Chapter 13 JEWS AND THE CULTURAL REVIVAL OF PHILADELPHIA

1. John E. Cooney, *The Annenbergs* (New York: Simon & Schuster, 1982); Gaeton Fonzi, *Annenberg: A Biography of Power* (New York: Weybright & Talley, 1970).
2. Source requested anonymity.
3. Daniel Webster, "An Impression Adapts to Change," *Philadelphia Inquirer,* October 30, 1983.
4. Samuel Lipman, "Out of the Ghetto," *Commentary,* March 1985.
5. Stephen Fried, "The Music Mann at 80," *Philadelphia,* July 1983; Michael Elkin, "The Music Mann of Philadelphia," *Jewish Exponent,* June 15, 1984; Leonard Boasberg, "The Mann Who's Behind the Music," *Philadelphia Inquirer,* June 17, 1984.
6. Julia Klein, "Unsettled Times at Settlement Music School," *Philadelphia Inquirer Magazine,* December 12, 1982.
7. Daniel Webster, "Ballet Halts, and All Sides Ask What's Wrong," *Philadelphia Inquirer,* January 17, 1982; "Founder of Ballet Reigns as Director," *Philadelphia Inquirer,* February 27, 1982; "Is the Ballet in Danger of Becoming a Minor Ensemble?" *Philadelphia Inquirer,* March 15, 1982. Valerie Scher, "Back on Its Toes, Ballet Struggles," *Philadelphia Inquirer,* May 30, 1982. "Barbara Weisberger Tells Her Side of the Story," *Philadelphia Inquirer,* July 25, 1982. Anna Kisselgoff, "A Cosby and Nureyev Gala," *New York Times,* June 8, 1984.
8. Ernest L. Schier, "Inside Look at 'New' Old Walnut," Philadelphia *Bulletin,* February 11, 1971; Harold J. Weigand, "Phil Klein Plans 'New' Old Walnut," *Philadelphia Inquirer,* March 3, 1971; Daniel Webster, "Beset by Delays, Walnut Theater Hurries to Meet Fall Opening Date," *Philadelphia Inquirer,* March 7, 1971.
9. Marc Duvoisin, "The Light Behind People's Light," *Philadelphia Inquirer Magazine,* March 31, 1985.
10. Cooney, *The Annenbergs,* pp. 282, 370, 371.
11. Edgar Williams, "Gil Guben, Prominent in Restaurant Revival," *Philadelphia Inquirer* December 7, 1978.
12. Marilyn Lois Polak, "Steve Poses: He Catered to the Kennedys," *Philadelphia Inquirer Magazine,* March 25, 1977; Douglas Campbell, "Proven Recipe," *Philadelphia Inquirer,* February 25, 1980; Steven X. Rea, "The Succulent World of Steven Poses," *Philadelphia Inquirer Magazine,* November 11, 1984.
13. Marilyn Lois Polak, "Interview: Larry Magid," *Philadelphia Inquirer Magazine,* December 12, 1976.
14. Rod Nordland, "Isaac D. Levy, 85, Radio Pioneer. . . ." *Philadelphia Inquirer,* November 30, 1975.
15. Harry M. Gould, Jr., "The Power and the Juice," *Philadelphia Inquirer Magazine,* August 14, 1983; Hank Klibanoff, "A 'Scary' Chapter in WDAS's Past," *Philadelphia Inquirer Magazine,* August 14, 1983; Burr Van Atta, "Max M. Leon, 80, Businessman, Civic and Cultural Leader," *Philadelphia Inquirer,* 1984.
16. Cooney, *The Annenbergs,* pp. 204–206.
17. "Battling Bill Goldman," *Greater Philadelphia Magazine,* February 1960.
18. Joe Baltake, "The Doylestown Dream," *Daily News,* October 29, 1974.
19. Richard A. Sabatini, "Samuel Shapiro . . . Founder of Sameric Theater Chain," *Philadelphia Inquirer,* May 20, 1977.
20. Robin L. Palley, "A Miser of Old Buildings," *Daily News,* June 15, 1984.
21. Thomas Hine, "Yesterday's Guru of Building Design," *Philadelphia Inquirer,* March 11, 1984; "Philadelphia's Best Buildings," *Philadelphia Inquirer Magazine,* December 9, 1984.
22. Marilyn Lois Polak, "Interview: Marian Locks," *Philadelphia Inquirer Magazine,* September 7, 1974.
23. Maryanne Conheim, "She's the Catalyst for the Art of Crafts," *Philadelphia Inquirer,* October 13, 1978; Sharon Sexton. "The Frenetic Queen of Crafts," *Philadelphia Inquirer Magazine,* November 25, 1984.
24. Cooney, *The Annenbergs,* pp. 266–268.
25. Douglas Keating, "Jewish Museum Is a First in Many Ways," *Philadelphia Inquirer,* July 9, 1976.

26. Maryanne Conheim, "He Gets Things Done by Keeping the Money Coming," *Philadelphia Inquirer,* May 25, 1978.

27. Gloria Hayes Kremer, "Fathers and Daughters in Business Together," *Philadelphia Inquirer,* November 28, 1982.

28. Marilyn Lois Polak, "David Schlessinger, the Pinballing Bookseller," *Philadelphia Inquirer Magazine,* July 10, 1983; Peter F. Binzen, "High Volume—A New Idea Succeeds," *Philadelphia Inquirer,* December 7, 1982.

29. Diane Levenberg, "Jewish Publication Society," *Inside Magazine,* Winter 1984.

30. Cooney, *The Annenbergs,* pp. 234–239.

31. D. Herbert Lipson, "Off the Cuff," *Philadelphia* magazine, September, 1984.

32. Other sources for this essay are Murray Friedman, "Religion and Politics in an Age of Pluralism . . . ," *Publius;* David Brenner, *Soft Pretzels with Mustard* (New York: Arbor House, 1983); Marilyn Lois Polak, "He Can Take a Joke," *Philadelphia Inquirer Magazine,* July 31, 1983; Daniel Webster, "Orchestra Executive Director Quits," *Philadelphia Inquirer,* February 20, 1982; Jack Lloyd, "In Picking Hits, He's a Superstar," *Philadelphia Inquirer,* January 29, 1980; Steven Salisbury, "A Gallery for Today in a Bastion of Art," *Philadelphia Inquirer,* March 25, 1984. The author acknowledges the kind cooperation and contributions of Fredric R. Mann, Moe Septee, Larry Magid, Nessa R. Forman, Edwin A. Wolf II, Sam Bushman, Morris Yuter, Dr. Charles Lee, Judith Karp, Barbara Weisberger, Abe Rosen, Joseph Carlin, William Collins, and Daniel C. Webster.

About the Contributors

RON AVERY, a native Philadelphian and graduate of Penn State University, has been a newspaper reporter for many years and served as the New Jersey reporter for the Philadelphia *Daily News.*

E. DIGBY BALTZELL, deceased, was among the nation's most honored sociologists. As a member of the faculty of the University of Pennsylvania, he set the standard for his discipline during over three decades of teaching and through such landmark works as *Puritan Boston and Quaker Philadelphia* (1979); *The Protestant Establishment* (1964), and *Philadelphia Gentlemen* (1958).

CAROLYN BECK received her Ph.D. from Bryn Mawr College. She has been project director of the Self-Study of Mother Bethel's Museum Program, funded by the William Penn Foundation, and consultant to the Mother Bethel's Preservation and Restoration Project.

PETER BINZEN has been a distinguished reporter, columnist, and editor in Philadelphia for more than fifty years. He is author of *Whitetown U.S.A.* (1970) and co-author of *The Wreck of the Penn Central* (1976) and *The Cop Who Would Be King* (1977).

DENNIS CLARK, deceased, received his Ph.D. from Temple University and authored many books on Philadelphia's Irish community, urban development, and race relations, including *The Irish in Philadelphia: Ten Generations of Urban Experience* (Temple University Press, 1973). He was editor of *The Interracial Review* and contributed many articles on the ethnic history of Jews, blacks, and Irish immigration to journals and collections.

MURRAY FRIEDMAN, editor of this volume, served as Middle Atlantic States Director of the American Jewish Committee for more than forty years and directs the Myer and Rosaline Feinstein Center for American Jewish History at Temple University. He has contributed articles on human relations and Jewish life for many of the nation's outstanding periodicals; has authored several books on public issues, including *The Utopian Dilemma* (1985) and *What Went Wrong: The Creation and Collapse of the Black Jewish Alliance* (1995); and edited *Jewish Life in Philadelphia, 1830–1940* (1983). In September 1986, Dr. Friedman was appointed vice chairman of the U.S. Commission on Civil Rights by President Ronald Reagan and served for three years.

DAVID GROSS is a former reporter for the Philadelphia *Jewish Exponent.* In July 1985 he made *aliyah* and now lives in Jerusalem.

ANDREW HARRISON, PH.D., received a B.A. in history from The George Washington University in 1988. He graduated Magna Cum Laude from that school and was admitted into its Phi Beta Kappa chapter. Following undergraduate school, Harrison attended Temple University, where he received a Ph.D. in history. Currently, he works as the archivist for the Robert Wood Johnson Foundation and teaches as an adjunct professor at Philadelphia University and Community College of Philadelphia. Harrison has published a book on the Philadelphia Soviet Jewry movement entitled *Passover Revisited* and has written a number of articles on Philadlphiia's Jewish community.

DON HARRISON is currently the editor of *Milestones,* published by the Philadelphia Corporation for Aging, and senior editor of *Real Philly* magazine. He retired from the Philadelphia *Daily News* after nineteen years as deputy editor of the Opinion pages. His career in journalism has included nineteen years on the Philadelphia *Bulletin* editorial staff; ten years as managing editor of the *News of Delaware Country;* and a tenure as city editor of the Philadelphia *Jewish Times.*

ERNEST M. KAHN, PH.D., is the retired associate executive of the Jewish Federation of Greater Philadelphia. He served the Federation in various positions, including several periods as its acting executive vice president. He has also held positions as assistant dean and associate professor at the University of Maryland School of Social Work and in Jewish Community Centers, Hillel, and Jewish education. Since retirement, he has been the interim president of Gratz College and a consultant to several national agencies. He is currently a member of the faculty of the Reconstructionist Rabbinical College and of the boards and committees of several national and local agencies.

DIANE A. KING received her Ph.D. in education and history from Dropsie University and her Teachers Diploma from Gratz College. For many years, she was a master teacher at Germantown Jewish Centre Religious School and taught at Gratz College. She has co-authored original teaching materials produced under the auspices of the Gratz College Division of Community Services and the Board of Jewish Education in Philadelphia.

THOMAS A. KOLSKY, a native of Buzuluk, Russia, attended Rutgers University, the University of Hawaii, the University of Pennsylvania, and George Washington University. He is author of *Jews against Zionism: The American Council for Judaism 1942–1948* (Temple University Press, 1990). He is currently professor of history and political science at Montgomery County Community College in Blue Bell, Pennsylvania.

WILLIAM B. LAKRITZ, deceased, held a Ph.D. in Jewish education from Dropsie College. His distinguished career in Jewish education included twenty years as educational director of the Board of Jewish Education, Philadelphia Branch, United Synagogue of America; many published articles, academic positions, and professional affiliations; and the 1971 Philadelphia Board of Jewish Education Award.

NORA LEVIN, deceased, was associate professor of Jewish history at Gratz College and founder and director of the Gratz College Holocaust Archive. Among her outstanding works are *Jewish Socialist Movements: 1871–1917* (1978) and *The Jews in the Soviet Union Since 1917*, 2 vols. (1987).

PAUL LYONS teaches history at Stockton College in New Jersey. He is the author of *Philadelphia Communists, 1936–1956; Class of '66; New Left, New Right, and the Legacy of the Sixties* (all at Temple University Press); and *A History of the Movement in Philadelphia, the New Left and the 1960's*.

PHILIP ROSEN received a doctorate in immigrant and ethnic studies from Carnegie Mellon University. He is the author of *The Neglected Dimension* (1979) and has taught in the Philadelphia school system.

DAN ROTTENBERG is editor of *Family Business* magazine and the author of eight books, most recently *The Man Who Made Wall Street* (2002). He has been executive editor of *Philadelphia* magazine, a columnist for the *Philadelphia Inquirer,* a contributing editor to *Town & Country,* and editor of three Philadelphia publications: the *Welcomat, Seven Arts* magazine, and the *Philadelphia Forum.*

SIDNEY H. SCHWARTZ is the founder/president of PANIM: The Institute for Jewish Leadership and Values. A trained Reconstructionist rabbi, he is the author of *Finding a Spiritual Home: How a New Generation of Jews Can Transform the American Synagogue* (2000).

ROBERT TABAK received his M.A. in religion from Temple University, and has his Ph.D. in history from Temple. His dissertation is entitled, "The Transformation of Jewish Identity: The Philadelphia Experience, 1920–1945."

DAVID P. VARADY received his Ph.D. in city planning from the University of Pennsylvania and served as a member of the faculty of the School of Planning at the University of Cincinnati. He is the author of *Ethnic Minorities in Urban Areas* (1983) and *Neighborhood Upgrading: A Realistic Assessment* (1984), as well as numerous articles on neighborhood revitalization, housing for the elderly, and Jewish demography. Between 1980 and 1982, he was Visiting Scholar in the Community Conservation Research Division of the U.S. Department of Housing and Urban Development.

SAUL P. WACHS is Rosaline B. Feinstein Professor of Education and Liturgy and chair of education at Gratz College. A native of Philadelphia, he received a Ph.D. in education and Jewish history from Ohio State University. Among his many contributions to Jewish education have been his many years as teacher, principal, and educational director at various institutions across the country and as dean of Gratz College. He was the first recipient of the Aaron Zachs Award of the American Association of Jewish Education. He was also awarded an honorary doctorate by the Jewish Theological Seminary. He has lectured in over four hundred communities on five continents and has authored over seventy publications.

Index

Smukler, Joseph, 188
Snellenburg, Harry, Jr., 55
Snider, Ed, 205
Socialist party, 58–59. *See also* Left-wing politics
Social organizations
    admission of Jews into, xxxvi–xxxvii
    admission of women into, xxxvix, 80
    Jewish, xxxi–xxxii
Social services
    for Soviet Jews, 129–130, 129–131, 135–137, 180, 182
    for WW II refugees, 4–5, 17–18, 20–21, 23, 28–29
Society for the Advancement of Judaism, 228–229, 230
Society Hill, xxxv, xl
Society Hill Synagogue, 230
Solis-Cohen, D. Hays, xxx, xxxii–xxxiii, 172–173
Solis-Cohen, Leon, 61
Solomon, Morton, 116
Solomon Schechter School, 109, 110, 147, 169–170, 173–174, 175
Sonneborn Institute, 30, 31, 32, 33, 36
South Philadelphia, migration from, xv–xviii
South Philadelphia Hebrew Association basketball team, 191–194
Soviet Jewry Council, 136
Soviet Jews, xix, xli, 119, 127–141
    adjustment problems of, 129–130
    assimilation of, 137–138, 139–141
    assistance for, 129–131, 135–137, 139, 180, 182
    characteristics of, 127
    children's programs for, 138–139
    cities of origin of, 127
    community attitudes toward, 136–137, 139–140
    cultural programs for, 138–139
    culture shock among, 129–131, 138
    economic status of, 132, 134–135
    elderly, 129–131
    employment problems of, 133, 134–135
    family conflicts among, 131, 137
    financial problems of, 132, 134
    health problems of, 132–133
    Jewish identity of, 127–128, 134, 137–139, 140
    language problems of, 133
    March on Washington for, 187
    population of, 127
    self-help programs of, 135–136, 139
    status of, 128–129
Soviet Newcomers Organization, 135
Soviet Union
    aid to, 5–6
    immigrants from. *See* Soviet Jews
    Israel and, 68
Specter, Arlen, xvii, xxxix, 77–79
Specter, Joan, 79–80
Spivak, Allen, 217
Spivak, Herbert, 217
Sports, xxvi, xl, 191–205
    anti-Semitism in, 193, 197, 201
    assimilation and, 191
    athletes in, 197–204
    baseball, 198–200
    basketball, 191–195, 205

    boxing, 195–197, 201, 205
    fencing, 201
    football, 200–201, 205
    gymnastics, 203
    horse racing, 204, 205
    ice hockey, 204, 205
    Olympic, 201–203
    owners and promoters in, 204–205
    Ping-Pong, 203–204
    rowing, 202
    track and field, 202, 203
    weightlifting, 201–202
    yachting, 203
Sprafkin, Benjamin, 130
Stanley-Warner, 219
Starr, Susan, 211
Stein, Fred, 117
Stein, Louis, 86
Stelmakh, Menasha, 135–136
Stern, Horace, xxv, xxxiii, 29
Stern, I. Jerome, xxxix, 187–188
Stern, J. David, xxviii, 12, 24, 74, 225
Strauss, Lewis L., 40
Street, John, xix
Struma, 12
Suburban Jewish Folkshul, relocation of, 110
Suburban migration, xv–xvi, xxix, xxxvii–xxxviii, xli
    Federation of Jewish Agencies and, 180
    from Germantown, 148
    from Northeast, xvi, 124–125. *See also* Northeast Philadelphia
    political power and, 80–81
    racial factors in, xxxvii–xxxviii, 80. *See also* White flight
    synagogue relocation and, xxix, xxx, xxxvii, 106–109, 145–146, 147, 149
    from Wynnefield, 101–111, 147. *See also* Wynnefield
Sulzberger, Mayer, 144
Summer camps, 161–162, 166, 181
Sunday schools, 159
Sunstein, Emily, xxxiii, 80
Sunstein, Leon, 15
Supplementary schools, 149, 155, 159, 160. *See also* Schools, Conservative *and* Reform
Sylk, Harry, xxviii
Sylk, William, xxviii, 15, 30, 36
Synagogues. *See also* specific synagogues
    neighborhood vs. commuter, 149
    relocation of, xxix, xxx, xxxvii, 106–108, 145–146, 147, 149

𝒯

Talmudical Yeshiva, 110, 169, 174
Talmud Torahs, xxx, 155, 159
Tannenbaum, Myles, xxviii, 205
Tate, James H. J., xxxviii, xlii, 77–78
Taylor, Herman "Muggsy," 195, 197
Taylor, Joseph, 178
Teachers' unions, xxxii
Television, 209, 218–219
Temple Israel, 109, 165
Temple Judea, 149, 166
Temple Sholom, 117

Temple University, xxi, xxxix, 11, 66, 99, 165, 193, 194, 208
Tendler, Lew, 197
Tennis, 203–204
Theater
    dramatic, 209, 213–215
    musical, 209, 215–216
Theaters, movie, xvii, 209, 219
Tigay, Jeffrey, 165
Tobin, Gary, xvi
Toobin, Jerome, 63
    firing of, 57
Torah Academy, 169, 174
    relocation of, 110
Tose, Leonard, 205
Toubin, Isaac, 57, 65, 68
Track and field, 202, 203
Tribune, 83, 98, 99
Turoff, Fred, 203
TV Guide, 224

𝒰

Ullman, David, 88
Union League, xxxvi–xxxvii
Union of American Hebrew Congregations, 166
Unions. *See* Labor unions
United Hebrew Schools, 162
United Hebrew Trades, 85
United HIAS, Soviet Jews and, 127, 129
United Jewish Appeal, 178–179, 181
United Jewish Communities, 183
United Nations, Palestine and, 31–32, 34, 51
United Synagogues of America, 145, 147
    Board of Jewish Education of, 161–162
United Way, 177
University of Pennsylvania, xxi, xxxix, 53, 54, 98, 99, 165, 208, 219, 220
    Annenberg Center of, 207, 215
University of the Air, 218
Urban renewal, xxxiv–xxxv

𝒱

Vaad Hatzalah, 6–7, 23, 29
Valley Forge Music Fair, 215–216
Varady, David P., 106
Vincurov, Josef, 139
Visual arts, 220–221

𝒲

Wachman, Marvin, xxxix
Wallach, Sidney, 44, 48, 53
Walnut Street Theater, 213–215
War crimes trials, 25, 29
Ward politics, 71–72
War Refugee Board, 17, 18
WASPs, decline of, xlii
WDAS, 95, 99, 209, 212, 218
Weightlifting, 201–202
Weinberg, Manny, 74
Weiner, Charles, 75, 91
Weinrott, Leo, xxxiii, 79
Weisberger, Barbara, 212